D0397635

Ralph R. Loffmark

PRINCIPLES OF ACCOUNTING
ADVANCED

PRENTICE-HALL ACCOUNTING SERIES

H. A. Finney, Editor

PRINCIPLES OF ACCOUNTING

ADVANCED

by

H. A. FINNEY, Ph.B., C.P.A.

Member of the firm of Baumann, Finney & Co., Certified Public Accountants; formerly Professor of Accounting, Northwestern University.

THIRD EDITION

NEW YORK

PRENTICE-HALL, INC.

Copyright, 1924, 1928, 1934, 1946, by
PRENTICE-HALL, INC.
70 Fifth Avenue, New York

ALL RIGHTS RESERVED. NO PART OF THIS BOOK MAY BE REPRODUCED IN ANY FORM, BY MIMEOGRAPH OR ANY OTHER MEANS, WITHOUT PERMISSION IN WRITING FROM THE PUBLISHERS.

First Printing.............................September, 1946
Second Printing..........................September, 1946
Third Printing..............................February, 1947
Fourth Printing.................................April, 1947
Fifth Printing..............................September, 1948
Sixth Printing................................January, 1949
Seventh Printing..........................September, 1949
Eighth Printing................................October, 1950

PRINTED IN THE UNITED STATES OF AMERICA

Preface

In this, the third, edition of *Principles of Accounting, Advanced*, an effort has been made to give full recognition to the developments in accounting theory, the enactment of legislation affecting accounting, and the changes in the relative importance of the different subjects discussed, which have occurred during the somewhat more than ten years since the publication of the second edition.

In response to requests, some transfers of chapters have been made between the Intermediate and the Advanced texts. To provide additional, alternative, and more diversified assignment material, more questions and problems have been included in this edition than in preceding editions.

The author is indebted to Professor Norman B. Clark of Woodbury College, Los Angeles, California, for the preparation of progress tests and numerous short problems dealing, as far as practicable, exclusively with the subject matter of the chapters to which they are assigned. He is also indebted, for assistance in the preparation of certain chapters, to the following: Professor John C. Teevan, Northwestern University, Chapter 39; Dr. Emanuel Saxe, College of the City of New York, Chapters 55 and 56; Professor Lloyd Morey, University of Illinois, Chapter 58; Mr. Herbert Levy, partner in the firm of Paine, Webber, Jackson & Curtis, and Mr. Joseph A. Driscoll of the firm of Crook & Driscoll, Chapter 60.

For reading the entire manuscript and for offering helpful criticisms and suggestions, the author wishes to thank Professor Lyle Dieterlie, Indiana University; Professor Ralph C. Jones, Yale University; Professor A. C. Littleton, University of Illinois; Professor Charles J. Rowland, State College, Pennsylvania; and Lt. Comdr. Robert M. Trueblood, U. S. N. R. Grateful recognition is also given to all those who have taught from previous editions of the text, and who have responded to the author's request for advice.

Any similarity of names appearing in this text with names of persons or business entities is purely a coincidence.

H. A. FINNEY

Contents

CHAPTER 31

Partnerships

Retirement of a Partner

Adjustment of asset values. When a partner retires, he has a right to be paid the amount of his equity in the business. But the question arises whether his equity is fairly measured by the balance of his capital account. Three classes of adjustments in the asset values may be necessary to produce a balance in the retiring partner's capital account which is a fair amount for him to demand and receive.

In the first place, improper provision for bad debts, depreciation, and other shrinkages in asset values may have been made during the years of operation. The provisions may have been insufficient or excessive, and this fact becomes significant when one partner is to withdraw. If the provisions have been insufficient, a hardship will be worked on the remaining partners unless an adjustment is made; if the provisions have been excessive, an adjustment should be made to avoid working a hardship on the retiring partner.

In the second place, the rules which properly govern the valuation of assets in a going concern may not be the proper rules to apply in valuing the assets of a partnership which is about to dissolve. For instance, in figuring the profits of a going concern, it is a conservative practice to value the inventory at cost or market, whichever is lower; but when a partner is about to retire, he is virtually selling his interest in the inventory to the remaining partners, and justice would seem to require that he receive the benefit of any increase in the market value of the merchandise which took place before his retirement.

Fixed assets provide another illustration. From the standpoint of a going concern, fluctuations in the market value of fixed assets need not be recorded in the accounts. An increase in value is an unrealized profit, and a decrease in value need not be put on the books if there is no intention to sell the assets and to take the loss. But when a partner is retiring, the partnership of which he is a member is selling the assets to the remaining partner or partners, and equity requires that the transfer be made at market values prevailing at the date of sale.

In the third place, the partners may agree to place a goodwill account on the books. This subject is treated in the next section.

If any adjustments are made in the asset values, the gain should be credited, or the loss debited, to the partners in the profit and loss ratio.

Goodwill. The partnership articles may provide that a goodwill account shall be placed on the books in the event of the retirement of a partner. In such instances, the articles usually stipulate how the goodwill shall be computed. Or, at the time of the retirement, the partners may agree to place goodwill on the books, and may agree upon the method of computing it.

The general rule is that the credit for goodwill thus placed on the books should be divided among the partners in the profit and loss ratio existing at the time the entry is made, and this rule governs unless the partners agree to some other division.

It is sometimes contended that when the profit and loss ratio has changed during the existence of the partnership, the credit for goodwill should be divided on the basis of an average of these past ratios. There does not seem to be sufficient argument to support this view. Goodwill exists when there is reason to believe that future profits will provide more than an average return on the investment. Past profits may serve as an evidence of this probability, but the value placed on the goodwill is the purchase price of future, not past, profits. If the retiring partner had chosen to remain in the partnership, he would have shared in these future profits in the present profit and loss ratio, not in the average ratio of the past. At least, the present ratio would continue unless he consented to a change. The retiring partner takes an allowance for goodwill at the date of retirement, instead of continuing as a member of the firm and taking his share of future profits. It seems logical, therefore, that he should be credited with a share of the goodwill based on the profit and loss ratio at the date of his retirement, since that ratio would presumably have governed the distribution of future profits had he chosen to remain.

After the amount of the goodwill and its division in the profit and loss ratio are determined, the question remains concerning the method of recording it. Two conflicting views are held regarding the proper method of putting the goodwill on the books. These methods will be illustrated by an assumed case in which *C* is to retire from the firm of *A*, *B*, and *C*, who share profits equally. A goodwill value of $6,000.00 has been agreed upon.

First method. Place the entire goodwill on the books, crediting all of the partners in their profit and loss ratio, by the following journal entry:

Goodwill	$6,000.00	
A, capital		$2,000.00
B, capital		2,000.00
C, capital		2,000.00
To place on the books the agreed value of the goodwill, crediting the partners therefor in their profit and loss ratio.		

Second method. Place on the books only the share of goodwill to be credited to the retiring partner, by the following journal entry:

Goodwill	$2,000.00	
C, capital		$2,000.00
To place on the books *C*'s one third of the goodwill, which has been valued by agreement at $6,000.00.		

The second method is the more conservative, because it conforms to the rule that goodwill should be placed on the books only when it has been paid for. If *A* and *B* are to continue the business, their books will not conform to this rule if a goodwill account of $6,000.00 is shown. Only $2,000.00 was paid for goodwill on the retirement of *C*.

Implied goodwill or bonus. Assume that *A*, *B*, and *C* have capitals of $10,000.00 each and share profits equally. *C* is to retire and is to be paid $12,000.00 from partnership assets. The $2,000.00 excess of the payment to *C* over his capital may be recorded as a bonus or it may be regarded as indicative of the existence of goodwill.

If it is considered a bonus, the entry will be:

A, capital	$ 1,000.00	
B, capital	1,000.00	
C, capital	10,000.00	
Cash		$12,000.00

If the $2,000.00 excess payment is set up as goodwill, the entries will be:

Goodwill	$ 2,000.00	
C, capital		$ 2,000.00
C, capital	12,000.00	
Cash		12,000.00

If it is considered that a goodwill of $2,000.00 appertains to *C*'s interest, and a similar goodwill to the interests of *A* and *B*, and the total goodwill of $6,000.00 is to be recorded, the entries will be:

Goodwill	$ 6,000.00	
A, capital		$ 2,000.00
B, capital		2,000.00
C, capital		2,000.00
C, capital	12,000.00	
Cash		12,000.00

If the remaining partners continue to share profits in the same ratio as before, their relative capital interests are not affected by the choice of method. If the $2,000.00 is regarded as a bonus, chargeable $1,000.00 each to *A* and *B*, their resulting capitals will be $9,000.00 each. If a goodwill of $2,000.00 is placed on the books and subsequently written off, the result will be:

	A Capital	*B* Capital
Balances before *C*'s withdrawal	$10,000.00	$10,000.00
Write off goodwill	1,000.00	1,000.00
Resulting balances	$ 9,000.00	$ 9,000.00

If a goodwill of $6,000.00 is placed on the books and subsequently written off, the effect on the capitals of *A* and *B* is:

	A Capital	*B* Capital
Balances before *C*'s withdrawal	$10,000.00	$10,000.00
Credits for goodwill	2,000.00	2,000.00
Balances after *C*'s withdrawal	$12,000.00	$12,000.00
Write off goodwill	3,000.00	3,000.00
Resulting balances	$ 9,000.00	$ 9,000.00

However, even though the remaining partners share their profits immediately after the withdrawal in the same ratio as before, it cannot be assumed that the choice between the bonus and goodwill treatments is immaterial. If a goodwill is placed on the books and the remaining partners change their profit and loss ratio before the goodwill is written off, the result will not be the same as that produced by regarding the excess payment as a bonus.

Liability of retiring partner. After retirement, a partner is liable for firm debts incurred while he was a partner, unless the creditors release him. Furthermore, unless he was a secret partner, he is liable to former creditors for debts incurred after his retirement if such creditors have no notice of his retirement and extend credit on the assumption that he is still a partner. Therefore, it is advisable for a retiring partner to give notice to all parties with whom the firm has had dealings.

Settlement with retiring partner. The cash or other assets given to the withdrawing partner should be charged to his account. If he is paid in full, the account will, of course, be closed. In some instances, however, full payment is deferred, either because of the inadequacy of funds, or because an agreement cannot be reached regarding the value of certain assets, such as accounts receivable, and it is decided to postpone payment until the assets have been converted into cash and the losses ascertained.

When settlement is thus postponed, the capital account of the retiring partner should be closed, because he is no longer a partner; and the balance of the capital account should be transferred to a personal account or a note payable account, as the case may be. This account should be given a title which will clearly distinguish it from the trade accounts and notes payable.

If the settlement is postponed, pending the realization of doubtful assets, such as accounts receivable, the accounts with these assets should be kept entirely distinct from the accounts with similar assets obtained after the partner's retirement. Otherwise there may be difficulty in determining whether or not a loss should be charged in part to the former partner.

Death of a partner. The death of a partner automatically dissolves the partnership, and it becomes the duty of the surviving partners to wind up the affairs of the partnership and to make a settlement with the deceased partner's estate.

If the articles of partnership contain no provisions with respect to the death of a partner, the surviving partners should realize that the partnership has been dissolved and that the estate of the deceased partner is entitled to receive the amount of his interest in the firm at the date of his death. Therefore, the surviving partners should immediately take an inventory and close the books, to determine the capital interest of the deceased partner, including his share of the profits to the date of his death. As the decedent is no longer a partner, the balance of his capital account should be transferred to a personal account, pending settlement.

The articles of partnership may, however, contain provisions intended to avoid the necessity of taking an inventory and closing the books at the date of death. If the determination of the actual profits to the date of death and the determination of current values of assets as of that date are not required for estate or inheritance tax purposes, the following procedures may be effective:

(A) There may be an agreement that the estate or an heir of the decedent shall succeed him as a partner.

When such an agreement has been made, it is not necessary to close the books and to ascertain the profits to the date of death. It is necessary only to close the deceased partner's drawing account, and to transfer his capital credit to a capital account with the estate or the heir. At the next regular closing, the share of profits credited to the estate or to the heir will include the profits earned to the date of death, as well as those earned subsequently. The questions of goodwill and the realizable values of assets at the date of the partner's decease may be ignored, because the estate or heir merely steps into the decedent's place as a partner of a going business.

(B) If the deceased partner's interest is to be paid to his estate, the articles may contain an agreement that the profits to the date of death shall be estimated in some manner, instead of being actually computed by taking an inventory and by closing the books. The methods of making the estimate may be divided into two general classes, as follows:

(1) The profits to the date of death may be estimated on the basis of an average of the profits of a number of years preceding the year of death. For instance, *A*, *B*, and *C*, sharing profits equally, agreed that, in the event of the death of a partner, the deceased partner's share of profits from the date of the last closing until the date of death should be estimated by averaging the profits of the past four years and multiplying this average by the fraction of the year between the date of the last closing and the date of death. *A* died on March 31, 1946, and his share of the profits earned since the preceding December 31 was estimated as follows:

Year	Profits
1942	$18,500.00
1943	17,625.00
1944	18,346.00
1945	18,297.00
Total	$72,768.00
Average	$18,192.00
Fraction of year since last closing	¼
Estimated profits for three months	$ 4,548.00
A's fractional interest	⅓
A's estimated share of profits	$ 1,516.00

These estimated profits should be credited to *A* by a journal entry similar to the following:

A's estimated profits	$1,516.00	
A, capital		$1,516.00
To credit *A* with his share of the estimated profit for the three months ended March 31, 1946.		

The account called "*A*'s estimated profits" should remain open until the closing of the books on December 31, 1946, when it should be closed to profit and loss as a division of the profits.

(2) The articles may provide that settlement with the deceased partner's estate shall be postponed until the next regular closing, at which time his account shall be credited with a share of the profits.

Various methods may be agreed upon for computing the deceased partner's portion of the profit. Since the partnership retained his capital during the full period, he may receive a share of the profits for the full period. Or his account may be credited with a share of the profits for the full period minus an allowance for the loss of his services. Or the credit may be for the proper fraction of the period's profits, plus interest on his capital and on his share of the profits from the date of death to the date of settlement.

When settlement is thus postponed, the balance of the deceased partner's capital account should be transferred to a personal account or to an account with the estate.

The articles of partnership may also contain an agreement regarding goodwill, and regarding the recognition of the market value of other assets as of the date of the death of a partner.

Sale of a Partnership Business

Valued assets or lump sum. When a business is sold, the seller and the purchaser may agree upon the valuation of each asset, or they may agree on a lump-sum price for the business as a whole. The method of recording the sale will depend upon which of these methods is adopted.

Several illustrations will be given, assuming the sale of a business with the following balance sheet:

A*, *B*, AND *C
Balance Sheet—April 30, 1946
Assets

Land		$ 1,000.00
Buildings	$6,000.00	
Less reserve for depreciation	800.00	5,200.00
Merchandise		4,800.00
Accounts receivable	$4,560.00	
Less reserve for bad debts	140.00	4,420.00
Cash		280.00
		$15,700.00

Liabilities	
Accounts payable	$ 1,000.00
Notes payable	500.00
A, capital	6,100.00
B, capital	5,100.00
C, capital	3,000.00
	$15,700.00

Profits and losses are shared equally.

Valued assets. It is first assumed that the assets are sold to J. G. Burroughs at the following agreed values:

Land	$1,500.00
Buildings	5,000.00
Merchandise	4,500.00
Accounts receivable	4,000.00

The cash is not sold, and the liabilities are not assumed by the purchaser.

The procedure for recording the sale may be summarized as follows:

Adjust the asset values, closing out the various reserves, and taking up the net gain or loss to the partners' capitals in the profit and loss ratio. The gain or loss may be entered directly in the capital accounts or carried through a capital adjustment account.

Close out the asset accounts, charging the purchaser's account.

Record the collection from the purchaser.

Record the payment of the liabilities.

Record the final distribution of assets among the partners.

The journal entries to record the sale, in accordance with the terms stated in the illustration, the payment of the liabilities, and the distribution to the partners, are as follows:

(1)	Land	$ 500.00	
	Capital adjustment account		$ 500.00
	To write up the land to the agreed value of $1,500.00.		
(2)	Reserve for depreciation—buildings	800.00	
	Capital adjustment account	200.00	
	Buildings		1,000.00
	To write down the buildings to the agreed value of $5,000.00, closing the reserve and recording the loss of $200.00.		
(3)	Capital adjustment account	300.00	
	Merchandise		300.00
	To write down the merchandise from $4,800.00 to the agreed value of $4,500.00.		

(4)	Reserve for bad debts	$ 140.00	
	Capital adjustment account	420.00	
	Accounts receivable		$ 560.00
	To write down the accounts receivable from $4,560.00 to $4,000.00, closing the reserve and taking up the loss of $420.00.		
(5)	*A*, capital	140.00	
	B, capital	140.00	
	C, capital	140.00	
	Capital adjustment account		420.00
	To divide the loss on the sale in the profit and loss ratio.		
(6)	J. G. Burroughs	15,000.00	
	Land		1,500.00
	Buildings		5,000.00
	Merchandise		4,500.00
	Accounts receivable		4,000.00
	To record the sale of the assets at the agreed values.		
(7)	Cash	15,000.00	
	J. G. Burroughs		15,000.00
	To record the collection from Burroughs.		
(8)	Accounts payable	1,000.00	
	Notes payable	500.00	
	Cash		1,500.00
	To record the payment of the liabilities.		
(9)	*A*, capital	5,960.00	
	B, capital	4,960.00	
	C, capital	2,860.00	
	Cash		13,780.00
	To record the final distribution of cash.		

	A	*B*	*C*
Capitals	$6,100.00	$5,100.00	$3,000.00
Less loss on sale	140.00	140.00	140.00
Cash	$5,960.00	$4,960.00	$2,860.00

Lump-sum sale: At a loss. When the assets are sold for a lump sum, it is impossible to adjust the asset values. If the price is less than the book value of the assets transferred, the loss should be taken up in the entry for the sale.

To illustrate, assume that the assets of *A*, *B*, and *C*, exclusive of the cash, are sold to J. G. Burroughs for a lump sum of $15,000.00, without placing values on the individual assets. The entries for the transfer of the assets will be:

(1)	J. G. Burroughs	$15,000.00	
	Reserve for depreciation—buildings	800.00	
	Reserve for bad debts	140.00	
	Capital adjustment account	420.00	
	Land		$1,000.00
	Buildings		6,000.00
	Merchandise		4,800.00
	Accounts receivable		4,560.00
	To record the sale of the assets, exclusive of cash, for $15,000.00.		

(2) *A*, capital	$ 140.00	
B, capital	140.00	
C, capital	140.00	
Capital adjustment account		$ 420.00
To divide the loss on the sale.		

These entries will be followed by entries 7, 8, and 9, as in the preceding illustration.

Lump-sum sale: At a profit. The entries to be made when a business is sold at a profit will depend upon whether the profit is regarded as a payment for goodwill or as an adjustment of the value of other assets.

Illustration: PROFIT REGARDED AS A PAYMENT FOR GOODWILL. Assume that the assets of the firm of *A*, *B*, and *C* are sold to J. G. Burroughs at a lump-sum price of $18,000.00; the entries will be:

(1) Goodwill	$ 2,580.00	
Capital adjustment account		$ 2,580.00
To take up, by charge to goodwill, the excess of the sale price of the assets over their book value.		
(2) J. G. Burroughs	18,000.00	
Reserve for depreciation—buildings	800.00	
Reserve for bad debts	140.00	
Land		1,000.00
Buildings		6,000.00
Merchandise		4,800.00
Accounts receivable		4,560.00
Goodwill		2,580.00
To record the sale of the assets for $18,000.00.		
(3) Capital adjustment account	2,580.00	
A, capital		860.00
B, capital		860.00
C, capital		860.00
To divide the profit on the sale of the business.		
(4) Cash	18,000.00	
J. G. Burroughs		18,000.00
To record the collection from Burroughs.		
(5) Accounts payable	1,000.00	
Notes payable	500.00	
Cash		1,500.00
To record the payment of the liabilities.		
(6) *A*, capital	6,960.00	
B, capital	5,960.00	
C, capital	3,860.00	
Cash		16,780.00
To record the final distribution of cash to the partners.		

Illustration: PROFIT REGARDED AS AN ADJUSTMENT OF ASSET VALUES. The fact that the assets were sold for more than their book value is not conclusive evidence of the existence of a goodwill. The excess price may have been due to the fact that the book values of the assets were understated. On this assumption, the entries for the sale of the assets for $18,000.00 will be as follows:

(1) J. G. Burroughs	$18,000.00	
Reserve for depreciation—buildings	800.00	
Reserve for bad debts	140.00	
Land		$1,000.00
Buildings		6,000.00
Merchandise		4,800.00
Accounts receivable		4,560.00
Capital adjustment account		2,580.00
To record the sale of the assets, exclusive of cash, for $18,000.00.		

This entry will be followed by entries 3, 4, 5, and 6, as in the immediately preceding illustration.

Transfer of liabilities. If the purchaser assumes the liabilities, the entry transferring the assets will be followed by an entry transferring the liabilities, as follows:

Accounts payable	$1,000.00	
Notes payable	500.00	
J. G. Burroughs		$1,500.00
To record the assumption of our liabilities by the purchaser of the assets.		

When the liabilities are assumed by the purchaser of a business, the seller is not relieved from liability unless the creditors release him.

Division of profit or loss on sale. It cannot be too strongly emphasized that the agreed profit and loss ratio governs the division of gains or losses arising from the sale of a partnership's assets. Any agreement which the partners have made in regard to profits applies with equal force to losses, and the agreement concerning the sharing of profits or losses during operations applies also to profits or losses during liquidation, when the partnership is selling its assets and going out of business.

It is an error to assume that losses incurred at the dissolution of a partnership should be divided in the capital ratio. One writer has stated that such losses should be divided in the capital ratio and has supported this statement by the argument that when the partners decide to go out of business the partnership is dissolved, the partnership agreement is no longer binding, and, thereafter, losses are losses of capital and should be borne in the capital ratio.

There are several answers to this argument. In the first place, all losses are losses of capital. If operations result in a loss, the capital of the partners is reduced; but the loss is borne in the profit and loss ratio.

In the second place, the partnership is not dissolved merely by the decision to sell the business or to discontinue operations. The partners have placed their assets in a common fund for common operations, and they continue to be partners until the business is sold or until the assets are realized, and final distribution is made. Any losses on sale or realization are, therefore, partnership losses, and the agreement concerning the division of partnership losses governs their division.

In the third place, the profits or losses from operations which have been divided in the agreed ratio are merely periodical estimates; the true profit or loss on the partnership venture is not definitely determinable until the partnership is dissolved and the partnership fund is distributed among the partners. The depreciation, which affected the statement of operating profits, may have been incorrect; the provision for bad debts may have been incorrect; other assets may have been incorrectly valued. All of these things have affected the profits which have been divided in the profit and loss ratio; the loss or gain disclosed at dissolution is in a sense a correction of all of these errors, and it also should be divided in the profit and loss ratio.

In the fourth place, the agreement with respect to sharing of profits and losses is an unqualified agreement. Since the agreement is not expressly limited to operating profits or losses, it is incorrect to imply any such limitation.

CHAPTER 32

Partnerships (Continued)

Dissolution and Liquidation

Causes of dissolution. The causes of partnership dissolution are classified as follows:

(A) Act of the parties.

(1) Termination of the time agreed upon in the contract.

If, at the time of making the partnership contract, the parties agree upon the length of time the contract shall remain in force, the expiration of the agreed time dissolves the partnership. The partners may continue the partnership relation, but it is thereafter a "partnership at will" and any partner may withdraw at any time.

(2) Accomplishment of the purpose for which the partnership was formed.

If the partnership contract states that the partnership was formed for a definite purpose, as for the purchase and sale of a certain invoice of merchandise, or for the construction of a building, the accomplishment of the stated purpose discharges the contract and dissolves the partnership.

(3) Mutual agreement.

Since a partnership is based on a contract, the parties to the contract may, by mutual consent at any time, agree to terminate the contract.

(4) Withdrawal of a partner.

It has already been noted that a partner has the *right* to withdraw if (1) the agreed time has elapsed, (2) the stated purpose has been accomplished, or (3) a mutual agreement has been reached. A partner has the *power* to withdraw at any time even though he may have no right to do so. A partner's withdrawal without the right to withdraw is a violation of his contract, and renders him liable for any damages that may result from such violation. But his withdrawal nevertheless dissolves the partnership.

(B) Operation of law.

(1) Death of a partner.

The death of a partner automatically dissolves the partnership. The articles of partnership may provide that the deceased partner's estate or heirs may succeed him in the partnership. But such a provision results in the creation of a new partnership; it does not prevent the dissolution of the old partnership.

(2) Bankruptcy.

The bankruptcy of the firm or of a partner dissolves the partnership.

(3) War.

If the partners are citizens or subjects of different countries, the partnership is dissolved by war between these countries, or at least suspended during the continuance of the war.

(4) Illegality of object.

A partnership cannot be formed for an illegal purpose, and a legally organized partnership is dissolved by the subsequent enactment of legislation making the business of the firm illegal.

(C) Judicial decree.

A partner may appeal to a court for a decree dissolving the partnership for any of the following reasons:

(1) Insanity or other incapacity of one of the partners.
(2) Dissension among the partners.
(3) Misconduct of a partner, tending to interfere with the success of the business.
(4) Inability to make profits.
(5) Fraud in the inducement that caused him to become a partner.

Liquidation. In its narrower sense, liquidation means the payment of a liability. But in its broader sense, liquidation means the process of winding up a business, converting the assets into cash, paying the liabilities, and distributing the remaining cash among the partners or stockholders. While this process is going on, a business is said to be in liquidation.

Realization. Realization is the process of converting assets into cash. It is an incorrect use of accounting terminology to speak of liquidating assets. Assets are realized; liabilities are liquidated.

Recording liquidation. The process of liquidating a partnership requires entries to record the following facts:

Realization of the assets.
Division of the loss or gain on realization, by charges or credits to the partners' capitals.
Payment of the liabilities.
Payment of the partners' interests.

Order of distribution of cash. As a general rule, the cash should be distributed in the following order.

To outside creditors.
To partners for any loan accounts.
To partners for capital accounts.

This rule has some exceptions, which will be discussed in subsequent sections.

Distribution of loss or gain. There is one invariable rule which should be followed in partnership liquidations. *Any known loss or gain on realization should be recorded in the partners' accounts before any payments are made to the partners.* Put in another way: *Always distribute the loss or gain before distributing the cash.*

This rule cannot be too strongly emphasized, for it is frequently ignored and serious errors are thereby caused. The amount to which a partner is entitled when the business is liquidated, depends upon:

His capital contribution.
His loans to the firm.
His drawings.
His share of the profit or loss.

Unless all of these factors are taken into consideration, it is impossible to tell what a partner's equity is and what amount should be paid to him.

Typical cases. The illustrations in this chapter and in Chapter 33, while not embracing all possible cases of partnership liquidation, are fairly inclusive and show the principles involved in typical problems of partnership liquidation.

In every case in this chapter, it is assumed that no payments are made to the partners until all of the assets have been realized and the loss on realization has thus been fully determined. The cases in Chapter 33 are based on the assumption that payments are made to the partners before the assets have been fully realized and the loss ascertained.

Case 1. This case illustrates the following conditions:

Realization of assets completed before payments are made to partners.
Losses not sufficient to exhaust any partner's capital.
No loans from partners.

The following is a condensed trial balance of a partnership before realization and liquidation:

D, capital		$20,000.00
E, capital		10,000.00
Assets	$35,000.00	
Liabilities		5,000.00
	$35,000.00	$35,000.00

Profits and losses are shared equally. The assets are sold for $29,000.00 cash.

Cash	$29,000.00	
D, capital	3,000.00	
E, capital	3,000.00	
Assets		$35,000.00
To record the sale of the assets and the distribution of the loss of $6,000.00.		
Liabilities	5,000.00	
Cash		5,000.00
To record the payment of the liabilities.		
D, capital	17,000.00	
E, capital	7,000.00	
Cash		24,000.00
To record the final distribution to the partners in settlement of their capitals, as follows:		

	D	*E*
Capitals before sale	$20,000.00	$10,000.00
Loss on realization	3,000.00	3,000.00
Cash	$17,000.00	$ 7,000.00

The facts may be set up in a statement as follows:

Statement of Liquidation

	Assets	*D*, Capital	*E*, Capital	Liabilities
Balances before realization	$35,000	$20,000	$10,000	$5,000
Loss on realization	6,000	3,000	3,000	
Cash for division	$29,000			
Capital balances after realization		$17,000	$ 7,000	
Payment of creditors	5,000			5,000
Payment to partners	$24,000	17,000	7,000	

It is usually sufficient to submit a statement of the partners' capital accounts, for it is assumed that the liabilities are paid in full.

D* AND *E
Statement of Capital Accounts

	D	*E*	Together
Capitals before realization	$20,000.00	$10,000.00	$30,000.00
Deduct loss on realization	3,000.00	3,000.00	6,000.00
Balances paid in cash	$17,000.00	$ 7,000.00	$24,000.00

Wrong methods. The necessity of charging off the loss on realization before dividing the cash between the partners has already been emphasized. Students seem prone to overlook this rule and to make one of the following errors:

(1) Dividing the cash in the profit and loss ratio.
(2) Dividing the cash in the original capital ratio.

DIVIDING THE CASH IN THE PROFIT AND LOSS RATIO. The following statement (based on the preceding illustration) shows the effect of dividing the cash in the profit and loss ratio, instead of dividing the loss in the profit and loss ratio:

D* AND *E
Statement of Capital Accounts

	D	*E*	Together
Capitals before realization	$20,000.00	$10,000.00	$30,000.00
Cash (in P. & L. ratio)	12,000.00	12,000.00	24,000.00
Remaining balances	Cr. $ 8,000.00	Dr. $ 2,000.00	$ 6,000.00

This division of the cash makes *D* bear a loss of $8,000.00, while *E* actually gains $2,000.00; the loss of $6,000.00 should have been borne equally.

DIVIDING THE CASH IN THE ORIGINAL CAPITAL RATIO. The following statement shows the effect of dividing the cash in the original capital ratio, instead of first charging off the loss and then paying the partners their resulting balances:

D* AND *E
Statement of Capital Accounts

	D	*E*	Together
Capitals before realization	$20,000.00	$10,000.00	$30,000.00
Cash (in original capital ratio)	16,000.00	8,000.00	24,000.00
Remaining balances	$ 4,000.00	$ 2,000.00	$ 6,000.00

This incorrect procedure results in dividing the loss in the capital ratio instead of dividing it equally, as agreed.

Case 2. This case illustrates the following conditions:

Realization of assets completed before payments are made to partners.

Losses not sufficient to exhaust any partner's capital.
A loan from a partner.

The following is a condensed trial balance of a partnership prior to dissolution:

G, capital		$15,000.00
H, capital		10,000.00
G, loan		5,000.00
Assets	$35,000.00	
Liabilities		5,000.00
	$35,000.00	$35,000.00

The assets are sold for $30,000.00. Since nothing is said concerning the profit and loss ratio, it must be assumed that profits and losses are shared equally. The liquidation is shown below:

Statement of Liquidation

	Liabilities	*G*, Loan	*G*, Capital	*H*, Capital
Balances before realization	$5,000	$5,000	$15,000	$10,000
Loss on realization			2,500	2,500
Capital balances after realization			$12,500	$ 7,500
Distribution of cash:				
Liabilities	5,000			
G, loan		5,000		
Partners' capitals			12,500	7,500

This case illustrates the general rule that cash distributions should be made in the following order of priority: (1) to outside creditors, in payment of liabilities; (2) to partners, in payment of loans from them; and (3) to partners, in liquidation of their capital investments. However, this rule is subject to certain exceptions, which are illustrated in subsequent cases.

Case 3. This case illustrates the following conditions:

Realization of assets completed before payments are made to partners.
Partnership solvent and able to pay its creditors in full.
Two partners; one partner has a debit balance in his capital account after realization; the other partner has a credit balance. No partners' loans.

The illustration is based on the following condensed trial balance showing the condition before the realization of the assets.

I, capital		$15,000.00
J, capital		3,000.00
Assets	$30,000.00	
Liabilities		12,000.00
	$30,000.00	$30,000.00

Profits and losses are shared equally. The assets realize $22,000.00.

Statement of Liquidation

	Liabilities	*I*, Capital	*J*, Capital
Balances before realization......	$12,000.00	$15,000.00	$3,000.00
Loss on realization.............		4,000.00	4,000.00
Capitals after realization.......		$11,000.00	$1,000.00*
Distribution of cash:			
Liabilities....................	12,000.00		
I, capital.....................		10,000.00	
Balances......................		$ 1,000.00	$1,000.00*

* Debit balance.

In fulfillment of his agreement to bear one half of any loss, *J* should pay *I* the $1,000.00 balance of his account. Otherwise *I* will bear $5,000.00 of the loss and *J* will bear only $3,000.00.

Case 4. This case illustrates the following conditions:

Realization of assets completed before payments are made to partners.
Partnership solvent and able to pay its creditors in full.
Two partners; one partner has a debit balance in his capital account after realization; the other partner has a credit balance. Both partners have loan accounts with credit balances.

The credit balance in a partner's loan account should not be paid to him in full if there is a debit balance in his capital account. The debit balance in the capital account represents a debt owed by the partner to the partnership; the credit balance in the loan account represents a debt owed by the partnership to the partner. Enough of the loan should be transferred to the capital account to make good the debit balance in the capital account, and only the remainder of the loan should be paid to the partner. This is called *exercising the right of offset.*

If the entire credit balance in the loan account were paid to the partner, without making any offset, the partner might refuse, or be unable, to pay in the debit balance of his capital account.

The entire loan should not be transferred to the capital account. Loans take precedence over capitals and should be paid before the capitals. If the entire loan were transferred to the capital account, the priority of the unapplied balance of the loan would be disregarded.

X and *Y* share profits in the ratio of 70% and 30% respectively. Their trial balance prior to realization was:

X, capital		$20,000.00
Y, capital		18,000.00
Assets	$87,000.00	
Liabilities		15,000.00
X, loan		10,000.00
Y, loan		24,000.00
	$87,000.00	$87,000.00

The assets were sold for $55,000.00. Following are the journal entries to record the realization and liquidation:

Cash	$55,000.00	
X, capital	22,400.00	
Y, capital	9,600.00	
Assets		$87,000.00
To record the sale of assets, having a book value of $87,000.00, for $55,000.00, the resulting loss of $32,000.00 being divided between the partners in their profit and loss ratio of 70% and 30%.		
Liabilities	15,000.00	
Cash		15,000.00
To record the payment of the liabilities.		
X, loan	2,400.00	
X, capital		2,400.00
To exercise the right of offset, making good from *X*'s loan account the deficit in his capital account caused by: Loss on realization $22,400.00; Capital before realization 20,000.00; Debit balance $ 2,400.00		
X, loan	7,600.00	
Y, loan	24,000.00	
Cash		31,600.00
To record the payment of the partners' loans.		
Y, capital	8,400.00	
Cash		8,400.00
To record the payment of *Y*'s capital.		

The settlement could be shown in statement form as follows:

Statement of Liquidation

	Assets	Liabilities	*X*, Loan	*Y*, Loan	*X*, Capital	*Y*, Capital
Balances before realization	$87,000	$15,000	$10,000	$24,000	$20,000	$18,000
Loss on realization	32,000				22,400	9,600
Balances after realization	$55,000	$15,000	$10,000	$24,000	$ 2,400*	$ 8,400
Offset against loan			2,400		2,400	
Balances after offset	$55,000	$15,000	$ 7,600	$24,000	$ —	$ 8,400
Distribution of cash:						
Liabilities	$15,000	15,000				
Partners' loans	31,600		7,600	24,000		
Partner's capital	8,400					8,400
Total cash	$55,000					

* Capital deficit.

Case 5. This case illustrates the following conditions:

Realization of assets completed before payments are made to partners.

Partnership solvent and able to pay its creditors in full.

Three partners, one with a debit balance in his capital account after realization. No partners' loans.

This case is intended to illustrate the procedure to be followed when there are three or more partners, one of whom has a capital account which has been reduced to a debit balance by losses. In such a situation, it will be impossible to pay in full the partners who have credit balances, unless the partner with a debit balance pays in the amount thereof. But suppose that it is desired to distribute the cash on hand before the partner with a debit balance pays in the amount thereof, and before it is known whether he will be able to do so. The question is: How should the cash be divided?

The important thing to remember is that, if the partner with a debit balance fails to pay in, this debit balance will have to be charged off as a loss. The other partners will have to bear this loss in their profit and loss ratio. Therefore, the cash on hand should be distributed in such a way as to leave them with exactly the right balances to absorb the loss. In other words, the partners with credit balances should be paid *down to* the amounts with which they will be charged if the partner with the debit balance fails to make good this balance.

To illustrate, *R*, *S*, and *T* share profits in the ratio of 50%, 30%, and 20% respectively. After payment of their liabilities in full, preparatory to liquidation, their trial balance appears as follows:

R, capital		$10,000.00
S, capital		26,100.00
T, capital		23,900.00
Assets	$60,000.00	
	$60,000.00	$60,000.00

The assets are sold for $38,000.00. The following statement shows how the $38,000.00 should be distributed:

Statement of Capitals

	R	*S*	*T*	Together
Capitals before realization	$10,000.00	$26,100.00	$23,900.00	$60,000.00
Loss on realization	11,000.00	6,600.00	4,400.00	22,000.00
Balances after realization	$ 1,000.00*	$19,500.00	$19,500.00	$38,000.00
Cash distributed		18,900.00	19,100.00	38,000.00
Balances after distribution	$ 1,000.00*	$ 600.00	$ 400.00	

* Indicates debit balance.

The payments made to S and T were determined thus: The profit and loss ratio is: R, 50%; S, 30%; and T, 20%. If R fails to pay in his debit balance of $1,000.00, the loss will have to be divided between S and T in their ratio of 30 and 20, or three fifths and two fifths. Therefore S is paid down to three fifths of $1,000.00, or $600.00; and T is paid down to two fifths of $1,000.00, or $400.00. If R fails to pay in the $1,000.00, S and T will have balances in their accounts exactly equal to the losses with which they will be charged; if R does pay in the $1,000.00, S will be paid $600.00 and T will be paid $400.00.

Wrong methods. Problems of this type are frequently solved by actually charging off the debit balance and setting up a statement like the following one:

Statement of Capitals

	R	*S*	*T*	Together
Capitals before realization	$10,000	$26,100	$23,900	$60,000
Loss on realization	11,000	6,600	4,400	22,000
Balances after realization	$ 1,000*	$19,500	$19,500	$38,000
Debit balance charged off	Cr. 1,000	Dr. 600	Dr. 400	
Resulting balances	—	$18,900	$19,100	$38,000
Cash distributed		18,900	19,100	38,000

* Debit balance.

This method results in the same cash distribution as the correct method. The error lies in actually charging off R's debit balance before it is known positively that R will not pay it in.

Another wrong method is to pay the partners who have credit balances in the ratio of these credit balances. Thus:

Statement of Capitals

	R	*S*	*T*	Together
Capitals before realization	$10,000.00	$26,100.00	$23,900.00	$60,000.00
Loss on realization	11,000.00	6,600.00	4,400.00	22,000.00
Balances after realization	$ 1,000.00*	$19,500.00	$19,500.00	$38,000.00
Cash distributed		19,000.00	19,000.00	38,000.00
Resulting balances	$ 1,000.00*	$ 500.00	$ 500.00	

* Debit balance.

In this statement, the cash is divided equally because the capital balances of S and T are equal after the realization loss is charged off. But this procedure is incorrect. If R's account cannot be collected from him, S will be charged with $600.00 although he has only $500.00 in his account, and T will be charged with $400.00 although he has $500.00 in his account. T will then have to try to collect $100.00 from S, which he may not be able to do.

Case 6. This case illustrates the following conditions:

Realization of assets completed before payments are made to partners.
Partnership insolvent and unable to pay its creditors in full.
Two partners, both with debit balances in their capital accounts after realization. No partners' loans.

Assume the following trial balance before realization:

K, capital		$ 3,000.00
L, capital		2,000.00
Accounts payable		20,000.00
Assets	$25,000.00	
	$25,000.00	$25,000.00

Profits and losses are shared equally. The assets are sold for $17,000.00.

Statement of Liquidation

	Liabilities	*K*, Capital	*L*, Capital
Balances before realization	$20,000.00	$3,000.00	$2,000.00
Loss on realization		4,000.00	4,000.00
Resulting balances	$20,000.00	$1,000.00*	$2,000.00*
Cash payments to creditors	17,000.00		
Final balances	$ 3,000.00	$1,000.00*	$2,000.00*

* Debit balance.

The creditors have a claim against the partners for the $3,000.00 of unpaid liabilities. It is not necessary that they consider the debit balances of the two partners; that is, they have the right to enforce collection in full from either of the partners. Assuming that the creditors collect the entire amount from *K*, an entry should be made debiting the liability accounts and crediting *K*'s capital. Continuing the statement:

		Liabilities		*K*, Capital	*L*, Capital
Balances—as above		$3,000.00		$1,000.00*	$2,000 00*
Liabilities paid by *K*	Dr.	3,000.00	Cr.	3,000.00	
Resulting balances		—		$2,000.00	$2,000.00*

* Debit balance.

K, who now has a credit balance of $2,000.00, has a claim against *L* for this amount.

Case 7. This case illustrates the following conditions:

Realization of assets completed before payments are made to partners.
Partnership insolvent and unable to pay its creditors in full.
Some partners have debit balances and others have credit balances after charging off losses on realization. No partners' loans.

It is possible for one or more partners to have credit balances in their capital accounts, even though the partnership is insolvent; but at least one of the partners will, in that case, have a debit balance, and the capital account debit balances will exceed the capital account credit balances. To illustrate, *P*, *Q*, and *R* draw off the following trial balance preparatory to liquidation:

P, capital		$ 3,000.00
Q, capital		8,000.00
R, capital		9,000.00
Liabilities		20,000.00
Assets	$40,000.00	
	$40,000.00	$40,000.00

Profits and losses are shared equally. The assets are sold for $19,000.00. Following is the statement showing the liquidation:

Liquidation Statement

	Liabilities	*P*, Capital	*Q*, Capital	*R*, Capital
Balances before realization	$20,000.00	$3,000.00	$8,000.00	$9,000.00
Loss on realization		7,000.00	7,000.00	7,000.00
Balances after realization	$20,000.00	$4,000.00*	$1,000.00	$2,000.00
Cash payments to creditors	19,000.00			
Final balances	$ 1,000.00	$4,000.00*	$1,000.00	$2,000.00

* Debit balance.

In accordance with the partnership agreement concerning the sharing of profits and losses, *P* should pay in the $4,000.00 debit balance of his account. If he does so, the $4,000.00 will be sufficient to pay the creditors and the other two partners. But the creditors are not bound by the partnership agreement, and may attempt to enforce payment from any partner. Various conditions may therefore develop, some of which are illustrated below.

(1) *P* pays in the $4,000.00 debit balance in his account.

	Liabilities	*P*, Capital	*Q*, Capital	*R*, Capital
Balances—as above	$1,000 Cr.	$4,000 Dr.	$1,000 Cr.	$2,000 Cr.
P pays in		4,000 Cr.		
Final cash payments	1,000 Dr.		1,000 Dr.	2,000 Dr.

(2) The creditors collect $1,000.00 from *P*, and no further collections are received from him.

	Liabilities	*P*, Capital	*Q*, Capital	*R*, Capital
Balances—as above	$1,000 Cr.	$4,000 Dr.	$1,000 Cr.	$2,000 Cr.
P pays creditors	1,000 Dr.	1,000 Cr.		
P's account written off		3,000 Cr.	1,500 Dr.	1,500 Dr.
Balances			$ 500 Dr.	$ 500 Cr.

Q should pay *R* $500.00.

(3) The creditors collect \$1,000.00 from *Q*, and it is impossible to make any collection from *P*.

	Liabilities	*P*, Capital	*Q*, Capital	*R*, Capital
Balances—as above..	\$1,000 Cr.	\$4,000 Dr.	\$1,000 Cr.	\$2,000 Cr.
Q pays creditors.....	1,000 Dr.		1,000 Cr.	
P's account written off............		4,000 Cr.	2,000 Dr.	2,000 Dr.

Case 8. This case illustrates the following conditions:

Realization of assets completed before payments are made to partners.
Partnership insolvent and unable to pay its creditors in full.
One or more partners insolvent.

This case is intended to explain the legal rights of creditors of an insolvent partnership and the rights of creditors of an insolvent partner. The legal rules which apply may be stated as follows:

The creditors of the partnership have a right to be paid in full from the firm assets, before the creditors of the individual partners have any claim against the firm assets.
After the firm creditors have been paid, the creditors of a partner with a credit balance may have recourse against his partnership interest to the extent of such credit balance.
The creditors of a partner have a right to be paid in full from his private assets before the creditors of the firm have any claim against these assets.
After a partner's personal creditors have been paid, the creditors of the partnership have access to the residue of his assets regardless of whether he has a credit or a debit balance, provided the firm creditors have already exhausted the firm assets.

These rules may be summarized as follows:

The partnership assets must be applied first to the payment of partnership debts, and each partner's separate estate must be applied first to the payment of his own creditors.

To illustrate, assume that *A*, *B*, and *C*, sharing profits and losses equally, draw off the following trial balance preparatory to liquidation:

A, capital.............................		\$ 5,000.00
B, capital.............................		14,000.00
C, capital.............................		1,000.00
Liabilities.............................		40,000.00
Assets...................................	\$60,000.00	
	\$60,000.00	\$60,000.00

The assets are sold for $36,000.00. The liquidation statement shows the distribution of the loss, and the partial payment of the partnership creditors, as follows:

Liquidation Statement

	Liabilities	A, Capital	B, Capital	C, Capital
Balances before realization......	$40,000	$5,000	$14,000	$1,000
Loss on realization ($24,000.00)..		8,000	8,000	8,000
Balances after realization.......	$40,000	$3,000*	$ 6,000	$7,000*
Payment of creditors...........	36,000			
Final balances.................	$ 4,000	$3,000*	$ 6,000	$7,000*

* Debit balance.

An investigation of the partners' personal balance sheets discloses the following information:

	Assets	Liabilities
A..................................	$ 1,000.00	$ 1,000.00
B..................................	2,000.00	10,000.00
C..................................	15,000.00	1,000.00

Further rights of partnership creditors. The partnership creditors, who have had all of the firm assets applied to the payment of the firm debts and who still have claims of $4,000.00, cannot make any collections from *A* or *B*, because the private assets of these partners are only sufficient or are insufficient to pay their personal debts. They have a right, however, to collect the entire $4,000.00 from *C*. It is immaterial whether *C*'s capital account shows a debit or a credit balance. The only essential fact is that *C* will have $14,000.00 of assets after paying his private debts. Assuming that the partnership creditors collect the $4,000.00 from *C*, this fact would be shown on the liquidation statement as follows:

	Liabilities	A, Capital	B, Capital	C, Capital
Balances (as above).......	$4,000	$3,000*	$6,000	$7,000*
Payment of liabilities by *C*.	Dr. 4,000			Cr. 4,000
Resulting balances........		$3,000*	$6,000	$3,000*

* Debit balance.

Rights of creditors of A. *A* has $1,000.00 of personal assets and owes $1,000.00 of liabilities to separate creditors. But, after the partnership losses are charged off, *A* has a debit balance of $3,000.00 in his capital account. This means that *A* is obligated to pay $3,000.00 into the firm. This $3,000.00 is not a partnership debt, but is a personal obligation of *A* to make a contribution to the firm; the obligation arose from *A*'s profit and loss sharing agreement with his partners. Unless the $3,000.00 contribution is made by *A*, his partners will bear more than their agreed shares of the loss.

According to bankruptcy law and common-law decisions, *A*'s $1,000.00 of assets should be applied ratably toward the payment of his $3,000.00 debt to the firm and his debts of $1,000.00 to outsiders, as follows:

	Debt	Payment
To the firm	$3,000.00	$ 750.00
To outsiders	1,000.00	250.00
Total	$4,000.00	$1,000.00

However, the rule is different under the Uniform Partnership Law, in force in about half of the states, which provides that:

"Where a partner has become bankrupt or his estate is insolvent the claims against his separate property shall rank in the following order:

I. Those owing to separate creditors.
II. Those owing to partnership creditors.
III. Those owing to partners by way of contribution."

Under this rule, all of *A*'s assets would go to his separate creditors, who would be paid in full, and no contribution would be made by *A* to the partnership, in payment of his $3,000.00 debit balance.

Rights of creditors of B. The creditors of *B*, after receiving his assets of $2,000.00, will have a further claim of $8,000.00. Toward the satisfaction of this claim, *B*'s creditors can attach any interest which he may have in the partnership. The amount and nature of *B*'s interest in the partnership will depend upon whether or not a contribution is received from *A*.

If a $750.00 contribution is received from *A*, the accounts will stand as follows:

Statement of Capitals

	A	*B*	*C*
Balances (See page 26)	$3,000.00*	$6,000.00	$3,000.00*
Contribution from *A*	750.00		
Balances	$2,250.00*	$6,000.00	$3,000.00*
Loss on *A*'s account	2,250.00	1,125.00*	1,125.00*
Balances	—	$4,875.00	$4,125.00*

* Debit.

B has a partnership interest of $4,875.00, represented by the $750.00 of cash on hand, received from *A*, and his $4,125.00 claim against *C*. *B*'s private creditors are entitled to these amounts in payment of *B*'s liabilities to them.

However, if no contribution is received from *A*, the accounts will stand as follows:

Statement of Capitals

	A	*B*	*C*
Balances (See page 26)	$3,000.00*	$6,000.00	$3,000.00*
Loss on *A*'s account	3,000.00	1,500.00*	1,500.00*
Balances	—	$4,500.00	$4,500.00*

* Debit.

B now has a partnership interest of $4,500.00, represented by his claim against *C*. *B*'s private creditors are entitled to a contribution of $4,500.00 from *C*.

Rights of creditors of C. No problems arise with respect to *C*'s liabilities, because his assets are sufficient to meet all of the claims against him.

CHAPTER 33

Partnerships (Concluded)

Liquidation in Installments

Rule for installment payments to partners. In the illustrative cases in the preceding chapter, the assets were all realized before any payments were made to the partners. Hence all possible losses on the realization of the assets were known and could be charged to the partners before any cash payments were made to them.

But partnerships are sometimes liquidated in installments. That is, some of the assets are realized, the liabilities are paid, and the balance of the cash is distributed to the partners. More assets are then realized, and the cash thus obtained is distributed among the partners. This process continues until all of the assets have been realized and the proceeds thereof have been paid to the partners in installments.

When all assets are realized before any payments are made to partners (as in the cases in the preceding chapter), each partner is charged with his entire loss before receiving any money. But when payments are made to partners in installments, they receive money before it is known what losses will be incurred and charged to them. The question then is: How shall the installments be distributed among them? And the answer is: In such a way as to leave them, if possible, with capitals sufficient to bear any possible loss. As all of the remaining non-cash assets may be lost, the rule for installment payments should be: Pay the partners in such a way as to reduce their accounts to their profit and loss ratios of the remaining non-cash assets.

This procedure is illustrated by the following cases.

Case 9. This case illustrates the following conditions:

Payments are made to partners in installments before assets are fully realized.

Each partner's capital is in excess of his share of possible future losses.

A, *B*, *C*, and *D*, sharing profits and losses equally, draw off the following trial balance, preparatory to dissolution:

A, capital		$15,000.00
B, capital		13,000.00
C, capital		12,000.00
D, capital		10,000.00
Liabilities		5,000.00
Assets	$55,000.00	
	$55,000.00	$55,000.00

They sell for $24,000.00 assets carried at $25,000.00, pay the liabilities of $5,000.00, and have $19,000.00 to distribute among the partners. The distribution is shown below:

Statement of Partners' Capitals

	A	*B*	*C*	*D*	Together
Balances before realization	$15,000	$13,000	$12,000	$10,000	$50,000
Loss on realization	250	250	250	250	1,000
Balances	$14,750	$12,750	$11,750	$ 9,750	$49,000
Cash	7,250	5,250	4,250	2,250	19,000
Balances after first distribution	$ 7,500	$ 7,500	$ 7,500	$ 7,500	$30,000

It should be noted that the capital accounts are now reduced to the profit and loss ratio; as the partners share profits and losses equally, the capital accounts are reduced to equality. It was perfectly safe to distribute the cash in the manner shown, because, even if all of the $30,000.00 of non-cash assets are lost, each partner has been left with enough capital to bear his share of the loss.

To compute the amount of cash to give to each partner, it is advisable to prepare working papers (in addition to the statement of capitals) in the following form:

	A	*B*	*C*	*D*	Together
Profit and loss ratio	(25%)	(25%)	(25%)	(25%)	
Total of capitals after loss					$49,000
Cash for division					19,000
Possible loss—in P & L ratio	$7,500	$7,500	$7,500	$7,500	$30,000

These possible losses are then entered in the capital statement in the following manner, before the cash distribution is entered:

Statement of Partners' Capitals

	A	*B*	*C*	*D*	Together
Balances before realization	$15,000	$13,000	$12,000	$10,000	$50,000
Loss on realization	250	250	250	250	1,000
Balances	$14,750	$12,750	$11,750	$ 9,750	$49,000
Cash					19,000
Balances after first distribution	$ 7,500	$ 7,500	$ 7,500	$ 7,500	$30,000

The cash distribution is then entered, each partner receiving enough to reduce his account to the "balance after first distribution."

Each succeeding distribution should be made in such a manner as to leave the partners' balances in their profit and loss ratio. To illustrate, suppose that two more installments are paid in completing the liquidation, as follows:

Second installment:	
Assets realized—book value	$20,000.00
Loss on realization	2,000.00
Cash for division	$18,000.00
Third installment:	
Assets realized—book value	$10,000.00
Loss on realization	4,000.00
Cash for division	$ 6,000.00

The complete statement of the partners' capitals appears below:

Statement of Partners' Capitals

	A	B	C	D	Together
Balances before realization	$15,000	$13,000	$12,000	$10,000	$50,000
Loss on realization	250	250	250	250	1,000
Balances	$14,750	$12,750	$11,750	$ 9,750	$49,000
Cash—first distribution	7,250	5,250	4,250	2,250	19,000
Balances	$ 7,500	$ 7,500	$ 7,500	$ 7,500	$30,000
Loss on realization	500	500	500	500	2,000
Balances	$ 7,000	$ 7,000	$ 7,000	$ 7,000	$28,000
Cash—second distribution	4,500	4,500	4,500	4,500	18,000
Balances	$ 2,500	$ 2,500	$ 2,500	$ 2,500	$10,000
Loss on realization	1,000	1,000	1,000	1,000	4,000
Balances	$ 1,500	$ 1,500	$ 1,500	$ 1,500	$ 6,000
Cash—third distribution	1,500	1,500	1,500	1,500	6,000

No partner is defrauded in any way by this method of paying in installments. This fact may be shown by assuming that no payments had been made until after the realization was completed. The total loss and the total cash available for distribution would have been:

	Loss	Cash for Partners
First period	$1,000.00	$19,000.00
Second period	2,000.00	18,000.00
Third period	4,000.00	6,000.00
Totals	$7,000.00	$43,000.00

The distribution of the loss and of the total available cash would have been shown in the statement of capitals as follows:

Statement of Partners' Capitals

	A	B	C	D	Together
Balances before realization	$15,000	$13,000	$12,000	$10,000	$50,000
Loss on realization	1,750	1,750	1,750	1,750	7,000
Cash distribution	$13,250	$11,250	$10,250	$ 8,250	$43,000

By the installment method, the partners have been charged with exactly these losses and have been paid these amounts of cash, as shown below:

Losses Charged to Partners

	A	*B*	*C*	*D*	Together
First realization.	$ 250.00	$ 250.00	$ 250.00	$ 250.00	$1,000.00
Second realization.........	500.00	500.00	500.00	500.00	2,000.00
Third realization	1,000.00	1,000.00	1,000.00	1,000.00	4,000.00
Totals (as above).....	$1,750.00	$1,750.00	$1,750.00	$1,750.00	$7,000.00

Cash Distributed to Partners

	A	*B*	*C*	*D*	Together
First distribution...........	$ 7,250	$ 5,250	$ 4,250	$2,250	$19,000
Second distribution.........	4,500	4,500	4,500	4,500	18,000
Third distribution..........	1,500	1,500	1,500	1,500	6,000
Totals (as above)........	$13,250	$11,250	$10,250	$8,250	$43,000

Wrong method. The preceding illustration shows that no injustice is done by taking the precaution of making cash distributions in such a manner as to reduce the partners' accounts to the profit and loss ratio of the remaining assets. To show what danger is incurred by failing to take this precaution, let us take another case and assume that the first distribution is made in the ratio of the capitals after the realization loss has been charged off.

A, *B*, *C*, and *D* were partners sharing profits in the ratio of 40%, 25%, 25%, and 10% respectively. The following trial balance was drawn off in preparation for liquidation:

A, capital..........................		$24,000.00
B, capital..........................		27,500.00
C, capital..........................		22,500.00
D, capital..........................		16,000.00
Assets..........................	$90,000.00	
	$90,000.00	$90,000.00

Assets having a book value of $50,000.00 were sold for $40,000.00. The liquidator unwisely distributed the $40,000.00 in the ratio of the capitals after charging off the $10,000.00 loss. The statement of capitals, after the first distribution was made, appeared as follows:

Statement of Partners' Capitals

	A	*B*	*C*	*D*	Together
Balances before realization.	$24,000	$27,500	$22,500	$16,000	$90,000
Loss on realization........	4,000	2,500	2,500	1,000	10,000
Balances..................	$20,000	$25,000	$20,000	$15,000	$80,000
Cash—in ratio of capitals..	10,000	12,500	10,000	7,500	40,000
Resulting balances........	$10,000	$12,500	$10,000	$ 7,500	$40,000

In distributing the $40,000.00, the liquidator used the capital ratio after dividing the $10,000.00 loss, and paid each partner one half of the balance at his credit. The unwisdom of this procedure became evident when it was found that only $10,000.00 could be realized from the remaining assets. The liquidator then continued his statement, showing the distribution of the realization loss among the partners, as follows:

Statement of Partners' Capitals—(*Continued*)

	A	*B*	*C*	*D*	Together
Balances—as above	$10,000	$12,500	$10,000	$7,500	$40,000
Loss on realization	12,000	7,500	7,500	3,000	30,000
Balances	$ 2,000*	$ 5,000	$ 2,500	$4,500	$10,000

* Debit balance.

At this point *A*'s account had a debit balance of $2,000.00, and it was necessary to collect this $2,000.00 from *A* in order to pay the other three partners in full. But the liquidator was unable to collect the $2,000.00, and *B*, *C*, and *D* could hold the liquidator liable for causing them this loss by paying $10,000.00 to *A* instead of holding enough of a balance in *A*'s account to cover all possible loss on realization.

The liquidator should have safeguarded his own and the partners' interests by making the distribution as follows:

Statement of Partners' Capitals

	A	*B*	*C*	*D*	Together
Balances before realization	$24,000	$27,500	$22,500	$16,000	$90,000
Loss on realization	4,000	2,500	2,500	1,000	10,000
Balances after realization	$20,000	$25,000	$20,000	$15,000	$80,000
Cash	4,000	15,000	10,000	11,000	40,000
Balances in P & L ratio	$16,000	$10,000	$10,000	$ 4,000	$40,000

Each partner would thus have been left with enough capital to absorb his share of the loss, even if the entire $40,000.00 of non-cash assets had been lost. Assuming, as above, a final realization of $10,000.00 and a loss of $30,000.00, the final realization and distribution to the partners would be as indicated in the following statement:

Statement of Partners' Capitals—(*Continued*)

	A	*B*	*C*	*D*	Together
Balances—as above	$16,000	$10,000	$10,000	$4,000	$40,000
Loss on realization	12,000	7,500	7,500	3,000	30,000
Balances	$ 4,000	$ 2,500	$ 2,500	$1,000	$10,000
Cash	4,000	2,500	2,500	1,000	10,000

Case 10. This case illustrates the following conditions:

Payments are made to partners in installments before assets are fully realized.

One partner's capital is less than his possible future loss.

If any partner's capital, before a cash distribution is made, is less than his possible loss on the assets which will remain after the distribution, it is unwise to pay him anything.

In such instances the distribution of cash installments should be made as follows:

The partner with a capital smaller than his share of a total loss should be paid nothing.

The other partners should be left with capital balances sufficient to absorb:

(1) Their own shares of a total possible loss on the realization of the assets.

(2) Their shares of the loss which might result from a partner's failure to pay in a debit balance.

To illustrate, assume that four partners have capitals and share profits as follows:

Partner	Capitals	P & L Ratio
A	$20,000.00	25%
B	40,000.00	20%
C	50,000.00	25%
D	60,000.00	30%

All liabilities have been paid. The partnership is dissolved, and the process of realization and liquidation extends over five months, as follows:

	Assets Realized	Loss	Cash to Partners
First month	$50,000.00	$10,000.00	$40,000.00
Second month	40,000.00	2,000.00	38,000.00
Third month	30,000.00	4,000.00	26,000.00
Fourth month	35,000.00	5,000.00	30,000.00
Fifth month	15,000.00	6,000.00	9,000.00

The monthly cash distributions are computed as follows:

(1) Charge off the loss on realization, and show in the statement of capitals the balance at each partner's credit after dividing the loss.

(2) On working papers, set down the total capitals before distributing the cash; deduct the cash on hand for distribution; and thus compute the remaining non-cash assets, or total possible loss.

(3) Indicate on the working papers the loss which would be charged to each partner in case of a total loss.

(4) Compare each partner's capital before distributing the cash (per the statement of capitals) with his possible loss (per the working papers).

(5) If any partner's capital is less than his possible loss, indicate on the working papers how this debit balance would be charged to the other partners in case of a total loss and in case of the partner's inability to pay the debit balance.

(6) Add the possible losses shown in (3) and (5), and thus ascertain the total loss each partner may be called upon to bear for himself and for an insolvent partner with a debit balance.

(7) Enter these amounts in the statement of capitals, and pay the partners down to these balances.

If this method is applied to the present case, the partners will be charged with monthly losses and payments as indicated in the following statement:

Statement of Partners' Capitals

	A	*B*	*C*	*D*	Together
Original balances...	$20,000.00	$40,000.00	$50,000.00	$60,000.00	$170,000.00
First month:					
Loss............	2,500.00	2,000.00	2,500.00	3,000.00	10,000.00
Balances.........	$17,500.00	$38,000.00	$47,500.00	$57,000.00	$160,000.00
Cash (see working papers)........		10,666.67	13,333.33	16,000.00	40,000.00
Balances.........	$17,500.00	$27,333.33	$34,166.67	$41,000.00	$120,000.00
Second month:					
Loss............	500.00	400.00	500.00	600.00	2,000.00
Balances.........	$17,000.00	$26,933.33	$33,666.67	$40,400.00	$118,000.00
Cash (see working papers)........		10,133.33	12,666.67	15,200.00	38,000.00
Balances.........	$17,000.00	$16,800.00	$21,000.00	$25,200.00	$ 80,000.00
Third month:					
Loss............	1,000.00	800.00	1,000.00	1,200.00	4,000.00
Balances.........	$16,000.00	$16,000.00	$20,000.00	$24,000.00	$ 76,000.00
Cash (see working papers)........	3,500.00	6,000.00	7,500.00	9,000.00	26,000.00
Balances.........	$12,500.00	$10,000.00	$12,500.00	$15,000.00	$ 50,000.00
Fourth month:					
Loss............	1,250.00	1,000.00	1,250.00	1,500.00	5,000.00
Balances.........	$11,250.00	$ 9,000.00	$11,250.00	$13,500.00	$ 45,000.00
Cash............	7,500.00	6,000.00	7,500.00	9,000.00	30,000.00
Balances.........	$ 3,750.00	$ 3,000.00	$ 3,750.00	$ 4,500.00	$ 15,000.00
Fifth month:					
Loss............	1,500.00	1,200.00	1,500.00	1,800.00	6,000.00
Balances.........	$ 2,250.00	$ 1,800.00	$ 2,250.00	$ 2,700.00	$ 9,000.00
Cash............	2,250.00	1,800.00	2,250.00	2,700.00	9,000.00

As each partner's capital, after the third month's loss is charged off, exceeds his possible future loss, all partners can be paid, and the partners' capitals can be reduced to the profit and loss ratio. The distributions of the fourth and fifth months are then made in the profit and loss ratio, because that is also the capital ratio.

Working Papers—First Month

	A	*B*	*C*	*D*	Together
Profit and loss ratio	(25%)	(20%)	(25%)	(30%)	
Total capitals before distributing cash					$160,000
Less cash for distribution					40,000
Possible loss—P & L ratio	$30,000	$24,000.00	$30,000.00	$36,000	$120,000
Capital smaller than possible loss	17,500				
Additional possible loss to the other three partners	$12,500				
B—20/75 of $12,500.00		3,333.33			
C—25/75 of 12,500.00			4,166.67		
D—30/75 of 12,500.00				5,000	
Total possible losses, or balances to which partners are paid		$27,333.33	$34,166.67	$41,000	

Working Papers—Second Month

	A	*B*	*C*	*D*	Together
Total capitals before distributing cash					$118,000
Less cash for distribution					38,000
Possible loss—in P & L ratio	$20,000	$16,000	$20,000	$24,000	$ 80,000
Capital smaller than possible loss	17,000				
Additional possible loss to the other three partners	$ 3,000				
B—20/75 of $3,000.00		800			
C—25/75 of 3,000.00			1,000		
D—30/75 of 3,000.00				1,200	
Total possible losses, or balances to which partners are paid		$16,800	$21,000	$25,200	

Working Papers—Third Month

	A	*B*	*C*	*D*	Together
Total capitals before distributing cash					$76,000
Less cash for distribution					26,000
Possible loss—in P & L ratio	$12,500	$10,000	$12,500	$15,000	$50,000

Case 11. This case illustrates the following conditions:

Payments are made to partners in installments before assets are fully realized.

Two partners' capitals are less than their possible future losses.

This illustration involves no new principles. It merely shows how the safeguard principle is applied when two partners have capitals which are less than their shares of a possible future loss. Since no new principle is involved, the illustration is limited to the distribution of the first installment.

Given the following facts:

	A	B	C	D
Capitals before realization..	$40,000	$60,000	$70,000	$30,000
Profit and loss ratio.......	30%	20%	40%	10%
All liabilities paid.				
Book value of assets sold the first month..........				$30,000
Loss on realization........				6,000
Cash for distribution.....				$24,000

Required: a statement of the partners' capitals showing the distribution of the $24,000.00, and working papers showing the computation of the amounts paid to each partner.

Statement of Partners' Capitals

	A	B	C	D	Together
Capitals before realization.	$40,000	$60,000	$70,000	$30,000	$200,000
Loss on realization......	1,800	1,200	2,400	600	6,000
Balances after realization.	$38,200	$58,800	$67,600	$29,400	$194,000
Cash distributed.........		16,000		8,000	24,000
Balances after distribution	$38,200	$42,800	$67,600	$21,400	$170,000

Working Papers—First Month

	A	B	C	D	Together
Profit and loss ratio	(30%)	(20%)	(40%)	(10%)	
Total capitals before distributing cash.........					$194,000
Less cash for distribution.					24,000
Possible loss—in P & L ratio	$51,000	$34,000	$68,000	$17,000	$170,000
Capitals smaller than possible loss.............	38,200		67,600		
Additional possible loss to B & D...........	$12,800		$ 400		$ 13,200
B—20/30 of $13,200.00		8,800			
D—10/30 of 13,200.00				4,400	
Total possible losses, and balances to which partners are paid....		$42,800		$21,400	

Case 12. This case illustrates the following conditions:

Payments are made to partners in installments before assets are fully realized.

One partner has a capital less than his possible future loss.

Another partner has a capital sufficient to bear his own share of the possible future loss, but insufficient to bear also the charge if the first partner's account is thrown into a debit balance and written off.

Given the following facts:

	A	B	C	D	
Capitals	$20,000	$29,000	$36,000	$15,000	
Profit and loss ratio	30%	20%	40%	10%	
All liabilities paid.					
Book value of assets realized first month					$15,000
Loss on realization					3,000
Cash for distribution					$12,000

Required: a statement of the capitals showing the distribution of the $12,000.00, and working papers showing the computation of the amounts paid to the partners.

Working Papers—First Month

	A	B	C	D	Together
Profit and loss ratio	(30%)	(20%)	(40%)	(10%)	
Total capitals before distributing cash					$97,000
Less cash for distribution					12,000
Possible loss—in P & L ratio	$25,500	$17,000.00	$34,000.00	$ 8,500.00	$85,000
Capital smaller than possible loss	19,100				
Additional possible loss to *B*, *C*, and *D*	$ 6,400				
B—2/7 of $6,400.00		1,828.57			
C—4/7 of 6,400.00			3,657.14		
D—1/7 of 6,400.00				914.29	
Totals		$18,828.57	$37,657.14	$ 9,414.29	
Capital smaller than possible loss			34,800.00		
Additional possible loss to *B* and *D*			$ 2,857.14		
B—2/3 of $2,857.14		1,904.76			
D—1/3 of 2,857.14				952.38	
Total possible loss, and balances to which partners are paid		$20,733.33		$10,366.67	

Statement of Partners' Capitals

	A	B	C	D	Together
Capitals before realization	$20,000	$29,000.00	$36,000	$15,000.00	$100,000
Loss on realization	900	600.00	1,200	300.00	3,000
Balances after realization	$19,100	$28,400.00	$34,800	$14,700.00	$ 97,000
Cash		7,666.67		4,333.33	12,000
Balances after distribution	$19,100	$20,733.33	$34,800	$10,366.67	$ 85,000

Payment of partners' loans in installment liquidation. No cases have yet been considered in which partners have loan accounts as well as capital accounts, and in which liquidation is made in installments. In such instances the rule that partners' loans are to be paid before their capitals does not necessarily govern. The liquidator should consider the possible future loss, and remember that, by the right of offset, losses may be charged against a partner's loan account if his capital is not sufficient to cover his share of the loss. Hence the total possible future loss of each partner should be compared with the sum of his capital and loan account balances. One partner with a capital and no loan may receive a payment if his capital exceeds his possible loss; whereas another partner with a capital and a loan may receive nothing, because the sum of his capital and loan is insufficient to cover his possible loss.

If the liquidator proposes thus to make a payment on a partner's capital before making a payment on the loan account of another partner, the partner with the loan account may object on the basis of the general rule that partners' loans should be paid before distributions are made on capital accounts. In such an event the liquidator should explain that the proposed basis is the only one by which he can make any immediate payment without running the risk of causing one, or possibly more, of the partners to bear more than a proper share of the loss.

Case 13. This case illustrates the following conditions:

Payments are made to partners in installments before assets are fully realized.
Certain partners have loan accounts.
Each partner's capital is sufficient to absorb his possible future loss.

Four partners, sharing profits and losses equally, draw off the following trial balance preparatory to liquidation:

A, capital		$18,000.00
B, capital		16,000.00
C, capital		15,000.00
D, capital		15,000.00
C, loan		3,000.00
D, loan		5,000.00
Assets	$72,000.00	
	$72,000.00	$72,000.00

Assets having a book value of $22,000.00 are sold for $20,000.00. After the loss is divided, the capitals are:

A	$17,500.00
B	15,500.00
C	14,500.00
D	14,500.00

The non-cash assets amount to $50,000.00, and a total loss of these assets would result in a charge of $12,500.00 to each partner. As each partner has a capital account balance in excess of his possible loss, the loans can be paid in full, and payments can be made on the capitals, reducing them to $12,500.00 each.

Case 14. This case illustrates the following conditions:

Payments are made to partners in installments before assets are fully realized.

Certain partners have loans.

One partner's total capital and loan is less than his possible future loss.

The trial balance before liquidation is:

A, capital		$25,000.00
B, capital		15,000.00
C, capital		5,000.00
B, loan		3,000.00
C, loan		7,000.00
Assets	$55,000.00	
	$55,000.00	$55,000.00

Profits and losses are shared equally. Assets having a book value of $13,000.00 are sold for $10,000.00.

Although the cash on hand is exactly equal to the partners' loans of $10,000.00, the problem cannot be dismissed by the statement that partners' loans should be paid before the capitals, and that the entire $10,000.00 should therefore be used for the payment of the loans from *B* and *C*. It is necessary to determine the possible future loss, and pay only those partners who have capitals and loans in excess of their possible losses.

Working Papers

	A	*B*	*C*	Together
Profit and loss ratio	(⅓)	(⅓)	(⅓)	
Capitals—per trial balance	$25,000	$15,000	$ 5,000	$45,000
Loss on realization	1,000	1,000	1,000	3,000
Capitals after realization	$24,000	$14,000	$ 4,000	$42,000
Loans		3,000	7,000	10,000
Total capitals and loans	$24,000	$17,000	$11,000	$52,000
Cash for distribution				10,000
Possible loss—in P & L ratio	$14,000	$14,000	$14,000	$42,000
Capital and loan smaller than possible loss			11,000	
Additional possible loss to *A* and *B*.			$ 3,000	
A—½ of $3,000.00	1,500			
B—½ of 3,000.00		1,500		
Total	$15,500	$15,500		

These working papers show that *C* cannot safely be paid anything, because his loan and capital balances together amount to only $11,000.00, whereas he is in danger of being charged with a loss of $14,000.00. *A* and *B* can be paid amounts which will leave each with a capital (or total capital and loan) of $15,500.00. The cash should be distributed as follows:

	Balances After Charging off Loss	Cash Distributed	Balances After Distribution
A—Capital	$24,000.00	$ 8,500.00	$15,500.00
B—Capital	14,000.00	—	14,000.00
Loan	3,000.00	1,500.00	1,500.00
C—Capital	4,000.00	—	4,000.00
Loan	7,000.00	—	7,000.00
		$10,000.00	

Unpaid liabilities. If payments are made to partners in installments before the creditors are paid, the liquidator runs the risk of finding himself in a position where he cannot pay the creditors in full because of his inability to realize on the assets. He may be able to recover some of the payments made to the partners, and thus pay the creditors; but if he is unable to do this, he will be personally liable to the creditors. To avoid placing himself in such a position, the liquidator should either refuse to make payments to the partners until all creditors have been paid, or he should withhold sufficient cash to provide a fund with which the creditors can be paid in full, and should distribute only the remaining cash to the partners.

CHAPTER 34

Consignments

Definitions. A consignment is a transfer of possession of merchandise from the owner, called the *consignor*, to another party, called the *consignee*, who becomes the agent of the owner for the purpose of selling the goods. A consignment is a bailment, and the relation between the consignor and the consignee is one of bailment and agency; therefore, a consignment is governed by the laws of bailments and agencies.

From the standpoint of the consignor, a consignment is a consignment out; from the standpoint of the consignee it is a consignment in. A consignment out is sometimes referred to merely as a *shipment*, and a consignment in is sometimes referred to merely as a *consignment*. The use of the terms *shipment* and *consignment* with these special meanings is not general, nor is it to be recommended, because these terms are not self-explanatory and because the word *consignment* is thus given both a general meaning, denoting all consignments, and a special meaning, denoting only consignments in. The terms *consignment out* and *consignment in* are preferable.

Sale and consignment distinguished. The fundamental distinction between a sale and a consignment is this: In a sale the title to the goods passes from the seller to the buyer, whereas in a consignment the title to unsold goods remains with the consignor. This distinction must be borne in mind for three reasons.

First, since a consignment is not a sale, no profit results from the transaction, and none should be taken up until the goods have been sold by the consignee.

Second, since the title to the goods remains with the consignor, any goods out on consignment must be included in the consignor's inventory when his books are closed.

Finally, if the consignee becomes insolvent, the consignor can recover his goods, whereas if a sale was made instead of a consignment, the seller would have to take his place with the other creditors and accept a pro-rata settlement.

Reasons for consignments. The consignor may make a consignment instead of a sale for the following reasons:

(1) For credit purposes. There is less risk in a consignment than in a sale since the consignor retains title to the goods

until the consignee sells them. When a sale of the consigned goods is made, the consignee does not become a general debtor of the consignor; he must keep the proceeds of the sale separate as a trust fund, and must remit to the consignor according to the consignment agreement.

(2) To introduce a commodity. When the demand for the merchandise is so meager or uncertain that retailers hesitate to purchase, the consignment enables the owner to place his goods before the public.

(3) Sending out goods to consignees in various locations is an effective way of making market surveys in new territories.

(4) To control the selling price to the consumer.

From the consignee's standpoint, consignments may be preferable to purchases for the following reasons:

(1) Because of market fluctuations. When, as in the case of produce, market prices are subject to sudden, frequent, and considerable fluctuations, there is too much hazard in buying at quotations sent out several days before the goods are received and in selling at market prices prevailing after the goods have been received. The consignment method avoids this risk, because the consignee merely acts as the agent of the consignor, selling the goods at the market price and taking his compensation in commissions.

(2) Because of the danger of tying up capital in unsalable goods. A merchant may feel that the demand for a commodity is too uncertain to warrant purchasing it, although he may be willing to take the goods on consignment, paying for them only after they have been sold.

Consignment transactions are not as common as they formerly were. This decrease in consignment operations is due partly to the fact that the markets are more highly developed and retailers are more disposed to control their operation through purchases. Also, in recent years there has grown up a tendency to make sales with return privileges. Sometimes the purchaser is entitled to make unqualified return and receive a payment in cash; in other cases he is permitted to return the merchandise and obtain a credit against which subsequent purchases can be charged.

Also with the development of large-scale business operations, the extending of the market is more frequently accomplished by the establishment of sales agencies or branches.

Rights of the consignee. The principal rights of the consignee are:

(1) The right to be reimbursed for advances and expenses. In some instances, particularly where commission merchants handle grain, it is customary for the consignee to make advances to the consignor before the produce is sold. And in nearly all consignments, the consignee usually pays some expenses, cartage if nothing more. The consignee has a right to be reimbursed for these advances and expenses; in fact, he has a lien on the merchandise to the extent of the advances and the expenses, and he can sell the goods to satisfy the lien. He loses the lien on the goods when he parts with possession of them, but he has a lien on the proceeds of the sale.

(2) The right to compensation. Commission merchants usually take, as compensation, a percentage of the gross sales price. Merchants selling manufactured goods or other merchandise taken on consignment, may receive a commission computed on a percentage basis, or they may retain the amount by which the sale price exceeds a figure stated by the consignor.

(3) Right to warrant. The consignee, in making sales, has authority to make the usual, but not extraordinary, warranties, and the consignor will be bound by such warranties.

(4) Right to extend credit. If the extending of credit is a custom of the business, and if the consignor has not expressly restrained the consignee from extending credit, the consignee has a right to sell goods on account. The account thus created is the property of the consignor, and any loss on the collection of the account must be borne by the consignor. The consignee may, by special agreement, guarantee the accounts; if he makes such a guarantee, he is known as a "*del credere* agent" and is entitled to an extra compensation for the guarantee.

Duties of the consignee. The principal duties of the consignee are:

(1) To care for the consignor's property. It is sometimes said that the consignee must take as good care of the consignor's property as he takes of his own. This is not a good statement of the rule, since the consignee may not take reasonable care of his own goods. The consignee must give the consignor's property such care as an ordi-

narily prudent man would give them. Having done this, he is not liable for damages to the goods.

(2) To exercise prudence in granting credit and diligence in making collections. This is merely one requirement of the general rule that the consignee, in fulfilling the duties of his agency, must exercise ordinary prudence and diligence.

(3) To keep the consignor's property separate from his own. This duty may be discussed under two headings. First, the consignee must keep the merchandise separate from his own in order that it can be identified as the property of the consignor. This does not mean that there must be actual physical separation, but there must at least be records sufficient to show what property in the consignee's possession belongs to the consignor. Second, if the consignee sells goods on account, he must keep his records in such a way as to make a distinction between his own accounts receivable and accounts receivable originating from sales of consigned goods and thus belonging to the consignor.

(4) To make reports of and settlements for sales in accordance with the terms of the consignments. These terms may require settlement after the sale of the entire consignment, settlement after certain portions of the consignment have been sold, or settlements at stated intervals.

The report of the consignee is called an *account sales,* and is made in a form similar to the one following:

Account Sales

Of Shipment of 5 washing machines
Received from C. D. Jones & Co., Chicago, to be sold for his account and risk.

Rendered by Weston Co., Elgin, Illinois.

We have sold for your account 5 washing machines @ $125.00		$625.00
We deduct charges as follows:		
Freight	$ 15.00	
Drayage	3.00	
Commission—25% of $625.00	156.25	174.25
We enclose check for net proceeds		$450.75

Consignor's records. The entries to be made by a consignor will depend upon conditions which may be outlined as follows:

Profits on consignments are:
Kept separate from profits on regular sales;
Not kept separate from profits on regular sales.

The merchandising accounts are kept on:

A perpetual inventory basis;

A periodical inventory basis.

Regardless of these various conditions, the consignor will have an account with each consignment. These accounts may be kept in the general ledger, or there may be a controlling account in the general ledger and individual accounts in a subsidiary consignment ledger. The consignment accounts should not be kept in the accounts receivable ledger because consignees are not ordinary trade debtors.

Entries illustrating accounting procedures applicable to the four varying conditions mentioned above are given on pages 48, 49, and 50. The assumed facts are as follows:

C. D. Jones & Co. of Chicago consigned five washing machines to Weston Co. of Elgin, Illinois. The machines cost the consignor $60.00 each.

The drayage to the freight depot in Chicago, paid by the consignor, was $5.00.

Packing costs were estimated to be $6.00; the consignor charges all such costs to a packing expense account; the $6.00 regarded as applicable to this consignment is merely a portion of the total of such expenses.

The consignee remitted $450.75 as the proceeds of the consignment. (See account sales, page 46.)

Consignment out account. Although a consignment out account is kept in each of the methods illustrated, there is some difference in the nature of the accounts as used in the different methods. The nature of the account as used in each method is indicated below:

Consignment profits kept separate:

Perpetual inventory basis:

Periodical inventory basis:

On both bases the consignment out account is similar to an old fashioned merchandise account: It is charged with all costs and is credited with the proceeds of sales, and its balance, after all goods are sold, is the profit on the consignment.

Consignment profits not kept separate:

Perpetual inventory basis:

The account is essentially a perpetual inventory account showing the cost of goods on consignment.

Periodical inventory basis:

The account is merely one of the two offsetting memorandum accounts showing the cost of goods on consignment.

CONSIGNMENT PROFITS KEPT SEPARATE FROM PROFITS ON REGULAR SALES

Perpetual Inventory Basis			Periodical Inventory Basis		
Shipment:					
Consignment out—Weston Co	$300.00		Consignment out—Weston Co	$300.00	
Inventory		$300.00	Consignment shipments		$300.00
(This entry sets up the consignment asset account by direct transfer from the perpetual inventory controlling account.)			(This entry sets up the consignment asset account. The consignment shipments account will be closed at the end of the period in the manner shown below.)		
Cartage:					
Consignment out—Weston Co	5.00		Consignment out—Weston Co	5.00	
Cash		5.00	Cash		5.00
Packing expense:					
Consignment out—Weston Co	6.00		Consignment out—Weston Co	6.00	
Packing expense		6.00	Packing expense		6.00
Sales and proceeds:					
Cash	450.75		Cash	450.75	
Consignment out—Weston Co		450.75	Consignment out—Weston Co		450.75

(If the consignee reported a sale without remitting the proceeds, the debit would be to Weston Co.—consignee instead of to cash. If the sale was made for cash or on credit guaranteed by the consignee, it might be desirable to keep the consignee's account in the general ledger rather than in the subsidiary accounts receivable ledger, in order to indicate the peculiar status of the balance. If the sale was made on credit without guarantee, the account should be kept in the subsidiary ledger, because its balance represents the amount receivable from the purchaser of the goods, who is an ordinary debtor. The consignor may set up an account receivable in the name of the purchaser, rather than in the name of the consignee.)

Profit:

Perpetual Inventory Basis			Periodical Inventory Basis		
Consignment out—Weston Co.	139.75		Consignment out—Weston Co.	139.75	
Consignment profits		139.75	Consignment profits		139.75

(This entry, taking up the profit on the consignment, should be made when the account sales is received. Profits and losses on consignments will be accumulated in the consignment profits account until the end of the period, when the account will be closed to the profit and loss account.

Closing consignment shipments account:

Perpetual Inventory Basis			Periodical Inventory Basis		
			Consignment shipments	300.00	
			Cost of sales		300.00

(To determine the cost of goods sold on regular sales, cost of sales will be charged at the end of the period with the opening inventory and purchases—or cost of goods manufactured—and credited with the closing inventory. Cost of sales should also be credited with the cost of goods consigned, because these goods are not available for regular sales.)

CONSIGNMENT PROFITS NOT KEPT SEPARATE FROM PROFITS ON REGULAR SALES

Perpetual Inventory Basis	Dr.	Cr.	Periodical Inventory Basis	Dr.	Cr.
Shipment:					
Consignment out—Weston Co.	$300.00		Consignment out—Weston Co.	$300.00	
Inventory		$300.00	Consignment shipments		$300.00
(To set up the consignment asset account by direct transfer from the perpetual inventory controlling account.)			(This is purely a memorandum entry to be reversed when the goods are sold. See reversal entry below.)		
Cartage:					
Freight and cartage out	5.00		Freight and cartage out	5.00	
Cash		5.00	Cash		5.00

Packing expense:

No entry is required. The packing expense account already has been charged with the total expense of this nature, and, since profits on consignments are not to be shown separately, there is no need to set out as a separate item the portion of this expense which is applicable to the consignment.

Perpetual Inventory Basis	Dr.	Cr.	Periodical Inventory Basis	Dr.	Cr.
Sale and proceeds:					
Cash	450.75		Cash	450.75	
Sales		450.75	Sales		450.75
Cost of sales	300.00				
Consignment out—Weston Co.		300.00			
(To transfer the cost of goods on consignment to the general cost of sales account.)					

No entry is made for the profit at the time the account sales is received; the profit on consignments will never be determined separately from the profit on regular sales. The total of these profits will be determined at the end of the period when the sales, cost of sales, and expense accounts are closed.

Perpetual Inventory Basis	Dr.	Cr.	Periodical Inventory Basis	Dr.	Cr.
Reversal of memorandum entry for shipment:					
			Consignment shipments	300.00	
			Consignment out—Weston Co.		300.00
			(Since the goods have been sold, the memorandum record is no longer required.)		

Alternative entries for proceeds. When an account sales is received from the consignor, an entry may be made for the net proceeds only (as in the foregoing illustrations) or the entry may show the gross amount of the sale and the deductions made by the consignee. The alternative procedures are shown below:

(1) Consignment profits kept separate:

(*a*) Entry for net proceeds only:

Cash	$450.75	
Consignment out—Weston Co.		$450.75

Consignment Out—Weston Co.

5 washing machines	$300.00	Net proceeds	$450.75
Drayage	5.00		
Packing	6.00		
Consignment profits	139.75		
	$450.75		$450.75

(*b*) Entry for gross proceeds and expenses:

Cash	$450.75	
Consignment out—Weston Co.:		
Freight	15.00	
Drayage	3.00	
Commission	156.25	
Consignment out—Weston Co.		$625.00

Consignment Out—Weston Co.

5 washing machines	$300.00	Selling price	$625.00
Drayage	5.00		
Packing	6.00		
Freight	15.00		
Drayage	3.00		
Commission	156.25		
Consignment profits	139.75		
	$625.00		$625.00

(2) Consignment profits not kept separate:

(*a*) Entry for net proceeds only:

Cash	$450.75	
Sales		$450.75

(*b*) Entry for gross proceeds and expenses:

Cash	450.75	
Freight and cartage out	18.00	
Commission	156.25	
Sales		625.00

When recording the proceeds of sales by the consignee, it is preferable to follow the method of showing the gross sale price and the consignee's expenses, because of the additional information thus furnished by the accounts.

Consignor's inventory. If any goods sent out on consignment are unsold when the consignor closes his books, they should be included in the consignor's inventory. The inventory value should include the cost of the goods plus any expenses incurred which are applicable to the unsold goods.

If the accounts are kept in a manner to show profits on consignments separately (on either the perpetual or periodical inventory basis), the balance of the consignment out controlling account (or the sum of the balances of the individual accounts) will represent the inventory of consigned goods, because the consignment out account will have been charged with the cost of the goods and with applicable expenses. The balance of the account will therefore appear in the balance sheet as part of the inventory.

If profits on consignments are not kept separate from profits on regular sales, the consignment out account will be charged with only the cost of the goods on consignment, and expenses will be charged to the various expense accounts. It is advisable to make memorandum notations of expenses short in the consignment out accounts at the same time that the expense accounts are charged; reference to the unclosed consignment out accounts will then show the cost of unsold goods and the expenses applicable to these goods. When the expense accounts are closed, the portions applicable to goods on consignment can be transferred to an account called "deferred consignment expense" and included in the balance sheet valuation of the consigned goods inventory.

If the goods on consignment are a relatively small portion of the total inventory, the balance sheet need not show the consigned inventory separately. If it seems important to give details, they may be presented as follows:

Inventory:			
On hand		$10,000.00	
On consignment:			
Cost	$5,000.00		
Expenses	600.00	5,600.00	$15,000.00

Partial sales. If the consignee renders an account sales after selling a portion of the consignment, he has a right to deduct from the proceeds of the first sale all expenses incurred on the entire consignment. But the consignor, when recording the settlement, may properly carry forward as an element of the consigned goods inventory the expenses which are applicable to the unsold goods.

To illustrate, assume that Weston Co. sold one washing machine and rendered an account sales as follows:

We have sold for your account: 1 washing machine		$125.00
We deduct expenses as follows:		
Freight	$15.00	
Drayage	3.00	
Commission—25%	31.25	49.25
We enclose check for net proceeds		$ 75.75

If consignment profits are kept separate from profits on regular sales, the consignment out account, prior to recording the account sales, will be as follows:

Consignment Out—Weston Co.

Cost of 5 washing machines	$300.00		
Drayage	5.00		
Packing	6.00		

The entries to record the account sales are:

Cash	$75.75	
Consignment out—Weston Co.:		
Freight	15.00	
Drayage	3.00	
Commission	31.25	
Consignment out—Weston Co		$125.00
To record the account sales.		
Consignment out—Weston Co	27.95	
Consignment profits		27.95
To record the profit on sale of 1 machine, as follows:		

Sale price		$125.00
Less commission		31.25
Net		$ 93.75
Deduct cost:		
5 machines	$300.00	
Drayage	5.00	
Packing	6.00	
Freight	15.00	
Drayage	3.00	
Total	$329.00	
Less inventory value—4/5	263.20	
Costs applicable to machine sold		65.80
Profit		$ 27.95

The consignment out account, after the valuation of the four unsold machines has been brought down, appears as follows:

Consignment Out—Weston Co.

Cost of 5 washing machines	$300.00	Sale—1 machine	$125.00
Drayage	5.00	Inventory—down—4 machines	263.20
Packing	6.00		
Freight	15.00		
Drayage	3.00		
Commission—1 machine	31.25		
Profit	27.95		
	$388.20		$388.20

(Refer to page 49 and note that the last entry on the periodical inventory basis closes out the consignment shipments account; this entry should be made at the end of the period even though only one, or even none, of the machines has been sold.)

If the consignor does not keep consignment profits separate from profits on regular sales, his entries will be as shown on the following page.

CONSIGNMENT PROFITS NOT KEPT SEPARATE FROM PROFITS ON REGULAR SALES

Perpetual Inventory Basis			Periodical Inventory Basis		
Shipment:					
Consignment out—Weston Co.	$300.00		Consignment out—Weston Co.	$300.00	
Inventory		$300.00	Consignment shipments		$300.00
Cartage:					
Freight and cartage out	5.00		Freight and cartage out	5.00	
Cash		5.00	Cash		5.00
Packing:					
No entry.					
Sales and proceeds:					
Cash	75.75		Cash	75.75	
Freight and cartage out	18.00		Freight and cartage out	18.00	
Commission	31.25		Commission	31.25	
Sales		125.00	Sales		125.00
To record account sales.			To record account sales.		
Cost of sales	60.00				
Consignment out—Weston Co.		60.00			
Cost of machine sold.					
Reversal of memorandum entry for shipment:					
			Consignment shipments	60.00	
			Consignment out—Weston Co.		60.00
Inventory entries if books are closed at this point:					
Deferred consignment expense	23.20		Deferred consignment expense	23.20	
Freight and cartage out		18.40	Freight and cartage out		18.40
Packing expense		4.80	Packing expense		4.80
To defer 4/5 of expense—to be included in consigned goods inventory.			To defer 4/5 of expense—to be included in consigned goods inventory.		
			Inventory—consigned goods	240.00	
			Profit and loss		240.00
			To record the end-of-period inventory.		
(The inventory valuation is $263.20, the balance in the consignment out account plus the deferred expense.)			(The inventory valuation is $263.20, the cost set up by the above closing entry plus the deferred expense.)		

Advances from consignees. A consignor may, by agreement, draw on the consignee for a portion of the estimated sale price at the time of making the consignment. The amount of such an advance received by the consignor should be credited to the consignee and not to the consignment out account. The consignment out account should reflect an asset value of the goods on consignment, without netting a liability to the consignee for the advance received from him. The advance should be shown as a liability until it is applied in settlement for sales.

Consignee's entries. Following are the entries to be made by Weston Co. to record the transactions relative to the consignment received from C. D. Jones & Co.

Entry for receipt of goods:

Open a consignment in account and make a memorandum of the number and nature of the articles received, as follows:

Consignment In—C. D. Jones & Co.

5 washing machines	

Entry for expenses:

Consignment in—C. D. Jones & Co.	$18.00	
Cash (or expense accounts)		$18.00
For freight, $15.00, and drayage, $3.00.		

Entry for sales:

Cash	$625.00	
Consignment in—C. D. Jones & Co.		$625.00

Entry for commission:

Consignment in—C. D. Jones & Co	$156.25	
Commissions earned		$156.25

Entry for settlement:

Consignment in—C. D. Jones & Co	$450.75	
Cash		$450.75

After final settlement, the consignment account will appear as follows:

Consignment In—C. D. Jones & Co.

5 washing machines received		Sales—5 machines	$625.00
Freight	$ 15.00		
Drayage	3.00		
Commission	156.25		
Proceeds remitted	450.75		
	$625.00		$625.00

Any advances made by the consignee to the consignor may be charged to the consignment in account since the consignee is entitled to recover both expenses and advances.

Consignment in accounts in the balance sheet. When the consignee closes his books and prepares a balance sheet, some consignment in accounts may have debit balances, representing the excess of expenses, commissions, and advances over the proceeds of sales. These balances represent assets, and should be so shown in the balance sheet. Other accounts may have credit balances, representing the excess of the proceeds of sales over the expenses, commissions, and advances. These balances represent liabilities of the consignee to consignors, and should be so shown.

If a controlling account is kept with all consignments in, the balance of the controlling account will be the difference between the debit and the credit balances of the individual accounts. But the balance sheet should show the total debit balances and total credit balances of the individual consignment accounts as assets and liabilities respectively, and not merely the net balance of the controlling account.

Before the balances to be shown as assets or liabilities are obtained, any commissions which have been earned but not recorded should be put on the books.

To illustrate, assume that the controlling account and the individual accounts in the subsidiary ledger appear as follows:

Consignments In—Controlling Account

Expenses paid..........	$ 35.00	Sale—washing machine...	$125.00
Advances..............	150.00	Sale—2 ironing machines.	300.00

Consignment In—*A*

5 washing machines received		Sale of 1 machine......	$125.00
Freight................	$ 15.00		
Advances..............	150.00		

Consignment In—*B*

6 ironing machines received		Sale of 2 ironing machines................	$300.00
Freight................	$ 20.00		

No commissions have been taken up. The rate on both washing machines and ironing machines is 25%; therefore, before the books are closed, the following entry should be made:

Consignment in—*A*..............................	$31.25	
Consignment in—*B*..............................	75.00	
Commissions earned..........................		$106.25

After this entry is posted, the accounts will appear as follows:

Consignments In—Controlling Account

Expenses	$ 35.00	Sale—washing machine	$125.00
Advances	150.00	Sale—2 ironing machines	300.00
Commissions	106.25		

This account now has a credit balance of $133.75. But this balance should not appear in the balance sheet, because it is the difference between an asset and a liability. The balance sheet should show the asset represented by the balance of the consignment in—*A* account, and the liability represented by the balance of the consignment in—*B* account.

Consignment In—*A*

5 washing machines received		Sale of 1 machine	$125.00
Freight	$ 15.00	Balance—down	71.25
Advances	150.00		
Commission	31.25		
	$196.25		$196.25
Balance (to be shown as an asset)	$ 71.25		

Consignment In—*B*

6 ironing machines received		Sale of 2 machines	$300.00
Freight	$ 20.00		
Commission	75.00		
Balance—down	205.00		
	$300.00		$300.00
		Balance (to be shown as a liability)	$205.00

Separate account for each consignment. Both the consignor and the consignee should keep a separate account with each consignment. If there are several consignments between the same parties, each consignment must be settled for separately and the accounts should therefore clearly show the facts relative to each consignment.

CHAPTER 35

Venture Accounts

Nature of ventures. It is difficult to define a business venture, because ventures may be conducted in so many different ways. In general it may be said that a *venture* is a more or less speculative undertaking (usually not a part of the regular operations of the business) involving certain specific goods and terminating when these goods are disposed of.

Years ago, before the present methods of foreign trade were developed, a popular form of venture consisted of placing merchandise in charge of the captain of a vessel, to be sold or bartered at his discretion in some foreign port. With foreign trade now on a basis of regularly conducted purchases and sales, this form of venture is no longer common, but the idea that the term *venture* implies the shipment of merchandise still persists.

This idea is erroneous and places an unwarranted limitation on the term. While it is true that the merchandise which is the subject matter of the venture may be shipped, ventures may be conducted without making a shipment. Thus, the purchase of a piece of real estate in the hope of a sale at an increased value, or a speculation in stock, is a venture although there is no shipment.

Single and joint ventures. Just as a business may be conducted by an individual or by a partnership, so ventures may be *single* or *joint*. If the venture is conducted by one individual or business, it is a *single venture*, even though the business conducting the venture is a partnership or a corporation. If two or more individuals or businesses participate in the venture, it is a *joint venture*.

Single ventures. If a venture is conducted by one individual or business as sole owner, the accounting is usually very simple. An account may be opened with the venture, and charged with the cost of the merchandise and with all expenses, and credited with the proceeds. The balance of the account is the profit or loss. A consignment out is an illustration of a single venture.

Joint ventures. If two or more individuals or businesses engage in a venture, a partnership relation exists. Each participant may contribute merchandise or money, each may pay expenses, and each will share in the resulting profit or loss. As in any other partnership, profits will be shared in accordance with any agreement; if there is no agreement, they will be shared equally, regardless of relative investments.

Joint venture accounting. There are two distinct methods of recording the transactions of a joint venture, the method to be chosen depending upon whether the venture is to be of sufficient duration and complexity to warrant keeping a separate set of books for it. These two methods may be described as follows:

(1) No separate set of books for the venture.
Each participant records all of the venture transactions in his own books.

(2) A separate set of books for the venture.
All of the venture transactions are recorded in the venture books.
Each participant records in his own books only the transactions to which he is a party.

First method of accounting. As ventures are usually of short duration, the first method is commonly used. Each participant opens on his own books an account with the joint venture, and an account with each of the other participants. Transactions are recorded in the books of all parties as follows:

(1) Merchandise contributions:
The party contributing the merchandise debits joint venture and credits inventory (if the merchandising accounts are kept on a perpetual inventory basis) or merchandise contributed to joint venture (if the accounting is on a periodical inventory basis). Each of the other participants debits joint venture and credits the participant making the contribution.

(2) Cash payments for the venture:
The party making a payment, either for merchandise or for expense, debits the joint venture account and credits cash.
The other participants debit joint venture and credit the participant who made the payment.

(3) Cash given by one participant to another to be used for joint venture purposes:
The participant furnishing the money debits the account with the participant receiving it and credits cash.

The participant receiving the money debits cash and credits the participant providing the money.

Other participants debit the participant receiving the money and credit the participant furnishing it.

When this money is later spent for the venture, entries are made as indicated in (2).

(4) Sales for cash:

The participant making the sale debits cash and credits joint venture.

The other participants debit the participant who received the cash and credit joint venture.

(5) Sales on account:

The participant making the sale debits accounts receivable—joint venture and credits the joint venture account.

The other participants debit the participant making the sale and credit joint venture.

(6) Loss from bad debts:

The participant who made the sale and is carrying the account debits joint venture and credits accounts receivable—joint venture.

The other participants debit joint venture and credit the participant carrying the account.

(7) Expenses paid by participants:

If the expenses are paid in cash specifically for the venture, entries are made as in (2).

But the expense may have been part of a total payment charged by the participant to some expense account; in such a case, when the amount applicable to the venture is ascertained:

The participant who paid the expense debits the joint venture account and credits his expense account.

The other participants debit the joint venture account and credit the participant making the charge.

(8) Salary allowed to managing participant:

The participant receiving the salary debits joint venture and credits salary income.

The other participants debit joint venture and credit the participant who is allowed the salary.

(9) Commissions allowed to managing participant:

If commissions are allowed on purchases:

The managing participant debits joint venture for the cost of the merchandise plus the commission and credits cash and commissions earned.

The other participants debit joint venture for cost plus commission and credit the participant making the purchase.

If commissions are allowed on sales:

The managing participant debits cash (or accounts receivable), credits commissions earned, and credits joint venture for the net amount of the sale.

The other participants debit the participant making the sale and credit the joint venture account for the net amount.

(10) Withdrawals of cash:

The participant receiving the money debits cash and credits the participant sending the money.

The participant sending the money debits the participant receiving it and credits cash.

The other participants debit the participant receiving the cash and credit the participant sending it.

(11) Withdrawals of merchandise:

The participant receiving merchandise debits inventory (perpetual inventory basis) or merchandise received from joint venture (periodical inventory basis) and credits joint venture.

The other participants debit the one receiving the merchandise and credit joint venture.

(12) Interest:

It is sometimes considered equitable to allow interest on investments from the date of each investment to the date of settlement, and to charge interest on withdrawals from the date of each withdrawal to the date of settlement.

The net credit or debit is computed, and an entry is made on each participant's books as follows:

Debit joint venture for total.
Credit interest earned for own allowance.
Credit other participants for their allowances.

(13) Distribution of profit:

After the venture has been completed, the balance of the joint venture account will be the amount of the profit or loss. Assuming that a profit has been made, each participant will close the joint venture account by an entry as follows:

Debit joint venture for total profit.
Credit profit on joint venture for own share.
Credit other participants for their shares.

(14) Final settlement:

Each participant has an account with each other participant. To illustrate, assume that the books of three joint venture participants contain the following balances:

	X's Books	*Y*'s Books	*Z*'s Books
Account with *X*................		$1,000 Cr.	$1,000 Cr.
Account with *Y*................	$1,500 Cr.		1,500 Cr.
Account with *Z*................	2,500 Dr.	2,500 Dr.	

X is entitled to receive $1,000.00 in final settlement of the venture, and *Y* is entitled to receive $1,500.00; these amounts, totaling $2,500.00, should be paid to *X* and *Y* by *Z*. When *Z* makes the payments, the following entries are made:

	X's Books		*Y*'s Books		*Z*'s Books	
Debits:	Cash	1,000	*X*	1,000	*X*	1,000
	Y	1,500	Cash	1,500	*Y*	1,500
Credit:	*Z*	2,500	*Z*	2,500	Cash	2,500

Illustration. The following transactions of a joint venture will be used to illustrate the first method of making joint venture entries. (See pages 64 and 65.)

(1) June 1—*A* ships merchandise to *C*, who is to manage the venture. The merchandise is carried in the perpetual inventory at $3,000.00.

(2) " 1—*A* pays freight on the merchandise, $20.00.

(3) " 1—*A* makes a charge for delivery services of $10.00. As he uses his own delivery equipment, the $10.00 is credited to delivery expense.

(4) " 1—*B* sends *C* $2,000.00 in cash.

(5) " 1—*B* sends *C* a thirty-day draft for $1,000.00.

(6) " 5—*C* buys merchandise for the venture at a cost of $1,500.00, and is allowed a 2% commission.

(7) " 11—*C* discounts *B*'s draft, paying $3.33 discount.

(8) " 11—*C* purchases merchandise at a cost of $4,000.00, and is allowed a 2% commission.

(9) " 17—*C* pays expenses, $75.00.

(10) " 24—*C* sells merchandise for $3,600.00 and is allowed a 2% commission.

(11) " 26—*C* sends *A* and *B* each one third of the net proceeds of the sale, keeping one third himself.

(12) " 30—*C* sells the balance of the merchandise for $6,000.00, and is allowed a 2% commission.

(13) July 1—Interest at 6% is to be credited to all participants on credit entries in their accounts, and charged to

	A's Books			B's Books			C's Books		
(1) June 1	Joint venture	$3,000.00		Joint venture	$3,000.00		Joint venture	$3,000.00	
	Inventory		$3,000.00	*A*		$3,000.00	*A*		$3,000.00
	A contributes merchandise.								
(2) June 1	Joint venture	20.00		Joint venture	20.00		Joint venture	20.00	
	Cash		20.00	*A*		20.00	*A*		20.00
	A pays freight.								
(3) June 1	Joint venture	10.00		Joint venture	10.00		Joint venture	10.00	
	Delivery expense		10.00	*A*		10.00	*A*		10.00
	A charges for delivery.								
(4) June 1	*C*	2,000.00		*C*	2,000.00		Cash	2,000.00	
	B		2,000.00	Cash		2,000.00	*B*		2,000.00
	B sends cash to *C*.								
(5) June 1	*C*	1,000.00		*C*	1,000.00		Notes receivable	1,000.00	
	B		1,000.00	Notes payable		1,000.00	*B*		1,000.00
	B sends 30-day draft to *C*.								
(6) June 5	Joint venture	1,530.00		Joint venture	1,530.00		Joint venture	1,530.00	
	C		1,530.00	*C*		1,530.00	Cash		1,500.00
	C buys merchandise.						Commissions earned.		30.00
(7) June 11	*B*	3.33		Interest expense	3.33		Cash	996.67	
	C		3.33	*C*		3.33	*B*	3.33	
	C discounts *B*'s draft.						Notes rec. discounted.		1,000.00
(8) June 11	Joint venture	4,080.00		Joint venture	4,080.00		Joint venture	4,080.00	
	C		4,080.00	*C*		4,080.00	Cash		4,000.00
	Purchases by *C*.						Commissions earned		80.00
(9) June 17	Joint venture	75.00		Joint venture	75.00		Joint venture	75.00	
	C		75.00	*C*		75.00	Cash		75.00
	Payment of expenses by *C*.								
(10) June 24	*C*	3,528.00		*C*	3,528.00		Cash	3,600.00	
	Joint venture		3,528.00	Joint venture		3,528.00	Joint venture		3,528.00
	Sale by *C*, less commission.						Commissions earned		72.00
(11) June 26	Cash	1,176.00		*A*	1,176.00		*A*	1,176.00	
	B	1,176.00		Cash	1,176.00		*B*	1,176.00	
	C		2,352.00	*C*		2,352.00	Cash		2,352.00
	Remittances by *C* to *A* and *B*.								

Entry	Date	*A*'s Books	Dr.	Cr.	*B*'s Books	Dr.	Cr.	*C*'s Books	Dr.	Cr.
(12)	June 30	*C*....................	$5,880.00		*C*....................	$5,880.00		Cash..................	$6,000.00	
		Joint venture.......		$5,880.00	Joint venture.......		$5,880.00	Joint venture.......		$5,880.00
		Sale by *C*, less commission.						Commissions earned..		120.00
(13)	July 1	Joint venture..........	30.46		Joint venture..........	30.46		Joint venture..........	30.46	
		Interest earned.....		14.17	*A*................		14.17	*A*................		14.17
		B................		12.34	Interest earned......		12.34	*B*................		12.34
		C................		3.95	*C*................		3.95	Interest earned......		3.95
		Credits for net interest. See computation, page 66.								
(14)	July 1	Joint venture..........	662.54		Joint venture..........	662.54		Joint venture..........	662.54	
		Profit on venture....		220.85	*A*................		220.85	*A*................		220.85
		B................		220.85	Profit on venture....		220.85	*B*................		220.85
		C................		220.84	*C*................		220.84	Profit on venture....		220.84
		To close out profit. See venture account, page 66.								
(15)	July 1	Cash..................	2,089.02		*A*....................	2,089.02		*A*....................	2,089.02	
		B....................	2,053.86		Cash..................	2,053.86		*B*....................	2,053.86	
		C................		4,142.88	*C*................		4,142.88	Cash................		4,142.88
		Final settlement payments by *C* to *A* and *B*. See explanatory personal accounts—page 67.								

them on debit entries. Interest is to be computed from date of entry to July 1. [In the case of the draft given by *B* to *C*, *B* is to be credited and *C* is to be charged with interest on the proceeds of the draft ($996.67) from the date of discount (June 11) to July 1.]

(14) " 1—Profits are divided equally.

(15) " 1—Settlement is made; *C* sends checks to *A* and *B*.

Computation of Interest—(Explanatory of entry 13)

A—Credits:							
June	1	Merchandise	$3,000.00	30	days	$15.00	
"	1	Freight	20.00	30	"	.10	
"	1	Drayage	10.00	30	"	.05	$15.15
Debits:							
June	26	Cash	1,176.00	5	"		.98
							$14.17
B—Credits:							
June	1	Cash	$2,000.00	30	"	$10.00	
"	11	Proceeds of draft	996.67	20	"	3.32	$13.32
Debits:							
June	26	Cash	1,176.00	5	"		.98
							$12.34
C—Credits:							
June	5	Purchase and commission	$1,530.00	26	"	$ 6.63	
"	11	" " "	4,080.00	20	"	13.60	
"	17	Expenses	75.00	14	"	.18	
"	26	Cash to *A* and *B*	2,352.00	5	"	1.96	$22.37
Debits:							
June	1	Cash from *B*	2,000.00	30	"	$10.00	
"	11	Proceeds of *B*'s draft	996.67	20	"	3.32	
"	24	Sale less commission	3,528.00	7	"	4.12	
"	30	" " "	5,880.00	1	"	.98	18.42
							$ 3.95

Computation of Net Profit—(Explanatory of entry 14)

Following is the joint venture account after the profit has been computed, and distributed by entry 14.

Joint Venture Account

(As it will appear on books of *A*, *B*, and *C*)

June	1	Merchandise—*A*		$3,000.00	June	24	Sale—*C*	$3,528.00
"	1	Freight—*A*		20.00	"	30	" "	5,880.00
"	1	Delivery—*A*		10.00				
"	5	Purchase—*C*		1,530.00				
"	11	" "		4,080.00				
"	17	Expenses—*C*		75.00				
July	1	Interest		30.46				
"	1	Profit: *A*.	$220.85					
		B.	220.85					
		C.	220.84	662.54				
				$9,408.00				$9,408.00

Participants' Accounts

After posting the entries for the transactions of the venture (1 to 12), for the interest (13), and for the distribution of profit (14), *A*'s account on the books of *B* and *C* will have a credit balance of $2,089.02, which is the amount he is entitled to receive in settlement.

B's account on the books of *A* and *C* will have a credit balance of $2,053.86, which is the amount he is entitled to receive.

C's account on the books of *A* and *B* will have a debit balance of $4,142.88, which is the amount he must pay to *A* and *B*: $2,089.02 to *A*, and $2,053.86 to *B*. After these payments have been made and recorded by entry 15, the accounts will appear as follows:

Account with *A*
(As it will appear on books of *B* and *C*)

June 26	Cash from *C*......	$1,176.00	June 1	Merchandise to *C*...	$3,000.00
July 1	" " "......	2,089.02	" 1	Freight............	20.00
			" 1	Drayage..........	10.00
			July 1	Interest...........	14.17
			" 1	Profit.............	220.85
		$3,265.02			$3,265.02

Account with *B*
(As it will appear on the books of *A* and *C*)

June 11	Discount on draft..	$ 3.33	June 1	Cash to *C*..........	$2,000.00
" 26	Cash from *C*......	1,176.00	" 1	Draft to *C*.........	1,000.00
July 1	" " "......	2,053.86	July 1	Interest...........	12.34
			" 1	Profit.............	220.85
		$3,233.19			$3,233.19

Account with *C*
(As it will appear on books of *A* and *B*)

June 1	Cash from *B*.....	$ 2,000.00	June 5	Purchase and commission.......	$ 1,530.00
" 1	Draft from *B*....	1,000.00	" 11	Disc. on *B*'s draft.	3.33
" 24	Sale less commission..........	3,528.00	" 11	Purchase and commission........	4,080.00
" 30	Sale less commission..........	5,880.00	" 17	Expenses paid....	75.00
			" 26	Cash to *A* and *B*..	2,352.00
			July 1	Interest.........	3.95
			" 1	Profit...........	220.84
			" 1	Cash to *A*......	2,089.02
			" 1	" " *B*......	2,053.86
		$12,408.00			$12,408.00

Uncompleted ventures. If, at the time of closing the books, an account with an uncompleted venture appears on the books, the inventory may be entered in the account, the profit to date estimated, and the proper share taken up. If one participant makes such entries, all should do so in order to keep the joint venture accounts in agreement. However, if the venture is speculative in nature, it is hazardous to take up any profit until the completion of the venture; the conservative procedure is to leave the account unclosed, showing the facts in the balance sheet as follows, under the current asset caption if the assets of the venture are current:

Net investment in joint venture:		
Total investment	$1,500.00	
Less investments of other participants	950.00	$550.00

If the investment in the venture is relatively small in proportion to the total assets shown by the balance sheet, it is not necessary to indicate the amount of the investment of the other participants; in such instances it is sufficient to show the net investment as a single item in the balance sheet in the manner illustrated below:

Investment in joint venture	$550.00

Second method of accounting. While the method just described is the one usually followed, a separate set of books may be kept for the transactions of the venture.

With a separate set of books, it is not necessary to keep the joint venture account on the participants' books in a manner which will show the purchases, sales, and expenses of the venture. The profits will be determined from the books of the venture. Nor is it necessary for each participant to keep an account with each other participant, as the books of the venture will show the interest of each participant. Each participant keeps only a joint venture or an investment in joint venture account, charging it with what he puts into the venture and with his share of the profits, and crediting it with what he takes out. He makes no record of the investments, withdrawals, and expenses of the other participants.

Entries on pages 69 and 70 show how the illustrative transactions would be recorded in the books of the three participants and in the separate venture set. The entries are numbered to correspond with the statement of transactions beginning on page 60. All of the participants' books are assumed to be kept on a periodical inventory basis.

The venture accounts which will appear on the various participants' books are illustrated by the following account kept by *A*:

***A*'s Account with Joint Venture**

Merchandise	$3,000.00	Cash	$1,176.00
Expense	20.00	Cash—final settlement	2,089.02
"	10.00		
Interest	14.17		
Profit	220.85		
	$3,265.02		$3,265.02

	Venture Books			*A*'s Books			*B*'s Books			*C*'s Books		
(1)	Purchases.....	$3,000.00		Joint venture..	$3,000.00							
	A.........		$3,000.00	Mdse. contributed to J.V.		$3,000.00						
(2)	Expense......	20.00		Joint venture..	20.00							
	A.........		20.00	Cash........		20.00						
(3)	Expense......	10.00		Joint venture..	10.00							
	A.........		10.00	Expense.....		10.00						
(4)	Cash.........	2,000.00					Joint venture..	$2,000.00				
	B...........		2,000.00				Cash.......		$2,000.00			
(5)	Notes receivable	1,000.00					Joint venture..	1,000.00				
	B.........		1,000.00				Notes payable		1,000.00			
(6)	Purchases.....	1,500.00										
	Cash.......		1,500.00									
	Commissions..	30.00								Joint venture..	30.00	
	C.........		30.00							Commissions.		$ 30.00
(7)	Cash.........	996.67					Interest.......	3.33				
	B............	3.33					Joint venture		3.33			
	Notes rec. disc......		1,000.00									
(8)	Cash*........	2,503.33								Joint venture..	2,503.33	
	C.........		2,503.33							Cash.......		2,503.33
	Purchases.....	4,000.00										
	Cash.......		4,000.00									
	Commissions..	80.00								Joint venture..	80.00	
	C.........		80.00							Commissions.		80.00
(9)	Expense......	75.00								Joint venture..	75.00	
	C.........		75.00							Cash.......		75.00

* Amount which *C* must have contributed from his own funds to provide the cash necessary to make the $4,000.00 purchase.

	Venture Books			A's Books			B's Books			C's Books		
(10)	Cash.........	$3,528.00								Cash..........	$ 72.00	
	Commissions..	72.00								Commissions.		$ 72.00
	Sales.......		$3,600.00									
(11)	*A*............	1,176.00		Cash..........	$1,176.00		Cash..........	$1,176.00		Cash..........	1,176.00	
	B............	1,176.00		Joint venture		$1,176.00	Joint venture		$1,176.00	Joint venture		1,176.00
	C............	1,176.00										
	Cash.......		3,528.00									
(12)	Cash.........	5,880.00								Cash..........	120.00	
	Commissions..	120.00								Commissions.		120.00
	Sales.......		6,000.00									
	Sales..........	9,600.00										
	Purchases...		8,500.00									
	Expense....		105.00									
	Commissions		302.00									
	Profit & loss.		693.00									
(13)	Profit & loss...	30.46		Joint venture..	14.17		Joint venture..	12.34		Joint venture..	3.95	
	A..........		14.17	Interest.....		14.17	Interest.....		12.34	Interest.....		3.95
	B..........		12.34									
	C..........		3.95									
(14)	Profit & loss...	662.54		Joint venture..	220.85		Joint venture..	220.85		Joint venture..	220.84	
	A..........		220.85	Profit on J. V.		220.85	Profit on J. V.		220.85	Profit on J. V.		220.84
	B..........		220.85									
	C..........		220.84									
(15)	*A*............	2,089.02		Cash..........	2,089.02		Cash..........	2,053.86		Cash..........	1,737.12	
	B............	2,053.86		Joint venture		2,089.02	Joint venture		2,053.86	Joint venture		1,737.12
	C............	1,737.12										
	Cash.......		5,880.00									

(When *A* closes his books, the credit balance in the merchandise contributed to joint venture account will be closed to profit and loss as an offset to the charges closing the purchases and opening inventory accounts.)

The participants' accounts which will appear on the venture books are illustrated by the following account with *A*:

Joint Venture's Account with *A*

Cash	$1,176.00	Merchandise	$3,000.00
Cash—final settlement	2,089.02	Expense	20.00
		"	10.00
		Interest	14.17
		Profit	220.85
	$3,265.02		$3,265.02

In a similar way, *B*'s account with the venture would be reciprocal with the venture's account with *B*; and the same would apply to *C*'s accounts.

The first method is the one to be used when joint venture accounts are called for in problems and no accounting method is specified.

Interest. The computation of interest in the preceding illustrations of the two methods of accounting was based on the assumption that *C*, as manager of the venture, was permitted to merge the venture funds with his own, and was therefore properly chargeable with interest on advances made to him.

CHAPTER 36

Installment Sales

Distinguishing features. Many concerns have departed from, or supplemented, the long-established method of selling for cash or on relatively short credit, by the adoption of a selling policy that involves the collection of the sale price in periodical installments. A down payment is usually required, and the remainder of the sale price is payable in periodical installments, which may or may not be subject to interest. Some of the conditions peculiar to installment selling are discussed below:

(1) Since the seller's risk is greatly increased by the deferment of collections, one of the following devices is usually employed to enable the seller to recover the merchandise if collections are not received in accordance with the terms of the contract:

- (*a*) Retention of title by the seller (usually by the use of documents called *conditional sales contracts*) until the last installment is paid by the purchaser. A transaction in which the seller's protection is obtained in this manner is technically a contract of sale rather than a sale, but this technicality is usually disregarded so far as the accounting is concerned.
- (*b*) Immediate transfer of title subject to a mortgage for the uncollected installments.
- (*c*) Conveyance to a trustee until the final installment is collected.
- (*d*) The hire-purchase plan, or lease of the property until final payment.

(2) Installment sales may be subject to greater collection losses and expenses than are incurred on regular sales.

Collection losses are likely to be heavy because the opportunity to purchase luxuries on the installment plan appeals to people who are not in a financial position to pay for them outright, and who, in many cases, are unable to pay for them even in installments. The right of recovery of the merchandise is not always an adequate protection to the seller, because of the depreciation of the property as a result of use, because of style changes, and because of the status of the property as second-hand merchandise. Unless carefully guarded against, the period of payment may extend beyond the useful life of the article, and the purchaser therefore may have no incentive to complete the payments; this is particularly true of seasonal merchandise and articles subject to supersession.

Expenses are also likely to be heavy since the installment method involves additional collection and accounting costs. The seller may find himself obliged to make repairs over a long period, either because of the purchaser's demand enforced by a refusal to pay installments, or in order to protect the seller's equity in the property. Moreover, tying up capital over a long period in installment receivables involves an interest expense which may assume considerable proportions.

(3) Expenses applicable to the sale are incurred in accounting periods subsequent to the period of sale. The accounting procedure must be based upon a recognition of this fact, as it would be incorrect accounting to take up all of the profit during the period of sale without making provision for the expenses to be incurred in subsequent periods.

Taking up profits. Because losses and expenses incident to installment selling are incurred in large amounts in periods subsequent to the period of sale, there is considerable difficulty in devising a method of taking up profits in a logical and conservative way. The following methods have been used:

(1) Take up all of the profit in the period of sale, and set up reserves for losses on bad debts, collection expenses, and costs of reconditioning repossessed merchandise. Theoretically, this method is perhaps the best, because it takes up the profit in the period in which the sale is made, and, at the same time, it reserves out of this profit an amount sufficient to cover losses and expenses arising out of the sale. However, sometimes it is virtually impossible to estimate the bad debt losses and collection expenses with any reasonable degree of accuracy.

There is an additional practical disadvantage to this method: reserves for collection expenses and costs of reconditioning repossessed merchandise are not allowable deductions for income tax purposes; hence, a company which applies this method for general accounting purposes is required to report the expenses on an expenditure basis.

(2) Take up the profits in installments on a basis of cash collections. Three methods of taking up the profits in installments have been used, and are discussed below, but the first two are rarely desirable and not recognized for Federal income tax purposes.

(*a*) The first collections are considered a return of cost, and no profit is taken up until the collections exceed the cost. This method is usually too conservative, and is not justified unless the property cannot be recovered or unless it would have no net value if recovered.

(*b*) The first collections are considered profit and the last collections are considered a return of cost. This method is usually not sufficiently conservative, because of the danger of depreciation of recovered property.

(*c*) Each collection is regarded as including profit and a return of cost in the same proportion that these two elements were included in the total selling price. Thus, if a sale price of $150.00 included $100.00 cost and $50.00 profit, a collection of $15.00 would be regarded as including a $10.00 return of cost and $5.00 profit. This method is acceptable for tax purposes, and is discussed in the remaining pages of this chapter.

Illustration: SINGLE SALE. As a simple illustration of the accounting procedure applied in taking up profits on the basis of the profit element included in each collection, let us assume the following facts:

Sale—July 15:	
Selling price	$15,000.00
Cost	10,000.00
Profit	5,000.00
Ratio of profit to total selling price, 33⅓%	
Collections during the year of sale:	
Down payment	3,000.00
Monthly payment	1,500.00

The entire gross profit will be set up (immediately or at the end of the year, by entries discussed later) in a deferred gross profit account, as follows:

Deferred Gross Profit on Installment Sales

	Total gross profit..... $5,000.00

The collections are recorded by debits to cash and credits to the customer. The customer should be charged with the full sales price of the merchandise and credited with the down payment so as to leave a complete record of the transaction in his account. Assuming that installments are collected regularly on the first of each month, the customer's account at the end of the year will appear as follows:

A Customer

July 15	Sale........	$15,000.00	July 15	Cash........	$3,000.00
			Aug. 1	Cash........	1,500.00
			Sept. 1	Cash........	1,500.00
			Oct. 1	Cash........	1,500.00
			Nov. 1	Cash........	1,500.00
			Dec. 1	Cash........	1,500.00

Since $10,500.00 has been collected, and since the ratio of profit to selling price was 33⅓%, the profit regarded as realized is one third of $10,500.00, or $3,500.00. This realized portion of the gross profit is taken into income for the year by the following entry:

Dec. 31	Deferred gross profit on installment sales	$3,500.00	
	Profit and loss....................		$3,500.00
	To take up as income the portion of the gross profit on installment sales realized by collections.		

The result of this entry is indicated below:

Deferred Gross Profit on Installment Sales

To profit and loss......	$3,500.00	Total gross profit.......	$5,000.00

Profit and Loss

		Realized profit........	$3,500.00

After the remaining installments are collected, the balance in the deferred gross profit account will be transferred to profit and loss. A subsequent section in this chapter contains a discussion of the disposition in the periodical statements of any balance in the deferred profit account.

Setting up the deferred gross profit account. The procedure for setting up the deferred gross profit account will depend upon whether the merchandise accounting is on a perpetual inventory basis or a periodical inventory basis. Typical entries by both methods are illustrated below, it being assumed that three articles of the same kind were purchased and one was sold.

Perpetual Inventory Basis			Periodical Inventory Basis		
Purchase—July 1:					
Inventory....	$30,000.00		Purchases.....	$30,000.00	
Cash . .		$30,000.00	Cash...... .		$30,000.00

Perpetual Inventory Basis			Periodical Inventory Basis		
Sale—July 15:					
A Customer..	$15,000.00		A Customer....	$15,000.00	
Inventory..		$10,000.00	Installment sales......		$15,000.00
Def. G.P. on installment sales		5,000.00			
Closing—Dec. 31:					
			Inventory.....	20,000.00	
			Cost of inst. sales......	10,000.00	
			Purchases...		30,000.00
			Installment sales	15,000.00	
			Cost of inst. sales......		10,000.00
			Def. G.P. on inst. sales..		5,000.00
Def. G.P. on inst. sales	3,500.00		Def. G.P. on inst. sales..	3,500.00	
Profit and loss.....		3,500.00	Profit and loss.......		3,500.00

The periodical inventory basis is usually impracticable if merchandise charged to one purchases account is sold both on ordinary credit terms and on installments. The cost of goods sold, as determined by taking an end-of-year inventory, is the cost of all goods sold, and the cost of the portion sold on installments is not separately determined. Of course, if all kinds of merchandise are sold at the same rate of gross profit and if installment and regular sales are made at the same profit rate (conditions which are unlikely), the deferred gross profit on installment sales can be determined by multiplying the installment sales by the gross profit rate.

Trade-ins. Companies making sales on the installment plan frequently find it necessary to accept trade-ins as part of the down payment, and, as a matter of policy, they may give the customer a greater trade-in allowance for his property than it is worth at a fair market value. In such instances, the trade-in should be put on the books as an asset at a fair valuation, and the gross profit on the sale should be computed on the basis of that valuation.

Assume, for instance, that an article which cost $1,000.00 is sold for $1,500.00, and that an article with a fair value of $125.00 is accepted as part of the down payment at a valuation of $175.00. Entries may be made as follows:

Customer......................................	$1,500.00	
Inventory....................................		$1,000.00
Deferred gross profit.........................		500.00
To record the installment sale.		

Trade-in inventory	$ 125.00	
Deferred gross profit	50.00	
Customer		$ 175.00
To record the trade-in allowance.		

Illustration: NUMEROUS SALES. When numerous installment sales are made, it is impracticable to attempt to compute the rate of gross profit on each sale and to apply a separate rate of gross profit to the collections from each sale. Instead, an average rate of gross profit on all installment sales for a year may be applied to the collections on receivables resulting from the sales of that year. To illustrate, assume the following facts for the year 1944.

Installment sales	$150,000.00
Cost of installment sales	100,000.00
Gross profit	50,000.00
Ratio of gross profit to selling price	33⅓%
Collections during 1944	$105,000.00
Gross profit realized, 33⅓% of $105,000.00	35,000.00

The controlling account with installment receivables may be summarized as follows:

Installment Accounts Receivable

Sales	$150,000.00	Collections	$105,000.00

And the deferred gross profit account, after the books are closed at the end of the year, will appear as follows:

Deferred Gross Profit on Installment Sales

To profit and loss	$35,000.00	Total gross profit	$50,000.00

Operations for a series of years. Let us now assume that installment sales operations are conducted over a series of years, and that the transactions during three years were as follows:

Summary of Facts

	1944	1945	1946
Sales	$150,000	$200,000	$250,000
Cost of goods sold	100,000	120,000	125,000
Gross profit	$ 50,000	$ 80,000	$125,000
Rate of gross profit	33⅓%	40%	50%
Cash collections:			
On 1944 accounts	$105,000	$ 30,000	$ 15,000
On 1945 accounts		125,000	50,000
On 1946 accounts			175,000
Gross profits realized by collections:			
33⅓% of collections on 1944 accounts	$ 35,000	$ 10,000	$ 5,000
40 % of collections on 1945 accounts		50,000	20,000
50 % of collections on 1946 accounts			87,500

Two methods of determining and accounting for the gross profits regarded as realized at the end of each year are described below. The results obtained by the two methods are the same.

First method. To determine the collections applicable to receivables arising in different years and therefore subject to different gross profit rates, the cash receipts book may contain columns headed: accounts receivable—1944, accounts receivable—1945, and accounts receivable—1946. Separate subsidiary ledgers and controlling accounts may be kept with the receivables by years. Such controlling accounts would contain the following data:

Installment Accounts Receivable—1944

Sales..............	$150,000.00	Collections—1944....	$105,000.00
		Collections—1945....	30,000.00
		Collections—1946....	15,000.00

Installment Accounts Receivable—1945

Sales..............	$200,000.00	Collections—1945....	$125,000.00
		Collections—1946....	50,000.00

Installment Accounts Receivable—1946

Sales..............	$250,000.00	Collections—1946....	$175,000.00

Separate deferred profit accounts may be kept by years, and transfers from these accounts to profit and loss may be made on the basis of the collections shown by the several accounts receivable columns in the cash receipts book. Entries for taking up the realized portions of the gross profit, computed on the basis of cash collections as shown in the foregoing summary of facts, would be:

At the end of 1944:

Deferred gross profit on installment sales—1944.	$35,000.00	
Profit and loss........................		$35,000.00
Gross profit equal to 33⅓% of collections.		

At the end of 1945:

Deferred gross profit on installment sales—1944.	$10,000.00	
Deferred gross profit on installment sales—1945.	50,000.00	
Profit and loss........................		$60,000.00
33⅓% of collections on 1944 accounts, and 40% of collections on 1945 accounts.		

At the end of 1946:

Deferred gross profit on installment sales—1944	$ 5,000.00	
Deferred gross profit on installment sales—1945	20,000.00	
Deferred gross profit on installment sales—1946	87,500.00	
Profit and loss........................		$112,500.00
33⅓% of collections on 1944 accounts, 40% of collections on 1945 accounts, and 50% of collections on 1946 accounts.		

By the end of 1946, the deferred gross profit accounts would appear as shown on the following page.

Deferred Gross Profit on Installment Sales—1944

To profit and loss in 1944..	$35,000.00	Total gross profit..........	$50,000.00
To profit and loss in 1945..	10,000.00		
To profit and loss in 1946..	5,000.00		
	$50,000.00		$50,000.00

Deferred Gross Profit on Installment Sales—1945

To profit and loss in 1945..	$50,000.00	Total gross profit..........	$80,000.00
To profit and loss in 1946..	20,000.00		

Deferred Gross Profit on Installment Sales—1946

To profit and loss in 1946..	$87,500.00	Total gross profit.........	$125,000.00

Second method. One deferred profit account may be used instead of separate deferred profit accounts by years. Also a single accounts receivable controlling account may be used instead of separate accounts by years; this will avoid the necessity of separate columns in the cash receipts book for collections applicable to different years.

At the end of each year, the accounts receivable will be analyzed to determine the uncollected balances arising from sales in various years, and the deferred profit will be determined on the basis of this aging. To illustrate, using the same data as in the preceding illustration, a single controlling account with installment receivables would appear as follows:

Installment Accounts Receivable

	Debits	Credits	Balance
1944: Sales....................	$150,000.00		
Collections..............		$105,000.00	
Balance..................			$ 45,000.00
1945: Sales....................	200,000.00		
Collections..............		155,000.00	
Balance..................			90,000.00
1946: Sales....................	250,000.00		
Collections..............		240,000.00	
Balance..................			100,000.00

This controlling account gives no indication of the ages of the accounts making up the balance at the end of each year (except the first); an analysis of the subsidiary ledger, however, discloses the following information:

Age of Installment Receivables

At the end of 1944:

Balances of 1944 accounts	$45,000.00

At the end of 1945:

Balances of 1944 accounts	$15,000.00	
Balances of 1945 accounts	75,000.00	$90,000.00

At the end of 1946:

Balances of 1944 accounts	$ —	
Balances of 1945 accounts	25,000.00	
Balances of 1946 accounts	75,000.00	100,000.00

On the basis of this aging of the receivables, the amount to be *left* in the deferred gross profit account at the end of each year can be determined as follows:

At the end of 1944:

33⅓% of 1944 balances—$45,000.00		$15,000.00

At the end of 1945:

33⅓% of 1944 balances—$15,000.00	$ 5,000.00	
40 % of 1945 balances— 75,000.00	30,000.00	35,000.00

At the end of 1946:

40% of 1945 balances—$25,000.00	$10,000.00	
50% of 1946 balances— 75,000.00	37,500.00	47,500.00

The amounts to be left as deferred gross profit determine the amounts to be transferred to profit and loss, as shown below:

1944:	
Total gross profit	$ 50,000.00
Amount to be transferred to profit and loss	35,000.00
Balance required, as determined above	$ 15,000.00
1945:	
Total gross profit	80,000.00
Total	$ 95,000.00
Amount to be transferred to profit and loss	60,000.00
Balance required, as determined above	$ 35,000.00
1946:	
Total gross profit	125,000.00
Total	$160,000.00
Amount to be transferred to profit and loss	112,500.00
Balance required, as determined above	$ 47,500.00

The annual journal entries transferring realized gross profit to profit and loss will be as follows:

At the end of 1944:

Deferred gross profit on installment sales	$35,000.00	
Profit and loss		$35,000.00
Balance before transfer $50,000.00		
Amount still deferred 15,000.00		
To profit and loss $35,000.00		

At the end of 1945:

Deferred gross profit on installment sales	$60,000.00	
Profit and loss		$60,000.00
(With explanation of computation)		

At the end of 1946:

Deferred gross profit on installment sales	112,500.00	
Profit and loss		112,500.00
(With explanation of computation)		

The deferred gross profit account will appear as follows:

Deferred Gross Profit on Installment Sales

	Debit	Credit	Balance
1944: On 1944 sales		$ 50,000.00	
To profit and loss	$ 35,000.00		
Balance			$15,000.00
1945: On 1945 sales		80,000.00	
To profit and loss	60,000.00		
Balance			35,000.00
1946: On 1946 sales		125.000.00	
To profit and loss	112,500.00		
Balance			47,500.00

Departmental rates of gross profit. If a business is divided into several departments with widely differing rates of gross profit, and if the ratios of periodical collections to sales differ by departments, it may be desirable, in the interest of greater accuracy, to keep the records in such a manner that the gross profit rate for each department for each year can be applied to the cash collections on the departmental installment sales of each year. Such a procedure will, of course, involve a considerable amount of additional work, for it will be necessary to classify the collections not merely by years but by years and departments.

The use of an average rate of gross profit will produce the same results as the use of the different departmental rates if the ratio of annual collections to sales is the same in each department. This is shown by the following illustration, in which the departmental rates of gross profit differ, but the ratios of annual collections to sales are uniform: 75% the first year in each department, and 25% the second year.

	Departments			
	A	B	C	Total
1944 sales and gross profits:				
Sales	$100,000	$100,000	$60,000	$260,000
Gross profits	30,000	40,000	28,800	98,800
Rate of gross profit	30%	40%	48%	38%

Collections and realized profits	Departments A	B	C	Total
1943:				
Collections (75%)..........	$ 75,000	$ 75,000	$45,000	$195,000
Profit realized:				
Computed by multiplying departmental collections by departmental rates..	22,500	30,000	21,600	74,100
Computed by multiplying total collections by average rate..............				74,100
1944:				
Collections (25%)..........	$ 25,000	$ 25,000	$15,000	$ 65,000
Profit realized:				
Using departmental collections and rates........	7,500	10,000	7,200	24,700
Using total collections and average rate...........				24,700

The use of an average rate of gross profit will not produce the same results as the use of the departmental rates if the ratios of annual collections to sales are not the same in all departments. This is shown by the following illustration, which differs from the preceding one only in the amounts of annual collections.

	Departments A	B	C	Total
1944 sales and gross profits:				
Sales..........................	$100,000	$100,000	$60,000	$260,000
Gross profits.................	30,000	40,000	28,800	98,800
Rate of gross profit..........	30%	40%	48%	38%
Collections and realized profits:				
1944:				
Collections................	$ 75,000	$ 40,000	$15,000	$130,000
Profit realized:				
Using departmental collections and rates........	22,500	16,000	7,200	45,700
Using total collections and average rate..........				49,400
1945:				
Collections................	$ 25,000	$ 60,000	$25,000	$110,000
Profit realized:				
Using departmental collections and rates........	7,500	24,000	12,000	43,500
Using total collections and average rate..........				41,800
1946:				
Collections................			$20,000	$ 20,000
Profit realized:				
Using departmental collections and rates........			9,600	9,600
Using total collections and average rate..........				7,600

As indicated by these illustrations, the decision with regard to using departmental rates should depend on whether the variations in gross profit rates *and* collection periods are so great that the extra accounting labor is advisable in order to avoid material inaccuracies.

Defaults and repossessions. If a customer defaults in the payment of installments and if no further collections can be expected, both his account and the deferred profit applicable to the uncollectible installments should be written off.

A default by a customer usually results in a repossession of the merchandise by the seller, and the loss on the uncollectible account is reduced to the extent of the value of the property. In fact, the value of the repossessed property may be sufficient to produce a profit on the repossession.

Four methods of accounting for repossessed merchandise are discussed below:

(1) Do not take up the repossessed merchandise as an asset at the time it is repossessed, and charge as a loss the entire excess of the balance of the receivable over the related deferred gross profit; when the repossessed merchandise is sold, record the entire selling price as income.

This method is sometimes used if the repossessed property has little value, or if its realizable value cannot be determined with a reasonable degree of accuracy. It should be understood that, if this method is used, statements prepared before the disposal of repossessed property of value will misstate the profits or losses on repossessions and will understate the assets.

(2) Take up the repossessed property at an amount equal to the excess of the balance of the receivable over the related deferred gross profit. For example, assume these facts:

	Receivable	Deferred Gross Profit
Original selling price	$150.00	$150.00
Cost		100.00
Gross profit (33⅓%)		$ 50.00
Collections	60.00	
Gross profit applicable to collections (33⅓%)		20.00
Account balances at date of repossession	$ 90.00	$ 30.00

The entry for the default and repossession would be:

Repossessed merchandise inventory	$60.00	
Deferred gross profit	30.00	
Account receivable		$90.00

This method has little except convenience to recommend it. The repossessed merchandise is given an arbitrary value equal to the net balance of the receivable and deferred gross profit accounts, and the taking of a loss (or possible profit) on the default is postponed until the repossessed merchandise is resold.

(3) Take up the repossessed property at the unrecovered cost; that is, at the original cost minus all collections; in the above illustration, at $100.00 minus $60.00, or $40.00. This procedure necessitates reversing the portion of gross profit previously regarded as earned, and treating it as a reduction of the valuation of the repossession inventory. The entry for the default and repossession would be:

Repossessed merchandise inventory	$40.00	
Profit and loss (for profits previously taken up)	20.00	
Deferred gross profit	30.00	
Account receivable		$90.00

This method is also subject to the criticism that the amount of loss taken on the default is the result of a purely arbitrary valuation of the repossessed merchandise.

(4) Take up the repossessed property at its depreciated value or unrecovered cost, whichever is lower. The unrecovered cost, in this instance, is computed as follows:

Cost	$100.00
Ratio of cost to selling price—66⅔%	
Collections—$60.00	
Recovered cost—66⅔% of $60.00	40.00
Unrecovered cost	$ 60.00

Assuming a depreciated value of $55.00, the entry will be:

Repossessed merchandise inventory	$55.00	
Deferred gross profit	30.00	
Loss on defaults	5.00	
Account receivable		$90.00

This method appears to be the most logical and most conservative one. The procedure for determining the loss may be stated as follows:

Determine the gross profit or loss actually realized on the sale in the following manner:	
Collections	$ 60.00
Valuation of property recovered	55.00
Total	$115.00
Cost	100.00
Gross profit realized	$ 15.00
Deduct the amount of gross profit previously taken up	20.00
The difference represents the loss on repossession	$ 5.00

The account title, repossessed merchandise inventory, used in the foregoing illustrative journal entries presupposes that the perpetual inventory method of merchandise accounting is in operation. If the periodical inventory method is in operation, the word *inventory* should be omitted from the title, and the account should be understood to be of the same nature as a purchase account.

No entries are here given for resales of repossessed merchandise; if resales are made on an installment basis, entries similar to those previously described in this chapter would be made; the student is equally familiar with the entries to be made if sales are made for cash or on regular credit terms.

Default and repossession register. A register in somewhat the following form may be used for the recording of defaults and repossessions:

Default and Repossession Register

Date		Name	1944 Accounts (30%)	1945 Accounts (40%)	1946 Accounts (33⅓%)	Repossessed Merchandise
1946						
July	5	Customer *A* (see foregoing illustration)			$100.00	$ 55.00
July	11	Customer *B*	$ 100.00			20.00
July	12	Customer *C*		$ 150.00		60.00
		(*et cetera*)				
			$1,500.00	$1,200.00	$900.00	$1,350.00
		Deferred gross profit	$ 450.00	$ 480.00	$300.00	

The account balances to be written off as uncollectible are classified in columns showing the year of origin, so that the deferred gross profits applicable thereto can be determined in total by multiplying each column total by the gross profit rate applicable to the year of sale (shown in the column heading). This procedure assumes that transfers from the deferred gross profit accounts to income are made monthly, so that only the deferred gross profit applicable to the account balance at the date of default appears in the deferred gross profit account.

The receivable accounts in the subsidiary ledgers are written off by crediting them with the amounts shown opposite the customers' names.

At the end of the month, the following summary entry is posted to the accounts in the general ledger:

Repossessed merchandise inventory	$1,350.00	
Deferred gross profit—1944	450.00	
Deferred gross profit—1945	480.00	
Deferred gross profit—1946	300.00	
Loss on defaults (to balance the journal entry)	1,020.00	
Receivables—1944		$1,500.00
Receivables—1945		1,200.00
Receivables—1946		900.00

Alternative method of recording defaults. The following illustrative entries indicate an alternative procedure for recording defaults and repossessions. Entries for two conditions, both based on the illustration on pages 84 and 85, are given.

First, on the assumption that the default occurs in the year of the sale, before any profit has been taken up as realized. The sale is reversed, and the balance in the account receivable is closed out; the installments collected and forfeited are recorded as a separate class of income; the cost of the property is removed from the regular merchandise accounts, the valuation of the repossession is set up, and the difference between the original cost of the property and its valuation as a repossession is recorded as a loss.

Installment sales	$150.00	
Account receivable		$ 90.00
Income from forfeited contract		60.00
Repossessed merchandise inventory	55.00	
Loss on repossessions	45.00	
Merchandise inventory (or purchases)		100.00

The net income taken up is $60.00 minus $45.00, or $15.00.

Second, on the assumption that the default occurs in a year subsequent to that of the sale, after realized profit has been taken up at the end of the year. Referring to the foregoing illustration, and assuming that $45.00 was collected during the year of sale and $15.00 during the subsequent year, before default, the entries for the two years will be:

Year of sale:

Account receivable	$150.00	
Installment sales		$150.00
Cash	45.00	
Account receivable		45.00
Installment sales	150.00	
Purchases (or inventory)		100.00
Deferred gross profit		50.00
Deferred gross profit	15.00	
Profit and loss (33⅓% of $45.00)		15.00

Subsequent year:

Cash	$ 15.00	
Account receivable		$15.00
Repossessed merchandise inventory	55.00	
Deferred gross profit ($50.00 − $15.00)	35.00	
Loss on repossession	15.00	
Account receivable		90.00
Income from forfeited contract (collection)		15.00

The $15.00 loss on repossession is computed as follows:

Unrecovered cost:	
Cost	$100.00
Less cost recovery in first year's collections (the collections during the year of repossession are treated wholly as a special class of income)—66⅔% of $45.00	30.00
Unrecovered cost	$ 70.00
Valuation given to repossession	55.00
Loss on repossession	$ 15.00

Refunds to customers. In some states a defaulting customer is entitled to credit for the proceeds of the sale of the repossessed chattel, less costs of repossession and resale; and any credit balance finally remaining in his account is payable to him. Under such conditions, the seller is virtually acting as the customer's agent for the resale of the property, and it seems unnecessary to place any tentative valuation on the property for purposes of record prior to resale. Returning to the illustration in which the accounts appeared as follows at the date of repossession,

Customer *A*

Charge for sale	$150.00	Credits for cash	$60.00

Deferred Gross Profit

Taken into income	$20.00	Total	$50.00

and assuming that the repossessed property was resold for $110.00 and that the expenses of repossession and resale amounted to $15.00, we might make entries as follows:

Customer *A*	$ 15.00	
Cash		$ 15.00
Expenses of repossession and resale.		
Cash or account receivable	110.00	
Customer *A*		110.00
Entry for resale of property.		
Customer *A*	5.00	
Cash		5.00
Refund to customer.		
Deferred gross profit	30.00	
Profit and loss		30.00
Balance of deferred gross profit taken into income.		

If, after crediting the customer with the proceeds of resale and charging him with the repossession and resale expense, his account has a debit balance, this balance and the deferred gross profit applicable to his account should be written off, the difference between these two balances representing the loss or gain on the default.

Expenses and bad debt losses. Two questions arise with respect to expenses, namely:

(1) Since gross profits are deferred and taken into income on the basis of collections, should expenses of the period of sale be similarly deferred and charged to income on the basis of collections?

There is an element of inconsistency in deferring the profits from sales and not deferring the expenses incurred in making the sales; this inconsistency may be justified, however, because the realization of the profits is regarded as contingent upon the collection of the accounts, whereas the same contingency does not exist with respect to the expenses already incurred. Nevertheless, the immediate charge-off of expenses coupled with the deferring of the gross profit seems to result in a distortion of net profits between the accounting periods during which collections are made. To illustrate, assume that an article which cost $1,200.00 is sold for $1,500.00; that the expenses connected with the sale were $120.00; and that $250.00 of the sale price was collected during the year of sale and $1,250.00 was collected during the subsequent year. The net profits taken during the two years on the installment basis of accounting, if the expenses of the year of sale are charged off during that year, are computed below:

Sale price	$1,500.00
Cost	1,200.00
Gross profit—20%	$ 300.00

	First Year	Second Year
Collections	$ 250.00	$1,250.00
Gross profit	$ 50.00	$ 250.00
Expenses	120.00	—
Net loss	$ 70.00	
Net profit (before charges for any expenses incurred during the second year)		$ 250.00

If the expenses were deferred and charged off ratably with the gross profit taken up, the results for the two years would be:

	First Year	Second Year
Gross profit	$50.00	$250.00
Expenses	20.00	100.00
Net profit (subject to charges for expenses incurred in second year)	$30.00	$150.00

Although the deferring of expenses is thus indicated to have some theoretical justification, it would usually be difficult, as a practical matter, to determine the amount of expense which could be properly deferred as applicable to the installment sales.

(2) Expenses will be incurred in periods subsequent to the period in which the sale is made. For example, collection expenses will be incurred and sales commissions may be payable on the basis of amounts collected. Should reserves be provided for such expenses?

To set up such reserves by charges against the profits of the period in which the sales were made appears to be too severe; such a procedure would mean that the sale period would be deprived of the deferred portion of the gross profit but would, nevertheless, be charged with all past and prospective expenses connected with the sale. For this reason, current practice sanctions charging the sale period with the expenses incurred in that period, and charging subsequent periods with the expenses incurred in such subsequent periods. But reserves for bad debt losses and future expenses may be created by charges against the deferred profit, as discussed later.

Profit and loss statement. The computation of the realized gross profit may be shown in a schedule supporting the profit and loss statement, in the manner illustrated below.

Profit and Loss Statement
Year Ended December 31, 1946

Sales—other than installment sales	$ 60,000.00
Less cost thereof	40,000.00
Gross profit	$ 20,000.00
Realized gross profit on installment sales (Schedule 1):	
1944 sales	9,000.00
1945 sales	25,200.00
1946 sales	49,500.00
Total realized gross profit	$103,700.00
Loss on defaults	4,000.00
Gross profit less defaults	$ 99,700.00

Schedule of Realized Gross Profits on Installment Sales — Schedule 1

	1944	1945	1946
Installment sales	$150,000.00	$175,000.00	$190,000.00
Cost of goods sold	90,000.00	101,500.00	104,500.00
Gross profit	$ 60,000.00	$ 73,500.00	$ 85,500.00
Rate of gross profit	40%	42%	45%
Collections in 1946	$ 22,500.00	$ 60,000.00	$110,000.00
Profit applicable to collections	9,000.00	25,200.00	49,500.00

Or the profit and loss statement may be prepared as follows:

Profit and Loss Statement
Year Ended December 31, 1946

Sales	$250,000.00
Less cost of goods sold (Exhibit B)	144,500.00
Gross profit	$105,500.00
Less unrealized gross profit applicable to uncollected installment receivables	36,000.00
Gross profit realized on 1946 sales	$ 69,500.00
Add gross profit realized in 1946 on collections of:	
1944 sales	9,000.00
1945 sales	25,200.00
Total realized gross profit	$103,700.00
Loss on defaults	4,000.00
Gross profit less defaults	$ 99,700.00
Selling and general expenses (detailed and deducted in the usual manner)	

The balance sheet. If possible, the installment accounts receivable should be shown by years of maturity; those due more than one year from the balance sheet date should be excluded from the current assets, thus:

Balance Sheet—December 31, 1946

Current assets:		
Installment accounts receivable due in 1947		$57,800.00
Other assets:		
Installment accounts receivable due after 1947:		
Due in 1948	$54,500.00	
Due in 1949	24,000.00	78,500.00

If the major portion of the installment receivables is due within one year from the balance sheet date, custom seems to sanction including the total amount of the receivables under the current asset caption.

Although reserves for the estimated future expenses and for bad debts should not be set up by charges to profit and loss, there is no objection to making an apportionment of the deferred gross profit account to show what portions thereof represent estimated requirements for expenses and bad debts. In fact, such a procedure may be desirable. If such an apportionment is made, a clearer and more complete picture is presented by the balance sheet; and, since the reserves are set up out of the deferred profit rather than by charges to profit and loss, the portion of the profit regarded as realized during the sale period is not subjected to charges for subsequent expenses.

The deferred gross profit should be sufficient to cover bad debt losses and future expenses applicable to past sales, and still leave a margin of net profit. Therefore, if estimates can be made, the deferred gross profit should be divided into three elements for balance sheet presentation. Assume that a deferred gross profit balance of $50,000.00 is estimated to contain the following elements:

Provision for losses on bad debts	$10,000.00
Provision for future expenses applicable to past sales	15,000.00
Deferred net profit	25,000.00

These elements may be classified in the balance sheet thus:

Reserve for bad debts	$10,000.00
(To be deducted from the accounts receivable, to reduce the net balance to the estimated realizable value of the installment receivables.)	
Reserve for installment sales expenses	$15,000.00
(In the author's opinion, this reserve should appear under a reserve caption and should not be included among the liabilities because no liabilities for the estimated subsequent expenses exist at the balance sheet date.)	
Estimated net profit on installment sales	$25,000.00
(This portion of the deferred gross profit should be shown in the balance sheet under the caption of deferred credits.)	

It should be understood that, if the deferred gross profit is thus apportioned, the apportionment is made *for balance sheet purposes only:* if desired, reserves may be set up by adjusting entries as of the balance sheet date; reversing entries will then be required as of the beginning of the next period. The deferred gross profit should be transferred to income when the profit is realized, and bad debts and expenses should be charged to income.

The company's loss experience can be used as a basis for determining the amount of the bad debt reserve. If, for instance, the losses have been two per cent of the liquidation (liquidation meaning the amount of the credit to the receivables during the period), a two per cent rate may be applied to the balances of the accounts to estimate the total required reserve. If it is desired to inspect individual accounts to estimate probable losses, the seasoned accounts (those of sufficient age to have established an experience record) can be judged on the basis of collections. With respect to unseasoned accounts, consideration should be given to the customer's previous paying record, if any, and also to the amount of down payment and the length of time over which the account is to be collected. As a general rule, customers who have made small down payments are less likely to pay their accounts in full than those who have made a sufficient down payment to create a considerable equity in the property, which they wish to protect; also, if the installments run over a long period, and the property is subject to depreciation, there is the hazard that the depreciated value of the property, or secondhand value, may become less than the uncollected balance of the account, and that the customer will therefore cease making payments.

Contracts of sale. If title is retained until after all or a certain portion of the sale price is collected, the transaction is a contract to sell, and not a sale; and it may be desired to make this distinction in the accounts.

Assume that a company holds land which cost $50,000.00, and that it contracts to pass title to a certain parcel, which cost $1,000.00, after the sale price of $1,800.00 has been collected. When the contract is signed, the following entry may be made:

Contracts receivable	$1,800.00	
Land sold under contract		$1,000.00
Deferred gross profit on installment sale		800.00

Collections would be recorded and profits taken up in the manner already illustrated. Until title passes, the balances of the land account and the land sold under contract account should appear on the balance sheet as follows:

Land	$50,000.00	
Less land sold under contract—title not passed	1,000.00	
Land available for sale		$49,000.00

When the final installment is received, an entry should be made debiting land sold under contract and crediting land.

Interest. If installment sales contracts call for interest on uncollected balances, the interest should be taken into income during the period in which it accrues. Three typical conditions regarding interest are illustrated below; the illustrations are based on a contract requiring the payment of a principal sum of $500.00 in five annual installments, with interest at 6%.

(1) Long-end interest. This term signifies that, on each installment date, the debtor pays one period's interest on the unpaid balance of the debt. As the principal is diminished each period, the interest payments are correspondingly diminished. Contracts calling for the payment of long-end interest may provide for:

(*a*) The payment of an equal periodical sum to apply on the principal, plus an additional sum to cover the interest. Payments under such a contract are illustrated below:

End of Year	Collections Total	Collections Interest	Collections Principal	Balance of Principal
				$500.00
1	$130.00	$30.00	$100.00	400.00
2	124.00	24.00	100.00	300.00
3	118.00	18.00	100.00	200.00
4	112.00	12.00	100.00	100.00
5	106.00	6.00	100.00	

(*b*) The payment of an equal periodical sum to include the accrued interest and a payment on the principal. The computation of the annual payment and the reduction of the debt are shown below:

4.2123638 = Present value of annuity of 5 rents of 1 at 6%
$500.00 ÷ 4.2123638 = $118.70, annual payment

End of Year	Collections Total	Collections Interest	Collections Principal	Balance of Principal
				$500.00
1	$118.70	$30.00	$ 88.70	411.30
2	118.70	24.68	94.02	317.28
3	118.70	19.04	99.66	217.62
4	118.70	13.06	105.64	111.98
5	118.70	6.72	111.98	

(2) Short-end interest. The debtor pays, with each installment, the interest on that installment from the beginning of the contract period to the date of payment.

In the foregoing illustration, the debtor would pay $100.00 per annum on the principal; at the end of the first year, he would pay $100.00 plus one year's interest thereon; at the end of the second year he would pay $100.00 plus two years' interest thereon; and so on. It will be noted that, by the short-end interest method, the annual interest payments increase. The interest accruals and the payments on interest and principal are tabulated below:

End of Year	Interest: Accrued During Year	Interest: Paid	Interest: Unpaid End of Year	Principal: Payment	Principal: Balance
					$500.00
1	$30.00	$ 6.00	$24.00	$100.00	400.00
2	24.00	12.00	36.00	100.00	300.00
3	18.00	18.00	36.00	100.00	200.00
4	12.00	24.00	24.00	100.00	100.00
5	6.00	30.00		100.00	

It will be observed, with respect to long-end interest, that all interest accrued during the period is payable at the end of the period; the credits to interest income should therefore agree with the interest collections. For instance, in the first illustration of long-end interest, the entry for interest at the end of the first year will be a debit to cash and a credit to interest income for $30.00; at the end of the second year, a debit to cash and a credit to interest income for $24.00.

In the case of short-end interest, however, the interest collections do not agree annually with the interest earned. In the third illustration, the entries for interest should be:

First year:

Cash	$ 6.00	
Accrued interest receivable	24.00	
Interest income		$30.00

Second year:

Cash	$12.00	
Accrued interest receivable	12.00	
Interest income		$24.00

Third year:

Cash	$18.00	
Interest income		$18.00

Fourth year:

Cash	$24.00	
Accrued interest receivable		$12.00
Interest income		12.00

Fifth year:

Cash	$30.00	
Accrued interest receivable		$24.00
Interest income		6.00

CHAPTER 37

Insurance

Introduction. An insurance policy is a contract between an insurance company and the insured, by which the company agrees to pay the insured for a specified damage, loss, or liability, contingent upon the occurrence of some event.

Premiums are usually payable in advance. The rates represent the charge per $100.00 or $1,000.00 of insurance carried, and are usually computed on a standard basis which is adjusted, by local factors and indorsement clauses, to the requirements of particular cases. Policies, except those for life insurance, generally cover a period of from one to three years; rate advantages are usually obtained by purchasing policies covering a period of more than one year. Cancellation, if permissible, may be effected by either party upon notice to the other; a specified time must usually elapse before the cancellation becomes effective. If the policy is cancelled by the company, the premium refundable to the insured will be computed on a pro-rata basis; if the policy is cancelled by the insured, the premium refundable to him will be computed on a "short rate" basis, and will be less than the unexpired portion of the premium.

An accountant should have a knowledge of the types of insurance protection available; he should know whether changes in specific or total asset values will affect the coverage in force; he should understand the proper accounting treatment of accrued and unexpired premiums, rebates, dividends, and surrender and loan values; and he should know what accounts and records are necessary to prove an insured loss and to obtain settlement.

In this chapter especial consideration will be given to fire, life, and workmen's compensation insurance, which present the principal accounting problems; some of the distinguishing features of a few other important types of insurance will be mentioned.

Fire Insurance

General. Property insurable against fire may be classified as:

Buildings.
Building contents: merchandise, machinery, and so forth.
Miscellaneous property.

The rates for fire insurance depend upon construction, occupancy, exposure, and protection. *Construction* means the material used and the number of stories in the building insured, or in the building containing the property insured. *Occupancy* refers to any special hazards resulting from the nature of the business conducted. *Exposure* means the distance from other buildings, and any hazard which might arise from the proximity of dangerous buildings. *Protection* refers to such matters as distance from a fire hydrant, the efficiency of the fire department, the installation of automatic sprinklers, and the employment of watchmen.

The co-insurance clause. Because losses are often only partial, there is a tendency to insure for only a portion of the value of the property. To combat this tendency, policies may contain a co-insurance clause, in which the insured consents, in consideration of a reduction in the rate, to carry insurance in an amount equal to a stipulated per cent of the value of the property. The following is such a clause:

"In consideration of the premium for which this policy is issued, it is expressly stipulated that, in event of loss, this company shall be liable for no greater proportion thereof than the sum hereby insured bears to 80% of the cash value of the property described herein at the time when such loss shall happen."

If the insured does not carry insurance in an amount equal to the co-insurance requirements, he is regarded as being himself a co-insurer with the insurance company; that is, he carries a portion of the risk. For example, if, under an 80% co-insurance policy, the insured carries insurance equal to only 70% of the value of the property at the date of the loss, he is a co-insurer for 10%. Any loss will be borne seven eighths by the company and one eighth by the insured; however, the company will not be liable for more than the face of the policy. If the policy is 80% of the sound value of the property, the company will be liable for all losses up to the face of the policy.

The operation of this clause is illustrated below.

First illustration:

Value of property at date of loss	$10,000.00
Policy—80%	8,000.00

The company is liable for all losses up to $8,000.00.

Second illustration:

Value of property at date of loss	$10,000.00
Policy—more than 80%	8,500.00

The company is liable for all losses up to $8,500.00.

Third illustration:

Value of property at date of loss	$10,000.00
Policy—70%	7,000.00
Loss	4,000.00

The insured is a co-insurer for 1/8 of all losses, and the company's liability is 7/8 of $4,000.00, or $3,500.00.

Fourth illustration:

Value of property at date of loss	$10,000.00
Policy—65%	6,500.00
Loss	4,000.00

The insured is a co-insurer for 15/80 of all losses, and the company's liability is 65/80 of $4,000.00, or $3,250.00.

Fifth illustration:

Value of property at date of loss	$10,000.00
Policy—65%	6,500.00
Loss	Total

65/80 of $10,000.00 is $8,125.00, but the policy is for only $6,500.00; hence the company's liability is $6,500.00.

From these illustrations the following general rule may be derived. To determine the insurance company's liability under a policy with the 80% co-insurance clause: When the policy is less than 80% of the sound value of the property, multiply the loss by a fraction, the numerator of which is the face of the policy and the denominator of which is 80% of the sound value of the property. The product is the liability of the company, except that the liability cannot be more than the face of the policy.

If the insured amount is 80% or more of the sound value of the property, the co-insurance clause does not affect the settlement.

When the policy contains a co-insurance clause, it is important to watch changing values of the insured property, caused either by additional purchases or by increases in market value. To illustrate, assume that property was purchased at a cost of $5,000.00 and insured for $4,000.00 under a policy containing an 80% co-insurance clause. Later, when the property had a sound value of $8,000.00, it was destroyed, with a loss of $4,000.00. Settlement would be made as follows:

Sound value	$8,000.00
80% thereof	6,400.00

Company's liability: 40/64 of $4,000.00, or $2,500.00.

Although of particular importance in fire insurance, co-insurance clauses may be included in policies for other types of insurance. An 80% co-insurance rate was used in the preceding illustrations because it is the usual rate in fire insurance policies; other co-insurance rates are also used.

Contribution clause. If property is insured with several companies, each company whose policy contains a contribution clause assumes a liability for only a pro-rata portion of the loss; this portion is computed by multiplying the loss by a fraction, the numerator of which is the face of the policy, and the denominator of which is:

(1) The face of all policies, if the company's policy carries no co-insurance clause (see Company *A*, below) or if the insurance carried meets the requirements of the policy (see Company *B*, below).

(2) The insurance required under the co-insurance clause, if the company's policy contains such a clause and its requirements have not been met (see Company *C*, below).

To illustrate, assume that property having a sound value of $100,000.00 is insured under the policies described below, and that a loss of $75,000.00 is incurred. The amount collectible from each company is computed as follows:

		Insurance				
Company	Co-Insurance Clause	Required by C.-I. Clause	Carried	Fraction	Loss	Amount Collectible
A	None	—	$40,000.00	$\frac{40}{80}$	$75,000.00	$37,500.00
B	75%	$75,000.00	20,000.00	$\frac{20}{80}$	75,000.00	18,750.00
C	90%	90,000.00	20,000.00	$\frac{20}{90}$	75,000.00	16,666.67
Total			$80,000.00			$72,916.67

Floater policies. Under a floater policy, the insured property may be moved from one place to another for processing, storing, or other purposes. The property is insured, regardless of its location, within specified geographical limits, and with limitations upon the amount payable on a loss at any one location. Under this type of policy, inventory records showing the value of property at various locations are desirable for the purpose of proving losses.

Losses. Settlements for losses are usually based on the sound value of the property at the date of the loss; that is, cost or market value new, as of that date, less depreciation. Salvage is the sound value of property saved. The amount of the loss is the sound value of the property minus the salvage.

In the event of a loss, the insured should notify the company at once, and should file a formal proof of loss, usually within sixty days and usually on a form provided by the company, showing, among other things, the cash value of the property at the time of the loss and the amount of the recovery claimed.

If the insured and the company cannot agree on the amount of the loss, each may appoint a competent, disinterested appraiser; the appraisers then appoint an umpire; if the appraisers fail to agree upon a settlement, the umpire's decision is final.

Fire loss account. When a fire occurs, a fire loss account should be immediately set up. It should be charged with:

The carrying value of the fixed assets destroyed or damaged.
The estimated value of the inventories.
The unexpired insurance.

It should be credited with:

The value of the salvage.
The settlement received from the insurance company.

The balance of the account should not necessarily be regarded as a profit or loss from the fire; it is presumably a composite of several elements: adjustment of prior depreciation provisions, realization of changes in market values, and the difference between the sound value of the property lost and the insurance collected.

Carrying value of assets. If the fire occurs some time after the closing of the books, there will be accrued depreciation to record. This should be put on the books in the customary manner, by debiting depreciation accounts and crediting reserve accounts.

If all the fixed assets are destroyed, each depreciation reserve should be closed against its related fixed asset account, and the resulting balances of the fixed asset accounts should be closed to fire loss. If only a partial loss is sustained, the fixed asset accounts should be relieved of the cost of the property destroyed, and the depreciation reserves should be relieved of the depreciation provided on such property.

If the salvage is to be sold, no entries for salvage should be made until sales are effected; the fire loss account should be held open until that time in order to show the final surplus adjustment resulting from the fire. If the salvage is to be put back into use, the fixed asset accounts should be debited and fire loss credited with the estimated value.

Estimated values of inventories. The method of estimating the value of the merchandise inventories on hand at the date of the fire will depend upon the accounting records kept. If perpetual inventories are maintained, they usually furnish the best possible evidence of quantities. If there are no perpetual inventories, the gross profit method may be used. To illustrate, assuming an inventory of $30,000.00 at the last closing, purchases of $60,000.00 between the date of closing and the date of the fire, sales of $75,000.00, and an estimated gross profit of 33⅓%, the inventory at the date of the fire might be estimated as follows:

Inventory, at date of last closing		$30,000.00
Add purchases		60,000.00
Total		$90,000.00
Less estimated cost of sales:		
Sales	$75,000.00	
Less gross profit—33⅓%	25,000.00	50,000.00
Estimated inventory at date of fire		$40,000.00

The value thus ascertained may be subject to scaling down by the adjuster for depreciation in the value of goods which were shopworn, damaged prior to the fire, or out of style.

In this connection it is important to note the effect on the estimated inventory valuation if the inventory at the date of the last closing was written down to a market value below cost, or was marked down because of depreciation or obsolescence. Assume, for instance, that the inventory at the date of the last closing cost $30,000.00 but was written down to $25,000.00. Using all other figures in the preceding illustration, the inventory value at the date of the fire would be reduced $5,000.00, as shown below:

Inventory, at date of last closing		$25,000.00
Add purchases		60,000.00
Total		$85,000.00
Less estimated cost of sales:		
Sales	$75,000.00	
Less gross profit—33⅓%	25,000.00	50,000.00
Estimated inventory at date of fire		$35,000.00

It is apparent that the inventory value at the date of the fire is reduced $5,000.00. This is the amount of the conservative provision for decreases in market value or for other losses applicable to the inventory which was on hand at the date of the last closing. But all of these goods, or a large portion of them, may have been sold, so that the inventory at the date of the fire should be stated at $40,000.00 instead of at $35,000.00.

It would certainly be unfortunate if the fact that a merchant deducted $5,000.00 from his inventory on January 1, in order to state his profits conservatively, caused him to suffer an unwarranted loss in the estimated value of an inventory on hand at, say, the following September 1. To avoid such a loss, it is advisable to preserve inventory sheets showing both the cost and market, or depreciated, values.

The question remains concerning the entries to be made for the inventory. If desired, the books may be closed, but this would be an unusual procedure; after the inventories are set up in the usual manner, as an incident to such a closing, the value of the destroyed inventories may be transferred from the inventory accounts to the fire loss account. In making the closing entries and the entries transferring inventory values to the fire loss account, the accountant should use estimated values and not those allowed by the adjuster. If the adjuster's values were used, any extraneous loss resulting from his scaling down of values, or any extraneous profit resulting from an excess of market value at the date of the fire over cost, would be improperly merged in the operating accounts instead of being clearly shown as an extraneous item in the fire loss account, where it belongs.

If it is not desired to close the books at the date of the fire, the debits to fire loss for inventories destroyed may be offset by credits to raw materials burned, goods in process burned, and finished goods burned. These accounts will remain open until the next closing of the books.

Unexpired insurance. All insurance premiums expired between the date of the last closing and the date of the fire should be charged to the insurance expense account. If the loss is so great as to exhaust the policy and cause its cancellation, all insurance unexpired at the date of the fire should be charged to the fire loss account. If the loss is only partial, the payment will be indorsed on the policy and the remainder of the policy will continue in force. In such cases, the fire loss account should be charged with such a proportion of the unexpired insurance as the indorsement bears to the face of the policy.

To illustrate, assume that, on January 1, insurance policies of $40,000.00 were carried and that the unexpired insurance premiums were $600.00. All policies were to expire on the following December 31. A fire occurred on September 1, and $30,000.00 was received from the insurance company. The insurance premium entries should be:

Insurance	$400.00	
Unexpired insurance		$400.00
To charge operations with insurance premiums expired between January 1 and September 1.		
Fire loss	150.00	
Unexpired insurance		150.00
To charge fire loss with three fourths of the $200.00 insurance premiums unexpired on September 1, the insurance company having paid $30,000.00 on policies of $40,000.00.		

Desirable records. To facilitate the preparation of a proof of loss, the following books and records are desirable:

(1) A plant ledger, with a separate account for each item of fixed property, showing cost and depreciation taken.
(2) Vouchers and supporting bills which may be submitted to the adjuster, if demanded, in proof of cost.
(3) A perpetual inventory, or inventory sheets showing both cost and marked-down values.
(4) A record showing exactly what property is insured under each policy.

An appraisal of fixed assets is extremely important from an insurance standpoint, even though it is not recorded on the books. It is of service in determining insurance requirements, under co-insurance clauses and otherwise, and in effecting settlements in case of loss.

Life Insurance

Business uses. The following are some of the important reasons why a business may insure the lives of its owners or employees:

(1) To provide funds for the purchase of the shares of a deceased stockholder in a close corporation, and thus keep the stock under the control of interested parties.
(2) To provide funds for the payment of the capital interest of a deceased partner, without placing an undue strain on the working capital.
(3) To compensate for the loss which might result from the death of an important member of the organization.

Beneficiaries. If the insured or his estate is the beneficiary, the premiums are virtually additional salary, and should be so recorded. Such insurance, however, is not customary.

Usually the business is named as the beneficiary. To be so named, the business must have an insurable interest in the life of the person insured. An insurable interest exists if the business has a reasonable ground for expecting some benefit or advantage from the continued life of the insured.

Premiums, dividends, and cash and loan values. Life insurance premiums are payable in advance, usually at annual intervals, but sometimes semiannually, quarterly, or monthly. In the illustrations in this chapter, it is assumed that premiums are payable annually.

Dividends are distributions, to policy holders, of a portion of the earned surplus of mutual insurance companies. Various options may be exercised with respect to the use of dividends, but in business insurance they are probably applied most frequently as a deduction from the premiums payable. Dividends often are not payable on a policy before the end of the second year of its life.

The cash surrender value is the amount which the insurance company will pay to the insured upon cancellation of the policy; a policy usually has no cash surrender value until the end of the third policy year, although the policies of some companies provide for a surrender value at the end of the second year.

The loan value is the amount which the insurance company will loan on a policy maintained in force. The loan value at any date is equal to the cash surrender value at the end of the policy year, minus discount thereon from the loan date to the end of the policy year. If a policy has a cash surrender value at the end of the third year, it has a loan value at the beginning of the third year, after the payment of the third year's premium. The following table shows one company's cash surrender values on a $50,000.00 straight life policy taken at the age of thirty-five; values are given here for only the earlier years of the policy. The loan values at the beginning of each year were computed by discounting the end-of-year cash values at 6%; that is, the cash value which will be available one year after making the premium payment was divided by 1.06 to determine the loan value at the date of paying the premium.

Year	Cash Surrender Value at End of Year	Loan Value at Beginning of Year
1	—	—
2	—	—
3	$1,590.50	$1,500.47
4	2,151.00	2,029.25
5	2,908.00	2,743.40
6	3,647.00	3,440.57

The premium less any dividend applied in reduction thereof is the net amount payable to the insurance company. The net premium less the increase in the cash or loan value during the year is the net insurance expense for the year.

Accounting for insurance expense and asset values. The accounting relative to the carrying of life insurance policies requires a recognition of expense and investment elements. But what is the insurance expense for a year? For the policy year it is the amount of a premium, minus (in the case of a participating policy) a dividend (after the policy has aged), and minus (with certain types of policies and after, usually, three years) an increase in an investment value. But should a dividend received at the end of, say, the fifth year be applied as a reduction of the premium of the fifth year, or as a reduction of the premium of the sixth year? Should all of the premiums of the first three years be regarded as expense, if no cash surrender value is established until the end of the third year, or should the amount shown by the policy as the cash surrender value at the end of the third year be applied ratably as a reduction of the expense during the first three years? Or should the total premium payments during the first three years be carried in suspense until the asset and expense elements thereof are determined at the end of the third year?

These problems are further complicated by the fact that the policy year rarely coincides with the company's accounting year; hence in the company reports for any accounting year, consideration must be given to premiums, dividends, and increases in asset value during two policy years. What constitutes the asset value applicable to a life insurance policy at any date, for balance sheet purposes? Should it be based on the cash surrender value at the end of the preceding policy year, or on the cash surrender value at the end of the current policy year? Or should it be determined by an interpolation between these two values? Or should loan values be used? Since premiums are payable at the beginning of the policy year, should unexpired premiums on life insurance policies as well as on fire insurance policies be shown as prepaid expenses in the balance sheet? And, since compound interest computations enter into the insurance company's determination of premiums, cash surrender values, and loan values, should the company owning the policy give any consideration to interest in computing its expense and asset values?

With so many alternatives, it is scarcely surprising that there is no apparent unanimity of accounting opinion with respect to the recording of life insurance expense and asset values. The procedures described in this chapter are not presented as the only acceptable ones; however, they have been checked with, and have received the approval of, insurance company representatives.

Premiums paid should be charged to life insurance expense. Dividends received should be credited to the same account. If the dividends are applied in reduction of premiums, the net premium should be charged to life insurance expense.

The cash or loan value of the policy should be set up as an asset, and the annual increase therein should be credited to life insurance expense. When the initial value is placed on the books during the third year of the policy's life, two thirds of the value should be regarded as applicable to the first two years of the policy's life, and a surplus* adjustment should be made with respect thereto; the other one third should be regarded as a reduction of the current year's insurance expense. Term policies have no cash value.

Some companies take up the increase in cash surrender value at the end of the policy year; other companies take up the increase in loan value at the beginning of the policy year. Both methods are illustrated below. Dividends are ignored in the illustrations. In the first two illustrations it is assumed that the policy anniversary date coincides with the close of the accounting period.

Cash values taken up at end of year. This illustration is based on a straight life policy of $50,000.00, taken at the age of thirty-five, with an annual premium of $1,405.50. The cash values are those shown in the foregoing table. Entries for the first four years are given below.

First and second years:

Life insurance expense	$1,405.50	
Cash		$1,405.50
Entry at beginning of year for payment of premium.		
Profit and loss	1,405.50	
Life insurance expense		1,405.50
Entry at end of year to charge off expense.		

Third year:

Life insurance expense	$1,405.50	
Cash		$1,405.50
Entry at beginning of year for payment of premium.		
Cash surrender value of life insurance	1,590.50	
Surplus (⅔ of $1,590.50)		1,060.33
Life insurance expense		530.17
Entry to take up cash surrender value at end of year.		
Profit and loss ($1,405.50 − $530.17)	875.33	
Life insurance expense		875.33
Entry at end of year to charge off expense.		

---

* As stated in *Intermediate Accounting*, there is, at the time of this writing, a tendency in the direction of maintaining a "clean surplus"; that is, many accountants advocate an abandonment of the traditional procedure of recording in surplus the corrections of profits of prior years as well as extraneous profits and losses; such accountants advocate showing items of this nature in a combined profit and loss and surplus statement. When, in this text, a statement is made that surplus should be charged or credited for an extraneous item or for a correction of the profits of prior periods, the reader will understand that a clean surplus may be maintained by charging or crediting the item to a special account and showing it in a non-operating section of the profit and loss statement.

Fourth year:

Life insurance expense	$1,405.50	
Cash		$1,405.50
Entry at beginning of year for payment of premium.		
Cash surrender value of life insurance	560.50	
Life insurance expense		560.50
Entry at end of year for increase in cash surrender value from $1,590.50 to $2,151.00		
Profit and loss	845.00	
Life insurance expense		845.00
Entry at end of year to charge off expense.		

Loan values taken up at beginning of year. When loan values are taken up at the beginning of the year, precision in terminology might suggest the use of an account with some title such as loan value of life insurance, instead of cash surrender value of life insurance. However, such a distinction is not usually made. Moreover, as will be shown in the final illustration, the account may at times show surrender values as well as loan values.

First and second years:

Life insurance expense	$1,405.50	
Cash		$1,405.50
Entry at beginning of year for payment of premium.		
Profit and loss	1,405.50	
Life insurance expense		1,405.50
Entry at end of year to charge off expense.		

Third year:

Life insurance expense	$1,405.50	
Cash		$1,405.50
Entry at beginning of year for payment of premium.		
Cash surrender value of life insurance	1,500.47	
Surplus (⅔ of $1,500.47)		1,000.31
Life insurance expense		500.16
Entry at beginning of year to take up loan value.		
Profit and loss	905.34	
Life insurance expense		905.34
Entry at end of year to charge off expense.		

Fourth year:

Life insurance expense	$1,405.50	
Cash		$1,405.50
Entry at beginning of year for payment of premium.		

Cash surrender value of life insurance............	$528.78	
Life insurance expense....................		$528.78
Entry at beginning of year for increase in loan value from $1,500.47 to $2,029.25.		
Profit and loss................................	876.72	
Life insurance expense....................		876.72
Entry at end of year to charge off expense.		

Advantage of taking up loan values. Those who favor taking up loan values as of the beginning of the policy year, instead of cash values at the end of the policy year, do so for the following reasons:

(1) The asset value of the policy is more accurately reflected. It is particularly desirable to have the loan value of the policy reflected on the books and in the balance sheet if loans are made to the full amount of the available loan value. The following summary of loans and asset values shows this fact clearly:

Beginning of Policy Year	Loans	Asset Values: Loan Value	Asset Values: Cash Value
3	$1,500.47	$1,500.47	—
4	2,029.25	2,029.25	$1,590.50

Assume that the full amounts of available loans are taken, as shown in the first column; if the loan values are taken up at the beginning of each policy year, the accounts and the balance sheet will show that the asset values of the policy are equal to the loans. But if cash values are taken up at the end of each year, the books and the balance sheet will misrepresent the condition by indicating that the asset values of the policy are less than the liabilities on policy loans.

(2) A truer statement of the annual expense is obtained, particularly if the end of the policy year does not coincide with the end of the accounting period. The insurance expense for any year is the net premium paid, minus the increase in asset value during the year. However, if the books are closed during the policy year, after the premium payment has been recorded but before the increase in asset value resulting therefrom has been recorded, the true net insurance expense for the year will not be shown.

Closing the books during the policy year. Using the same figures as in the preceding illustration, assume that loan values are taken up at the beginning of the policy year, that September 30 is the end of the policy year, and that the books are closed on December 31. The entries are shown by the following statement; credits are indicated by asterisks.

	Insurance Expense	Cash Surrender Value	Profit and Loss	Surplus
First policy year:				
Oct. 1—Premium paid........	$1,405.50			
Dec. 31—Expense (Note 1).....	351.38*		$ 351.38	
Deferred............	$1,054.12			
Second policy year:				
Oct. 1—Premium paid........	1,405.50			
Dec. 31—Expense (Note 2).....	1,405.50*		$1,405.50	
Deferred............	$1,054.12			
Third policy year:				
Oct. 1—Premium paid........	1,405.50			
Loan value (Note 3)	875.27*	$1,500.47		$625.20*
Dec. 31—Expense (Note 4).....	905.34*		$ 905.34	
Deferred (Note 4).....	$ 679.01			
Fourth policy year:				
Oct. 1—Premium paid........	1,405.50			
Loan value increase....	528.78*	528.78		
Total loan value......		$2,029.25		
Dec. 31—Expense (Note 5).....	898.19*		$ 898.19	
Deferred............	$ 657.54			

Notes

Note 1. The payment of premium on October 1 covers the expense for the next twelve months; three months' proportion (one fourth) is charged to profit and loss, and nine months' proportion (three fourths) is deferred.

Note 2. Profit and loss should now be charged with a full year's premium; however, there is again a prepayment of premium for nine months, which should be deferred.

Note 3. The credit for the loan value is apportioned between surplus and life insurance expense on the following basis: The loan value was created by the payment of premiums for three years (thirty-six months). The expense for one year and three months (fifteen months) has already been charged to profit and loss, and thence to surplus; the charge for the premiums applicable to the remaining year and nine months (twenty-one months) remains in the life insurance expense account. Then:

$\frac{15}{36}$ of $1,500.47 = $625.20, credited to surplus.
$\frac{21}{36}$ of 1,500.47 = 875.27, credited to life insurance expense.

Note 4. The apportionment between expired and deferred expense at the end of the third year is determined as follows:

The balance in the insurance expense account represents the net cost of insurance for 21 months, as follows:	
For 9 months—deferred at beginning	$1,054.12
For 12 months—charged during the year	1,405.50
Total	$2,459.62
Less reduction for loan value, applicable ratably to the premiums for 21 months	875.27
Net cost for 21 months	$1,584.35
Cost for 12 months ($^{12}/_{21}$) written off	905.34
Cost for 9 months ($^{9}/_{21}$) deferred	$ 679.01

Note 5. The amount charged off on December 31 of the fourth policy year is determined as follows:

Amount deferred on preceding January 1, representing the cost for the first 9 months of the calendar year		$679.01
Cost for the last 3 months of the calendar year:		
Premium paid October 1, for next 12 months	$1,405.50	
Increase in loan value resulting from this payment	528.78	
Net cost for 12 months	$ 876.72	
Portion applicable to first 3 months of policy year = ¼ of	$876.72	219.18
Total expense for the calendar year		$898.19

The amount deferred is ¾ of $876.72, or $657.54.

The expense for subsequent years should be computed in the same manner as for the fourth year. The peculiar complication in the third year results from the fact that the loan value was put on the books during that year.

Amortization of discount. If the books are closed monthly or at a date other than the end of the policy year, strict accuracy should probably require the amortization of the discount which was deducted from end-of-year cash values to determine beginning-of-year loan values. In the preceding illustration, these discount deductions were:

	Third Year	Fourth Year
Cash surrender value—end of year	$1,590.50	$2,151.00
Loan value—beginning of year	1,500.47	2,029.25
Discount	$ 90.03	$ 121.75

The loan value on each December 31 will be greater than the loan value on the preceding October 1, because of the smaller discount which would be deducted. The computation of the loan value at any date by amortization of the discount for the expired portion of the policy year is illustrated on the next page.

Loan value, beginning of third policy year	$1,500.47
Loan value on following December 31:	
Add discount for three months—¼ of $90.03	22.51
Total	$1,522.98

The effect of such discount adjustments upon the loan values and insurance expense is shown by the following summary; variations from the preceding illustration are mentioned in the notes following the summary.

	Insurance Expense	Cash Surrender Value	Profit and Loss	Surplus
First policy year:				
Oct. 1—Premium paid	$1,405.50			
Dec. 31—Expense	351.38*		$ 351.38	
Deferred	$1,054.12			
Second policy year:				
Oct. 1—Premium paid	1,405.50			
Dec. 31—Expense	1,405.50*		$1,405.50	
Deferred	$1,054.12			
Third policy year:				
Oct. 1—Premium paid	1,405.50			
Loan value	875.27*	$1,500.47		$625.20*
Dec. 31—Discount adjustment (Note 1)	22.51*	22.51		
Total loan value		$1,522.98		
Expense (Note 2)	882.83*		$ 882.83	
Deferred	$ 679.01			
Fourth policy year:				
Oct. 1—Discount adjustment (Note 3)	67.52*	67.52		
Premium paid	1,405.50			
Loan value increase (Note 4)	438.75*	438.75		
Total loan value		$2,029.25		
Dec. 31—Discount adjustment (Note 5)	30.44*	30.44		
Total loan value		$2,059.69		
Expense (Note 6)	822.74*		$ 822.74	
Deferred	$ 725.06			

Notes

Note 1. The discount adjustment on December 31 of the third policy year is one fourth of the total discount ($90.03) deducted on October 1 from the end-of-year cash value to determine the beginning-of-year loan value.

Note 2. The charge to profit and loss on December 31 of the third policy year is the same as that in the preceding illustration ($905.34) minus the discount amortization ($22.51).

Note 3. The discount adjustment ($67.52) on October 1 (end of the third policy year) is the total discount for the year ($90.03) minus the discount previously amortized ($22.51).

Note 4. The increase in loan value ($438.75) is the same as that in the preceding illustration ($528.78) minus the two amortizations of the discount totaling $90.03.

Note 5. The discount amortization ($30.44) on December 31 of the fourth policy year is one fourth of the total discount ($121.75) for that year.

Note 6. The amount charged to profit and loss on December 31 of the fourth policy year was computed as follows:

Amount deferred on preceding January 1, representing cost for the first 9 months of the calendar year		$679.01
Less amortization of discount on October 1, applicable thereto.		67.52
Net cost for first 9 months of calendar year		$611.49
Cost for the last 3 months of the calendar year:		
Premium paid October 1, for 12 months	$1,405.50	
Immediate increase in loan value resulting therefrom	438.75	
Remainder—applicable to 12 months	$ 966.75	
Portion applicable to 9 months after December 31—9/12 of $966.75—deferred	725.06	
Remainder applicable to first 3 months	$ 241.69	
Less discount amortization for 3 months	30.44	
Net cost for 3 months		211.25
Cost for 12 months		$822.74

Effect of dividends. No consideration has been given to dividends in the preceding illustrations. If the dividends are applied in reduction of premiums, they simply reduce the charges to be made to the life insurance expense account for premium payments. If they are left with the insurance company for the purpose of increasing the insurance, they produce increases in the cash surrender and loan values. Consequently they do not affect the principles and methods discussed on the preceding pages; they merely affect the amounts of premiums and asset values.

Balance sheet values. The balance sheet should show the deferred premium and the cash or loan value of the insurance. Referring to the preceding illustration, the balance sheet on December 31 of the fourth policy year should show deferred premiums of $725.06, and the loan value of $2,059.69.

The deferred premiums should be shown under the deferred charge caption, as a separate item or combined with unexpired premiums on other types of insurance. There is some difference of opinion concerning where the cash or loan value should be shown. It is often contended that the cash or loan value should be shown under the current asset caption because it is a source of immediately available funds. On the other hand, business life insurance is not customarily carried primarily for the purpose of providing available funds through surrender values. From the standpoint of theoretical definitions, the cash or loan value is a current asset if current assets are defined as: cash and other assets which may be converted into cash without interfering with the operations of the business; it is not a current asset if current assets are defined as: cash and other assets which will normally be converted into cash in the near future through the regular operations of the business. Bankers probably look with some disfavor upon the classification of cash and loan values as current assets because current realization is not to be presumed, and prefer to see them classified under captions of investments or other assets.

A policy loan from the insurance company is probably more properly regarded as a withdrawal of, or against, the equity in the policy rather than as a liability, and is therefore properly deductible from the cash surrender or loan value on the asset side of the balance sheet. In recent years banks have been making loans against the security of insurance policies; in such cases the notes should probably be regarded as obligations to be shown on the liability side of the balance sheet; if they are classified as current liabilities, it appears that the cash surrender or loan values of the policies should be classified as current assets.

Settlements. The collection of a policy by a corporation will be recorded by crediting surplus with the entire amount received, if no cash surrender value account appears on the books. If a cash surrender value account has been set up, this account should be credited with a sufficient amount to close it, and the balance should be credited to surplus.

The entries to be made on the books of a partnership to record the collection of a policy on the life of a partner will depend upon whether the partnership is the beneficiary or only the surviving partners are beneficiaries. If the partnership is the beneficiary, the credit will be divided among the capital accounts (including the account of the deceased partner) in the profit and loss ratio. If only the surviving partners are beneficiaries, they alone will share in the proceeds, and their accounts will be credited in their profit and loss ratio.

Workmen's Compensation and Employers' Liability Insurance

Nature of risk. Under the common law, employees had great difficulty in recovering from employers for accidents suffered in the course of their employment, but most of the states now have workmen's compensation laws which provide that, for various specific accidents sustained during employment, the employee or his family shall be entitled to receive from his employer a certain fixed sum and/or a percentage of the wages which he would have earned during the period of disability. There is also a tendency to include occupational diseases among the hazards for which the employee shall be compensated. A specific statement of risks and compensations cannot be made, because of the diversity of laws.

Under workmen's compensation insurance, the insurance company assumes the employer's entire liability arising from the workmen's compensation law of the state. Employers' liability insurance gives the employer coverage against common-law suits brought by employees to obtain damages for personal injuries. The two related risks are usually covered by the same policy.

Premiums. The premium is based upon the amount of the pay roll during the policy period. The previous accident experience of the insured and the safety measures and devices used in his plant are factors affecting the rates to be charged. All of the classes of employees of the insured may be covered by one policy; the rate per $100.00 of pay roll will be determined for each class separately on the basis of the hazard incident to the nature of the work.

At the beginning of the policy period, an advance premium is paid on the basis of the estimated pay roll. The actual pay roll is determined by an audit made by representatives of the insurance company, and the actual premium is thereby determined. If the policy provides for an annual pay roll audit, the advance premium will cover the estimated pay roll for the year; at the end of the year, the insured will pay an additional premium or receive a refund, depending upon whether the advance premium was less or more than the actual premium. If the policy is for a year, and the audit is made more frequently (say quarterly), the advance premium will cover the estimated pay roll for one quarter; at the end of the first, second, and third quarters, a payment will be made for the actual premium for the expired quarter; at the end of the fourth quarter, an additional premium payment or refund will be made, based on the difference between the original advance premium and the actual premium for the fourth quarter. The policy usually provides that a certain minimum portion of the advance premium shall not be refundable to the insured.

Since the rate applicable to each class of employees and the total estimated pay roll therefor are stated in the policy, the pay roll records must be kept separately for each class or in such a manner that a summary may be prepared by classifications. Computations of earned premiums are made separately for each class of employees.

Accounting. The advance premium should be charged to prepaid workmen's compensation insurance, and this account should be written off to workmen's compensation insurance expense accounts by periodical entries based on the actual pay rolls. To illustrate the procedure, assume that the non-refundable advance premium is $175.00, and that the total advance premium is $206.80, computed thus:

Classification	Estimated Payroll for the Year	Rate per $100.00	Advance Premium
Factory	$20,000.00	$.80	$160.00
Shipping	4,000.00	.42	16.80
Office	10,000.00	.06	6.00
Salesmen	15,000.00	.16	24.00
Total			$206.80

The entry for the advance premium payment would be:

Prepaid workmen's compensation insurance	$206.80	
Cash		$206.80

A summary may be kept to show the earned premium based on the pay roll for each pay roll period, as follows:

		July		August	
Classification	Rate	Pay Roll	Premium	Pay Roll	Premium
Factory	.80	$2,000.00	$16.00	$1,960.00	$15.68
Shipping	.42	350.00	1.47	365.00	1.53
Office	.06	900.00	.54	1,015.00	.61
Salesmen	.16	1,000.00	1.60	1,100.00	1.76
Total		$4,250.00	$19.61	$4,440.00	$19.58

The entry for the premium earned in July might be:

Workmen's compensation insurance	$19.61	
Prepaid workmen's compensation insurance		$19.61

Or the charge might be classified, as follows:

Workmen's compensation insurance—factory	$16.00	
Workmen's compensation insurance—shipping	1.47	
Workmen's compensation insurance—office	.54	
Workmen's compensation insurance—salesmen	1.60	
Prepaid workmen's compensation insurance		$19.61

To illustrate the final premium settlement, let us assume that the total premiums payable, based on actual pay rolls for the year, were $221.30. The prepaid workmen's compensation insurance account would have been charged with $206.80 (the prepaid premium) and credited with $221.30 (the premium based on actual pay rolls) and would therefore have a credit balance of $14.50, representing the liability for additional premium. If the premiums based on actual pay rolls were $195.00, the prepaid workmen's compensation insurance account would have a debit balance of $11.80, representing the refund receivable from the insurance company. If the actual premiums were only $160.00, the account would have a debit balance of $46.80, but the recoverable refund would be only $31.80, the $206.80 advance premium minus the $175.00 minimum premium.

Miscellaneous Types cf Insurance

Use and occupancy. This type of insurance indemnifies the insured for loss of net profits during a period of plant shutdown, for fixed charges which continue during that period, for extraordinary expenses incurred to hasten the replacement of machinery, for extra compensation for overtime, for extra cost of having product manufactured elsewhere while the plant is inoperative, and for other similar costs.

The forms of use and occupancy insurance available are based on the nature of the earning power of the insured; for example:

Straight per diem form, which is suitable if the earning power is distributed evenly throughout the year. The recovery per day is limited to 1/300 of the full amount of the policy.

Fluctuating or seasonal per diem form, which is suitable if periods of fluctuation in operations can be predetermined. The daily limit of recovery is determined by the fluctuating character of the business.

Use and occupancy insurance may be obtained in connection with fire, riot and civil commotion, sprinkler leakage, water damage, boiler explosion, tornado, and other types of insurance.

If one manufacturer is dependent upon another for a continuous and uninterrupted supply of materials or parts, he can obtain contingent use and occupancy insurance against the loss which would be caused by the supplier's inability to furnish goods.

Explosion; riot and civil ccmmotion. This type of insurance protects the insured against loss or damage due to riot, insurrection, and explosion resulting from the foregoing or other causes, whether originating on the insured's premises or elsewhere. It does not cover damages done at the direction of governmental or civil authorities, explosions coverable by boiler explosion insurance, fires resulting from such explosions, or loss or damage caused by the military or naval forces of foreign enemies.

Sprinkler leakage. Such policies insure against loss or damage due to sprinkler leakage, but do not cover loss or damage to the sprinkler system itself. Losses of books of account, money, notes, evidences of indebtedness, and patterns are excluded or the underwriter's liability therefor is greatly limited.

Boiler explosion. The coverage under policies of this type includes loss of, or damage to, property of the insured, or property of others for which the insured is liable, caused directly by the accident; personal injuries caused by the accident; and items of cost for temporary repairs. The coverage does not include explosions caused by fire, or fire resulting from any cause.

Fidelity bonds. Fidelity bonds, under which a surety company obligates itself to reimburse the insured for losses resulting from the dishonesty of employees, are issued in the following forms:

Individual bonds, covering one or a few employees.
Position schedule bonds, covering anyone holding any of the positions scheduled.
Name schedule bonds, covering named employees occupying named positions.

The insured must notify the company promptly upon the discovery of a loss, and time limits are placed upon the filing of claims and the filing of suits against the insurer for losses suffered during the policy period.

Plate glass. This insurance covers loss due to breakage of glass, and usually the cost of lettering and ornamentation on the glass. It does not cover damage caused by fire, by earthquake, or by workmen engaged in construction or repairs.

Marine insurance. This type of protection is indispensable for all shippers engaged in foreign commerce. Protection may be obtained under policies as mentioned on the next page.

A special policy, covering one shipment only.

An open policy, covering all shipments made during a specified period, a premium being charged for each shipment.

A blanket policy, which is similar to an open policy, except that an estimated annual premium is payable in advance.

Public liability and property damage. Such policies protect the insured against losses resulting from liability for injury to another, or against damage to the property of another, due to negligence of the insured or of his employees or agents. Public liability insurance may be written to cover various types of hazard, such as a contractor's liability for injuries to persons passing a building under construction; a building owner's liability for injury to persons riding in an elevator; an automobile owner's liability for injury to others; physicians' and dentists' liability for malpractice; and so forth. Property damage insurance may be obtained by indorsement to public liability policies.

Public liability policies usually provide that the insurance company shall reimburse the insured for the cost of first aid, defend the insured against damage suits, pay all expenses incurred in connection therewith, and satisfy judgments rendered against the insured—all subject to the limits of the policy. A limit is placed upon the amount to be paid to any one person or to two or more persons as the result of one accident. Damages resulting from liabilities imposed by workmen's compensation laws are excluded.

Profit insurance. This type of insurance indemnifies for the profit which would have been made from the sale of finished goods destroyed. For instance, ordinary fire insurance will protect the insured to the extent of the actual cash value of the goods destroyed; profit insurance will further protect him to the extent of the profit which could have been made by the sale of the goods.

Under certain circumstances and on payment of an additional premium, a profit insurance clause may be included in other insurance policies, such as fire, riot and civil commotion, sprinkler leakage, and water damage. The reputation of the applicant may be fully investigated before such insurance is written.

Insurance Register

Form and purpose. A register of insurance policies is desirable for two purposes: first, to show the policies in force, and the amount of each class of coverage; and second, to show the distribution of the insurance premium expense by months or years. Insurance registers are obtainable with various rulings. The following information should be shown:

Policy number.
Date of policy.
Date of expiration.
Name of insurance company.
Nature of coverage.
Amount of insurance.
Total premium.
Distribution of premium expense by periods.

The nature of the coverage and the amount of the insurance may be shown as follows:

Coverage	Insured Amount
Fire—building	$150,000.00
Fire—contents	60,000.00
Elevator	50,000.00
Steam boiler	50,000.00

If coverage for one risk is carried in several policies, it may be desirable to provide columns in the register so that the coverages may be shown as follows:

Coverage					
Fire Building	Fire Contents	Elevator	Steam Boiler	Etc.	Etc.
$150,000.00					
	$60,000.00				
		$50,000.00			
			$50,000.00		
90,000.00					
	35,000.00				

The columns to be provided for distribution of premium expense by periods will depend upon whether it is desired to show distributions by years or by months. If distribution by years is sufficient, four or five year columns will suffice. If distribution is desired by months, a column must be provided for each month of the year, for the unexpired premiums at the beginning of the year and for the unexpired premiums at the end of the year, thus:

Unexpired	Monthly Expiration					Unexpired
Jan. 1	Jan.	Feb.	Mar.	Apr.	Dec.	Dec. 31

The totals of the monthly expiration columns will show the amounts to be charged monthly to insurance expense and credited to unexpired insurance. At the end of each year, a new page must be opened, and all policies in force forwarded to it.

CHAPTER 38

Correction of Statements and Books

Correction of profits and surplus. The profits of a given period and the surplus at the end of the period may be misstated because of the omission or the improper inclusion of income or expense, the failure to take accruals and deferred items into consideration, an incorrect computation of the inventory, a failure to make a proper distinction between capital and revenue charges, and almost innumerable other errors.

After the expiration of several periods, it may be desired to prepare amended profit and loss statements in which the profits of each period are correctly stated. For the purpose of illustrating the working papers used in arriving at adjusted figures for profits and surplus, the various errors may be classified in three groups:

(1) Errors made in computing the profits of one period, which are offset by counterbalancing errors in a subsequent period, thus eventually correcting the surplus, but leaving the profits incorrectly stated by periods.

(2) Errors made in computing the profits of one period, which are not offset by counterbalancing errors in subsequent periods, and which leave the surplus (and one or more other accounts) permanently misstated.

(3) Errors in surplus, resulting from:

  (*a*) Recording items in profit and loss which should have gone directly to surplus, or vice versa.*

  (*b*) Recording items directly in surplus in a wrong period.

---

* It was long regarded as preferable procedure to show (1) corrections of prior periods' profits and (2) extraneous profits and losses in the surplus statement; many accountants now advocate showing such items in the income statement. This difference of opinion was discussed at length in *Intermediate Accounting*. Since this chapter is concerned with the preparation of *corrected* profit and loss statements for a series of periods, the debated question of whether corrections of prior periods' profits should appear in the income or surplus statement does not arise; the income statements for the several periods are adjusted to give effect to the corrections in the periods to which they are applicable.

Extraneous profits and losses are shown in the illustrations in this chapter as charges and credits to surplus solely for the purpose of clearly identifying them. If desired, they can be shown in the income statement or in the surplus section of a combined income and surplus statement.

Illustration. In the following illustration, no attempt will be made to show all possible errors, as that would complicate the illustration and make it more confusing than clarifying. A few typical errors in each of the three groups in the foregoing outline will be sufficient to illustrate the methods employed in preparing a statement of adjusted profits and surplus.

The following statement shows the surplus per books of a company which finds that errors have been made in the computation of its profits:

THE *A. B.* COMPANY
Statement of Surplus Account
December 31, 1944 to December 31, 1946

Balance—December 31, 1944		$10,000.00
Add profits of 1945		7,500.00
Total		$17,500.00
Deduct:		
Fire loss	$ 700.00	
Dividends paid in 1945	6,000.00	6,700.00
Balance—December 31, 1945		$10,800.00
Add profits of 1946		6,850.00
Total		$17,650.00
Deduct dividends paid in 1946		6,000.00
Balance—December 31, 1946		$11,650.00

Errors subsequently counterbalanced. The following errors were made, which resulted in misstatements of the profits of one year and of the surplus at the end of the year, but which were counterbalanced in later years, leaving the surplus eventually correct. The errors are numbered to correspond with the corrections in the working papers on page 123.

(1) The accounts receivable on December 31, 1944 contained bad debts of $365.00 which should have been charged against the profits of 1944 by setting up a reserve. Such a reserve was not set up, and the losses were charged against the profits of 1945 when the accounts were written off.

Thus the profits of 1944 and the surplus on December 31, 1944 were overstated; the profits of 1945 were correspondingly understated. However, the errors of the two years counterbalanced each other, with the result that (so far as these errors were concerned) the surplus on December 31, 1945 was correct. A similar comment might be made in regard to the following errors.

(2) Bad debts of $415.00 on December 31, 1945 were written off in 1946.

THE *A. B.* COMPANY
Working Papers Adjusting Profits and Surplus
December 31, 1944 to December 31, 1946

	Surplus Dec. 31, 1944		Profit and Loss 1945		Profit and Loss 1946	
Balance per books		$10,000.00		$7,500.00		$6,850.00
(1) Bad debts, Dec. 31, 1944, written off in 1945	$ 365.00			365.00		
(2) " " Dec. 31, 1945, " " " 1946			$ 415.00			415.00
(3) Inventory, Dec. 31, 1944 overstated	500.00			500.00		
(4) " Dec. 31, 1945 understated				390.00	$ 390.00	
(5) Wages accrued Dec. 31, 1944	175.00			175.00		
(6) " " Dec. 31, 1945			215.00			215.00
Balances as adjusted	8,960.00		8,300.00		7,090.00	
	$10,000.00	$10,000.00	$8,930.00	$8,930.00	$7,480.00	$7,480.00

(3) The inventory on December 31, 1944 was overstated $500.00.

(4) The inventory on December 31, 1945 was understated $390.00.

(5) On December 31, 1944 there were accrued wages of $175.00. No attention was paid to this accrual at the end of 1944, and the payment was charged as an expense in 1945.

(6) Accrued wages on December 31, 1945 charged as an expense in 1946, $215.00.

The working papers on page 123 show:

The surplus on December 31, 1944 and the profits of 1945 and 1946 per the books.

The transfers between years, correcting the six errors.

The surplus on December 31, 1944 and the profits of 1945 and 1946 as adjusted.

Errors not counterbalanced. Other errors were made, which were not counterbalanced in subsequent years, and which resulted in misstatements of the surplus and some other accounts on December 31, 1946, the end of the period under review. These errors may be divided into two groups, as follows:

(A) Errors and omissions of the final year, which would be counterbalanced in the succeeding year:

(7) Bad debts of $505.00 from 1946 sales, for which a reserve should be provided.

(8) The inventory on December 31, 1946 was overstated $610.00.

(9) Accrued wages on December 31, 1946, $230.00.

(B) Errors of prior years, which are of such a nature that they are not automatically counterbalanced:

(10) Too much depreciation was provided in 1944; excess amounted to $160.00.

(11) Too little depreciation was provided in 1945; the deficiency was $255.00.

The working papers on page 125 show:

The corrections already made in the first working papers, for errors 1 to 6, inclusive.

The corrections (checked) for errors 7 to 11, inclusive. These errors affect other accounts as well as profits and surplus; these balance sheet corrections are indicated at the right.

THE *A. B.* COMPANY
Working Papers Adjusting Profits and Surplus
December 31, 1944 to December 31, 1946

	Surplus Dec. 31, 1944		Profit & Loss 1945		Profit & Loss 1946		Balance Sheet Adjustments		
							Account	Debit	Credit
Balances per books		$10,000		$7,500		$6,850			
(1) Bad debts, Dec. 31, 1944 written off in 1945	$ 365			365					
(2) " " Dec. 31, 1945 " " " 1946			$ 415			415			
√(7) " " Dec. 31, 1946					$ 505		Reserve for Bad Debts		$505
(3) Inventory, Dec. 31, 1944 overstated	500			500					
(4) " Dec. 31, 1945 understated				390	390				
√(8) " Dec. 31, 1946 overstated					610		Inventory		610
(5) Wages accrued, Dec. 31, 1944	175			175					
(6) " " Dec. 31, 1945			215			215			
√(9) " " Dec. 31, 1946					230		Accrued Wages		230
√(10) Too much depreciation charged in 1944		160					Reserve for Depreciation	$160	
√(11) " little " " " 1945			255				" " "		255
Balances as adjusted	9,120		8,045		5,745				
	$10,160	$10,160	$8,930	$8,930	$7,480	$7,480			

Errors in surplus entries. As already stated, errors in entries made directly in the surplus account may be divided into two groups; one error in each group is illustrated below:

(A) Items entered in profit and loss instead of in surplus, or vice versa.

(12) Fixed assets were sold in 1946 at a profit of $750.00, and the profit was entered in profit and loss instead of in surplus.

(B) Items properly recorded directly in surplus, but entered in that account in a wrong year.

(13) Plant property carried in the asset account at $3,000.00 was destroyed by fire on December 24, 1944. A settlement of $2,000.00 was agreed upon with the insurance company on December 29, 1944, but no entry for the fire loss and the settlement was made until a check was received on January 20, 1945, when the following entry was made:

Cash	$2,000.00	
Reserve for depreciation	300.00	
Surplus	700.00	
Plant account		$3,000.00

Those accountants who believe that extraneous profits and losses should be shown in the profit and loss statement would make no adjustment for item 12, and would charge profit and loss rather than surplus with the adjustment for item 13.

In the working papers (which repeat corrections for errors 1 to 11, inclusive) the profit on the sale of fixed assets in 1946 is transferred from profit and loss to surplus as a direct credit; and the error of charging the 1944 fire loss to surplus in 1945 is corrected by charging surplus of 1944 and crediting surplus of 1945.

Adjusted statements. It should be understood, of course, that one set of working papers is sufficient to adjust all errors; the three illustrations were given merely to make the explanation of the subject as clear as possible, and not to include too much in the first illustration.

After the working papers have been completed, the adjusted surplus statement on page 128 may be drawn up. This statement is made up from the adjusted balances of opening surplus and annual profits, and all direct charges and credits to surplus except those which are offset in the same year (such as the $700.00 items).

THE *A. B.* COMPANY
Working Papers Adjusting Profits and Surplus
December 31, 1944 to December 31, 1946

	Surplus Dec. 31, 1944		Profit & Loss 1945		Profit & Loss 1946		Balance Sheet Adjustments: Account	Debit	Credit
Balances per books		$10,000		$7,500		$6,850			
(1) Bad debts, Dec. 31, 1944 written off in 1945	$ 365			365					
(2) " " " 31, 1945 " " " 1946			$ 415			415			
(7) " " " 31, 1946					$ 505		Reserve for bad debts		$505
(3) Inventory, Dec. 31, 1944 overstated	500			500					
(4) " " 31, 1945 understated				390	390				
(8) " " 31, 1946 overstated					610		Inventory		610
(5) Wages accrued, Dec. 31, 1944	175			175					
(6) " " " 31, 1945			215			215			
(9) " " " 31, 1946					230		Accrued wages		230
(10) Too much depreciation charged in 1944		160					Reserve for depreciation	$160	
(11) " little " " " 1945			255				" "		255
√(12) Profit on sale of fixed assets, credited to profit and loss					750				
√(13) Fire loss charged in 1945 instead of 1944	700								
Balances as adjusted	8,420		8,045		4,995				
	$10,160	$10,160	$8,930	$8,930	$7,480	$7,480			

	Surplus—1945		Surplus—1946	
Direct charges and credits to surplus:				
Per books				
Fire loss	$ 700			
Dividends	6,000		$6,000	
Adjustments:				
√(12) Profit on sale of fixed assets				$ 750
√(13) Entry to correct 1945 surplus debit for fire loss		$ 700		

THE *A. B.* COMPANY
Statement of Surplus Account
December 31, 1944 to December 31, 1946

Balance—Dec. 31, 1944		$ 8,420.00
Add profits of 1945		8,045.00
Total		$16,465.00
Deduct dividends		6,000.00
Balance—Dec. 31, 1945		$10,465.00
Add: Profits of 1946 from operations	$4,995.00	
Profit on sale of fixed assets	750.00	5,745.00
Total		$16,210.00
Deduct dividends		6,000.00
Balance—Dec. 31, 1946		$10,210.00

Reconciliation

Surplus per books—Dec. 31, 1946			$11,650.00
Adjustments reducing surplus:			
Bad debts, Dec. 31, 1946	$505.00		
Inventory overstated, Dec. 31, 1946	610.00		
Accrued wages, Dec. 31, 1946	230.00		
Additional depreciation, 1945	255.00	$1,600.00	
Adjustment increasing surplus:			
Reduction of depreciation 1944		100.00	1,440.00
Surplus as adjusted—Dec. 31, 1946			$10,210.00

Balance sheet adjustments. The preceding illustrations dealt only with the profits and surplus. But if the profit and loss statements prepared at the end of each year were incorrect, the balance sheets were also incorrect. The following illustrations show how to prepare working papers to correct the several balance sheets. The balance sheets drawn from the books of The *A. B.* Company (same company as that in preceding illustration) at the end of 1944, 1945, and 1946 are as follows:

THE *A. B.* COMPANY
Balance Sheets

Assets	Dec. 31, 1944	Dec. 31, 1945	Dec. 31, 1946
Cash	$ 2,000.00	$ 2,800.00	$ 3,150.00
Accounts receivable	9,000.00	7,100.00	8,950.00
Inventories	15,000.00	15,700.00	16,100.00
Plant	40,000.00	42,000.00	43,000.00
	$66,000.00	$67,600.00	$71,200.00
Liabilities and Net Worth			
Accounts payable	$12,000.00	$11,500.00	$12,800.00
Reserve for depreciation	4,000.00	5,300.00	6,750.00
Capital stock	40,000.00	40,000.00	40,000.00
Surplus	10,000.00	10,800.00	11,650.00
	$66,000.00	$67,600.00	$71,200.00

It is desired to prepare adjusted balance sheets as of each of the three dates. The summary on page 129 shows the adjustments in the working papers on pages 130 and 131, required to correct the thirteen errors already mentioned, and the balance sheets which the adjustments affect:

			Balance Sheet at End of		
			1944	1945	1946
(1)	Bad debts, December 31, 1944: $365.00				
	Debit surplus; credit reserve for bad debts....		x		
(2)	Bad debts, December 31, 1945: $415.00				
	Debit surplus; credit reserve for bad debts....			x	
(3)	Inventory, December 31, 1944 overstated $500.00				
	Debit surplus; credit inventory..............		x		
(4)	Inventory, December 31, 1945 understated $390.00				
	Debit inventory; credit surplus.............				
(5)	Wages accrued, December 31, 1944, $175.00				
	Debit surplus; credit accrued wages..........		x		
(6)	Wages accrued, December 31, 1945, $215.00				
	Debit surplus; credit accrued wages..........			x	
(7)	Bad debts, December 31, 1946, $505.00				
	Debit surplus; credit reserve for bad debts....				x
(8)	Inventory, December 31, 1946 overstated $610.00				
	Debit surplus; credit inventory..............				x
(9)	Wages accrued, December 31, 1946, $230.00				
	Debit surplus; credit accrued wages..........				x
(10)	Too much depreciation in 1944, $160.00				
	Debit reserve for depreciation; credit surplus.		x	x	x
(11)	Too little depreciation in 1945, $255.00				
	Debit surplus; credit reserve for depreciation.			x	x
(12)	No adjustment in balance sheet				
(13)	Fire loss recorded in 1945 instead of 1944......		x		
	Debit: Due from insurance company.........	$2,000.00			
	Reserve for depreciation.............	300.00			
	Surplus.............................	700.00			
	Credit: Plant account......................	3,000.00			

The working papers should be prepared as follows:

Enter the figures in the balance sheets per books columns.

Make the necessary adjustments, with offsetting debits and credits, in the adjustments columns.

Carry out the adjusted figures into the balance sheets as adjusted columns.

It should be noted that some errors affect one balance sheet only, as they have been counterbalanced in subsequent years, whereas other errors affect all balance sheets subsequent to the date of the error.

Correcting the books. When errors have been made during a series of years, and when the books are to be corrected at the close of this series, it is usually better to correct such errors as exist at that time, and to ignore errors which have been automatically corrected by counterbalancing errors.

THE *A. B.* COMPANY
Balance Sheet Adjustment Working Papers
December 31, 1944, 1945, and 1946

	Balance Sheets Per Books		Adjustments Debit	Adjustments Credit	Balance Sheets As Adjusted	
Dec. 31, 1944:						
Cash	$ 2,000.00				$ 2,000.00	
Accounts receivable	9,000.00				9,000.00	
Inventories	15,000.00			$ 500.00(3)	14,500.00	
Plant	40,000.00			3,000.00(13)	37,000.00	
Due from insurance company			$2,000.00(13)		2,000.00	
Accounts payable		$12,000.00				$12,000.00
Reserve for depreciation		4,000.00	{160.00(10) {300.00(13)			3,540.00
Capital stock		40,000.00				40,000.00
Surplus		10,000.00	365.00(1) 500.00(3) 175.00(5) 700.00(13)	160.00(10)		8,420.00
Reserve for bad debts				365.00(1)		365.00
Accrued wages				175.00(5)		175.00
	$66,000.00	$66,000.00	$4,200.00	$4,200.00	$64,500.00	$64,500.00
Dec. 31, 1945:						
Cash	$ 2,800.00				$ 2,800.00	
Accounts receivable	7,100.00				7,100.00	
Inventories	15,700.00		$ 390.00(4)		16,090.00	
Plant	42,000.00				42,000.00	

Accounts payable		$11,500.00				$11,500.00
Reserve for depreciation		5,300.00	160.00(10)	$ 255.00(11)		5,395.00
Capital stock		40,000.00				40,000.00
Surplus		10,800.00	415.00(2)	390.00(4)		10,465.00
			215.00(6)	160.00(10)		
			255.00(11)			
Reserve for bad debts				415.00(2)		415.00
Accrued wages				215.00(6)		215.00
	$67,600.00	$67,600.00	$1,435.00	$1,435.00	$67,990.00	$67,990.00
Dec. 31, 1946:						
Cash	$ 3,150.00				$ 3,150.00	
Accounts receivable	8,950.00				8,950.00	
Inventories	16,100.00			$ 610.00(8)	15,490.00	
Plant	43,000.00				43,000.00	
Accounts payable		$12,800.00				$12,800.00
Reserve for depreciation		6,750.00	$ 160.00(10)	255.00(11)		6,845.00
Capital stock		40,000.00				40,000.00
Surplus		11,650.00	505.00(7)	160.00(10)		10,210.00
			610.00(8)			
			230.00(9)			
			255.00(11)			
Reserve for bad debts				505.00(7)		505.00
Accrued wages				230.00(9)		230.00
	$71,200.00	$71,200.00	$1,760.00	$1,760.00	$70,590.00	$70,590.00

To correct the books on December 31, 1946, it is sufficient to make only those entries that are necessary to change the December 31, 1946 balance sheet from the figures per books to the figures as adjusted in the balance sheet working papers. This entry should be followed by a complete explanation, showing when and how the errors occurred which necessitated the adjustments.

The following journal entry will correct the books of The *A. B.* Company on December 31, 1946:

Surplus			$1,440.00	
Inventories				$610.00
Reserve for depreciation				95.00
Reserve for bad debts				505.00
Accrued wages				230.00
To correct the books as of Dec. 31, 1946, for the following matters:				
Inventory overstated on Dec. 31, 1946		$ 610.00		
Depreciation:				
Insufficient provision in 1945	$255.00			
Excess " " 1944	160.00	95.00		
Reserve for bad debts required Dec. 31, 1946		505.00		
Accrued wages on Dec. 31, 1946		230.00		
Total deduction from surplus		$1,440.00		

If an attempt were made on December 31, 1946, to reopen the books as of December 31, 1944, and to set up an accrued wages account and a reserve for bad debts, a great deal of confusion would result, because the omission of these items on December 31, 1944 was offset by their inclusion as expenses in 1945, and the books were therefore correct, so far as these items were concerned, on December 31, 1945. The same may be said in regard to all errors subsequently counterbalanced.

CHAPTER 39

The Statement of Affairs*

Insolvency. The word *insolvent* has two meanings. First, the popular meaning: A person who is not able to pay his debts as they mature in the regular order of business, is said to be insolvent. He may have assets greatly in excess of his liabilities, but these assets may be tied up in such a manner that they cannot be realized promptly enough to meet current liabilities. Second, the definition in the Bankruptcy Act: "A person is 'insolvent' when the present fair salable value of his property is less than the amount required to pay his debts."

Procedures available for businesses in financial difficulty. A business which cannot pay its debts as they mature may have recourse to the following procedures:

(A) Non-judicial procedures (without court action):
- (1) Extension of time of payment.
- (2) Composition settlement.
- (3) Creditor committee management.
- (4) Voluntary assignment.

(B) Judicial procedures (with court action):
- (1) Equity receivership.
- (2) Procedures under the Bankruptcy (Chandler) Act:
  - (*a*) Liquidation.
  - (*b*) Corporate reorganization.
  - (*c*) Arrangement.

Extension of time of payment. In a case where a debtor is temporarily embarrassed but has assets sufficient to pay his debts over an extended period, his creditors or a sufficient majority of them may grant him additional time. This arrangement obviously frees the debtor from financial pressure for the time being, and is designed to allow him time for an orderly realization of sufficient of his assets, without undue losses incident to forced sales, to meet his obligations at the extended maturity dates. The debtor is also

---

* The author is indebted to Professor John C. Teevan of Northwestern University for assistance with respect to matters of law discussed in this chapter.

enabled to carry on and maintain his business more efficiently than he could under the threat of more drastic action on the part of his creditors. Extensions usually are practical only in the case of relatively small businesses or where the creditors are comparatively few in number. From the standpoint of the debtor, the purpose of extensions is the preservation rather than the liquidation of the business.

Composition settlements. A *composition agreement* is one in which all or a sufficient number of the creditors of an insolvent debtor agree to accept from him a stated percentage of their respective claims in full settlement and satisfaction of such claims. Usually, in such cases, the debtor is insolvent in the bankruptcy meaning of the term; that is, his liabilities are in excess of his assets. As in the case of extensions, this procedure is practicable only in the case of small businesses or where the number of creditors is not large. If there are non-assenting creditors, but their number is not too large or the amount of their claims is not too large, the assenting creditors may allow the debtor to pay them either in full or in a greater amount than they would receive if they were parties to the composition. In order that the agreement be binding on the creditors, the debtor must have made full disclosure of all of his assets, and he must not have made any secret preferential arrangement with any creditor. If the debtor fails to disclose all of his assets or if he secretly prefers any creditor, the other creditors may repudiate the agreement, retain such payments on account as they may have received, and take appropriate legal action against the debtor for the recovery of their claims to the fullest possible extent. In composition agreements, the debtor usually makes a part payment in cash and gives notes or other instruments for the balance payable in the future. If they choose, the creditors may allow the debtor to retain some of his assets, in which case he may continue the operation of his business. If the composition agreement is faithfully carried out by the debtor, he is discharged from all his debts.

Creditor committee management. This form of coöperation between creditors and a distressed debtor originates in an agreement whereby control of the debtor's business is turned over to a committee chosen by the creditors. The agreement usually provides for an extension of payment of existing debts. Sometimes, if the committee deems it advisable, the creditors will put fresh capital into the business. The personnel of the debtor's organization is usually left intact, except insofar as the committee may decide that changes are necessary. In any case, the control and management of the business rests with the committee. The agreement usually provides for the return of the business to the debtor when payment of the creditors' claims has been made or satisfactorily provided for. Sometimes, in the case of a corporate debtor, the committee will effect or supervise a reorganization. If, in the course of time, it appears that rehabilitation or reorganization is impracticable, the committee may liquidate the business.

Voluntary assignment. Under common law (that is, in the absence of a statute) an insolvent debtor may make a general assignment of all his assets to a designated trustee or assignee for the benefit of his creditors. Upon the execution of such an assignment, it becomes the duty of the assignee to realize on the assets and distribute the proceeds pro rata among the creditors. Ordinarily, an assignment is made with the understanding that the debtor is thereby discharged of all his debts. It should be noted that a general assignment by a debtor for the benefit of his creditors constitutes an act of bankruptcy; consequently, creditors who refuse to participate in the assignment may file a petition in bankruptcy against the debtor. The matter of voluntary assignments is now regulated by statutes in most states. These statutes vary, but, in general, provide for the supervision of assignments by some designated court, and require the assignee to file an inventory, furnish a bond, publish notice of the assignment, and so forth. In general, the voluntary assignment is falling into disuse.

Equity receiverships. A receivership of an insolvent business comes within the general jurisdiction of a court of equity, whether federal or state. However, in most, if not all, states statutes now provide for a variety of receiverships, mostly in connection with insolvent corporations. Such receiverships may be had for various reasons and by various parties, as by stockholders, the corporation itself, or groups of stockholders. Receiverships are usually involuntary, but may be procured voluntarily at the instance of the debtor. Procuring, permitting, or suffering a receivership, either voluntary or involuntary, when a debtor is insolvent in either meaning of the term, is an act of bankruptcy, and may be availed of as such by any creditors who so desire. If they do, and the debtor is adjudged a bankrupt, the effect is to terminate the receivership proceedings.

Briefly, in receivership proceedings, the property, business, and affairs of the debtor are brought before the court, which in its discretion may appoint a receiver. The receiver may be a natural person or a corporation. A receiver is an officer of the court, and enjoys the protection, and is subject to the orders, of the court. The immediate effect of the appointment of a receiver is to place the assets of the debtor under the control of the court. This prevents a race on the part of the creditors against the assets by levy, attachment, forced sales, and other normal legal procedures, which might be disastrous to many of the creditors as well as to the business itself. The receiver is thus given time to proceed to rehabilitate the business if possible, or, if not, to proceed with an orderly liquidation. The creditors' rights and claims remain intact, but their satisfaction is postponed until rehabilitation, reorganization, or liquidation is effected.

Equity receiverships involving large corporations, including railroads and other public utilities, generally are instituted in the federal courts. The proceedings are usually begun by a friendly creditor in another state, diversity of citizenship being necessary in order to bring the proceedings under the jurisdiction of a federal court. The debtor will then admit insolvency and a willingness to have a receiver appointed. Such receiverships, though technically involuntary, are known as *friendly* or *consent receiverships*. Upon the appointment of the receiver, the various groups of creditors (bondholders and other secured and unsecured creditors), as well as the stockholders, proceed to form their respective protective committees. Conflict of interest may arise among the various groups and unduly delay the proceedings. Sometimes minorities have to be bought off, and sometimes they are frozen out. Usually, complete reorganization is necessary and a new corporation is formed for this purpose. The various groups will then receive the securities of the new corporation, with or without part payment in cash, as the case may be. The expenses of a receivership are usually excessive, and the procedure dilatory, extending sometimes as long as twenty or thirty years. Since the amendment of the Bankruptcy Act in 1933 by the debtor relief provisions, which furnish more efficient, less expensive, and more speedy relief, federal equity receiverships are largely falling into disuse.

The Chandler Act. The Bankruptcy Act was amended in 1933 and 1934 by provisions known as *debtor relief legislation.* This was done to meet grave financial problems in the business world caused by the then existing depression. The best known of these provisions was Section 77B. In 1938, the act including both bankruptcy and debtor relief provisions was considerably revised and amended by the Chandler Act. The Bankruptcy Act, as so revised and amended, contains thirteen chapters. The first seven chapters cover bankruptcy proper, the object being liquidation. The remaining six chapters pertain, not to bankruptcy, but to the relief of debtors, and the object here is the preservation or rehabilitation of the embarrassed business.

Liquidation under Bankruptcy Act. *Bankruptcy* is the legal status of a debtor who, pursuant to his voluntary petition or an involuntary petition filed by creditors, has been adjudicated a bankrupt by a federal district court, known for this purpose as a *court of bankruptcy.* Municipal, railroad, insurance, and banking corporations, and building and loan associations cannot be adjudged bankrupt. A farmer or wage earner cannot be adjudged an involuntary bankrupt, but may become a voluntary bankrupt. A wage earner is one employed by another person and whose compensation does not exceed $1,500.00 per year.

The purpose of bankruptcy is to effect a speedy and fair distribution of the bankrupt's assets among his creditors and to discharge the bankrupt from his debts. The act provides that certain debts are not dischargeable.

Shortly after the adjudication, the creditors elect a trustee, or they may elect three. The trustee takes title to, and control of, the bankrupt's estate. The assets are realized by him, and the proceeds are distributed among the creditors. Under Section 64 of the act, quoted on page 142, certain debts have priority. The general control of the bankruptcy proceedings is in the hands of the referee, an officer appointed by the court for a period of two years, and who functions as an arm of the court. In summary, bankruptcy proceedings imply complete and final liquidation of the bankrupt's entire estate, the distribution of the proceeds among the creditors as provided by the act, and the discharge of the bankrupt from all his general business debts.

Debtor relief under Bankruptcy Act. The following are the titles of the chapters of the Bankruptcy Act providing for the relief of debtors:

Chapter VIII:	
Section 75	Agricultural Compositions and Extensions.
Section 77	Reorganization of Railroads Engaged in Interstate Commerce.
Chapter IX	Readjustment of Debts of Taxing Districts (expired June 30, 1940).
Chapter X	Corporate Reorganization.
Chapter XI	Arrangements.

Chapter XII Real Property Arrangements by Persons Other Than Corporations.

Chapter XIII Wage Earners' Plans.

Of these chapters, only Chapters X and XI will be considered.

To obtain relief by a corporate reorganization or an arrangement, the debtor must be insolvent, either in the sense that his liabilities exceed his assets, or because of an inability to pay debts as they mature. The debtor is not adjudged a bankrupt, and is known not as a *bankrupt* but simply as the *debtor*.

Corporate reorganization. Chapter X, covering corporate reorganizations, replaces Section 77B enacted in 1934. This chapter applies only to corporations seeking reorganization by means of a revision of capital structure, with or without an adjustment of its unsecured debts. Where a corporation seeks adjustment of its unsecured debts only, it comes within the provisions of Chapter XI on arrangements.

The petition to effect a reorganization may be filed by the corporation itself, or by creditors or an indenture trustee. A petition may be filed even though bankruptcy proceedings are pending against the corporation. If the judge finds that the petition was filed in good faith and in accordance with the act, he enters an order approving it. If the indebtedness, certain with regard to amount and not contingent with regard to liability, exeeds $250,000.00, the judge must appoint one or more trustees. If such indebtedness is less than $250,000.00, the judge may appoint one or more trustees or may continue the debtor in possession.

Until changed by the judge, the order approving the petition operates as a stay of any prior pending bankruptcy, mortgage foreclosure, equity receivership proceeding, or any other act or proceeding to enforce a lien against the debtor's property. Certain schedules and lists must then be filed by the debtor in possession or by the trustee. In due time, a plan of reorganization is filed by the trustee, debtor in possession, stockholders, or an examiner appointed by the court, according to various circumstances.

A hearing on the plan then takes place. If the judge finds the plan fair, equitable, and feasible, he enters an order approving it. It is then submitted for acceptance to all creditors and stockholders affected by it. It must be accepted by creditors holding two thirds in amount of claims filed and allowed in each class. If the corporation is solvent, the plan must also be accepted by a majority of stockholders in each class. If the plan is accepted by the necessary majorities, a further hearing on the plan takes place, at which all interested parties may be present. If the judge finds the plan to be fair, equitable, and feasible, and in compliance with the act, he enters an order confirming it. The plan then becomes binding upon the corporation and all creditors and stockholders, and on any other corporation formed or to be formed for the purpose of carrying out the plan. Distribution of cash, other assets, or stocks and bonds, as the case may be, is then made to creditors and stockholders. Upon the consummation of the plan, the judge enters an order discharging the debtor corporation from its liabilities, discharging the trustee, and closing the estate. In the event no plan is proposed, or if no plan is approved by the judge, or if an approved plan is not accepted, or if a confirmed plan is not consummated, the judge may dismiss the reorganization proceeding, and direct that bankruptcy be proceeded with against the debtor corporation. Chapter X has done away with federal equity receiverships to a very considerable extent.

Arrangements. An *arrangement* means any plan of a debtor for the settlement, satisfaction, or extension of the time of payment of his unsecured debts. *Debtor* includes an individual, partnership, or corporation. A petition for an arrangement can be filed only by the debtor, and must set forth the provisions of the arrangement proposed by him. A petition may be filed by a debtor against whom bankruptcy proceedings are already pending. The court may then appoint a receiver, unless a trustee in bankruptcy has already been appointed. If no receiver or trustee is appointed, the debtor remains in possession of his property and business.

The court then calls a meeting of creditors, to whom a copy of the proposed arrangement and a summary of the debtor's assets and liabilities have been furnished. To be effective, the plan of arrangement must be accepted by a majority in number of all creditors. After acceptance, the court appoints a receiver, trustee, or other person to receive the money and other consideration to be deposited by the debtor for distribution to creditors, fixes the time for such deposit, and also fixes the time for the hearing on the confirmation of the arrangement. On the hearing for confirmation, the court, if it finds that the plan of arrangement is fair, equitable, and feasible, and that the debtor has deposited the money and other consideration as agreed, confirms the arrangement. The arrangement then becomes binding on the debtor and all the creditors. The money and other consideration are then distributed to the creditors as provided by the arrangement. The confirmation of the arrangement operates to discharge the debtor of all his unsecured debts, except as provided by the arrangement. If the plan of arrangement fails because of non-acceptance, non-performance by the debtor, or otherwise, bankruptcy proceedings may be reinstated or begun against the debtor.

Statement of affairs. The statement of affairs is sometimes used to reflect the financial condition of an insolvent business. In England the bankruptcy laws require that a statement of affairs be furnished to the creditors of an insolvent debtor. Because of the influence of British accountants practicing in this country, problems requiring the preparation of such statements were frequently included in examinations, and the subject has therefore necessarily been covered in textbooks. The statement is of little, if any, importance in American practice, and problems dealing with it are now given infrequently in the examinations.

Both the balance sheet and the statement of affairs are statements of financial condition. The differences between the two statements are indicated below:

(1) The balance sheet is prepared from the viewpoint of a going concern; the statement of affairs is prepared from the viewpoint of liquidation.

(2) In the balance sheet, the assets and liabilities are classified on a going-concern basis, as *fixed*, *current*, *deferred*, and so forth; in the statement of affairs, the liabilities are classified as *prior*, *fully secured*, *partially secured*, and *unsecured*, and the assets are classified to indicate those which have been pledged with creditors and those which are free.

(3) In the balance sheet, the assets are stated at going-concern values; in the statement of affairs, they are stated both at going-concern values and at estimated realizable values.

Illustration. The statement of affairs on page 141 is based on the following balance sheet and supplementary information:

THE SMITH COMPANY

Balance Sheet—June 30, 1946

Assets		Liabilities	
Cash	$ 300.00	Accrued wages	$ 250.00
Accounts receivable	9,000.00	Accounts payable	25,000.00
Merchandise	18,000.00	Notes payable	4,000.00
Bonds of *X* Company	3,000.00	Mortgage payable	15,000.00
Land and buildings	25,000.00	Capital stock	10,000.00
		Surplus	1,050.00
	$55,300.00		$55,300.00

THE SMITH COMPANY

Statement of Affairs—June 30, 1946

Assets

Book Value			Expected to Realize
	Assets pledged with fully secured creditors:		
$25,000.00	Land and buildings:		
	Estimated value............	$18,000.00	
	Less mortgage payable—contra	15,000.00	$ 3,000.00
	Assets pledged with partially secured creditors:		
3,000.00	Bonds of *X* Company—deducted contra		
	Estimated value...........	$ 3,200.00	
	Free assets:		
300.00	Cash........................		300.00
9,000.00	Accounts receivable		
	$4,000 Good............		4,000.00
	3,000 Doubtful..........		1,500.00
	2,000 Bad..............		
	$9,000		
18,000.00	Merchandise................		13,500.00
	Total free assets................		$22,300.00
	Deduct liabilities having priority, per contra:		
	Accrued wages..............		250.00
	Net free assets..................		$22,050.00
	Deficiency to unsecured creditors		3,750.00
$55,300.00			$25,800.00

Liabilities

Book Value			Expected to Rank
	Liabilities having priority:		
$ 250.00	Accrued wages—deducted contra		
	Fully secured liabilities:		
15,000.00	Mortgage payable—deducted contra		
	Partially secured liabilities:		
4,000.00	Notes payable..........	$4,000.00	
	Deduct bonds of *X* Co.	3,200.00	$ 800.00
	Unsecured liabilities:		
25,000.00	Accounts payable.......		25,000.00
	Capital:		
10,000.00	Capital stock		
1,050.00	Surplus		
$55,300.00			$25,800.00

The accounts receivable have not been pledged with any of the creditors; their value is estimated as follows:

	Gross Value	Estimated Realizable Value
Good	$4,000.00	$4,000.00
Doubtful	3,000.00	1,500.00
Bad	2,000.00	—

The merchandise is not pledged, and its estimated realizable value is $13,500.00.

The bonds of *X* Company, carried at $3,000.00, are worth $3,200.00; they have been pledged as security to the notes payable of $4,000.00, which are therefore only partially secured.

The land and buildings, which are thought to be worth $18-000.00, serve as security to the $15,000.00 mortgage, which is therefore fully secured.

In the statement of affairs on page 141, the balance sheet values are shown in the book value columns. The expected to realize column shows the amounts which the receiver expects to obtain from these assets; this column is sometimes headed "free assets at realizable values." The expected to rank column shows the amounts of unsecured liabilities; this column is sometimes headed "unsecured claims." The treatment of the various assets and liabilities is discussed in the following sections.

Liabilities having priority. Section 64 of the Bankruptcy Act provides:

"a. The debts to have priority, in advance of the payment of dividends to creditors, and to be paid in full out of bankrupt estates, and the order of payment, shall be (1) the actual and necessary costs and expenses of preserving the estate subsequent to filing the petition; the filing fees paid by creditors in involuntary cases; where property of the bankrupt, transferred or concealed by him either before or after the filing of the petition, shall have been recovered for the benefit of the estate of the bankrupt by the efforts and at the cost and expense of one or more creditors, the reasonable costs and expenses of such recovery; the costs and expenses of administration, including the trustee's expenses in opposing the bankrupt's discharge, the fees and mileage payable to witnesses as now or hereafter provided by the laws of the United States, and one reasonable attorney's fee for the professional services actually rendered, irrespective of the number of attorneys employed, to the petitioning creditors in involuntary cases and to the bankrupt in voluntary and involuntary cases as the court may allow; (2) wages, not to exceed $600 to each claimant, which have been earned within three months before the date of the commencement of the proceeding, due to workmen, servants, clerks, or traveling or city salesmen on salary or commission basis, whole or part time, whether or not selling exclusively for the bankrupt; (3) where the confirmation of an arrangement or wage-earner plan or the bankrupt's discharge has been refused, revoked, or set aside upon the objection and through the efforts and at the cost and expense of one or more creditors, evidence shall have been adduced resulting in the conviction of any person of an offense under this Act, the reasonable costs and expenses of such creditors in obtaining such refusal, revocation, or setting aside, or in adducing such evidence; (4) taxes legally due and owing by the bankrupt to the United States or any State or any subdivision thereof: *Provided*, That no order shall be made for the payment of a tax assessed against any property of the bankrupt in excess of the value of the interest of the bankrupt estate therein as determined by the court; *And provided further*, That, in case any question arises as to the amount or legality of any taxes, such question shall be heard and determined by the court; and (5) debts owing to any person, including the United States, who by the laws of the United States in [*sic*] entitled to priority, and rent owing to a landlord who is entitled to priority by applicable state law: *Provided, however*, That such priority for rent to a landlord shall be restricted to the rent which is legally due and owing for the actual use and occupancy of the premises affected, and which accrued within three months before the date of bankruptcy.

"b. Debts contracted while a discharge is in force or after the confirmation of an arrangement shall, in the event of a revocation of the discharge or setting aside of the confirmation, have priority and be paid in full in advance of the payment of the debts which were provable in the bankruptcy or arrangement proceeding, as the case may be."

Liabilities having priority have usually been shown in the statement of affairs under the caption "preferred liabilities." However, "preference" has a different meaning under the Bankruptcy Act, which provides (Section 60):

"A preference is a transfer, as defined in this Act, of any of the property of a debtor to or for the benefit of a creditor for or on account of an antecedent debt, made or suffered by such debtor while insolvent and within four months before the filing by or against him of the petition in bankruptcy, or of the original petition under Chapters X, XI, XII, or XIII of this Act, the effect of which transfer will be to enable such creditor to obtain a greater percentage of his debt than some other creditor of the same class . . . . "

For purposes of precision in terminology, the author has taken the liberty of discontinuing the customary caption "preferred liabilities" in the statement of affairs and substituting the caption "liabilities having priority."

It will be noted that, in the statement of affairs, such liabilities are not extended to the expected to rank column, but are deducted from the total free assets in the expected to realize column, to indicate that they are a first claim against the free assets and that they must be settled in full before any assets are available for the payment of unsecured liabilities.

Fully secured liabilities and pledged assets. A fully secured liability is a debt secured by pledged assets having a realizable value equal to or greater than the amount of the debt. A fully secured creditor realizes on the pledged assets, deducts the amount of his claim, and pays any excess to the receiver or trustee; in the statement of affairs on page 141, the $15,000.00 fully secured mortgage and the $18,000.00 of pledged assets are shown as follows:

On the asset side:

The estimated value of the mortgaged land and buildings, $18,000.00, is entered at the left of the expected to realize column, the amount of the mortgage is deducted, and the $3,000.00 excess of the security over the liability is entered in the expected to realize column, to show the net amount which the trustee expects to obtain.

On the liability side:

The notation "deducted contra" and the omission of the amount from the expected to rank column indicate that the mortgage will be paid from the proceeds of the pledged assets and not from the proceeds of free assets.

Partially secured liabilities and pledged assets. A partially secured liability is a debt secured by assets having a realizable value less than the amount of the debt. Partially secured creditors realize on the pledged assets, apply the proceeds in reduction of their claims, and look to the free assets for payment of the unsecured balance. Therefore, as illustrated by the statement of affairs on page 141,

On the liability side:

The estimated value of the pledged bonds ($3,200.00) is deducted from the amount of the liability ($4,000.00), and the $800.00 excess, or unsecured portion of the liability, is extended to the expected to rank column, as a general claim against the free assets.

On the asset side:

The notation "deducted contra" and the omission of the estimated value from the expected to realize column indicate that the trustee will obtain no funds from the disposal of the bonds.

Unsecured liabilities and free assets. All unsecured liabilities are entered in the expected to rank column, and the realizable values of all free assets are entered in the expected to realize column.

Capital. The amounts of the capital stock and surplus are entered in the book value column on the liability side of the statement of affairs, to bring the two book value columns into balance and thus to indicate that no assets or liabilities shown by the balance sheet have been omitted from the statement of affairs.

Net free assets and deficiency to unsecured creditors. The $22,300.00 total of the expected to realize column is the amount of funds which the trustee expects will come into his possession. The liabilities having priority are deducted from this total to indicate that they are a first claim against the free assets, and to determine the $22,050.00 remainder, or net free assets, which it is estimated will be available for the payment of unsecured liabilities. The difference between the net free assets and the unsecured liabilities (shown by the total of the expected to rank column) is the deficiency to unsecured creditors.

The deficiency account. The statement of affairs may be accompanied by a statement called a *deficiency account*, showing the estimated loss or gain on the realization of the assets. This account, or statement, shows why it will be impossible to pay the unsecured creditors in full. The estimated losses and gains appear in the deficiency account as follows:

THE SMITH COMPANY

Deficiency Account—June 30, 1946

Estimated loss on:		Estimated gain on:	
Accounts receivable	$3,500.00	Bonds of *X* Company	$200.00
Merchandise	4,500.00		
Land and buildings	7,000.00		

The balance of this account now shows a loss of $14,800.00. The account is closed by entering on the credit side:

(1) The capital stock and surplus of the corporation, thus indicating the loss to be borne by the stockholders; and
(2) The deficiency to unsecured creditors, per the statement of affairs, thus indicating the probable loss to be borne by the creditors.

THE SMITH COMPANY

Deficiency Account—June 30, 1946

Estimated loss on:		Estimated gain on:	
Accounts receivable	$ 3,500.00	Bonds of *X* Company	$ 200.00
Merchandise	4,500.00	Capital stock	10,000.00
Land and buildings	7,000.00	Surplus	1,050.00
		Deficiency to creditors	3,750.00
	$15,000.00		$15,000.00

Illustration of special points. The statement of affairs and the deficiency account on pages 148 to 150 illustrate the treatment of a number of special points discussed in the following sections.

Reserves. The treatment of reserves depends upon their nature. For purposes of explanation and illustration, reserves may be classified in the three groups discussed on page 146.

(1) Valuation reserves, such as reserves for depreciation and for bad debts.

Such reserves are usually deducted from the gross book values of the assets, and the net book values are entered in the book value column on the asset side of the statement of affairs. This treatment is illustrated by the deduction of the reserves for depreciation of buildings and machinery. The deficiency account shows, as a loss, the difference between the net book value and the estimated realizable value.

In some cases one reserve may be set up against two or more assets. For instance, in the illustrative statement, there is one reserve for losses on both accounts and notes receivable. Since this reserve cannot be apportioned between the two assets, it cannot be deducted on the asset side of the statement, and is therefore shown under the reserve caption on the liability side of the statement. In the deficiency account, the reserve is deducted from the gross loss on the accounts and notes.

(2) Reserves for accrued liabilities.

Such reserves should be classified under the prior, fully secured, partially secured, or unsecured liabilities caption if any real liability exists. If there is no liability, the reserve may be shown under the reserve caption, with no amount extended to the expected to rank column. In the illustration, a reserve was provided for possible additional Federal income taxes of prior years; as it is expected that the tax will have to be paid, the item is classified as "a liability having priority."

(3) Contingent liabilities.

The three following contingent liabilities appear in the statement of affairs on pages 148 and 149.

The company was contingently liable in the amount of $400.00 on notes receivable discounted. The discounted notes will probably have to be paid by the indorser, and the $400.00 is therefore extended to the expected to rank column. This $400.00 is also, of course, included in the $1,200.00 debit balance of the notes receivable account. Since it is expected that the remaining notes receivable will be collectible, $800.00 is extended to the expected to realize column on the asset side.

The company had set up a $3,000.00 reserve for possible payments to be made as damages under a pending suit. A favorable issue of the suit now appears probable, and therefore no liability is extended to the expected to rank column.

On the other hand, the company is in default on a contract for the delivery of goods and will probably be required to pay $1,000.00 in settlement of damages. Although no reserve was set up, the item is shown under the contingent liabilities caption, with $1,000.00 extended to the expected to rank column.

(4) Unrealized profit reserves.

When the company's machinery was appraised, a reserve was set up for the unrealized profit of $5,000.00. This reserve is shown under the reserves caption in the statement of affairs. It might have been deducted from the book value of the property on the asset side, thus:

$18,700.00		Machinery
	$31,000.00	Appraised value
	7,300.00	Reserve for depreciation
	$23,700.00	Net book value
	5,000.00	Unrealized profit per appraisal
	$18,700.00	Cost less depreciation

(5) Surplus reserves.

The illustrative statement of affairs contains one surplus reserve—the sinking fund reserve. As it is a part of the net worth, it is classified under the capital caption.

Accrued interest. Accrued interest should appear in the statement of affairs immediately after the asset or liability on which the interest has accrued. If interest has accrued:

On an asset pledged as security, the interest as well as the principal should be shown as pledged. As an illustration, note the treatment of the accrued interest on the Fairview Company bonds under the caption, assets pledged with partially secured creditors.

On a fully secured liability, the interest as well as the principal of the liability should be deducted from the security. As an illustration, note (under the caption, assets pledged with fully secured creditors) the deduction of the bond principal and interest from the total security. (Continued on page 151.)

THE LUCAS MANUFACTURING COMPANY

Statement of Affairs—August 31, 1946

Assets

Book Value				Expected to Realize
	Assets pledged with fully secured creditors:			
$ 5,000	Land—estimated value		$ 5,350	
21,000	Buildings—estimated value		16,000	
	$27,500 Cost			
	6,500 Reserve for depreciation			
	$21,000 Net book value			
12,500	Sinking fund		12,250	
	Total security for bonds payable		$33,600	
	Deduct: Bonds payable	$25,000		
	Accrued interest	500	25,500	$ 8,100
	Assets pledged with partially secured creditors:			
5,000	Bonds of Fairview Company—estimated value		$ 4,850	
100	Accrued interest on bonds		100	
2,350	Finished goods		1,200	
	Total security for $10,000 of notes payable—deducted contra		$ 6,150	
	Free assets:			
495	Cash		$ 495	
	Less worthless checks held		210	285
32,375	Accounts receivable			19,800
1,200	Notes receivable			800

Liabilities

Book Value			Expected to Rank
	Liabilities having priority:		
$ 225	Accrued taxes—deducted contra		
425	Reserve for federal income tax—deducted contra		
	Fully secured liabilities:		
25,000	Bonds payable—deducted contra		
500	Accrued bond interest—deducted contra		
	Partially secured liabilities:		
10,000	Notes payable	$10,000	
120	Accrued interest on notes payable	120	
	Total	$10,120	
	Deduct security—detailed contra	6,150	$ 3,970
	Unsecured liabilities:		
25,000	Notes payable		25,000
355	Accrued interest on notes payable		355
32,350	Accounts payable		32,350
	Contingent liabilities:		
400	Notes receivable discounted		400
3,000	Reserve for damage suit		

18	Accrued interest on notes receivable			18
5,900	Goods in process			
	Estimated value when completed		$ 6,000	
	Less cost to complete:			
	Raw materials worth	$500		
	Other expenditures	200	700	5,300
7,000	Raw materials			
	$1,000 to be used in finishing goods in process			500
	$6,000 to be sold			3,000
5,000	Bonds of Fairview Company			4,850
100	Accrued interest on bonds			100
23,700	Machinery—estimated value			18,500
	$31,000 Appraised value			
	7,300 Reserve for depreciation			
	$23,700 Net book value			
10,000	Goodwill—No value			
125	Unexpired insurance			
500	Discount on stock			300
	Total free assets			$61,553
	Deduct liabilities having priority—per contra			650
	Net free assets			$60,903
	Deficiency to creditors			2,172
$132,363				$63,075

	Possible liability for non-delivery of merchandise	1,000
	Reserves:	
5,000	Unrealized profit on appraisal of machinery	
1,500	Reserve for doubtful receivables	
	Capital:	
25,000	Capital stock	
12,500	Sinking fund reserve	
9,012*	Deficit (in red)	
$132,363		$63,075

THE LUCAS MANUFACTURING COMPANY

Deficiency Account—August 31, 1946

Deficit from operations		$ 9,012.00	Estimated gain on land	$ 350.00
Estimated loss on:			Reserve for damage suit—not required	3,000.00
Buildings		5,000.00	Capital stock	25,000.00
Sinking fund		250.00	Sinking fund reserve	12,500.00
Bonds of Fairview Company		300.00	Deficiency to creditors	2,172.00
Finished goods		1,150.00		
Cash		210.00		
Receivables:				
Accounts receivable	$12,575.00			
Notes receivable	400.00			
Total	$12,975.00			
Less reserve for losses	1,500.00	11,475.00		
Goods in process		600.00		
Raw materials		3,500.00		
Machinery:				
Net book value	$23,700.00			
Less unrealized profit on appraisal	5,000.00			
Cost less depreciation	$18,700.00			
Less estimated realizable value	18,500.00	200.00		
Goodwill		10,000.00		
Unexpired insurance		125.00		
Discount on stock		200.00		
Possible liability for non-delivery of merchandise		1,000.00		
		$43,022.00		$43,022.00

On a partially secured liability, the security should be deducted from the sum of the liability on principal and interest. For an illustration, refer to the data shown under the partially secured liabilities caption.

Liabilities secured by more than one asset. The statement of affairs on pages 148 and 149 contains two illustrations of liabilities secured by more than one asset. Under the captions:

Assets pledged with fully secured creditors:
The company's land, buildings, and sinking fund are shown as security for the bonds payable.
Assets pledged with partially secured creditors:
Half of the company's Fairview bonds, the accrued interest thereon, and the finished goods are shown as security for the notes payable.

Unexpired insurance. There is a difference of opinion among accountants about whether the unexpired premiums on insurance policies should appear in the expected to realize column. While it is true that the unexpired premiums have a certain cash value at the time of preparing the statement of affairs, it is doubtful whether this value should be shown as a realizable asset. It cannot be realized without canceling the policies, and the policies cannot be safely canceled until the assets insured have been disposed of. As it is not certain when the policies can be canceled, there is no way of knowing what, if anything, can be realized from the policies, and it therefore seems more conservative to give them no realizable value. The total unexpired premium can properly be shown in the expected to realize column of a statement prepared in support of a request for a loan because of its going-concern value.

Assets partly pledged and partly free. The statement on pages 148 and 149 shows that $5,000.00 par value of the Fairview Company bonds are pledged with partially secured creditors, and that the other $5,000.00 par value are free and unpledged. In a balance sheet the $10,000.00 total would probably be shown under one caption, but in a statement of affairs the pledged and unpledged status should be clearly indicated.

Deficit. If a deficit appears in the balance sheet, it should not be shown on the asset side of the statement of affairs but should be deducted from the capital stock on the liability side, in the manner illustrated on page 149.

Stock discount. When a stock discount account appears on the books of a corporation, the creditors have a right to the payment of the discount, or as much thereof as is necessary to pay the liabilities in full. If it is possible to make collections from the stockholders, a value should be carried to the expected to realize column. The expected to realize column may show only the amount necessary to collect in order to avoid a deficiency to creditors. For instance, if there is a $10,000.00 stock discount account, and if, on the basis of the estimated realizable values of the assets, it appears necessary to collect $7,000.00 of the discount, only $7,000.00 need be entered in the expected to realize column. However, while it is true that no more will be collected from the stockholders than is necessary to pay the creditors in full, it seems desirable to show the full amount that can be collected, because of the possibility that the realizable values of the assets may have been overestimated. If this should prove to be true, there would be a corresponding increase in the amount to be collected from the stockholders, and it seems desirable to have the statement of affairs show the maximum amount which could be collected. The facts may therefore be shown as follows:

Book Value		Expected to Realize
$5,000.00	Discount on stock	
	Estimated amount collectible $4,000.00	
	Estimated amount required to pay creditors in full $2,000.00	

Additional costs before realizaticn. It is sometimes necessary to make additional expenditures on assets before they can be realized to the best advantage. As an example, the statement of affairs on page 149 shows, under the goods in process caption, that this inventory, when completed, will probably realize $6,000,00 but that raw materials worth $500.00 and other expenditures of $200.00 will be required for their completion. The proposed use, in the completion of goods in process, of raw materials having a realizable value of $500.00, is also shown under the raw materials caption.

Accounts and notes payable. There is a tendency to assume that notes payable rank ahead of accounts payable as liabilities. This is a false assumption. Notes do not rank ahead of accounts unless the notes are secured and the accounts are not.

Loss to partners. If the business is operated by a partnership, the deficiency to creditors may be brought down in the statement of affairs as shown in the illustration on page 153 because the creditors can collect from the partners' private resources.

	Deficiency to unsecured creditors—dcwn...			$ 3,750.00	
				$25,800.00	
	Estimated loss to partners................			$14,800.00	
	Division of loss, and resulting capitals:				
		Jones	Smith		
	Capitals per books	$8,000.00	$3,050.00		
	Loss............	7,400.00	7,400.00		
	Balance.........	$ 600.00	$4,350.00*		
$55,300.00				$14,800.00	$55,300.00

* Debit balance.

Total unsecured liabilities............	$25,800.00
Deficiency to creditors—down..........	$ 3,750.00
Capital:	
Jones, capital.....................	8,000.00
Smith, capital.....................	3,050.00
	$14,800.00

This form of statement may be used to advantage when one of the partners is insolvent and it is desired to show his personal creditors what equity he will have in the assets of the partnership after liquidation.

Statement for credit purposes. A statement of affairs may be submitted to a bank or other prospective creditor in support of a request for unsecured credit. The statement of affairs might be considered preferable to a balance sheet for that purpose because it shows the realizable values as well as the book values of the assets, and because the offsets of secured liabilities against pledged assets are clearly reflected.

If a statement of affairs is used for credit purposes, it will presumably show an excess of free assets over unsecured claims, thus indicating that the business is in such a good financial condition that all creditors may expect to be paid in full.

To illustrate the form of a statement of affairs for credit purposes, we may use the balance sheet of The Smith Company appearing on page 141 and increase the estimated realizable values of the assets. The illustrative statement appears on page 155.

THE SMITH COMPANY

Statement of Affairs—June 30, 1946

Assets

Book Value			Expected to Realize
	Assets pledged with fully secured creditors:		
$25,000.00	Land and buildings:		
	Estimated value	$26,500.00	
	Less mortgage payable—contra	15,000.00	$11,500.00
	Assets pledged with partially secured creditors:		
3,000.00	Bonds of *X* Company—deducted contra		
	Estimated value	$ 3,200.00	
	Free assets:		
300.00	Cash		300.00
9,000.00	Accounts receivable:		
	$7,000.00 Good		7,000.00
	2,000.00 Doubtful		1,500.00
	$9,000.00		
18,000.00	Merchandise		21,000.00
	Total free assets		$41,300.00
	Deduct liabilities having priority—per contra:		
	Accrued wages		250.00
$55,300.00			$41,050.00

Liabilities

Book Value			Expected to Rank
	Liabilities having priority:		
$ 250.00	Accrued wages—deducted contra		
	Fully secured liabilities:		
15,000.00	Mortgage payable—deducted contra		
	Partially secured liabilities:		
4,000.00	Notes payable	$4,000.00	
	Deduct bonds of *X* Company	3,200.00	$ 800.00
	Unsecured liabilities:		
25,000.00	Accounts payable		25,000.00
	Capital:		
10,000.00	Capital stock		
1,050.00	Surplus		
	Total unsecured liabilities		$25,800.00
	Excess of net free assets over unsecured liabilities		15,250.00
$55,300.00			$41,050.00

CHAPTER 40

Receiver's Accounts

Opening new books. It is rarely necessary to open new books for a company in financial difficulties unless the business is to be operated by a receiver in equity. The old books may be continued if the business is to be liquidated under bankruptcy proceedings or by an assignee under a voluntary assignment, or if the operations are to be continued under the supervision of a representative of the creditors.

If operations are to be continued under the direction of a receiver in equity, it is usually desirable to open new books, to indicate that there has been a transfer of assets to the receiver, and to distinguish clearly between liabilities incurred prior to the receivership, which will be left on the old books, and liabilities incurred by the receiver, which will be recorded on the new books.

The order of the court appointing the receiver usually states the assets to which he is to take title; these assets may include part or all of the corporation's property. The receiver should open his books by taking up these assets as well as any valuation reserves against them. But he should not take the liabilities onto his books. The liabilities existing prior to the receivership should remain on the corporation's books, so as to maintain a distinction between prior and subsequent debts.

The entries on both sets of books showing the transfer of the assets, are:

Receiver's Books	Corporation's Books
Assets taken over	*M*—receiver
Reserves against assets	Reserves against assets
X Y Z Co.—in receivership	Assets

Payment of prior liabilities. Although the receiver does not take the liabilities onto his books, he may be ordered by the court to pay them. In that case he should debit the corporation and credit cash. But his debit entry should not be made in the account which was credited with the assets; temporary accounts with the corporation should be set up to furnish detailed information which the receiver will need in preparing his reports. The entries on both sets of books showing the payment of liabilities existing prior to the receivership, are shown on the next page.

Receiver's Books	Corporation's Books
X Y Z Co.—bonds paid Cash	Bonds payable *M*—receiver

Since the liabilities appear on the corporation's books instead of on the receiver's books, the accrued interest should be recorded on the corporation's books. The receiver, however, will be expected to pay the interest, and the entries should be made in such a way as to distinguish between interest accrued prior to the receivership and interest accrued during the receivership. This is done as follows:

Receiver's Books	Corporation's Books
X Y Z Co.—accrued interest paid Cash	Accrued interest *M*—receiver
X Y Z Co.—interest paid Cash	Interest *M*—receiver

Recording operations. The expenses and income of operations should be recorded on the receiver's books, and so far as possible the receiver should follow the same classification of accounts as the corporation formerly used, in order that comparative statements can be made for the receivership and prior periods.

Receiver's Books	Corporation's Books
Various expense accounts Cash or Accounts payable	
Cash or Accounts receivable Sales	
Cash or Accounts receivable Other income accounts	

Closing the books. At the end of the regular accounting periods, and more frequently if desired, the receiver's books should be closed. This closing follows the regular routine, and no special points are involved except that the profit and loss account is closed to the account with the company in receivership. After the receiver has made up his statements, the special accounts with the company showing liabilities carried on the company books but paid by the receiver, should be closed to the main account with the company.

The profit or loss shown by the receiver is taken into the corporation's books by a debit to the receiver's account and a credit to profit and loss for a profit, or by a debit to profit and loss and a credit to the receiver if a loss is incurred. Any nominal accounts on the corporation's books are then closed to profit and loss, and the net profit or loss thus determined is closed to surplus.

Periodical statements. The statements prepared at the end of each accounting period should include a profit and loss statement and a balance sheet, which should embody the information recorded in both the company's books and the receiver's books. The balances shown by the two sets of books may be assembled on working papers provided with columns for the trial balances of the two ledgers, as illustrated on page 166.

Close of the receivership. When the receivership is terminated, the receiver should close his books by recording the return to the corporation of such assets as he holds. Entries recording the termination of the receivership should be made on both sets of books as follows:

Receiver's Books	Corporation's Books
X Y Z Co.—in receivership	Assets
Reserves	Reserves
Assets	*M*—receiver

If any unpaid liabilities appear on the receiver's books, they should also be transferred to the company's books.

Illustration

Basis of illustration. The *C* Company found itself in financial difficulties, and F. C. White was appointed receiver as of June 30, 1945. The books were closed, and the following balance sheet was prepared.

C COMPANY
Balance Sheet—June 30, 1945

Assets

Current assets:			
Cash		$ 1,800.00	
Accounts receivable	$50,000.00		
Less reserve for bad debts	1,500.00	48,500.00	
Notes receivable		15,000.00	
Inventory		60,000.00	
Total current assets			$125,300.00
Marketable securities			7,500.00
Fixed assets:			
Land		$10,000.00	
Building	$80,000.00		
Less reserve for depreciation	15,000.00	65,000.00	
Furniture and fixtures	$10,000.00		
Less reserve for depreciation	3,000.00	7,000.00	
Total fixed assets			82,000.00
Deferred charges:			
Unexpired insurance			900.00
			$215,700.00

Liabilities

Current liabilities:		
Accounts payable	$95,000.00	
Notes payable	25,000.00	
Accrued mortgage interest	500.00	
Total current liabilities		$120,500.00
Fixed liabilities:		
Mortgage payable		50,000.00
Net worth:		
Capital stock	$50,000.00	
Less deficit	4,800.00	
Net worth		45,200.00
		$215,700.00

On pages 162 to 165 will be found the entries, in journal form, recording the following facts on the books of the receiver and the books of the company. The transactions cover a period of a year.

(a) The receiver, under order of the court, took over all of the assets shown by the foregoing balance sheet. Note that the receiver, in taking up the accounts receivable, debits accounts receivable—old, to distinguish them from accounts receivable which will result from sales during the receivership.

(b) Merchandise purchases on account, $120,000.00.

(c) Sales on account, $200,000.00.

(d) Cash collections amounting to $47,500.00 were obtained on the old accounts receivable. The remaining accounts were written off as worthless, by charges to the reserve for bad debts and to a special loss account.

(e) The notes receivable, $15,000.00, were collected in full.

(f) Interest in the amount of $300.00 was collected on these notes.

(g) New accounts receivable amounting to $160,000.00 were settled by cash collections of $157,700.00 and the allowance of cash discounts of $2,300.00.

(h) Interest in the amount of $120.00 was collected on the marketable securities.

(i) The marketable securities were sold for $7,350.00, or at a loss of $150.00.

(j) Prior liabilities were paid as follows:

Accounts payable	$95,000.00
Notes payable	25,000.00
Mortgage installment	5,000.00
Mortgage interest accrued on June 30, 1945	500.00

(k) The mortgage interest accrued from June 30, 1945 to June 30, 1946, was $2,950.00.

(l) The receiver paid the accrued mortgage interest from June 30, 1945 to April 30, 1946, in the amount of $2,500.00.

(m) Receiver's accounts payable for merchandise purchases, in the amount of $75,000.00, were settled as follows: Cash payments were made in the amount of $73,600.00; and cash discounts were taken in the amount of $1,400.00.

(n) The following expenses were paid in cash:

Salaries and wages	$17,000.00
Freight in	350.00
Delivery expense	1,000.00
Taxes	1,200.00
General expense	7,500.00

(o) Depreciation for the year was provided in the following amounts:

Building	$3,200.00
Furniture and fixtures	1,000.00

(p) A reserve for bad debts in the amount of $1,200.00 was provided against the new accounts receivable.

(q) The insurance premium expiration for the year, chargeable to operations, was $550.00.

The merchandise inventory on June 30, 1946 was $23,000.00.

Receiver's Books

		Debit	Credit
(a)	Cash	$ 1,800.00	
	Accounts receivable—old	50,000.00	
	Notes receivable	15,000.00	
	Inventory	60,000.00	
	Marketable securities	7,500.00	
	Land	10,000.00	
	Building	80,000.00	
	Furniture and fixtures	10,000.00	
	Unexpired insurance	900.00	
	Reserve for bad debts—old		$ 1,500.00
	Reserve for depreciation—building		15,000.00
	Reserve for depreciation—furniture and fixtures		3,000.00
	C Company—in receivership		215,700.00
	To open the receiver's books.		
(b)	Purchases	120,000.00	
	Accounts payable		120,000.00
	Purchases of merchandise.		
(c)	Accounts receivable—new	200,000.00	
	Sales		200,000.00
	Sales on account.		
(d)	Cash	47,500.00	
	Reserve for bad debts—old	1,500.00	
	Loss on accounts receivable—old	1,000.00	
	Accounts receivable—old		50,000.00
	Collections on old accounts receivable.		
(e)	Cash	15,000.00	
	Notes receivable		15,000.00
	Collection of notes in full.		
(f)	Cash	300.00	
	Interest income		300.00
	Interest collected on notes.		
(g)	Cash	157,700.00	
	Discount on sales	2,300.00	
	Accounts receivable—new		160,000.00
	Collections on new accounts receivable.		
(h)	Cash	120.00	
	Interest income		120.00
	Collected on securities.		
(i)	Cash	7,350.00	
	Loss on securities	150.00	
	Marketable securities		7,500.00
	Sale of securities.		
(j)	*C* Company—accounts payable paid	95,000.00	
	C Company—notes payable paid	25,000.00	
	C Company—mortgage payments	5,000.00	
	C Company—mortgage interest paid	500.00	
	Cash		125,500.00
	Payment of prior liabilities.		

Company's Books

(a)	F. C. White—receiver	$215,700.00	
	Reserve for bad debts	1,500.00	
	Reserve for depreciation—building	15,000.00	
	Reserve for depreciation—furniture and fixtures	3,000.00	
	Cash		$ 1,800.00
	Accounts receivable		50,000.00
	Notes receivable		15,000.00
	Inventory		60,000.00
	Marketable securities		7,500.00
	Land		10,000.00
	Building		80,000.00
	Furniture and fixtures		10,000.00
	Unexpired insurance		900.00
	To charge the receiver with the assets taken over.		

(j)	Accounts payable	95,000 00	
	Notes payable	25,000.00	
	Mortgage payable	5,000.00	
	Accrued mortgage interest	500.00	
	F. C. White—receiver		125,500.00
	Liabilities paid by receiver.		

Receiver's Books

(l)	*C* Company—mortgage interest paid	$ 2,500.00	
	Cash		$ 2,500.00
	Payment of interest from June 30, 1945 to April 30, 1946.		
(m)	Accounts payable	75,000.00	
	Cash		73,600.00
	Discount on purchases		1,400.00
	Payment for purchases.		
(n)	Salaries and wages	17,000.00	
	Freight in	350.00	
	Delivery expense	1,000.00	
	Taxes	1,200.00	
	General expense	7,500.00	
	Cash		27,050.00
	Payment of expenses.		
(o)	Depreciation—building	3,200.00	
	Depreciation—furniture and fixtures	1,000.00	
	Reserve for depreciation—building		3,200.00
	Reserve for depreciation—furniture and fixtures		1,000.00
	Depreciation provisions for the year.		
(p)	Bad debts—receiver's sales	1,200.00	
	Reserve for bad debts—new		1,200.00
	Provision for losses.		
(q)	Insurance	550.00	
	Unexpired insurance		550.00
	To write off insurance expired during year.		

Company's Books

(k) Mortgage interest	$ 2,950.00	
Accrued mortgage interest		$ 2,950.00
Interest for year ended June 30, 1946.		
(l) Accrued mortgage interest	2,500.00	
F. C. White—receiver		2,500.00
Payment of interest from June 30, 1945 to April 30, 1946.		

Working papers. The working papers assembling the balances on the receiver's books and on the company's books appear on page 166. These working papers contain the information required for the balance sheet and the profit and loss statement on pages 167 and 168.

C COMPANY—IN RECEIVERSHIP
Working Papers
For the Year Ended June 30, 1946

	Receiver's Trial Balance		Company's Trial Balance		Eliminations		Profit and Loss		Balance Sheet	
Cash	$ 1,120								$ 1,120	
Accounts receivable—new	40,000								40,000	
Reserve for bad debts—new		$ 1,200								$ 1,200
Inventory—June 30, 1945	60,000						$ 60,000			
Land	10,000								10,000	
Building	80,000								80,000	
Reserve for depreciation—building		18,200								18,200
Furniture and fixtures	10,000								10,000	
Reserve for depreciation—furniture and fixtures		4,000								4,000
Unexpired insurance	350								350	
Accounts payable		45,000								45,000
Accrued mortgage interest				$ 450						450
Mortgage payable				45,000						45,000
Capital stock				50,000						50,000
Surplus			$ 4,800						4,800	
F. C. White—receiver			87,700		$ 87,700					
C Company—in receivership		215,700				$215,700				
C Company—accounts payable paid	95,000				95,000					
C Company—notes payable paid	25,000				25,000					
C Company—mortgage payments	5,000				5,000					
C Company—mortgage interest paid	3,000				3,000					
Sales		200,000						$200,000		
Purchases	120,000						120,000			
Freight in	350						350			
Salaries and wages	17,000						17,000			
Delivery expense	1,000						1,000			
Taxes	1,200						1,200			
Insurance	550						550			
General expense	7,500						7,500			
Depreciation—building	3,200						3,200			
Depreciation—furniture and fixtures	1,000						1,000			
Bad debts	1,200						1,200			
Discount on sales	2,300						2,300			
Discount on purchases		1,400						1,400		
Interest income		420						420		
Mortgage interest			2,950				2,950			
Loss on accounts receivable—old	1,000						1,000			
Loss on securities	150						150			
	$485,920	$485,920	$95,450	$95,450	$215,700	$215,700				
Inventory—June 30, 1946								23,000	23,000	
Net income							5,420			5,420
							$224,820	$224,820	$169,270	$169,270

Balance sheet. The balance sheet as of June 30, 1946, prepared from the working papers, appears below.

C COMPANY—IN RECEIVERSHIP
F. C. WHITE—RECEIVER
Balance Sheet—June 30, 1946

Assets

Current assets:			
Cash		$ 1,120.00	
Accounts receivable—new	$40,000.00		
Less reserve for bad debts	1,200.00	38,800.00	
Inventory		23,000.00	
Total current assets			$ 62,920.00
Fixed assets:			
Land		$10,000.00	
Building	$80,000.00		
Less reserve for depreciation	18,200.00		
Depreciated value		61,800.00	
Furniture and fixtures	$10,000.00		
Less reserve for depreciation	4,000.00	6,000.00	
Total fixed assets			77,800.00
Deferred charges:			
Unexpired insurance			350.00
			$141,070.00

Liabilities

Current liabilities:			
Accounts payable		$45,000.00	
Accrued mortgage interest		450.00	
Total current liabilities			$ 45,450.00
Fixed liabilities:			
Mortgage payable			45,000.00
Net worth:			
Capital stock		$50,000.00	
Surplus:			
Deficit, June 30, 1945	$ 4,800.00		
Surplus for the year	5,420.00	620.00	50,620.00
			$141,070.00

Profit and loss statement. The profit and loss statement for the year ended June 30, 1946 follows:

C COMPANY—IN RECEIVERSHIP
F. C. WHITE—RECEIVER
Profit and Loss Statement
For the Year Ended June 30, 1946

Sales			$200,000.00
Less cost of goods sold:			
Inventory, June 30, 1945		$ 60,000.00	
Purchases	$120,000.00		
Freight in	350.00	120,350.00	
Total		$180,350.00	
Less inventory, June 30, 1946		23,000.00	
Remainder—cost of goods sold			157,350.00
Gross profit on sales (forward)			$ 42,650.00

Gross profit on sales (brought forward)			$ 42,650.00
Less operating expenses:			
Salaries and wages		$ 17,000.00	
Delivery expense		1,000.00	
Taxes		1,200.00	
Insurance		550.00	
General expense		7,500.00	
Depreciation:			
Building		3,200.00	
Furniture and fixtures		1,000.00	
Bad debts—receiver's sales		1,200.00	
Total operating expenses			32,650.00
Net operating profit			$ 10,000.00
Interest and discount—receiver's operations:			
Discount on sales		$ 2,300.00	
Deduct:			
Discount on purchases	$ 1,400.00		
Interest income	420.00	1,820.00	480.00
Net income before realization losses and mortgage interest			$ 9,520.00
Deduct realization losses:			
Marketable securities		$ 150.00	
Accounts receivable—old		1,000.00	1,150.00
Net income before mortgage interest			$ 8,370.00
Deduct mortgage interest			2,950.00
Net increase in surplus during the year			$ 5,420.00

Closing the books. The following entries show the procedure of closing both sets of books.

Receiver's Books

Sales	$200,000.00	
Profit and loss		$200,000.00
To close the sales account.		
Profit and loss	180,350.00	
Inventory—June 30, 1945		60,000.00
Purchases		120,000.00
Freight in		350.00
To close accounts showing merchandise costs.		
Inventory—June 30, 1946	23,000.00	
Profit and loss		23,000.00
To set up the inventory at the end of the year.		
Profit and loss	32,650.00	
Salaries and wages		17,000.00
Delivery expense		1,000.00
Taxes		1,200.00
Insurance		550.00
General expense		7,500.00
Depreciation—building		3,200.00
Depreciation—furniture and fixtures		1,000.00
Bad debts		1,200.00
To close the expense accounts.		

Discount on purchases	$1,400.00	
Interest income	420.00	
Profit and loss	480.00	
Discount on sales		$2,300.00
To close the interest and cash discount accounts.		
Profit and loss	1,150.00	
Loss on accounts receivable—old		1,000.00
Loss on securities		150.00
To close out the realization losses.		
Profit and loss	8,370.00	
C Company—in receivership		8,370.00
To close the profit and loss account.		
C Company—in receivership	128,000.00	
C Company—accounts payable paid		95,000.00
C Company—notes payable paid		25,000.00
C Company—mortgage payments		5,000.00
C Company—mortgage interest paid		3,000.00
To close the temporary accounts showing liability payments.		

Corporation's Books

F. C. White—receiver	$8,370.00	
Profit and loss		$8,370.00
To take up the net profit before mortgage interest, as shown by the receiver's books.		
Profit and loss	2,950.00	
Mortgage interest		2,950.00
To close the interest account.		
Profit and loss	5,420.00	
Surplus		5,420.00
To close net income to surplus.		

Reconciliation of reciprocal accounts. After the two sets of books have been closed, trial balances should be drawn off and a statement should be prepared to reconcile the reciprocal accounts and to prove that the accounts on the two sets of books agree with the balance sheet.

Working Papers After Closing

Debits	Receiver's Books	Company's Books	Eliminations	Combined
Cash	$ 1,120			$ 1,120
Accounts receivable—new	40,000			40,000
Inventory	23,000			23,000
Land	10,000			10,000
Building	80,000			80,000
Furniture and fixtures	10,000			10,000
Unexpired insurance	350			350
F. C. White—receiver		$96,070	$96,070	
	$164,470	$96,070	$96,070	$164,470

Credits	Receiver's Books	Company's Books	Eliminations	Combined
Accounts payable	$ 45,000			$ 45,000
Accrued mortgage interest		$ 450		450
Mortgage payable		45,000		45,000
Reserve for bad debts	1,200			1,200
Reserve for depreciation—building	18,200			18,200
Reserve for depreciation—furniture and fixtures	4,000			4,000
C Company—in receivership	96,070		$96,070	
Capital stock		50,000		50,000
Surplus		620		620
	$164,470	$96,070	$96,070	$164,470

Closing the receivership. If the receivership is terminated at this point, an entry should be made on the receiver's books as follows:

Accounts payable	$45,000	
Reserve for bad debts	1,200	
Reserve for depreciation—building	18,200	
Reserve for depreciation—furniture and fixtures	4,000	
C Company—in receivership	96,070	
Cash		$ 1,120
Accounts receivable—new		40,000
Inventory		23,000
Land		10,000
Building		80,000
Furniture and fixtures		10,000
Unexpired insurance		350
To close the receiver's books, recording the termination of the receivership.		

The company's books should contain a contra entry, debiting the assets, crediting the liabilities and reserves, and crediting F. C. White—receiver for the net assets.

CHAPTER 41

Realization and Liquidation Reports

Realization and Liquidation Account

Purpose. The statement called a *realization and liquidation account* may be used to show a court or the creditors of an insolvent business what has been done, during a stated period of time, in the realization of assets and the liquidation of liabilities; what expenses have been incurred; and what income has been earned. The statement is usually supplemented by a cash account, a profit and loss statement, and a balance sheet.

The statement is called an *account* because it is drawn up in account form with debit and credit sides; it should be called a *statement* because it does not appear in the ledger.

Elements of the statement. As shown by the illustration on the following page, this statement shows the following facts:

With respect to assets:	
Assets to be realized (Assets at the opening date of the statement)	Assets realized (Proceeds from disposal of assets)
Assets acquired (Additional assets discovered or acquired)	Assets not realized (Assets at closing date of statement)
With respect to liabilities:	
Liabilities liquidated (Payments to creditors)	Liabilities to be liquidated (At opening date of statement)
Liabilities not liquidated (At closing date)	Liabilities assumed (Discovered or incurred)
With respect to expense and income:	
Supplementary charges (Expenses)	Supplementary credits (Income)

Components of loss or gain. It is usually difficult to understand why this statement, which shows facts with respect to assets and liabilities as well as facts with respect to income and expense,

JAMES BUTLER
F. S. MONTGOMERY—TRUSTEE IN BANKRUPTCY
Realization and Liquidation Account
June 16, 1946 to August 31, 1946

Assets to be realized:			Liabilities to be liquidated:		
(a) Land and buildings	$14,500.00		(a) Accounts payable		$28,000.00
(a) Merchandise	8,000.00				
(a) Accounts receivable	7,000.00		Liabilities assumed:		
(a) Notes receivable	3,000.00	$32,500.00	(b) Accounts payable		500.00
Assets acquired:			Supplementary credits:		
(b) Merchandise		500.00	(f) Interest on notes receivable		10.00
Supplementary charges:			Assets realized:		
(g) Expense		200.00	(c) Merchandise	$ 5,500.00	
			(d) Accounts receivable	4,500.00	
Liabilities liquidated:			(e) Notes receivable	2,000.00	12,000.00
(h) Accounts payable		11,000.00			
Liabilities not liquidated:			Assets not realized:		
Accounts payable		17,500.00	Accounts receivable	$ 2,500.00	
			Land and buildings	14,500.00	17,000.00
			Loss on realization		4,190.00
		$61,700.00			$61,700.00

should have a balance showing a loss or a gain. The reason should be apparent from the following regrouping of the major items of the statement:

Facts about assets:			
Debit side of statement:			
Assets to be realized	$32,500.00		
Assets acquired	500.00	$33,000.00	
Credit side of statement:			
Assets realized	$12,000.00		
Assets not realized	17,000.00	29,000.00	
Loss on realization of assets			$4,000.00
Facts about liabilities:			
Credit side of statement:			
Liabilities to be liquidated	$28,000.00		
Liabilities assumed	500.00	$28,500.00	
Debit side of statement:			
Liabilities liquidated	$11,000.00		
Liabilities not liquidated	17,500.00	28,500.00	
Gain or loss—none		—	
Facts about expense and income:			
Supplementary charges—expenses		$ 200.00	
Supplementary credits—income		10.00	
Net expense			190.00
Net loss			$4,190.00

Trustee's cash account. The cash account to accompany the statement on page 172 is shown below:

JAMES BUTLER
F. S. MONTGOMERY—TRUSTEE IN BANKRUPTCY
Cash Account
June 16, 1946 to August 31, 1946

(a) Balance—June 16	$ 700.00	(g) Expense	$ 200.00
(c) Merchandise	5,500.00	(h) Accounts payable	11,000.00
(d) Accounts receivable	4,500.00	Balance—August 31	1,510.00
(e) Notes receivable	2,000.00		
(f) Int. on notes receivable	10.00		
	$12,710.00		$12,710.00

Procedure in preparing statements. The letters in the cash account and in the realization and liquidation account on page 172 are included merely for purposes of explanation in this chapter.

The preparation of the realization and liquidation account and the accompanying cash account will not be found difficult or confusing if it is accomplished by making offsetting debit and credit entries. The following entries should be traced to the statements:

(a) The assets, liabilities, and capital as of June 16 are "journalized" in the statements as follows:

Debits: Under assets to be realized—all assets other than cash.

In the cash account—the opening cash balance.

Credits: Under liabilities to be liquidated—all liabilities.

In a memorandum capital account—the opening net worth, thus:

Memorandum Capital Account

	(a) Net worth June 16..... $5,200.00

(b) Merchandise was purchased at a cost of $500.00:

Debit: Under assets acquired—the cost of the merchandise.

Credit: Under liabilities assumed—the amount of the account payable.

(c) Merchandise was sold for cash, $5,500.00:

Debit: In the cash account.

Credit: Under assets realized.

(d) Accounts receivable were collected in the amount of $4,500.00:

Debit: In the cash account.

Credit: Under assets realized.

(e) Notes receivable were collected in the amount of $2,000.00:

Debit: In the cash account.

Credit: Under assets realized.

(f) Interest on notes receivable was collected in the amount of $10.00:

Debit: In the cash account.

Credit: Under supplementary credits.

(g) Expenses were paid in the amount of $200.00:

Debit: Under supplementary charges.

Credit: In the cash account.

(h) Accounts payable were paid in the amount of $11,000.00:

Debit: Under liabilities liquidated.

Credit: In the cash account.

To complete the realization and liquidation account, the assets (other than cash) at the end of the period were entered under the assets not realized caption; the unpaid liabilities were entered under the liabilities not liquidated caption; and the loss on realization was entered to balance the statement.

To prove the loss shown in the realization and liquidation account, the following realization profit and loss statement was prepared:

JAMES BUTLER
F. S. MONTGOMERY—TRUSTEE IN BANKRUPTCY
Realization Profit and Loss Statement
July 16, 1946 to August 31, 1946

Losses on realization:		
Merchandise	$3,000.00	
Notes receivable	1,000.00	
Total		$4,000.00
Expense		200.00
Total loss and expense		$4,200.00
Deduct interest on notes receivable		10.00
Net loss		$4,190.00

This loss was then deducted from the $5,200.00 credit in the memorandum capital account (which showed the net worth at the beginning of the period) to determine the net worth of $1,010.00 at the end of the period; and the following balance sheet was prepared from the data shown by the assets not realized and the liabilities not liquidated sections of the realization and liquidation account, by the balance in the cash account, and by the balance in the memorandum capital account.

JAMES BUTLER
F. S. MONTGOMERY—TRUSTEE IN BANKRUPTCY
Balance Sheet—August 31, 1946

Assets		Liabilities	
Accounts receivable	$ 2,500.00	Accounts payable	$17,500.00
Land and buildings	14,500.00	James Butler, capital	1,010.00
Cash	1,510.00		
	$18,510.00		$18,510.00

Reserves. If reserves have been set up against the assets, they should be deducted from the assets in the assets to be realized section, thus:

Assets to be realized:		
Timber lands	$300,000.00	
Less reserve for depletion	75,000.00	$225,000.00
Machinery	$ 15,000.00	
Less reserve for depreciation	3,000.00	12,000.00
Accounts receivable	$ 1,250.00	
Less reserve for bad debts	350.00	900.00

When the assets not realized are entered at the close of the statement, the reserves should again be deducted. Assuming that the operations of the business have been continued, that $5,000.00

depletion and $600.00 depreciation have been charged off, and that $700.00 of the accounts receivable have been collected, while $100.00 has been charged to the reserve, the accounts would be shown thus:

Assets not realized:		
Timber lands	$300,000.00	
Less reserve for depletion	80,000.00	$220,000.00
Machinery	$ 15,000.00	
Less reserve for depreciation	3,600.00	11,400.00
Accounts receivable	$ 450.00	
Less reserve for bad debts	250.00	200.00

The $5,000.00 depletion and the $600.00 depreciation would appear in the realization profit and loss statement, but the $100.00 loss on accounts receivable would not appear in the profit and loss statement, because the loss was absorbed in the reserve.

Sales and purchases. If business operations are continued, the materials or merchandise purchased may be shown in the realization and liquidation account as assets acquired or as supplementary charges, and sales may be shown as assets realized or as supplementary credits.

Accruals. The question of accruals presents some difficulty. To illustrate, assume that $15.00 of accrued interest on notes receivable is shown in the assets to be realized section. By the time the notes are collected, $5.00 additional interest has accrued, so that $20.00 is collected. The accrual and the collection of interest may be handled in either of two ways:

First method:

Cash	$20.00	
Assets realized		$15.00
Supplementary credits		5.00

Second method:

Assets acquired (accrued interest)	5.00	
Supplementary credits		5.00
Cash	20.00	
Assets realized		20.00

Similar methods may be used for accrued expenses.

Discounts. Two methods are available for dealing with discounts and allowances, either to customers or from creditors. To illustrate, assume that $8,000.00 of accounts receivable are taken over by the receiver, who continues operations. Discounts of $75.00 and allowances of $150.00 are given to the customers, and the balance is collected in full. The two methods of dealing with the discounts and allowances are shown below.

First method:

Assets to be realized:		Assets realized:	
Accounts receivable. .	$8,000.00	Accounts receivable.	$7,775.00

By this method, the discounts and allowances are not shown, but the $225.00 excess of debits over credits will be included in the loss on realization.

Second method:

Assets to be realized:					
Accounts receivable.		$8,000.00			
Supplementary charges:			Assets realized:		
Discounts to customers.	$ 75.00		Accounts receivable:		
			Discounts. . .	$ 75.00	
Allowances to customers.	150.00	225.00	Allowances. .	150.00	
			Cash.	7,775.00	$8,000.00

Similar methods may be used for discounts and allowances from creditors.

Premium or discount on securities. If securities owned are sold at a profit or a loss, the profit or the loss is not shown as a separate item. The book value is shown under assets to be realized, and the price received is shown under assets realized. But if outstanding bonds or other liabilities are redeemed at a premium or a discount, the face of the liability should be shown under liabilities liquidated; any discount on redemption should be shown under supplementary credits, and any premium on redemption should be shown under supplementary charges.

To illustrate, assume that a company holds $5,000.00 of bonds for which it paid par; these bonds are sold for $4,960.00. The company also has $20,000.00 of bonds outstanding which are redeemed for $19,000.00. The facts may be shown thus:

Realization and Liquidation Account

Assets to be realized:		Liabilities to be liquidated:	
Bonds of *X* Company. . . .	$ 5,000.00	Bonds payable.	$20,000.00
Liabilities liquidated:		Supplementary credits:	
Bonds payable.	20,000.00	Discount on bonds payable.	1,000.00
		Assets realized:	
		Bonds of *X* Company. . . .	4,960.00

Composition with creditors. If creditors agree to accept a certain number of cents on the dollar, the old indebtedness is, according to law, canceled by the agreement and a new indebtedness takes its place. Assume that there were $20,000.00 of accounts payable, that the creditors agreed to accept seventy-five cents on the dollar, and that twenty cents (of the seventy-five) had been paid at the time of preparing the realization and liquidation account; the facts would be shown as follows:

		Liabilities to be liquidated:	
		Accounts payable...........	$20,000
Liabilities liquidated:		Liabilities incurred:	
Accounts payable—settled at 75¢ on the dollar..........	$20,000	Accounts payable—composition agreement to accept 75¢ on the dollar in settlement of accounts payable..	15,000
Accounts payable—payments under composition agreement....................	4,000		
Liabilities not liquidated:		Supplementary credits:	
Accounts payable...........	11,000	Composition gain...........	5,000

Old and new accounts. If the receiver continues operations, any liabilities which he incurs should be kept entirely separate from the old liabilities, because of the prior rights which the receiver's creditors enjoy. The two classes may be designated as old accounts payable, and receiver's accounts payable or receiver's certificates.

Accounts receivable should be similarly separated, not because of any difference in the claims against the two classes of debtors, but because, with respect to old accounts receivable, the receiver is responsible only for diligence in collection, whereas, with respect to new accounts, he is responsible also for the exercise of good judgment in granting credits.

Continued operations. When operations are continued by a receiver, the realization and liquidation account is more complicated, because of the necessity of showing operating transactions. However, the "journalizing" procedure can still be used effectively in the preparation of the statements. The statements on pages 180 to 182 are based on the illustration, in the preceding chapter, of the operations of F. C. White, as receiver for the *C* Company. Letters have again been inserted in the statements for reference purposes. The following details should be traced to the statements:

(a) The assets, liabilities, and net worth as of June 30, 1945, the beginning of the receivership, are entered in the statement as follows:

Debits: Cash—in the cash account.
Other assets—under assets to be realized.
Credits: Liabilities—under liabilities to be liquidated.
Capital stock and deficit—in the memorandum capital account.

(b) Purchases on account, $120,000.00:
Debit: Supplementary charges—purchases.
Credit: Liabilities assumed—accounts payable.

(c) Sales on account, $200,000.00:
Debit: Assets acquired—accounts receivable.
Credit: Supplementary credits—sales.

(d) Cash, $47,500.00, was collected on old accounts receivable; the remaining accounts were uncollectible:
Debit: Cash.
Credit: Assets realized.

(e) The notes receivable, $15,000.00, were collected in full:
Debit: Cash.
Credit: Assets realized.

(f) Interest in the amount of $300.00 was collected on the notes:
Debit: Cash.
Credit: Supplementary credits—interest.

(g) New accounts receivable amounting to $160,000.00 were settled by cash collections of $157,700.00, and the allowance of cash discounts of $2,300.00:
Debits: Cash, $157,700.00.
Supplementary charges—discount on sales, $2,300.00.
Credit: Assets realized—accounts receivable, $160,000.00.

(h) Interest of $120.00 was collected on the marketable securities:
Debit: Cash.
Credit: Supplementary credits.

(i) The marketable securities were sold for $7,350.00.
Debit: Cash.
Credit: Assets realized.

(j) Prior liabilities were paid as follows: accounts payable, $95,000.00; notes payable, $25,000.00; mortage installment, $5,000.00; mortage interest accrued to June 30, 1945, $500.00:
Debit: Liabilities liquidated.
Credit: Cash.

(Continued on page 183.)

THE *C* COMPANY—IN RECEIVERSHIP
F. C. WHITE—RECEIVER
Realization and Liquidation Account
July 1, 1945 to June 30, 1946

Assets to be realized:			
(a) Accounts receivable—old	$50,000		
(a) Less reserve for bad debts	1,500	$ 48,500	
(a) Notes receivable—old		15,000	
(a) Inventory		60,000	
(a) Marketable securities		7,500	
(a) Land		10,000	
(a) Building	$80,000		
(a) Less reserve for depreciation	15,000	65,000	
(a) Furniture and fixtures	$10,000		
(a) Less reserve for depreciation	3,000	7,000	
(a) Unexpired insurance		900	$213,900
Assets acquired:			
(c) Accounts receivable—new			200,000
Supplementary charges:			
(b) Purchases		$120,000	
(g) Discount on sales		2,300	
(k) Mortgage interest—June 30, 1945 to June 30, 1946		2,950	
(n) Salaries and wages		17,000	
(n) Freight in		350	
(n) Delivery expense		1,000	
(n) Taxes		1,200	
(n) General expense		7,500	152,300

Liabilities to be liquidated:			
(a) Accounts payable—old		$ 95,000	
(a) Notes payable		25,000	
(a) Accrued mortgage interest		500	
(a) Mortgage payable		50,000	$170,500
Liabilities assumed:			
(b) Accounts payable—purchases		$120,000	
(k) Accrued mortgage interest—from June 30, 1945 to June 30, 1946		2,950	122,950
Supplementary credits:			
(c) Sales		$200,000	
(f) Interest on notes receivable		300	
(h) Interest on securities		120	
(m) Discount on purchases		1,400	201,820
Assets realized:			
(d) Accounts receivable—old		$ 47,500	
(e) Notes receivable		15,000	
(g) Accounts receivable—new		160,000	
(i) Marketable securities		7,350	229,850
Assets not realized:			
Accounts receivable—new	$40,000		
Less reserve for bad debts	1,200	$ 38,800	

			Inventory		23,000	
Liabilities liquidated:			Land		10,000	
(j) Accounts payable—old	$ 95,000		Building	$80,000		
(j) Notes payable—old	25,000		Less reserve for depreciation	18,200	61,800	
(j) Mortgage interest accrued—June 30, 1945	500		Furniture and fixtures	$10,000		
(j) Mortgage installment	5,000		Less reserve for depreciation	4,000	6,000	
(l) Mortgage interest—June 30, 1945 to April 30, 1946	2,500		Unexpired insurance		350	139,950
(m) Accounts payable—receiver's purchases	75,000	203,000				
Liabilities not liquidated:						
Accounts payable	$ 45,000					
Mortgage payable	45,000					
Accrued interest on mortgage	450	90,450				
Net profit on realization		5,420				
		$865,070				$865,070

THE *C* COMPANY—IN RECEIVERSHIP
F. C. WHITE—RECEIVER
Cash Account
July 1, 1945 to June 30, 1946

(a)	Balance—June 30, 1945	$ 1,800	(j)	Accounts payable—old	$ 95,000
(d)	Accounts receivable—old	47,500	(j)	Notes payable—old	25,000
(e)	Notes receivable	15,000	(j)	Mortgage installment	5,000
(f)	Interest on notes receivable	300	(j)	Mortgage interest accrued—June 30, 1945	500
(g)	Accounts receivable—new	157,700	(l)	Mortgage interest—June 30, 1945 to April 30, 1946	2,500
(h)	Interest on securities	120	(m)	Accounts payable—new	73,600
(i)	Marketable securities	7,350	(n)	Salaries and wages	17,000
			(n)	Freight in	350
			(n)	Delivery expense	1,000
			(n)	Taxes	1,200
			(n)	General expense	7,500
				Balance—June 30, 1946	1,120
		$229,770			$229,770

Memorandum Capital Account

(a)	Deficit—June 30, 1945	$ 4,800.00	(a)	Capital stock	$50,000.00
	Net worth—June 30, 1946	50,620.00		Net profit	5,420.00
		$55,420.00			$55,420.00

(k) The mortgage interest accrued from June 30, 1945 to June 30, 1946, was $2,950.00:
Debit: Supplementary charges.
Credit: Liabilities assumed.

(l) The receiver paid the accrued interest from June 30, 1945 to April 30, 1946, in the amount of $2,500.00.
Debit: Liabilities liquidated.
Credit: Cash.

(m) Receiver's accounts payable for merchandise purchases were settled in the amount of $75,000.00 as follows: cash payment, $73,600.00; cash discounts taken, $1,400.00:
Debit: Liabilities liquidated—accounts payable, $75,000.00.
Credits: Cash, $73,600.00.
Supplementary credits—discount on purchases, $1,400.00.

(n) The receiver paid expenses, as detailed in the statements:
Debit: Supplementary charges.
Credit: Cash.

The assets as of June 30, 1946 (after providing for depreciation of the building and of the furniture and fixtures and for losses on bad debts, and after writing off the insurance premiums expired during the year) were next entered under assets not realized; the liabilities at the end of the period were entered under liabilities not liquidated; and the statement was balanced by entering the net profit for the year. This net profit should also be entered in the memorandum capital account to determine whether the resulting net worth will balance the net assets.

In addition to the realization and liquidation account and the cash account, the receiver should prepare a profit and loss statement similar to the one on pages 167 and 168 of the preceding chapter, and a balance sheet similar to the one on page 167 of the preceding chapter.

Realization and Liquidation Statement

Purpose. The realization and liquidation account illustrated in the preceding portion of this chapter is the traditional form for the presentation of data with respect to realization and liquidation, but it is somewhat confusing, and is not admirably adapted to its purpose.

An alternative statement which seems to present the information more clearly is illustrated in the remainder of the chapter.

(First Illustration)

JAMES BUTLER
F. S. MONTGOMERY—TRUSTEE
Statement of Realization, Liquidation, and Operations
June 16, 1946 to August 31, 1946

		Balances, June 16, 1946	Miscellaneous		Cash		Profit and Loss		Balances, August 31, 1946
			Charges	Credits	Receipts	Payments	Charges	Credits	
Assets:									
Cash:									
Balance, June 16, 1946	$ 700	$ 700							
Total receipts	12,010								
Total	$12,710								
Total payments	11,200								
Balance, August 31, 1946	$ 1,510								$ 1,510
Merchandise		8,000							
Purchases			$ 500						
Proceeds of sales					$ 5,500				
Loss on sales							$ 3,000		
Accounts receivable		7,000							
Collections					4,500				
Balance									2,500
Notes receivable		3,000							
Collections					2,000				
Losses							1,000		
Interest on notes receivable					10			$ 10	
Land and building		14,500							14,500
Total assets		$33,200							$18,510
Liabilities:									
Accounts payable		$28,000							
Incurred for purchases				$ 500					
Paid						$11,000			
Unpaid									$17,500
Expenses						200	200		
Total liabilities		$28,000							$17,500
Net Worth:									
James Butler, capital		$ 5,200							
Net loss								4,190	
Balance, August 31, 1946									$ 1,010
			$ 500	$ 500	$12,010	$11,200	$ 4,200	$ 4,200	

First illustration. The statement on page 184 is based on the same facts as those used in the illustration on page 172. Attention is directed to the following matters:

The financial condition at the beginning of the period is shown in the first column; the financial condition at the end of the period is shown in the last column.

The cash receipts and disbursements are detailed in the two cash columns. After these two columns are footed, their totals are entered in the cash summary at the top of the statement, to determine the cash balance at the end of the period.

The changes in the other assets are fully described. For example, starting with merchandise valued at $8,000.00, the trustee made purchases of $500.00, received $5,500.00 as proceeds of sales, lost $3,000.00 on sales, and had no merchandise at the end of the period.

The changes in each liability are similarly described. Starting with accounts payable of $28,000.00, the trustee incurred $500.00 of additional liabilities for purchases, made payments of $11,000.00, and had $17,500.00 of unpaid accounts at the end of the period.

The net worth section shows the net worth at the beginning of the period, the net loss for the period (as a balancing figure in the profit and loss columns), and the net worth at the end of the period.

The miscellaneous columns include all items not classified in the cash and the profit and loss columns. The debits and credits in these columns are equal.

The profit and loss columns show the details accounting for the net loss of $4,190.00. Glancing down these columns, we find that $3,000.00 was lost on sales of merchandise, and $1,000.00 on uncollectible notes receivable; that $200.00 of expenses were incurred; and that $10.00 of interest was earned on notes receivable.

Second illustration. The statement on pages 186 and 187 is based on the same facts as the illustration on pages 180 and 181.

Attention is directed to the method of introducing income items into the asset section of the statement. It will be noted that the interest on notes receivable and on securities is shown immediately below the notes and the securities. Income should be shown in the asset section even if there were no accrued items to appear in the balance columns at either the beginning or end of the period. (Continued on page 187.)

(Second Illustration)

THE *C* COMPANY—IN RECEIVERSHIP
F. S. WHITE—RECEIVER
Statement of Realization, Liquidation, and Operations
Year Ended June 30, 1946

		Balances, June 30, 1945	Miscellaneous		Cash		Profit and Loss		Balances, June 30, 1946
			Charges	Credits	Receipts	Payments	Charges	Credits	
Assets:									
Cash:									
Balance, June 30, 1945	$ 1,800	$ 1,800							
Total receipts	227,970								
Total	$229,770								
Total payments	228,650								
Balance, June 30, 1946	$ 1,120								$ 1,120
Accounts receivable—old		50,000							
Collections					$ 47,500				
Losses charged to the reserve				$ 1,500					
Losses charged to profit and loss							$ 1,000		
Reserve for bad debts		1,500*							
Charges for losses			$ 1,500						
Accounts receivable—new—from sales								$200,000	
Collections and cash discounts					157,700		2,300		
Balance uncollected									40,000
Reserve for bad debts—for new accounts							1,200		1,200*
Notes receivable—old		15,000			15,000				
Interest on notes receivable					300			300	
Merchandise		60,000							
Purchases			120,000						
Cost of goods sold							157,000		
Inventory, June 30, 1946									23,000
Marketable securities		7,500							
Proceeds of sale and loss					7,350		150		
Interest on securities					120			120	
Land		10,000							10,000
Building		80,000							80,000
Reserve for depreciation—building		15,000*							
Depreciation for the year							3,200		
Reserve, June 30, 1946									18,200*
Furniture and fixtures		10,000							10,000

Reserve for depreciation—furniture and fixtures	3,000*							
Depreciation for the year						1,000		
Reserve, June 30, 1946								4,000*
Unexpired insurance	900							
Expired during the year						550		
Balance—unexpired								350
Total assets	$215,700							$141,070
LIABILITIES:								
Accounts payable—old	$ 95,000							
Payments					$ 95,000			
Accounts payable—new—from purchases			$120,000					
Payments and discounts					73,600		1,400	
Balance								$ 45,000
Notes payable—old	25,000							
Payments					25,000			
Mortgage payable	50,000							
Payments					5,000			
Balance								45,000
Mortgage interest:								
Accrued, June 30, 1945	500				500			
Accrued during the year					2,500	2,950		450
Salaries and wages					17,000	17,000		
Freight in					350	350		
Delivery expense					1,000	1,000		
Taxes					1,200	1,200		
General expense					7,500	7,500		
Total liabilities	$170,500							$ 90,450
NET WORTH:								
Capital stock	$ 50,000							$ 50,000
Deficit, June 30, 1945	4,800*							
Net profit for the year						5,420		
Surplus, June 30, 1946								620
Total net worth	$ 45,200							$ 50,620
		$121,500	$121,500	$227,970	$228,650	$201,820	$201,820	

* Deduction.

Attention is also directed to the method of introducing expense items into the liability section of the statement. Interest on the mortgage is shown immediately below the mortgage. The absence of balances on the lines for salaries and wages, freight in, delivery expense, taxes, and general expense shows that there were no unpaid liabilities for such expenses at either the beginning or end of the period.

(Third Illustration—See page 191)

MARTIN AND DUNCAN
Statement of Realization, Liquidation, and Operations
Year Ended December 31, 1946

		Balances, December 31, 1945	Miscellaneous		Cash		Profit and Loss		Balances, December 31, 1946
			Charges	Credits	Receipts	Payments	Charges	Credits	
Assets:									
Cash:									
Balance, December 31, 1945	$ 500	$ 500							
Total receipts	354,770								
Total	$355,270								
Total payments	354,420								
Balance, December 31, 1946	$ 850								$ 850
Accounts receivable—old		60,000							
Collections					$ 48,000				
Discounts allowed							$ 600		
Written off to reserve				$ 3,200					
Balance									8,200
Reserve for bad debts		5,000*							
Charges for accounts written off			$ 3,200						
Balance									1,800*
Notes receivable—old		40,000							
Collections					29,300				
Securities accepted in settlement				10,000					
Losses							700		
Balance									—
Securities—taken for notes			10,000						10,000
Reserve to reduce to market value							1,500		1,500*
Interest on securities:									
Collected					120			$ 120	
Accrued but not collected								130	130
Accounts receivable—new:									
Sales								300,000	
Collected					260,000				
Discounts allowed							1,150		
Settled by notes				25,000					
Written off to reserve				1,000					
Balance									12,850
Reserve for bad debts:									
Amount credited to reserve							3,000		
Charges for accounts written off			1,000						
Balance									2,000*
Notes receivable—new:									
Taken in settlement of new accounts			25,000						
Collections					15,000				
Balance									10,000

Interest on notes receivable:								
Collected				350			350	
Accrued							250	250
Finished goods	50,000							
Decrease during year						12,000		
Balance								38,000
Goods in process	7,700							
Increase during year							2,000	
Balance								9,700
Raw materials	35,000							
Purchases		95,000						
Used						105,000		
Balance								25,000
Land	20,000							20,000
Buildings	60,000							60,000
Reserve for depreciation	9,800*							
Depreciation for the year						1,800		
Balance								11,600*
Building rental income				2,000			2,000	
Machinery	80,000							
Purchases					$ 3,500			
Fully depreciated—written off			6,000					
Balance								77,500
Reserve for depreciation	25,000*							
Charge for fully depreciated assets		6,000						
Depreciation for the year						4,000		
Balance								23,000*
Prepaid insurance	850							
Payments					2,300			
Amount expired						1,600		
Unexpired								1,550
Advertising	2,500							
Payments					3,000			
Charged to expense						5,500		
Total assets	$316,750							$234,130
LIABILITIES:								
Bonds payable	$ 50,000							
Bonds retired at a discount					4,850		150	
Balance								$ 45,000
Interest on bonds						2,250		2,250
Notes payable—old	35,000				35,000			
Interest on notes payable	270				270			
Accrued during the year					150	150		
Accounts payable—old	105,000							
Payment and discounts taken					103,850		1,150	
Accounts payable—new—for purchases			95,000					
Payments and discounts taken					45,000		800	
Notes given in settlement		25,000						
Balance								24,200
Forward	$190,270	$165,200	$140,200	$354,770	$197,920	$139,250	$306,950	$ 71,450

Statement of Realization, Liquidation, and Operations—(*Continued*)

	Balances, December 31, 1945	Miscellaneous		Cash		Profit and Loss		Balances, December 31, 1946
		Charges	Credits	Receipts	Payments	Charges	Credits	
Forward	$190,270	$165,200	$140,200	$354,770	$197,920	$139,250	$306,950	$ 71,450
Notes payable—given on account			25,000					25,000
Accrued interest on notes payable						120		120
Direct labor	900				75,000	75,200		1,100
Indirect labor					6,500	6,500		
Manufacturing expenses					18,300	18,300		
Salesmen's salaries					35,000	35,800		800
Office salaries	600				8,100	7,500		
General expenses					3,600	3,600		
Receiver's charges					5,000	5,000		
Total liabilities	$191,770							$ 98,470
Net Worth:								
James Martin, capital	$ 61,900							
Net profit—one half						7,840		
Drawings					2,500			
Balance, December 31, 1946								$ 67,240
Frank Duncan, capital	63,080							
Net profit—one half						7,840		
Drawings					2,500			
Balance, December 31, 1946								68,420
Total net worth	$124,980	$165,200	$165,200	$354,770	$354,420	$306,950	$306,950	$135,660

Third illustration. The statement on pages 188, 189, and 190 is based on assumed facts not used in any previous illustration. It is presented without any preliminary listing of the facts, as they are shown clearly by the statement itself.

In the solution of problems which require the preparation of statements of this nature, space should be left after each asset and liability sufficient to provide for the requirements of the problem.

CHAPTER 42

Home Office and Branch Accounting

Agencies and branches. Although agencies and branches differ in several particulars, the two words are often used indiscriminately. Agencies and branches both are means of projecting the sales organization into territory at a distance from the home office, and setting up a sales establishment in the buyers' territory; but aside from this common feature, the agency and the branch differ very widely in organization, management, and control. The points of difference may be summarized as follows:

Agency	Branch
Carries a line of samples for inspection, but does not carry a full stock for making deliveries to customers. Orders are sent to the home office and deliveries are made by the home office.	Carries a stock of merchandise, most of which is usually obtained from the home office, but part of which may be purchased from outsiders. Deliveries are made from the branch stock.
Credits passed on by the home office; accounts receivable carried on the home office books; collections made by the home office.	Credits passed on by the branch; accounts receivable carried on the branch books; collections made by the branch.
Working fund for agency expenses provided by the home office, and replenished by the home office when exhausted. No other cash handled by the agency.	Receipts from sales and collections deposited in local bank to the credit of the branch; checks for expenses drawn by the branch manager.

It is evident from this summary that an agency exercises about the same functions as a traveling salesman, while the branch exercises most of the functions of an independent business, subject only to the supervision and control of the home office.

The foregoing summary is descriptive of the true agency and the true branch, but extensions may be made whereby the agency is vested with some of the powers of a branch. For instance, the agency may carry a stock of merchandise and make deliveries, although credits are passed on by the home office and the accounts receivable are carried on the home office books.

On the other hand, some restrictions may be placed on a branch. For instance, although the branch may be allowed to pass on its own credits, the accounts may be carried on the home office books. A very common restriction has to do with cash. The branch manager may be required to deposit all receipts from sales and all collections in a bank account in the name of the home office, subject to check by the home office only; a working fund for expenses is then provided from the home office by a deposit in a separate bank account which may be drawn against by the branch manager, and which is replenished by another check from the home office.

Thus, in addition to true agencies and true branches, other establishments exist having some of the characteristics of both—agencies exercising some of the functions of branches, and branches subject to some of the restrictions which apply to agencies. It is neither possible nor necessary to consider here all of the variations from the true agency and the true branch. The accounting methods used by the typical agency and the typical branch will be illustrated, and it will be understood that, if an agency exercises some of the functions of a branch, or if a branch is subject to some restrictions which usually apply only to agencies, their accounting systems will necessarily be modified to suit the conditions.

Agency accounts. An agency does not need to keep a double entry system of accounts. All that is necessary is a cash book in which to record money received from the home office for its working fund, and the disbursements made therefrom for expenses. The disbursement record is usually kept in duplicate. When the working fund runs low and a replenishing check is desired, one copy of the disbursement sheet is sent to the home office, together with the vouchers, as evidence of the nature and propriety of the disbursements, and the other copy is retained by the agency.

The home office, on the other hand, must keep its records in such a manner as to show:

(1) The merchandise sent to the agency for sample purposes.
(2) The cash sent to the agency for the establishment of the working fund.
(3) The sales made by the agency.
(4) The cost of goods sold by the agency.
(5) The expenses of the agency.
(6) The profits of the agency.

The following illustration shows how these records are kept on the home office books; it is understood that the agency keeps only a cash book.

(1) Samples to the value of $1,000.00 sent to the agency:

Agency samples	$1,000.00	
Purchases		$1,000.00

(2) Working fund of $500.00 established:

Agency working fund	$500.00	
Cash		$500.00

(3) Sales of $10,000.00 reported by the agency and delivered by the home office:

Accounts receivable	$10,000.00	
Agency sales		$10,000.00

Collections of accounts receivable arising from agency sales are recorded in the usual way.

(4) Cost of agency sales, $7,000.00:

Cost of agency sales	$7,000.00	
Purchases		$7,000.00

This entry may be made at the end of the period for the total cost of sales, but a memorandum record must be kept during the period when sales orders are filled. This memorandum record will furnish the information for the above entry at the end of the period.

(5) When the agency reports its cash disbursements for expenses, the home office issues a check to the agency to replenish its working fund, and makes an entry similar to the following:

Agency expenses (detailed as desired)	$1,400.00	
Cash		$1,400.00

(6) Entry to close the accounts showing agency profit:

Agency sales	$10,000.00	
Cost of agency sales		$7,000.00
Agency expenses		1,400.00
Profit and loss		1,600.00

If it is not desired to keep the records in such a way as to show the profit of the agency as a separate amount, the agency sales may be credited to the regular sales account, entry (4) for cost of sales may be omitted, and the expenses may be charged to the regular expense accounts.

Branch accounts. The accounting for a branch is more complex. The branch keeps a complete set of books in which to record goods received from the home office and purchased from outsiders, sales, accounts receivable, accounts payable, and expenses. The ledger contains an account called home office current, which is credited with everything received from the home office and charged with everything sent to the home office. The home office current account is thus a proprietorship account, showing the investment made by the home office in the branch. When the branch closes its books, a net profit is transferred from profit and loss to the home office current account, as an increase in the investment, while a net loss is closed to the debit of the home office current account.

The methods used by the home office depend, to some extent, on the price at which goods are billed to the branch. Three illustrations are therefore given, dealing with the three typical methods of billing:

(1) Goods billed to the branch at cost.
This is the simplest method.

(2) Goods billed to the branch at an arbitrary value between cost and selling price. This method is sometimes used in order to keep the branch manager in ignorance of the cost of goods sold and hence of the profits of the branch.

(3) Goods billed to the branch at selling price.
This method is based on the theory that if the branch charges its merchandise accounts with the selling price of goods received and credits its merchandise accounts with sales at the same price, the net balance of the merchandise accounts on the books of the branch should represent the selling price of the goods on hand. In other words, this method is supposed to provide a perpetual inventory of branch merchandise at selling price, and thus furnish a check on the goods, which will prevent or detect carelessness or fraud. The method works well unless frequent changes are made in selling prices; if selling prices fluctuate frequently, it is necessary to make so many adjustments that the work involved usually outweighs the advantages.

First illustration: Shipments at cost. Assume the following transactions:

(1) Cash sent to the branch, $500.00.
(2) Merchandise sent to the branch, $5,000.00.

(3) Merchandise purchased by the branch from outsiders on account, $1,000.00.

(4) Sales by branch:

Cash	$2,000.00.
On account	5,000.00.

(5) Collections from accounts receivable, $4,200.00.

(6) Payments of accounts payable, $750.00.

(7) Expenses paid, $1,200.00.

(8) Cash sent to home office, $4,000.00.

The following journal entries show the accounts debited and credited by the home office and the branch:

Branch Books			Home Office Books		
(1) Cash	$ 500		Branch Current	$ 500	
Home office current		$ 500	Cash		$ 500
(2) Mdse. from H. O.	5,000		Branch current	5,000	
Home office current		5,000	Shipments to branch (to be closed to purchases)		5,000
(3) Purchases	1,000				
Accounts pay.		1,000			
(4) Cash	2,000				
Accounts receivable	5,000				
Sales		7,000			
(5) Cash	4,200				
Accounts rec.		4,200			
(6) Accounts payable	750				
Cash		750			
(7) Expenses	1,200				
Cash		1,200			
(8) H. O. current	4,000		Cash	4,000	
Cash		4,000	Branch current		4,000

The branch is now ready to close its books. Assuming that its inventory is $1,500.00, the closing entries on the branch books are:

Profit and loss	$7,200.00	
Merchandise from home office		$5,000.00
Purchases		1,000.00
Expenses		1,200.00
Inventory	1,500.00	
Sales	7,000.00	
Profit and loss		8,500.00
Profit and loss	1,300.00	
Home office current		1,300.00

After closing its books, the branch draws off the following balance sheet:

Branch Balance Sheet

Cash	$ 750.00	Accounts payable	$ 250.00
Accounts receivable	800.00	Home office current	2,800.00
Inventory	1,500.00		
	$3,050.00		$3,050.00

The home office takes up the profit by the following entry:

Branch current account	$1,300.00	
Branch profit and loss		$1,300.00

The branch current account now appears as follows:

Branch Current

Cash (sent to branch)	$ 500.00	Cash (received from branch)	$4,000.00
Merchandise (sent to branch)	5,000.00	Balance	2,800.00
Net profit of branch	1,300.00		
	$6,800.00		$6,800.00
Balance—down	$2,800.00		

Combined statements. At the end of the period, statements should be made combining the profit and loss statements of the branch and the home office, and the balance sheets of the branch and the home office. Using assumed figures for the home office, these statements are illustrated below:

The *X Y* COMPANY
Profit and Loss Statement
For the Year Ended December 31, 1945

	Branch		Home Office		Total	
Sales		$7,000		$18,000		$25,000
Less cost of goods sold:						
Inventory—January 1			$ 4,000		$ 4,000	
Purchases and shipments from home office	$6,000		13,000		19,000	
Total	$6,000		$17,000		$23,000	
Inventory—December 31	1,500	4,500	5,000	12,000	6,500	16,500
Gross profit on sales		$2,500		$ 6,000		$ 8,500
Less expenses		1,200		2,700		3,900
Net profit		$1,300		$ 3,300		$ 4,600

THE *X Y* COMPANY
Balance Sheet
December 31, 1945

Assets		Liabilities	
Cash	$ 3,950.00	Accounts payable	$ 1,650.00
Accounts receivable	3,700.00	Capital stock	7,500.00
Inventory	6,500.00	Surplus	5,000.00
	$14,150.00		$14,150.00

This balance sheet was prepared from the following working papers, in which similar assets and liabilities are combined, and the reciprocal current accounts are eliminated.

Combined Balance Sheet Working Papers
December 31, 1945

	Home Office	Branch	Eliminations	Balance Sheet
Assets				
Cash	$ 3,200.00	$ 750.00		$ 3,950.00
Accounts receivable	2,900.00	800.00		3,700.00
Inventory	5,000.00	1,500.00		6,500.00
Branch current	2,800.00		$2,800.00	
	$13,900.00	$3,050.00	$2,800.00	$14,150.00
Liabilities				
Accounts payable	$ 1,400.00	$ 250.00		$ 1,650.00
Home office current		2,800.00	$2,800.00	
Capital stock	7,500.00			7,500.00
Surplus	5,000.00			5,000.00
	$13,900.00	$3,050.00	$2,800.00	$14,150.00

Second illustration: SHIPMENTS AT ARBITRARY VALUE. In this illustration it is assumed that the home office bills all goods to the branch at 10% above cost, in order to keep the branch manager uninformed concerning the true profits of the branch. The following transactions are recorded:

(1) Cash sent to branch, $500.00.
(2) Merchandise sent to branch, cost $5,000.00, billed at $5,500.00.
(3) Branch sales (all for cash) $6,000.00.
(4) Expenses paid, $1,200.00.
(5) Cash sent to home office, $4,000.00.
The branch inventory at the end of the period is $1,650.00, at billed prices.

Branch Books			Home Office Books		
(1) Cash	$ 500		Branch current	$ 500	
Home office current		$ 500	Cash		$ 500
(2) Mdse. from H. O.	5,500		Branch current	5,500	
Home office current		5,500	Shipments to branch		5,500
(3) Cash	6,000				
Sales		6,000			
(4) Expense	1,200				
Cash		1,200			
(5) Home office current	4,000		Cash	4,000	
Cash		4,000	Branch current		4,000

Closing Entries

Profit and loss	$6,700				
Mdse. from H. O.		$5,500			
Expense		1,200			
Inventory	1,650				
Sales	6,000				
Profit and loss		7,650			
Profit and loss	950		Branch current	$ 950	
H. O. current		950	Branch profit & loss		$ 950
			Shipments to branch	5,500	
			Purchases		5,000
			Branch profit & loss		350
			Reserve for unrealized profit in branch inventory		150

These illustrative entries show that the practice of billing at an arbitrary figure above cost does not affect the accounting methods or the books of the branch in any way except that the profit and loss account on the branch books does not show the true profit of the branch.

The home office books are kept in the same manner as in the first illustration, the only difference being in the entry closing out the shipments to branch account. The purchases account is credited with the cost of the goods shipped to the branch, $5,000.00; the branch profit and loss account is credited with the 10% profit realized by the sale of goods costing $3,500.00; and a reserve is credited with $150.00, the 10% unrealized profit on the goods in the branch inventory, which cost $1,500.00 and which are inventoried by the branch at the billed price of $1,650.00.

This reserve is deducted from the inventory, as shown in the following working papers.

Combined Profit and Loss Statement Working Papers

	Home Office	Branch	Eliminations	Combined
Sales	$19,000	$6,000		$25,000
Less cost of goods sold:				
Inventory, January 1	$ 4,800			$ 4,800
Purchases	19,000			19,000
Shipments to branch	5,000*	$5,500	$500	
Total	$18,800	$5,500	$500	$23,800
Inventory, December 31	6,200	1,650	150	7,700
Cost of goods sold	$12,600	$3,850	$350	$16,100
Gross profit on sales	$ 6,400	$2,150	$350	$ 8,900
Expenses	3,900	1,200		5,100
Net profit	$ 2,500	$ 950	$350	$ 3,800

* Deduction.

Combined Balance Sheet Working Papers

	Home Office	Branch	Eliminations	Balance Sheet
Assets				
Cash	$ 3,500.00	$1,300.00		$ 4,800.00
Accounts receivable	2,950.00			2,950.00
Inventory	6,800.00	1,650.00	$ 150.00	8,300.00
Branch current	2,950.00		2,950.00	
	$16,200.00	$2,950.00	$3,100.00	$16,050.00
Liabilities				
Accounts payable	$ 2,000.00			$ 2,000.00
Reserve for unrealized profit in inventory	150.00		$ 150.00	
Home office current		$2,950.00	2,950.00	
Capital stock	10,000.00			10,000.00
Surplus	4,050.00			4,050.00
	$16,200.00	$2,950.00	$3,100.00	$16,050.00

Third illustration: SHIPMENTS AT SELLING PRICE. In this illustration it is assumed that the home office bills all goods to the branch at selling price, to keep the branch manager uninformed about the profits of the branch, and also to maintain a control over the branch merchandise. This control is based on the fact that the debits to merchandise from home office, on the branch books, minus the credits to sales, on the branch books, should equal the inventory at the branch at selling prices. The following transactions are recorded:

(1) Cash sent to branch, $500.00.
(2) Merchandise sent to branch, cost $5,000.00, selling price $7,500.00. (While the total selling price is 150% of the cost, it must not be assumed that this rate applies to each commodity, as there may be different rates of mark-up.)
(3) Branch sales, all for cash, $6,000.00.
(4) Expenses paid, $1,200.00.
(5) Cash sent to home office, $4,000.00.

The inventory at the branch at the end of the period is valued at selling prices totaling $1,400.00. Therefore, goods marked to sell at $100.00 are unaccounted for. ($7,500.00 shipments minus $6,000.00 sales should leave an inventory of $1,500.00 instead of $1,400,00.)

	Branch Books			Home Office Books		
(1)	Cash	$ 500		Branch current	$ 500	
	Home office current		$ 500	Cash		$ 500
(2)	Mdse. from H. O.	7,500		Branch current	7,500	
	H. O. current		7,500	Shipments to branch		7,500

A memorandum record of the cost of the goods should be kept in the shipments account, the credit side of which would appear as follows:

Shipments to Branch

		Cost	Selling Price
	Date..........	$5,000.00	$7,500.00

Branch Books			Home Office Books		
(3) Cash..............	$6,000				
Sales..........		$6,000			
(4) Expense...........	1,200				
Cash..........		1,200			
(5) H. O. current.......	4,000		Cash.................	$4,000	
Cash..........		4,000	Branch current.....		$4,000

When the branch closes its books, there is no object in setting up a profit and loss account, because no profit can possibly be shown. The following entry is sufficient to effect the closing:

Sales.................	$6,000	
Inventory..............	1,400	
H. O. current..........	1,300	
Mdse. from H. O..		$7,500
Expense..........		1,200

The charge to the home office current account is the sum of the expenses and the $100.00 merchandise shortage.

The home office takes up the apparent, or book, loss shown by the branch books, as follows:

Branch profit & loss....	$1,300	
Branch current.....		$1,300

The branch inventory is sent to the home office, and all items are repriced at cost (or market, if lower than cost). If we assume that the cost of the inventory (selling price $1,400.00) is found to be $975.00, a reserve must be set up for the $425.00 unrealized profit in the inventory, and the remaining profit of $2,075.00 ($2,500.00 profit added to shipments minus $425.00 unrealized profit) may be credited to branch profit and loss, because it has been realized by branch sales.

Shipments to branch....	$7,500	
Purchases..........		$5,000
Reserve for unrealized profit in branch inventory.		425
Branch profit & loss.		2,075

The branch profit and loss account on the home office books now stands:

Credited with profits realized by branch sales	$2,075.00
Debited with book loss, per branch books	1,300.00
Net credit, or branch profit	$ 775.00

This is the true branch profit, as shown by the following profit and loss statement:

Branch sales		$6,000.00
Less cost of goods sold:		
Shipments—at cost	$5,000.00	
Less inventory—at cost	975.00	4,025.00
Gross profit on sales		$1,975.00
Less expense		1,200.00
Net profit		$ 775.00

The reserve for unrealized profit in the branch inventory is deducted from the inventory in the working papers for the combined balance sheet, in the manner illustrated on page 201.

Fixed assets. The fixed assets of a branch are usually carried on the home office books. If this method is followed, a purchase of fixed assets by the home office for the branch is recorded on the home office books by a debit to branch furniture and fixtures (or other fixed asset account) and a credit to cash. No entries will appear on the branch books. If the fixed assets are purchased by the branch, the entry on the branch books debits the home office current account and credits cash. The branch will report the purchase to the home office, which will debit branch furniture and fixtures (or other fixed asset account) and credit branch current account.

Branch expenses on home office books. Some expenses applicable to the branch operations may appear on the home office books instead of on the branch books. For instance, if the fixed assets are carried on the home office books, the depreciation provision will be recorded on these books. After taking up the profit as shown by the branch, the home office should make an entry on its books debiting branch profit and loss and crediting the reserve for depreciation. If any of the home office expenses are to be apportioned in part to the branch, entries may be made debiting the branch profit and loss account and crediting the expense accounts. The balance of the branch profit and loss account will then represent the net profit of the branch, and this balance will be transferred to the general profit and loss account.

Reconciliation of reciprocal accounts. The branch current account on the home office books, and the home office current account on the branch books, are supposed to be reciprocal, but in actual practice this condition rarely exists, because entries made by the home office for remittances of cash and shipments of merchandise are not taken up on the branch books until some time later, when the cash and merchandise are received; and because entries on the branch books for cash remitted to the home office may not be taken up by the home office for several days, while the cash is in transit.

At closing time, therefore, it is necessary to make adjustments to bring the two current accounts into agreement. Any shipments made by the home office and not received by the branch at the closing date, should be taken up on the branch books by a debit to merchandise in transit and a credit to home office current. This merchandise in transit should be included in the inventory. Any remittances made by the branch and not received by the home office at the closing date should be taken up on the home office books by debiting cash in transit and crediting the branch current account. Other necessary adjustments should be made in a similar manner.

Interbranch transfers. If merchandise is shipped from one branch to another, or if other assets are transferred between branches, the branch parting with the asset should debit the home office current account and credit the asset. The branch receiving it should debit the asset and credit its home office current account. The home office should debit the current account of the branch receiving the asset, and credit the current account of the branch parting with the asset. No branch should carry an account with any other branch; all interbranch transfers should be cleared through the home office current accounts.

Freight. Freight on goods received by the branch can properly be included in the branch inventory, on the basis of the same principles which apply to freight in. But if goods are shipped from one branch to another, it is conservative for the branch receiving the goods to include in the inventory valuation only such an amount of freight as would have been paid if the goods had been shipped directly from the home office, and to charge off any excess freight as an expense.

To illustrate, assume that \$500.00 worth of goods are shipped from the home office to Branch *A* at a freight cost of \$25.00. These goods are reshipped by Branch *A* to Branch *B* at an additional freight cost of $20.00, which is paid by Branch *A*. If the goods had been shipped from the home office to Branch *B*, the freight cost would have been $30.00. The entries on the various books should be:

For shipment to Branch *A*:

Home office:			
	Branch *A*	$525.00	
	Shipments to Branch *A*		$500.00
	Cash		25.00
Branch *A*:			
	Merchandise from home office	500.00	
	Freight in	25.00	
	Home office current		525.00

For shipment from Branch *A* to Branch *B*:

Branch *A*:			
	Home office current	$525.00	
	Merchandise from home office		$500.00
	Freight in		25.00
	Home office current	20.00	
	Cash		20.00
Branch *B*:			
	Merchandise from home office	500.00	
	Freight in	30.00	
	Home office current		530.00
Home Office:			
	Shipments to Branch *A*	500.00	
	Shipments to Branch *B*		500.00
	Branch *B* current	530.00	
	Interbranch excess freight	15.00	
	Branch *A* current		545.00

Branch records on home office books. The foregoing illustrations of branch and home office entries are based on the assumption that a detailed double entry set of records is maintained by the branch. This is not always the case. Some companies prefer to have the branch make daily reports to the home office from which the records of sales, collections, purchases, expenses, and so on, can be made directly on the home office books. When this is done, the entries become similar to those discussed at the beginning of this chapter under the title of "Agencies"; whether or not the home office maintains a classified record of sales by branches and other records sufficient to permit the determination of gross and net profit by branches is purely a matter of preference to be determined by the management.

CHAPTER 43

Parent and Subsidiary Accounting—Consolidated Balance Sheets at Date of Acquisition

Investment in branches and subsidiaries. Let us assume that Company *P* established an unincorporated branch, with an investment of $10,000.00 in cash and $20,000.00 in merchandise. The following combined balance sheet working papers were prepared immediately after the establishment of the branch:

COMPANY *P* AND BRANCH *S*
Combined Balance Sheet Working Papers
July 31, 1945

	Company *P*	Branch *S*	Eliminations	Combined Balance Sheet
Assets				
Cash	$ 25,000.00	$10,000.00		$ 35,000.00
Merchandise inventory	60,000.00	20,000.00		80,000.00
Accounts receivable	35,000.00			35,000.00
Branch current	30,000.00		$30,000.00	
	$150,000.00	$30,000.00	$30,000.00	$150,000.00
Liabilities and Net Worth				
Accounts payable	$ 40,000.00			$ 40,000.00
Home office current		$30,000.00	$30,000.00	
Capital stock	100,000.00			100,000.00
Surplus	10,000.00			10,000.00
	$150,000.00	$30,000.00	$30,000.00	$150,000.00

In these working papers, the balances of the two reciprocal current accounts are eliminated because they represent mere interrelationships between the home office and the branch.

Let us now assume that Branch *S* was incorporated as a separate company on July 31, 1945, and issued $30,000.00 of capital stock to Company *P* for the cash and merchandise received. Company *P* is a parent company; Company *S* is a subsidiary.

A *parent company* is one which holds all of, or a controlling interest in, the stock of another company. If a parent company conducts no operations other than those incident to the ownership of subsidiary shares, it is referred to as a *holding company*. Thus, parent companies are of two classes: operating companies and holding companies.

Although the parent and subsidiary companies are separate corporate entities, they constitute a single business organization, and a consolidated balance sheet should be prepared to show their combined assets and liabilities. The working papers for the consolidation of the balance sheets of this parent company and its subsidiary are similar to those of a home office and branch, except for the change in the names of the reciprocal accounts.

COMPANY *P* AND SUBSIDIARY *S*
Consolidated Balance Sheet Working Papers
July 31, 1945

	Company *P*	Company *S*	Intercompany Eliminations	Consolidated Balance Sheet
Assets				
Cash	$ 25,000	$10,000		$ 35,000
Merchandise inventory	60,000	20,000		80,000
Accounts receivable	35,000			35,000
Investment in stock of Company *S*	30,000		$30,000	
	$150,000	$30,000	$30,000	$150,000
Liabilities and Net Worth				
Accounts payable	$ 40,000			$ 40,000
Capital stock:				
Company *P*	100,000			100,000
Company *S*		$30,000	$30,000	
Surplus	10,000			10,000
	$150,000	$30,000	$30,000	$150,000

COMPANY *P* AND SUBSIDIARY *S*
Consolidated Balance Sheet
July 31, 1945

Assets		**Liabilities and Net Worth**		
Cash	$ 35,000	Accounts payable		$ 40,000
Inventory	80,000	Net worth:		
Accounts receivable	35,000	Capital stock	$100,000	
		Surplus	10,000	110,000
	$150,000			$150,000

Intercompany eliminations. The elimination of intercompany accounts in the foregoing working papers may be expressed by the following rule:

Elimination of reciprocals:
Subsidiary's capital stock account.
Parent company's investment account.

Purpose of the consolidated balance sheet. The parent company and its subsidiary, although legally separate entities, constitute a single business organization. Each company's balance sheet shows its own assets and liabilities, but a consolidated balance sheet is required if it is desired to show the total assets and liabilities of the combined organization.

Subsidiary surplus or deficit. Let us now assume that a company which has been in operation for some time has net assets of $65,000.00, represented by capital stock of $50,000.00 and surplus of $15,000.00. Its stock is acquired by another corporation at book value, $65,000.00. The reciprocal balances on the books of the two companies are:

On parent company's books:

Investment in stock of Company *S* (debit).....		$65,000.00

On subsidiary's books:

Capital stock (credit)........................	$50,000.00	
Surplus (credit)..............................	15,000.00	$65,000.00

Obviously, the elimination of reciprocal balances will not be complete unless the subsidiary's surplus, as well as its capital stock, is eliminated.

Or let us assume that a company has net assets of $45,000.00, represented by capital stock of $60,000.00 and a deficit of $15,000.00. Its stock is acquired by another corporation at book value, $45,000.00. The reciprocal balances on the books of the two companies are:

On parent company's books:

Investment in stock of Company *S* (debit).....		$45,000.00

On subsidiary's books:

Capital stock (credit)........................	$60,000.00	
Deficit (debit)...............................	15,000.00	$45,000.00

Again it is obvious that the elimination of reciprocals will require the elimination of the subsidiary's deficit as well as its capital stock.

We must therefore expand our original rule for the elimination of intercompany balances by the addition of the words shown below in italics:

Elimination of reciprocals:
  Subsidiary's capital stock *and surplus or deficit accounts.*
  Parent company's investment account.

Two illustrations are given involving a subsidiary surplus or deficit.

First illustration: Subsidiary surplus. The following working papers show the elimination of a subsidiary's capital stock and surplus accounts, which (together) are reciprocal to the investment account:

COMPANY *P* AND SUBSIDIARY *S*
Consolidated Balance Sheet Working Papers
(Date of Acquisition)

	Company *P*	Company *S*	Eliminations	Consolidated Balance sheet
Assets				
Investment in stock of Company *S*.........	$65,000		$65,000	
Cash..	20,000	$70,000		$90,000
	$85,000	$70,000	$65,000	$90,000
Liabilities and Net Worth				
Accounts payable........................	$10,000	$ 5,000		$15,000
Capital stock:				
Company *P*............................	75,000			75,000
Company *S*............................		50,000	$50,000	
Surplus:				
Company *S*............................		15,000	15,000	
	$85,000	$70,000	$65,000	$90,000

Second illustration: SUBSIDIARY DEFICIT. The following working papers show the elimination of a subsidiary's capital stock and deficit accounts, which (net) are reciprocal to the investment account:

COMPANY *P* AND SUBSIDIARY *S*
Consolidated Balance Sheet Working Papers
(Date of Acquisition)

	Company *P*	Company *S*	Eliminations	Consolidated Balance Sheet
Assets				
Investment in stock of Company *S*.......	$45,000		$45,000	
Cash.......................................	35,000	$55,000		$90,000
	$80,000	$55,000	$45,000	$90,000
Liabilities and Net Worth				
Accounts payable........................	$20,000	$10,000		$30,000
Capital stock:				
Company *P*...........................	50,000			50,000
Company *S*...........................		60,000	$60,000	
Surplus (deficit*):				
Company *P*...........................	10,000			10,000
Company *S*...........................		15,000*	15,000*	
	$80,000	$55,000	$45,000	$90,000

Minority interest. If the parent company acquires less than 100% of the stock of the subsidiary, it shares the ownership of the subsidiary with the outsiders whose stock it does not purchase. These outsiders are called the *minority stockholders* of the subsidiary. The capital stock and surplus (or deficit) accounts of the subsidiary then include two elements:

The holding company's percentage of the subsidiary stock and surplus (or deficit). These items are reciprocal to the parent company's investment account, and should therefore be eliminated.

The minority stockholders' interest in the subsidiary stock and surplus (or deficit). These items are not reciprocal to any balances on the parent company's books, and they are therefore carried out to the consolidated balance sheet column.

We must therefore again expand our original rule for the elimination of intercompany balances, by the addition of the words shown below in italics:

Elimination of reciprocals:
- Subsidiary's capital stock and surplus or deficit accounts.
  - *Eliminate reciprocal element—parent company's proportion.*
  - *Extend non-reciprocal element (minority interest)* to *consolidated balance sheet column.*
- Parent company's investment account.

Three illustrations are given involving a minority interest in the subsidiary.

First illustration: No subsidiary surplus or deficit. In this illustration it is assumed that the subsidiary had a capital stock of $50,000.00 and no surplus or deficit at the date when the parent company acquired 90% of its stock at book value, $45,000.00.

COMPANY *P* AND SUBSIDIARY *S*
Consolidated Balance Sheet Working Papers
(Date of Acquisition)

	Company *P*	Company *S*	Eliminations	Consolidated Balance Sheet
Assets				
Cash	$ 65,000	$60,000		$125,000
Investment in stock of Company *S*	45,000		$45,000	
	$110,000	$60,000	$45,000	$125,000
Liabilities and Net Worth				
Accounts payable	$ 20,000	$10,000		$ 30,000
Capital stock:				
Company *P*	75,000			75,000
Company *S*		50,000		
Eliminate parent company's 90%			$45,000	
Minority interest—10%				5,000M
Surplus—Company *P*	15,000			15,000
	$110,000	$60,000	$45,000	$125,000

COMPANY *P* AND SUBSIDIARY *S*
Consolidated Balance Sheet
(Date of Acquisition)

Assets		Liabilities and Net Worth	
Cash	$125,000	Accounts payable	$ 30,000
		Minority interest—Company S (10%)	5,000
		Capital stock	75,000
		Surplus	15,000
	$125,000		$125,000

Second illustration: SUBSIDIARY SURPLUS. In this illustration it is assumed that the subsidiary had a capital stock of $50,000.00 and a surplus of $10,000.00, making a total net worth of $60,000.00, at the date when the parent company acquired 90% of its stock at book value, $54,000.00.

COMPANY *P* AND SUBSIDIARY *S*
Consolidated Balance Sheet Working Papers
(Date of Acquisition)

	Company *P*	Company *S*	Eliminations	Consolidated Balance Sheet
Assets				
Investment in stock of Company *S*	$ 54,000		$54,000	
Cash	46,000	$75,000		$121,000
	$100,000	$75,000	$54,000	$121,000
Liabilities and Net Worth				
Accounts payable	$ 10,000	$15,000		$ 25,000
Capital stock:				
Company *P*	75,000			75,000
Company *S*		50,000		
Eliminate parent company's 90%			$45,000	
Minority interest—10%				5,000M
Surplus:				
Company *P*	15,000			15,000S
Company *S*		10,000		
Eliminate parent company's 90%			9,000	
Minority interest—10%				1,000M
	$100,000	$75,000	$54,000	$121,000

COMPANY *P* AND SUBSIDIARY *S*
Consolidated Balance Sheet
(Date of Acquisition)

Assets		Liabilities and Net Worth		
Cash	$121,000	Accounts payable		$ 25,000
		Minority interest in Company *S* (10%):		
		Capital stock	$ 5,000	
		Surplus	1,000	6,000
		Capital:		
		Capital stock	$75,000	
		Surplus	15,000	90,000
	$121,000			$121,000

The minority interest may be shown in one amount, as below.

COMPANY *P* AND SUBSIDIARY *S*
Consolidated Balance Sheet
(Date of Acquisition)

Assets		Liabilities and Net Worth		
Cash	$121,000	Accounts payable		$ 25,000
		Minority interest in Co. *S* (10%)		6,000
		Capital:		
		Capital stock	$75,000	
		Surplus	15,000	90,000
	$121,000			$121,000

Third illustration: SUBSIDIARY DEFICIT. The subsidiary had a capital stock of $50,000.00 and a deficit of $10,000.00, or a net worth of $40,000.00, at the date when the parent company acquired 90% of its stock at book value, $36,000.00.

COMPANY *P* AND SUBSIDIARY *S*
Consolidated Balance Sheet Working Papers
(Date of Acquisition)

	Company *P*	Company *S*	Eliminations	Consolidated Balance Sheet
Assets				
Investment in stock of Company *S*	$ 36,000		$36,000	
Cash	64,000	$55,000		$119,000
	$100,000	$55,000	$36,000	$119,000
Liabilities and Net Worth				
Accounts payable	$ 10,000	$15,000		$ 25,000
Capital stock:				
Company *P*	75,000			75,000
Company *S*		50,000		
Eliminate parent company's 90%			$45,000	
Minority interest—10%				5,000M
Surplus (deficit*):				
Company *P*	15,000			15,000S
Company *S*		10,000*		
Eliminate parent company's 90%			9,000*	
Minority interest—10%				1,000*M
	$100,000	$55,000	$36,000	$119,000

COMPANY *P* AND SUBSIDIARY *S*
Consolidated Balance Sheet
(Date of Acquisition)

Assets		Liabilities and Net Worth		
Cash	$119,000	Accounts payable		$ 25,000
		Minority interest in Company *S* (10%)		4,000
		Capital:		
		Capital stock	$75,000	
		Surplus	15,000	90,000
	$119,000			$119,000

Goodwill. If one company acquires the assets and liabilities of another company (instead of its stock), any payment in excess of the value of the net assets acquired is regarded as goodwill. Similarly, if one company acquires control of another company by purchasing its stock, any payment in excess of the book value of the stock acquired (as shown by the books of the subsidiary) may be regarded as a payment for goodwill.

Therefore, if the stock of a subsidiary is purchased at a price in excess of its book value, the balance of the investment account on the parent company's books will consist of two elements:

(1) The book value of the stock acquired.
(2) The excess payment, or goodwill.

To illustrate, assume that a company paid $65,000.00 for all of the stock of a subsidiary which had a capital stock of $50,000.00 and a surplus of $10,000.00. The balance of the investment account may be regarded as consisting of the following elements:

$60,000.00—representing the book value of the stock acquired. This element is reciprocal to, and is eliminated against, the capital stock and surplus accounts of the subsidiary.

$5,000.00—representing a payment for goodwill. This element is not reciprocal to any balance on the subsidiary's books and therefore is not eliminated, but is extended to the consolidated balance sheet column, and is shown in the consolidated balance sheet as goodwill, either as a separate item or added to the goodwill on the books of the parent or subsidiary.

It therefore becomes necessary again to expand our rule for the elimination of intercompany accounts, by adding the words shown below in italics.

Elimination of reciprocals:
- Subsidiary's capital stock and surplus or deficit accounts:
  - Eliminate reciprocal element—parent company's proportion.
  - Extend non-reciprocal element (minority interest) to consolidated balance sheet column.
- Parent company's investment account:
  - *Eliminate reciprocal element—parent company's proportion of subsidiary's stock and surplus.*

Extend non-reciprocal element (goodwill) to the consolidated balance sheet column.

Three illustrations involving goodwill are presented; they differ in the percentage of stock ownership by the parent company and in the matter of the existence of a surplus or deficit on the books of the subsidiary.

First illustration. At the date of acquisition, the subsidiary has a capital stock of $50,000.00 and no surplus or deficit. The parent company acquires all of the stock, paying $57,000.00 therefor.

COMPANY *P* AND SUBSIDIARY *S*
Consolidated Balance Sheet Working Papers
(Date of Acquisition)

	Company *P*	Company *S*	Eliminations	Consolidated Balance Sheet
Assets				
Investment in stock of Company *S* (100%)	$ 57,000			
Eliminate book value:				
Capital stock			$50,000	
Goodwill				$ 7,000
Cash	43,000	$60,000		103,000
	$100,000	$60,000	$50,000	$110,000
Liabilities and Net Worth				
Accounts payable	$ 10,000	$10,000		$ 20,000
Capital stock:				
Company *P*	75,000			75,000
Company *S*		50,000		
Eliminate parent company's 100%			$50,000	
Surplus—Company *P*	15,000			15,000
	$100,000	$60,000	$50,000	$110,000

COMPANY *P* AND SUBSIDIARY *S*
Consolidated Balance Sheet
(Date of Acquisition)

Assets		**Liabilities and Net Worth**		
Cash	$103,000	Accounts payable		$ 20,000
Goodwill	7,000	Capital:		
		Capital stock	$75,000	
		Surplus	15,000	90,000
	$110,000			$110,000

Second illustration. At the date of acquisition, the subsidiary has a capital stock of $50,000.00 and a surplus of $10,000.00, making a total book value of $60,000.00. The parent company acquires a 90% interest, the book value of which is $54,000.00 and the purchase price, $57,000.00. Hence there is a goodwill element of $3,000.00 in the price paid by the parent company for its 90% interest in the subsidiary stock.

COMPANY *P* AND SUBSIDIARY *S*
Consolidated Balance Sheet Working Papers
(Date of Acquisition)

	Company *P*	Company *S*	Eliminations	Consolidated Balance Sheet
Assets				
Investment in stock of Company *S* (90%)	$ 57,000			
Eliminate book value:				
Capital stock: 90% of $50,000.00			$45,000	
Surplus: 90% of $10,000.00			9,000	
Goodwill				$ 3,000G
Cash	43,000	$75,000		118,000
	$100,000	$75,000	$54,000	$121,000
Liabilities and Net Worth				
Accounts payable	$ 10,000	$15,000		$ 25,000
Capital stock:				
Company *P*	75,000			75,000
Company *S*		50,000		
Eliminate parent company's 90%			$45,000	
Minority interest—10%				5,000M
Surplus:				
Company *P*	15,000			15,000
Company *S*		10,000		
Eliminate parent company's 90%			9,000	
Minority interest—10%				1,000M
	$100,000	$75,000	$54,000	$121,000

COMPANY P AND SUBSIDIARY S
Consolidated Balance Sheet
(Date of Acquisition)

Assets		**Liabilities and Net Worth**		
Cash	$118,000	Accounts payable		$ 25,000
Goodwill	3,000	Minority interest—Company *S* (10%)		6,000
		Capital:		
		Capital stock	$75,000	
		Surplus	15,000	90,000
	$121,000			$121,000

Third illustration. At the date of acquisition, the subsidiary has a capital stock of $50,000.00 and a deficit of $10,000.00, making a net book value of $40,000.00. The parent company acquires a 90% interest, the book value of which is $36,000.00, and the purchase price, $38,000.00. Hence there is a goodwill element of $2,000.00 in the purchase price. The working papers and consolidated balance sheet appear on page 217.

Deduction from goodwill. If the subsidiary has a goodwill account on its books at the date when the parent company acquires its stock interest, and if the parent company pays less than book value for the stock, the presumption is that the parent company does not recognize the subsidiary's goodwill as conservatively

COMPANY *P* AND SUBSIDIARY *S*
Consolidated Balance Sheet Working Papers
(Date of Acquisition)

	Company *P*	Company *S*	Eliminations	Consolidated Balance Sheet
Assets				
Investment in stock of Co. *S* (90%)	$ 38,000			
Eliminate book value:				
Capital stock: 90% of $50,000.00			$45,000	
Less deficit: 90% of $10,000.00			9,000*	
Goodwill				$ 2,000G
Cash	62,000	$55,000		117,000
	$100,000	$55,000	$36,000	$119,000
Liabilities and Net Worth				
Accounts payable	$ 10,000	$15,000		$ 25,000
Capital stock:				
Company *P*	75,000			75,000
Company *S*		50,000		
Eliminate parent company's 90%			$45,000	
Minority interest—10%				5,000M
Surplus (deficit*):				
Company *P*	15,000			15,000S
Company *S*		10,000*		
Eliminate parent company's 90%			9,000*	
Minority interest—10%				1,000*M
	$100,000	$55,000	$36,000	$119,000

* Indicates a deduction.

COMPANY *P* AND SUBSIDIARY *S*
Consolidated Balance Sheet
(Date of Acquisition)

Assets		Liabilities and Net Worth		
Cash	$117,000	Accounts payable		$ 25,000
Goodwill	2,000	Minority interest—Company *S* (10%)		4,000
		Capital:		
		Capital stock	$75,000	
		Surplus	15,000	90,000
	$119,000			$119,000

valued and is therefore unwilling to pay book value for the stock. Therefore, when the purchase price is less than the book value of the acquired stock, the deficiency in price should be deducted from the goodwill appearing on the subsidiary's books.

For example, if the subsidiary has a capital stock of $100,000.00 and a surplus of $50,000.00, or a total net worth of $150,000.00, of which $10,000.00 is represented by a goodwill account, and if the parent company acquires all of the stock of this subsidiary at a cost of $142,000.00, it appears that the parent company refused to recognize the existence of a goodwill of $10,000.00, but based its purchase price on a goodwill of $2,000.00. In the consolidated working papers, the $8,000.00 excess of the book value of the subsidiary stock over the purchase price should be regarded as a deduction from the $10,000.00 goodwill shown by the subsidiary books.

One more addition to our rule is therefore required:

Elimination of reciprocals:
- Subsidiary's capital stock and surplus or deficit accounts:
  - Eliminate reciprocal element—parent company's proportion.
  - Extend non-reciprocal element (minority interest) to consolidated balance sheet column.
- Parent company's investment account:
  - Eliminate reciprocal element—parent company's proportion of subsidiary's stock and surplus.
  - Extend non-reciprocal element (goodwill *or deduction from goodwill*) to the consolidated balance sheet column.

Three illustrations involving deductions from goodwill are presented. In each case the subsidiary has a goodwill account.

First illustration. At the date of acquisition the subsidiary has a capital stock of $50,000.00 and no surplus or deficit. The parent company acquires all of the stock, paying $49,000.00 therefor, or $1,000.00 less than the book value.

COMPANY *P* AND SUBSIDIARY *S*
Consolidated Balance Sheet Working Papers
(Date of Acquisition)

	Company *P*	Company *S*	Eliminations	Consolidated Balance Sheet
Assets				
Investment in stock of Co. *S* (100%)	$ 49,000			
Eliminate book value:				
Capital stock			$50,000	
Deduction from goodwill				$ 1,000*G
Goodwill		$ 3,000		3,000
Cash	51,000	57,000		108,000
	$100,000	$60,000	$50,000	$110,000
Liabilities and Net Worth				
Accounts payable	$ 15,000	$10,000		$ 25,000
Capital stock:				
Company *P*	75,000			75,000
Company *S*		50,000		
Eliminate parent company's 100%			$50,000	
Surplus—Company *P*	10,000			10,000
	$100,000	$60,000	$50,000	$110,000

* Indicates a deduction.

COMPANY *P* AND SUBSIDIARY *S*
Consolidated Balance Sheet
(Date of Acquisition)

Assets		Liabilities and Net Worth		
Cash	$108,000	Accounts payable		$ 25,000
Goodwill	2,000	Capital:		
		Capital stock	$75,000	
		Surplus	10,000	85,000
	$110,000			$110,000

Second illustration. At the date of acquisition the subsidiary has a capital stock of $50,000.00 and a surplus of $10,000.00. The parent company acquires a 90% interest for $53,000.00.

COMPANY *P* AND SUBSIDIARY *S*
Consolidated Balance Sheet Working Papers
(Date of Acquisition)

	Company *P*	Company *S*	Eliminations	Consolidated Balance Sheet
Assets				
Investment in stock of Company *S* (90%)	$ 53,000			
Eliminate book value:				
Capital stock: 90% of $50,000.00			$45,000	
Surplus: 90% of $10,000.00			9,000	
Deduction from goodwill				$ 1,000*G
Cash	47,000	$72,000		119,000
Goodwill		3,000		3,000G
	$100,000	$75,000	$54,000	$121,000
Liabilities and Net Worth				
Accounts payable	$ 10,000	$15,000		$ 25,000
Capital stock:				
Company *P*	75,000			75,000
Company *S*		50,000		
Eliminate parent company's 90%			$45,000	
Minority interest—10%				5,000M
Surplus:				
Company *P*	15,000			15,000
Company *S*		10,000		
Eliminate parent company's 90%			9,000	
Minority interest—10%				1,000M
	$100,000	$75,000	$54,000	$121,000

* Indicates a deduction.

COMPANY *P* AND SUBSIDIARY *S*
Consolidated Balance Sheet
(Date of Acquisition)

Assets		Liabilities and Net Worth		
Cash	$119,000	Accounts payable		$ 25,000
Goodwill	2,000	Minority interest—Company *S* (10%)		6,000
		Capital:		
		Capital stock	$75,000	
		Surplus	15,000	90,000
	$121,000			$121,000

Third illustration. At the date of acquisition the subsidiary has a capital stock of $50,000.00 and a deficit of $10,000.00, making a net book value of $40,000.00. The parent company acquires a 90% interest, the book value of which is $36,000.00 and the purchase price, $35,000.00.

COMPANY *P* AND SUBSIDIARY *S*
Consolidated Balance Sheet Working Papers
(Date of Acquisition)

	Company *P*	Company *S*	Eliminations	Consolidated Balance Sheet
Assets				
Investment in stock of Co. *S* (90%) ..	$ 35,000			
Eliminate book value:				
Capital stock: 90% of $50,000.00			$45,000	
Deficit: 90% of $10,000.00			9,000*	
Deduction from goodwill				$ 1,000*G
Cash	65,000	$52,000		117,000
Goodwill		3,000		3,000G
	$100,000	$55,000	$36,000	$119,000
Liabilities and Net Worth				
Accounts payable	$ 10,000	$15,000		$ 25,000
Capital stock:				
Company *P*	75,000			75,000
Company *S*		50,000		
Eliminate parent company's 90%			$45,000	
Minority interest—10%				5,000M
Surplus (deficit*):				
Company *P*	15,000			15,000S
Company *S*		10,000*		
Eliminate parent company's 90%			9,000*	
Minority interest—10%				1,000*M
	$100,000	$55,000	$36,000	$119,000

COMPANY *P* AND SUBSIDIARY *S*
Consolidated Balance Sheet
(Date of Acquisition)

Assets		Liabilities and Net Worth		
Cash	$117,000	Accounts payable		$ 25,000
Goodwill	2,000	Minority interest—Company *S* (10%)		4,000
		Capital:		
		Capital stock	$75,000	
		Surplus	15,000	90,000
	$119,000			$119,000

In a subsequent chapter we shall consider the treatment of any excess of the book value of stock acquired over the purchase price, if no goodwill appears on the books of the subsidiary whose stock is acquired at less than book value.

Intercompany receivables and payables. A consolidated balance sheet shows the financial condition of a group of companies with all intercompany relationships eliminated.

Related companies frequently buy from and sell to each other on credit, so that the accounts receivable of one company and the accounts payable of another company contain reciprocal intercompany accounts. The amounts of such reciprocal intercompany receivables and payables should be eliminated in the eliminations column of the consolidated working papers, and the consolidated balance sheet should include only amounts receivable from and payable to others.

If the capital of one company is inadequate, one of the other related companies may make more or less permanent advances to it. The reciprocal accounts with these advances should also be eliminated in the consolidated working papers.

If the intercompany indebtedness takes the form of a note, the amount thereof should also be eliminated from the receivables and payables in the consolidated working papers.

The following partial working papers show the method of making such eliminations.

Consolidated Balance Sheet Working Papers

	Company *P*	Company *S*	Eliminations	Consolidated Balance Sheet
Assets				
Accounts receivable	$165,000	$60,000	$12,000	$213,000
Notes receivable—Company *S*	25,000		25,000	
Liabilities				
Accounts payable	90,000	30,000	12,000	108,000
Notes payable—Company *P*		25,000	25,000	

Company *S* owes Company *P* $12,000.00 for merchandise; this amount is included in Company *P*'s accounts receivable (which total $165,000.00) and in Company *S*'s accounts payable (which total $30,000.00). The $12,000.00 is eliminated from the accounts receivable and accounts payable, so that the consolidated balance sheet shows only the amounts of the accounts with outsiders.

Company *S* also owes Company *P* $25,000.00 on a note; the amount receivable appears as an asset in Company *P*'s balance sheet and as a liability in Company *S*'s balance sheet; this intercompany obligation is also eliminated.

CHAPTER 44

Parent and Subsidiary Accounting (Continued) Consolidated Balance Sheets if Parent Records Share of Subsidiary Profits and Losses

Parent's entries for subsidiary profits, losses, and dividends. Before dealing with the preparation of consolidated balance sheets at dates subsequent to the acquisition of the subsidiary stock by the parent company, it will be desirable to consider the entries which may be made by the parent company in recording the profits, losses, and dividends of the subsidiary.* For purposes of illustration, we shall assume the following facts:

Company *P* acquired all of the stock of Company *S* on January 1, 1946.

During the six months ended June 30, 1946, Company *S* made a profit of $20,000.00.

During the six months ended December 31, 1946, Company *S* lost $10,000.00, and paid a dividend of $5,000.00.

(1) Subsidiary profit—$20,000.00: The parent company's entry for the subsidiary's profit of the first six months is:

Investment in stock of Company *S*............	$20,000.00	
Income from Company *S*................		$20,000.00
To take up the subsidiary's profit for the six months ended June 30, 1946.		

Explanation of debit: Subsidiary profits increase the net assets of the subsidiary, which are represented on the parent company's books by the debit balance of the investment account. The increase in the net assets of the subsidiary is reflected on the parent company's books by a debit to the investment account.

Explanation of credit: Profits earned by the subsidiary are earned for the benefit of the parent company; the parent company takes up the profit by a credit to an income account.

* The methods described on the following pages are not used by all parent companies; the relative merits of these and alternative procedures are discussed in chapter 48.

(2) Subsidiary loss—$10,000.00: The parent company's entry for the subsidiary's loss of the second six months is:

Loss of Company *S*	$10,000.00	
Investment in stock of Company *S*		$10,000.00
To take up the subsidiary's loss for the six months ended December 31, 1946.		

Explanation of debit: If the parent company takes up the subsidiary's profit by a credit to an income account, it should take up the subsidiary's loss by a debit to a loss account.

Explanation of credit: Subsidiary losses decrease the net assets of the subsidiary, which are represented on the parent company's books by the debit balance of the investment account. The decrease in the net assets of the subsidiary, therefore, is reflected on the parent company's books by a credit to the investment account.

(3) Subsidiary dividend—$5,000.00: The parent company's entry for the subsidiary's dividend is:

Cash	$5,000.00	
Investment in stock of Company *S*		$5,000.00
To record the receipt of a dividend from the subsidiary.		

Explanation of debit: The debit to cash records the increase in the cash in the parent company's possession.

Explanation of credit: The subsidiary's net assets are decreased by the payment of a dividend. The balance in the investment account, which represents the net assets of the subsidiary, is therefore correspondingly reduced by a credit.

If time elapses between the declaration and the payment of the dividend, the parent company may debit dividends receivable and credit the investment account, to record the declaration of the dividend. Subsequently, it will debit cash and credit dividends receivable, to record the collection of the dividend.

If the parent company had owned only 90% of the subsidiary stock, its entries to record its proportion of the subsidiary's profits, losses, and dividends would have been:

Investment in stock of Company *S*	$18,000.00	
Income from Company *S*		$18,000.00
To take up 90% of the profit of Company *S* for the six months ended June 30, 1946.		

Loss of Company *S*	$9,000.00	
Investment in stock of Company *S*		$9,000.00
To take up 90% of the loss of Company *S* for the six months ended December 31, 1946.		
Cash	4,500.00	
Investment in stock of Company *S*		4,500.00
To record the dividend received from Company *S*.		

Rule for eliminations. The rule for making eliminations in consolidated balance sheet working papers at the date of acquisition, as developed in the preceding chapter, was stated as follows:

Subsidiary's capital stock and surplus accounts:
Eliminate reciprocal element—parent company's proportion.
Extend non reciprocal element (minority interest, if any) to the consolidated balance sheet column.

Parent company investment account:
Eliminate reciprocal element—parent company's proportion of subsidiary's stock and surplus.
Extend non reciprocal element (goodwill or deduction from goodwill, if any) to the consolidated balance sheet column.

The same rule for eliminations can be applied at all balance sheet dates subsequent to acquisition, if the parent company has taken up subsidiary profits, losses, and dividends in the manner illustrated by the preceding journal entries.

Four illustrative cases are presented in this chapter. All are based on the following facts:

Company *P* acquired a stock interest in Company *S* on January 1, 1946.

At that date Company *S* had capital stock of $100,000.00 and a surplus of $50,000.00, or a total book value of $150,000.00.

The amounts of subsidiary profits, losses, and dividends during 1946 were the same as those in the preceding journal entries, namely:

During the first six months—a profit of $20,000.00;
During the second six months—a loss of $10,000.00 and a dividend of $5,000.00.

Consolidated balance sheet required on December 31, 1946.

The four cases differ with respect to the goodwill and minority interest.

Case A: No minority interest; no goodwill. In this case it is assumed that Company *P* acquired all of the stock of Company *S*, paying exactly book value, $150,000.00; hence there is no minority interest and no goodwill element in the purchase price.

The changes in the subsidiary's surplus and the parent's investment account during the year are shown below:

	Subsidiary's Surplus	Parent's Investment Account
Balances, January 1, 1946	$50,000.00	$150,000.00
First six months:		
Subsidiary profit	20,000.00	20,000.00
Second six months:		
Subsidiary loss	10,000.00*	10,000.00*
Subsidiary dividend	5,000.00*	5,000.00*
Balances, December 31, 1946	$55,000.00	$155,000.00

* Denotes deduction.

The working papers and the consolidated balance sheet are presented below.

COMPANY *P* AND SUBSIDIARY *S*
Consolidated Balance Sheet Working Papers
December 31, 1946

	Company *P*	Company *S*	Eliminations	Consolidated Balance Sheet
Assets				
Cash	$ 45,000	$ 20,000		$ 65,000
Accounts receivable	95,000	75,000		170,000
Inventory	125,000	70,000		195,000
Investment in stock of Company *S*	155,000			
Eliminate book value:				
Capital stock			$100,000	
Surplus			55,000	
Goodwill		10,000		10,000
	$420,000	$175,000	$155,000	$440,000
Liabilities and Net Worth				
Accounts payable	$ 40,000	$ 20,000		$ 60,000
Capital stock:				
Company *P*	300,000			300,000
Company *S*		100,000		
Eliminate Company *P*'s 100%			$100,000	
Surplus:				
Company *P*	80,000			80,000
Company *S*		55,000		
Eliminate Company *P*'s 100%			55,000	
	$420,000	$175,000	$155,000	$440,000

COMPANY *P* AND SUBSIDIARY *S*
Consolidated Balance Sheet
December 31, 1946

Assets		Liabilities and Net Worth		
Cash	$ 65,000	Accounts payable		$ 60,000
Accounts receivable	170,000	Net worth:		
Inventory	195,000	Capital stock	$300,000	
Goodwill	10,000	Surplus	80,000	380,000
	$440,000			$440,000

Case B: MINORITY INTEREST; NO GOODWILL. In this case it is assumed that Company *P* acquired only 90% of the stock of Company *S*; hence there is a 10% minority interest. The book value of the stock acquired was 90% of $150,000.00, or $135,000.00; the stock was purchased for $135,000.00; hence there was no goodwill. The changes in the subsidiary's surplus and the parent's investment account during the year are shown below:

	Subsidiary's Surplus	Parent's Investment Account
Balances, January 1, 1946	$50,000.00	$135,000.00
First six months:		
Subsidiary profit	20,000.00	18,000.00
Second six months:		
Subsidiary loss	10,000.00*	9,000.00*
Subsidiary dividend	5,000.00*	4,500.00*
Balances, December 31, 1946	$55,000.00	$139,500.00

* Denotes deduction.

The working papers and the consolidated balance sheet are presented below.

COMPANY *P* AND SUBSIDIARY *S*
Consolidated Balance Sheet Working Papers
December 31, 1946

	Company *P*	Company *S*	Eliminations	Consolidated Balance Sheet
Assets				
Cash	$ 59,500	$ 20,000		$ 79,500
Accounts receivable	95,000	75,000		170,000
Inventory	125,000	70,000		195,000
Investment in stock of Company *S*	139,500			
Eliminate book value—90%:				
Capital stock			$ 90,000	
Surplus			49,500	
Goodwill		10,000		10,000
	$419,000	$175,000	$139,500	$454,500
Liabilities and Net Worth				
Accounts payable	$ 40,000	$ 20,000		$ 60,000
Capital stock:				
Company *P*	300,000			300,000
Company *S*		100,000		
Eliminate Company *P*'s 90%			$ 90,000	
Minority interest—10%				10,000M
Surplus:				
Company *P*	79,000			79,000
Company *S*		55,000		
Eliminate Company *P*'s 90%			49,500	
Minority interest—10%				5,500M
	$419,000	$175,000	$139,500	$454,500

COMPANY *P* AND SUBSIDIARY *S*
Consolidated Balance Sheet
December 31, 1946

Assets		Liabilities and Net Worth		
Cash	$ 79,500	Accounts payable		$ 60,000
Accounts receivable	170,000	Minority interest in Co. *S*		15,500
Inventory	195,000	Net worth:		
Goodwill	10,000	Capital stock	$300,000	
		Surplus	79,000	379,000
	$454,500			$454,500

Case C: Minority interest; goodwill. In this case it is again assumed that there is a 10% minority interest. When the 90% interest was acquired on January 1, 1946, the subsidiary had a book value of $150,000.00; the 90% interest had a book value of $135,000.00; the purchase price was $138,000.00; hence there was a goodwill payment of $3,000.00. The changes in the subsidiary surplus and the parent's investment account during the year are shown below:

	Subsidiary's Surplus	Parent's Investment Account
Balances, January 1, 1946	$50,000.00	$138,000.00
First six months:		
Subsidiary profit	20,000.00	18,000.00
Second six months:		
Subsidiary loss	10,000.00*	9,000.00*
Subsidiary dividend	5,000.00*	4,500.00*
Balances, December 31, 1946	$55,000.00	$142,500.00

The working papers and the consolidated balance sheet are presented below.

COMPANY *P* AND SUBSIDIARY *S*
Consolidated Balance Sheet Working Papers
December 31, 1946

	Company *P*	Company *S*	Eliminations	Consolidated Balance Sheet
Assets				
Cash	$ 56,500	$ 20,000		$ 76,500
Accounts receivable	95,000	75,000		170,000
Inventory	125,000	70,000		195,000
Investment in stock of Company *S*	142,500			
Eliminate book balue—90%:				
Capital stock			$ 90,000	
Surplus			49,500	
Goodwill				3,000G
Goodwill		10,000		10,000G
	$419,000	$175,000	$139,500	$454,000

	Company P	Company S	Eliminations	Consolidated Balance Sheet
Liabilities and Net Worth				
Accounts payable	$ 40,000	$ 20,000		$ 60,000
Capital stock:				
Company *P*	300,000			300,000
Company *S*		100,000		
Eliminate Company *P*'s 90%			$ 90,000	
Minority interest—10%				10,000M
Surplus:				
Company *P*	79,000			79,000
Company *S*		55,000		
Eliminate Company *P*'s 90%			49,500	
Minority interest—10%				5,500M
	$419,000	$175,000	$139,500	$454,500

Note that the goodwill on the books of Company *S* and the goodwill payment made in the acquisition of its stock are combined in the following consolidated balance sheet:

COMPANY *P* AND SUBSIDIARY *S*
Consolidated Balance Sheet
December 31, 1946

Assets		**Liabilities and Net Worth**		
Cash	$ 76,500	Accounts payable		$ 60,000
Accounts receivable	170,000	Minority interest in Co. *S*—10%		15,500
Inventory	195,000	Net worth:		
Goodwill	13,000	Capital stock	$300,000	
		Surplus	79,000	379,000
	$454,500			$454,500

Case D: MINORITY INTEREST; DEDUCTION FROM GOODWILL. In this case it is again assumed that the parent company acquired only 90% of the subsidiary stock. The book value was $135,000.00, and the purchase price was $130,000.00; hence there was a $5,000.00 goodwill deduction. The changes in the subsidiary surplus and the parent's investment account during the year are shown below.

	Subsidiary's Surplus	Parent's Investment Account
Balances, January 1, 1946	$50,000.00	$130,000.00
First six months:		
Subsidiary profit	20,000.00	18,000.00
Second six months:		
Subsidiary loss	10,000.00*	9,000.00*
Subsidiary dividend	5,000.00*	4,500.00*
Balances, December 31, 1946	$55,000.00	$134,500.00

* Denotes deduction.

The working papers and the consolidated balance sheet appear below.

COMPANY *P* AND SUBSIDIARY *S*
Consolidated Balance Sheet Working Papers
December 31, 1946

	Company *P*	Company *S*	Eliminations	Consolidated Balance Sheet
Assets				
Cash	$ 64,500	$ 20,000		$ 84,500
Accounts receivable	95,000	75,000		170,000
Inventory	125,000	70,000		195,000
Investment in stock of Company *S*	134,500			
Eliminate book value—90%:				
Capital stock			$ 90,000	
Surplus			49,500	
Deduction from goodwill				5,000*G
Goodwill		10,000		10,000G
	$419,000	$175,000	$139,500	$454,500
Liabilities and Net Worth				
Accounts payable	$ 40,000	$ 20,000		$ 60,000
Capital stock:				
Company *P*	300,000			300,000
Company *S*		100,000		
Eliminate Company *P*'s 90%			$ 90,000	
Minority interest—10%				10,000M
Surplus:				
Company *P*	79,000			79,000
Company *S*		55,000		
Eliminate Company *P*'s 90%			49,500	
Minority interest—10%				5,500M
	$419,000	$175,000	$139,500	$454,500

Note that, in the following consolidated balance sheet, the amount shown as goodwill is the $10,000.00 balance on the books of Company *S* minus the $5,000.00 goodwill deduction resulting from the purchase of the stock of Company *S* at less than book value.

COMPANY *P* AND SUBSIDIARY *S*
Consolidated Balance Sheet
December 31, 1946

Assets		**Liabilities and Net Worth**		
Cash	$ 84,500	Accounts payable		$ 60,000
Accounts receivable	170,000	Minority interest in Co. *S*—10%		15,500
Inventory	195,000	Net worth:		
Goodwill	5,000	Capital stock	$300,000	
		Surplus	79,000	379,000
	$454,500			$454,500

Consolidated balance sheets without formal working papers. Although students should be thoroughly familiar with the method of preparing the consolidated working papers previously presented, it is often a simple matter to prepare a consolidated balance sheet without formal working papers. To show how this is done, the four cases presented in this chapter will be repeated.

Case A: NO MINORITY INTEREST; NO GOODWILL. Following are the balance sheets of the two companies used in Case A.

Balance Sheets—December 31, 1946

	Company *P*	Company *S*
Assets		
Cash	$ 45,000.00	$ 20,000.00
Accounts receivable	95,000.00	75,000.00
Inventory	125,000.00	70,000.00
Investment in stock of Company *S*—100%	155,000.00	
Goodwill		10,000.00
	$420,000.00	$175,000.00
Liabilities and Net Worth		
Accounts payable	$ 40,000.00	$ 20,000.00
Capital stock	300,000.00	100,000.00
Surplus	80,000.00	55,000.00
	$420,000.00	$175,000.00

We can enter immediately in the consolidated balance sheet:

The totals of the following assets: cash, accounts receivable, inventory.
The total of the following liabilities: accounts payable.
The parent company's capital stock and surplus.

COMPANY *P* AND SUBSIDIARY *S*
Consolidated Balance Sheet
December 31, 1946

Assets		**Liabilities and Net Worth**		
Cash	$ 65,000	Accounts payable		$ 60,000
Accounts receivable	170,000	Net worth:		
Inventory	195,000	Capital stock	$300,000	
		Surplus	80,000	380,000

The balances of the parent's investment account and the subsidiary's capital stock and surplus accounts are not entered immediately in the consolidated balance sheet, because eliminations are to be made therefrom to determine any minority interest and goodwill element in the stock purchase price. The balance of the subsidiary's goodwill account is not entered until it is determined whether any goodwill from consolidation is to be added thereto. Any minority interest and goodwill from consolidation can be easily determined by simple working papers in the following form, in which the 100% interest in the book value of the subsidiary is eliminated from the subsidiary's net worth accounts and from the parent's investment account.

	Subsidiary's Capital Stock	Subsidiary's Surplus	Parent's Investment Account (100%)
Balances	$100,000	$55,000	$155,000
Deduct reciprocal element—100%	100,000	55,000	155,000
Nonreciprocal elements	—	—	—

The consolidated balance sheet can be completed by entering the goodwill shown in the subsidiary balance sheet.

COMPANY *P* AND SUBSIDIARY *S*
Consolidated Balance Sheet
December 31, 1946

Assets		Liabilities and Net Worth		
Cash	$ 65,000	Accounts payable		$ 60,000
Accounts receivable	170,000	Net worth:		
Inventory	195,000	Capital stock	$300,000	
Goodwill	10,000	Surplus	80,000	380,000
	$440,000			$440,000

Case B: Minority interest; no goodwill. The parent company owns 90% of the stock of the subsidiary.

	Company *P*	Company *S*
Assets		
Cash	$ 59,500.00	$ 20,000.00
Accounts receivable	95,000.00	75,000.00
Inventory	125,000.00	70,000.00
Investment in stock of Company *S*—90%	139,500.00	
Goodwill		10,000.00
	$419,000.00	$175,000.00
Liabilities and Net Worth		
Accounts payable	$ 40,000.00	$ 20,000.00
Capital stock	300,000.00	100,000.00
Surplus	79,000.00	55,000.00
	$419,000.00	$175,000.00

The consolidated balance sheet appears on page 233. It was prepared as follows:

(1) The reciprocal element was eliminated to determine any goodwill and minority interest, thus:

	Subsidiary's Capital Stock	Subsidiary's Surplus	Parent's Investment Account (90%)
Balances	$100,000	$55,000	$139,500
Deduct reciprocal element—90%	90,000	49,500	139,500
Nonreciprocal elements:			
Minority interest—10%	$ 10,000	$ 5,500	
Goodwill			

(2) The following amounts were entered in the consolidated balance sheet:

(a) Combined balances of asset accounts: cash, accounts receivable, inventory, goodwill. (No adjustment of goodwill.)

(b) Combined balances of liability accounts: accounts payable.

(c) Minority interest determined in (1).

(d) Net worth: parent company's capital stock and surplus.

COMPANY *P* AND SUBSIDIARY *S*
Consolidated Balance Sheet
December 31, 1946

Assets		Liabilities and Net Worth		
Cash	$ 79,500	Accounts payable		$ 60,000
Account receivable	170,000	Minority interest in Co. *S*—10%		15,500
Inventory	195,000	Net worth:		
Goodwill	10,000	Capital stock	$300,000	
		Surplus	79,000	379,000
	$454,500			$454,500

Case C: MINORITY INTEREST; GOODWILL. Following are the balance sheets used in the third case. The parent company owns 90% of the subsidiary stock.

	Company *P*	Company *S*
Assets		
Cash	$ 56,500.00	$ 20,000.00
Accounts receivable	95,000.00	75,000.00
Inventory	125,000.00	70,000.00
Investment in stock of Company *S*—90%	142,500.00	
Goodwill		10,000.00
	$419,000.00	$175,000.00
Liabilities and Net Worth		
Accounts payable	$ 40,000.00	$ 20,000.00
Capital stock	300,000.00	100,000.00
Surplus	79,000.00	55,000.00
	$419,000.00	$175,000.00

(1) Determination of minority interest and goodwill:

	Subsidiary's Capital Stock	Subsidiary's Surplus	Parent's Investment Account (90%)
Balances	$100,000.00	$55,000.00	$142,500.00
Reciprocals to be eliminated—90%	90,000.00	49,500.00	139,500.00
Nonreciprocals:			
Minority interest	$ 10,000.00	$ 5,500.00	
Goodwill			$ 3,000.00

(2) The following amounts were entered in the consolidated balance sheet:

(*a*) Combined balances of asset accounts: cash, accounts receivable, inventory. The amount shown as goodwill in the consolidated balance sheet is the sum of the $10,000.00 account on the books of Company *S* and the $3,000.00 goodwill element determined in (1) above.

(*b*) Combined amounts of liability accounts.

(*c*) Minority interest of $15,500.00, as determined in (1) above.

(*d*) Net worth: parent's capital stock and surplus.

COMPANY *P* AND SUBSIDIARY *S*

Consolidated Balance Sheet

December 31, 1946

Assets		Liabilities and Net Worth		
Cash	$ 76,500	Accounts payable		$ 60,000
Accounts receivable	170,000	Minority interest in Co. *S*—10%		15,500
Inventory	195,000	Net worth:		
Goodwill	13,000	Capital stock	$300,000	
		Surplus	79,000	379,000
	$454,500			$454,500

Case D: MINORITY INTEREST; DEDUCTION FROM GOODWILL. Following are the balance sheets used in the fourth case. The parent company owns 90% of the subsidiary stock.

	Company *P*	Company *S*
Assets		
Cash	$ 64,500.00	$ 20,000.00
Accounts receivable	95,000.00	75,000.00
Inventory	125,000.00	70,000.00
Investment in stock of Company *S*—90%	134,500.00	
Goodwill		10,000.00
	$419,000.00	$175,000.00
Liabilities and Net Worth		
Accounts payable	$ 40,000.00	$ 20,000.00
Capital stock	300,000.00	100,000.00
Surplus	79,000.00	55,000.00
	$419,000.00	$175,000.00

(1) Determination of minority interest and goodwill:

	SUBSIDIARY'S Capital Stock	SUBSIDIARY'S Surplus	Parent's Investment Account (90%)
Balances	$100,000.00	$55,000.00	$134,500.00
Reciprocals to be eliminated—90%	90,000.00	49,500.00	139,500.00
Nonreciprocal elements:			
Minority interest—10%	$ 10,000.00	$ 5,500.00	
Deduction from goodwill			$ 5,000.00*

(2) The following amounts were entered in the consolidated balance sheet below:

(*a*) Combined balances of asset accounts: cash, accounts receivable, inventory. The goodwill in the consolidated balance sheet is the amount shown in the balance sheet of Company *S*, minus the goodwill deduction determined in (1) above.

(*b*) Combined balances of liability accounts: accounts payable.

(*c*) Minority interest of $15,500.00, as determined in (1) above.

(*d*) Net worth: parent company's capital stock and surplus.

COMPANY *P* AND SUBSIDIARY *S*
Consolidated Balance Sheet
December 31, 1946

Assets		Liabilities and Net Worth		
Cash	$ 84,500	Accounts payable		$ 60,000
Accounts receivable	170,000	Minority interest in Co. *S*—10%		15,500
Inventory	195,000	Net worth:		
Goodwill	5,000	Capital stock	$300,000	
		Surplus	79,000	379,000
	$454,500			$454,500

CHAPTER 45

Parent and Subsidiary Accounting (Continued)—Consolidated Balance Sheet Subsequent to Acquisition if Investment Is Carried at Cost

Carrying investment at cost. The preceding chapter explained the journal entries by which a parent company may debit its investment account with subsidiary profits, and credit its investment account with subsidiary losses and dividends.

Some parent companies, however, make no entries in the investment account except those to record the cost of the stock purchased. No entries whatever are made for subsidiary profits and losses; dividends from the subsidiary are recorded by debiting cash and crediting dividends from subsidiary (or some similar account), which is regarded as an income account and is closed to profit and loss.

These two methods of accounting used by parent companies are compared below.

	Profits, Losses, and Dividends Recorded Through Investment Account (First Method)			Investment Carried at Cost Dividends Recorded as Income (Second Method)		
Cost:	Investment in Company *S*	$100,000		Investment in Company *S*	$100,000	
	Cash		$100,000	Cash		$100,000
Profit:	Investment in Company *S*	20,000		No entry.		
	Income from *S*		20,000			
Loss:	Loss from *S*	10,000		No entry.		
	Investment in Company *S*		10,000			
Dividend:	Cash	5,000		Cash	5,000	
	Investment in Company *S*		5,000	Dividends from Company *S*		5,000
	The income and loss accounts are closed to profit and loss and thence to surplus.			The dividends account is closed to profit and loss and thence to surplus.		

Differences in account balances. The parent company's investment and surplus accounts resulting from the two methods of accounting are compared below:

	First Method		Second Method	
	Investment Account	Surplus	Investment Account	Surplus
Cost of stock.............	$100,000		$100,000	
Subsidiary profit..........	20,000	$20,000		
Subsidiary loss............	10,000*	10,000*		
Subsidiary dividend........	5,000*			$ 5,000
Balances.................	$105,000	$10,000	$100,000	$ 5,000

* Denotes deduction.

Observe that the balances of the investment and surplus accounts under the first method are $5,000.00 larger than the balances of these accounts under the second method. This $5,000.00 difference is the increase in the subsidiary surplus since acquisition.

Consolidating procedure: investment carried at cost. If the investment in the subsidiary is carried at cost, consolidated working papers can be prepared by the following procedure:

Adjust the parent company's investment and surplus accounts for its share of the increase or decrease in the subsidiary surplus since acquisition, by applying adjusting entries in the working papers, as follows:

If the subsidiary surplus has increased: debit the investment account and credit surplus.

If the subsidiary surplus has decreased: debit surplus and credit the investment account.

The account balances will then be the same as those resulting from the accounting method described in Chapter 44, and eliminations can be made in the manner described in Chapter 44.

Several illustrations are given in the remaining sections of this chapter. The balance sheets of the parent and subsidiary companies are shown in the first two columns of the working papers. In all cases it is assumed that:

(1) The subsidiary had a capital stock of $100,000.00 and a surplus of $50,000.00 on January 1, 1946, when the parent company acquired its stock.

(2) The investment is carried at cost on the parent company's books.

(3) The parent company has a surplus of $30,000.00 from its own operations, and has taken up as income (and included in its surplus) the dividends received from the subsidiary.

First illustration. The parent company purchased all of the subsidiary stock; hence there is no minority interest. The price paid was book value, $150,000.00; hence there was no goodwill payment.

As shown by the working papers on page 240, the subsidiary has a surplus of $54,000.00 at the end of the year; therefore, the subsidiary suplus increased $4,000.00 since acquisition. (This is the result of a $10,000.00 profit and a $6,000.00 dividend.) The adjustment applied to the parent company's accounts in the consolidated working papers is:

Investment in Company *S*	$4,000.00	
Surplus		$4,000.00
For increase in subsidiary's net assets and surplus since acquisition.		

COMPANY *P* AND SUBSIDIARY *S*
Consolidated Balance Sheet
December 31, 1946

Assets		Liabilities and Net Worth		
Cash	$ 55,000	Accounts payable		$ 61,000
Accounts receivable	145,000	Net worth:		
Inventory	191,000	Capital stock	$300,000	
Goodwill	10,000	Surplus	40,000	340,000
	$401,000			$401,000

A consolidated balance sheet can be prepared without formal working papers, thus:

(1) In the following simple working papers, adjust the parent company's investment and surplus accounts. Then make the customary eliminations from the investment account and from the subsidiary's capital stock and surplus accounts, to determine the amounts (if any) of goodwill and minority interest.

	Subsidiary's		Parent's	
	Capital Stock	Surplus	Investment	Surplus
Balances before adjustment	$100,000	$54,000	$150,000	$36,000
Add increase in subsidiary's net assets and surplus since date of acquisition			4,000	4,000
Adjusted balances			$154,000	$40,000
Deduct reciprocal element—100%	100,000	54,000	154,000	
Nonreciprocal elements	—	—	—	

COMPANY *P* AND SUBSIDIARY *S*
Consolidated Balance Sheet Working Papers
December 31, 1946

	Company *P*	Company *S*	Adjustments Debit	Adjustments Credit	Eliminations	Consolidated Balance Sheet
Assets						
Cash	$ 35,000.00	$ 20,000.00				$ 55,000.00
Accounts receivable	80,000.00	65,000.00				145,000.00
Inventory	111,000.00	80,000.00				191,000.00
Investment in Company *S*—100% (cost)	150,000.00					
Adjustment—increase in Company *S* net assets since acquisition			$4,000.00			
Eliminate book value:						
Capital stock					$100,000.00	
Surplus					54,000.00	
Goodwill		10,000.00				10,000.00
	$376,000.00	$175,000.00			$154,000.00	$401,000.00
Liabilities and Net Worth						
Accounts payable	$ 40,000.00	$ 21,000.00				$ 61,000.00
Capital stock:						
Company *P*	300,000.00					300,000.00
Company *S*		100,000.00				
Eliminate Company *P*'s 100%					$100,000.00	
Surplus:						
Company *P*	36,000.00					
Adjustment—increase in Company *S* surplus since acquisition				$4,000.00		40,000.00
Company *S*		54,000.00				
Eliminate Company *P*'s 100%					54,000.00	
	$376,000.00	$175,000.00	$4,000.00	$4,000.00	$154,000.00	$401,000.00

(2) Enter in the consolidated balance sheet:
- (a) Combined balances of asset accounts.
- (b) Combined balances of liability accounts.
- (c) Minority interest: none.
- (d) Net worth: parent company's capital stock and the $40,000.00 adjusted balance of its surplus.

Second illustration. This illustration is the same as the preceding one, with two exceptions: the parent company purchased only a 90% interest, leaving a 10% minority interest; the book value of the stock purchased was 90% of $150,000.00 or $135,000.00 and the purchase price was $138,000.00, including a goodwill payment of $3,000.00.

As in the preceding illustration, the subsidiary surplus increased $4,000.00 since acquisition; the adjustment of the parent company's investment and surplus accounts is for 90% of $4,000.00, or $3,600.00. The working papers for this illustration are on page 242.

The consolidated balance sheet may be prepared without formal working papers thus:

(1) Adjust the parent company's investment and surplus accounts, and determine the minority interest and goodwill.

	Subsidiary's		Parent's	
	Capital Stock	Surplus	Investment	Surplus
Balances before adjustment	$100,000	$54,000	$138,000	$35,400
Add 90% of $4,000 increase in subsidiary surplus since acquisition			3,600	3,600
Adjusted balances			$141,600	$39,000
Deduct reciprocal elements—90%	90,000	48,600	138,600	
Nonreciprocal elements:				
Minority interest—10%	$ 10,000	$ 5,400		
Goodwill			$ 3,000	

(2) Enter in the consolidated balance sheet:
- (a) Combined balances of asset accounts; add the $3,000 goodwill from consolidation to the goodwill in the balance sheet of Company *S*.
- (b) Combined balances of liability accounts.
- (c) Minority interest of $15,400.00 as determined in (1).
- (d) Net worth: parent company's capital stock and the $39,000.00 adjusted balance of its surplus account.

The consolidated balance sheet is on page 243.

COMPANY *P* AND SUBSIDIARY *S*
Consolidated Balance Sheet Working Papers
December 31, 1946

	Company *P*	Company *S*	Adjustments Debit	Adjustments Credit	Eliminations	Consolidated Balance Sheet
Assets						
Cash	$ 46,400.00	$ 20,000.00				$ 66,400.00
Accounts receivable	80,000.00	65,000.00				145,000.00
Inventory	111,000.00	80,000.00				191,000.00
Investment in Company *S*—90% (cost)	138,000.00					
Adjustment—90% of increase in Company *S* net assets since acquisition			$3,600.00			
Eliminate book value:						
Capital stock—90%					$ 90,000.00	
Surplus—90%					48,600.00	
Goodwill						3,000.00G
Goodwill		10,000.00				10,000.00G
	$375,400.00	$175,000.00			$138,600.00	$415,400.00
Liabilities and Net Worth						
Accounts payable	$ 40,000.00	$ 21,000.00				$ 61,000.00
Capital stock:						
Company *P*	300,000.00					300,000.00
Company *S*		100,000.00				
Eliminate Company *P*'s 90%					$ 90,000.00	
Minority interest—10%						10,000.00M
Surplus:						
Company *P*	35,400.00					
Adjustment—90% of increase in Company *S* surplus since acquisition				$3,600.00		39,000.00
Company *S*		54,000.00				
Eliminate Company *P*'s 90%					48,600.00	
Minority interest—10%						5,400.00M
	$375,400.00	$175,000.00	$3,600.00	$3,600.00	$138,600.00	$415,400.00

COMPANY *P* AND SUBSIDIARY *S*
Consolidated Balance Sheet
December 31, 1946

Assets		Liabilities and Net Worth		
Cash	$ 66,400	Accounts payable		$ 61,000
Accounts receivable	145,000	Minority int. in Co. *S*—10%		15,400
Inventory	191,000	Net worth:		
Goodwill	13,000	Capital stock	$300,000	
		Surplus	39,000	339,000
	$415,400			$415,400

Third illustration. The parent company purchased a 90% interest in the subsidiary stock. The book value of the stock purchased was 90% of $150,000.00, or $135,000.00, and the purchase price was $138,000.00.

As shown by the working papers on page 244, the subsidiary surplus decreased from $50,000.00 at the date of acquisition to $34,000.00 on December 31, 1946. (This was the result of a $10,000.00 loss and a $6,000.00 dividend.) The adjustment therefore decreases the parent company's investment and surplus accounts 90% of $16,000.00, or $14,400.00.

Following is the consolidated balance sheet.

COMPANY *P* AND SUBSIDIARY *S*
Consolidated Balance Sheet
December 31, 1946

Assets		Liabilities and Net Worth		
Cash	$ 66,400	Accounts payable		$ 81,000
Accounts receivable	145,000	Minority int. in Co. *S*—10%		13,400
Inventory	191,000	Net worth:		
Goodwill	13,000	Capital stock	$300,000	
		Surplus	21,000	321,000
	$415,400			$415,400

The consolidated balance sheet could be prepared without formal working papers thus:

(1) Adjust the parent company's investment and surplus accounts and determine the minority interest and goodwill.

	Subsidiary's		Parent's	
	Capital Stock	Surplus	Investment	Surplus
Balances before adjustment	$100,000	$34,000	$138,000	$35,400
Deduct 90% of $16,000 decrease in subsidiary surplus since acquisition			14,400	14,400
Adjusted balances			$123,600	$21,000
Deduct reciprocal elements—90%	90,000	30,600	120,600	
Nonreciprocal elements:				
Minority interest—10%	$ 10,000	$ 3,400		
Goodwill			$ 3,000	

COMPANY *P* AND SUBSIDIARY *S*
Consolidated Balance Sheet Working Papers
December 31, 1946

	Company *P*	Company *S*	Adjustments Debit	Adjustments Credit	Eliminations	Consolidated Balance Sheet
Assets						
Cash	$ 46,400.00	$ 20,000.00				$ 66,400.00
Accounts receivable	80,000.00	65,000.00				145,000.00
Inventory	111,000.00	80,000.00				191,000.00
Investment in Company *S*—90% (cost)	138,000.00					
Adjustment—90% of $16,000 decrease in subsidiary net assets since acquisition				$14,400.00		
Eliminate book value:						
Capital stock—90%					$ 90,000.00	
Surplus—90% of $34,000					30,600.00	
Goodwill						3,000.00G
Goodwill		10,000.00				10,000.00G
	$375,400.00	$175,000.00			$120,600.00	$415,400.00
Liabilities and Net Worth						
Accounts payable	$ 40,000.00	$ 41,000.00				$ 81,000.00
Capital stock:						
Company *P*	300,000.00					300,000.00
Company *S*		100,000.00				
Eliminate Company *P*'s 90%					$ 90,000.00	
Minority interest—10%						10,000.00M
Surplus:						
Company *P*	35,400.00					
Adjustment—90% of $16,000 decrease in subsidiary surplus since acquisition			$14,400.00			21,000.00
Company *S*		34,000.00				
Eliminate Company *P*'s 90%					30,600.00	
Minority interest—10%						3,400.00M
	$375,400.00	$175,000.00	$14,400.00	$14,400.00	$120,600.00	$415,400.00

(2) Enter in the consolidated balance sheet:
- (*a*) Combined balances of asset accounts; add the $3,000.00 goodwill element to the goodwill in the balance sheet of Company *S*.
- (*b*) Combined balances of liability accounts.
- (*c*) Minority interest of $13,400.00, as determined in (1).
- (*d*) Net worth: parent company's capital stock and adjusted surplus of $21,000.00.

Fourth illustration. The parent company purchased a 90% interest in the subsidiary. The book value of the stock acquired was $135,000.00 and the purchase price was $131,000.00; hence there is a $4,000.00 goodwill deduction.

As shown by the subsidiary's balance sheet in the working papers on page 246, its surplus decreased to $34,000.00 on December 31, 1946. The adjustment is therefore for 90% of the $16,000.00 decrease, or $14,400.00.

Following is the consolidated balance sheet:

COMPANY *P* AND SUBSIDIARY *S*
Consolidated Balance Sheet
December 31, 1946

Assets		Liabilities and Net Worth		
Cash	$ 73,400	Accounts payable		$ 81,000
Accounts receivable	145,000	Minority int. in Co. *S*—10%		13,400
Inventory	191,000	Net worth:		
Goodwill	6,000	Capital stock	$300,000	
		Surplus	21,000	321,000
	$415,400			$415,400

The consolidated balance sheet may be prepared without formal working papers, thus:

(1) Adjust the parent company's investment and surplus accounts, and determine the minority interest and the goodwill.

	Subsidiary's		Parent's	
	Capital Stock	Surplus	Investment	Surplus
Balances before adjustment	$100,000	$34,000	$131,000	$35,400
Deduct 90% of $16,000 decrease in subsidiary surplus since acquisition			14,400	14,400
Adjusted balances			$116,600	$21,000
Deduct reciprocal elements—90%	90,000	30,600	120,600	
Nonreciprocal elements:				
Minority interest—10%	$ 10,000	$ 3,400		
Deduction from goodwill			$ 4,000*	

COMPANY *P* AND SUBSIDIARY *S*
Consolidated Balance Sheet Working Papers
December 31, 1946

	Company *P*	Company *S*	Adjustments Debit	Adjustments Credit	Eliminations	Consolidated Balance Sheet
Assets						
Cash	$ 53,400.00	$ 20,000.00				$ 73,400.00
Accounts receivable	80,000.00	65,000.00				145,000.00
Inventory	111,000.00	80,000.00				191,000.00
Investment in Company *S*—90% (cost)	131,000.00					
Adjustment—90% of $16,000 decrease in subsidiary net assets since acquisition				$14,400.00		
Eliminate book value:						
Capital stock—90%					$ 90,000.00	
Surplus—90% of $34,000					30,600.00	
Deduction from goodwill						4,000.00*G
Goodwill		10,000.00				10,000.00G
	$375,400.00	$175,000.00			$120,600.00	$415,400.00
Liabilities and Net Worth						
Accounts payable	$ 40,000.00	$ 41,000.00				$ 81,000.00
Capital stock:						
Company *P*	300,000.00					300,000.00
Company *S*		100,000.00				
Eliminate Company *P*'s 90%					$ 90,000.00	
Minority interest—10%						10,000.00M
Surplus:						
Company *P*	35,400.00					
Adjustment—90% of $16,000 decrease in subsidiary surplus since acquisition			$14,400.00			21,000.00
Company *S*		34,000.00				
Eliminate Company *P*'s 90%					30,600.00	
Minority interest—10%						3,400.00M
	$375,400.00	$175,000.00	$14,400.00	$14,400.00	$120,600.00	$415,400.00

(2) Enter in the consolidated balance sheet:
- (*a*) Combined balances of asset accounts; deduct the \$4,000.00 negative goodwill item from the \$10,000.00 goodwill shown in the balance sheet of Company *S*.
- (*b*) Combined balances of liability accounts.
- (*c*) Minority interest of \$13,400.00.
- (*d*) Net worth: parent company's capital stock and adjusted surplus of \$21,000.00.

CHAPTER 46

Parent and Subsidiary Accounting (Continued)—Intercompany Accounts. Miscellaneous Matters

Intercompany Accounts

Intercompany notes discounted. The elimination of intercompany accounts receivable and payable and intercompany notes receivable and payable has been illustrated. The situation is more complex when one company has discounted notes receivable taken from a related company. To illustrate, assume that Company *A* has given a $5,000.00 note to Company *B*. Company *B* has discounted this note with its bankers. At the date of the consolidated balance sheet, the note has not matured.

Since the note is in the hands of the bankers, the liability is no longer an intercompany one, and hence it must be shown as a liability on the consolidated balance sheet. The notes payable account on Company *A*'s books should be offset in the working papers against the notes receivable account on Company *B*'s books, and the notes receivable—Company *A*—discounted account should be carried to the consolidated balance sheet column, thus:

	Company *A*	Company *B*	Eliminations	Consolidated Balance Sheet
Assets				
Notes receivable—Co. *A*........		$5,000	$5,000	
Liabilities				
Notes payable—Co. *B*..........	$5,000		5,000	
Notes rec.—Co. *A*—discounted..		5,000		5,000

There is a difference of opinion among accountants about whether the $5,000.00 liability to outsiders should be shown in the consolidated balance sheet as notes receivable—Company *A*—discounted, or as notes payable. Those who favor the former title contend that the note is a direct liability of one of the related companies and a secondary liability of the other company, and hence is an obligation different in nature from a note signed by one company only. Showing the liability as a note payable would not indicate the liability of both companies.

The author's opinion is that the "notes payable" title is preferable. In the first place, the consolidated balance sheet is based on the assumption that the related companies are a single organization, and the legal fact of separate corporate entities is ignored. From the viewpoint of the consolidated balance sheet, therefore, a note signed by one company is as much a liability of the organization as a note signed by one company and indorsed by another related company. In the second place, since *notes receivable discounted* suggests merely a contingent liability, the term is likely to be misleading.

Customers' notes transferred. If one of the related companies discounts its customers' notes, no peculiar difficulties arise. Its accounts may contain, for example, the following balances:

Notes receivable	$20,000.00	
Notes receivable discounted		$5,000.00

The consolidated balance sheet will include the $15,000.00 of undiscounted notes, and the $5,000.00 contingent liability on discounted notes will be mentioned in a footnote.

If Company *A* transferred the $5,000.00 of customers' notes to Company *B*, an affiliated company, the accounts of the two companies might contain the following balances:

Company *A*'s Books		
Notes receivable	$20,000.00	
Notes receivable discounted		$5,000.00
Company *B*'s Books		
Notes receivable	$ 5,000.00	

Since the $5,000.00 of discounted notes are carried in the notes receivable accounts of both companies, and since the $5,000.00 credit to notes receivable discounted does not represent a contingent liability to outsiders, $5,000.00 of the notes receivable balance and the total notes receivable discounted credit balance should be eliminated.

But suppose that Company *B* has rediscounted $3,000.00 of the notes at the bank. The account balances and the eliminations in the working papers will be as follows:

	Company *A*	Company *B*	Eliminations	Consolidated Balance Sheet
Assets				
Notes receivable	$20,000	$5,000	$5,000	$20,000
Liabilities				
Notes receivable discounted	5,000	3,000	5,000	3,000

The $5,000.00 contingent liability on the books of Company *A* should be eliminated, with an offsetting elimination against the notes receivable on the books of Company *B*. The $3,000.00 contingent liability to outsiders, shown by the books of Company *B*, should be extended to the consolidated column so that it will not be overlooked when preparing the consolidated balance sheet; the balance sheet should show as an asset the $17,000.00 of notes not discounted with outsiders, and the contingent liability of $3,000.00 to outsiders should be mentioned in a footnote.

Intercompany bond holdings. When one company holds bonds of a related company, the bonds held as an asset by one company are sometimes offset against the bond liability of the other company, and only the net amount outstanding in the hands of the public is shown as a liability. It is preferable, however, to extend the balance of the asset account and the balance of the liability account to the balance sheet columns of the working papers, and deduct the intercompany holdings from the total liability in the consolidated balance sheet.

The situation is somewhat analogous to that of a corporation with an authorized bond issue of, say, $500,000.00, of which only $400,000.00 has been issued: such facts should be shown on the balance sheet thus:

Bonds payable—authorized	$500,000.00	
Less treasury bonds	100,000.00	
Bonds outstanding		$400,000.00

Similarly, in the case of intercompany bond holdings, the bonds are virtually treasury bonds of the organization, available for issuance or for use as collateral.

Premium or discount on intercompany bond holdings. If the company which purchased the bonds paid more or less than par for them, it may have written off the premium or discount immediately. From the individual company standpoint, it is better to charge the bond investment account with the purchase cost and to amortize the premium or discount. From the consolidated standpoint, the premium or discount on issuance by one company and the premium or discount on repurchases by another related company should probably be disposed of as they would be if the bonds were issued and retired by the same company.

To illustrate, assume that Company *B* issued bonds of a par value of $100,000.00 at a discount of $2,000.00, and that Company *A* acquired $10,000.00 of the bonds at a discount of $150.00, before any of the discount had been amortized by Company *B*. In the consolidated working papers, the cost of the bonds acquired may be detailed, the discount on purchase may be offset against the discount on sale applicable thereto, and the net discount applicable to the reacquired bonds may be written off against the parent company's surplus, as illustrated below:

	Company A	Company B	Adjustments Debit	Adjustments Credit	Consolidated
Assets					
Bonds of Company *B*—par.....	$10,000				$ 10,000
Discount on purchase of bonds..	150*		$150		
Discount on issuance of bonds...		$ 2,000		$200	1,800
Liabilities					
Bonds payable..................		100,000			100,000
Surplus—Company *A*..........	5,000		50		4,950

* Red.

The adjusting entry writes off $200.00 (or one tenth of the discount on issuance), as applicable to the 10% portion of the bonds reacquired; it also writes off the $150.00 discount on repurchase; and it charges the difference, $50.00, to surplus of the parent company so as to deduct it from the consolidated surplus.

Such an adjustment is conservative if it results in a net debit to surplus; but it would not be so conservative if the discount on purchase was greater than the discount on issuance, so that the adjustment involved a net credit to surplus. In such a case, it would be more conservative, but not obligatory, to include the net credit as a deferred credit in the consolidated balance sheet.

A theoretical objection may be raised against the illustrated treatment if the parent company does not own 100% of the stock of the company which issued the bonds and of the company which reacquired them. Assume that Company *A* owns 75% of the stock of Company *B* and 90% of the stock of Company *C*. Company *B* issued $100,000.00 of bonds at a discount and Company *C* acquired, at a discount of $4,000.00, all of these bonds at a date when Company *B* was still carrying $5,000.00 of unamortized discount. The elimination of the discounts by the method illustrated above would result as follows:

	Company A	Company B	Company C	Adjustments Debit	Adjustments Credit	Consolidated Balance Sheet
Assets						
Bonds of Co. *B*—par.			$100,000			$100,000
Discount on purchase of bonds..........			4,000*	$4,000		
Discount on issuance of bonds.........		$ 5,000			$ 5,000	
Liabilities						
Bonds payable......		100,000				100,000
Surplus	$25,000			1,000		24,000

* Red.

The $1,000.00 charge against the surplus of Company *A* is theoretically incorrect because it ignores the minority interests in Companies *B* and *C*. The gradual amortization of the discounts would affect the consolidated surplus (or surplus of Company *A*) and the minority interests as follows:

	Total	Surplus of Company *A*	Minority Interests
Discount on issuance—75% to Company *A* and 25% to minority of *B*	$5,000	$3,750	$1,250
Discount on repurchase—90% to Company *A* and 10% to minority of *C*	4,000	3,600	400
Net charges to surplus and to minority	$1,000	$ 150	$ 850

Greater accuracy, therefore, would result from an adjustment charging the surplus of Company *A* with only the $150.00 by which its surplus will ultimately be reduced. The facts would be shown in the consolidated working papers in the manner illustrated below:

	Company *A*	Company *B*	Company *C*	Adjustments Debit	Adjustments Credit	Consolidated Balance Sheet
Assets						
Bonds owned—par			$100,000			$100,000
Discount on purchase			4,000*	$3,600		400*
Discount on issuance		$ 5,000			$3,750	1,250
Liabilities						
Bonds payable		100,000				100,000
Surplus	$25,000			150		24,850

* Red.

The facts would be shown in the consolidated balance sheet as follows:

Assets

Deferred charges:		
Issuance discount on intercompany bonds—portion to be amortized by charges to minority interest in Company *B*		$1,250.00

Liabilities and Net Worth

Deferred credits:		
Acquisition discount on intercompany bonds—portion to be amortized by credits to minority interest in Company *B*		$ 400.00
Fixed liabilities:		
Bonds payable—Company *B*	$100,000.00	
Less intercompany owned bonds	100,000.00	
Outstanding		—

Accrued interest. If there are intercompany bonds or notes, the balance sheet of the company issuing the paper may show a liability for accrued interest. The company holding the paper should then show an asset of accrued interest receivable. The accrued interest receivable should be offset against the accrued interest payable, and only the net amount due to the outside creditors should be shown as a liability.

Declared dividends unpaid. If the subsidiary has declared dividends which are unpaid at the date of the balance sheet, its books will show a liability of dividends payable. The parent company's books should show an asset of dividends receivable, which should be offset against the dividends payable. The consolidated balance sheet will then show only the liability for dividends declared and payable to the outside, or minority, stockholders.

If, at the date of acquisition of the subsidiary stock, a dividend had been declared by the subsidiary but had not been paid, and the parent company became a stockholder of record to participate in the dividend, a portion of the purchase price equal to the declared dividend applicable to the shares acquired should be charged to dividends receivable and only the remainder should be charged to the stock investment account.

Adjusting intercompany accounts. All intercompany relations should be shown on the books of both related companies, so that the same amounts may be eliminated from the assets and the liabilities. If any intercompany transactions have been recorded on the books of one company only, they should be taken up on the books of the other company before the consolidated balance sheet is prepared.

Goods may have been sold by one company to another immediately prior to the close of the year and recorded in the current account of the selling company, but not taken up on the books of the purchasing company. These goods should be added to the purchasing company's inventory and credited to its current account with the selling company.

If services have been rendered by one company and recorded by a charge to the current account and by a credit to income, and if the balance sheet of the other company was drawn up before the transaction was recorded, an adjustment should be made debiting surplus and crediting the current account of the company rendering the service.

If a company holding bonds of a related company has not taken up its share of the accrued interest on these bonds, an adjustment should be made debiting bond interest receivable and crediting surplus.

If the subsidiary has declared a dividend which is unpaid at the date of the balance sheet and which is shown on its books as dividends payable, the holding company should take up its share by a debit to dividends receivable. The offsetting credit will depend upon the method adopted by the parent company for carrying its investment in the subsidiary stock. If it has taken up its share of subsidiary profits and losses, the offsetting credit for the dividend will be made in the investment account. If the investment is carried at cost, the credit will be made to surplus.

Illustration. Company *A* owns 90% of the stock of Company *B* and 95% of the stock of Company *C*. Company *A* has taken up its share of the profits and losses of Company *B*, but is carrying its investment in Company *C* at cost. The balance sheets on December 31, 1946, appear in the working papers on pages 256 and 257. The adjustments and eliminations in the working papers are described below.

Adjustment A. Company *A* acts as a selling agent for Company *B* on a commission basis. On December 31, 1946, Company *A* charged Company *B* $1,000.00 as commission on sales made during December, but this commission expense and liability have not been taken up on the books of Company *B*. Adjustment A, for $1,000.00, debits the surplus account of Company *B* and credits Company *B*'s current account with Company *A*.

Adjustment B. Company *A* has taken up its 90% interest in the profits of Company *B* for 1946, by a debit to investment in stock of Company *B* and a credit to surplus. Company *B*'s failure to record the $1,000.00 commission charge resulted in a $1,000.00 overstatement of Company *B*'s profit. The 90% portion of Company *B*'s profit taken up by Company *A* was therefore overstated $900.00. This overstatement is corrected by adjustment B, which debits the surplus of Company *A* and credits investment in stock of Company *B*, $900.00.

Adjustment C. On December 30, 1946, Company *B* drew a draft on Company *A* for $3,000.00 and deposited the proceeds. Company *B* debited cash and credited Company *A*. The draft was not presented to Company *A* until January 1947, and the transaction was not recorded by Company *A* before drawing up its balance sheet. Adjustment C, applicable to the accounts of Company *A*, debits the current account of Company *B* and credits cash, $3,000.00.

COMPANY *A* AND SUBSIDIARIES *B* AND *C*

Consolidated Balance Sheet Working Papers

December 31, 1946

Assets		Company *A*	Company *B*	Company *C*	Adjustments Debit	Adjustments Credit	Eliminations	Consolidated Balance Sheet
Investment in stock of Company *B*—90%		$ 64,000						
Overstatement of *B*'s profit						$ 900(B)		
Dividends declared by Company *B*						2,700(D)		
Eliminate book value:								
Capital stock—90% of $50,000							$ 45,000(a)	
Surplus (as adjusted) 90% of $15,500							13,950(b)	
Goodwill								$ 1,450(G)
Investment in stock of Company *C*—95% (at cost)		68,000						
Adjustment—95% of decrease in Company *C* surplus:								
Surplus at acquisition	$30,000							
Present surplus	18,000							
95% of decrease	$12,000					11,400(H)		
Eliminate book value:								
Capital stock—95% of $40,000							38,000(c)	
Surplus—95% of $18,000							17,100(d)	
Goodwill								1,500(G)
Cash		5,000	$ 20,000	$ 3,000		3,000(C)		25,000
Company *B* current		6,000			$ 3,000(C)		9,000(e)	
Advances to Company *C*		10,000					10,000(f)	
Investment in bonds of Company *B*:								
Par of bonds		40,000						40,000
Unamortized premium		1,000				1,000(G)		
Merchandise inventory			40,000	62,000				102,000
Notes receivable				11,000				11,000
Notes receivable—Company *C*			15,000				15,000(g)	
Plant			75,000	14,000				89,000
Dividends receivable:								
Company *B* stock—90% of $3,000					2,700(D)		2,700(i)	
Company *C* stock—95% of $2,000					1,900(E)		1,900(j)	
Bond interest receivable (on $40,000 Company *B* bonds)					1,200(F)		1,200(h)	
		$194,000	$150,000	$90,000			$153,850	$269,950

Liabilities and Net Worth							
Accounts payable	$ 25,000	$ 13,000	$ 5,000				$ 43,000
Bond interest accrued		1,500				$ 1,200(h)	300
Company *A* current		8,000			$ 1,000(A)	9,000(c)	
Notes receivable—Company *C*—discounted		6,000					6,000
Dividends payable:							
Company *B*		3,000				2,700(i)	300
Company *C*			2,000			1,900(j)	100
Advances from Company *A*			10,000			10,000(f)	
Notes payable—Company *B*			15,000			15,000(g)	
Bonds payable		50,000					50,000
Unamortized premium on bonds		2,000		$ 1,440(G)			560
Capital stock:							
Company *A*	100,000						100,000
Company *B*		50,000					
Eliminate Company *A*'s 90%						45,000(a)	
Minority interest—10%							5,000(M)
Company *C*			40,000				
Eliminate Company *A*'s 95%						38,000(c)	
Minority interest—5%							2,000(M)
Surplus:							
Company *A*	69,000						
Deduct 90% of overstatement of Company *B*'s profit				900(B)			
Add dividends on Company *C* stock					1,900(E)		
Add bond interest accrued					1,200(F)		
Deduct 95% of decrease in Company *C* surplus since acquisition				11,400(H)			
Add bond premium adjustment					440(G)		
Adjusted balance							60,240(S)
Company *B*		16,500					
Deduct commissions				1,000(A)			
Eliminate Company *A*'s 90% of $15,500						13,950(b)	
Minority interest—10%							1,550(M)
Company *C*			18,000				
Eliminate Company *A*'s 95%						17,100(d)	
Minority interest—5%							900(M)
	$194,000	$150,000	$90,000	$23,540	$23,540	$153,850	$269,950

Adjustment D. Company *B* has declared a dividend of $3,000.-00, of which amount $2,700.00 represents Company *A*'s 90%. The dividend liability is shown in the balance sheet of Company *B*, but the dividend receivable has not been taken up on the books of Company *A*. Adjustment D debits dividends receivable, $2,700.00; since Company *A* has recorded the profits, losses, and past dividends of Company *B* through the investment account, the offsetting credit of $2,700.00 is made in the investment account.

Adjustment E. Company *C* has declared a dividend of $2,-000.00, of which amount Company *A*'s 95%, or $1,900.00, has not been taken up on its books; adjustment E debits dividends receivable, $1,900.00. Since the parent company is carrying its investment in Company *C* at cost and regards dividends as income, this dividend is taken up by a credit to Company *A*'s surplus.

Adjustment F. Company *A* owns $40,000.00 par value of bonds issued by Company *B*; the accrued interest, $1,200.00 (at 6% per annum for six months), has not been taken up on Company *A*'s books. This adjustment debits bond interest receivable and credits Company *A*'s surplus, $1,200.00.

Adjustment G. The bonds of $40,000.00 par value owned are carried at $41,000.00; this latter amount includes $1,000.00 of unamortized premium on purchase. The balance sheet of Company *B* shows $2,000.00 of unamortized premium applicable to the total issue of $50,000.00 of bonds. Since Company *A* owns only 90% of the stock of Company *B* and 80% of its bonds, the adjustment of the two premium accounts is made as follows:

Unamortized premium on issuance (books of Company *B*)	$1,440.00	
($1,440 is 90% of 80% of the $2,000 balance in the premium account on *B*'s books.)		
Unamortized premium (books of Co. *A*)		$1,000.00
Surplus of Company *A*		440.00

Adjustment H. Company *A* is carrying its investment in Company *C* at cost. Company *C* had a surplus of $30,000.00 on the date at which its stock was acquired by Company *A*. Company *C*'s surplus on December 31, 1946 is $18,000.00. Company *A*'s 95% of the $12,000.00 decrease, or $11,400.00, should be debited to Company *A*'s surplus and credited to its investment in the stock of Company *C*.

Eliminations a *and* b. Ninety per cent of Company *B*'s capital stock and 90% of its surplus (as adjusted) on December 31, 1946 are eliminated from the parent company's investment account and from the subsidiary's stock and surplus accounts: $45,000.00 from capital stock and $13,950.00 from surplus.

Eliminations c *and* d. Ninety-five per cent of Company *C*'s capital stock and 95% of its surplus are eliminated from the parent company's investment account and from the subsidiary's capital stock and surplus accounts: $38,000.00 from capital stock and $17,100.00 from surplus.

Elimination e. Intercompany current accounts of Companies *A* and *B*, $9,000.00.

Elimination f. Advance from Company *A* to Company *C*, $10,000.00.

Elimination g. Company *B* has received $15,000.00 of notes from Company *C*. The intercompany notes receivable and notes payable accounts are eliminated; $6,000.00 of the notes have been discounted with outsiders, as shown by the credit balance of the notes receivable discounted account, which is extended to the consolidated column.

Elimination h. Accrued bond interest, $1,200.00, payable by Company *B* to Company *A*.

Eliminations i *and* j. Intercompany dividends.

COMPANY *A* AND SUBSIDIARY COMPANIES *B* AND *C*
Consolidated Balance Sheet
December 31, 1946

Assets

Current assets:		
Cash	$ 25,000.00	
Notes receivable	11,000.00	
Merchandise inventory	102,000.00	$138,000.00
Fixed assets:		
Plant	$ 89,000.00	
Goodwill	2,950.00	91,950.00
		$229,950.00

Liabilities and Net Worth

Current liabilities:		
Accounts payable	$ 43,000.00	
Notes payable	6,000.00	
Accrued bond interest	300.00	
Dividends payable	400.00	$ 49,700.00
Fixed liabilities:		
Bonds payable	$ 50,000.00	
Less intercompany owned bonds	40,000.00	10,000.00
Unamortized bond premium		560.00
Minority interests:		
Company *B*—10%	$ 6,550.00	
Company *C*—5%	2,900.00	9,450.00
Net worth:		
Capital stock	$100,000.00	
Surplus	60,240.00	160,240.00
		$229,950.00

Miscellaneous Matters

Minority column in working papers. If there are a number of subsidiaries, the liability and net worth section of the working papers may be somewhat simplified by including a minority column, as illustrated on page 261.

Minority interest; subsidiary deficit. In all working papers thus far prepared, the minority interest has been shown at an amount equal to the minority's share of the subsidiary's stock plus its share of the subsidiary's surplus, or minus its share of the subsidiary's deficit, at the date of the consolidated balance sheet; in other words, the minority interest has been shown at the book value of the minority stock. This treatment is shown by the following illustration, in which it is assumed that the parent company has taken up its share of subsidiary gains and losses; the minority interest is reduced by its share of the subsidiary's deficit.

	Company *P*	Company *S*	Eliminations	Consolidated Balance Sheet
Assets				
Investment in stock of Co. *S* (90%)	$ 38,000			
Eliminate book value:				
Capital stock—90% of $50,000.00			$45,000	
Deficit—90% of $10,000.00			9,000*	
Goodwill				$ 2,000G
Cash	22,000	$20,000		42,000
Merchandise	80,000	45,000		125,000
	$140,000	$65,000	$36,000	$169,000
Liabilities				
Accounts payable	$ 15,000	$25,000		$ 40,000
Capital stock:				
Company *P*	100,000			100,000
Company *S*		50,000		
Eliminate 90%			$45,000	
Minority—10%				5,000M
Surplus (deficit*):				
Company *P*	25,000			25,000S
Company *S*		10,000*		
Eliminate 90%			9,000*	
Minority—10%				1,000*M
	$140,000	$65,000	$36,000	$169,000

* Red.

Some accountants would show the minority interest at the par of the stock, without deducting the minority's share of the deficit.

If the minority's interest is not to be diminished by its $1,000.00 share of the subsidiary's deficit, the $1,000.00 shown in the foregoing working papers as a deduction from the minority's interest would be deducted from the parent company's surplus; as a result,

COMPANY *A* AND SUBSIDIARIES *B* AND *C*
Consolidated Balance Sheet Working Papers—(*Continued*)
December 31, 1946

Liabilities and Net Worth	Company *A*	Company *B*	Company *C*	Adjustments Debit	Adjustments Credit	Eliminations	Minority	Consolidated Balance Sheet
Adjustment column totals brought forward.				$ 8,800	$19,000			
Accounts payable	$ 25,000	$ 13,000	$ 5,000					$ 43,000
Bond interest accrued		1,500				$ 1,200(h)		300
Company *A* current		8,000			1,000(A)	9,000(e)		
Notes receivable—Company *C*—discounted		6,000						6,000
Dividends payable:								
Company *B*		3,000				2,700(i)		300
Company *C*			2,000			1,900(j)		100
Advances from Company *A*			10,000			10,000(f)		
Notes payable—Company *B*			15,000			15,000(g)		
Bonds payable		50,000						50,000
Unamortized premium on bonds		2,000		1,440(G)				560
Capital Stock:								
Company *A*	100,000							100,000
Company *B*		50,000				45,000(a)	$5,000(B)	
Company *C*			40,000			38,000(c)	2,000(C)	
Surplus:								
Company *A*	69,000							
Deduct 90% of overstatement in Co. *B* profit				900(B)				
Add dividends on Company *C* stock					1,900(E)			
Add bond interest accrued					1,200(F)			
Deduct 95% of decrease in Company *C* surplus since acquisition				11,400(H)				
Add bond premium adjustment					440(G)			
Adjusted balance								60,240(S)
Company *B*		16,500		1,000(A)		13,950(b)	1,550(B)	
Company *C*			18,000			17,100(d)	900(C)	
Total minority interest							$9,450	9,450(M)
	$194,000	$150,000	$90,000	$23,540	$23,540	$153,850		$269,950

the minority interest would be shown at $5,000.00, the par of the stock held by the minority, and the consolidated surplus would be shown at $24,000.00.

Accountants who follow this latter method do so on the theory that, while the minority will share in profits, the parent company will be obliged to "absorb the losses" of the subsidiary.

Although it is true that the subsidiary may be such an essential part of the organization that the parent company will consider it expedient to retain its ownership of the stock in spite of these losses, it does not seem necessary for the parent company to assume the magnanimous position of allowing the minority stockholders to share in subsidiary profits while relieving them from any reduction in the book value of their stock caused by subsidiary losses. As long as the subsidiary is able to pay its debts, the losses merely reduce the value of all shares proportionately. If the subsidiary becomes unable to pay its debts, the parent company may advance the funds necessary to prevent the creditors from forcing the subsidiary into liquidation.

As an extreme illustration, let us assume that the subsidiary losses have resulted in a deficit equal to the capital stock, and that the parent company has not seen fit to make advances in order to keep the business out of the hands of the creditors. The creditors therefore take possession, and the parent company loses its stock and the minority stockholders lose theirs. But the parent company does not bear the minority's loss.

On the other hand, assume that the parent company has made advances, so that the subsidiary's condition is as follows:

Subsidiary Balance Sheet

Net assets	$ 50,000.00	Advances from parent	$ 50,000.00
Deficit	100,000.00	Capital stock	100,000.00

The parent company may now take over the assets of the subsidiary in settlement of the advances; again the parent company loses its portion of the stock and the minority stockholders lose theirs.

The purpose of a balance sheet is to show the present financial condition of a business organization. It appears that a consolidated balance sheet fulfills this purpose if it shows all of the assets and liabilities of the combined companies, and the actual present interests of the parent company and of the minority stockholders in these net assets. Regardless of what the parent company may have to do in the future (and it is difficult to see how it can be obliged to bear more than its share of the loss), it cannot be denied that the present book value of the minority's interest in the net assets of the organization is measured by the minority's percentage of the subsidiary's capital stock and surplus or deficit.

The propriety of stating the minority interest at a net amount after deduction of a proportion of the deficit has been questioned on the ground that the controlling company sometimes finds it desirable to buy out minority stockholders, and that the minority stockholders may not be willing to sell at the book value of their holdings. This does not seem to be a pertinent argument because the consolidated balance sheet is prepared from the standpoint of a going concern; the market values of a corporation's stock are not properly given consideration in the preparation of its balance sheet.

Detailing minority interests. Custom differs with regard to the detailing of minority interests in the consolidated balance sheet; sometimes the capital stock and surplus elements of each minority interest are shown; in other instances, the aggregate of the minority interests in all companies is shown in a single amount.

Since a consolidated balance sheet is essentially a balance sheet of the parent company, prepared on the assumption that the legal fact of separate corporate entities can be ignored for the specific purposes of the statement, and that underlying assets and liabilities can be stated in lieu of the investments, it follows that the minority stockholders should not look to consolidated statements for information about balance sheet facts relative to their investments, but should look to the balance sheets of the subsidiaries. For this reason, the detailing of the minority interests in the consolidated balance sheet seems unnecessary.

Stock dividends. To illustrate some of the problems which may arise in connection with stock dividends paid by a subsidiary, assume that Company *S* had a capital stock of $100,000.00 and a surplus of $50,000.00 on January 1, 1946, and that Company *P* purchased 90% of the stock on that date. The book value of the stock acquired was 90% of $150,000.00, or $135,000.00 and the purchase price was $140,000.00. Hence there was a goodwill payment of $5,000.00. During 1946, the subsidiary made a profit of $25,000.00, and issued a stock dividend of $40,000.00, of which Company *P* received stock of a par value of $36,000.00. Various conditions with respect to the parent company's method of accounting may be encountered; in all cases, it will be assumed that the parent company has no surplus from its own operations.

It is also assumed that the parent company made no entry for the stock dividend; none should be made, because the stock dividend merely converts a portion of the subsidiary surplus into capital stock, without affecting the parent company's interest.

First, assume that the parent company takes up its $22,500.00 share of the profit of Company *S* for 1946 by a debit to the investment account and a credit to surplus.

Eliminations will be made in the consolidated working papers as follows:

	Company *P*	Company *S*	Eliminations	Consolidated Balance Sheet
Assets				
Investment in stock of Company *S*....	$162,500			
Eliminate book value:				
Capital stock—90% of $140,000.00			$126,000	
Surplus—90% of $35,000.00......			31,500	
Goodwill..........................				$ 5,000G
Liabilities				
Capital stock—Company *S*..........		$140,000	126,000	14,000M
Surplus:				
Company *P*......................	22,500			22,500S
Company *S*......................		35,000	31,500	3,500M

Note that the goodwill is $5,000.00, the minority interest is $17,500.00, and the consolidated surplus is $22,500.00.

Second, let us assume that the parent company is carrying the investment at cost, and has made no entry for the stock dividend. It will be necessary to make an adjustment of Company *P*'s investment and surplus accounts, by taking up its $22,500.00 share of the profit of Company *S*; eliminations can then be made as in the preceding case.

	Company *P*	Company *S*	Adjustments Debit	Adjustments Credit	Eliminations	Consolidated Balance Sheet
Assets						
Investment in stock of Co. *S*—90%..	$140,000					
Add 90% of *S*'s net profit since acquisition.......			$22,500A			
Eliminate book value:						
Capital stock—90%........					$126,000	
Surplus—90%..					31,500	
Goodwill..........						$ 5,000G
Liabilities						
Capital stock—Co. *S*		$140,000			126,000	14,000M
Surplus:						
Company *P*......	—					
Add 90% of Company *S* profit........				$22,500A		22,500S
Company *S*......		35,000			31,500	3,500M

Note that the goodwill, the minority interest, and the consolidated surplus are the same as those shown in the statements in the preceding case.

In the preceding illustrations it was assumed that the stock dividend paid by the subsidiary was less than the subsidiary surplus at the date of acquisition and, consequently, the parent company's interest in the subsidiary earnings since acquisition is still carried in the subsidiary's surplus account.

Let us now assume that, at the date of acquisition of a 90% interest for $140,000.00, the subsidiary had a surplus of $50,000.00, that it made a profit of $25,000.00 during the following year, and that it issued a stock dividend of $60,000.00. The parent company has taken up its 90% of the subsidiary profits and has made no entry for the stock dividend. The working papers will be as follows:

	Company *S*		Company *P*	
	Capital Stock	Surplus	Investment in Co. *S*	Surplus
Balances	$160,000	$15,000	$162,500	$22,500
Eliminate reciprocals (90%)	144,000	13,500	157,500	
Minority interest	$ 16,000	$ 1,500		
Goodwill			$ 5,000	
Consolidated surplus				$22,500

Although the consolidated surplus is $22,500.00 (representing 90% of the subsidiary's earnings since acquisition), it must be noted that the stock dividend was $10,000.00 in excess of the subsidiary surplus at acquisition, and that this $10,000.00 must be regarded as a capitalization of earnings since acquisition. The $10,000.00 cannot be used for cash dividends; the parent company's proportion of this is $9,000.00; and hence $9,000.00 of the $22,500.00 consolidated surplus is restricted with regard to its availability for dividends by the subsidiary to the parent company, and by the parent company to its stockholders. Therefore, the surplus should be shown in the consolidated balance sheet in some manner similar to the following:

Surplus:		
Restricted—surplus earned by subsidiary since acquisition capitalized by stock dividend	$ 9,000.00	
Free	13,500.00	$22,500.00

Or the restriction may be stated in a balance sheet footnote.

Holdings of no-par stock. The method of making eliminations is not affected by the fact that the subsidiary's stock is without par value. The book value of the parent company's ownings is determined by ascertaining the per cent of subsidiary stock owned, and by multiplying the subsidiary's capital stock and surplus account balances by this per cent. To illustrate, assume that the subsidiary has an issue of 3,000 shares of no-par value stock, for which $250,000.00 was received and credited to capital stock. The subsidiary also has a surplus of $60,000.00. The parent company acquires 2,400 shares at a cost of $260,000.00.

Consolidated Working Papers

	Company *P*	Company *S*	Eliminations	Consolidated Balance Sheet
Assets				
Investment in stock of Company *S* (80%) 2,400 shares of a total issue of 3,000	$260,000			
Eliminate book value:				
Capital stock—80% of $250,000.00			$200,000	
Surplus—80% of $60,000.00			48,000	
Goodwill				$12,000G
Liabilities				
Capital stock—Company *S*		$250,000		
Eliminate parent company's 80%			200,000	
Minority—20%				50,000M
Surplus—Company *S*		60,000		
Eliminate parent company's 80%			48,000	
Minority—20%				12,000M

Holdings of both common and preferred stock. When the parent company owns both common and preferred stock, it may be necessary to divide the subsidiary surplus into the portions applicable to the two classes of stock, in order to determine their book values and to make proper eliminations. In making this division, it is necessary to consider whether the subsidiary's preferred stock is cumulative or non-cumulative, and participating or non-participating, and whether there are any cumulative dividends in arrears. In the following illustrations, it is assumed that the parent company bought 80% of the preferred stock for $48,000.00 (par value $40,000.00) and 90% of the common stock for $106,000.00 (par value $90,000.00). The subsidiary had no surplus at the date of acquisition. The total goodwill was therefore $8,000.00 + $16,000.00, or $24,000.00. At the end of one year the subsidiary had made a profit of $18,000.00.

First, it is assumed that the preferred stock is non-cumulative and non-participating, and that the year's dividend of $3,000.00 has been paid on the preferred stock. The preferred, therefore, has no further claim on the surplus of the subsidiary, which was reduced to $15,000.00 by the payment of the preferred dividend, and the entire $15,000.00 is applicable to the common stock. The parent company should have taken up 90% of this amount, or $13,500.00, as well as the $2,400.00 dividend on its holdings of preferred stock.

Consolidated Working Papers

	Company *P*	Company *S*	Eliminations	Consolidated Balance Sheet
Assets				
Investment in preferred stock of Company *S* (80%)	$ 48,000			
Eliminate book value:				
Capital stock—80% of $50,000.00			$40,000	
Goodwill				$ 8,000G
Investment in common stock of Company *S* (90%)	119,500			
Eliminate book value:				
Capital stock—90% of $100,000.00			90,000	
Surplus—90% of $15,000.00			13,500	
Goodwill				16,000G
Liabilities and Net Worth				
Capital stock preferred—Company *S*		$ 50,000		
Eliminate parent company's 80%			40,000	
Minority—20%				10,000M
Capital stock common—Company *S*		100,000		
Eliminate parent company's 90%			90,000	
Minority—10%				10,000M
Surplus—Company *S* (applicable to common stock)		15,000		
Eliminate parent company's 90%			13,500	
Minority—10%				1,500M
Surplus—Company *P*	15,900			15,900S

Second, it is assumed that the preferred stock is cumulative and non-participating, and that there are no dividends in arrears. The rights of the preferred stockholders in the subsidiary surplus have thus been satisfied by the payment of the dividend, and the entire surplus is applicable to the common stock. Therefore, the working papers would be identical with those just shown.

Third, it is assumed that the preferred stock is cumulative but non-participating, and that one year's dividend of 6% is in arrears. The surplus is therefore $18,000.00. As the profits have been earned, the preferred stockholders have a claim against them to the extent of $3,000.00, and the parent company might take up its 80% thereof by a debit to the preferred stock investment account and a credit to earnings. The subsidiary surplus is divided into two parts: $3,000.00 applicable to preferred stock, and $15,000.00 applicable to common stock.

Consolidated Working Papers

	Company P	Company S	Eliminations	Consolidated Balance Sheet
Assets				
Investment in preferred stock of Company S (80%)	$ 50,400			
Eliminate book value:				
Capital stock—80% of $50,000.00			$40,000	
Surplus—80% of $3,000.00			2,400	
Goodwill				$ 8,000G
Investment in common stock of Company S (90%)	119,500			
Eliminate book value:				
Capital stock—90% of $100,000.00			90,000	
Surplus—90% of $15,000.00			13,500	
Goodwill				16,000G
Liabilities and Net Worth				
Capital stock—preferred—Company S		$ 50,000		
Eliminate parent company's 80%			40,000	
Minority—20%				10,000M
Capital stock—common—Company S		100,000		
Eliminate parent company's 90%			90,000	
Minority—10%				10,000M
Surplus—Company S (applicable to preferred stock)		3,000		
Eliminate parent company's 80%			2,400	
Minority—20%				600M
Surplus—Company S (applicable to common stock)		15,000		
Eliminate parent company's 90%			13,500	
Minority—10%				1,500M
Surplus—Company P ($2,400 + $13,500)	15,900			15,900S

Fourth, it is assumed that the preferred stock is cumulative and participating, and that no dividends have been paid on either preferred or common stock. Since the preferred stock is participating, $6,000.00 of the earnings are applicable to the preferred and $12,000.00 are applicable to the common. The parent company might make the following entry:

Investment in preferred stock of Co. S (80% of $6,000.00)	$ 4,800	
Investment in common stock of Co. S (90% of $12,000.00)	10,800	
Surplus		$15,600
To take up our share of the earnings of Company S.		

The goodwill, minority interest, and consolidated surplus are computed in the working papers on page 269.

If the subsidiary has an outstanding issue of preferred stock and the parent company acquires none of it, or acquires different percentages of preferred and common stocks, very troublesome questions may arise in the determination of the book values of the stocks acquired. The surplus applicable to the common stock is the remainder after having allotted to the preferred stock what-

Consolidated Working Papers

	Company P	Company S	Eliminations	Consolidated Balance Sheet
Assets				
Investment in preferred stock of Company S (80%)	$ 52,800			
Eliminate book value:				
Capital stock—80% of $50,000.00			$40,000	
Surplus—80% of $6,000.00			4,800	
Goodwill				$ 8,000G
Investment in common stock of Company S (90%)	116,800			
Eliminate book value:				
Capital stock—90% of $100,000.00			90,000	
Surplus—90% of $12,000.00			10,800	
Goodwill				16,000G
Liabilities and Net Worth				
Capital stock preferred—Company S		$ 50,000		
Eliminate parent company's 80%			40,000	
Minority—20%				10,000M
Capital stock common—Company S		100,000		
Eliminate parent company's 90%			90,000	
Minority—10%				10,000M
Surplus—Company S		18,000		
Applicable to preferred—$6,000.00:				
Eliminate parent company's 80%			4,800	
Minority—20%				1,200M
Applicable to common—$12,000.00:				
Eliminate parent company's 90%			10,800	
Minority—10%				1,200M
Surplus—Company P	15,600			15,600S

ever interest it may have in the subsidiary surplus. The preferred stock interest in surplus is affected not only by the cumulative or non-cumulative features and by the participating or non-participating features, but also by dividends in arrears. Moreover, the subsidiary may have a deficit and preferred dividends may be in arrears, or the preferred stock may be entitled in liquidation to par, or to par plus dividends in arrears. Also, there is some question whether the apportionment of a surplus should be made purely on the basis of the provisions of the preferred stock or whether dividend policies should be recognized. For instance, if a subsidiary has outstanding 6% preferred stock of $100,000.00 and outstanding common stock of $100,000.00, the preferred being cumulative and participating with no dividends in arrears, consideration of only the terms of issuance of the preferred stock would result in apportioning the surplus in equal amounts between the preferred and common stocks, because the preferred is participating. However, the participation rights govern only dividends distributed and do not necessarily mean that a certain portion of the undistributed earnings appertains to the preferred stock. For instance, if the subsidiary has long followed the policy of paying only 6% dividends on the preferred and common shares, there is a question, from a practical point of view, whether the preferred stockholders will ever participate in the accumulated surplus.

Arbitrary entries in investment account. In some instances, a parent company will not take up the profits and losses of its subsidiary but will, at intervals, make entries of an arbitrary amount to raise or lower the balance of the investment account to an amount regarded as representing the value of the stock owned. If the entry adjusts the balance of the account to the book value of the stock, as measured by the capital stock and surplus accounts of the subsidiary, the elimination of book value at the balance sheet date will have the effect of eliminating from the consolidated balance sheet any goodwill in the stock purchase. To illustrate, Company *P* purchased 90% of the stock of Company *S*, paying $115,000.00 therefor. At the date of acquisition, Company *P* had a capital stock of $100,000.00 and a surplus of $20;000.00, so that its book value was $120,000.00. As 90% of $120,000.00 is $108,000.00, there was a goodwill element of $7,000.00 in the purchase. The investment was carried at cost until the end of the year, at which time the subsidiary had a surplus of $50,000.00, and a total net worth of $150,000.00. Ninety per cent of this amount is $135,000.00, and Company *P* erroneously made an entry debiting the investment account and crediting surplus with $20,-000.00, to raise the balance of the investment account from $115,-000.00 to $135,000.00. The following working papers show that the $7,000.00 goodwill payment was thus, in effect, written off.

	Company *P*	Company *S*	Eliminations	Consolidated Balance Sheet
Assets				
Investment in stock of Company *S* (90%)	$135,000			
Eliminate book value:				
Capital stock—90% of $100,000.00.			$90,000	
Surplus—90% of $50,000.00.......			45,000	
Liabilities				
Capital stock—Company *S*............		$100,000		
Eliminate parent company's 90%....			90,000	
Minority interest—10%............				$10,000M
Surplus:				
Company *P*......................	20,000			20,000S
Company *S*......................		50,000		
Eliminate parent company's 90%..			45,000	
Minority interest—10%.........				5,000M

These working papers show that the goodwill of $7,000.00 has been written off and that the parent company's surplus is only $20,000.00, although it should be 90% of the subsidiary's $30,000.00 profits for the year, or $27,000.00. Because such arbitrary entries produce erroneous results, it is advisable to reverse them by adjusting entries in the consolidated working papers, and proceed with the adjustments and eliminations in the usual manner.

CHAPTER 47

Parent and Subsidiary Accounting (Continued)—Miscellaneous Matters

Profits in inventories. When one company sells goods at a profit to a related company, the minority stockholders of the selling company have a right to consider that the profit has been realized, since the goods have been sold to a company in which they have no interest. The parent company, which controls the organization and looks upon the various subsidiaries virtually as departments of the organization, should not regard the profit as realized until the goods have been resold to a purchaser outside of the organization.

Therefore, if, at the date of the consolidated balance sheet, the inventories of any of the related companies contain goods that were purchased from other related companies after the selling companies' stocks were acquired by the parent company, the inventories should be analyzed to determine how much of their present carrying value is composed of profits added by the selling companies. After this unrealized profit has been ascertained, a reserve should be created, out of the parent company's surplus, for the parent company's portion of such unrealized profit.

To illustrate, it is assumed that Company *P* owns 90% of the stock of Company *S*. Company *S* has sold goods to Company *P* during the year at a profit, and the inventory of Company *P* at the end of the year includes goods purchased from Company *S* on which the latter company made a profit of \$1,000.00. Since Company *P*, in taking up its share of the profits of Company *S*, has taken up \$900.00 of this profit, a reserve should be created by deducting \$900.00 from the parent company's surplus and transferring it to a reserve.

The reserve for unrealized profits may be shown on the consolidated balance sheet as a deduction from the inventories. Inventories should be priced at cost (unless market is lower), and cost should not include the organization's share of unrealized profits resulting from transfers from one related company to another. Or the inventories may be shown at the net amount after the intercompany profit has been deducted, without showing the reserve on the balance sheet.

If inventory values have been reduced from cost to market, and the amount of this reduction is at least equal to the intercompany profit included in the gross value, it appears unnecessary to create a reserve for the intercompany profit.

Some accountants have advocated that a 100% reserve should be created for unrealized profits taken by a subsidiary on intercompany sales, even though there is a minority interest. Those who advocate this procedure state that a reserve less than 100% does not reduce the inventories to cost as cost would be stated if all of the companies were, in fact, one company.

This seems to raise a fundamental question: What is the purpose of a consolidated balance sheet? Is it a statement based on the theoretical assumption that a group of related companies are, in effect, one company? Or is it essentially a parent company balance sheet in which underlying assets and liabilities take the place of stock investments? The answer to these questions can be found in the answer to another question: What is customarily shown as net worth in a consolidated balance sheet? Since the consolidated net worth does not include the minority interest, it appears obvious that the consolidated balance sheet is essentially a parent company statement;* the net worth is the parent company's

* The statement that a consolidated balance sheet is essentially a parent company statement, appears to be true if one accepts current practice in the preparation of consolidated statements as the correct procedure. Or stated conversely: If a consolidated balance sheet is essentially a parent company statement, then (*a*) the net worth shown therein should be the parent company's net worth, adjusted by the parent's share of the undistributed earnings of the subsidiaries since acquisition, (*b*) reserves for intercompany profit should be in amounts equal to the parent's share of such profits, (*c*) the minority interests should be shown at amounts determined wholly from the balance sheets of the subsidiaries and without modification as the result of the consolidating procedure; and (*d*) the consolidated balance sheet should include as goodwill the balances of the goodwill accounts on the books of the related companies plus any goodwill elements in the cost to the parent company of its investments in subsidiaries. In 1944, the American Accounting Association published a monograph, *The Entity Theory of Consolidated Statements*, by Maurice Moonitz, Ph.D., which advocated the preparation of consolidated balance sheets in a manner based on a different concept of the nature and purpose of consolidated statements. In this monograph Doctor Moonitz maintains, in effect, that a consolidated balance sheet is not essentially a parent company statement; that it is a balance sheet of a business entity with two classes of proprietary interests—the majority interest and the minority interest; and that, in the preparation of the consolidated balance sheet, these interests should be treated consistently. Starting with this entity concept and arguing for consistency, he advocates certain procedures not in accord with present general practice. Two such procedures are: (1) the creation of reserves for 100% of intercompany profit, by reduction of the minority interest as well as of the consolidated surplus; (2) an adjustment of the minority interest by an addition for goodwill applicable to the minority holdings of subsidiary stock if the parent company's acquisition cost included a goodwill element—for instance, if the parent company acquired 80% of the subsidiary stock at a price which included a goodwill element of $8,000.00, a goodwill element of $2,000.00 would be regarded as applicable to the minority holdings, and the consolidated goodwill and minority interest would be

net worth on a consolidated basis, and the minority interest is a liability, or quasi liability.

If, then, Company *P* owns 90% of the stock of Company *S*, and if Company *P*'s inventory contains goods purchased from Company *S* on which Company *S* made a profit of $10,000.00, the customary procedure of setting up only a 90% reserve, or $9,000.00, seems correct. It does not seem proper to set up an additional $1,000.00 out of the parent company, or consolidated, surplus; if the parent company has taken up only 90% of the subsidiary's profit, including $9,000.00 derived from the intercompany transaction, there seems to be no propriety in charging the consolidated surplus with $10,000.00. If a 100% reserve is created, $1,000.00 thereof should be charged against the minority interest; but the intercompany profit should be regarded as realized, so far as the minority stockholders are concerned, because the goods have been sold to a company in which they have no interest. Moreover, since the minority interest is tantamount to a liability for consolidated balance sheet purposes, there seems to be no propriety in reducing the liability by the deduction of profits to which the minority stockholders are entitled.

But assume that Company *P* sold the goods to Company *S*, making a $10,000.00 profit. What should be the amount of the reserve? It might appear that, since there is a 10% minority interest in Company *S*, 10% of the profit could be regarded as realized in the sense that Company *P* sold 10% of the goods to the minority interest in Company *S*. However, Company *P*'s surplus has been increased by the entire $10,000.00 profit; unless the parent company were obliged to remove the entire $10,000.00 from its surplus by the creation of a reserve, the parent company would be in a position arbitrarily to inflate its profits by forcing the subsidiary to purchase merchandise at such a profit as the parent company might dictate.

Care must be exercised in determining the amount of the reserve if the parent company owns several subsidiaries. To illustrate, assume that Company *P* owns 90% of the stock of Company *S* and 75% of the stock of Company *T*. If Company *S*'s inventory contains goods on which Company *T* made a $10,000.00 profit, the reserve should be 75% of $10,000.00, because the parent company takes up 75% of the profit of Company *T*. On the other hand, if Company *T* holds merchandise which it has purchased from Company *S*, the reserve should be 90% of the profit, because the parent company takes up 90% of the profit of Company *S*.

---

increased by $2,000.00. It will be interesting to see whether the accounting profession accepts this entity theory and changes current practices accordingly.

The situation may be further complicated by assuming that Company *P* owns merchandise that it bought from Company *S*, which made a profit of $10,000.00 on the sale to Company *P*; furthermore, Company *S* acquired the merchandise from Company *T*, which made a profit of $6,000.00 on the sale. Since Company *P* owns 90% of the stock of Company *S* and 75% of the stock of Company *T*, the reserve should be:

90% of $10,000.00 profit made by *S* on sale to *P*	$ 9,000.00
75% of $6,000.00 profit made by *T* on sale to *S*	4,500.00
Total reserve	$13,500.00

Reserve based on net profit. It has been suggested by some accountants that the reserve for intercompany profits in inventories should be determined on the basis of the selling affiliate's rate of net profit instead of on its rate of gross profit. This procedure would, of course, result in the establishment of a smaller reserve. The procedure probably would be justified if all expenses varied in exact proportion to the sales; this, however, is not the normal condition. Many expenses are fixed; others vary, but not in direct proportion to the sales; and it is therefore incorrect to assume that the elimination of the intercompany sales would result in a corresponding reduction in the expenses. Neither is it practicable to undertake to allocate expenses between intercompany and outside sales. Under the circumstances, therefore, the expedient and conservative procedure is to compute the reserve for intercompany profit on the basis of the rate of gross profit.

Profits from sales before stock acquisition. If the inventories contain goods which were sold by one company to another prior to their affiliation, should a reserve for intercompany profit be created? Most accountants appear to believe that no reserve should be provided. The companies were not related when the sale was made; hence the profit was not intercompany profit.

If the sale was made by a company which subsequently became a subsidiary, the creation of a reserve would require a charge to the parent company, or consolidated, surplus, or a charge to the subsidiary surplus as of the date of acquisition. There seems to be no propriety in reducing the parent company or consolidated surplus by the amount of a profit which has not been included therein. Of course, the reduction will be only temporary and the reserve will be restored to surplus after the goods are sold; but even a temporary deduction does not appear warranted, particularly if the effect is to add into consolidated earnings subsequent to acquisition a profit made by a subsidiary prior to acquisition. The creation of a reserve by charge to the surplus of the subsidiary as of the date of acquisition is even less justifiable, since it causes a reduction in the book value of the subsidiary at the date of acquisition, and thus increases any goodwill arising from consolidation; moreover, it results in throwing the profit into the consolidated earnings of the period between the date of acquisition of the subsidiary and the date of sale of the goods to outsiders.

If the sale was made by the parent company, one might take the position that, from the consolidated standpoint, the parent company is reacquiring its merchandise and any profit on the sale should be canceled upon the reacquisition. Moreover, since the sale was made by the parent company, the profit is in the parent company's surplus; therefore, the creation of a reserve from the parent company's surplus does not involve a surplus charge without a preceding surplus credit. Nevertheless, the creation of a reserve appears to be improper because of the effect on the consolidated income of subsequent periods. For, if a parent company or one of its subsidiaries sells merchandise to another company which subsequently becomes a subsidiary, the creation of a reserve for profit in the inventory of the new subsidiary at the date of acquisition results in a reduction of the consolidated earnings for the prior period and an addition to the consolidated earnings of a subsequent period. If a transaction is not an intercompany transaction when it occurs, there seems to be no propriety in retroactively classifying it as such and thereby transferring a non-intercompany profit of one year to consolidated profits of a subsequent year.

Intercompany sales at a loss. A reserve for intercompany profits in inventories is intended to produce two results: adjust the inventories to intercompany cost, and eliminate intercompany profits from consolidated income. Consistency, therefore, seems to require that, if intercompany sales are made at a loss, the inventory valuation should be increased to intercompany cost, and the consolidated income should not be affected by the intercompany loss.

Some accountants advocate that no adjustments should be made for intercompany losses; they support this position on the general ground of conservatism, or on the specific ground that sales at a loss may indicate a decline in market value and that such a decline should be recognized by valuing the inventory at the reduced intercompany sales price. The answer appears to be: If there has been no decline in market value, conservatism is not justified and merely introduces a secret reserve into the consolidated balance sheet. If there has been a decline in market value, the proper treatment is to keep the consolidating procedure on a consistent basis by eliminating the intercompany loss, and then reducing the inventory valuation from cost to market.

Intercompany profits on construction. When one company produces fixed assets for another related company and makes a profit on the construction, a reserve should be created to eliminate the parent company's proportion of such profit and reduce the fixed assets to cost. As already shown in connection with inventories, the cost may properly include the profit applicable to the minority interest of the selling company. The parent company cannot equitably ask the minority stockholders of its subsidiary to forego their share of the profit on work done for a company in which they have no interest; nor can the parent company reasonably be called upon to set up a reserve for the total profit made by a subsidiary, if the parent company owns only 90% of the stock and has taken up only 90% of the profit on the construction.

To illustrate, assume that Company *P* owns 90% of the stock of Company *S*. After the combination is effected, the latter company sells fixed assets to Company *P* at a profit of $1,000.00. At the end of the year, Company *P* will take up $900.00 of the profit which Company *S* made on the sale, and it should therefore create a reserve of $900.00 for unrealized profit in fixed assets.

The question of intercompany profits on the construction of fixed assets is a much more complex one than that of intercompany profits in inventories. Intercompany profits in inventories will become realized profits when the goods are sold to outsiders, and the reserve will disappear when the goods are disposed of. In the case of fixed assets, however, the property is not ordinarily disposed of through sale, and it might seem, therefore, that the reserve should be kept intact and appear as a deduction on the balance sheet at the original amount so long as the fixed assets are owned. But since fixed assets are virtually disposed of gradually through use and depreciation, it seems logical to reduce the depreciation charges to a basis of intercompany cost. This view is strengthened when it is remembered that depreciation should be based on cost, which cannot be two different things for two different purposes. If cost for consolidated balance sheet purposes is purchase price less intercompany profit, then cost for depreciation purposes should be the same amount. If manufacturing expense is charged with depreciation on the intercompany purchase price, the costs of manufacture on a consolidated basis are overstated, because depreciation is computed on a value in excess of the cost to the organization.

It is not difficult to put this theory into practice if the parent company owns the asset on which the intercompany profit was made. Two methods are available:

(1) The parent company may write down the asset to intercompany cost by debiting surplus and crediting the asset account instead of crediting a reserve for intercompany profit. Depreciation will then be computed on the carrying value of the property as shown by the asset account. This procedure will produce satisfactory results from a consolidated standpoint, but not from the standpoint of the parent company as a separate corporate entity, because it will not reflect the cost of the property to the parent company.

(2) The parent company may carry the reserve and compute depreciation for consolidated balance sheet purposes on the carrying value of the property as measured by the debit balance in the asset account minus the credit balance in the reserve for intercompany profit.

To illustrate, assume that Company *P* owns 90% of the stock of Company *S*, and that, during the year, Company *S* manufactured for Company *P* machinery which it delivered to Company *P* at the end of the year, billing that company $25,000.00. The profit made by Company *S* was $5,000.00. Company *P*, in taking up its share of the profits of Company *S*, took up 90% of this amount, or $4,500.00. If Company *P* follows the first method suggested above, it will debit its surplus and credit the machinery account $4,500.00, thus reducing the asset to $20,500.00, which is intercompany cost after the minority stockholders of Company *S* are allowed their 10% of the profit. Depreciation will then be computed on $20,500.00. If Company *P* follows the second method suggested above, it will debit surplus and credit a reserve for unrealized profit in fixed assets, $4,500.00; it will then compute depreciation on the $25,000.00 balance in the asset account minus the $4,500.00 balance in the reserve for intercompany profit.

The theory is not so easily put into practice if the company making the profit sold the assets to another affiliated company instead of to the parent company. To illustrate, assume that Company *P* owns 90% of the stock of Company *S* and 80% of the stock of Company *T*. Company *T* has sold to Company *S* for $50,000.00 machinery which cost $40,000.00. When Company *P* takes up its 80% of the profits of Company *T*, it takes up $8,000.00 of this unrealized intercompany profit and should therefore create a reserve of $8,000.00. The first method suggested above is not practicable in this case; the asset is on the books of Company *S* while the unrealized profit reserve must be set up in the consolidated working papers out of the surplus of Company *P*. It is impossible to write down the asset on the books of Company *S*, because such a write-down would involve a debit to the surplus of Company *S*, a procedure which would be improper because the intercompany profit went into *P*'s surplus. The asset will therefore go on to the books of Company *S* at $50,000.00, and the reserve will be set up at $8,000.00 out of *P*'s surplus.

For consolidated balance sheet purposes, the cost of the asset was $42,000.00, but Company *S* will compute depreciation on a basis of $50,000.00, which was the cost to Company *S* as a separate corporation. If the rate of depreciation is 10%, the depreciation on a straight-line basis will be $5,000.00 annually. But, from the consolidated standpoint, Company *S* has overstated its manufacturing costs by 10% of $8,000.00, or $800.00, and if all of the goods manufactured by Company *S* during the year have been sold outside the organization, the profits of the organization have been understated $800.00. In other words, since depreciation of machinery used in manufacturing is a manufacturing expense, 10% of the machinery (from an accounting standpoint) has now been converted into finished goods and sold. Ten per cent of the unrealized profit on fixed assets has thereby been realized by converting the fixed assets into finished goods and selling them. At the end of the year, the parent company would therefore be justified, in the author's opinion, in transferring 10% of the $8,000.00 reserve, or $800.00, to its surplus account, thus reducing the reserve on its books to $7,200.00. The asset would then appear on the consolidated balance sheet as follows:

Machinery		$50,000
Less: Reserve for intercompany profit on construction	$7,200	
Reserve for depreciation	5,000	12,200
Depreciated cost		$37,800

This treatment seems theoretically correct, since it produces the same result that would be produced by either the first or second method if the parent company had itself purchased the asset from Company *T*. In that case, Company *P* would carry the asset on its own books at $42,000.00. The depreciation at 10% would be $4,200.00, and the carrying value at the end of the first year would be:

Machinery (at cost less intercompany profit)	$42,000.00
Less depreciation	4,200.00
Depreciated cost	$37,800.00

There is a still further complication if the finished goods have not been sold or have been sold to another company within the organization. In such an instance the intercompany profit on construction has merely been converted into an unrealized intercompany profit in inventories, for which a proper reserve should be created.

Illustration of working papers. The treatment of intercompany profits in the consolidated balance sheet working papers will depend upon whether or not reserves have been set up on the books of the parent company. If they have been set up, they will appear in the balance sheet of the parent company and will be merely carried out to the consolidated balance sheet columns. If they have not been set up on the parent company's books, they will be created by deductions from the parent company's surplus, as illustrated below:

Consolidated Balance Sheet Working Papers

	Company *P*	Company *S*	Eliminations	Consolidated Balance Sheet
Surplus—Company *P*	$40,000			
Reserve for intercompany profit in inventories				$ 900R
Reserve for intercompany profit in construction				4,500R
Surplus				34,600S

Stock acquired from the subsidiary. In all illustrations heretofore presented, it has been assumed that the parent company acquired its stock by purchase from former stockholders of the subsidiary. Sometimes the stock is acquired directly from the subsidiary. The difference in the method of acquiring the stock has no effect on the method of making eliminations from the investment account. If the investment account has been charged with subsidiary profits and credited with subsidiary losses and dividends, the book value of the stock at the date of the balance sheet should be eliminated. If the investment is carried at cost, the parent company's investment and surplus accounts will be subject to the customary adjustment for the parent company's percentage of any increase or decrease in subsidiary surplus since the date of acquisition.

But it should be understood that the subsidiary surplus at the date of acquisition includes any premium paid by the parent company in acquiring the subsidiary stock. To illustrate, assume that Company *A* had an issue of $50,000.00 of stock, all of which was outstanding in the hands of individual owners, and a surplus of $10,-000.00. An additional issue of $70,000.00 was authorized and sold at 150, or for $105,000.00, to Company *B*, which thus became Company *A*'s parent. The purchase cost to the parent company includes a goodwill element of $8,750.00, computed as follows:

Cost of stock to parent		$105,000.00
Book value of stock acquired:		
Net worth before issuance of additional stock:		
Capital stock	$ 50,000.00	
Surplus	10,000.00	
Additional capital paid in by parent:		
Capital stock	70,000.00	
Paid-in surplus	35,000.00	
Total	$165,000.00	
7/12 thereof		96,250.00
Goodwill		$ 8,750.00

Issuance of subsidiary shares to outsiders. Assume that subsidiary Company *S* has capital stock of $100,000.00 and surplus of $40,000.00, and that Company *P* acquires ninety per cent of the stock for $131,000.00. Since the book value of the stock acquired is $126,000.00, the goodwill element of the purchase cost is $5,-000.00. During the first year after the acquisition, Company *B* made a profit of $30,000.00, of which Company *A* took up ninety per cent, and the accounts stand as follows:

Company *P*:		
Investment in Company *S*	$158,000.00	
Surplus		$ 27,000.00
Company *S*:		
Capital stock		100,000.00
Surplus		70,000.00

If a consolidated balance sheet is prepared at this date, the minority interest, goodwill, and consolidated surplus will be computed as follows:

	Company *S*		Company *P*	
	Capital Stock	Surplus	Investment in Co. *S*	Surplus
Balances	$100,000	$70,000	$158,000	$27,000
Eliminate reciprocals (90%)	90,000	63,000	153,000	
Minority interest	$ 10,000	$ 7,000		
Goodwill			$ 5,000	
Consolidated surplus				$27,000

Let us now assume that the subsidiary issues $20,000.00 par value of stock to outsiders. If the sale is made at book value, $170.00 per share, no special problems will arise; the working papers will be:

	Company *S*		Company *P*	
	Capital Stock	Total Surplus	Investment in Co. *S*	Surplus
Balances	$120,000	$84,000	$158,000	$27,000
Eliminate reciprocals (75%)	90,000	63,000	153,000	
Minority interest	$ 30,000	$21,000		
Goodwill			$ 5,000	
Consolidated surplus				$27,000

The goodwill and the consolidated surplus are not affected, and the minority interest is increased by the amount which the company received for the additional stock sold to outsiders.

But let us now assume that the additional shares were sold at a price different from book value, say at $150.00 per share, thus increasing surplus by only $10,000.00. If no adjustments are made in the parent company's accounts, the working papers will appear as follows:

	Company *S*		Company *P*	
	Capital Stock	Total Surplus	Investment in Co. *S*	Surplus
Balances	$120,000	$80,000	$158,000	$27,000
Eliminate reciprocals (75%)	90,000	60,000	150,000	
Minority interest	$ 30,000	$20,000		
Goodwill			$ 8,000	
Consolidated surplus				$27,000

The minority interest is correctly stated, at twenty-five per cent of the subsidiary's net worth, but there is a question of whether the goodwill and consolidated surplus are correctly stated. When the parent company made the entry debiting the investment account and crediting surplus $27,000.00, it did so on the basis of a ninety per cent interest in the subsidiary. But the issuance of additional stock to outsiders diluted the parent company's interest to seventy-five per cent, so that it now has only a seventy-five per cent interest in the undistributed profits of $30,000.00 earned by the subsidiary since acquisition. A seventy five per cent interest is $22,500.00; therefore, the parent company should make the following entry:

Surplus	$4,500.00	
Investment in Co. *B*		$4,500.00

The working papers will then be:

	Company *S*		Company *P*	
	Capital Stock	Total Surplus	Investment in Co. *S*	Surplus
Balances	$120,000	$80,000	$153,500	$22,500
Eliminate reciprocals (75%)	90,000	60,000	150,000	
Minority interest	$ 30,000	$20,000		
Goodwill			$ 3,500	
Consolidated surplus				$22,500

Investments carried at cost—alternative working paper procedure. Assume that Company *P* acquired 90% of the stock of Company *S*; at the date of acquisition, the subsidiary had $100,000.00 of capital stock and $50,000.00 of surplus; the acquired stock therefore had a book value of 90% of $150,000.00, or $135,000.00; the purchase price was $140,000.00. The parent company carries the investment at cost. A consolidated balance sheet is to be prepared at a date subsequent to acquisition, when the subsidiary has a surplus of $60,000.00. The parent company has $100,000.00 of surplus from its own operations.

The procedure explained in Chapter 45 for preparing a consolidated balance sheet when the investment is carried at cost is:

Adjust the parent company's investment and surplus accounts by taking up its percentage of the increase or decrease in the subsidiary's surplus since the date of acquisition.

Eliminate the parent company's percentage of the subsidiary's capital stock and surplus as of the balance sheet date.

	Company *P*	Company *S*	Adjustments Debit	Adjustments Credit	Eliminations	Consolidated Balance Sheet
Assets						
Investment in Company *S*—at cost	$140,000					
Adjustment—90% of increase in surplus of Company *S* since acquisition			$9,000A			
Eliminate present book value:						
Capital stock—90% of $100,000.00					$90,000	
Surplus—90% of $60,000.00					54,000	
Goodwill						$ 5,000G
Liabilities						
Capital stock:						
Company *P*	500,000					500,000
Company *S*		$100,000				
Eliminate Company *P*'s 90%					90,000	
Minority—10%						10,000M
Surplus:						
Company *P*	100,000					
Adjustment—as above				$9,000A		
Adjusted balance						109,000S
Company *S*		60,000				
Eliminate Company *P*'s 90%					54,000	
Minority—10%						6,000M

Note that the goodwill is $5,000.00, the minority interest is $16,000.00, and the consolidated surplus is $109,000.00.

As an alternative procedure, the adjustment of the parent company's investment and surplus accounts may be omitted, and the intercompany eliminations may be based on the subsidiary's capital stock and surplus *as of the date of acquisition,* as illustrated by the following working papers.

		Company *P*	Company *S*	Eliminations	Consolidated Balance Sheet
Assets					
Investment in Company *S*—at cost		$140,000			
Eliminate book value at acquisition:					
Capital stock—90% of $100,000.00				$90,000	
Surplus—90% of $50,000.00				45,000	
Goodwill					$ 5,000G
Liabilities					
Capital stock:					
Company *P*		500,000			500,000
Company *S*			$100,000		
Eliminate 90%				90,000	
Minority—10%					10,000M
Surplus:					
Company *P*		100,000			100,000S
Company *S*			60,000		
Minority—10% of present surplus	$60,000				6,000M
Eliminate—90% of surplus at acquisition	50,000			45,000	
Add to consolidated surplus —90% of increase	$10,000				9,000S

The goodwill is $5,000.00 and the minority interest is $16,000.00, as before. By the first procedure, the consolidated surplus was $109,000.00, as shown by the adjusted balance of Company *P*'s surplus account. By the second procedure, the consolidated surplus is again $109,000.00, consisting of the $100,000.00 balance in Company *P*'s surplus, plus $9,000.00 carried to the consolidated column from the surplus of the subsidiary.

Investment acquired by parent's stock. If the subsidiary stock is acquired by issuance of shares of parent company stock, the par of the parent company shares may not represent the true cost of the investment in the subsidiary. On the one hand, it is possible that the par value of the parent company stock is in excess of its real cash value, and that the parent company stock is in reality issued at a discount. On the other hand, the parent company's stock may have a cash issuance value in excess of par, in which case the parent company would appear justified in recording the stock as having been issued at a premium. If a cash issuance price for the parent's shares is definitely ascertainable, it seems proper for the parent company to take cognizance of the premium or discount implicit in the transaction, with respect to the entries recording the cost of the investment and the issuance of its shares. However, the general inclination of accountants to be conservative may deter them from setting up a premium on the parent company's stock, particularly if it is offset in the consolidated balance sheet by an intangible element of goodwill.

File of consolidating information. The preparation of a consolidated statement frequently requires a knowledge of certain events which occurred in prior periods, and other data not required for individual company statements. For instance, if the investments are carried at cost, it is essential to retain in available form complete information relative to the book value of the subsidiary stocks at the dates of acquisition. This, of course, is especially important if the subsidiary stock was acquired by purchases at several dates. If fixed assets are transferred from one affiliated company to another at a profit, it is necessary to have information about the profit and the applicable depreciation rate so long as the asset remains in the accounts. For these, and often other, reasons it is advisable to retain a file of required consolidating information.

When to consolidate. The relation of parent and subsidiary exists if one company owns a majority of the voting stock of another company. However, the existence of a mere majority control does not necessarily justify the preparation of consolidated statements.

A consolidated balance sheet is, in a sense, an extra-legal balance sheet of the parent company; the legal reality of separate corporate entities is ignored, and the investment account on the parent company's books is assumed to represent the net assets of the subsidiary. If a parent owns 100% of a subsidiary's stock, the parent has no legal ownership of the subsidiary's assets, but a condition exists which, for consolidated balance sheet purposes, is assumed to represent effective ownership. If the parent company owns only 95% of the subsidiary stock, there is a 5% error in the assumption of effective ownership; but this error is regarded as insignificant and is adequately indicated by the inclusion of the minority interest as a separate item in the consolidated balance sheet. But if there is a 49% minority interest, the degree of error in the assumption is so great that many accountants believe the accounts of such a subsidiary should not be included in consolidated statements. Unfortunately, there is no well-accepted rule concerning the percentage of ownership required to justify the inclusion of a subsidiary's accounts in a consolidated balance sheet. Some accountants appear to believe that a 60% interest is sufficient; others regard a 75% or an 80% interest as a minimum.

Matters other than the percentage of voting stock ownership should be considered. In the first place, consideration should be given to the size of the subsidiary in relation to the size of the parent company. If a subsidiary is so small that a 40% minority interest is insignificant in comparison with the net worth of the parent company, there appears to be no serious objection to consolidating its accounts. On the other hand, a 25% minority interest in the voting stock of a large subsidiary might be so large in proportion to the net worth of the parent company as to raise a serious question of the propriety of consolidating its accounts.

In the second place, the voting stock may represent only a portion of the net worth, and the minority interest applicable to the other classes of stock may require consideration. Thus, if a subsidiary's net worth consists of $100,000.00 of voting common stock (75% owned by the parent company) and $100,000.00 of non-voting preferred stock (none of which is owned by the parent company), the 75% voting control represents only a 37½% interest in the net assets of the subsidiary, and the outside interest represents 62½%. In this connection, it may also be necessary to give consideration to the preference rights of the preferred stockholders, particularly if they have a disproportionate interest in the surplus because of dividends in arrears.

In the third place, if the assets and operations of the parent company and those of the subsidiary are not homogeneous, consolidated statements may be more confusing than enlightening. For instance, automobile finance companies frequently have subsidiaries which carry the insurance on the cars which serve as collateral to the parent company's loans; consolidated statements of a finance company and an insurance company would be of little significance.

In the fourth place, special problems arise with respect to foreign subsidiaries. Under normal conditions, the consolidation of the accounts of foreign subsidiaries is usually regarded as permissible, but if the subsidiary's operations are conducted in a country at war or if any exchange restrictions exist, consolidated statements usually are undesirable.

If a subsidiary is being controlled only temporarily, or for any reason is about to be disposed of, it should probably be excluded from the consolidation.

It has recently been advocated that, if the cost of the stock is greatly in excess of the book value as shown by the subsidiary's accounts, and there is any probability that the excess may be a recognition of an understatement in the book values of subsidiary assets (instead of a recognition of earning power), the accounts of the subsidiary should not be consolidated, since a consolidation might greatly misstate the values of tangibles and intangibles.

If the accounts of any subsidiary are omitted from the consolidated statements, information should be given, in footnotes or elsewhere, concerning the reasons for the omission, the financial condition and operating results of the subsidiary, and the relation of profits earned by the subsidiary and dividends paid by it during the period. If the subsidiary not consolidated is of material size, the annual report of the parent company should include the omitted subsidiary's balance sheet and operating statement.

Consolidated statements sometimes are prepared when there is no intercompany stock control. For instance, control may be effectively exercised by means of a long term lease. Or, if a company owns a substantial portion of the stock, but less than control, of a company which is operating at a serious loss, and if the investment represents a substantial portion of the assets of the company holding the stock, consolidated statements may be helpful in indicating that the holding company's financial condition is in jeopardy. Under modern conditions, with numerous holders of small blocks of shares, and the extensive use of proxies, effective control is often exercised without majority ownership of stock; if, under such conditions, one company actually exercises control of another, a consolidated balance sheet may be justified for special purposes. If, under any circumstances, a consolidated balance sheet is prepared when there is no control through ownership of at least a majority of the voting stock, full disclosure of the conditions should be made in a balance sheet footnote.

If the stocks of two or more companies are owned by the same shareholders, an affiliation exists although there is no parent-subsidiary relationship. It may be desirable to prepare a balance sheet of all companies so affiliated; such a statement is properly called a *combined balance sheet*, rather than a *consolidated balance sheet*.

CHAPTER 48

Parent and Subsidiary Accounting—Miscellaneous Matters (Continued)

Excess of cost over book value. In the preceding illustrations, any excess of the cost of the investment to the parent company over the book value of the investment as shown by the accounts of the subsidiary has been included in the consolidated balance sheet as *goodwill.* This was the almost universal practice until recently; however, it should in many instances be regarded as a convenient expedient rather than a logically correct procedure, and there is a tendency to adopt one of two alternative treatments.

First alternative procedure. The excess of cost over book value may be a recognition of an undervaluation of the net assets of the subsidiary as shown by its accounts. Errors of accounting principle may have been committed by the subsidiary; for instance, capital expenditures may have been charged to revenue, excess depreciation may have been provided, or excess loss reserves may have been created. Or, since the acquisition of the subsidiary stock may be regarded, from the consolidated standpoint, as an acquisition of subsidiary net assets, it may be proper to give recognition to increased market values in the consolidated balance sheet, although such recognition might not be permissible in the balance sheet of the subsidiary. Or the excess may reflect the existence of other intangibles, such as patents or franchises. For any or all of these reasons there is much to be said in favor of discontinuing the traditional procedure of applying the title of goodwill to the excess of cost over book value, and adopting a new procedure of scrutinizing the subsidiary balance sheet valuations to determine the extent, if any, to which this excess should be applied to the valuation of other assets.

Second alternative procedure. Although the first alternative may be theoretically correct, there may be no information about the amounts by which the book values of subsidiary assets should be adjusted; moreover, the purchase cost of the subsidiary stock may be determined by its market value, which is affected by the earning power of the subsidiary. It may therefore be impractica-ble to apportion the excess, and apply portions thereof as adjust-ments of book values of tangibles and to recognize other portions as representative of intangibles. A second alternative procedure may therefore be adopted; it consists of showing the excess as a separate item in the consolidated balance sheet, with some title such as "Excess of cost of subsidiary stock over book value thereof at date of acquisition." This procedure is a frank acknowledgement of an inability to determine just what the excess does represent with respect to subsidiary asset valuations.

Excess of book value over cost. The traditional treatment, for consolidated balance sheet purposes, of an excess of the book value, at the date of acquisition, of the subsidiary stock over the cost to the parent company, is stated below:

If a goodwill appears in the balance sheet of the subsidiary, apply the excess of book value over cost as a reduction or elimination of the subsidiary goodwill.

If no goodwill appears in the balance sheet of the subsidiary, the excess may be applied in reduction of any goodwill appearing elsewhere in the consolidated working papers: that is, from goodwill in the balance sheet of the parent company or any other subsidiary, or so-called goodwill represented by the excess of cost over book value of investments in other subsidiaries.

If the excess of book value over cost cannot be absorbed against goodwill elements, it should be shown in the consolidated balance sheet as capital surplus.

In the preceding chapters there were several illustrative cases in which the book value of the subsidiary stock at the date of acquisition was in excess of the cost to the parent company. In all of these illustrations there was a goodwill account on the books of the subsidiary, and the excess was deducted from the subsidiary goodwill in accordance with the above-stated traditional procedure, which is based on the assumption that the parent company, in paying less than book value for the stock, refused to recognize the propriety of the stated book value of the goodwill. It is now coming to be recognized that this assumption is not necessarily true; the goodwill may be reasonably valued on the books of the subsidiary, and other assets may be overvalued. However, in the absence of definite information which will justify a downward adjustment of the valuation of other assets, it seems desirable to continue the traditional procedure and reduce the subsidiary's goodwill for consolidated balance sheet purposes; otherwise, the consolidated balance sheet will include a subsidiary goodwill of at least doubtful value, offset by a credit to capital surplus.

Let us now assume that no goodwill appears in the balance sheet of the subsidiary whose stock was acquired at less than book value, and that there is no knowledge of overvaluation in any of its other assets. If goodwill items appear in the balance sheets of other companies in the group or arise from the purchase of other subsidiary stocks, it is customary, as stated above, to deduct the excess of book value over cost from goodwill appearing anywhere in the consolidated working papers. Although this practice has been customary, it does not seem to be theoretically correct, for the following reasons.

(1) It is difficult to see how the purchase of the stock of a subsidiary at less than book value can reduce the goodwill of the consolidation, unless that subsidiary is making very small profits or is incurring losses which will reduce the consolidated earnings. But even in that case,

(2) It is a well-recognized accounting convention that, while the real value of a company's goodwill is dependent upon its earnings, the amount which may be shown in its balance sheet as goodwill is determined by the price paid for goodwill. This convention appears to warrant retaining in the consolidated balance sheet all goodwill paid for by the parent company or by other subsidiaries and appearing in their balance sheets, or paid for by the parent company in acquiring the stock of other subsidiaries, regardless of the meager earnings or the losses of a subsidiary acquired at less than book value. Moreover,

(3) While it may be regarded as conservative to offset an excess of book value over cost against any goodwill appearing in the consolidated working papers, the accountant should recognize that, in doing so, he is in effect writing off goodwill presumably paid for in other transactions. If such a conservative action is to be taken, it would seem to require the authorization of the directors of the parent company.

For these reasons the author believes that, if a subsidiary with no goodwill account and no assets known to be overvalued is acquired at less than book value, the excess of book value over cost should not be offset against goodwill appearing elsewhere in the consolidated working papers.

Because of the practical difficulty of determining whether an excess of book value over cost should be reflected by an adjustment of goodwill, an adjustment of the book values of other subsidiary assets, or a credit to consolidated capital surplus, there is a growing tendency among accountants to set such items out separately in the consolidated balance sheet with some title such as "Excess of book value of subsidiary stock at date of acquisition over cost thereof." If this procedure is followed, the accountant is still faced with the necessity of classifying the item in the balance sheet; it is usually shown under the net worth caption, but this procedure is correct only if all assets of the subsidiary are properly valued; if the excess of book value over cost really means an overstatement of the book value of subsidiary assets, the item should be excluded from consolidated net worth.

Excess shown net or otherwise. The traditional procedure for the treatment of differences between the cost of the investment and the underlying book value may be summarized as follows:

Any excess of cost over book value is added to goodwill.

Any excess of book value over cost is deducted from goodwill wherever found; any such excesses that cannot be absorbed against goodwill are shown in the consolidated balance sheet as capital surplus.

The traditional consolidated balance sheet showed *either* a goodwill *or* a capital surplus (or perhaps neither), but not both. The present tendency is toward the following treatment:

Show as goodwill the aggregate amounts thereof shown by the books.

Show as excess of costs of subsidiary stocks over book values thereof at dates of acquisition the total of such excesses.

Show on the liability side as excess of book values of subsidiary stocks at dates of acquisition over costs thereof the total of such excesses.

This procedure has not been adopted as standard practice; the traditional form is still generally used; moreover, there is some tendency to favor adjustments of subsidiary asset values.

Adjustment of asset values. If a difference between the book value of the subsidiary stock at the date of acquisition and the cost of the stock is to be dealt with by adjustment of asset values, the adjustment may be made on the subsidiary's books or in the consolidated working papers.

Adjustments of the subsidiary's books may be appropriate if the overvaluation or undervaluation of its assets is the result of errors of accounting which cause a misstatement of values from the standpoint of a going concern. But if the adjustments of asset values represent differences between correct going-concern values and market values, it does not appear correct to adjust the subsidiary's books. The purchase of a subsidiary's stock may be tantamount, from a consolidated standpoint, to a purchase of subsidiary assets, and market values of subsidiary assets may therefore be regarded as a permissible basis for consolidated balance sheet presentation; but from the non-consolidated, separate corporate entity standpoint, going-concern values should prevail, and the book value of a subsidiary's assets should not be predicated on the market price of its stock.

To illustrate the procedure to be applied in adjusting asset values in consolidated working papers, assume that Company *P* acquired all of the stock of Company *S* at a cost of $165,000.00; the book value at the date of acquisition was $150,000.00. The $15,000.00 excess of cost over book value is stated by company officials to be the net amount of the following:

Undervaluation of land	$10,000.00
Overvaluation of patents	8,000.00*
Goodwill	13,000.00
Net	$15,000.00

* Deduction.

Adjustments and eliminations may be made in the working papers as shown on the next page.

Although adjusting subsidiary asset values may be theoretically more nearly correct than showing on the asset side of the consolidated balance sheet such items as goodwill or excess of cost over book value of subsidiary stock at acquisition, or on the liability side such items as capital surplus, surplus arising from consolidation, or excess of book value of subsidiary stock at acquisition over cost, it must be recognized that adjustments of asset values bring in their train new and difficult problems of consolidated balance sheet construction. No especial difficulties arise in the preparation of a consolidated balance sheet at the date of acquisition, if we assume that the adjusted asset values can be definitely ascertained. But difficulties arise subsequently. For instance, if fixed asset values are adjusted on the books of the subsidiary, revised depreciation schedules will have to be established, and their application will involve reconciliations of depreciation charges for general accounting and tax purposes; on the other hand, if the adjustments are applied in the consolidated working papers, similar adjustments will be required in subsequent consolidated balance sheet working papers, and additional adjustments will be required for the difference between depreciation on the basis of subsidiary book value and depreciation on the basis

Partial Consolidated Working Papers

	Co. *P*	Co. *S*	Adjustments Debit	Adjustments Credit	Eliminations	Consolidated Balance Sheet
Assets						
Investment in Company *S*	$165,000					
Eliminate book value:						
Capital stock					$100,000A	
Surplus—as adjusted					52,000B	
Goodwill						$13,000
Land		$ 15,000	$10,000(a)			25,000
Patents		8,000		$ 8,000(b)		
Net Worth						
Capital stock		100,000			100,000A	
Surplus		50,000				
Adjustment for undervaluation of land				10,000(a) }	52,000B	
Adjustment for overvaluation of patents			8,000(b)	}		

of the consolidated valuation. Or, assume that, at the date of acquisition, the market value of the subsidiary's inventory was in excess of cost, and the price paid for the subsidiary stock was based on the market value of the inventory. To treat the excess of the cost over the book value of the subsidiary stock as goodwill would obviously be wrong because no goodwill exists; moreover, since the parent company in effect paid market value for the inventory, the consolidated profit from the sale of the inventory should be computed on the basis of the market value at acquisition. If the adjustment of the inventory is made on the books of the subsidiary, the write-up would have to be recognized as an unrealized profit; for subsidiary accounting purposes it should be taken into income as the inventory is disposed of, but for consolidated statement purposes it should never find its way into income or surplus.

If an excess of cost over book value at acquisition does not represent a payment for goodwill, but represents in effect a payment for subsidiary assets at a price in excess of their book value, the traditional treatment of the excess as goodwill (or the more recently recommended procedure of showing it as excess of cost over book value) will probably result in an ultimate overstatement of consolidated net assets. Assume, for purposes of illustration, that a parent company acquired all of the stock of a subsidiary at a cost of $150,000.00; the book value of the subsidiary assets at the date of acquisition was $135,000.00; the excess of cost over book value was $15,000.00; and the market value of the subsidiary inventory was $15,000.00 in excess of cost. If this excess is shown permanently in the consolidated balance sheet as goodwill (or as excess of cost over book value of subsidiary stock at acquisition), there will be a permanent overstatement of the consolidated assets, and the consolidated earnings and surplus will be overstated because the profit on the sale of the subsidiary inventory will be overstated from a consolidated standpoint.

Or assume that the $15,000.00 should properly be treated by an upward adjustment of a depreciating asset, such as a building. Depreciation charges and disposal entries will ultimately eliminate this asset from the accounts, and the $15,000.00 should ultimately be eliminated from the consolidated balance sheet. But if the $15,000.00 is shown as goodwill (or excess of cost over book value) it will not be so eliminated.

Adjustments subsequent to acquisition. If subsidiary assets are not adjusted at the date of acquisition, either on the subsidiary's books or in the consolidated working papers, but adjustments are made on the subsidiary's books at a subsequent date, consideration should be given to the effect, if any, upon the goodwill appearing in the consolidated balance sheet.

To illustrate, let us assume that a parent company acquired subsidiary stock at a price \$20,000.00 in excess of book value, and that the consolidated balance sheet at the date of acquisition shows a goodwill of \$20,000.00. Assume, further, that the subsidiary's fixed assets are appraised immediately after the date of acquisition and the appraised valuation is \$20,000.00 in excess of the book value. Obviously, consolidated balance sheets subsequently prepared should not include the subsidiary plant at the appraised value and also include a goodwill of \$20,000.00. Such a balance sheet would contain a \$20,000.00 asset duplication; or, more precisely, it would show a consolidated goodwill when none existed.

Or assume that the plant was appraised several years after the date of acquisition, and a \$30,000.00 increase in value was disclosed by the appraisal. If it should be ascertained that \$15,000.00 of the increase had taken place at the date of acquisition of the subsidiary stock, an adjustment of the goodwill to \$5,000.00 would be in order.

Similarly, if the subsidiary net assets and surplus were misstated at the date of acquisition because of accounting errors discovered after that date, the correction of the subsidiary's accounts as of the date of acquisition should carry with it an adjustment of the consolidated goodwill. For instance, assume that a goodwill of \$50,000.00 was determined on the basis of subsidiary book values at the date of acquisition, and that it was subsequently discovered that depreciation of fixed assets up to the date of acquisition was overstated \$10,000.00; an adjustment of the subsidiary's accounts to correct the overdepreciation would result in a \$10,000.00 increase in the subsidiary surplus as of the date of acquisition, and an equal reduction in the consolidated goodwill.

If, by reason of any such adjustments, the goodwill shown in the consolidated balance sheet at the date of acquisition differs materially from that shown in a consolidated balance sheet at a subsequent date, it may be desirable to append a footnote to the balance sheet stating the reason for the change.

Adjustment of minority interest for implied goodwill. If a parent company acquires less than the total subsidiary stock, and a goodwill element is included in the purchase price, it is customary to compute the goodwill element as only the excess of the cost to the parent company over the book value of the stock acquired. For instance, if a subsidiary's net assets have a book value of \$100,000.00

and an 80% interest in the subsidiary stock cost the parent company $84,000.00, the goodwill element is computed as $4,000.00. However, some accountants have contended, and with some theoretical justification, that if there is a $4,000.00 goodwill applicable to 80% of the subsidiary stock, there is a corresponding goodwill element of $1,000.00 applicable to the minority's 20% interest, that a total of $5,000.00 should be included in the consolidated goodwill, and that the book value of the minority interest should be increased $1,000.00.

While there seems to be some theoretical basis for this contention, the procedure is not in conformity with present practice, and the facts may negative the assumption on which the contention is based. It may be that the parent company paid the premium to obtain control of the subsidiary in order to increase the profits of other companies in the group; if this is true, the premium was not paid for a goodwill inherent in the new subsidiary as a separate corporation and the minority shareholders are therefore not entitled to participate in it. Moreover, the addition of a goodwill element to the minority interest is contrary to the general opinion that goodwill should not be stated at an amount in excess of its cost. In the foregoing illustration, the only payment made for goodwill was $4,000.00.

As indicated in preceding discussions, the excess of the cost of the parent's investment over the underlying book value may be a recognition of the undervaluation of assets on the subsidiary's books. If the evidence of such undervaluation is sufficient to justify adjusting entries on the subsidiary's books, the minority interest will be increased by the portion of the adjustment applicable thereto. If, with evidence relative to undervaluations of tangible assets adequate to support adjustments of the subsidiary's books, the adjustments are not made therein but are applied to the consolidating working papers, it seems proper to give the minority interest the benefit of its share of the adjustments.

Economic and Legal Bases of Parent Company Accounting

The economic basis. For purposes of reference in this chapter, the method of parent company accounting for subsidiary investments and for profits, losses, and dividends thereon described in Chapter 44, will be called the *economic basis of accounting*, because it derives from business concepts of underlying asset values and operating profits and losses rather than from legal considerations of separate corporate entities.

If a company organizes a subsidiary and acquires its entire stock issue by an investment of $100,000.00, and if the subsidiary, during the first year of its operations, makes a profit of $30,000.00, the subsidiary's net assets are increased to $130,000.00 and it is obvious that the value of the parent company's investment, based on underlying net assets, also has increased to $130,000.00. It also seems obvious that, since the subsidiary is owned by the parent company, the subsidiary's operations are conducted for the benefit of the parent company, and the $30,000.00 profit made by the subsidiary during the year was made for the benefit of the parent company. If this reasoning determines the parent company's accounting procedure, an entry similar to the following will be made, as described in Chapter 44:

Investment in stock of subsidiary Company *S*..	$30,000.00	
Income from operations of subsidiary *S*.....		$30,000.00

Assume that, at the close of the first year of operations, the subsidiary pays a dividend of $5,000.00. Since the parent company has taken up as income the profit made by the subsidiary, it cannot also regard the dividend as income. It will recognize the dividend as merely a conversion of part of its subsidiary investment into cash, and will record this conversion as follows:

Cash....................................	$5,000.00	
Investment in stock of subsidiary Company *S*..		$5,000.00

If, during the second year, the subsidiary suffers a loss of $15,000.00 and pays the parent company a dividend of $5,000.00 from the profits of the prior year, the parent company will record the loss and the consequent decrease in the underlying asset value of the investment and the dividend by the following entries:

Loss from operations of subsidiary Company *S*.	$15,000.00	
Investment in stock of subsidiary Company *S*		$15,000.00
Cash....................................	5,000.00	
Investment in stock of subsidiary Company *S*		5,000.00

The following summary shows the effect of the foregoing entries on the parent company's investment and surplus accounts; it also shows the subsidiary's net worth accounts.

	Subsidiary's Accounts		Parent's Accounts	
	Capital Stock	Surplus	Investment	Surplus
Stock issued..............	$100,000		$100,000	
First year:				
Profit..................		$30,000	30,000	$30,000
Dividend................		5,000*	5,000*	
Second year:				
Loss....................		15,000*	15,000*	15,000*
Dividend................		5,000*	5,000*	
Balances................	$100,000	$ 5,000	$105,000	$15,000

* Decrease.

It is obvious from the foregoing illustration that this method of parent company accounting conforms with the economic realities: The $105,000.00 balance in the investment account is equal to the underlying subsidiary net assets, and the parent company has taken as earnings the $15,000.00 net profit made by the subsidiary during the two years.

The only objection to this accounting procedure is that it does not conform with the legal realities.

The legal basis. From a legal standpoint a parent and its subsidiary must be recognized as separate corporate entities, and the profits earned by the subsidiary are not profits available for parent company dividends until the parent company receives them as subsidiary dividends.

If this legal reality is to govern the accounting procedure, the methods described in Chapter 45 will be used. The parent company will make no entries for subsidiary profits or losses, and will record dividends received as income, regardless of the relation of the dividends to the subsidiary's profits or losses. Referring to the preceding illustration, the parent company's entries will be:

Cash	$5,000.00	
Dividend income		$5,000.00
To record the dividend of the first year.		
Cash	5,000.00	
Dividend income		5,000 00
To record the dividend of the second year.		

The accounts of the parent and subsidiary will stand as follows:

	Subsidiary's Accounts		Parent's Accounts	
	Capital Stock	Surplus	Investment	Surplus
Stock issued	$100,000		$100,000	
First year:				
Profit		$30,000		
Dividend		5,000*		$ 5,000
Second year:				
Loss		15,000*		
Dividend		5,000*		5,000
Balances	$100,000	$ 5,000	$100,000	$10,000

* Deduction.

This procedure conforms strictly to the legal realities of separate corporate entities. However, it does not reflect underlying asset values and operating results. The investment is carried at cost, $100,000.00, although the underlying net assets total $105,000.00. And of more serious consequence is the fact that the parent company shows a uniform income of $5,000.00 per year, although the subsidiary earned $30,000.00 in the first year and lost $15,000.00 in the second.

Since the parent company is in a position to dictate the dividend policy of the subsidiary, so long as a subsidiary surplus exists, the dividends paid to the parent company need bear no relation to annual profits or losses. And subsidiary dividends can be paid from surplus earned prior to acquisition.

Adherence to the legal basis of parent company accounting thus often places the parent company in a position to show as annual income such amounts as it may arbitrarily decide to have transferred to it as dividends, instead of the profit or loss which results from the subsidiary's operations.

Changing bases. It is regrettable that the two bases of accounting described above exist. For one reason, one cannot safely undertake to interpret the statements of a parent company unless he knows which basis of accounting has been used. For another reason, cases have been known where a parent company has jumped from one basis to another in succeeding years, in order to make the best picture: showing subsidiary earnings as parent company income in a year when the earnings exceeded the dividends, and showing dividends as income in a year when the subsidiary dividends exceeded the subsidiary earnings.

Reconciling the bases. Various suggestions have been made to effect a reconciliation or compromise between the two accounting bases. Most of these start with the premise that the legal concept should serve as the basis, but that some modifications should be made.

Some accountants advocate adhering strictly to the legal basis in the accounts, but supplementing the statements by parenthetical remarks or footnotes. By this procedure, the parent company's balance sheet would show the cost of the investment, and supplementary comments would state the underlying net asset value as shown by the books of the subsidiary; the income statement would show subsidiary dividends as parent company earnings, and the subsidiary's profit or loss for the period would be shown as supplementary information.

It has been suggested in some quarters that the legal basis should be applied as long as the subsidiary's earnings since acquisition are at least equal to its dividends, but that the economic basis should be applied when the subsidiary's losses and/or dividends have exceeded its earnings since acquisition. That is: If the subsidiary had a surplus of $50,000.00 at the date of acquisition, the investment should be carried at cost and dividends should be taken as income regardless of any increase of subsidiary surplus over $50,000.00; but if losses and/or dividends reduce the subsidiary surplus to, say, $40,000.00, the parent company should write down its investment, $10,000.00. What justification there is for such a procedure lies in its conservatism, but it is a hybrid accounting method.

The author suggests the following procedure, which seems to have the advantages of the economic basis of recognizing on the parent company's books the increases or decreases in underlying asset values and the operating results, while at the same time recognizing the legal restriction against regarding undistributed subsidiary earnings as parent company surplus available for dividends. It accepts the economic concept as the proper accounting basis, and introduces modifications to reflect the legal restrictions on parent company dividends from undistributed subsidiary profits. The procedure is illustrated by the following entries.

During the first year after acquisition the subsidiary made a profit of $20,000.00 and paid a dividend of $6,000.00:

Investment in stock of subsidiary *S*	$20,000.00	
Undistributed subsidiary earnings		$20,000.00
Subsidiary profit.		
Cash	6,000.00	
Investment in stock of subsidiary *S*		6,000.00
Subsidiary dividend.		
Undistributed subsidiary earnings	6,000.00	
Surplus		6,000.00
Subsidiary earnings made available for parent company dividends.		

Surplus can be shown in the parent company's balance sheet in two amounts, as illustrated below. It is assumed that the parent company's surplus includes $50,000.00 realized from its own operations.

Surplus:		
Not available for dividends—undistributed subsidiary earnings	$14,000.00	
Free	56,000.00	$70,000.00

Some may object to showing the undistributed earnings of the subsidiary under the surplus caption in the parent company's balance sheet; for this reason it may be preferable to separate it from surplus, thus:

Net worth:		
Capital stock	$500,000.00	
Surplus	56,000.00	
Undistributed subsidiary earnings	14,000.00	$570,000.00

Such a procedure is somewhat comparable to showing under the net worth caption an unrealized increment in plant values disclosed by an appraisal; the essential thing in both cases is to indicate that the credit is not available for dividends.

Continuing the illustration, it is assumed that, during the second year, the subsidiary made a profit of $2,500.00 and paid a dividend of $6,000.00.

Investment in stock of subsidiary *S*............	$2,500.00	
Undistributed subsidiary earnings..........		$2,500.00
Subsidiary profit.		
Cash....................................	6,000.00	
Investment in stock of subsidiary *S*........		6,000.00
Subsidiary dividend.		
Undistributed subsidiary earnings..............	6,000.00	
Surplus............................		6,000.00
Subsidiary earnings made available for parent company dividends.		

The undistributed earnings to be shown in the balance sheet are now $10,500.00, which represents the $14,000.00 balance at the end of the first year, plus $2,500.00 earnings, and minus the $6,000.00 dividend. (It is equal to the undistributed earnings of the subsidiary since acquisition: $20,000.00 and $2,500.00, minus dividends of $12,000.00.)

During the third year, the subsidiary lost $13,000.00, but nevertheless paid a $6,000.00 dividend from surplus accumulated prior to acquisition.

Undistributed subsidiary earnings............	$10,500.00	
Surplus..................................	2,500.00	
Investment in stock of subsidiary *S*.......		$13,000.00
Subsidiary loss.		
Cash....................................	6,000.00	
Investment in stock of subsidiary *S*.......		6,000.00
Subsidiary dividend.		

The dividend during the third year does not justify any transfer from undistributed subsidiary earnings to surplus, because the loss during the third year more than offset the undistributed earnings since acquisition; in fact, the subsidiary has suffered a net loss of $2,500.00 since acquisition, and this is reflected in the $2,500.00 debit to the parent company's surplus account.

What amounts should be shown in the parent company's income statement in each of the three years? The facts were as follows:

	Profit Loss*	Dividend
First year..............................	$20,000.00	$6,000.00
Second year.............................	2,500.00	6,000.00
Third year..............................	13,000.00*	6,000.00

If we adopt the legal basis, we will show income of $6,000.00 during each year. This may be regarded as conservative during the first year; it is not conservative during the second year, when the earnings were less than the dividends; and there seems to be no accounting propriety in taking up $6,000.00 of income during the third year, thus making a total of $18,000.00 since acquisition although the total profits were only $8,500.00.

The economic basis seems more truly to reflect the facts. On this basis, the parent company's income statement for the first year could show the facts as follows:

Earnings of subsidiary:		
Received as a dividend	$ 6,000.00	
Undistributed	14,000.00	$20,000.00

The statement for the second year would show an income of $2,500.00 and the statement for the third year would show a loss of $13,000.00. Information relative to the dividends received during the second and third year could be given in footnotes.

From the accounting standpoint of reflecting the true earnings of the parent company on its investment in the subsidiary, this procedure must surely be regarded as preferable to statements showing as income the dividends received regardless of subsidiary profits and losses during the period. Does the suggested procedure violate any legal requirements which should govern the accountant? The legal fact of separate corporate entities seems merely to effect a restriction on the profits available for parent company dividends. The presentation of income facts as illustrated above for the first year seems, therefore, to be in accord with both economic realities and legal requirements, for the parent company's income statement and balance sheet say in effect: The subsidiary operations during the year produced an income of $20,000.00 on our investment; however, only $6,000.00 of this amount has been transferred to us as a dividend and thus made available for our dividend payments.

This proposed compromise accounting procedure enables the parent company to take up true economic profits and losses; it results in adjustments of the carrying value of the stock investment to reflect changes in underlying net assets; and yet, by the segregation of undistributed subsidiary profits, it indicates the amount not legally available for parent company dividends.

While the suggested method does not seem to be in conflict with any legal *requirement*, it does, in the interest of sound and conservative accounting, deprive the parent company of what is probably a legal *privilege*. From the legal standpoint, dividends received from a subsidiary are income—presumably even those dividends which are in excess of subsidiary earnings since acquisition

Consolidated working papers. The adoption of the procedure just described for reconciling the economic and legal concepts of parent company accounting creates no complications in the consolidated balance sheet working papers. For example, assume that Company *P* on January 1, 1946 purchased for $155,000.00 all of the stock of Company *S*, which on that date had $100,000.00 of capital stock and $50,000.00 of surplus. The subsidiary earned a profit of $20,000.00 during 1946, and paid a dividend of $6,000.00. The parent company's surplus on December 31, 1946, from its own operations, was $100,000.00.

If the parent company used the accounting procedure described in Chapter 44, the consolidated balance sheet working papers would contain amounts shown below:

Partial Consolidated Working Papers
December 31, 1946

Assets	Company *P*	Company *S*	Eliminations	Consolidated
Investment in Co. *S*	$169,000			
Eliminate:				
Capital stock.........			$100,000A	
Surplus..........			64,000B	
Goodwill..............				$ 5,000
Liabilities and net worth				
Capital stock:				
Company *S*............		$100,000	100,000A	
Surplus:				
Company *P*..........	120,000			120,000
Company *S*...........		64,000	64,000B	

If the parent company used the compromise procedure described in this chapter, the working papers would include the following amounts:

Partial Consolidated Working Papers
December 31, 1946

Assets	Company *P*	Company *S*	Eliminations	Consolidated
Investment in Co. *S*	$169,000			
Eliminate:				
Capital stock.........			$100,000A	
Surplus..............			64,000B	
Goodwill..............				$ 5,000
Liabilities and net worth				
Capital stock:				
Company *S*............		$100,000	100,000A	
Surplus:				
Company *P*:				
Undistributed earnings —Co. *S*...........	14,000			} 120,000
Free..................	106,000			}
Company *S*............		64,000	64,000B	

CHAPTER 49

Purchases and Sales of Subsidiary Stock—Major and Minor Parent Companies—Reciprocal Stockholdings

First illustration: Several purchases. It is assumed that the parent company acquires its interest in the subsidiary by several purchases. The dates and amounts of these purchases are shown in the statement on page 306 which also shows the profits, losses, and dividends of the two companies for four years.

Since the statement on page 306 shows the investment and surplus accounts of the parent company after having taken up the profits, losses, and dividends of the subsidiary, the minority interest, goodwill, and consolidated surplus can be easily computed, as follows:

	Company *S*		Company *P*	
	Capital Stock	Surplus	Investment in Co. *S*	Surplus
Balances	$100,000	$66,000	$160,400	$163,000
Eliminate reciprocals (90%)	90,000	59,400	149,400	
Minority interest	$ 10,000	$ 6,600		
Goodwill			$ 11,000	
Consolidated surplus				$163,000

The statement on page 307 shows the accounts of the parent and subsidiary on the assumption that the parent company has carried the investment at cost, and has taken subsidiary dividends as income. Under these conditions it becomes necessary to make an adjustment of the parent company's accounts to take up the increases in the subsidiary surplus. (To simplify the illustrations somewhat, it is assumed that entries are made by the parent company in its surplus account rather than in an undistributed subsidiary earnings account.)

The amount of the adjustment for increases in the subsidiary surplus is computed as follows:

	Subsidiary Surplus			Per Cent of Stock	Parent's Share of
Year	Dividends	Profit	Increase	Owned	Increase
1943	$6,000	$10,000	$4,000	60%	$ 2,400
1944	6,000	10,000	4,000	70	2,800
1945	6,000	10,000	4,000	90	3,600
1946	6,000	10,000	4,000	90	3,600
Total adjustment					$12,400

COMPANY *P* AND SUBSIDIARY *S*

Statement of Surplus and Investment Accounts

(Subsidiary Profits and Dividends Taken Up)

	Company *S*	Company *P*		
		Investment in Company *S*		
	Surplus	Per Cent	Amount	Surplus
December 31, 1942—purchase, 600 shares	$50,000.00	60%	$ 99,000.00	$100,000.00
1943: Profits: Company *S*	10,000.00		6,000.00	6,000.00
Company *P*				20,000.00
Dividends: Company *S*	6,000.00*		3,600.00*	
Company *P*				12,000.00*
Purchase—December 31, 100 shares		10	16,000.00	
Balances	$54,000.00	70%	$117,400.00	$114,000.00
1944: Profits: Company *S*	10,000.00		7,000.00	7,000.00
Company *P*				20,000.00
Dividends: Company *S*	6,000.00*		4,200.00*	
Company *P*				12,000.00*
Purchase—December 31, 200 shares		20	33,000.00	
Balances	$58,000.00	90%	$153,200.00	$129,000.00
1945: Profits: Company *S*	10,000.00		9,000.00	9,000.00
Company *P*				20,000.00
Dividends: Company *S*	6,000.00*		5,400.00*	
Company *P*				12,000.00*
Balances	$62,000.00	90%	$156,800.00	$146,000.00
1946: Profits: Company *S*	10,000.00		9,000.00	9,000.00
Company *P*				20,000.00
Dividends: Company *S*	6,000.00*		5,400.00*	
Company *P*				12,000.00*
Balances	$66,000.00	90%	$160,400.00	$163,000.00

* Deductions.

COMPANY *P* AND SUBSIDIARY *S*

Statement of Surplus and Investment Accounts

(*Investment Carried at Cost*)

	Company S	Company P		
		Investment in Company S		
	Surplus	Per Cent	Cost	Surplus
December 31, 1942—purchase, 600 shares	$50,000.00	60%	$ 99,000.00	$100,000.00
1943: Profits	10,000.00			20,000.00
Dividends: Company S	6,000.00*			3,600.00
Company P				12,000.00*
Purchase—December 31, 100 shares		10	16,000.00	
Balances	$54,000.00	70%	$115,000.00	$111,600.00
1944: Profits	10,000.00			20,000.00
Dividends: Company S	6,000.00*			4,200.00
Company P				12,000.00*
Purchase—December 31, 200 shares		20	33,000.00	
Balances	$58,000.00	90%	$148,000.00	$123,800.00
1945: Profits	10,000.00			20,000.00
Dividends: Company S	6,000.00*			5,400.00
Company P				12,000.00*
Balances	$62,000.00	90%	$148,000.00	$137,200.00
1946: Profits	10,000.00			20,000.00
Dividends: Company S	6,000.00*			5,400.00
Company P				12,000.00*
Balances	$66,000.00	90%	$148,000.00	$150,600.00

* Deductions.

The goodwill, minority interest, and consolidated surplus can now be computed as follows:

	Company *S*		Company *P*	
	Capital Stock	Surplus	Investment in Co. *S*	Surplus
Balances before adjustment..	$100,000	$66,000	$148,000	$150,600
Adjustment for increases in subsidiary surplus since dates of acquisition........			12,400	12,400
Adjusted balances...........	$100,000	$66,000	$160,400	$163,000
Eliminate reciprocals (90%)..	90,000	59,400	149,400	
Minority interest............	$ 10,000	$ 6,600		
Goodwill....................			$ 11,000	
Consolidated surplus........				$163,000

Several purchases—control not originally obtained. Assume that a company makes more than one purchase of the stock of a company before control is obtained, as in the following illustration:

January 1, 1945:
  Company *A* purchases 25% of the stock of Company *B* for $28,000.00. At that date Company *B* has capital stock of $100,000.00 and no surplus.
Year ended December 31, 1945:
  Company *B* earns $20,000.00, and pays no dividends.
January 1, 1946:
  Company *A* purchases the remaining 75% of the stock of Company *B* for $96,000.00.
Year ended December 31, 1946:
  Company *B* earns $20,000.00, and pays no dividends.

Should the parent company take up 25% of the profit of Company *B* for 1945, during which time the parent company did not own a controlling interest in Company *B*'s stock?

On December 31, 1945, Company *A* would not have been justified in taking up 25% of the profit of Company *B* because the condition of parent and subsidiary did not exist.

But after Company *A* acquired the remaining 75% interest in the stock, the relation of parent and subsidiary did exist, and the parent company would then have been justified in taking up the profits of the subsidiary applicable to its previously held minority interest from the date of acquisition thereof to the date of the acquisition of control. In fact, if it did not do so, any subsequent consolidated balance sheet would misstate the goodwill and the consolidated surplus. To demonstrate this fact, let us return to the illustration.

The goodwill elements in the costs of the two stock acquisitions are shown on the following page.

First purchase—25% interest:			
Cost		$28,000.00	
Book value of stock acquired:			
Capital stock	$100,000.00		
Surplus	—		
Total	$100,000.00		
25% thereof		25,000.00	
Goodwill			$3,000.00
Second purchase—75% interest:			
Cost		$96,000.00	
Book value of stock acquired:			
Capital stock	$100,000.00		
Surplus	20,000.00		
Total	$120,000.00		
75% thereof		90,000.00	
Goodwill			6,000.00
Total goodwill			$9,000.00

Company *A*'s shares of the earnings of Company *B* applicable to its investments are:

For 1945—25% of $20,000.00, which benefited the parent company, although the parent company was not justified in actually taking up this profit before acquiring control	$ 5,000.00
For 1946—100% of $20,000.00	20,000.00
Total	$25,000.00

The following working papers show entries in the accounts of the two companies on the assumption that Company *A* did not take up its 25% interest in the profits of Company *B* at the end of 1945 because control did not then exist, but did take up the profit on this minority holding on the date when the purchase was made which established control. The working papers also show the computation of the goodwill and consolidated surplus at the end of 1946.

	Company *A*		Company *B*	
	Investment Account	Surplus	Capital Stock	Surplus
January 1, 1945:				
Subsidiary's account balances.			$100,000.00	$ —
Cost of 25% stock interest	$ 28,000.00			
December 31, 1945:				
Profit for year				20,000.00
January 1, 1946:				
Cost of 75% stock interest	96,000.00			
Profit applicable to 25% interest since date of acquisition.	5,000.00	$ 5,000.00		
December 31, 1946:				
Profit for year	20,000.00	20,000.00		20,000.00
Account balances	$149,000.00	$25,000.00	$100,000.00	$40,000.00
Eliminate reciprocals	140,000.00		100,000.00	40,000.00
Nonreciprocals:				
Goodwill	$ 9,000.00			
Consolidated surplus		$25,000.00		

The amounts of goodwill and consolidated surplus shown in the working papers are the amounts previously indicated as correct.

Let us now assume that the parent company kept its accounts on the incorrect premise that it could take up no profits other than those for periods subsequent to the date when control was established.

	Company *A*		Company *B*	
	Investment Account	Surplus	Capital Stock	Surplus
January 1, 1945:				
Subsidiary's account balances.			$100,000.00	$ —
Cost of 25% stock interest...	$ 28,000.00			
December 31, 1945:				
Profit for year.............				20,000.00
January 1, 1946:				
Cost of 75% stock interest...	96,000.00			
December 31, 1946:				
Profit for year.............	20,000.00	$20,000.00		20,000.00
Account balances.......	$144,000.00	$20,000.00	$100,000.00	$40,000.00
Eliminate reciprocals..........	140,000.00		100,000.00	40,000.00
Nonreciprocals:				
Goodwill..................	$ 4,000.00			
Consolidated surplus........		$20,000.00		

It is obvious that these working papers misstate the goodwill (excess of costs of stock acquisitions over book values thereof at dates of acquisition) and the consolidated surplus. The amount shown for consolidated surplus can be regarded as correct only on the theory that Company *A* earned nothing on its $28,000.00 investment during 1945; and the amount shown for goodwill can be regarded as correct only on the theory that the $5,000.00 profit applicable to the 25% holding in 1945 was not income but was a return of part of the cost of the investment.

Additional acquisition by subscription. If a parent company acquires additional subsidiary stock by subscription, the acquisition may be regarded as a purchase for purposes of determining any goodwill cost included in the price. But, since the subscription price is paid to the subsidiary, the price affects the book value of the total outstanding stock. Therefore, the book value of the stock acquired should be based on the total net worth of the subsidiary immediately after the issuance of the new stock.

Second illustration: Purchases and sales. In this illustration it is assumed that the parent company made several purchases of subsidiary stock and also made two sales. All facts relative to purchases, sales, profits, and dividends are shown in the statement on the following page.

COMPANY *P* AND SUBSIDIARY *S*
Statement of Surplus and Investment Accounts
(Subsidiary Profits and Dividends Taken Up)

	Company *S*	Company *P*		
		Investment In Company *S*		
	Surplus	Per Cent	Amount	Surplus
December 31, 1942—purchase, 600 shares	$50,000.00	60%	$ 99,000.00	$100,000.00
1943: Profits: Company *S*	10,000.00		6,000.00	6,000.00
Company *P*				20,000.00
Dividends: Company *S*	6,000.00*		3,600.00*	
Company *P*				12,000.00*
Purchase—December 31—100 shares		10	16,000.00	
Balances	$54,000.00	70%	$117,400.00	$114,000.00
1944: Profits: Company *S*	10,000.00		7,000.00	7,000.00
Company *P*				20,000.00
Dividends: Company *S*	6,000.00*		4,200.00*	
Company *P*				12,000.00*
Purchase—December 31—200 shares		20	33,000.00	
Balances	$58,000.00	90%	$153,200.00	$129,000.00
1945: Sale—January 1—50 shares		5 *	8,650.00*	1,350.00
Profits: Company *S*	10,000.00		8,500.00	8,500.00
Company *P*				20,000.00
Dividends: Company *S*	6,000.00*		5,100.00*	
Company *P*				12,000.00*
Balances	$62,000.00	85%	$147,950.00	$146,850.00
1946: Sale—June 30—50 shares		5 *	8,850.00*	1,150.00
Purchase—September 30—100 shares		10	19,000.00	
Profits: Company *S*	10,000.00			
80% for year			8,000.00	8,000.00
10% for ¼ year			250.00	250.00
Company *P*				20,000.00
Dividends: Company *S*	6,000.00*		5,400.00*	
Company *P*				12,000.00*
Balances	$66,000.00	90%	$160,950.00	$164,250.00

* Deductions.

All sales are regarded as having been made from the first stock purchased,† and the investment account is relieved of the carrying value of the stock sold—that is, the cost plus the net increase resulting from taking up profits, losses, and dividends. As the first purchase consisted of 600 shares, and as each sale disposed of 50 shares, each sale represented $\frac{5}{60}$ of the first stock purchased. The amounts credited to the investment account and the profits on the sales are determined as follows:

First sale—January 1, 1945:

Sale price			$10,000
Less carrying value:			
Cost—$\frac{5}{60}$ of $99,000.00		$8,250	
Increase since purchase:			
1943—Profits less dividends on 600 shares owned	$2,400		
$\frac{5}{60}$ thereof		200	
1944—Profits less dividends on 700 shares owned	2,800		
$\frac{5}{70}$ thereof		200	
Total carrying value (credited to investment)			8,650
Profit (credited to surplus)			$ 1,350

Second sale—June 30, 1946:

Sale price			$10,000
Less carrying value:			
Cost—$\frac{5}{60}$ of $99,000.00		$8,250	
Increase—1943 (computed as above)		200	
Increase—1944 (computed as above)		200	
Increase—1945—Profits less dividends on 850 shares owned	$3,400		
$\frac{5}{85}$ thereof		200	
Total carrying value (credited to investment)			8,850
Profit (credited to surplus)			$ 1,150

In connection with the second sale, it will be noted that the subsidiary's profit to June 30, 1946, the date of the sale, has not been taken up by the parent company. If it were known that the profit of Company *S* for the first six months of 1946 was (for example) $5,000.00 (half of the profit for the year), the entries to be made by Company *P* at the time of the sale could be:

	Investment in Company *S*	Surplus
To take up 5% of profit of Company *S* for the first 6 months of 1946	$ 250.00	$250.00
Sale of 50 shares	9,100.00*	900.00

* Deduction.

† The first-in, first-out basis is not the only one which could be used; other possible bases are last-in, first-out, average cost, and specific identification of stock certificates. Only the first-in, first-out, and the specific identification bases are recognized for tax purposes.

The net effect of the two methods is the same: In the second method, the investment account is debited with $250.00 and credited with $9,100.00, making a net credit of $8,850.00, as in the first method. In the second method, the $1,150.00 credit to surplus consists of two parts: the $250.00 share of income applicable to the stock to June 30, 1946 (the date of sale), and $900.00 profit on the sale.

One hundred shares of stock (10% interest) were purchased on September 30, 1946. The investment account was charged with the cost. The subsidiary profits for 1946 were taken up in amounts computed as follows:

Applicable to 800 shares owned during the entire year:	
80% of $10,000.00	$8,000.00
Applicable to 100 shares owned during last quarter of year:	
¼ of 10% of $10,000.00	250.00
Total	$8,250.00

The minority interest, goodwill, and consolidated surplus to appear in a consolidated balance sheet on December 31, 1946, are computed below:

	Subsidiary		Parent	
	Capital Stock	Surplus	Investment in Co. *S*	Surplus
Balances	$100,000	$66,000	$160,950	$164,250
Eliminate reciprocals (90%)	90,000	59,400	149,400	
Minority interest	$ 10,000	$ 6,600		
Goodwill			$ 11,550	
Consolidated surplus				$164,250

It will be of interest to note the effect of the stock sales upon the goodwill. The goodwill of $11,550.00 should represent the goodwill payments made in connection with the various stock purchases, minus the goodwill payments applicable to the stock sold. By the first-in, first-out theory, the stock sold is taken from the first stock purchased; the goodwill payment on the first purchase was $15.00 per share, as shown below; therefore, the goodwill payment applicable to the stock sold is regarded as $15.00 per share.

As shown in the statement of the parent company's accounts on page 311, the parent company took up (as applicable to the stock purchased on September 30, 1946) only the portion of the profit applicable to the three months subsequent to purchase. Therefore, the profits for the first nine months should be included in the book value of the subsidiary stock on September 30, for purposes of determining the goodwill applicable to the stock purchase on that date.

Purchase—December 31, 1942:			
Cost of 600 shares—60%		$99,000	
Book value:			
Stock and surplus of Company *S* (page 311)	$150,000		
60% thereof		90,000	
Goodwill ($15.00 per share)			$ 9,000
Purchase—December 31, 1943:			
Cost of 100 shares—10%		$16,000	
Book value:			
Stock and surplus of Company *S* (page 311)	$154,000		
10% thereof		15,400	
Goodwill ($6.00 per share)			600
Purchase—December 31, 1944:			
Cost of 200 shares—20%		$33,000	
Book value:			
Stock and surplus of Company *S* (page 311)	$158,000		
20% thereof		31,600	
Goodwill ($7.00 per share)			1,400
Sale—January 1, 1945—50 shares—regarded (by first-in, first-out theory) as purchased December 31, 1930; hence the goodwill was $15.00 per share. $15.00 × 50			750*
Sale—June 30, 1946—$15.00 × 50			750*
Purchase—September 30, 1946:			
Cost of 100 shares		$19,000	
Book value:			
Stock and surplus of Company *S*—December 31, 1945 (page 311)	$162,000		
Add profits to September 30, 1946—¾ of $10,000	7,500		
Total	$169,500		
10% thereof		16,950	
Goodwill—$20.50 per share			2,050
Total goodwill			$11,550

* Deductions.

The statement on page 315 shows the parent company's accounts on the basis of carrying the investment at cost and taking subsidiary dividends as income.

The amount of the required adjustment for changes in the subsidiary surplus is computed below:

Year	Subsidiary Surplus: Dividends	Subsidiary Surplus: Profit	Subsidiary Surplus: Increase Decrease*	Per Cent of Stock Retained	Parent's Share of Increase Decrease*
1943	$6,000	$10,000	$4,000	50%	$ 2,000
1944	6,000	10,000	4,000	60	2,400
1945	6,000	10,000	4,000	80	3,200
1946					
First nine months		7,500	7,500	80	6,000
Last three months	6,000	2,500	3,500*	90	3,150*
Total					$10,450

COMPANY *P* AND SUBSIDIARY *S*
Statement of Surplus and Investment Accounts
(Investment Carried at Cost)

	Company *S* Surplus	Company *P* — Investment In Company *S* — Per Cent	Company *P* — Investment In Company *S* — Cost	Company *P* — Surplus
December 31, 1942—Purchase, 600 shares	$50,000.00	60%	$ 99,000.00	$100,000.00
1943: Profits	10,000.00			20,000.00
Dividends: Company *S*	6,000.00*			3,600.00
Company *P*				12,000.00*
Purchase—December 31—100 shares		10	16,000.00	
Balances	$54,000.00	70%	$115,000.00	$111,600.00
1944: Profits	10,000.00			20,000.00
Dividends: Company *S*	6,000.00*			4,200.00
Company *P*				12,000.00*
Purchase—December 31—200 shares		20	33,000.00	
Balances	$58,000.00	90%	$148,000.00	$123,800.00
1945: Sale—January 1—50 shares (see note)		5 *	8,250.00*	1,750.00
Profits	10,000.00			20,000.00
Dividends: Company *S*	6,000.00*			5,100.00
Company *P*				12,000.00*
Balances	$62,000.00	85%	$139,750.00	$138,650.00
1946: Sale—June 30—50 shares (see note)		5 *	8,250.00*	1,750.00
Purchase—September 30—100 shares		10	19,000.00	
Profits	10,000.00			20,000.00
Dividends: Company *S*	6,000.00*			5,400.00
Company *P*				12,000.00*
Balances	$66,000.00	90%	$150,500.00	$153,800.00

* Deduction.

Note.—Since the investment is carried at cost, only the cost of the stock sold is credited to the investment account. The stock sold is regarded as a part of the first stock purchased. The profits on the sales are computed as follows:

Sale price	$10,000.00
Cost—5/60 of $99,000.00	8,250.00
Profit	$ 1,750.00

Observe that, in the worksheet on page 314, the adjustment for each year is based, not on the percentage of stock owned during the year, but on the percentage of stock owned and *retained to the end of the period.* For instance, the parent company owned 60% of the subsidiary stock during 1943, but it subsequently sold 10%; therefore, the 1943 adjustment is for only 50% of the increase in the subsidiary's surplus during that year. The operating income applicable to the 10% sold should be ignored, because, since the investment was carried at cost, the amounts taken into the parent company's surplus as profits on sales of stock really include the parent company's share of the subsidiary's earnings (minus dividends received) applicable to the stock sold. This can be proved by comparing the entries for profit on stock sales under the two methods of accounting.

	Investment Carried at Cost (See page 315)	Subsidiary Profits Taken Up (See page 311)
Profit on first sale	$1,750.00	$1,350.00
Profit on second sale	1,750.00	1,150.00
Total	$3,500.00	$2,500.00

The excess $1,000.00 recorded as profit on sales (if the investment is carried at cost) is really the excess of subsidiary profits over dividends (on the 100 shares sold) during the period that the shares were owned by the parent company, as shown below (the annual profits were $10.00 per share and the dividends were $6.00 per share, leaving a net increase in surplus of $4.00 per share):

1943—100 shares	$ 400.00
1945—100 shares	400.00
1946— 50 shares	200.00
Total	$1,000.00

The minority interest, goodwill, and consolidated surplus are computed below:

	Subsidiary		Parent	
	Capital Stock	Surplus	Investment in Co. *S*	Surplus
Balances before adjustment	$100,000	$66,000	$150,500	$153,800
Adjustment for net increase in subsidiary surplus since acquisition			10,450	10,450
Balances after adjustment	$100,000	$66,000	$160,950	$164,250
Eliminate reciprocals (90%)	90,000	59,400	149,400	
Minority interest	$ 10,000	$ 6,600		
Goodwill			$ 11,550	
Consolidated surplus				$164,250

Third illustration: Major and minor parents. In this illustration, the following stockholdings are assumed:

Company *A* (the major parent) owns an 80% interest in the stock of Company *B*.

Company *B* (the minor parent) owns a 90% interest in the stock of Company *C*.

Thus Company *A*, through its ownership in Company *B*, has a 72% interest in Company *C*.

The statement on page 318 shows accounts of the three companies on the assumption that subsidiary profits, losses, and dividends are taken up by the parent companies. Note that Company *B* takes up 80% of the changes in Company *C*'s surplus, and that Company *A* includes the applicable portions of these adjustments when taking up its 90% of the changes in Company *B*'s surplus.

The minority interests, goodwill, and consolidated surplus to be shown in a consolidated balance sheet, if one is prepared at this time, are computed on page 319.

If the investments are carried at cost, the accounts will be as shown on page 320, and the amounts of the adjustments for changes in subsidiary surpluses will be computed in the manner shown below. (It will be remembered that *B* purchased the stock of *C* on December 31, 1941, and *A* purchased the stock of *B* on December 31, 1943.)

	Surplus per Books		Surplus Adjustments	
	Company *C*	Company *B*	Company *B*	Company *A*
1942–1943:				
Surplus—end of period......	$72,000			
Surplus—beginning of period	50,000			
Increase..................	$22,000			
B's 90% of $22,000 increase			$19,800	
1944–1945:				
Surplus—end of period.....	$57,000	$120,800		
Surplus—beginning of period	72,000	129,400		
Decrease—Co. *C*..........	$15,000*			
B's 90% of $15,000*.....			13,500*	
A's 80% of $13,500*.....				$10,800*
Decrease—Co. *B*..........		$ 8,600*		
A's 80% of $8,60C*......				6,880*
Total adjustments..........			$ 6,300	$17,680*

The minority interests, goodwill, and consolidated surplus will then be computed as shown in the working papers appearing on page 321.

COMPANY *A* AND SUBSIDIARIES *B* AND *C*

Statement of Surplus and Investment Accounts

(Subsidiary Profits, Losses, and Dividends Taken Up)

	Company *C*	Company *B*			Company *A*		
		Investment In Company *C*			Investment In Company *B*		
	Surplus	Per Cent	Amount	Surplus	Per Cent	Amount	Surplus
1941: Purchase—December 31	$50,000	90%	$140,000	$100,000			
1942: Profits: Company *C*	20,000		18,000	18,000			
Company *B*				20,000			
Dividends: Company *C*	8,000*		7,200*				
Company *B*				10,000*			
Balances	$62,000	90%	$150,800	$128,000			
1943: Profits: Company *C*	18,000		16,200	16,200			
Company *B*				15,000			
Dividends: Company *C*	8,000*		7,200*				
Company *B*				10,000*			
Purchase—December 31					80%	$284,360	$150,000
Balances	$72,000	90%	$159,800	$149,200	80%	$284,360	$150,000
1944: Profits: Company *C*	6,000		5,400	5,400		4,320	4,320
Company *B*				3,000		2,400	2,400
Company *A*							30,000
Dividends: Company *C*	8,000*		7,200*				
Company *B*				10,000*		8,000*	
Company *A*							25,000*
Balances	$70,000	90%	$158,000	$147,600	80%	$283,080	$161,720
1945: Profits (losses*): Company *C*	5,000*		4,500*	4,500*		3,600*	3,600*
Company *B*				6,000*		4,800*	4,800*
Company *A*							6,000
Dividends: Company *C*	8,000*		7,200*				
Company *B*				10,000*		8,000*	
Company *A*							25,000*
Balances	$57,000	90%	$146,300	$127,100	80%	$266,680	$134,320

* Deduction.

	Company C		Company B			Company A	
	Capital Stock	Surplus	Investment in Co. C	Capital Stock	Surplus	Investment in Co. B	Surplus
Balances	$100,000	$57,000	$146,300	$200,000	$127,100	$266,680	$134,320
Eliminate reciprocals:							
Company B's 90% in Company C	90,000	51,300	141,300				
Company A's 80% in Company B				160,000	101,680	261,680	
Minority interests:							
In Company C	$ 10,000	$ 5,700					
In Company B				$ 40,000	$ 25,420		
Goodwill			$ 5,000			$ 5,000	
Consolidated surplus							$134,320

COMPANY *A* AND SUBSIDIARIES *B* AND *C*

Statement of Surplus and Investment Accounts

(*Investments Carried at Cost*)

		Company B			Company A		
		Investment In Company *C*			Investment In Company *B*		
	Company *C* Surplus	Per Cent	Amount	Surplus	Per Cent	Amount	Surplus
1941: Purchase—December 31	$50,000.00	90%	$140,000.00	$100,000.00			
1942: Profits	20,000.00			20,000.00			
Dividends: Company *C*	8,000.00*			7,200.00			
Company *B*				10,000.00*			
Balances	$62,000.00	90%	$140,000.00	$117,200.00			
1943: Profits	18,000.00			15,000.00			
Dividends: Company *C*	8,000.00*			7,200.00			
Company *B*				10,000.00*			
Purchase—December 31					80%	$284,360.00	$150,000.00
Balances	$72,000.00	90%	$140,000.00	$129,400.00	80%	$284,360.00	$150,000.00
1944: Profits	6,000.00			3,000.00			30,000.00
Dividends: Company *C*	8,000.00*			7,200.00			
Company *B*				10,000.00*			8,000.00
Company *A*							25,000.00*
Balances	$70,000.00	90%	$140,000.00	$129,600.00	80%	$284,360.00	$163,000.00
1945: Profits (Losses*)	5,000.00*			6,000.00*			6,000.00
Dividends: Company *C*	8,000.00*			7,200.00			
Company *B*				10,000.00*			8,000.00
Company *A*							25,000.00*
Balances	$57,000.00	90%	$140,000.00	$120,800.00	80%	$284,360.00	$152,000.00

* Deduction.

	Company C		Company B			Company A	
	Capital Stock	Surplus	Investment in Co. C	Capital Stock	Surplus	Investment in Co. B	Surplus
Balances before adjustment	$100,000	$57,000	$140,000	$200,000	$120,800	$284,360	$152,000
Adjustments for changes in subsidiary surpluses since acquisition:							
For increase in Co. C surplus			6,300		6,300		
For decrease in Co. B surplus						17,680*	17,680*
Balances after adjustment	$100,000	$57,000	$146,300	$200,000	$127,100	$266,680	$134,320
Eliminate reciprocals:							
Co. B's investment in Co. C—90%	90,000	51,300	141,300				
Co. A's investment in Co. B—80%				160,000	101,680	261,680	
Minority interests:							
Co. C	$ 10,000	$ 5,700					
Co. B				$ 40,000	$ 25,420		
Goodwill			$ 5,000			$ 5,000	
Consolidated surplus							$134,320

* Deduction.

Fourth illustration: Control through minor parent and direct. In this illustration it is assumed that, as a result of stock purchases by Company *A* and Company *B* at various dates, the intercompany holdings were as follows:

	Per Cent of Stock of	
	Company *B*	Company *C*
1941–1942:		
Co. *A* owned	60%	
1943:		
Co. *A* owned	60%	
Co. *B* owned		70%
1944:		
Co. *A* owned	60%	20%
Co. *B* owned		70
1945:		
Co. *A* owned	80%	20%
Co. *B* owned		70
1946:		
Co. *A* owned	80%	25%
Co. *B* owned		75

Company *A*'s control of Company *C* is based largely on its ownership of the stock of the minor parent, Company *B*, but partly also upon direct ownership by Company *A* of stock of Company *C*.

The statement on page 323 shows the accounts of the three companies on the assumption that the parent companies (Company *A* and Company *B*) take up their percentages of the profits, losses, and dividends of their subsidiaries. Note that, with respect to the profits of Company *C*:

In 1943, Company *B* takes up 70% of the profit of Company *C*, or $4,200.00; Company *A* then takes up 60% of this $4,200.00.

In 1944, Company *B* takes up (by debit to investment in *C*) 70% of *C*'s $2,000.00 profit, or $1,400.00.

Company *A* takes up (by debit to investment in *B*) 60% of the $1,400.00.

Company *A* also takes up (by debit to investment in *C*) 20% of *C*'s $2,000.00 profit, or $400.00. Since the 20% interest is a minority holding, the entry would not be justified except for the fact that Company *A* exercises control of Company *C* through its ownership of a controlling interest in the stock of the minor parent company, *B*.

Entries for profits and losses of Company *C* in subsequent years are made in a similar manner.

COMPANY *A* AND SUBSIDIARIES *B* AND *C*

Statement of Surplus and Investment Accounts

(Subsidiary Profits, Losses, and Dividends Taken Up)

		Company *B*			Company *A*				
	Company *C* Surplus	Investment In Company *C* Per Cent	Investment In Company *C* Amount	Surplus	Investment In Company *C* Per Cent	Investment In Company *C* Amount	Investment In Company *B* Per Cent	Investment In Company *B* Amount	Surplus
1940: Purchase—December 31				$50,000			60%	$100,000	$150,000
1941: Profits: Company *B*				15,000				9,000	9,000
Company *A*									25,000
Dividends: Company *B*				6,000*				3,600*	
Company *A*									9,000*
Balances				$59,000			60%	$105,400	$175,000
1942: Profits: Company *B*				12,000				7,200	7,200
Company *A*									20,000
Dividends: Company *B*				6,000*				3,600*	
Company *A*									9,000*
Purchase—December 31	$30,000	70%	$60,000						
Balances	$30,000	70%	$60,000	$65,000			60%	$109,000	$193,200
1943: Profits: Company *C*	6,000		4,200	4,200				2,520	2,520
Company *B*				10,000				6,000	6,000
Company *A*									15,000
Dividends: Company *C*	3,000*		2,100*						
Company *B*				6,000*				3,600*	
Company *A*									9,000*
Purchase—December 31					20%	$18,000			
Balances forward	$33,000	70%	$62,100	$73,200	20%	$18,000	60%	$113,920	$207,720

COMPANY *A* AND SUBSIDIARIES *B* AND *C*

Statement of Surplus and Investment Accounts—(*Continued*)

(*Subsidiary Profits, Losses, and Dividends Taken Up*)

	Company *C*	Company *B*			Company *A*				
		Investment In Company *C*			Investment In Company *C*		Investment In Company *B*		
	Surplus	Per Cent	Amount	Surplus	Per Cent	Amount	Per Cent	Amount	Surplus
Balances (brought forward)	$33,000	70 %	$62,100	73,200	20 %	$18,000	60 %	$113,920	$207,720
1944: Profits: Company *C*	2,000		1,400	1,400		400		840	1,240
Company *B*				5,000				3,000	3,000
Company *A*									10,000
Dividends: Company *C*	3,000*		2,100*			600*			
Company *B*				6,000*				3,600*	
Company *A*									9,000*
Purchase—December 31							20 %	36,000	
Balances	$32,000	70 %	$61,400	$73,600	20 %	$17,800	80 %	$150,160	$212,960
1945: Profits (losses*): Company *C*	3,000*		2,100*	2,100*		600*		1,680*	2,280*
Company *B*				2,000*				1,600*	1,600*
Company *A*									5,000
Dividends: Company *C*	3,000*		2,100*			600*			
Company *B*				6,000*				4,800*	
Company *A*									9,000*
Purchase—December 31		5	4,000		5	4,000			
Balances	$26,000	75 %	$61,200	$63,500	25 %	$20,600	80 %	$142,080	$205,080
1946: Losses: Company *C*	2,000*		1,500*	1,500*		500*		1,200*	1,700*
Company *B*				4,000*				3,200*	3,200*
Company *A*									3,000*
Dividends: Company *C*	3,000*		2,250*			750*			
Company *B*				6,000*				4,800*	
Company *A*									9,000*
Balances	$21,000	75 %	$57,450	$52,000	25 %	$19,350	80 %	$132,880	$188,180

* Deductions.

The minority interests, goodwill, and consolidated surplus are computed below:

	Company *C*		Company *B*			Company *A*		
	Capital Stock	Surplus	Investment in Co. *C*	Capital Stock	Surplus	Investment in Co. *B*	Investment in Co. *C*	Surplus
Balances	$50,000	$21,000	$57,450	$100,000	$52,000	$132,880	$19,350	$188,180
Eliminate reciprocals:								
Company *A*'s 80% interest in Company *B*				80,000	41,600	121,600		
Company *B*'s 75% interest in Company *C*	37,500	15,750	53,250					
Company *A*'s 25% interest in Company *C*	12,500	5,250					17,750	
Minority interest in Company *B*				$ 20,000	$10,400			
Goodwill			$ 4,200			$ 11,280	$ 1,600	
Consolidated surplus								$188,180

The following statement shows the accounts of the three companies on the assumption that the investments are carried at cost.

COMPANIES *A*, *B*, AND *C*

Statement of Surplus and Investment Accounts

(*Investments Carried at Cost*)

	Company *C*	Company *B*			Company *A*				
		Investment In Company *C*			Investment In Company *C*		Investment In Company *B*		
	Surplus	Per Cent	Cost	Surplus	Per Cent	Cost	Per Cent	Cost	Surplus
1940: Purchase—December 31				$50,000.00			60%	$100,000.00	$150,000.00
1941: Profits				15,000.00					25,000.00
Dividends: Company *B*				6,000.00*					3,600.00
Company *A*									9,000.00*
Balances				$59,000.00			60%	$100,000.00	$169,600.00
1942: Profits				12,000.00					20,000.00
Dividends: Company *B*				6,000.00*					3,600.00
Company *A*									9,000.00*
Purchase—December 31	$30,000.00	70%	$60,000.00						
Balances	$30,000.00	70%	$60,000.00	$65,000.00			60%	$100,000.00	$184,200.00
1943: Profits	6,000.00			10,000.00					15,000.00
Dividends: Company *C*	3,000.00*			2,100.00					
Company *B*				6,000.00*					3,600.00
Company *A*									9,000.00*
Purchase—December 31					20%	$18,000.00			
Balances	$33,000.00	70%	$60,000.00	$71,100.00	20%	$18,000.00	60%	$100,000.00	$193,800.00
1944: Profits	2,000.00			5,000.00					10,000.00
Dividends: Company *C*	3,000.00*			2,100.00					600.00
Company *B*				6,000.00*					3,600.00
Company *A*									9,000.00*
Purchase—December 31							20%	36,000.00	
Balances	$32,000.00	70%	$60,000.00	$72,200.00	20%	$18,000.00	80%	$136,000.00	$199,000.00
1945: Profits (Losses*)	3,000.00*			2,000.00*					5,000.00
Dividends: Company *C*	3,000.00*			2,100.00					600.00
Company *B*				6,000.00*					4,800.00
Company *A*									9,000.00*
Purchase—December 31		5	4,000.00		5	4,000.00			
Balances	$26,000.00	75%	$64,000.00	$66,300.00	25%	$22,000.00	80%	$136,000.00	$200,400.00
1946: Profits (Losses*)	2,000.00*			4,000.00*					3,000.00*
Dividends: Company *C*	3,000.00*			2,250.00					750.00
Company *B*				6,000.00*					4,800.00
Company *A*									9,000.00*
Balances	$21,000.00	75%	$64,000.00	$58,550.00	25%	$22,000.00	80%	$136,000.00	$193,950.00

* Deductions.

The adjustments for changes in subsidiaries' surpluses since acquisition dates are computed below:

Acquisition Dates	Subsidiaries' Surplus Accounts—Per Books		Company B		Company A			
			Investment In Company C		Investment In Company C		Investment In Company B	
	Company C	Company B	Per Cent	Amount	Per Cent	Amount	Per Cent	Amount
Dec. 31, 1940—*A* buys 60% of *B*		$50,000					60%	$9,000
1941–1942—Increase		15,000						
Dec. 31, 1942—*B* buys 70% of *C*	$30,000	$65,000						
1943: Increase—Co. *C*	3,000		70%	$2,100			60	1,260
Increase—Co. *B*		6,100					60	3,660
Dec. 31, 1943—*A* buys 20% of *C*	$33,000	$71,100						
1944: Decrease—Co. *C*	1,000*		70	700*	20%	$ 200*	60	420*
Increase—Co. *B*		1,100					60	660
Dec. 31, 1944—*A* buys 20% of *B*	$32,000	$72,200						
1945: Decrease—Co. *C*	6,000*		70	4,200*	20	1,200*	80	3,360*
Decrease—Co. *B*		5,900*					80	4,720*
Dec. 31, 1945—*A* and *B* each buys 5% of *C*	$26,000	$66,300						
1946: Decrease—Co. *C*	5,000*		75	3,750*	25	1,250*	80	3,000*
Decrease—Co. *B*		7,750*					80	6,200*
Balances—December 31, 1946	$21,000	$58,550						
Total adjustments: Company *B*				$6,550*				
Company *A*						$2,650*		$3,120*

* Deductions.

The minority interest, goodwill, and consolidated surplus are computed in the following working papers:

	Company *C*			Company *B*		Company *A*		
	Capital Stock	Surplus	Investment in Co. *C*	Capital Stock	Surplus	Investment in Co. *B*	Investment in Co. *C*	Surplus
Balances before adjustment	$50,000	$21,000	$64,000	$100,000	$58,550	$136,000	$22,000	$193,950
Adjustments—decreases in surplus:								
Co. *B*'s investment in Co. *C*			6,550*		6,550*			
Co. *A*'s investment in Co. *B*						3,120*		3,120*
Co. *A*'s investment in Co. *C*							2,650*	2,650*
Adjusted balances	$50,000	$21,000	$57,450	$100,000	$52,000	$132,880	$19,350	$188,180
Eliminate reciprocals:								
Co. *B*'s investment in Co. *C*	37,500	15,750	53,250					
Co. *A*'s investment in Co. *B*				80,000	41,600	121,600		
Co. *A*'s investment in Co. *C*	12,500	5,250					17,750	
Minority interest in Co. *B*				$ 20,000	$10,400			
Goodwill			$ 4,200			$ 11,280	$ 1,600	
Consolidated surplus								$188,180

* Deduction.

Fifth illustration: Reciprocal stockholdings. In this illustration we shall assume that three companies were organized on January 1, 1946, and that their stocks were issued on that date as follows:

	Company *A*	Company *B*	Company *C*
Par of stock	$500,000	$250,000	$150,000
Issued to:			
Company *A*		70%	75%
Company *B*			20
Company *C*		18	
Outsiders	100%	12	5
Total	100%	100%	100%

The profits of the several companies for 1946 were:

Company *A*	$50,000.00
Company *B*	20,000.00
Company *C*	15,000.00
Total	$85,000.00

How should the total surplus of $85,000.00 be apportioned to consolidated surplus and minority interests? To answer this question we must remember that the profits shown by the individual companies are not their total profits, because they must be adjusted for interests in the profits of other companies. Representing the adjusted profits of the three companies by *A*, *B*, and *C*, we have the following equations:

$$A = \$50{,}000.00 + .70B + .75C$$
$$B = \$20{,}000.00 + .20C$$
$$C = \$15{,}000.00 + .18B$$

It is advisable to compute the profits of Companies *B* and *C*, before computing those of Company *A*. Starting with the equation for Company *B*,

$$B = \$20{,}000.00 + .20C$$

and substituting for *C* the valuation of *C*,

$$B = \$20{,}000.00 + .20\ (\$15{,}000.00 + .18B)$$
$$B = \$20{,}000.00 + \$3{,}000.00 + .036B$$
$$.964B = \$23{,}000.00$$
$$B = \$23{,}858.93$$

$$C = \$15{,}000.00 + .18B$$
$$C = \$15{,}000.00 + (.18 \times \$23{,}858.93)$$
$$C = \$15{,}000.00 + \$4{,}294.61$$
$$C = \$19{,}294.61$$
$$A = \$50{,}000.00 + .70B + .75C$$
$$A = \$50{,}000.00 + (.70 \times \$23{,}858.93) + (.75 \times \$19{,}294.61)$$
$$A = \$50{,}000.00 + \$16{,}701.25 + \$14{,}470.96$$
$$A = \$81{,}172.21$$

We can now determine the consolidated surplus and the minority interests in the surpluses of the two subsidiaries, as shown on page 330.

Consolidated surplus:	
100% of Company *A* profits	$81,172.21
Minority interest in Company *B*:	
12% of Company *B*'s profits of $23,858.93	2,863.07
Minority interest in Company *C*:	
5% of Company *C*'s profits of $19,294.61	964.72
Total—equal to surplus of three companies	$85,000.00

The adjustments to be made in the working papers will depend upon how the intercompany investments are carried. Let us assume, first, that they are carried at cost, as follows:

A's investment in *B* (70% of $250,000.00)	$175,000.00
A's investment in *C* (75% of $150,000.00)	112,500.00
B's investment in *C* (20% of $150,000.00)	30,000.00
C's investment in *B* (18% of $250,000.00)	45,000.00

The adjustments and eliminations in the working papers are shown on page 331.

Let us now assume that Company *A* has taken up its share of the profits of Company *B* and Company *C*, as shown by their books, but the subsidiaries have not taken up the profits applicable to their reciprocal stockholdings; the surplus accounts of the three companies will then stand as follows:

Company *A*:	
Own profits	$50,000.00
70% of *B*'s $20,000.00 profit	14,000.00
75% of *C*'s $15,000.00 profit	11,250.00
Total	$75,250.00
Company *B*—own profits	$20,000.00
Company *C*—own profits	$15,000.00

The necessary adjustments and eliminations are shown in the working papers on page 331.

Sixth illustration: Circular stockholdings. In this illustration, the following stockholdings are assumed:

Company *A* owns 90% of Company *B*.
Company *B* owns 80% of Company *C*.
Company *C* owns 10% of Company *A*.

All stock acquisitions were made on January 1, 1946, the date on which all companies were organized. The profits of the three companies for 1946 were: Company *A*, $30,000.00; Company *B*, $20,000.00; Company *C*, $15,000.00. How should the surplus of the three companies, totaling $65,000.00, be apportioned to the minority interests and the consolidated surplus in a consolidated balance sheet on December 31, 1946?

	Company A			Company B			Company C		
Investments carried at cost	Investment in B	Investment in C	Surplus	Investment in C	Capital Stock	Surplus	Investment in B	Capital Stock	Surplus
Balances before adjustment	$175,000.00	$112,500.00	$50,000.00	$30,000.00	$250,000.00	$20,000.00	$45,000.00	$150,000.00	$15,000.00
Adjustment for intercompany profits:									
A's interest in *B* and *C*	16,701.25	14,470.96	31,172.21						
B's interest in *C*				3,858.93		3,858.93			
C's interest in *B*							4,294.61		4,294.61
Adjusted balances	$191,701.25	$126,970.96	$81,172.21	$33,858.93	$250,000.00	$23,858.93	$49,294.61	$150,000.00	$19,294.61
Eliminate reciprocals:									
A's 70% interest in *B*	$191,701.25				$175,000.00	$16,701.25			
A's 75% interest in *C*		$126,970.96						$112,500.00	$14,470.96
B's 20% interest in *C*				$33,858.93				30,000.00	3,858.93
C's 18% interest in *B*					45,000.00	4,294.61	$49,294.61		
Total eliminations	$191,701.25	$126,970.96		$33,858.93	$220,000.00	$20,995.86	$49,294.61	$142,500.00	$18,329.89
Non-reciprocals:									
Consolidated surplus			$81,172.21						
Minority interests:									
Company *B*					$ 30,000.00	$ 2,863.07			
Company *C*								$ 7,500.00	$ 964.72
Profits taken up by Company *A*									
Balances before adjustment	$189,000.00	$123,750.00	$75,250.00	$30,000.00	$250,000.00	$20,000.00	$45,000.00	$150,000.00	$15,000.00
Adjustments:									
B's 20% interest in *C*				3,858.93		3,858.93			
C's 18% interest in *B*							4,294.61		4,294.61
A's 70% interest in *B*'s $3,858.93 interest in *C*	2,701.25		2,701.25						
A's 75% interest in *C*'s $4,294.61 interest in *B*		3,220.96	3,220.96						
Adjusted balances	$191,701.25	$126,970.96	$81,172.21	$33,858.93	$250,000.00	$23,858.93	$49,294.61	$150,000.00	$19,294.61
Eliminate reciprocals:									
A's 70% interest in *B*	$191,701.25				$175,000.00	$16,701.25			
A's 75% interest in *C*		$126,970.96						$112,500.00	$14,470.96
B's 20% interest in *C*				$33,858.93				30,000.00	3,858.93
C's 18% interest in *B*					45,000.00	4,294.61	$49,294.61		
Total eliminations	$191,701.25	$126,970.96		$33,858.93	$220,000.00	$20,995.86	$49,294.61	$142,500.00	$18,329.89
Non-reciprocals:									
Consolidated surplus			$81,172.21						
Minority interests:									
Company *B*					$ 30,000.00	$ 2,863.07			
Company *C*								$ 7,500.00	$ 964.72

The adjusted earnings of the three companies, after giving recognition to the profits applicable to stockholdings, are computed as follows:

$$A = \$30{,}000.00 + .90B$$
$$B = \$20{,}000.00 + .80C$$
$$C = \$15{,}000.00 + .10A$$

These equations are solved as follows:

$$A = \$30{,}000.00 + .9B$$

Substituting for B, the value of B in the second equation,

$$A = \$30{,}000.00 + .9\ (\$20{,}000.00 + .8C)$$
$$A = \$30{,}000.00 + \$18{,}000.00 + .72C$$

Substituting for C, the value of C in the third equation,

$$A = \$48{,}000.00 + .72\ (\$15{,}000.00 + .1A)$$
$$A = \$48{,}000.00 + \$10{,}800.00 + .072A$$
$$A - .072A = \$58{,}800.00$$
$$A = \$63{,}362.07$$

$$C = \$15{,}000.00 + .1A$$
$$C = \$15{,}000.00 + (.1 \times \$63{,}362.07)$$
$$C = \$15{,}000.00 + \$6{,}336.21$$
$$C = \$21{,}336.21$$

$$B = \$20{,}000.00 + .8C$$
$$B = \$20{,}000.00 + (.8 \times \$21{,}336.21)$$
$$B = \$20{,}000.00 + \$17{,}068.97$$
$$B = \$37{,}068.97$$

The apportionment of the total surplus of $65,000.00 among the minority interests and the consolidated surplus on December 31, 1946, is as follows:

Minority interests:	
Company *B*—10% of $37,068.97 adjusted profit	$ 3,706,90
Company *C*—20% of $21,336.21 adjusted profit	4,267.24
Consolidated surplus—90% of $63,362.07	57,025.86
Total	$65,000.00

There is a trend in corporation laws to place a dividend restriction on surplus to the extent of the cost of treasury stock acquired. This suggests the following questions: If a subsidiary acquires part of the parent company's stock, is this tantamount to the parent company's purchase of its own shares; and should the consolidated balance sheet show a restriction of consolidated surplus? Presumably, a court would decide such questions from the legal standpoint of separate corporate entities, which is not the standpoint from which the consolidated balance sheet is prepared.

Reciprocal stockholdings: Intercompany profit reserve. Assume that Company *A* owns 85% of the stock of Company *B*, and that A holds goods in its inventory on which B made a profit of \$10,000.00. The reserve for intercompany profit in inventories would be 85% of \$10,000.00, or \$8,500.00.

But let us now assume a reciprocal stockholding situation: A owns 85% of B and B owns 10% of A. The reserve should not be \$8,500.00 because the minority stockholders of B have an interest in the profits of A. Representing Company A's profits by A, and Company B's profits by B, we have the following equations:

$$A = .85B$$
$$B = \$10{,}000.00 + .10A$$
Then
$$A = .85\,(\$10{,}000.00 + .10A)$$
$$A = \$8{,}500.00 + .085A$$
$$.915A = \$8{,}500.00$$
$$A = \$9{,}289.62$$

And, since only 90% of Company A's stock is in the hands of the public, the reserve should be 90% of \$9,289.62, or \$8,360.66.

This can be checked by computing Company B's minority interest in the \$10,000.00 profit, and noting that the reserve plus the minority interest equals the total profit.

$$B = \$10{,}000.00 + .10A$$
$$B = \$10{,}000.00 + (.10 \times \$9{,}289.62)$$
$$B = \$10{,}000.00 + \$928.96$$
$$B = \$10{,}928.96$$

The minority interest is 15% of \$10,928.96, or \$1,639.34.

Reserve for intercompany profit	\$ 8,360.66
Minority interest in intercompany profit	1,639.34
Total	\$10,000.00

Let us now assume that the profit was made by Company A and that the goods remain in the inventory of Company B. The equations are:

$$A = \$10{,}000.00 + .85B$$
$$B = .10A$$
$$A = \$10{,}000.00 + (.85 \times .10A)$$
$$A = \$10{,}000.00 + .085A$$
$$.915A = \$10{,}000.00$$
$$A = \$10{,}928.96$$

The reserve for intercompany profit is 90% of \$10,928.96, or \$9,836.06. The computation of the minority interest is shown below:

$$B = .10A$$
$$B = \tfrac{1}{10} \text{ of } \$10{,}928.96$$
$$B = \$1{,}092.90$$
$.15B = \$163.94$ which is the minority interest in the intercompany profit.

Proof

Reserve for intercompany profit	\$ 9,836.06
Minority interest in intercompany profit	163.94
Total	\$10,000.00

CHAPTER 50

Consolidated Balance Sheet, Surplus Statement, and Profit and Loss Statement

Working papers—facilitating conditions. The consolidated balance sheet is frequently accompanied by a consolidated surplus statement and a consolidated profit and loss statement.

In the chapters dealing with the consolidated balance sheet it was shown that the preparation of the working papers is facilitated if the parent company follows the accounting practice of recording its share of subsidiary profits, losses, and dividends in the investment account. If a consolidated profit and loss statement also is required, it is advisable to prepare the working papers before the parent company has made an entry taking up its share of the subsidiary profit or loss for the current period. If such an entry has been made, subsidiary profits will be recorded on the books of both companies, and an adjustment will be required to eliminate the duplication.

If a consolidated surplus statement also is required, the preparation of the working papers will be facilitated if the parent and subsidiary companies' surplus accounts show the balances at the beginning of the current period, and if changes during the period (required for the statement) are shown as balances of separate accounts, or as separate items.

For purposes of reference in this text, the conditions mentioned above will be called "facilitating conditions." They may be summarized as follows:

(A) The parent company has recorded, in its investment account, its share of subsidiary profits, losses, and dividends from the date of acquisition to the end of the current period, except that

(B) The parent company has not made an entry to take up its share of the subsidiary profit or loss for the current period.

(C) The parent and subsidiary companies' surplus accounts show the balances at the beginning of the current period, and any changes during the period are shown in separate accounts.

In the illustrations in this chapter, these conditions will be assumed to exist; subsequent illustrations will show the adjustments to be made if they do not exist.

Case 1. This illustration is based on the following facts:

Consolidated statements are required for the year 1945.

Company *P* owns 90% of the stock of Company *S*, which it acquired on January 1, 1945.

No dividends were paid by either company during 1945.

The principal working papers appear on page 337; supplementary working papers appear on page 338. The procedure for preparing the working papers is explained in detail below.

Enter the trial balances, leaving lines for eliminations after the investment account in the debit section. Add the trial balance columns to detect any errors in copying.

Enter the adjustments. In the working papers on page 337, the only adjustment is for the inventories at the end of the year, which are:

Company *P*	$27,000.00
Company *S*	16,000.00
Total	$43,000.00

Enter the eliminations.

Eliminations A and B are for the parent company's 90% of the capital stock of the subsidiary and 90% of its surplus at the beginning of the year.

If any nominal accounts contain debits or credits for intercompany transactions, the amounts of such intercompany items must be eliminated so that the consolidated statements will reflect the results of transactions with outsiders only. In the illustration, it is assumed that Company *S* made sales of $25,000.00 to Company *P*; elimination C takes this amount out of the sales and purchases accounts.

Foot the adjustments and eliminations columns.

Extend the trial balance amounts, as modified by the adjustments and eliminations, to the appropriate columns.

Determine the subsidiary's net profit, and the apportionment thereof between the minority and the parent company, by the following procedure:

Add the profit and loss columns of the debit and credit sections;

From the total profit and loss credits, deduct the total profit and loss debits; the remainder is the combined profit of the parent company and the subsidiary.

COMPANY *P* AND SUBSIDIARY *S*

Consolidated Working Papers

For the Year Ended December 31, 1945

	Company *P*	Company *S*	Adjustments Dr.	Adjustments Cr.	Eliminations	Profit and Loss	Surplus	Minority	Balance Sheet
Debits									
Cash	$ 39,500	$ 29,000							$ 68,500
Accounts receivable	50,000	40,000							90,000
Investment in Company *S*—90%	61,500								
Eliminate:									
Capital stock					$45,000A				
Surplus					13,500B				
Goodwill									3,000
Inventory, December 31, 1944	25,000	15,000				$ 40,000			
Purchases	100,000	80,000			25,000C	155,000			
Expense	15,000	11,000				26,000			
	$291,000	$175,000							
Inventory, December 31, 1945			$43,000a						43,000
					$83,500				
Column total deducted contra						$221,000	$ —	$ —	
									$204,500
Credits									
Accounts payable	$ 22,500	$ 10,000							$ 32,500
Capital stock:									
Company *P*	100,000								100,000
Company *S*		50,000			$45,000A			$5,000	
Surplus, December 31, 1944:									
Company *P*	43,500						$43,500		
Company *S*		15,000			13,500B			1,500	
Sales	125,000	100,000			25,000C	$200,000			
	$291,000	$175,000							
Inventory, December 31, 1945				$43,000a		43,000			
			$43,000	$43,000	$83,500				
Profit and loss:									
Credits						$243,000			
Debits—per contra						221,000			
Net profit						$ 22,000			
Minority interest in Company *S*—see page 338						1,000		1,000	
Parent company's share						$ 21,000	21,000		
Surplus							$64,500		64,500
Minority interest								$7,500	7,500
									$204,500

On a separate work sheet compute the minority interest in the profit of the subsidiary.

The computation may be detailed in the manner illustrated below:

Minority Interest in Subsidiary Net Profit

Profit and loss credits:		
Per trial balance:		
Sales		$100,000.00
Inventory at end of year		16,000.00
Total		$116,000.00
Profit and loss debits:		
Per trial balance:		
Inventory at beginning of year	$15,000.00	
Purchases	80,000.00	
Expenses	11,000.00	
Total		106,000.00
Net profit		$ 10,000.00
Minority interest:		
Per cent		10%
Amount		$ 1,000.00

Or, instead of repeating account balances already detailed in the trial balance columns of the main working papers, totals thereof may be shown, thus:

Minority Interest in Subsidiary Net Profit

Profit and loss credits:	
Detailed in trial balance	$100,000.00
Inventory at end of year	16,000.00
Total	$116,000.00
Profit and loss debits:	
Detailed in trial balance	106,000.00
Net profit	$ 10,000.00
Minority interest:	
Per cent	10%
Amount	$ 1,000.00

From the total net profit shown in the main working papers, deduct the minority interest in the profit of the subsidiary; the remainder is the parent company's share of the total net income.

Determine the consolidated surplus balance by extending the parent company's share of the net income to the surplus column and totaling that column.

Determine the total minority interest by extending the minority's share of the net income to the minority column and totaling that column.

Extend the totals of the surplus and minority columns to the balance sheet column, and determine the debit and credit totals of that column.

Statements for Case 1. The following statements were prepared from the working papers on page 337.

COMPANY *P* AND SUBSIDIARY *S* Exhibit *C*

Consolidated Statement of Profit and Loss

For the Year Ended December 31, 1945

Sales		$200,000.00
Deduct cost of goods sold:		
Inventory, December 31, 1944	$ 40,000.00	
Purchases	155,000.00	
Total	$195,000.00	
Deduct inventory, December 31, 1945	43,000.00	
Cost of goods sold		152,000.00
Gross profit on sales		$ 48,000.00
Deduct expenses		26,000.00
Total net profit		$ 22,000.00
Deduct minority interest in subsidiary profit		1,000.00
Consolidated net profit		$ 21,000.00

COMPANY *P* AND SUBSIDIARY *S* Exhibit *B*

Consolidated Statement of Surplus

For the Year Ended December 31, 1945

Balance, December 31, 1944	$43,500.00
Add net profit—Exhibit C	21,000.00
Balance, December 31, 1945	$64,500.00

COMPANY *P* AND SUBSIDIARY *S* Exhibit *A*

Consolidated Balance Sheet

December 31, 1945

Assets		Liabilities and Net Worth		
Cash	$ 68,500.00	Accounts payable		$ 32,500.00
Accounts receivable	90,000.00	Minority interest—Company *S*		7,500.00
Inventory	43,000.00	Net worth:		
Goodwill	3,000.00	Capital stock	$100,000.00	
		Surplus—Exhibit B	64,500.00	164,500.00
	$204,500.00			$204,500.00

Case 2. This case is the same as the preceding one except that it is now assumed that dividends were paid by both companies in 1945. The facilitating conditions exist because:

(1) The parent company, having adopted the accounting procedure of recording subsidiary profits, losses, and dividends, has credited the investment account with the dividend received during the year.

(2) The parent company has not yet taken up its share of the subsidiary's profit for the year.

(Case 2)

COMPANY *P* AND SUBSIDIARY *S*
Consolidated Working Papers
For the Year Ended December 31, 1945

Debits	Company *P*	Company *S*	Adjustments Dr.	Adjustments Cr.	Eliminations	Profit and Loss	Surplus	Minority	Balance Sheet
Cash	$ 36,200	$ 26,000							$ 62,200
Accounts receivable	50,000	40,000							90,000
Investment in Company *S*—90%	58,800								
Eliminate:									
Capital stock					$45,000A				
Surplus					10,800B				
Goodwill									3,000
Inventory, December 31, 1944	25,000	15,000				$ 40,000			
Purchases	100,000	80,000			25,000C	155,000			
Expense	15,000	11,000				26,000			
Dividends paid:									
Company *P*	6,000						$ 6,000		
Company *S*		3,000			2,700B			$ 300	
	$291,000	$175,000							
Inventory, December 31, 1945			$43,000a						43,000
					$83,500				
Column totals deducted contra						$221,000	$ 6,000	$ 300	
									$198,200

Credits									
Accounts payable	$ 22,500	$ 10,000							$ 32,500
Capital stock:									
Company *P*	100,000								100,000
Company *S*		50,000			$45,000A			$5,000	
Surplus, December 31, 1944:									
Company *P*	43,500						$43,500		
Company *S*		15,000			13,500B			1,500	
Sales	125,000	100,000			25,000C	$200,000			
	$291,000	$175,000							
Inventory, December 31, 1945				$43,000a		43,000			
			$43,000	$43,000	$83,500				
Profit and loss:									
Credits						$243,000			
Debits—per contra						221,000			
Net profit						$ 22,000			
Minority interest in Company *S*—see page 342						1,000		1,000	
Parent company's share						$ 21,000	21,000		
Surplus:									
Credits							$64,500		
Debits—per contra							6,000		
Balance							$58,500		58,500
Minority:									
Credits								$7,500	
Debits—per contra								300	
Balance								$7,200	7,200
									$198,200

(3) The surplus accounts of both companies show the balances at the beginning of the year, and the dividend payments are shown as debits to dividends paid accounts.

The working papers appear on pages 340 and 341. Attention is directed to elimination B, applicable to the subsidiary's surplus and the parent company's investment account:

Elimination from subsidiary surplus:	
From the surplus account: 90% of the $15,000.00 balance at the beginning of the year	$13,500.00
From the dividends paid account: 90% of $3,000.00	2,700.00
Net elimination from subsidiary surplus, and offsetting elimination from the parent's investment account	$10,800.00

Minority Interest in Subsidiary Net Profit

Profit and loss credits:	
Detailed in trial balance	$100,000.00
Inventory, end of year	16,000.00
Total	$116,000.00
Profit and loss debits:	
Detailed in trial balance	106,000.00
Net profit	$ 10,000.00
Minority interest:	
Per cent	10%
Amount	$ 1,000.00

Statements for Case 2. Since this case differs from Case 1 only in the payment of dividends, the statement of profit and loss for the two illustrations is the same. This statement appears on page 339.

Exhibit B

COMPANY *P* AND SUBSIDIARY *S*
Consolidated Surplus Statement
For the Year Ended December 31, 1945

Surplus, December 31, 1944	$43,500.00
Add net profit (Exhibit C)	21,000.00
Total	$64,500.00
Deduct dividends paid	6,000.00
Surplus, December 31, 1945	$58,500.00

Exhibit A

COMPANY *P* AND SUBSIDIARY *S*
Consolidated Balance Sheet
December 31, 1945

Assets		Liabilities and Net Worth		
Cash	$ 62,200.00	Accounts payable		$ 32,500.00
Accounts receivable	90,000.00	Minority interest—Company *S*		7,200.00
Inventory	43,000.00	Net worth:		
Goodwill	3,000.00	Capital stock	$100,000.00	
		Surplus (Exhibit B)	58,500.00	158,500.00
	$198,200.00			$198,200.00

Case 3. In the preceding cases, statements were prepared for 1945; in this case, statements for the same parent and subsidiary are prepared for 1946. The inventories at the end of 1946 were: Company *P*, $30,000.00; Company *S*, $19,000.00. No dividend was paid by either company in 1946.

The parent company takes up subsidiary profits, losses, and dividends through the investment account; the parent company has made no entry for the subsidiary profit for 1946; the surplus accounts show the balances at the beginning of the year; therefore, the facilitating conditions exist.

The working papers appear on page 344.

Minority Interest in Subsidiary Net Profit

Profit and loss credits:	
Detailed in trial balance	$120,000.00
Inventory—end of year	19,000.00
Total	$139,000.00
Profit and loss debits:	
Detailed in trial balance	128,000.00
Net profit	$ 11,000.00
Minority interest:	
Per cent	10%
Amount	$ 1,100.00

Statements for Case 3. The following statements were prepared from the working papers on page 344.

COMPANY *P* AND SUBSIDIARY *S* Exhibit C

Consolidated Statement of Profit and Loss

For the Year Ended December 31, 1946

Sales		$250,000.00
Deduct cost of goods sold:		
Inventory, December 31, 1945	$ 43,000.00	
Purchases	200,000.00	
Total	$243,000.00	
Deduct inventory, December 31, 1946	49,000.00	
Cost of goods sold		194,000.00
Gross profit on sales		$ 56,000.00
Deduct expenses		32,000.00
Total net profit		$ 24,000.00
Deduct minority interest in subsidiary profit		1,100.00
Consolidated net profit		$ 22,900.00

COMPANY *P* AND SUBSIDIARY *S* Exhibit B

Consolidated Statement of Surplus

For the Year Ended December 31, 1946

Balance, December 31, 1945	$58,500.00
Add net profit—Exhibit C	22,900.00
Balance, December 31, 1946	$81,400.00

Case 3

COMPANY *P* AND SUBSIDIARY *S*
Consolidated Working Papers
For the Year Ended December 31, 1946

	Company *P*	Company *S*	Adjustments Debit	Adjustments Credit	Eliminations	Profit and Loss	Surplus	Minority	Balance Sheet
Debits									
Cash	$ 44,700	$ 34,000							$ 78,700
Accounts receivable	54,000	45,000							99,000
Investment in Company *S*—90%	67,800								
Eliminate:									
Capital stock					$45,000A				
Surplus					19,800B				
Goodwill									3,000
Inventory, December 31, 1945	27,000	16,000				$ 43,000			
Purchases	120,000	100,000			20,000C	200,000			
Expense	20,000	12,000				32,000			
	$333,500	$207,000							
Inventory, December 31, 1946			$49,000a						49,000
					$84,800				
Column totals deducted contra						$275,000	$ —	$ —	
									$229,700
Credits									
Accounts payable	$ 25,000	$ 15,000							$ 40,000
Capital stock:									
Company *P*	100,000								100,000
Company *S*		50,000			$45,000A			$5,000	
Surplus, December 31, 1945:									
Company *P*	58,500						$58,500		
Company *S*		22,000			19,800B			2,200	
Sales	150,000	120,000			20,000C	$250,000			
	$333,500	$207,000							
Inventory, December 31, 1946				$49,000a		49,000			
			$49,000	$49,000	$84,800				
Profit and loss:									
Credits						$299,000			
Debits—per contra						275,000			
Net profit						$ 24,000			
Minority interest in Company *S*—see page 343						1,100		1,100	
Parent company's share						$ 22,900	22,900		
Surplus							$81,400		81,400
Minority interest								$8,300	8,300
									$229,700

Exhibit A

COMPANY *P* AND SUBSIDIARY *S*
Consolidated Balance Sheet
December 31, 1946

Assets		Liabilities and Net Worth		
Cash	$ 78,700.00	Accounts payable		$ 40,000.00
Accounts receivable	99,000.00	Minority interest—Company *S*		8,300.00
Inventory	49,000.00	Net worth:		
Goodwill	3,000.00	Capital stock	$100,000.00	
		Surplus—Exhibit B	81,400.00	181,400.00
	$229,700.00			$229,700.00

Case 4. This case is the same as the preceding one except that it is now assumed that both companies paid dividends in 1946. The facilitating conditions exist because (1) the parent company has recorded its share of subsidiary profits and dividends since acquisition, (2) except the subsidiary profit for the current year; and (3) the surplus accounts of both companies show the balances at the beginning of the year.

The working papers appear on pages 346 and 347. Observe the B eliminations: from the parent's investment account and from the subsidiary's surplus and dividends paid accounts.

Statements for Case 4. Since this case differs from Case 3 only in the payment of dividends, the statement of profit and loss is the same for both cases. This statement appears on page 343. The remaining statements appear below.

Exhibit B

COMPANY *P* AND SUBSIDIARY *S*
Consolidated Surplus Statement
For the Year Ended December 31, 1946

Balance, December 31, 1945	$58,500.00
Add net profit—Exhibit C	22,900.00
Total	$81,400.00
Deduct dividends paid	6,000.00
Balance, December 31, 1946	$75,400.00

Exhibit A

COMPANY *P* AND SUBSIDIARY *S*
Consolidated Balance Sheet
December 31, 1946

Assets		Liabilities and Net Worth		
Cash	$ 72,400.00	Accounts payable		$ 40,000.00
Accounts receivable	99,000.00	Minority interest—Company *S*		8,000.00
Inventory	49,000.00	Net worth:		
Goodwill	3,000.00	Capital stock	$100,000.00	
		Surplus—Exhibit B	75,400.00	175,400.00
	$223,400.00			$223,400.00

COMPANY *P* AND SUBSIDIARY *S*
Consolidated Working Papers
For the Year Ended December 31, 1946

Debits	Company *P*	Company *S*	Adjustments Debit	Adjustments Credit	Eliminations	Profit and Loss	Surplus	Minority	Balance Sheet
Cash	$ 41,400	$ 31,000							$ 72,400
Accounts receivable	54,000	45,000							99,000
Investment in Company *S*—90%	65,100								
Eliminate:									
Capital stock					$45,000A				
Surplus					17,100B				
Goodwill									3,000
Inventory, December 31, 1945	27,000	16,000				$ 43,000			
Purchases	120,000	100,000			20,000C	200,000			
Expense	20,000	12,000				32,000			
Dividends paid:									
Company *P*	6,000						$ 6,000		
Company *S*		3,000			2,700B			$ 300	
	$333,500	$207,000							
Inventory, December 31, 1946			$49,000a						49,000
					$84,800				
Column totals deducted contra						$275,000	$ 6,000	$ 300	
									$223,400

Credits									
Accounts payable	$ 25,000	$ 15,000							$ 40,000
Capital stock:									
Company *P*	100,000								100,000
Company *S*		50,000			$45,000A			$5,000	
Surplus, December 31, 1945:									
Company *P*	58,500						$58,500		
Company *S*		22,000			19,800B			2,200	
Sales	150,000	120,000			20,000C	$250,000			
	$333,500	$207,000							
Inventory, December 31, 1946				$49,000a		49,000			
			$49,000	$49,000	$84,800				
Profit and loss:									
Credits						$299,000			
Debits—per contra						275,000			
Net profit						$ 24,000			
Minority interest in Company *S*—see page 343						1,100		1,100	
Parent company's share						$ 22,900	22,900		
Surplus:									
Credits							$81,400		
Debits—per contra							6,000		
Balance							$75,400		75,400
Minority:									
Credits								$8,300	
Debits—per contra								300	
Balance								$8,000	8,000
									$223,400

CHAPTER 51

Consolidated Balance Sheet, Surplus Statement, Profit and Loss Statement, and Supporting Statements (Continued)

Variations from facilitating conditions. The facilitating conditions described in the preceding chapter may not exist for the following reasons:

(1) The parent company may carry the subsidiary investment at cost.

(2) The parent company, pursuing the policy of recording subsidiary profits, losses, and dividends in the investment account, may have taken up the subsidiary profit or loss for the current period.

(3) Dividend payments (or other surplus changes during the current period) may have been recorded in the surplus accounts instead of in separate accounts.

Variation 1. If the investment is carried by the parent company at cost, the investment and surplus accounts of the parent should be adjusted by taking up the parent's share of the change in the subsidiary's surplus since acquisition, except the profit or loss for the current period. Cases 3–Variation 1 and Case 4–Variation 1 (based on Cases 3 and 4 in the preceding chapter) illustrate adjustments required for this variation.

Case 3–Variation 1. This case is the same as Case 3, except that it is now assumed that the investment is carried at cost. The investment and surplus account balances on December 31, 1946 are shown below:

	Debit	Credit
Parent:		
Investment in Company *S*—90%	$61,500.00	
Surplus		$52,200.00
Subsidiary:		
Surplus		22,000.00

The parent company's share of the change in the subsidiary surplus since acquisition (except for subsidiary profits for the current year) is computed on the following page.

Balance as above	$22,000.00
Balance at acquisition (see Case 1)	15,000.00
Increase in surplus (except profit for 1946)	$ 7,000.00
Parent company's 90%	$ 6,300.00

Compare the following partial working papers for Case 3 and Case 3–Variation 1. After applying the $6,300.00 adjustment in Case 3–Variation 1, the investment account has a balance of $67,800.00 and the parent's surplus account has a balance of $58,500.00—as in Case 3. The same eliminations can therefore be made in both cases.

Partial Working Papers—Case 3

	Co. *P*	Co. *S*	Adjustments Debit	Adjustments Credit	Eliminations
Debits					
Investment in Co. *S*—90%	$67,800				
Eliminate:					
Capital stock					$45,000A
Surplus					19,800B
Credits					
Capital stock:					
Company *S*		$50,000			45,000A
Surplus:					
Company *P*	58,500				
Company *S*		22,000			19,800B

Partial Working Papers—Case 3–Variation 1

	Co. *P*	Co. *S*	Adjustments Debit	Adjustments Credit	Eliminations
Debits					
Investment in Co. *S*—90%	$61,500				
Add 90% of increase in Co. *S* surplus since acquisition			$6,300b		
Eliminate:					
Capital stock					$45,000A
Surplus					19,800B
Credits					
Capital stock:					
Company *S*		$50,000			45,000A
Surplus:					
Company *P*	52,200			$6,300b	
Company *S*		22,000			19,800B

Case 4–Variation 1. This case is the same as Case 4, except that the investment is carried at cost; it illustrates the adjustment to be made if a subsidiary dividend has been paid during the period. The investment, surplus, and dividends paid account balances on December 31, 1946 are shown on the next page.

	Debit	Credit
Parent:		
Investment in Company *S*—90%	$61,500.00	
Surplus		$54,900.00
Dividends paid	6,000.00	
Subsidiary:		
Surplus		22,000.00
Dividends paid	3,000.00	

The parent company's share of the change in the subsidiary surplus since acquisition (except for subsidiary profits for the current year) is computed below:

Balance as above	$22,000.00
Deduct dividends paid	3,000.00
Net balance, December 31, 1946—before profits for the year	$19,000.00
Surplus at acquisition	15,000.00
Increase	$ 4,000.00
Parent company's 90% thereof	$ 3,600.00

Partial Working Papers—Case 4

	Co. *P*	Co. *S*	Adjustments Debit	Adjustments Credit	Eliminations
Debits					
Investment in Co. *S*—90%	$65,100				
Eliminate:					
Capital stock					$45,000A
Surplus					17,100B
Dividends paid:					
Company *S*		$ 3,000			2,700B
Credits					
Capital stock:					
Company *S*		50,000			45,000A
Surplus:					
Company *P*	58,500				
Company *S*		22,000			19,800B

Partial Working Papers—Case 4–Variation 1

	Co. *P*	Co. *S*	Adjustments Debit	Adjustments Credit	Eliminations
Debits					
Investment in Co. *S*—90%	$61,500				
Add 90% of increase in Co. *S* surplus since acquisition			$3,600c		
Eliminate:					
Capital stock					$45,000A
Surplus					17,100B
Dividends paid:					
Company *S*		$ 3,000			2,700B
Credits					
Capital stock:					
Company *S*		50,000			45,000A
Surplus:					
Company *P*	54,900			$3,600c	
Company *S*		22,000			19,800B

Compare the foregoing partial working papers for Case 4 and Case 4–Variation 1. After the $3,600.00 adjustment has been applied in Case 4–Variation 1, the investment account has a balance of $65,100.00 and the parent company's surplus has a balance of $58,500.00—as in Case 4. The same eliminations are therefore made in both cases.

Variation 2. If the parent company, pursuing the policy of recording subsidiary profits, losses, and dividends in the investment account, has taken up the subsidiary profit or loss for the current period, an adjustment should be made to reverse the entry.

Case 4–Variation 2. This case is the same as Case 4, except that it is now assumed that the parent company has made an entry taking up its $9,900.00 share of the subsidiary's $11,000.00 profit for 1946. Compare the following partial working papers for Case 4 and Case 4–Variation 2. After applying the $9,900.00 adjustment to reverse the parent company's entry taking up the subsidiary profit for 1946, the account balances in the two cases are identical, and the same eliminations can be made.

Partial Working Papers—Case 4

	Co. *P*	Co. *S*	Adjustments: Debit	Adjustments: Credit	Eliminations
Debits					
Investment in Co. *S*—90%	$65,100				
Eliminate:					
Capital stock					$45,000A
Surplus					17,100B
Dividends paid:					
Company *S*		$ 3,000			2,700B
Credits					
Capital stock:					
Company *S*		50,000			45,000A
Surplus:					
Company *P*	58,500				
Company *S*		22,000			19,800B

Partial Working Papers—Case 4–Variation 2

	Co. *P*	Co. *S*	Adjustments: Debit	Adjustments: Credit	Eliminations
Debits					
Investment in Co. *S*—90%	$75,000				
Reverse entry for 1946 profit				$9,900d	
Eliminate:					
Capital stock					$45,000A
Surplus					17,100B
Dividends paid:					
Company *S*		$ 3,000			2,700B

	Co. P	Co. S	Adjustments Debit	Adjustments Credit	Eliminations
Credits					
Capital stock:					
Company *S*............		50,000			45,000A
Surplus:					
Company *P*............	58,500				
Company *S*............		22,000			19,800B
Income from Company *S*.	9,900		$9,900d		

Variation 3. If dividend payments have been charged to surplus accounts, or if any other direct charges or credits have been made to surplus during the period, adjustments should be made to set these items out separately; this is done merely for convenience in assembling the information required for the consolidated surplus statement.

Case 4–Variation 3. This case is the same as Case 4 except that it is now assumed that dividend payments were charged to the surplus accounts instead of to dividend paid accounts.

Partial Working Papers—Case 4

	Co. P	Co. S	Adjustments Debit	Adjustments Credit	Eliminations
Debits					
Investment in Co. *S*—90%.	$65,100				
Eliminate:					
Capital stock.........					$45,000A
Surplus...............					17,100B
Dividends paid:					
Company *P*............	6,000				
Company *S*............		$ 3,000			2,700B
Credits					
Capital stock:					
Company *S*............		50,000			45,000A
Surplus:					
Company *P*............	58,500				
Company *S*............		22,000			19,800B

Partial Working Papers—Case 4–Variation 3

	Co. P	Co. S	Adjustments Debit	Adjustments Credit	Eliminations
Debits					
Investment in Co. *S*—90%.	$65,100				
Eliminate:					
Capital stock.........					$45,000A
Surplus...............					17,100B
Dividends paid:					
Company *P*............			$6,000e		
Company *S*............			3,000f		2,700B
Credits					
Capital stock:					
Company *S*............		$50,000			45,000A
Surplus:					
Company *P*............	52,500			$6,000e	
Company *S*............		19,000		3,000f	19,800B

Two variations. The variations discussed on the preceding pages have to do with the following matters:

The investment account:

(1) The investment is carried at cost.

(2) Pursuing the policy of taking up its share of the subsidiary profits, losses, and dividends, the parent company has taken up its share of the profit for the current period.

The surplus accounts:

(3) Entries for dividends (or other charges and credits) have been made in the surplus accounts rather than in separate accounts.

It is therefore possible to have combinations of two variations, as follows: Variations 1 and 3; and Variations 2 and 3.

Case 4–Variations 1, 3. This case is the same as Case 4 except that adjustments are required for Variations 1 and 3. In the following partial working papers,

Adjustment c (required because the investment is carried at cost) is the same as in Case 4–Variation 1.

Adjustments e and f (required because dividends have been charged to surplus) are the same as in Case 4–Variation 3.

Partial Working Papers—Case 4–Variations 1, 3

	Co. *P*	Co. *S*	Adjustments Debit	Adjustments Credit	Eliminations
Debits					
Investment in Co. *S*—90% at cost	$61,500				
Add 90% of increase in Co. *S*. surplus since acquisition			$3,600c		
Eliminate:					
Capital stock					$45,000A
Surplus					17,100B
Dividends paid:					
Company *P*			6,000e		
Company *S*			3,000f		2,700B
Credits					
Capital stock:					
Company *S*		$50,000			45,000A
Surplus:					
Company *P*	48,900				
Add adjustment for increase in Co. *S*. surplus				$3,600c	
Add adjustment for dividends				6,000e	
Company *S*		19,000		3,000f	19,800B

Case 4–Variations 2, 3. This case is the same as Case 4 except that adjustments are required for Variations 2 and 3.

Adjustment d is required because the parent company has taken up its share of the subsidiary's profit for the current period. This is the same adjustment as in Case 4–Variation 2.

Adjustments e and f (required because dividends have been charged to surplus) are the same as in Case 4–Variation 3.

Partial Working Papers—Case 4–Variations 2, 3

	Co. *P*	Co. *S*	Adjustments Debit	Adjustments Credit	Eliminations
Debits					
Investment in Co. *S*—90%	$75,000				
Reverse entry for 1946 profit				9,900d	
Eliminate:					
Capital stock					$45,000A
Surplus					17,100B
Dividends paid:					
Company *P*			$6,000e		
Company *S*			3,000f		2,700B
Credits					
Capital stock:					
Company *S*		$50,000			45,000A
Surplus:					
Company *P*	52,500				
Add adjustment for dividends				6,000e	
Company *S*		19,000		3,000f	19,800B
Income from Company *S*	9,900		9,900d		

Stock purchases during the period. A slight complication arises if subsidiary stock is purchased at an interim date during the year for which the consolidated statements are being prepared.

To illustrate, assume that Company *B* had a capital stock of $100,000.00 and a surplus of $50,000.00 on January 1, 1945; that Company *A* purchased 90% of the stock on April 1, 1945 for $140,000.00; and that Company *B* made a profit of $20,000.00 during 1945, in equal quarterly amounts of $5,000.00.

The profits of the subsidiary for 1945 accruing to the parent company were:

Total profit of Company *B*	$20,000.00
Deduct minority interest—10% of $20,000.00	2,000.00
Balance—applicable to parent company	$18,000.00
Portion earned prior to acquisition—90% of $5,000.00	4,500.00
Balance—applicable to parent company and earned since acquisition	$13,500.00

The working papers on page 356 illustrate a method of dealing with the $4,500.00, which must be recognized as part of the book

COMPANY *A* AND SUBSIDIARY *B*
Consolidated Working Papers
For the Year Ended December 31, 1945

	Company *A*	Company *B*	Adjustments Debit	Adjustments Credit	Eliminations	Profit and Loss	Surplus	Minority	Balance Sheet
Debits									
Cash	$ 45,000	$ 30,000							$ 75,000
Accounts receivable	200,000	130,000							330,000
Investment in Company *B*—90%	140,000			$ 4,500g					
Eliminate:									
Capital stock					$ 90,000A				
Surplus					45,000B				
Goodwill									500
Inventory, December 31, 1944	50,000	35,000				$ 85,000			
Purchases	400,000	215,000			25,000C	590,000			
Expenses	75,000	80,000				155,000			
	$910,000	$490,000							
Inventory, December 31, 1945			$100,000a						100,000
					$160,000				
Column total deducted contra						$830,000	$ —	$ —	
									$505,500
Credits									
Accounts payable	$ 60,000	$ 40,000							$100,000
Capital stock:									
Company *A*	250,000								250,000
Company *B*		100,000			$ 90,000A			$10,000	
Surplus, December 31, 1944:									
Company *A*	100,000						$100,000		
Company *B*		50,000			45,000B			5,000	
Sales	500,000	300,000			25,000C	$775,000			
	$910,000	$490,000							
Inventory, December 31, 1945				100,000a		100,000			
Profit and loss:									
Credits						$875,000			
Debits—per contra						830,000			
Net profit						$ 45,000			
Minority interest in Company *B*—see page 356						2,000*		2,000	
Parent company's share:									
Earned prior to acquisition—¼ of 90% of $20,000 subsidiary profit			4,500g			4,500*			
Consolidated net profit						$ 38,500	38,500		
			$104,500	$104,500	$160,000				
Surplus							$138,500		138,500
Minority interest								$17,000	17,000
									$505,500

* Deductions.

value of the stock at acquisition, and which must therefore be applied against the cost rather than included in the consolidated earnings for the year.

Computation of Minority Interest in Subsidiary Net Profit

Profit and loss credits:	
Detailed in trial balance	$300,000.00
Inventory, end of year	50,000.00
Total	$350,000.00
Profit and loss debits:	
Detailed in trial balance	330,000.00
Net profit	$ 20,000.00
Minority interest:	
Per cent	10%
Amount	$ 2,000.00

The consolidated profit and loss statement prepared from the working papers on page 356, illustrating the treatment of the portion of the year's profit earned prior to acquisition, is shown below:

COMPANY *A* AND SUBSIDIARY *B*
Consolidated Statement of Profit and Loss
For the Year Ended December 31, 1945

Sales		$775,000.00
Deduct cost of goods sold:		
Inventory, December 31, 1944	$ 85,000.00	
Purchases	590,000.00	
Total	$675,000.00	
Deduct inventory, December 31, 1945	100,000.00	
Cost of goods sold		575,000.00
Gross profit on sales		$200,000.00
Deduct expense		155,000.00
Net profit		$ 45,000.00
Deduct:		
Subsidiary profits applicable to minority	$ 2,000.00	
Subsidiary profits applicable to parent company's holdings, but earned prior to acquisition	4,500.00	6,500.00
Consolidated net profit		$ 38,500.00

Intercompany profits in inventories. This illustration shows the treatment of intercompany profits in inventories, and incidentally shows the use of a cost of sales column, which is a convenience when a considerable number of items are involved in the computation of the cost of sales. It also illustrates the use of separate debit and credit sheets and the forwarding of the adjustment column totals. The working papers are on pages 358 and 359.

This case is identical with Case 4, except for the intercompany profits in the inventories at the beginning and end of the year. It will be remembered that Company *P* purchased goods from Com-

COMPANY *P* AND SUBSIDIARY *S*
Consolidated Working Papers
For the Year Ended December 31, 1946

Debits	Company *P*	Company *S*	Adjustments Debit	Adjustments Credit	Eliminations	Cost of Sales	Profit and Loss	Surplus	Minority	Balance Sheet
Cash	$ 41,400	$ 31,000								$ 72,400
Accounts receivable	54,000	45,000								99,000
Investment in Company *S*—90%	65,100									
Eliminate:										
Capital stock					$45,000A					
Surplus					17,100B					
Goodwill										3,000
Inventory, December 31, 1945	27,000	16,000		$1,800h		$ 41,200				
Purchases	120,000	100,000			20,000C	200,000				
Expense	20,000	12,000					$ 32,000			
Dividends paid:										
Company *P*	6,000							$6,000		
Company *S*		3,000			2,700B				$300	
	$333,500	$207,000								
Inventory, December 31, 1946			$49,000a	900i						48,100
			$49,000	$2,700	$84,800					
Cost of sales:										
Debits						$241,200				
Credits—per contra						48,100				
Balance						$193,100	193,100			
Column totals deducted contra							$225,100	$6,000	$300	
										$222,500

COMPANY *P* AND SUBSIDIARY *S*
Consolidated Working Papers—Continued
For the Year Ended December 31, 1946

Credits	Company *P*	Company *S*	Adjustments Debit	Adjustments Credit	Eliminations	Cost of Sales	Profit and Loss	Surplus	Minority	Balance Sheet
Adjustment column totals brought forward			$49,000	$ 2,700						
Accounts payable	$ 25,000	$ 15,000								$ 40,000
Capital stock:										
Company *P*	100,000									100,000
Company *S*		50,000			$45,000A				$5,000	
Surplus, December 31, 1945:										
Company *P*	58,500		1,800h					$56,700		
Company *S*		22,000			19,800B				2,200	
Sales	150,000	120,000			20,000C		$250,000			
	$333,500	$207,000								
Inventory, December 31, 1946			900i	49,000a		$48,100				
			$51,700	$51,700	$84,800					
Column total deducted contra						$48,100	—			
Profit and loss:										
Credits							$250,000			
Debits—per contra							225,100			
Total net profit							$ 24,900			
Minority interest in Company *S* —see page 343							1,100		1,100	
Parent company's share							$ 23,800	23,800		
Surplus:										
Credits								$80,500		
Debits—per contra								6,000		
Balance								$74,500	—	74,500
Minority:										
Credits									$8,300	
Debits—per contra									300	
Balance									$8,000	8,000
										$222,500

pany *S*. It is now assumed that Company *P*'s inventories contained goods purchased from Company *S* on which the intercompany profits were as follows:

	Total Intercompany Profit	Company *P*'s 90% Thereof
December 31, 1945	$2,000.00	$1,800.00
December 31, 1946	1,000.00	900.00

We shall first consider the adjustment required for the intercompany profit in the inventory on December 31, 1945. In the consolidated working papers at the end of 1945, the inventory would have been reduced $1,800.00, and the consolidated surplus would have been correspondingly reduced; to be consistent, the same adjustment should be made at the end of 1946. See adjustment h, debiting Company *P*'s surplus as of December 31, 1945 and crediting the inventory.

The inventories at the end of 1946 were put into the working papers by adjustment a; observe how adjustment i reduces the inventory, on both the debit and credit sheets, by the $900.00 of intercompany profit.

Adjustments of subsidiary's profits. If the working papers contain adjustments which affect a subsidiary's earnings, these must be given proper consideration in the computation of the minority interest in the subsidiary profit.

The following illustration is based on Case 4, with the addition of required adjustments for the following unrecorded transactions:

	Company *P*	Company *S*
Sales on account	$1,500.00	
Purchases on account		$500.00
Accrued expense	800.00	700.00

Minority Interest in Subsidiary Net Profit

Profit and loss credits:		
Detailed in trial balance		$120,000.00
Inventory, end of year		19,000.00
Total		$139,000.00
Profit and loss debits:		
Detailed in trial balance	$128,000.00	
Adjustments:		
Unrecorded purchases	500.00	
Unrecorded expenses	700.00	
Total		129,200.00
Net profit		$ 9,800.00
Minority interest:		
Per cent		10%
Amount		$ 980.00

COMPANY *P* AND SUBSIDIARY *S*
Consolidated Working Papers
For the Year Ended December 31, 1946

Debits	Company *P*	Company *S*	Adjustments Debit	Adjustments Credit	Eliminations	Cost of Sales	Profit and Loss	Surplus	Minority	Balance Sheet
Cash	$ 41,400	$ 31,000								$ 72,400
Accounts receivable	54,000	45,000	$ 1,500j							100,500
Investment in Company *S*—90%	65,100									
Eliminate:										
Capital stock					$45,000A					
Surplus					17,100B					
Goodwill										3,000
Inventory, December 31, 1945	27,000	16,000		$ 1,800h		$ 41,200				
Purchases	120,000	100,000	500k		20,000C	200,500				
Expense	20,000	12,000	1,500l				$ 33,500			
Dividends paid:										
Company *P*	6,000							$ 6,000		
Company *S*		3,000			2,700B				$ 300	
	$333,500	$207,000								
Inventory, December 31, 1946			49,000a	900i						48,100
			$52,500	$ 2,700	$84,800					
Cost of sales:										
Debits						$241,700				
Credits—per contra						48,100				
Balance						$193,600	193,600			
Column totals deducted contra							$227,100	$ 6,000	$ 300	$224,000

COMPANY *P* AND SUBSIDIARY *S*
Consolidated Working Papers—Continued
For the Year Ended December 31, 1946

Credits	Company *P*	Company *S*	Adjustments Debit	Adjustments Credit	Eliminations	Cost of Sales	Profit and Loss	Surplus	Minority	Balance Sheet
Adjustment column totals brought forward			$52,500	$ 2,700						
				500k						
Accounts payable	$ 25,000	$ 15,000		1,500l						$ 42,000
Capital stock:										
Company *P*	100,000									100,000
Company *S*		50,000			$45,000A				$5,000	
Surplus, December 31, 1945:										
Company *P*	58,500		1,800h					$56,700		
Company *S*		22,000			19,800B				2,200	
Sales	150,000	120,000		1,500j	20,000C		$251,500			
	$333,500	$207,000								
Inventory, December 31, 1946			900i	49,000a		$48,100				
			$55,200	$55,200	$84,800					
Column total deducted contra						$48,100				
Profit and loss:										
Credits							$251,500			
Debits—per contra							227,100			
Net profit							$ 24,400			
Minority interest in Company *S*—see page 360							980		980	
Parent company's share							$ 23,420	23,420		
Surplus:										
Credits								$80,120		
Debits—per contra								6,000		
Balance								$74,120		74,120
Minority:										
Credits									$8,180	
Debits—per contra									300	
Balance									$7,880	7,880
										$224,000

Subsidiary earnings not available to parent. A subsidiary may have made earnings during the year, but in an amount less than that required to meet the full dividends on its preferred stock in the hands of outsiders. The entire earnings would, in such a case, be wholly excluded from the consolidated net income because they would be entirely applicable to outsiders.

If, for any reason, subsidiary earnings are not available for transfer to the parent company as dividends, the consolidated statements should indicate this fact, by footnotes or otherwise. Earnings applicable to the parent company's stockholdings may not be available for dividends to the parent company because of conditions such as the following: the subsidiary may have made profits during the year, but not enough to offset a deficit; the surplus may be restricted because of treasury stock purchases; surplus may have been used for the issuance of a stock dividend; appropriations may have been made to a sinking fund reserve, or to a reserve for the retirement of preferred stock.

The foregoing are legal or contractual restrictions upon the payment of dividends. In considering the availability of subsidiary profits for dividend purposes, it may also be pertinent to consider the current position, since profits may have been tied up in capital assets or in required working capital. If the profits are legally available for dividends, it is not necessary to mention self-imposed dividend limitations.

CHAPTER 52

Consolidated Balance Sheet, Surplus Statement, Profit and Loss Statement, and Supporting Statements (Concluded)

Case 1. This illustration is somewhat more complex than any in the preceding chapters, because:

(1) There are two subsidiaries. Company *A*, the parent company, owns:
  90% of the stock of Company *B*, which it acquired on January 1, 1942; the surplus of Company *B* on that date was $15,000.00.
  80% of the stock of Company *C*, which it acquired on January 1, 1946; the surplus of Company *C* on that date was $20,000.00.

(2) Numerous additional adjustments and eliminations are illustrated.

Consolidated statements are required for the year 1946, and it is assumed that the facilitating conditions described in Chapter 50 exist.

The adjustments and eliminations in the working papers on pages 366 and 367 are explained below and on pages 368 to 370.

Adjustment a—End-of-year inventories. The inventories on December 31, 1946, are detailed below:

	Company *A*	Company *B*	Company *C*	Total
Finished goods	$ 45,000.00	$ 50,000.00		$ 95,000.00
Goods in process	55,000.00	25,000.00		80,000.00
Raw materials	50,000.00	25,000.00	$11,000.00	86,000.00
Total	$150,000.00	$100,000.00	$11,000.00	$261,000.00

These inventories are entered in the working papers by adjustment a.

Adjustment b—Intercompany profit in opening inventories. The inventories on December 31, 1945 (the end of the preceding year) contained profits made on intercompany sales during 1945, as shown on page 368.

COMPANY *A* AND SUBSIDIARIES *B* AND *C*
Consolidated Working Papers
For the Year Ended December 31, 1946

Debits	Company *A*	Company *B*	Company *C*	Adjustments Debit	Adjustments Credit	Eliminations	Cost of Sales	Profit and Loss	Surplus	Minority	Balance Sheet
Cash	$ 40,000	$ 16,000	$ 16,500								$ 72,500
Accounts receivable	53,700	17,000	25,000			$ 11,500E					84,200
Inventories, December 31, 1945:											
Finished goods		30,000					$ 30,000				
Goods in process	25,000	30,000			$ 1,350b		53,650				
Raw materials	40,000	15,000	15,000		1,800b		68,200				
Land	50,000	20,000	25,000								95,000
Buildings—less depreciation	140,000	35,000	60,000								235,000
Equipment—less depreciation	90,000	40,000	15,000								145,000
Investment in stock of Company *B*—90%	117,500										
Eliminate:											
Capital stock						90,000A					
Surplus						22,50CB					
Goodwill											5,000
Investment in stock of Company *C*—80%	66,000										
Eliminate:											
Capital stock						40,000C					
Surplus						16,00CD					
Goodwill											10,000
Investment in bonds of Company *C*	40,000										40,000
Returned sales and allowances	3,000	2,000	1,000					$ 6,000			
Purchases—materials	145,000	95,000	76,000			170,000F	146,000				
Direct labor	85,000	65,000					150,000				
Manufacturing expense	70,000	40,000				3,000G	107,000				
Selling expense	23,000	22,000	15,000					60,000			
General expense	24,000	9,000	3,000					36,000			
Bond interest	6,000		2,500			2,000H		6,500			
	$1,018,200	$436,000	$254,000								
Inventories, December 31, 1946:											
Finished goods				$ 95,000a	3,860c						91,140
Goods in process				80,000a	1,680c						78,320
Raw materials				86,000a	3,610c						82,390
				$261,000	$12,300	$355,000					
Cost of sales:											
Debits							$554,850				
Credits—per contra							251,850				
Balance							$303,000	303,000			
Column total deducted contra								$411,500	$ —	$ —	$938,550

COMPANY *A* AND SUBSIDIARIES *B* AND *C*
Consolidated Working Papers—Continued
For the Year Ended December 31, 1946

Credits	Company *A*	Company *B*	Company *C*	Adjustments Debit	Adjustments Credit	Eliminations	Cost of Sales	Profit and Loss	Surplus	Minority	Balance Sheet
Adjustment column totals brought forward				$261,000	$ 12,300						
Accounts payable	$ 78,200	$ 86,000	$ 14,000			$ 11,500E					$166,700
Bonds payable:											
Company *A*—6%	100,000										100,000
Company *C*—5%			50,000								50,000
Capital stock:											
Company *A*	500,000										500,000
Company *B*		100,000				90,000A				$10,000	
Company *C*			50,000			40,000C				10,000	
Surplus, December 31, 1945:											
Company *A*	35,000			3,150b					$31,850		
Company *B*		25,000				22,500B				2,500	
Company *C*			20,000			16,000D				4,000	
Sales	300,000	225,000	120,000			170,000F		$475,000			
Rent of equipment to Company *B*	3,000					3,000G					
Bond interest from Company *C*	2,000					2,000H					
	$1,018,200	$436,000	$254,000								
Inventories, December 31, 1946:											
Finished goods				3,860c	95,000a		$ 91,140				
Goods in process				1,680c	80,000a		78,320				
Raw materials				3,610c	86,000a		82,390				
				$273,300	$273,300	$355,000					
Column total deducted contra							$251,850				
Profit and loss:											
Credits								$475,000			
Debits—per contra								411,500			
Net profit								$ 63,500			
Minority interests—see page 370:											
Company *B*								1,700*		1,700	
Company *C*								3,700*		3,700	
Parent company's share								$ 58,100	58,100		
Surplus									$89,950		89,950
Minority										$31,900	31,900
											$938,550

* Deduction.

	Profit Made by		
	Company *B*		
	Total	Co. *A*'s 90%	Company *C*
On goods in Company *A*'s inventory:			
Goods in process	$1,500.00	$1,350.00	$ 800.00
Raw materials	2,000.00	1,800.00	1,000.00
On goods in Company *B*'s inventory:			
Finished goods			250.00
Goods in process			800.00
Raw materials			500.00
Total intercompany profit		$3,150.00	

Since Company *A* did not own the stock of Company *C* during 1945, the profits made by Company *C* on sales to Companies *A* and *B* during that year were not intercompany profits.

Adjustment is made for the intercompany profit of $3,150.00, as follows:

Surplus of Company *A*, December 31, 1945	$3,150.00	
Inventories—December 31, 1945:		
Goods in process		$1,350.00
Raw materials		1,800.00

Adjustment c—Intercompany profit in closing inventories. The inventories on December 31, 1946, contained intercompany profits, made on sales during 1946, as follows:

	Profit Made by	
	Company *B*	Company *C*
On goods in Company *A*'s inventory:		
Finished goods	$1,800.00	$1,500.00
Goods in process	800.00	200.00
Raw materials	2,500.00	1,200.00
On goods in Company *B*'s inventory:		
Finished goods		1,300.00
Goods in process		1,000.00
Raw materials		500.00
Total	$5,100.00	$5,700.00
Per cent of subsidiary stock owned by Company *A*	90%	80%
Deductions to be made for intercompany profit	$4,590.00	$4,560.00

The total deduction for intercompany profit is thus found to be $9,150.00, but separate deductions must be made from finished goods, goods in process, and raw materials. The amounts of these deductions are determined as follows:

	In Inventory of	Sold by	Total Profit	Per Cent of Selling Company's Stock Owned by Company *A*	Deduction
Finished goods:	Co. *A*	Co. *B*	$1,800.00	90%	$1,620.00
	Co. *A*	Co. *C*	1,500.00	80	1,200.00
	Co. *B*	Co. *C*	1,300.00	80	1,040.00
	Total				$3,860.00

Goods in process:	Co. *A*	Co. *B*	$ 800.00	90%	$ 720.00
	Co. *A*	Co. *C*	200.00	80	160.00
	Co. *B*	Co. *C*	1,000.00	80	800.00
	Total				$1,680.00
Raw materials:	Co. *A*	Co. *B*	$2,500.00	90%	$2,250.00
	Co. *A*	Co. *C*	1,200.00	80	960.00
	Co. *B*	Co. *C*	500.00	80	400.00
	Total				$3,610.00
Total					$9,150.00

The adjustment for this intercompany profit is made by deductions from the gross inventory valuations in both the debit and credit sections of the working papers.

Elimination A—*Company A's interest in stock of Company B:*

Company *B* has $100,000.00 of capital stock, of which Company *A* owns 90%, or $90,000.00.

Elimination B—*Company A's interest in surplus of Company B:*

Since Company *A* has a 90% interest in Company *B*, 90% of Company *B*'s $25,000.00 surplus, or $22,500.00, is eliminated.

Elimination C—*Company A's interest in stock of Company C:*

Company *C* has $50,000.00 of capital stock, of which Company *A* owns 80%, or $40,000.00.

Elimination D—*Company A's interest in surplus of Company C:*

Company *C*'s surplus balance is $20,000.00; Company *A*'s interest therein is 80%, or $16,000.00.

Elimination E—*Intercompany receivables and payables:*

Following are the intercompany accounts receivable and accounts payable on December 31, 1946:

Owed to Company *B*:	
By Company *A*	$ 5,000.00
Owed to Company *C*:	
By Company *A*	2,900.00
By Company *B*	3,600.00
Total	$11,500.00

Elimination F—*Intercompany sales:*

The intercompany sales during 1946 were as follows:

By	To	Amount
Company *B*	Company *C*	$ 75,000.00
Company *C*	Company *A*	35,000.00
Company *C*	Company *B*	60,000.00
Total		$170,000.00

Elimination G—*Intercompany rent:*

Company *A* leases certain equipment to Company *B* at an annual rent of $3,000.00. This amount appears as an item of income in the trial balance of Company *A*, and is included in the manufacturing expenses of Company *B*.

Elimination H—*Bond interest:*

Company *C* has an issue of $50,000.00 of 5% bonds, of which Company *A* owns $40,000.00. The $2,000.00 of interest collected by Company *A* is eliminated against the $2,500.00 of interest expense shown by the accounts of Company *C*.

Minority Interests in Subsidiaries' Net Profits

	Company *B*	Company *C*
Profit and loss credits:		
Detailed in trial balance	$225,000.00	$120,000.00
Inventories at end of year	100,000.00	11,000.00
Total	$325,000.00	$131,000.00
Profit and loss debits:		
Detailed in trial balance	308,000.00	112,500.00
Net profit	$ 17,000.00	$ 18,500.00
Minority interests:		
Per cent	10%	20%
Amount	$ 1,700.00	$ 3,700.00

Consolidated statements: Case 1. The following consolidated statements were prepared from the working papers on pages 366 and 367.

Exhibit D

COMPANY *A* AND SUBSIDIARIES *B* AND *C*
Consolidated Statement of Cost of Goods Sold
For the Year Ended December 31, 1946

Materials:	
Inventory, December 31, 1945	$ 68,200.00
Purchases	146,000.00
Total	$214,200.00
Less inventory, December 31, 1946	82,390.00
Cost of materials used or sold	$131,810.00
Direct labor	150,000.00
Manufacturing expense	107,000.00
Total	$388,810.00
Add goods in process, December 31, 1945	53,650.00
Total	$442,460.00
Deduct goods in process, December 31, 1946	78,320.00
Cost of goods manufactured, and materials sold	$364,140.00
Add finished goods, December 31, 1945	30,000.00
Total	$394,140.00
Deduct finished goods, December 31, 1946	91,140.00
Cost of goods sold	$303,000.00

Exhibit C

COMPANY *A* AND SUBSIDIARIES *B* AND *C*
Consolidated Profit and Loss Statement
For the Year Ended December 31, 1946

Gross sales	$475,000.00
Less returned sales and allowances	6,000.00
Net sales	$469,000.00
Less cost of goods sold (Exhibit D)	303,000.00
Gross profit on sales	$166,000.00
Less selling expenses	60,000.00
Net profit on sales	$106,000.00
Less general expenses	36,000.00
Net profit on operations	$ 70,000.00
Less bond interest	6,500.00
Total net profit	$ 63,500.00
Less minority interests in net income	5,400.00
Consolidated net profit	$ 58,100.00

Exhibit A

COMPANY *A* AND SUBSIDIARIES *B* AND *C*
Consolidated Balance Sheet
December 31, 1946

Assets

Current assets:			
Cash		$ 72,500.00	
Accounts receivable		84,200.00	
Inventories:			
Finished goods	$91,140.00		
Goods in process	78,320.00		
Raw materials	82,390.00	251,850.00	
Total current assets			$408,550.00
Fixed assets:			
Land		$ 95,000.00	
Buildings—less depreciation		235,000.00	
Machinery—less depreciation		145,000.00	
Total fixed assets			475,000.00
Goodwill			15,000.00
			$898,550.00

Liabilities and Net Worth

Current liabilities:			
Accounts payable			$166,700.00
Fixed liabilities:			
Bonds payable—6%		$100,000.00	
Bonds payable—5%	$50,000.00		
Less intercompany owned bonds	40,000.00	10,000.00	
Total fixed liabilities			110,000.00
Minority interests			31,900.00
Net worth:			
Capital stock		$500,000.00	
Surplus (Exhibit B)		89,950.00	
Total net worth			589,950.00
			$898,550.00

Exhibit B

COMPANY *A* AND SUBSIDIARIES *B* AND *C*
Consolidated Surplus Statement
For the Year Ended December 31, 1946

Surplus, December 31, 1945	$31,850.00
Net profit for 1946	58,100.00
Surplus, December 31, 1946	$89,950.00

Variations from facilitating conditions. As stated in Chapter 51, adjustments of the investment and/or surplus accounts may be required for the following reasons:

(1) The parent company may carry the subsidiary investment at cost.

(2) The parent company, pursuing the policy of taking up subsidiary profits, losses, and dividends through the investment account, may have taken up the subsidiary profit or loss for the current period.

(3) Dividend payments during the current period may have been charged to surplus accounts instead of to separate accounts.

As no dividends were paid during the current year in Case 1 of this chapter, it is possible to modify that case with respect to only variations 1 and 2.

Variation 1—Investments carried at cost. We shall now assume that Company *A* is carrying the subsidiary investments at cost; adjustments should therefore be made for the parent company's proportions of all changes in subsidiary surpluses since acquisition except the profits for the current year.

The adjustment with respect to Company *B* is computed below:

Subsidiary surplus:	
December 31, 1945 (and, since no dividends were paid in 1946, this is also the surplus on December 31, 1946, before crediting the profit for 1946)	$25,000.00
At date of acquisition—as stated on page 365	15,000.00
Increase	$10,000.00
Parent company's 90% thereof (adjustment x)	9,000.00

No adjustment is required with respect to the investment in Company *C*; this subsidiary's stock was acquired at the beginning of the current year, and there have been no changes in Company *C*'s surplus during 1946 except the profit.

Partial working papers showing the adjustment appear on the following page.

PARTIAL WORKING PAPERS
(Case 1, with Variation 1)

	Company *A*	Company *B*	Company *C*	Adjustments Debit	Adjustments Credit
Debits					
Investment in stock of Company *B*—90%	$108,500.00				
90% of increase in Company *B* surplus				$9,000.00x	
Investment in stock of Company *C*—80%	66,000.00				
Credits					
Surplus, December 31, 1945:					
Company *A*	26,000.00				$9,000.00x

Variation 2—Current profits taken up. We shall now assume that the parent company has taken up its share of all changes in the subsidiaries' surpluses since acquisition, including the profits for the current year. The following partial working papers contain adjustments to reverse the entries taking up the current year's profits.

PARTIAL WORKING PAPERS
(Case 1, with Variation 2)

	Company *A*	Company *B*	Company *C*	Adjustments Debit	Adjustments Credit
Debits					
Investment in stock of Company *B*—90%	$132,800.00				
Reverse entry for 1946 profit					$15,300.00y
Investment in stock of Company *C*—80%	80,800.00				
Reverse entry for 1946 profit					14,800.00z
Credits					
Surplus, December 31, 1945:					
Company *A*	35,000.00				
Company *B* profit.	15,300.00			$15,300.00y	
Company *C* profit.	14,800.00			14,800.00z	

Case 2. This case is the same as Case 1, except that it is now assumed that dividends were paid by all companies in 1946. The facilitating accounting conditions exist. The working papers appear on pages 374 and 375.

COMPANY *A* AND SUBSIDIARIES *B* AND *C*

Consolidated Working Papers

For the Year Ended December 31, 1946

Debits	Company *A*	Company *B*	Company *C*	Adjustments Debit	Adjustments Credit	Eliminations	Cost of Sales	Profit and Loss	Surplus	Minority	Balance Sheet
Cash	$ 17,800	$ 10,000	$ 13,500								$ 41,300
Accounts receivable	53,700	17,000	25,000			$ 11,500F					84,200
Inventories, December 31, 1945:											
Finished goods		30,000					$ 30,000				
Goods in process	25,000	30,000			$ 1,350b		53,650				
Raw materials	40,000	15,000	15,000		1,800b		68,200				
Land	50,000	20,000	25,000								95,000
Buildings—less depreciation	140,000	35,000	60,000								235,000
Equipment—less depreciation	90,000	40,000	15,000								145,000
Investment in stock of Company *B*—90%	112,100										
Eliminate:											
Capital stock						90,000A					
Surplus						17,100B					
Goodwill											5,000
Investment in stock of Company *C*—80%	63,600										
Eliminate:											
Capital stock						40,000C					
Surplus						13,600D					
Goodwill											10,000
Investment in bonds of Company *C*	40,000										40,000
Returned sales and allowances	3,000	2,000	1,000					$ 6,000			
Purchases—materials	145,000	95,000	76,000			170,000F	146,000				
Direct labor	85,000	65,000					150,000				
Manufacturing expense	70,000	40,000				3,000G	107,000				
Selling expense	23,000	22,000	15,000					60,000			
General expense	24,000	9,000	3,000					36,000			
Bond interest	6,000		2,500			2,000H		6,500			
Dividends paid:											
Company *A*	30,000								$30,000		
Company *B*		6,000				5,400B				$ 600	
Company *C*			3,000			2,400D				600	
	$1,018,200	$436,000	$254,000								
Inventories, December 31, 1946:											
Finished goods				$ 95,000a	$ 3,860c						91,140
Goods in process				80,000a	1,680c						78,320
Raw materials				86,000a	3,610c						82,390
				$261,000	$12,300	$355,000					
Cost of sales:											
Debits							$554,850				
Credits—per contra							251,850				
Balance							$303,000	303,000			
Column totals—deducted contra								$411,500	$30,000	$ 1,200	$907,350

COMPANY *A* AND SUBSIDIARIES *B* AND *C*

Consolidated Working Papers—Continued

For the Year Ended December 31, 1946

Credits	Company *A*	Company *B*	Company *C*	Adjustments Debit	Adjustments Credit	Eliminations	Cost of Sales	Profit and Loss	Surplus	Minority	Balance Sheet
Adjustment column totals brought forward				$261,000	$ 12,300						
Accounts payable	$ 78,200	$ 86,000	$ 14,000			$ 11,500E					$166,700
Bonds payable:											
Company *A*—6%	100,000										100,000
Company *C*—5%			50,000								50,000
Capital stock:											
Company *A*	500,000										500,000
Company *B*		100,000				90,000A				$10,000	
Company *C*			50,000			40,000C				10,000	
Surplus, December 31, 1945:											
Company *A*	35,000			3,150b					$31,850		
Company *B*		25,000				22,500B				2,500	
Company *C*			20,000			16,000D				4,000	
Sales	300,000	225,000	120,000			170,000F		$475,000			
Rent of equipment to Company *B*	3,000					3,000G					
Bond interest from Company *C*	2,000					2,000H					
	$1,018,200	$436,000	$254,000								
Inventories, December 31, 1946:											
Finished goods				3,860c	95,000a		$ 91,140				
Goods in process				1,680c	80,000a		78,320				
Raw materials				3,610c	86,000a		82,390				
				$273,300	$273,300	$355,000					
Column total—deducted contra							$251,850				
Profit and loss:											
Credits								$475,000			
Debits—per contra								411,500			
Net profit								$ 63,500			
Minority interests—see page 370:											
Company *B*								1,700*		1,700	
Company *C*								3,700*		3,700	
Parent company's share								$ 58,100	58,100		
Surplus:											
Credits									$89,950		
Debits—per contra									30,000		
Balance									$59,950		59,950
Minority:											
Credits										$31,900	
Debits—per contra										1,200	
Balance										$30,700	30,700
											$907,350

* Deduction.

Consolidated statements: Case 2. The statement of cost of goods sold and the statement of profit and loss would be the same as those in Case 1. The two cases differ only because of the payment of dividends, and this affects only the cash, minority interest, and consolidated surplus.

Exhibit B

COMPANY *A* AND SUBSIDIARIES *B* AND *C*
Consolidated Surplus Statement
For the Year Ended December 31, 1946

Surplus, December 31, 1945	$31,850.00
Net profit for 1946	58,100.00
Total	$89,950.00
Less dividends paid	30,000.00
Surplus, December 31, 1946	$59,950.00

Exhibit A

COMPANY *A* AND SUBSIDIARIES *B* AND *C*
Consolidated Balance Sheet
December 31, 1946

Assets

Current assets:			
Cash		$ 41,300.00	
Accounts receivable		84,200.00	
Inventories:			
Finished goods	$91,140.00		
Goods in process	78,320.00		
Raw materials	82,390.00	251,850.00	
Total current assets			$377,350.00
Fixed assets:			
Land		$ 95,000.00	
Buildings—less depreciation		235,000.00	
Machinery—less depreciation		145,000.00	
Total fixed assets			475,000.00
Goodwill			15,000.00
			$867,350.00

Liabilities and Net Worth

Current liabilities:			
Accounts payable			$166,700.00
Fixed liabilities:			
Bonds payable—6%		$100,000.00	
Bonds payable—5%	$50,000.00		
Less intercompany owned bonds	40,000.00	10,000.00	
Total fixed liabilities			110,000.00
Minority interest			30,700.00
Net worth:			
Capital stock		$500,000.00	
Surplus		59,950.00	
Total net worth			559,950.00
			$867,350.00

Variations 1 and 3. If, in Case 2, the investments had been carried at cost and dividend payments by both companies had been charged directly to surplus, adjustments would be required as shown in the following partial working papers. These adjustments are:

x—For increase in surplus of Company *B*:

Surplus, December 31, 1945	$25,000.00
Dividend paid—1946	6,000.00
Surplus, December 31, 1946, before 1946 profit	$19,000.00
Surplus at acquisition	15,000.00
Increase	$ 4,000.00
Parent company's 90%	$ 3,600.00

y—For decrease in surplus of Company *C*:

Surplus, December 31, 1945	$20,000.00
Dividend paid—1946	3,000.00
Surplus, December 31, 1946, before 1946 profit	$17,000.00
Surplus at acquisition	20,000.00
Decrease	$ 3,000.00
Parent company's 80%	$ 2,400.00

z—To transfer charges for dividend payments of both companies from surplus account to separate accounts.

Partial Working Papers
(Case 2—with Variations 1 and 3)

	Company *A*	Company *B*	Company *C*	Adjustments Debit	Adjustments Credit
Debits					
Investment in Company *B*—90%—at cost	$108,500				
90% of increase in Company *B* surplus				$ 3,600x	
Investment in Company *C*—80%—at cost	66,000				
90% of decrease in Company *C* surplus					$ 2,400y
Dividends paid:					
Company *A*				30,000z	
Company *B*				6,000z	
Company *C*				3,000z	
Credits					
Surplus:					
Company *A*	3,800			$2,400y	3,600x 30,000z
Company *B*		$19,000			6,000z
Company *C*			$17,000		3,000z

Variations 2 and 3. It is now assumed that the parent company, in following the policy of taking up subsidiary profits, losses, and dividends through the investment account, has taken up its percentages of the 1946 profits of Companies *B* and *C*. It is also assumed that dividend payments by all companies in 1946 have been charged to the surplus accounts. The adjustments are shown in the partial working papers on the following page.

Partial Working Papers
(Case 2, with Variations 2 and 3)

	Company *A*	Company *B*	Company *C*	Adjustments Debit	Adjustments Credit
Debits					
Investment in stock of Company *B*—90%....	$127,400.00				
Reverse entry for 1946 profit.....					$15,300.00v
Investment in stock of Company *C*—80%....	78,400.00				
Reverse entry for 1946 profit.....					14,800.00w
Dividends paid:					
Company *A*..				$30,000.00z	
Company *B*..				6,000.00z	
Company *C*..				3,000.00z	
Credits					
Surplus:					
Company *A*..	35,100.00			15,300.00v 14,800.00w	30,000.00z
Company *B*..		$19,000.00			6,000.00z
Company *C*..			$17,000.00		3,000.00z

Intercompany profit in construction. To illustrate the adjustments required if one company sells fixed assets to another related company at a profit, let us assume the following facts: Machinery sold by the parent company to the subsidiary on January 1, 1945 for $50,000.00; cost to parent company, $40,000.00; depreciation rate, 10%.

If a consolidated balance sheet is prepared on January 1, 1945, the only required adjustment is one setting up a $10,000.00 reserve for the intercompany profit. This is accomplished in the working papers as follows:

Partial Working Papers—January 1, 1945

	Co. *P*	Co. *S*	Adjustments Debit	Adjustments Credit
Debits				
Machinery..................		$50,000		
Credits				
Profit on sale of machinery....	$10,000		$10,000a	
Reserve for intercompany profit				$10,000a

At the end of 1945, the adjustments will be somewhat more complex because Company *S* will have provided $5,000.00 for depreciation (10% of $50,000.00) whereas, from a consolidated standpoint, the depreciation should be $4,000.00 (10% of the $40,000.00 cost to Company *P*). The required adjustments are shown in the partial working papers on the following page.

Partial Working Papers—December 31, 1945

	Co. *P*	Co. *S*	Adjustments Debit	Adjustments Credit
Debits				
Machinery..................		$50,000		
Depreciation expense.........		5,000		$ 1,000b
Credits				
Reserve for depreciation......		5,000	$ 1,000b	
Profit on sale of machinery....	$10,000		10,000a	
Reserve for intercompany profit				10,000a

At the end of 1946, the conditions will be still more complex. A reserve for the entire intercompany profit of $10,000.00 should be set up; the charge should be to Company *P*'s surplus since the profit made in 1945 will have been closed to surplus. The depreciation reserve should be reduced $2,000.00 representing the excess depreciation from a consolidated standpoint for 1945 and 1946; offsetting this $2,000.00 debit adjustment there should be a $1,000.00 credit to surplus as of December 31, 1945 (representing the excess depreciation charge in 1945) and a $1,000.00 credit to depreciation expense (to reduce the depreciation expense for 1946 to a basis of intercompany cost). The required adjustments are shown below.

Partial Working Papers—December 31, 1946

	Co. *P*	Co. *S*	Adjustments Debit	Adjustments Credit
Debits				
Machinery..................		$50,000		
Depreciation expense.........		5,000		$ 1,000b
Credits				
Reserve for depreciation......		$10,000	$ 2,000b	
Surplus.....................	10,000		10,000a	1,000b
Reserve for intercompany profit				10,000a

Let us now assume the same facts as before except that the sale of the fixed assets was made by the subsidiary to the parent company, and that there is a 10% minority interest in the subsidiary.

If a consolidated balance sheet is prepared on January 1, 1945, the date of the sale, the only required adjustment is one setting up a reserve for the intercompany profit. Although the subsidiary made a total profit of $10,000.00, the parent company's portion thereof is only $9,000.00.

Partial Working Papers—January 1, 1945

	Co. *P*	Co. *S*	Adjustments Debit	Adjustments Credit
Debits				
Machinery....................	$50,000			
Credits				
Profit on sale of machinery......		$10,000		
Surplus—Co. *P*...............			$9,000a	
Reserve for intercompany profit..				$9,000a

At the end of 1945 Company *P* will have provided $5,000.00 for depreciation (10% of $50,000.00). From a consolidated standpoint, the depreciation should be 10% of $41,000.00, the intercompany cost. The required adjustments are shown below.

Partial Working Papers—December 31, 1945

			Adjustments	
Debits	Co. P	Co. S	Debit	Credit
Machinery	$50.000			
Depreciation expense	5,000			$ 900b
Credits				
Reserve for depreciation	5,000		$ 900b	
Profit on sale of machinery		$10,000		
Surplus—Co. *P*			9,000a	
Reserve for intercompany profit				9,000a

As a result of these adjustments the $9,000.00 of intercompany profit is eliminated from consolidated surplus; the $50,000.00 balance in the machinery account minus the $9,000.00 balance in the reserve for intercompany profit is the $41,000.00 intercompany cost at which the asset should be stated in the balance sheet; the depreciation reserve to be shown in the consolidated balance sheet is $4,100.00; and the depreciation expense to be shown in the consolidated profit and loss statement is $4,100.00.

At the end of 1946, a reserve of $9,000.00 should again be set up to eliminate the intercompany profit. The depreciation reserve should be reduced $1,800.00, representing the excess depreciation from a consolidated standpoint for 1945 and 1946; offsetting this $1,800.00 debit to the depreciation reserve there should be a $900.00 credit to consolidated surplus (representing the excess depreciation charge in 1945) and a $900.00 credit to depreciation expense (to reduce the depreciation charge for 1946 to a basis of intercompany cost).

Partial Working Papers—December 31, 1946

			Adjustments	
Debits	Co. *P*	Co. *S*	Debit	Credit
Machinery	$50,000			
Depreciation expense	5,000			$ 900b
Credits				
Reserve for depreciation	10,000		$1,800b	
Surplus—Co. *P*			9,000a	900b
Reserve for intercompany profit				9,000a

Alternative working papers—first illustration. In the following working papers a separate section is provided for each statement.

The first illustration is based on the same facts, and the adjustments and eliminations are the same as those in the working papers on pages 358 and 359.

COMPANY *P* AND SUBSIDIARY *S*
Consolidated Working Papers
For the Year Ended December 31, 1946

	Company *P*	Company *S*	Adjustments and Eliminations: Debit	Adjustments and Eliminations: Credit	Minority	Consolidated
Cost of Goods Sold						
Debits:						
Inventory, December 31, 1945	$ 27,000	$ 16,000		$ 1,800b		$ 41,200
Purchases	120,000	100,000		20,000C		200,000
Total debits	$147,000	$116,000				$241,200
Credits:						
Inventory, December 31, 1946	30,000a	19,000a	$ 900c			48,100
Cost of goods sold—forward	$117,000	$ 97,000	$ 900	$21,800		$193,100
Profit and Loss						
Credits:						
Sales	$150,000	$120,000	$20,000C			$250,000
Debits:						
Cost of goods sold—brought forward	$117,000	$ 97,000	900	$21,800		$193,100
Expense	20,000	12,000				32,000
Total debits	$137,000	$109,000				$225,100
Net profit—forward:						
Total	$ 13,000	$ 11,000	$20,900	$21,800		$ 24,900
Minority interest—10% of $11,000					$1,100	1,100
Consolidated net profit						$ 23,800
Surplus						
Credits:						
Balance, December 31, 1945:						
Company *P*	$ 58,500		$ 1,800b			$ 56,700
Company *S*		$ 22,000	19,800B		$2,200	
Net profit—brought forward	13,000	11,000	20,900	$21,800	1,100	23,800
Total credits	$ 71,500	$ 33,000			$3,300	$ 80,500
Debits:						
Dividends paid:						
Company *P*	6,000					6,000
Company *S*		3,000		2,700B	300	
Balance, December 31, 1946—forward	$ 65,500	$ 30,000	$42,500	$24,500	$3,000	$ 74,500

COMPANY *P* AND SUBSIDIARY *S*
Consolidated Working Papers—Continued
For the Year Ended December 31, 1946

Balance Sheet	Company *P*	Company *S*	Adjustments and Eliminations Debit	Adjustments and Eliminations Credit	Minority	Consolidated
Assets:						
Cash	$ 41,400	$ 31,000				$ 72,400
Accounts receivable	54,000	45,000				99,000
Inventory	30,000a	19,000a		$ 900c		48,100
Investment in Company *S*—90 %	65,100					
Eliminate:						
Capital stock				45,000A		
Surplus				17,100B		
Goodwill						3,000
	$190,500	$ 95,000				$222,500
Liabilities and net worth:						
Accounts payable	$ 25,000	$ 15,000				$ 40,000
Capital stock:						
Company *P*	100,000					100,000
Company *S*		50,000	$45,000A		$5,000	
Surplus—brought forward	65,500	30,000	42,500	24,500	3,000	74,500
Total minority interest					$8,000	8,000
	$190,500	$ 95,000	$87,500	$87,500		$222,500

Working papers in the alternative form are prepared as follows:

Enter amounts in the company columns in the statement sequence; cost of sales debits, cost of sales credits; profit and loss credits, profit and loss debits; and so on.

Enter the adjustments and eliminations. In the illustration, adjustments are indicated by lower case reference letters; eliminations are indicated by capitals. Adjustments affecting individual company statements are entered in the company columns so that these columns will correctly reflect the operations and financial condition of the individual companies. They are not also entered in the adjustment columns, as such a procedure would involve a duplication.

Complete each successive section of the working papers and make forwardings to the succeeding section in the manner illustrated.

Alternative working papers—second illustration. The working papers on pages 384 and 385 are based on the same facts as those on pages 381 and 382, and are intended to further illustrate the treatment of adjustments affecting the statements by companies, as distinguished from those that affect only the consolidated statements. In addition to the adjustment for the end-of-year inventory, there are adjustments for the following unrecorded transactions:

	Company *P*	Company *S*
Sales on account	$1,500.00	
Purchases on account		$500.00
Accrued expense	800.00	700.00

Observe that these adjustments affect the company statements and therefore appear in the company columns and not in the adjustment columns.

COMPANY *P* AND SUBSIDIARY *S*
Consolidated Working Papers
For the Year Ended December 31, 1946

	Company *P*	Company *S*	Adjustments and Eliminations Debit	Adjustments and Eliminations Credit	Minority	Consolidated
Cost of Goods Sold						
Debits:						
Inventory, December 31, 1945	$ 27,000	$ 16,000		$ 1,800b		$ 41,200
Purchases	120,000	500y 100,000		20,000C		200,500
Total debits	$147,000	$116,500				$241,700
Credits:						
Inventory, December 31, 1946	30,000a	19,000a	$ 900c			48,100
Cost of goods sold—forward	$117,000	$ 97,500	$ 900	$21,800		$193,600
Profit and Loss						
Credits:						
Sales	$ 1,500x 150,000	$120,000	$20,000C			$251,500
Debits:						
Cost of goods sold—brought forward	$117,000	$ 97,500	900	$21,800		$193,600
Expense	800z 20,000	700z 12,000				33,500
Total debits	$137,800	$110,200				$227,100
Net profit—forward:						
Total	$ 13,700	$ 9,800	$20,900	$21,800		$ 24,400
Minority interest—10% of $9,800					$ 980	980
Consolidated net profit						$ 23,420
Surplus						
Credits:						
Balance, December 31, 1945:						
Company *P*	$ 58,500		$ 1,800b			$ 56,700
Company *S*		$ 22,000	19,800B		$2,200	
Net profit—brought forward	13,700	9,800	20,900	$21,800	980	23,420
Total credits	$ 72,200	$ 31,800			$3,180	$ 80,120
Debits:						
Dividends paid:						
Company *P*	6,000					6,000
Company *S*		3,000		2,700B	300	
Balance, December 31, 1946—forward	$ 66,200	$ 28,800	$42,500	$24,500	$2,880	$ 74,120

COMPANY *P* AND SUBSIDIARY *S*
Consolidated Working Papers—Continued
For the Year Ended December 31, 1946

Balance Sheet	Company *P*	Company *S*	Adjustments and Eliminations: Debit	Adjustments and Eliminations: Credit	Minority	Consolidated
Assets:						
Cash	$ 41,400	$31,000				$ 72,400
Accounts receivable	{ 1,500x 54,000	45,000				100,500
Inventory	30,000a	19,000a		$ 900c		48,100
Investment in Company *S*—90%	65,100					
Eliminate:						
Capital stock				45,000A		
Surplus				17,100B		
Goodwill						3,000
	$192,000	$95,000				$224,000
Liabilities and net worth:						
Accounts payable	{ $ 800z 25,000	$ 500y 700z 15,000				$ 42,000
Capital stock:						
Company *P*	100,000					100,000
Company *S*		50,000	$45,000A		$5,000	
Surplus—brought forward	66,200	28,800	42,500	24,500	2,880	74,120
Total minority interest					$7,880	7,880
	$192,000	$95,000	$87,500	$87,500		$224,000

Alternative working papers—third illustration. This illustration is based on the same facts as those on pages 374 and 375.

COMPANY *A* AND SUBSIDIARIES *B* AND *C*
Consolidated Working Papers
For the Year Ended December 31, 1946

Cost of Goods Sold	Company *A*	Company *B*	Company *C*	Adjustments and Eliminations Debit	Adjustments and Eliminations Credit	Minority	Consolidated
Debits:							
Inventories, December 31, 1945:							
Finished goods		$ 30,000.00					$ 30,000.00
Goods in process	$ 25,000.00	30,000.00			$ 1,350.00b		53,650.00
Raw materials	40,000.00	15,000.00	$ 15,000.00		1,800.00b		68,200.00
Purchases—materials	145,000.00	95,000.00	76,000.00		170,000.00F		146,000.00
Direct labor	85,000.00	65,000.00					150,000.00
Manufacturing expense	70,000.00	40,000.00			3,000.00G		107,000.00
Total debits	$365,000.00	$275,000.00	$ 91,000.00				$554,850.00
Credits:							
Inventories, December 31, 1946:							
Finished goods	$ 45,000.00a	$ 50,000.00a		$ 3,860.00c			$ 91,140.00
Goods in process	55,000.00a	25,000.00a		1,680.00c			78,320.00
Raw materials	50,000.00a	25,000.00a	$ 11,000.00a	3,610.00c			82,390.00
Total credits	$150,000.00	$100,000.00	$ 11,000.00				$251,850.00
Cost of goods sold—forward	$215,000.00	$175,000.00	$ 80,000.00	$ 9,150.00	$176,150.00		$303,000.00
Profit and Loss							
Credits:							
Sales	$300,000.00	$225,000.00	$120,000.00	$170,000.00F			$475,000.00
Rent of equipment to Company *B*	3,000.00			3,000.00G			
Bond interest from Company *C*	2,000.00			2,000.00H			
Total credits	$305,000.00	$225,000.00	$120,000.00				$475,000.00
Debits:							
Returned sales and allowances	$ 3,000.00	$ 2,000.00	$ 1,000.00				$ 6,000.00
Cost of goods sold—brought forward	215,000.00	175,000.00	80,000.00	9,150.00	$176,150.00		303,000.00
Selling expense	23,000.00	22,000.00	15,000.00				60,000.00
General expense	24,000.00	9,000.00	3,000.00				36,000.00
Bond interest	6,000.00		2,500.00		2,000.00H		6,500.00
Total debits	$271,000.00	$208,000.00	$101,500.00				$411,500.00
Net profit—forward:							
Total	$ 34,000.00	$ 17,000.00	$ 18,500.00	$184,150.00	$178,150 00		$ 63,500.00
Minority interests:							
Company *B*—10% of $17,000.00						$ 1,700.00	
Company *C*—20% of $18,500.00						3,700.00	
Total						$ 5,400.00	5,400.00
Consolidated net profit							$ 58,100.00

COMPANY *A* AND SUBSIDIARIES *B* AND *C*
Consolidated Working Papers—Continued
For the Year Ended December 31, 1946

Surplus	Company *A*	Company *B*	Company *C*	Adjustments and Eliminations Debit	Adjustments and Eliminations Credit	Minority	Consolidated
Credits:							
Balance, December 31, 1945:							
Company *A*	$ 35,000.00			$ 3,150.00b			$31,850.00
Company *B*		$ 25,000.00		22,500.00B		$ 2,500.00	
Company *C*			$20,000.00	16,000.00D		4,000.00	
Net profit—brought forward	34,000.00	17,000.00	18,500.00	184,150.00	$178,150.00	5,400.00	58,100.00
Total credits	$ 69,000.00	$ 42,000.00	$38,500.00			$11,900.00	$89,950.00
Debits:							
Dividends paid:							
Company *A*	$ 30,000.00						$30,000.00
Company *B*		$ 6,000.00			5,400.00B	$ 600.00	
Company *C*			$ 3,000.00		2,400.00D	600.00	
Total debits	$ 30,000.00	$ 6,000.00	$ 3,000.00			$ 1,200.00	$30,000.00
Balance, December 31, 1946—forward	$ 39,000.00	$ 36,000.00	$35,500.00	$225,800.00	$185,950.00	$10,700.00	$59,950.00

COMPANY *A* AND SUBSIDIARIES *B* AND *C*

Consolidated Working Papers—Continued

For the Year Ended December 31, 1946

Balance Sheet	Company *A*	Company *B*	Company *C*	Adjustments and Eliminations: Debit	Adjustments and Eliminations: Credit	Minority	Consolidated
Assets:							
Cash	$ 17,800.00	$ 10,000.00	$ 13,500.00				$ 41,300.00
Accounts receivable	53,700.00	17,000.00	25,000.00		$ 11,500.00E		84,200.00
Inventories:							
Finished goods	45,000.00a	50,000.00a			3,860.00c		91,140.00
Goods in process	55,000 00a	25,000.00a			1,680.00c		78,320.00
Raw materials	50,000.00a	25,000.00a	11,000.00a		3,610.00c		82,390.00
Land	50,000.00	20,000.00	25,000.00				95,000.00
Buildings—less depreciation	140,000.00	35,000.00	60,000.00				235,000.00
Equipment—less depreciation	90,000.00	40,000.00	15,000.00				145,000.00
Investment in stock of Company *B*—90%	112,100.00						
Eliminate:							
Capital stock					90,000.00A		
Surplus					17,100.00B		
Goodwill							5,000.00
Investment in stock of Company *C*—80%	63,600.00						
Eliminate:							
Capital stock					40,000.00C		
Surplus					13,600.00D		
Goodwill							10,000.00
Investment in bonds of Company *C*	40,000.00						40,000.00
	$717,200.00	$222,000.00	$149,500.00				$907,350.00
Liabilities and net worth:							
Accounts payable	$ 78,200.00	$ 86,000.00	$ 14,000.00	$ 11,500.00E			$166,700.00
Bonds payable:							
Company *A*—6%	100,000.00						100,000.00
Company *C*—5%			50,000.00				50,000.00
Capital stock:							
Company *A*	500,000.00						500,000.00
Company *B*		100,000.00		90,000.00A		$10,000.00	
Company *C*			50,000.00	40,000.00C		10,000.00	
Surplus—brought forward	39,000.00	36,000.00	35,500.00	225,800.00	185,950.00	10,700.00	59,950.00
Total minority interest						$30,700.00	30,700.00
	$717,200.00	$222,000.00	$149,500.00	$367,300.00	$367,300.00		$907,350.00

Acquisitions at interim dates. If a parent company acquires stock at an interim date when no subsidiary balance sheet is available from which to determine the book value of the stock acquired, the subsidiary surplus at the date of acquisition may be approximated by prorating the change in surplus between a date preceding and one succeeding the date of acquisition. Although such an approximation is obviously arbitrary, it can be assumed to be more accurate in most cases than would be the acceptance of a book value at a date prior or subsequent to the date of acquisition.

The transfer of the subsidiary stock may be made on one date, but as of a preceding date. Two questions then arise: Which date should be used for determining the book value of the subsidiary stock for purposes of computing the consolidated goodwill? Should the subsidiary earnings for the period between the two dates be regarded as accruing to the parent company and be included in consolidated earnings? If negotiations are started in May for the acquisition of a business as of the end of the preceding December, there is a presumption that the purchase price includes an allowance for the earnings of the intervening period, and in the absence of a specific contract provision to the contrary, it is doubtful whether the parent company is justified in taking the interim earnings into consolidated income. However, if the price is specifically based on the conditions existing on December 31, and the transfer is postponed because of the time required for audits or other verifications of the stated conditions, the goodwill computation could be based on the subsidiary book value at the end of December, and the consolidated earnings could include the results of operations subsequent to that date.

If the earnings of a subsidiary for a portion of a fiscal period prior to acquisition are to be excluded from the consolidated net income, the best practical procedure is to consolidate the subsidiary's operating statement for the entire fiscal period and, from the resulting total net income, deduct an amount representing the subsidiary's net income for the portion of the period prior to acquisition. This procedure has two advantages: first, it avoids the necessity of preparing a subsidiary profit and loss statement for a fractional period, which may be difficult because of the absence of inventories; second, the statement gives a better picture of the earning power of the group than would be presented by a statement consolidating the operations of the parent company for the entire period and those of the subsidiary for a fraction thereof.

Limitations of consolidated statements. Although consolidated statements have a very real usefulness for purposes of presenting a composite picture of the financial condition and operating results of a group of affiliated corporations, they cannot be regarded as properly taking the place of statements for the individual companies.

Minority stockholders of a subsidiary can obtain very little information of value to them from consolidated statements, for such statements do not detail the assets, liabilities, income, and expenses of the subsidiary. Minority stockholders should be supplied with subsidiary company statements. Moreover, the minority stockholders should be interested in information relative to the volume of business conducted with the parent company and other affiliates; the continuance or discontinuance of such business is under the control of the parent company, and decisions with respect thereto may be determined from the standpoint of the parent company and to the detriment of the minority.

The creditors of each company are primarily concerned with the financial condition and earnings of the specific debtor company. It is obvious that creditors of a subsidiary cannot obtain from consolidated statements the information they require relative to the subsidiary. It is perhaps less obvious, but it is equally true, that the creditors of the parent company are not adequately informed by such statements. The pool of assets shown by a consolidated balance sheet is not available ratably for the payment of the liabilities shown in the balance sheet. Subsidiary assets are available for the payment of parent company liabilities only after the satisfaction of the subsidiary's obligations; in fact, all outside stockholders of the subsidiary, whether holders of preferred or common shares, would rank with, or before, the parent's creditors in liquidation.

It is often difficult to show, in a consolidated balance sheet, the liens which affect the rights of creditors. Assume, for example, that the parent company has pledged the stock of a subsidiary as security to a parent company debt. As a consequence, the net assets of the subsidiary do not constitute the same potential debt-paying resource for all creditors of the parent company. This condition is not reflected by a consolidated balance sheet in which all parent and subsidiary assets are merged in a pool which purports to be available ratably for the payment of all parent and subsidiary liabilities. The pledge of the subsidiary stock may be stated in a footnote, but this does not suffice because the consolidated balance sheet does not show the subsidiary's assets affected by the pledge, nor the subsidiary liabilities, which rank ahead of the parent company's liabilities to creditors holding the pledged stock.

Since a consolidated statement is a composite, a weak current position of one company may be bolstered by a strong current position in another company: for this and other reasons, the consolidated balance sheet cannot be regarded as reflecting the current position of the parent company.

If assets of foreign subsidiaries represent a considerable portion of the consolidated total, very misleading conclusions may be reached if the consolidated balance sheet includes foreign cash subject to widely fluctuating exchange rates or to exchange restrictions, or if it includes foreign receivables subject to extraordinary collection hazards, or if it includes merchandise manufactured and/or labeled specifically for foreign sales.

It is customary to show as finished goods inventory in the consolidated statements the total finished goods inventories of all companies, and to combine the other inventories in a similar manner. However, if intercompany sales are made and finished goods of one company become raw materials of another company, the extent of such intercompany transactions has a bearing on the liquidity of the inventories. If such intercompany transfers are of inconsequential amount, the customary procedure results in only a negligible distortion; but if substantial inventories properly classified as finished goods from the individual company standpoint are in reality raw materials or goods in process from the consolidated standpoint, the consolidated balance sheet will give a false impression of the liquidity of the inventories.

Bond indentures frequently require the maintaining of specified ratios of current assets to current liabilities, and provide penalties for non-conformance. A consolidated balance sheet does not give the bondholders of individual companies information from which they can determine whether the requirements are being fulfilled, nor can the stockholders see whether their company is in any jeopardy because of a default.

The bondholders and preferred stockholders are interested in the relation of separate company earnings to interest and preferred dividend requirements, and the common stockholders are interested in the remaining earnings on common shares. Consolidated statements do not provide this information. Moreover, because of the customary procedure of combining bond interest and preferred dividends of all companies, the statements do not show, with respect to any company, the number of times its bond interest or preferred dividend is earned. Also, the custom of deducting all bond interest before any preferred or common dividends, tends to create the false impression that all bond interest ranks ahead of any dividends; actually, the bond interest and preferred and common dividends of subsidiaries must be paid before any subsidiary earnings become available for the payment of parent company bond interest.

It is, of course, obvious that a consolidated income statement does not show the operating results of individual companies. Such information may be extremely important, not only from the standpoint of minority stockholders of subsidiaries, but from the standpoint of the parent company as well. A family of companies may be able to carry a weak sister, but the strength of the organization is enhanced if each affiliate carries itself. A weak subsidiary may be a real source of danger. Assume, for instance, that an essential subsidiary is operating at a loss—a fact which is not disclosed because the group as a whole operates at a profit; control of the subsidiary has been exercised through ownership of the common stock, since the preferred stock has no vote as long as dividends are paid; here, obviously, is a situation in which control of an essential subsidiary may be lost to outside preferred stockholders, and the integrated operations of the entire group are therefore in jeopardy.

Ratio analyses based on consolidated data are not reliable. In the first place, such ratios are composites, and the good and bad features of individual companies are not disclosed. For instance, assume the following facts regarding sales and a certain expense:

	Sales	Expense	Per Cent
Company *A*	$ 300,000	$33,000	11%
Company *B*	700,000	42,000	6
Total	$1,000,000	$75,000	7.5

Let us further assume that 7.5% is a satisfactory ratio and that 11% is unsatisfactory; a bad feature of Company *A* is not disclosed.

In the second place, the ratios are affected by intercompany eliminations. Assume that there are intercompany sales of $250,000.00; the sales shown in the consolidated profit and loss statement are therefore $750,000.00, and the expense ratio is stated as 10%. If an expense should bear a certain relation to sales, the per cent should be computed by using the total sales as well as the total expenses; since intercompany sales are eliminated from the base, the per cent is distorted.

On the other hand, it should be recognized that statements of the parent company alone are not wholly satisfactory. A parent company balance sheet in which the assets consist principally of investments in subsidiaries can hardly be regarded as an adequate indication of the parent company's financial condition, unless it is supplemented by information about the assets and liabilities underlying the investments. And a parent company's income statement in which subsidiary dividends are taken as earnings reflects income only from the legal, and not from the economic, standpoint. Although the dividends received from the subsidiary are legal income to the parent company, the income statement showing such dividends as income should also show, by footnotes or other memoranda, the profit or loss of the subsidiary during the period.

It is of particular importance to direct attention to any dividends taken by the parent company as income but paid by the subsidiary out of surplus earned prior to the date of acquisition. It has recently been suggested that, even in a non-consolidated profit and loss statement, profits made by a parent company on sales to a subsidiary should be eliminated from the parent company income if the goods remain in the subsidiary's inventory. The legal fact of separate corporate entities probably makes it impossible for an accountant to insist on such a procedure; however, since the parent company may be in a position to inflate its profits by sales to a subsidiary, it might be in order to append a footnote to the unconsolidated income statement indicating the amount of parent company profit remaining in the subsidiary's inventory.

CHAPTER 53

Consolidations, Mergers, and Financing

Purposes of combinations. The modern trend of business organization has been toward the combining of competing firms and corporations into consolidated or affiliated companies. Some doubt has been raised by economists, and particularly by sociologists, regarding the desirability of this trend, and many combinations have been forced to dissolve because the Federal courts have regarded them as "combinations in restraint of trade" and hence in violation of the Sherman Anti-Trust law. At the date of this writing, there appears to be less assurance of the social benefits of free competition, and an increasing inclination to increase the governmental control over industry.

Industrialists have generally held, although not without some dissenting voices, that combinations reduce costs and expenses, and hence increase profits. It is claimed that these advantages result from:

(1) The reduction of competition in the buying market, thus tending to give the combination a certain measure of control over the costs of material and labor.

(2) The enlargement of the scope of production, enabling the combination to:

- (*a*) Own and operate the sources of its raw materials.
- (*b*) Carry manufacture through successive stages, as in the case of a company owning timber lands, producing lumber, and manufacturing furniture.
- (*c*) Process and market its own by-products.
- (*d*) Obtain the benefits of division of labor among workmen and among plants, which is an incident of large-scale production.

(3) The elimination of duplicate sales effort and expense.

(4) The elimination of duplicate administrative effort and expense.

(5) The increase in the control of sales prices which results from the elimination of competition in the selling market.

(6) The increase in financing ability resulting from the increase in the amount of capital controlled and the more ready access to large sources of credit.

Methods of combining. The devices which have been most frequently used in combining two or more corporations into a coördinated organization with a centralized control, or into a single company, are:

(1) Methods of obtaining centralized control of several companies:
  (*a*) Interlocking directorates.
  (*b*) Voting trusts.
  (*c*) Parent companies.
(2) Methods of combining several companies into one company:
  (*a*) Consolidation.
  (*b*) Merger.

Interlocking directorates. If companies have boards of directors which include members serving on more than one board, a certain degree of common control may be obtained. If there are enough directors in common, the policies of the several companies will be subject to the same direction, and may be determined on a basis of their mutual benefit.

Voting trusts. At the beginning of the era of great combinations, the voting trust was one of the most popular methods of effecting a unified control of competing businesses. The stockholders of each company, or a majority thereof, transferred their stock certificates to trustees in exchange for certificates of beneficial interest in the trust. The trustees, holding voting control of the corporations, elected the directors of the corporations, and were thus able to control the activities of the companies as effectively as if the corporations were a single company.

Parent companies. A *parent company* is a corporation which owns all, or a voting majority, of the stock of another corporation, and is thus in a position to control that corporation by electing its board of directors.

If several companies are to be combined by means of a parent company, a new corporation may be organized to act in that capacity, or one of the old companies may acquire the stock of the other companies. The stockholders who sell their stock to the parent company may be paid in cash or in securities of the parent company. In either case, the parent company purchases the stock of the companies to be controlled, but does not purchase their assets or assume their liabilities. Therefore, the controlled companies remain in existence and in the possession of their properties; so far as they are concerned, the only change made is the change in the personnel of their stockholders.

Consolidations and mergers. If the combination is effected by a consolidation or a merger, several companies may be replaced by a single company which will own all of the assets formerly owned by the old companies, and owe the debts which the old companies formerly owed. Certain assets and liabilities may be left with the old companies, but this does not affect the general nature of the consolidation or the merger. Payment for the net assets acquired may be made in cash or by the issuance of stock or other securities.

A distinction is sometimes made between a consolidation and a merger, as follows:

A consolidation is effected if a new corporation is organized which buys the assets and assumes the liabilities of the old companies.

A merger is effected if one of the old corporations buys the assets and assumes the liabilities of the others.

This distinction, however, is not usually recognized, and the two terms are generally used interchangeably.

Net assets and net earnings. If a combination of two or more companies is contemplated, it may be promoted by outsiders who desire to obtain the companies, or it may be promoted by the companies themselves. In either instance, consideration should be given to the value of the net assets and the amounts of the net earnings of the several companies.

If the combination is being promoted by the companies themselves, a consolidation committee should be organized, consisting of members from all of the companies. This committee, with the assistance of an appraiser, an accountant, and an attorney, should submit a report embodying statements of the net assets and the net earnings of each company, and the proposed method of effecting the combinations.

The accountant, after making audits of all companies, should submit a balance sheet of each company, stating the values at which it is proposed to take over the assets, and the liabilities to be assumed. The balance sheet should show the fixed assets at values determined by the appraiser, and the inventories at values determined by the appraiser or the committee.

The accountant should also submit income and surplus statements for the several companies. In preparing the income statements, the accountant should give consideration to the following matters:

(1) Number of years to be covered.
Profit and loss statements should be submitted for several years, in order to show the trend of profits; the value of the goodwill of each company depends, to some extent, upon whether its profits have been uniform year after year, or have steadily increased or decreased, or have fluctuated from year to year. Moreover, one year's statement may not be a fair basis for goodwill valuation because the year may have been characterized by extraordinary conditions.

(2) Correctness of the profits.
Adjustments may have to be made in the statements prepared by the companies themselves because errors have been made, such as:
(*a*) Incorrect distributions between capital and revenue.
(*b*) Failure to make provision for depreciation, bad debts, and other expenses.
(*c*) Failure to provide adequate repairs.
(*d*) Anticipation of profits on consignments, and so forth.

(3) Uniformity of bases of computing profits.
(*a*) Methods of computing manufacturing costs may have differed in the several companies; if possible, the cost statements should be revised and put on a uniform basis.
(*b*) Depreciation may have been computed by different methods. For instance, one company may have used the straight-line method and another the diminishing-value method; each may eventually provide adequate depreciation, but the annual charges will not be on a uniform basis.
(*c*) Management salaries may have differed widely in amount, and may require adjustment to a common basis. If one of the business units going into the merger is a partnership, care should be exercised to see that partner's salaries which have been treated as a distribution of profits are restated as management expense on a basis comparable with similar expenses of the merging corporations.

(*d*) If a partnership is to be included in the consolidation, and if interest on capital has been treated as an expense in the profit and loss statements, the interest should be added back to the profits.

(4) Adjustments from a historical basis to a prospective basis. The actual operating profits of the past may differ from those which can be expected in the future under consolidated conditions. For example:

(*a*) Depreciation charges in the past have presumably been based on cost; in the future they will be based on the appraised values at which the assets are acquired by the consolidated company. If the depreciation charges are thereby increased, the profits will be correspondingly decreased; it would seem, therefore, that the prospective depreciation charges should be applied retroactively to the statements for prior years.

(*b*) It is often stated that interest on borrowed capital should not be included as an expense, in determining the profits which are to be taken as a basis for goodwill valuation. If this theory is accepted, the statements should show the net income before deduction of interest. However, the author questions this theory, for reasons fully discussed in Chapter 19 of *Intermediate Accounting*.

Payments for acquired companies. After an agreement has been reached by all companies concerning the net asset values and the earnings of each company to be used as a basis for consolidation, the manner of payment remains for consideration. Payment may be made, in whole or in part, in:

Common stock.
Preferred stock.
Bonds.
Cash.
Short-term obligations.

Some matters to be borne in mind before a decision is made regarding the mode of payment are discussed and illustrated on the following pages.

Basis of illustration. For purposes of illustration let us assume the facts with respect to three companies as shown on the following page.

	Company *A*	Company *B*	Company *C*	Total
Net assets:				
Assets:				
Fixed	$150,000	$150,000	$100,000	$ 400,000
Other	150,000	275,000	575,000	1,000,000
Total assets	$300,000	$425,000	$675,000	$1,400,000
Liabilities	100,000	125,000	175,000	400,000
Net assets	$200,000	$300,000	$500,000	$1,000,000
Per cent of each company's net assets to total net assets	20%	30%	50%	100%
Annual net earnings:				
Amount of net earnings	$ 30,000	$ 30,000	$ 40,000	$ 100,000
Per cent of each company's net earnings to total net earnings	30%	30%	40%	100%
Per cent of each company's net earnings to its net assets	15	10	8	

Interest in net assets and net earnings. To effect an equitable consolidation of the three companies, consideration should be given to the portion of the total net assets and the portion of the total net earnings contributed by each company. These portions are:

	Company *A*	Company *B*	Company *C*
Per cent of total net assets	20%	30%	50%
Per cent of total net earnings	30	30	40

But how can the stockholders of Company *A*, for instance, obtain a 20% interest in the net assets of the consolidation and a 30% interest in its earnings? And how can the stockholders of Company *C* obtain a 50% interest in the consolidated net assets but only a 40% interest in its net earnings?

Such a theoretically desirable distribution of equities in the consolidated company may be impracticable or impossible, but it should always be remembered that consolidating companies are contributing net assets and net earnings, and that the ratio of each company's net assets to the total net assets, and the ratio of each company's net earnings to the total net earnings, should be given full consideration in determining the payments, in securities or otherwise, to be made to each company or its stockholders.

Illustrations. The following cases illustrate some of the principles involved in the distribution of securities incident to a consolidation. The securities may be issued to the consolidating companies, or directly to their stockholders; in the discussion of the cases, we may therefore refer to the stockholders, or to the companies as representative of their stockholders. In testing the equity of the stock distributions from the standpoint of interests in net earnings, we shall assume that all of the annual earnings of the consolidation are distributed in dividends.

Payment in common stock only. If payment to the consolidating companies is made in common stock only, proper recognition cannot be given to the fact that a company does not contribute the same per cent of net assets and of net earnings. This point is demonstrated by the first three cases.

Case 1: Common stock issued in the ratio of net assets. If common stock of a par or stated value of $1,000,000.00 is issued to the three companies (see foregoing statement of assumed facts) in amounts proportionate to their net assets, each old company will receive an equitable interest in the net assets of the consolidation. But the interests in future earnings will not be proportionate to the past earnings of the three companies, as shown by a comparison of the future and past distributions of earnings of $100,000.00:

	Company *A*	Company *B*	Company *C*	Total
Per cent of stock held	20%	30%	50%	100%
Distribution of consolidated earnings	$20,000	$30,000	$50,000	$100,000
Distribution of past earnings	30,000	30,000	40,000	100,000
Disadvantage to Company *A*	$10,000			
Advantage to Company *C*			$10,000	

Case 2: Common stock equal to net assets, issued in ratio of former earnings. If we now assume that common stock of a par or stated value of $1,000,000.00, the amount of the net assets, is issued to the old companies in amounts proportionate to their net earnings (instead of in proportion to their net assets, as in Case 1), the old companies will obtain equitable interests in the future eanings of the consolidation. But their interests in the consolidated net assets will not be equal to the net assets contributed by them, as shown below:

	Company *A*	Company *B*	Company *C*	Total
Stock acquired, and interest in consolidated net assets	$300,000	$300,000	$400,000	$1,000,000
Net assets contributed	200,000	300,000	500,000	1,000,000
Advantage to Company *A*	$100,000			
Disadvantage to Company *C*			$100,000	

Case 3: Common stock issued to each company for its net assets and goodwill. The inequities resulting from using common stock only cannot be eliminated by basing the common stock issue upon the amount of the net assets plus an allowance for goodwill based on earnings. To illustrate, let us assume that the

goodwill of each company is determined by capitalizing its net earnings at, say, 8%, and by deducting the net assets from the capitalized value thus obtained, as follows:

	Earnings	Divide by	Capitalized Value of Earnings	Deduct Net Assets	Goodwill
Company *A*....	$30,000	.08	$ 375,000	$ 200,000	$175,000
Company *B*....	30,000	.08	375,000	300,000	75,000
Company *C*....	40,000	.08	500,000	500,000	—
			$1,250,000	$1,000,000	$250,000

And let us further assume that common stock is issued for the total of the net assets and goodwill of each company, or, in other words, in amounts equal to the capitalized value of the earnings. Since these amounts are proportionate to the net earnings, an equitable distribution of stock from the earnings standpoint will be obtained. But an equitable distribution of stock from the net assets standpoint is not obtained, as may be proved by the following table showing the distribution of assets in liquidation, on the assumption that the net assets at that time total $1,000,000.00, or the amount of the net assets contributed.

	Company *A*	Company *B*	Company *C*	Total
Stock owned......................	$375,000	$375,000	$500,000	$1,250,000
Per cent of stock owned...........	30%	30%	40%	100%
Distribution of assets, in ratio of stock owned..........	$300,000	$300,000	$400,000	$1,000,000
Net assets contributed............	200,000	300,000	500,000	1,000,000
Advantage to Company *A*..........	$100,000			
Disadvantage to Company *C*........			$100,000	

Preferred and common stocks. Since common stock cannot be issued in both the net asset ratio and the net earnings ratio, it may be desirable to issue preferred and common stocks in amounts determined as follows:

(1) The total preferred and common shares should be allotted to the companies in the ratio of their net earnings.

(2) The preferred stock should be preferred as to assets as well as to dividends; it should be fully participating with the common; and it should be allotted to the several companies in the ratio of their contributed net assets.

(3) The number of shares of common stock to be allotted to each company should be determined by subtracting the number or par value of preferred shares to be allotted to it (as determined in 2) from the total number or par value of shares to be allotted to it (as determined in 1).

Case 4: PREFERRED STOCK FOR NET ASSETS; COMMON STOCK FOR GOODWILL. One illustration of the above-described procedure is shown by the following allotment of 5% preferred stock and common stock, both with a par value of \$100.00 per share. The total par value of the stock to be issued is determined by capitalizing the earnings at the 5% rate applicable to the preferred stock.

	Company *A*	Company *B*	Company *C*	Total
Net earnings	\$ 30,000	\$ 30,000	\$ 40,000	\$ 100,000
Total par value of preferred and common stocks to be issued, computed by capitalizing the earnings at 5%	\$600,000	\$600,000	\$800,000	\$2,000,000
Deduct preferred stock—to be issued for net assets	200,000	300,000	500,000	1,000,000
Common stock—to be issued for goodwill	\$400,000	\$300,000	\$300,000	\$1,000,000

Since the preferred stock is preferred as to assets, and is issued in amounts proportionate to the net assets contributed, the stockholders of the three companies are given equitable interests in the net assets. Liquidation of the consolidated company at a time when its net assets equaled \$1,000,000.00, the amount contributed, would result in returning to the stockholders of the three companies assets equal to the net assets contributed by them.

Let us now see whether the stock allotment also results in an equitable distribution of earnings, remembering that the earnings were contributed in the following amounts:

	Amount	Per Cent of Total
Company *A*	\$ 30,000.00	30%
Company *B*	30,000.00	30
Company *C*	40,000.00	40
Total	\$100,000.00	100%

First, we shall assume that the earnings after consolidation were exactly equal to those before consolidation. The distribution of earnings would be:

	Company *A*	Company *B*	Company *C*	Total
Preferred dividends:				
5% of \$200,000	\$10,000			
5% of 300,000		\$15,000		
5% of 500,000			\$25,000	
Total preferred dividends				\$ 50,000
Common dividends:				
5% of \$400,000	20,000			
5% of 300,000		15,000		
5% of 300,000			15,000	
Total common dividends				50,000
Total, equal in each case to the earnings of the predecessor company	\$30,000	\$30,000	\$40,000	\$100,000

Second, let us assume that the earnings after consolidation were 50% greater than those before consolidation. Since the preferred stock would participate fully with the common, the earnings would provide for a 7½% dividend on each class of stock.

	Company *A*	Company *B*	Company *C*	Total
Preferred dividends:				
7½% of $200,000	$15,000			
7½% of 300,000		$22,500		
7½% of 500,000			$37,500	
Total preferred dividends				$ 75,000
Common dividends:				
7½% of $400,000	30,000			
7½% of 300,000		22,500		
7½% of 300,000			22,500	
Total common dividends				75,000
Total, equal in each case to 150% of the earnings of the predecessor company	$45,000	$45,000	$60,000	$150,000

It thus appears that an equitable distribution of earnings will be obtained if the earnings after consolidation are equal to, or in excess of, those of the predecessor companies. If the earnings after consolidation are less than those before consolidation, a lack of equity may develop in the distribution of profits, because the preferred dividends, constituting a first claim against the earnings, are distributed in the net asset ratio instead of in the earnings ratio.

To illustrate, assume that the earnings after consolidation were only $80,000.00. This amount would provide for a 5% dividend on the preferred stock, but only a 3% dividend on the common stock. The distribution of earnings would be:

	Company *A*	Company *B*	Company *C*	Total
Preferred dividends:				
5% of $200,000	$10,000			
5% of 300,000		$15,000		
5% of 500,000			$25,000	
Total preferred dividends				$50,000
Common dividends:				
3% of $400,000	12,000			
3% of 300,000		9,000		
3% of 300,000			9,000	
Total common dividends				30,000
Total	$22,000	$24,000	$34,000	$80,000
Share of earnings after consolidation	27.5%	30%	42.5%	100%
Share of earnings before consolidation	30.0	30	40.0	100
Disadvantage to Company *A*	2.5%			
Advantage to Company *C*			2.5%	

This inequitable distribution of earnings could be avoided by making the preferred stock preferred as to assets only, with no preference as to dividends, but with the right to full participation with the common in all dividends. If the preferred stock were of this nature, the distribution of $80,000.00 of earnings would be:

	Company *A*	Company *B*	Company *C*	Total
Preferred dividends at 4%	$ 8,000	$12,000	$20,000	$40,000
Common dividends at 4%	16,000	12,000	12,000	40,000
Total	$24,000	$24,000	$32,000	$80,000
Share of earnings after consolidation	30%	30%	40%	100%
Share of earnings before consolidation	30	30	40	100

It may be contended, however, that the issuance of such preferred stock would not be equitable, because adequate recognition is not given to assets contributed unless the preferred stock issued therefor assures its holders dividends at a reasonable rate, even though the consolidated earnings are not sufficient to pay a comparable dividend on the common stock issued for goodwill. And, from the standpoint of practical considerations, it would probably be undesirable to eliminate the feature of preference as to dividends, because of the adverse effect upon the marketability of the stock.

Preferred stock should be fully participating. If the preferred stock is non-participating, an inequitable distribution of earnings may result.

Case 5: NON-PARTICIPATING PREFERRED STOCK. Assuming the same distribution of preferred and common stocks as in Case 4, except that the preferred stock is non-participating, and assuming that the profits after consolidation are 150% of those before consolidation, we will find the distribution of earnings to be as follows:

	Company *A*	Company *B*	Company *C*	Total
Preferred dividends:				
5% of $200,000	$10,000			
5% of 300,000		$15,000		
5% of 500,000			$25,000	
Total preferred dividends				$ 50,000
Common dividends:				
10% of $400,000	40,000			
10% of 300,000		30,000		
10% of 300,000			30,000	
Total common dividends				100,000
Total	$50,000	$45,000	$55,000	$150,000
Share of earnings after consolidation	33⅓%	30%	36⅔%	100%
Share of earnings before consolidation	30	30	40	100
Advantage to Company *A*	3⅓%			
Disadvantage to Company *C*			3⅓%	

Use of stock without par value. The use of par value common stock in Case 4 resulted in placing a very large value on the goodwill. The balance sheet in Case 4, immediately after the consolidation was effected, would appear as follows:

Balance Sheet

Net assets	$1,000,000.00	Preferred stock	$1,000,000.00
Goodwill	1,000,000.00	Common stock	1,000,000.00
	$2,000,000.00		$2,000,000.00

Such a disproportionate goodwill valuation may be avoided by using common stock without par value.

Case 6: COMMON STOCK WITHOUT PAR VALUE. Instead of 10,000 shares of par value common stock being issued, as in Case 4, the same number of shares might be issued without par value, but with a small stated value, such as $1.00 or $5.00 per share. But, to insure an equitable distribution of earnings, the no-par common stock should have the same dividend rights per share as those of the par value stock issued in Case 4.

Determining total preferred and common shares. Any method may be used for determining the total preferred and common shares to be issued, provided that:

(1) The aggregate dividend rights of the total shares allotted to the several companies are proportionate to the earnings contributed.
(2) The par or liquidating value of the preferred stock issued to each company is equal to the net assets contributed.

In Case 4, the total stock to be issued was determined by capitalizing the earnings of each company at 5%, the preference rate of the preferred stock. Other rates may, of course, be used for the preferred stock, and for capitalizing the net income, but:

The rate used in capitalizing the earnings should be not less than the preferred dividend rate, nor more than the lowest rate earned by any company on its net assets.

Case 7: PREFERRED RATE, 6%; EARNINGS CAPITALIZED AT 8%. This case conforms to the rule just stated; the capitalization rate, 8%, is not less than the 6% preferred dividend rate, nor more than the lowest rate earned by any company. (Company *C* earned 8%.) It will be assumed that the stock is given a par value of $100.00 per share; previous cases have shown that no-par stock might be used. The stock distribution is shown on page 407.

	Company A	Company B	Company C	Total
Net earnings	$ 30,000	$ 30,000	$ 40,000	$ 100,000
Total par of preferred and common stocks to be issued, computed by capitalizing net earnings at 8%	$375,000	$375,000	$500,000	$1,250,000
Preferred stock—for net assets	200,000	300,000	500,000	1,000,000
Common stock—for goodwill	$175,000	$ 75,000	—	$ 250,000

Equitable interests in the net assets are given to the three companies, because the preferred stock issued to them is equal to the net assets contributed. Let us now test the equity of the stock allotment from the earnings standpoint.

First, assume that the earnings after consolidation are the same as before, $100,000.00. The preferred and common stocks will total 12,500 shares; since the preferred participates fully with the common, the earnings will provide for dividends of $8.00 per share on the two classes of stock.

	Company A	Company B	Company C	Total
Preferred dividends:				
8% of $200,000	$16,000			
8% of 300,000		$24,000		
8% of 500,000			$40,000	
Total preferred dividends				$ 80,000
Common dividends:				
8% of $175,000	14,000			
8% of 75,000		6,000		
Total common dividends				20,000
Total—equal in each case to earnings before consolidation	$30,000	$30,000	$40,000	$100,000

Second, assume that the earnings after consolidation are $150,-000.00. The distribution thereof will be:

	Company A	Company B	Company C	Total
Preferred dividends:				
12% of $200,000	$24,000			
12% of 300,000		$36,000		
12% of 500,000			$60,000	
Total preferred dividends				$120,000
Common dividends:				
12% of $175,000	21,000			
12% of 75,000		9,000		
Total common dividends				30,000
Total	$45,000	$45,000	$60,000	$150,000
Share of earnings after consolidation	30%	30%	40%	100%
Share of earnings before consolidation	30	30	40	100

Case 8: PREFERRED RATE, 6%; EARNINGS CAPITALIZED AT 5%. This case does not conform to the stated rule; the capitalization

rate is less than the preferred dividend rate. The distribution of stock will be as follows:

	Company *A*	Company *B*	Company *C*	Total
Net earnings	$ 30,000	$ 30,000	$ 40,000	$ 100,000
Total par of preferred and common stocks to be issued, computed by capitalizing net earnings at 5%	$600,000	$600,000	$800,000	$2,000,000
Preferred stock—for net assets	200,000	300,000	500,000	1,000,000
Common stock—for goodwill	$400,000	$300,000	$300,000	$1,000,000

Since the preferred stock is issued on the basis of net assets, equitable interests in the net assets are maintained. To test the equity of the distribution of earnings, assume that the consolidated profits are $100,000.00, as they were before the consolidation. These would be sufficient to pay an average dividend of 5% on the total stock. But the preferred rate is 6%, and hence only 4% can be paid on the common stock.

	Company *A*	Company *B*	Company *C*	Total
Preferred dividends:				
6% of $200,000	$12,000			
6% of 300,000		$18,000		
6% of 500,000			$30,000	
Total preferred dividends				$ 60,000
Common dividends:				
4% of $400,000	16,000			
4% of 300,000		12,000		
4% of 300,000			12,000	
Total common dividends				40,000
Totals—shares of consolidated income	$28,000	$30,000	$42,000	$100,000
Net earnings contributed	30,000	30,000	40,000	100,000
Disadvantage to Company *A*	$ 2,000			
Advantage to Company *C*			$ 2,000	

To obtain an equitable distribution of earnings, the profits must be adequate to provide for a dividend at a uniform rate on both classes of stock; since the preferred bears 6%, the required profits are 6% of $2,000,000.00, or $120,000.00. If profits of that amount are made, the distribution will be:

	Company *A*	Company *B*	Company *C*	Total
Dividends on both classes of stocks at 6%:				
6% of $600,000	$36,000			
6% of 600,000		$36,000		
6% of 800,000			$48,000	
Total				$120,000
Share of earnings after consolidation	30%	30%	40%	100%
Share of earnings before consolidation	30	30	40	100

Case 9: PREFERRED RATE, 6%; EARNINGS CAPITALIZED AT 10%. This case also fails to conform to the stated rule, because the capitalization rate, 10%, is greater than the 8% rate earned by Company *C* on its net assets. The distribution of stock will be as follows:

	Company *A*	Company *B*	Company *C*	Total
Net earnings	$ 30,000	$ 30,000	$ 40,000	$ 100,000
Total par of preferred and common stocks to be issued, computed by capitalizing earnings at 10%	$300,000	$300,000	$400,000	$1,000,000
Preferred stock—for net assets	200,000	300,000	500,000	1,000,000

The inequity of this procedure immediately becomes apparent. Company *C* is entitled to preferred stock of a par (or liquidating) value of $500,000.00 for its net assets; but since the earnings were capitalized at a rate greater than that earned by Company *C*, the total stock allotted to it was only $400,000.00.

Problem of a company with low earnings. A difficult problem arises if one company's rate of earnings has been considerably less than a reasonable preferred dividend rate. Assume, for example, the following facts with respect to Company *D*:

Net assets	$300,000.00
Net earnings	6,000,00
Rate of net earnings on net assets	2%

If the consolidated company issues 6% preferred stock for the net assets, the allotment to this company of $300,000.00 of preferred stock for its net assets will entitle it to dividends of $18,000.00, although it contributed only $6,000.00 of earnings to the consolidation. If the company is given only $100,000.00 of preferred stock, an amount sufficient to entitle it to dividends of $6,000.00, it will not receive adequate consideration for the net assets contributed.

This condition might be met by the issuance of a special class of preferred stock with a low dividend rate, but such a solution would usually be impracticable. Some compromise probably would be necessary, such as the issuance of preferred stock of a smaller amount than that indicated by the net assets, but of a larger amount than that indicated by the earnings. For instance, in the above case, the company might receive 6% preferred stock of a par value of $200,000.00, carrying a dividend right of $12,000.00. As a compensation for its sacrifice from the net asset standpoint, the company would obtain an advantage from the earnings standpoint.

The use of bonds. Stockholders considering the consolidation of their company with other companies sometimes desire to be paid partly in bonds secured by the fixed assets. The bonds rank ahead of general, unsecured creditors; they entitle their holders to interest regardless of profits; and they may be sold to obtain funds without parting with stock interests. While these may be advantages, the use of bonds involves a difficulty in maintaining an equitable distribution of earnings if the consolidated earnings differ from those of the predecessor companies.

We have seen that an equitable distribution of earnings requires that the preferred stock be fully participating with the common. Unless the bonds are similarly participating (a most unusual feature of bonds), a stockholder who accepts a 6% bond instead of a share of 6% participating preferred stock, is giving up a right to participate in excess profits. If the bonds bear a lower rate than the preferred stock, a further loss of income is suffered.

Case 10: BONDS, PREFERRED STOCK, AND COMMON STOCK. Let us assume that Companies *A*, *B*, and *C* consolidate by issuance of:

5% bonds, of a par value equal to 80% of the fixed assets.
6% preferred stock for the remainder of the net assets.
Common stock for goodwill, based on the profits contributed in excess of bond interest and preferred dividends to be received.

The allotment of securities may be determined as follows:

	Company *A*	Company *B*	Company *C*	Total
Fixed assets	$150,000	$150,000	$100,000	$ 400,000
Net assets	200,000	300,000	500,000	1,000,000
Earnings	30,000	30,000	40,000	100,000
Bonds—80% of fixed assets	$120,000	$120,000	$ 80,000	$ 320,000
Preferred stock—remainder of net assets	80,000	180,000	420,000	680,000
Common stock	320,000	220,000	180,000	720,000

The computation of the allotment of common stock is shown below:

	Company *A*	Company *B*	Company *C*	Total
Net earnings	$ 30,000	$ 30,000	$ 40,000	$ 100,000
Deduct: Bond interest—5%	$ 6,000	$ 6,000	$ 4,000	$ 16,000
Preferred dividend—6%	4,800	10,800	25,200	40,800
Total	$ 10,800	$ 16,800	$ 29,200	$ 56,800
Remainder of earnings contributed—distribution thereof to be provided by issuance of common stock	$ 19,200	$ 13,200	$ 10,800	$ 43,200
Par value of common stock, computed by capitalizing remaining earnings at 6%	$320,000	$220,000	$180,000	$ 720,000

A 6% capitalization rate is used in determining the par value of the common stock to be issued, because this is the preference rate for the preferred stock.

If the earnings after consolidation are the same as those prior to consolidation, the earnings distributed to the former stockholders of the three companies will be the same as the former earnings of the three companies, as shown below:

	Company A	Company B	Company C	Total
Bond interest:				
5% of $120,000	$ 6,000			
5% of 120,000		$ 6,000		
5% of 80,000			$ 4,000	
Total bond interest				$ 16,000
Preferred dividends:				
6% of $ 80,000	4,800			
6% of 180,000		10,800		
6% of 420,000			25,200	
Total preferred dividends				40,800
Common dividends:				
6% of $320,000	19,200			
6% of 220,000		13,200		
6% of 180,000			10,800	
Total common dividends				43,200
Totals—same as before consolidation	$30,000	$30,000	$40,000	$100,000

But let us now assume that the profits after consolidation increase to $296,000.00, and note the effect of the bonds (which bear 5% interest, without further participation in profits) upon the distribution of the earnings.

	Company A	Company B	Company C	Total
Bond interest:				
5% of $120,000	$ 6,000			
5% of 120,000		$ 6,000		
5% of 80,000			$ 4,000	
Total bond interest				$ 16,000
Preferred dividends:				
20% of $ 80,000	16,000			
20% of 180,000		36,000		
20% of 420,000			84,000	
Total preferred dividends				136,000
Common dividends:				
20% of $320,000	64,000			
20% of 220,000		44,000		
20% of 180,000			36,000	
Total common dividends				144,000
Total	$86,000	$86,000	$124,000	$296,000
Share of earnings after consolidation	29%	29%	42%	100%
Share of earnings before consolidation	30	30	40	100

The bond interest totals $16,000.00, leaving $280,000.00 for dividends on the preferred and common stocks. Since these two classes of stock have an aggregate par value of $1,400,000.00, and since the preferred is fully participating, each class of stock has earned 20%.

Cash and short-term obligations. In all of the preceding cases it was assumed that the stockholders of the old companies became stockholders of the consolidated company; the problem of settlement therefore involved a distribution of securities in such a manner as to give the stockholders equitable interests in the assets and the earnings. If the old stockholders are bought out, and are paid immediately in cash, or partly in cash and partly in short-term obligations, their subsequent sharing of profits will be eliminated, and the settlement will be based on acceptable offers from the purchasers. However, the amounts to be paid should still be governed by the amounts of net assets and net earnings.

If the stockholders of the old companies wish to retain stock control of the consolidated company, but to obtain certain amounts of cash immediately or in the near future through the payment of short-term obligations issued by the consolidated company, or if certain assets are not to be transferred to the consolidated company, proper consideration should be given to the effect of such cash withdrawals or asset withholdings upon the net assets for which preferred stock is to be issued, and the effect upon the earnings taken as a basis for the allotment of common stock.

Modifications. The procedures discussed and illustrated in the preceding pages are merely indicative of the principles to be borne in mind in effecting consolidations; they cannot be accepted as procedures to be invariably followed.

The general desirability of issuing both preferred and common stocks to the stockholders of the predecessor companies has been emphasized; however, if new funds are required, the old stockholders may have to accept common stock only, in order that the preferred stock may be reserved for issuance to the suppliers of new capital.

The general desirability of making the preferred stock issued to the old stockholders fully participating has been discussed; but the poor profit record of certain companies may make this provision in the preferred stock impracticable.

In the cases illustrated, the stockholders of all companies shared ratably in all classes of securities issued; but the stockholders of one or more companies may desire to withdraw from the management, leaving the control to others, and taking cash, bonds, or preferred stock for their interests.

These and other matters almost invariably require modifications in the methods described, but the illustrations serve to indicate the basic principles involved in safeguarding the stockholders of several consolidating companies in their interests in the assets and earnings of the consolidation.

Balance sheets giving effect to financing. When securities are offered to the public in connection with a consolidation of several companies, or otherwise, accountants are usually asked to prepare a balance sheet of the issuing company giving effect to the financing. To illustrate, assume that investment bankers have agreed to purchase, as of March 1, 1946, a company's bonds of a par value of $100,000.00 at 95. To indicate the financial condition of the company after the financing, an accountant may be asked to apply the financing to his most recent audited balance sheet of the company, possibly that of December 31, 1945. Assuming that $75,000.00 of the proceeds of the financing is to be used in liquidating notes payable, the accountant's working papers may be similar to those shown below.

COMPANY *A*
Working Papers for Balance Sheet Giving Effect to Financing
As of December 31, 1945

	Before Financing	Financing Adjustments Debit	Financing Adjustments Credit	After Financing
Assets				
Current assets:				
Cash	$ 4,000	$ 95,000(a)	$ 75,000(b)	$ 24,000
Accounts receivable	75,000			75,000
Inventory	125,000			125,000
Fixed assets:				
Land and buildings	150,000			150,000
Machinery and equipment	90,000			90,000
Prepaid expenses:				
Unexpired insurance	2,000			2,000
Bond discount		5,000(a)		5,000
	$446,000			$471,000
Liabilities and Net Worth				
Current liabilities:				
Accounts payable	$ 50,000			$ 50,000
Notes payable	$ 75,000	75,000(b)		
Fixed liabilities:				
6% bonds payable			100,000(a)	100,000
Net worth:				
Capital stock	250,000			250,000
Surplus	71,000			71,000
	$446,000	$175,000	$175,000	$471,000

The balance sheet giving effect to the financing (sometimes called a "pro forma balance sheet") will embody the figures in the last column of the working papers.

Propriety of "giving effect" statements. A "giving effect" balance sheet portrays a financial condition which never, in fact, exists, because the balance sheet at a stated date is adjusted to give effect to certain transactions which may have occurred at a subsequent date (such as a consummated issuance of securities), or to transactions which are only in prospect (such as the proposed purchase of securities by an investment banker in accordance with a contract, and the application of the proceeds as forecast by the management of the issuing company). Is an accountant justified in issuing and certifying to such a balance sheet?

It is usually regarded as permissible for him to do so if: (1) the period between the date of the balance sheet and the date of the financing transaction is not too great—possibly not in excess of three or four months; (2) no other transactions have, in the meantime, materially affected the company's financial condition; and (3) the financing transaction is definitely determinable and based on a contract between the issuing company and the security underwriters or investment bankers.

The heading of the "giving effect" balance sheet, and the appended certificate, should indicate the nature of the transactions to which effect has been given. For instance, the heading of the balance sheet might read somewhat as follows:

THE *X Y* COMPANY

Balance Sheet—December 31, 1945

Giving effect as of that date to the proposed issuance of $1,000,000.00 of first mortgage bonds, and the application of the proceeds to the retirement of preferred stock and to an increase in working capital.

And the accompanying opinion might read somewhat as follows:

We have audited the accounts of The *X Y* Company as of December 31, 1945, and have examined a contract providing for the issuance of $1,000,000.00 of first mortgage bonds.

In our opinion, the foregoing balance sheet fairly reflects the financial condition of the company on December 31, 1945, after giving effect as of that date to the proposed issuance of the above-described bonds, and to the application of the proceeds thereof in retiring preferred stock and increasing the working capital.

CHAPTER 54

Foreign Exchange

Scope of discussion. Foreign exchange is of interest and importance to:

- Banks and brokers dealing in foreign exchange.
- Business concerns exporting and importing merchandise, holding foreign investments, operating foreign branches or subsidiaries, or engaged in other activities involving receipts from, or remittances to, other countries.

At the time of writing this chapter, foreign exchange is in a chaotic and uncertain condition. The gold standard has been abandoned. Although monetary systems may still be actually or theoretically based on coins containing gold of a legally established weight and fineness, nations have suspended their obligation to sell gold at the legal monetary par or to redeem their paper money in gold at par. After a pre-war period during which government embargoes or other restrictions or limitations were placed on gold shipments, we are now suffering the restrictions upon international trade and exchange settlements incident to the post-war period, and are facing the possibility that some wholly new machinery may be set up for handling international transfers of funds.

Under these conditions, little can be attempted in this book beyond a review of the traditional accounting procedures incident to foreign exchange, with a full realization of the extent to which they have been (perhaps only temporarily) modified and to which they may be (perhaps permanently) modified or even abandoned in a turbulent world.

Foreign money; par rates. Coinages are based on actual or theoretical monetary units containing gold (or silver) of a legally established weight and fineness. For example:

	Total Grains	Fraction Fine	Gold Grains
United States dollar:			
Prior to January 31, 1934	25.8	$\frac{9}{10}$	23.22
Established by Presidential proclamation of January 31, 1934	$15\frac{5}{21}$	$\frac{9}{10}$	13.7143
British pound sterling	123.274	$\frac{11}{12}$	113.0011

Mint par rates applicable to the coins of two countries, both of which are based on gold, are computed by determining the relative amounts of pure gold in the two coins. The par rate for the pound on the old basis was determined thus:

$$\frac{113.0011}{23.22} = 4.8665$$

The par rate on the new basis is determined as follows:

$$\frac{113.0011}{13.7143} = 8.2397$$

So long as there is no change in the metallic content of the coins of two countries which are both on a gold basis, the mint par rates applicable to their coins will not change. But when the gold content of either coin changes, the par rate changes.

If the coin of one country is based on gold, and the coin of another on silver, the mint par rate will fluctuate with changes in the price of silver in terms of gold.

Conversions at par. There are two types of conversion problems. Illustrations are given below, using par rates for conversion purposes.

(1) Converting a foreign value into a domestic value:

Problem: Convert £1,200 8s. 6d. to dollars.

Solution: Reduce shillings and pence to decimals of a pound, and multiply by the dollar value per pound.

Pounds	1,200.000
Shillings: 8s = 8/20 of a pound	.400
Pence: 6d = 1/2 of 1/20 of a pound	.025
Total	1,200.425
Multiply by	$8.2397
Dollar value	$ 9,891.14

(2) Converting a domestic value to a foreign value.

Problem: Convert $2,000.00 to pounds.

Solution: Divide the number of dollars by the dollar value per pound, and reduce fractions of a pound to shillings and pence.

$$\begin{aligned} 2{,}000 \div 8.2397 &= £242.727 \\ &= £242\ 14.54s \\ &= £242\ 14s\ 6d \end{aligned}$$

Cable transfers. A *cable transfer* is an order, transmitted by cable, usually upon a bank, to pay a certain sum of money to a designated payee. In a sense, therefore, a cable transfer is a draft.

Thus, if D in New York must remit £1,000 to E in London, D may purchase a draft drawn by a New York bank on its London correspondent and mail this draft to E; or D may purchase from his bank a cable transfer which will order the London bank to pay £1,000 to E. The effect of the two methods is identical except for the time required to make the payment and the somewhat higher price which will be charged by the bank for the cable transfer.

Bills of exchange. A *bill of exchange* is an unconditional order in writing, addressed by one person to another, to pay to a designated person or to his order, a sum certain in money on demand or at a fixed or determinable future time. Bills of exchange may be classified as:

Banker's bills, drawn by a bank or banker upon another bank or banker; such bills, as used in foreign exchange, are comparable to the bank drafts used in domestic exchange.

Commercial bills, drawn by a merchant on another merchant or a bank, or drawn by a bank on a merchant.

Bills of exchange may be classified according to the time when payment is ordered, as follows:

Sight bills, payable upon presentation.

Time bills, which may be further classified as:

Short bills, drawn for less than thirty days after sight.

Long bills, drawn for thirty or more days after sight.

Bills of exchange may also be classified with respect to any attached security, as follows:

Clean bills, drawn against deposits or previously arranged credits, and without any documents or collateral attached.

Secured or documentary bills, to which are attached documents serving as collateral to the bills.

For instance, if an American has sold stocks or bonds to a foreign purchaser, the securities sold may be attached to a bill drawn on the purchaser; the securities serve as collateral to the bill until it is paid or accepted by the foreign purchaser, when they are detached and delivered to him. If the bill is drawn for collection of a debt arising from a sale of merchandise, the attached documents will include a bill of lading, consular invoice, seller's invoice, insurance certificate, and so forth.

Secured or documentary bills may be further classified according to the requirements for the release of the documents, as shown on the following page.

Documentary acceptance bills: The documents accompanying such a bill are released to the drawee immediately upon his acceptance of the bill, which thereupon becomes a clean bill.

Documentary payment bills: The documents accompanying such a bill are not released to the drawee until the bill is paid.

Letters of credit. A letter of credit is an instrument addressed by the issuing bank to all or some of its foreign correspondents, introducing the holder, certifying that he is authorized to draw a stated aggregate sum of money, and requesting that his drafts be honored up to that amount. It is used by travelers for the payment of expenses and sometimes for the financing of purchases. To obtain funds, the holder of such a letter presents it and the accompanying letter of identification to a named correspondent bank, and draws a draft against the letter. The paying bank indorses the amount of the draft on the letter, to show how much of the credit has been utilized, and sends the draft to the issuing bank for credit. The issuing bank may receive its payment for the letter of credit either at the time of its issuance or after the payment of the drafts drawn against it.

Current rates. Current exchange rates for cable transfers, drafts, and so forth may be quoted directly or indirectly.

Direct quotations are stated in the domestic currency.

All quotations are now made on this basis in the United States. The rates state the value of the foreign unit in cents (or dollars); for example, the following rates are stated in cents:

For pounds: 510.875
For francs: 6.61

Paris quotes pounds and dollars directly; the rates state the value of the foreign unit in francs; thus, for example:

For pounds: 77.29
For dollars: 15.129

Indirect quotations are stated in the foreign currency.

London quotes francs and dollars indirectly; that is, in terms of francs and dollars per pound; thus, for example:

For francs: 77.29
For dollars: 5.10875

Current rates differ according to the nature of the exchange; that is, rates for cable transfers are higher than those for checks, and rates for checks are higher than those for time drafts. For simplicity of presentation, however, we shall give only minor consideration to these differences in the following discussion.

Fluctuations in current exchange rates. Current exchange rates vary from day to day as the result of changes in the supply of and demand for foreign bills. To understand why this is so, let us put ourselves in the position of a New York foreign exchange banker with a correspondent in London. We buy drafts and other forms of exchange payable in pounds, and send them to our correspondent for credit; against this credit we sell drafts or other forms of exchange payable in pounds. We are dealing in a commodity called *pounds.* The supply of the commodity is furnished by those who hold receivables collectible in pounds; the demand is created by those who owe debts which must be paid in pounds. If the supply is greater than the demand, the price will be low, or below par. If the demand is greater than the supply, the price will be high, or above par.

The demand for and the supply of foreign exchange between two countries are affected by the relative volumes of intercountry transactions. They are also affected by transactions involving debtors and creditors in other countries. For instance, an American exporter, shipping goods to China, may be paid by a draft on a London bank. Or a French banker with a larger dollar balance in New York than he desires, and with a smaller pound balance in London than he desires, may use his dollar balance to buy pounds in New York and direct that they be transferred to his London correspondent, to increase his pound balance in London.

Foreign purchases. An American importer, buying goods abroad, may be billed in dollars or in the foreign currency. If the American importer is billed in dollars, the foreign exporter will make the gain or bear the loss resulting from any fluctuation in exchange rates between the date of purchase and the date of settlement. For if an American importer purchases goods billed to him at $1,000.00, no fluctuation in exchange can cause him to remit more or less than $1,000.00 in settlement; any fluctuations in exchange rates will affect the amount of foreign money which the exporter will obtain for the $1,000.00 draft.

But if the importer is billed in terms of foreign currency, the fluctuations in exchange rates will affect the settlement. To illustrate, assume that a Chicago merchant purchases an invoice of goods billed to him at £1,000. The rate at the date of purchase is 5.12. The entry for the purchase will be:

Purchases	$5,120.00	
London manufacturer		$5,120.00

When the entry is posted to the London manufacturer's account, a notation will have to be made of the amount of the bill in pounds, or the account may be kept with pound and dollar columns on both sides.

If, at the date of settlement, the rate is 5.10, a draft for £1,000 will cost $5,100.00, and the entry to record the settlement will be:

London manufacturer	$5,120.00	
Cash		$5,100.00
Exchange (or Purchases)		20.00

On the other hand, if the rate at the date of settlement is 5.15, the entry to record the settlement will be:

London manufacturer	$5,120.00	
Exchange (or Purchases)	30.00	
Cash		$5,150.00

If the Chicago merchant desires to protect himself against speculative risks from exchange fluctuations, he may, at the time of purchasing the goods, buy future exchange on London, the delivery of the future to be made to him at the date when he will require it for the settlement of his invoice.

Foreign sales. An American, selling goods abroad, may bill in dollars or in foreign currency. If the American bills in dollars, the foreign purchaser will make the gain or bear the loss resulting from any exchange fluctuation. If the American bills in the foreign currency, he will make the gain or bear the loss. To illustrate, assume that a Chicago manufacturer sells a bill of goods to a London merchant for £1,000. The rate at the date of sale is 5.12, and the sale is recorded as follows:

London merchant	$5,120.00	
Sales		$5,120.00

A memorandum of the pound amount must be made in the London merchant's account on the Chicago manufacturer's books, or this account may be kept in both pounds and dollars.

If the rate is 5.15 when the Chicago manufacturer receives the London merchant's draft for £1,000, the Chicago merchant's bank will pay $5,150.00 for the draft, and the entry will be:

Cash	$5,150.00	
London merchant		$5,120.00
Exchange (or Sales)		30.00

If the rate at settlement time is 5.10, the entry will be:

Cash	$5,100.00	
Exchange (or Sales)	20.00	
London merchant		$5,120.00

If the Chicago merchant who sells goods and bills them in pounds, wishes to protect himself against exchange fluctuations, he may sell future exchange on London for £1,000 for delivery at the date when he expects to receive the draft for £1,000.

Foreign branches. The methods of accounting for foreign branches are similar to the methods described in the chapter on domestic branches; but the problem is complicated by the fact that the home office books are kept in terms of the domestic currency whereas the branch books are kept in terms of the foreign currency.

Illustration. The following transactions form the basis of the illustration:

(1) The home office, in Chicago, opens a London branch, sending it a draft for £1,000, which the home office purchases when the rate is 5.18.

(2) The home office sends the branch a draft for $2,600.00. When the branch receives this draft and deposits it, the rate is 5.20; the London bank therefore credits the branch with £500.

(3) The home office sends to the branch goods valued at $51,900.00, which is cost. The shipment is made when the exchange rate is 5.19, and the goods are therefore taken up on the branch books at £10,000.

(4) Purchases on account, made by the branch in England, £3,000.

(5) Payment made to creditors on account of above purchases, £2,500.

(6) Sales on account, £16,000.

(7) Collections on account, £15,000.

(8) Expenses paid, £2,000.

(9) The branch sends the home office a draft for £5,000, which the home office sells at 5.21, realizing $26,050.00.

(10) The branch sends the home office a draft for $31,140.00, which it purchased at 5.19, the cost being £6,000.

The branch inventory at the end of the year is valued at £2,000.

Entries during the period. Entries for transactions which are recorded only on the branch books present no new features and no difficulties. Reference to the following illustrative entries will show that transactions 4, 5, 6, 7, and 8, which appear on the branch books only, are recorded in the manner described in the chapter on domestic branches; the entries are recorded in the foreign currency only and the problem of conversion to domestic currency does not arise.

When cash is sent from the home office to the branch, the home office records the dollar cost of the remittance, and the branch records the pounds received. In transaction 1, the home office buys a £1,000 draft for 5.18. The cost is therefore $5,180.00, and the remittance is recorded on the home office books at this figure and is taken up on the branch books at £1,000. In transaction 2, the home office sends a draft for $2,600.00, and the branch records the receipt of the funds at the number of pounds received when the draft is deposited. Thus, in the first transaction, the rate at the date of purchase governs the conversion; whereas, in the second transaction, the rate at the date of deposit by the branch governs the conversion.

	Branch Books			Home Office Books		
(1)	Cash..........	£ 1,000		Remittances to branch	$ 5,180	
	Remittances from home office....		£ 1,000	Cash..........		$ 5,180
(2)	Cash..........	500		Remittances to branch	2,600	
	Remittances from home office.....		500	Cash..........		2,600
(3)	Merchandise from home office	10,000		Branch current.......	51,900	
	Home office current...		10,000	Shipments to branch.......		51,900
(4)	Purchases......	3,000				
	Accounts payable..		3,000			
(5)	Accounts payable	2,500				
	Cash......		2,500			
(6)	Accounts receivable.....	16,000				
	Sales......		16,000			
(7)	Cash..........	15,000				
	Accounts receivable..		15,000			
(8)	Expense.......	2,000				
	Cash.....		2,000			

	Branch Books			Home Office Books		
(9)	Remittances to home office	5,000		Cash...............	26,050	
	Cash.......		5,000	Remittances from branch........		26,050
(10)	Remittances to home office	6,000		Cash...............	31,140	
	Cash.......		6,000	Remittances from branch........		31,140

It should be noted that, in the illustrative entries, the home office debits remittances to branch, instead of debiting the branch current account; and the branch credits remittances from home office, instead of crediting the home office current account. These entries are made so that reciprocal accounts on the two books will show the value, in dollars and in pounds, of funds sent from the home office to the branch. These reciprocal accounts will be found useful when the branch trial balance is converted into domestic currency at the end of the period.

The goods sent by the home office to the branch (transaction 3) are credited by the home office to shipments to branch at cost, and are taken up on the branch books at the current exchange value at the date of shipment or date of arrival depending on the accounting policy adopted by the company.

Cash remittances from the branch to the home office are illustrated by the last two transactions. In 9, the branch buys a £5,000 draft, and the dollar value is determined when the home office sells it. In 10, the branch buys a draft for $31,140.00, paying for it at the rate of 5.19, the pound and dollar values both being known at the date of purchase. It should be noted that the branch charges remittances to home office instead of the home office current account, and the home office credits remittances from branch instead of branch current, for the purpose of providing reciprocal accounts showing the dollar and pound values of the remittances.

Branch closing and statements. At the close of the accounting period, the branch draws off the following trial balance:

Cash..	£ 1,000	
Accounts receivable........................	1,000	
Remittances to home office.................	11,000	
Accounts payable...........................		£ 500
Remittances from home office...............		1,500
Home office current........................		10,000
Sales......................................		16,000
Merchandise from home office...............	10,000	
Purchases..................................	3,000	
Expense....................................	2,000	
	£28,000	£28,000

Inventory—£2,000.

The branch then closes its books and prepares statements, as follows:

Profit and loss	£15,000	
Merchandise from home office		£10,000
Purchases		3,000
Expense		2,000
Inventory	2,000	
Sales	16,000	
Profit and loss		18,000
Profit and loss	3,000	
Home office current		3,000
Home office current	11,000	
Remittances to home office		11,000
Remittances from home office	1,500	
Home office current		1,500

Branch Profit and Loss Statement
For the Year Ended December 31, 194-

Sales		£16,000
Less cost of goods sold:		
Merchandise from home office	£10,000	
Purchases	3,000	
Total	£13,000	
Less inventory—December 31	2,000	11,000
Gross profit on sales		£ 5,000
Less expense		2,000
Net profit		£ 3,000

Statement of Home Office Current Account
(On Branch Books)

Remittances to home office	£11,000	Merchandise from home office	£10,000
Balance, December 31	3,500	Remittances from home office	1,500
		Net profit	3,000
	£14,500		£14,500

Branch Balance Sheet
December 31, 194-

Assets		Liabilities	
Cash	£ 1,000	Accounts payable	£ 500
Accounts receivable	1,000	Home office current	3,500
Inventory	2,000		
	£ 4,000		£ 4,000

Conversion of branch trial balance. The branch sends the home office copies of its trial balance, inventory, closing entries, profit and loss statement, statement of the home office current account, and balance sheet. As the trial balance and inventory furnish the basis for all of the other statements, the home office proceeds to convert the trial balance and inventory from pounds to dollars, so that:

(1) The net profit can be taken up on the home office books.
(2) The home office and branch profit and loss statements can be combined.
(3) The home office and branch balance sheets can be combined.

Under the old and long established foreign exchange accounting procedures, the following rules came to be accepted as standard practice for making conversions from foreign to domestic currency:

Current assets (including the final inventory) and current liabilities: at the rate which is current at the end of the period. This rate is used because it furnishes the best evidence of the present value of the assets (which presumably will shortly be converted into cash that may be remitted to the home office) and the present liability on current debts.

Fixed assets: at the rate which was current at the time when the assets were purchased. The reason for using this rate is fully discussed in a later section of this chapter.

Inventory at the beginning of the period: at the rate which was current at that date. This rate is used because, at the beginning of the period, the inventory was a current asset and was converted at the then current rate; as this inventory was the closing inventory in one statement and will be the opening inventory in the next statement, it should appear in the two statements at the same dollar value, and such a value can be obtained only by converting the inventory at the same rate for both statements.

Nominal accounts: at an average rate for the period. This average rate may be determined in several ways: by averaging the daily rates for the year; by averaging twelve monthly rates; by using a weighted average which gives more importance to the rates prevailing during busy seasons than to the rates prevailing during slack seasons; or by dividing the balance of the branch account, remittances to home office (pounds), into the balance of the home office account, remittances from branch (dollars), thus determining the average rate at which profits were transferred to the home office in the form of cash.

Accrued expense and income, and deferred charges and expenses. These items have two aspects: On the one hand, they affect the nominal items that appear in the profit and loss statement; and on the other hand, they enter into the balance sheet. As nominal items they should be converted at an average rate, while as assets and liabilities they should be converted at the current rate. But it is impossible to convert them at both rates. As the items are generally so small in amount that they are relatively insignificant, it is usually satisfactory to convert them at the current rate for both purposes. Or an adjusted trial balance in the foreign currency may be prepared, in which the expense and income accounts will have been charged and credited with the adjusting items; the nominal accounts, as adjusted, can then be converted at an average rate; and the accrued and deferred items, which will appear in the balance sheet, can be converted at the current rate.

Reserves. The rate at which a reserve should be converted will depend on the nature of the reserve. If it represents a current liability, it should be converted at the current rate. If it is a valuation reserve set up against a current asset, as the reserve for bad debts, it should be converted at the current rate, since the asset is converted at that rate. The reserves for depreciation should be converted at the same rates as the fixed asset accounts. But since a fixed asset account may contain charges for purchases made at various dates (so that the balance will have to be divided into several portions, and each converted at a different rate), it is better to compute the dollar, or converted, reserve on a percentage basis. Thus, if the reserve on the foreign books is 15% of the asset, the reserve may be converted into dollars by multiplying the dollar value of the asset by 15%, instead of using an exchange rate.

Reciprocal accounts: at the dollar balances of the accounts on the home office books, without using any rate; thus:

Remittances from home office, at the dollar balance of the home office account, remittances to branch.

Remittances to home office, at the dollar balance of the home office account, remittances from branch.

Merchandise from home office, at the dollar balance of the home office account, shipments to branch.

Home office current account, at the dollar balance of the branch current account on the home office books.

The branch trial balance, stated in pounds, will balance when sent by the branch to the home office, but it will not balance after the home office has converted the amounts into dollars, because the items will have been converted at different rates. Therefore, an adjusting figure must be entered on the smaller side of the branch trial balance after conversion. This adjustment is supposed to measure the profit or the loss due to exchange fluctuations. If the figure must be entered on the debit side of the branch trial balance, it is a loss; if it must be entered on the credit side of the trial balance, it is a gain. The final disposition of this adjustment in the home office closing entries is discussed on page 430.

Branch Trial Balance
December 31, 194-

	Pounds		Rate	Dollars	
Cash	£ 1,000		C	$ 5,200	
Accounts receivable	1,000		C	5,200	
Remittances to home office	11,000		R	57,190	
Accounts payable		£ 500	C		$ 2,600
Remittances from home office		1,500	R		7,780
Home office current		10,000	R		51,900
Sales		16,000	A		83,040
Merchandise from home office	10,000		R	51,900	
Purchases	3,000		A	15,570	
Expense	2,000		A	10,380	
	£28,000	£28,000		$145,440	$145,320
Exchange adjustment					120
				$145,440	$145,440
Inventory—December 31	£ 2,000		C	$ 10,400	

Rate symbols:
- C = Current rate: 5.20.
- A = Average rate: 5.19.
- R = Balance of reciprocal account on home office books. See home office trial balance, page 428.

Branch profit and loss statement. From the figures in the converted trial balance, the following profit and loss statement may be prepared in dollars:

Branch Profit and Loss Statement
For the Year Ended December 31, 194-

Sales		$83,040.00
Less cost of goods sold:		
Merchandise from home office	$51,900.00	
Purchases	15,570.00	
Total	$67,470.00	
Less inventory, December 31	10,400.00	57,070.00
Gross profit on sales		$25,970.00
Less expense		10,380.00
Net profit		$15,590.00

Branch balance sheet. The converted trial balance and final inventory furnish the information for the branch balance sheet:

Branch Balance Sheet
December 31, 194-

Assets:		
Cash	$ 5,200.00	
Accounts receivable	5,200.00	
Merchandise inventory	10,400.00	$20,800.00
Liabilities:		
Accounts payable		2,600.00
Net assets		$18,200.00

Home office closing entries. The home office trial balance at the end of the year is shown below:

Cash	$ 27,410.00	
Accounts receivable	31,000.00	
Branch current	51,900.00	
Remittances to branch	7,780.00	
Accounts payable		$ 6,000.00
Remittances from branch		57,190.00
Capital stock		50,000.00
Sales		150,000.00
Shipments to branch		51,900.00
Purchases	175,000.00	
Expense	22,000.00	
	$315,090.00	$315,090.00

Inventory, December 31, $10,000.00.

The home office closing entries may be divided into three groups:

(*a*) Entries to determine the profit from home office operations.

(*b*) Entries to take up the branch profit and to close the temporary accounts with the branch.

(*c*) Entries to adjust the balance of the branch current account to bring it into agreement with the net assets at the branch.

These entries are illustrated below.

(*a*) *Entries to determine the profit from home office operations.*

Shipments to branch	$ 51,900.00	
Purchases		$ 51,900.00
To credit purchases with the cost of goods sent to branch.		
Profit and loss	145,100.00	
Purchases		123,100.00
Expense		22,000.00
Inventory, December 31	10,000.00	
Sales	150,000.00	
Profit and loss		160,000.00

The balance of the profit and loss account is now $14,900.00, the amount of the home office profit from operations.

(*b*) *Entries to take up the branch profit and to close the temporary accounts with the branch.*

Branch current	$15,590.00	
Branch profit and loss		$15,590.00
To take up the net profit of the branch, as shown by the branch profit and loss statement converted into dollars.		
Branch current	7,780.00	
Remittances to branch		7,780.00
To close the temporary remittances account.		
Remittances from branch	57,190.00	
Branch current		57,190.00
To close.		

Finally, the home office will close both the home office profits and the branch profits into surplus by the following entry:

Profit and loss	$14,900.00	
Branch profit and loss	15,590.00	
Surplus		$30,490.00

(*c*) *Entries to adjust the balance of the branch current account to bring it into agreement with the net assets at the branch.* After the foregoing entries affecting the branch current account have been made, this account on the home office books will appear as follows:

Branch Current

Shipments to branch	$51,900.00	Remittances from branch	$57,190.00
Branch profit	15,590.00		
Remittances to branch	7,780.00		

The balance of this account is now $18,080.00, but the branch balance sheet on page 428 shows that the net assets at the branch are valued at $18,200.00. In other words, the balance of the branch current account is $120.00 smaller than the value of the net assets at the branch. When the combined balance sheet of the home office and the branch is prepared, the balance of the branch current account on the home office books will be eliminated, and will be replaced by the assets and liabilities of the branch. This cannot be done unless the balance of the branch current account on the home office books is exactly equal to the net assets at the branch.

It therefore becomes necessary to debit the branch current account, $120.00. It will be noted that this $120.00 is the amount of the adjustment entered in the branch trial balance after conversion (see page 427), and attention has already been called to the fact that this adjustment represents the profit or loss on exchange. The question now arises concerning the proper offsetting entry. Two common methods are in use.

First, the exchange adjustments may be made through branch profit and loss. If the branch current account balance must be increased to make it agree with the branch net assets, the offsetting credit may be made to branch profit and loss before the balance of that account is transferred to surplus. If the current account balance must be decreased, the offsetting debit may be to branch profit and loss.

Second, the exchange adjustment may be made through a reserve for exchange, on the theory that the exchange fluctuation is an unrealized and an uncertain matter, and that any profits which seem to have been made by a favorable fluctuation during one year may be offset by losses from unfavorable fluctuations in a succeeding year. Therefore, it is more conservative to credit the exchange adjustment to a reserve, where it will be available to absorb exchange losses in the future. If no reserve exists, an exchange loss should be charged to profit and loss; and if the loss exceeds the reserve, the excess should be charged to profit and loss.

Adopting the second procedure as the more conservative, the closing of the home office books would be continued by the following entry:

Branch current	$120.00	
Reserve for exchange		$120.00

Combined statements. The following exhibits show the working papers from which the combined balance sheet is prepared, and the combined profit and loss statement.

THE *X Y Z* COMPANY
Combined Balance Sheet Working Papers
December 31, 194-

	Home Office	Branch	Eliminations	Combined Balance Sheet
Assets				
Cash	$27,410.00	$ 5,200.00		$32,610.00
Accounts receivable	31,000.00	5,200.00		36,200.00
Inventory	10,000.00	10,400.00		20,400.00
Branch current	18,200.00		$18,200.00	
	$86,610.00	$20,800.00	$18,200.00	$89,210.00
Liabilities and Net Worth				
Accounts payable	$ 6,000.00	$ 2,600.00		$ 8,600.00
Reserve for exchange	120.00			120.00
Capital stock	50,000.00			50,000.00
Surplus	30,490.00			30,490.00
Home office current		18,200.00	$18,200.00	
	$86,610.00	$20,800.00	$18,200.00	$89,210.00

THE *X Y Z* COMPANY
Home Office and Branch Profit and Loss Statement
For the Year Ended December 31, 194-

	Home Office		Branch		Combined	
Sales		$150,000.00		$83,040.00		$233,040.00
Less cost of goods sold:						
Purchases	$175,000.00		$15,570.00		$190,570.00	
Transfers from home office to branch	51,900.00		51,900.00			
Net and total	$123,100.00		$67,470.00			
Less inventory, December 31	10,000.00		10,400.00		20,400.00	
Cost of goods sold		113,100.00		57,070.00		170,170.00
Gross profit on sales		$ 36,900.00		$25,970.00		$ 62,870.00
Less expense		22,000.00		10,380.00		32,380.00
Net profit		$ 14,900.00		$15,590.00		$ 30,490.00

Branch fixed assets. There is a general accounting principle which requires that profits and surplus shall not be affected by valuing fixed assets at market prices. According to this principle, it is improper to convert branch fixed assets at current exchange rates, if such rates are higher or lower than the rates prevailing at the dates of acquisition of the fixed assets, because the assets would thus be virtually written up or down as the result of a market fluctuation.

Since branch fixed assets should always be converted at the rate which prevailed at the date of acquisition, it is necessary to provide some accounting method by which the dollar value of foreign currency expenditures for fixed assets can be easily ascertained. For, if expenditures for branch fixed assets are made frequently, many different rates will exist because of different acquisition dates, and each rate will apply to a portion of the fixed asset account.

If the fixed asset accounts are kept on the branch books, two money columns should appear on each side. Expenditures made by the branch should be charged to the account in pounds, with a memorandum in the inner, or dollar, column, showing the current value of the pounds spent. If fixed assets are purchased by the home office and sent to the branch, the home office should charge the branch current account with the dollars spent, and notify the branch of the equivalent pound and dollar values at the date the expenditure was made. The branch will then debit the fixed asset accounts at both the dollar and pound values, and credit the home office current account at the pound value. The fixed asset account will thus show the dollar cost of the fixed assets, as well as the pound cost; and the dollar cost thus shown will be used when the branch trial balance is converted into dollars.

The problems of conversion can be simplified by carrying the branch fixed assets in dollars on the home office books. If this practice is followed, any expenditure made by the branch for fixed assets will be charged to the home office current account in pounds. The branch will notify the home office of the expenditure and of the rate prevailing at the date of the expenditure, and the home office will debit branch fixed assets (in properly classified accounts) and credit the branch current account at the dollar value obtained by converting at the stated rate. Any expenditures made by the home office will be charged to the branch fixed asset accounts on the home office books.

When the fixed assets are carried on the home office books, the depreciation reserves will also be set up on these books; after the home office has taken up the profit reported by the branch, an entry will be made debiting branch profit and loss and crediting the depreciation reserve.

Expenses incurred by the home office for the benefit of the branch may be charged against the branch profit and loss account in a similar manner, or may be charged to the branch current account and taken up on the branch books by debits to expense accounts and a credit to the home office current account.

The foreign subsidiary. Foreign operations may be, and frequently are, conducted by subsidiaries incorporated under the laws of a foreign country. In such instances the parent company should charge the investment in foreign subsidiary account with the dollar cost of the stock, and may debit the account with the parent's share of the subsidiary profit, and credit the account with the dollar proceeds of drafts received as dividends. When the balance sheets are consolidated, the subsidiary capital stock account should be converted at the dollar price paid by the parent company, and the subsidiary surplus account should be arbitrarily stated at an amount which will bring the subsidiary balance sheet into balance after conversion into dollars. If the parent company's investment account (exclusive of any goodwill element in the cost of the investment) does not agree with the subsidiary's capital stock plus surplus as thus converted (assuming 100% ownership), an adjusting journal entry should be made debiting or crediting the investment account with an offsetting debit or credit to profit and loss or to a reserve for exchange.

The parent company will bill goods to the subsidiary and will keep a current account to record such charges, crediting the current account with payments made against invoices. The parent company may bill in dollars or in the foreign currency. If the parent company bills in dollars, the foreign subsidiary will convert the invoice to foreign currency at the rate prevailing at the date the goods are received, recording the dollar liability in an inner column of the parent company current account. If invoices are paid by dollar drafts, and if there has been a change in rate between the date of receipt of the goods and the date of payment, the cost of the draft in foreign currency will be more or less than the foreign currency credit to the parent company made by the subsidiary at the time of receiving the goods. This difference will be a debit or a credit to exchange on the foreign subsidiary's books.

If the parent company bills in the foreign currency, it will be necessary to keep the foreign subsidiary current account on the home office books in both currencies; any loss or gain due to fluctuations in exchange between the date of shipment and the date of collection will be taken up on the parent company's books.

The fixed asset accounts of the foreign subsidiary should be kept in both currencies, and the dollar value of expenditures entered in an inner memorandum column at the rate prevailing at the date of the expenditure. This inner column will furnish the information required to convert the fixed assets from foreign to domestic currency.

The consolidation of the statements will be made in much the same manner as is followed in the consolidation of the statements of a parent and subsidiary both of which are incorporated in the same country.

Illustration. Following are a number of typical transactions, with journal entries, indicating how the transactions would be recorded on the books of the domestic parent company and the foreign subsidiary. The parent company's entries are at the left, and the subsidiary's entries at the right.

(1) The United States Company organized a foreign subsidiary called the London Company, with a capital stock of £10,000. The United States Company paid for this stock with a £10,000 draft purchased at 5.20.

(Note. It is desirable to make a memorandum in the foreign capital stock account showing the cost of this stock to the parent company in dollars, because the parent company's investment account will receive other entries for earnings, dividends, and exchange adjustments, so that the balance will not be the dollar cost of the stock. This dollar memorandum, to be made on the subsidiary's books, is indicated in the following entry.)

Investment in London Co.	$52,000		Cash	£10,000	
Cash		$52,000	Capital stock ($52,000)		£10,000

(2) The London Company purchased a plant for £7,000; the current exchange rate at the date of purchase of the plant was 5.19.

(Note. The London Company should show, parenthetically in the fixed asset accounts, the dollar cost of the plant, converted at the rate current at the date of making the expenditure.)

			Plant ($36,330.00)	£ 7,000	
			Cash		£ 7,000

(3) The United States Company shipped goods to the subsidiary, billing at cost, $134,680.00.

(Note. The invoices were made out in dollars and are payable in dollars. The rate at the date of arrival was 5.20, and the London Company took up the goods at £25,900, showing the dollar liability short in the United States Company current account.)

London Co. current	$134,680		Purchases	£25,900	
Sales to London Co.		$134,680	U.S. Co. current ($134,680.00)		£25,900

(4) Sales on account by London Company, £21,000.

			Accounts receivable	£21,000	
			Sales		£21,000

(5) Collections on account by London Company, £19,000.

			Cash	£19,000	
			Accounts receivable		£19,000

(6) The London Company paid half of its indebtedness to the United States Company (on current account for purchases) by sending a draft for $67,340.00 ($134,680.00 ÷ 2). The cost of this draft at 5.18 was £13,000 ($67,-340.00 ÷ 5.18).

(Note. The total liability of the London Company for purchases, stated in pounds, was £25,900. Half of this amount is £12,950. Since the draft cost £13,000, the foreign subsidiary incurred an exchange loss of £50.

Cash	$67,340		U.S. Co. current ($67,-340.00)	£12,950	
London Co. current		$67,340	Exchange	50	
			Cash		£13,000

(7) The London Company paid expenses of £2,000.

			Expense	£ 2,000	
			Cash		£ 2,000

(8) The London Company provided depreciation at 4% on its plant.

			Depreciation	£ 280	
			Res. for dep'n		£ 280

(9) The London Company paid a dividend of £2,000 to the United States Company. The United States Company sold the draft at 5.19, receiving $10,380.00.

Cash	$10,380		Dividend	£ 2,000	
Investment in London Co.		$10,380	Cash		£ 2,000

Conversion of subsidiary's accounts. Following are the trial balance, profit and loss statement, and surplus statement of the subsidiary both in pounds and in dollars as converted by the parent company.

Trial Balance

	Pounds		Rate	Dollars	
Cash	5,000		B	25,925.00	
Accounts receivable	2,000		B	10,370.00	
U. S. Co. current		12,950	A		67,340.00
Plant	7,000		A	36,330.00	
Reserve for depreciation (4%)		280	F		1,453.20
Capital stock		10,000	A		52,000.00
Sales		21,000	C		108,990.00
Purchases	25,900		D	134,680.00	
Expense	2,000		C	10,380.00	
Depreciation	280		F	1,453.20	
Exchange	50		C	259.50	
Dividend	2,000		E	10,380.00	
	44,230	44,230		229,777.70	229,783.20
Exchange Adjustment				5.50	
				229,783.20	229,783.20

Inventory: £10,000 @ 5.185, $51,850.00.

Explanation of conversions:

A = Dollar balance shown in dollar memorandum column on London Company books.
B = Current rate on December 31: 5.185.
C = Average rate for year: 5.19.
D = Balance of reciprocal account (Sales to London Co.)
E = Amount credited to investment account on U.S. books.
F = At 4% of gross dollar value of plant.

LONDON COMPANY
Balance Sheet, December 31, 194-

Assets			Liabilities and Net Worth		
Cash	£ 5,000	$ 25,925.00	U. S. Co. current	£12,950	$ 67,340.00
Accts. receivable	2,000	10,370.00	Capital stock	10,000	52,000.00
Inventory	10,000	51,850.00	Surplus	770	3,681.80
Plant less depreciation	6,720	34,876.80			
	£23,720	$123,021.80		£23,720	$123,021.80

LONDON COMPANY
Profit and Loss Statement
Year Ended December 31, 194-

	Pounds		Dollars	
Sales		£21,000		$108,990.00
Less cost of goods sold:				
Purchases	£25,900		$134,680.00	
Less inventory, December 31	10,000	15,900	51,850.00	82,830.00
Gross profit on sales		£ 5,100		$ 26,160.00
Deduct:				
Expenses	£ 2,000		$ 10,380.00	
Depreciation	280	2,280	1,453.20	11,833.20
Net profit on operations		£ 2,820		$ 14,326.80
Exchange loss		50		259.50
Net profit		£ 2,770		$ 14,067.30

LONDON COMPANY
Surplus Statement
Year Ended December 31, 194-

Profits for the year	£2,770	$14,067.30
Less dividends	2,000	10,380.00
Balance, December 31	£ 770	$ 3,687.30
Less exchange adjustment—required to make the capital stock and surplus in dollars equal to the converted value of the London subsidiary's net assets		5.50
Adjusted balance of surplus		$ 3,681.80

Parent company's trial balance. Following is the trial balance of the parent company:

UNITED STATES COMPANY
Trial Balance
December 31, 194-

Cash	$ 17,720.00	
Accounts receivable	10,000.00	
London Company current	67,340.00	
Investment in London Company	41,620.00	
Plant	60,000.00	
Reserve for depreciation		$ 3,000.00
Accounts payable		9,000.00
Capital stock		150,000.00
Sales		200,000.00
Sales to London Company		134,680.00
Material purchases	100,000.00	
Direct labor	90,000.00	
Manufacturing expense	85,000.00	
Depreciation	3,000.00	
Expense	22,000.00	
	$496,680.00	$496,680.00

Parent company's investment account. Following is a statement of the parent company's account with its investment in the London subsidiary after the subsidiary profit has been taken up.

Statement of Account
Investment in London Company
Year Ended December 31, 194-

Cost		$52,000.00
Add profit		14,067.30
Total		$66,067.30
Deduct:		
Dividend	$10,380.00	
Exchange adjustment	5.50	10,385.50
Balance, December 31, 194-		$55,681.80

Consolidated statements. The consolidated profit and loss statement of the parent company and its foreign subsidiary, and the consolidated balance sheet working papers, appear on pages 438 and 439.

UNITED STATES COMPANY AND LONDON SUBSIDIARY
Consolidated Statement of Profit and Loss
For the Year Ended December 31, 194-

	United States Company		London Company		Consolidated	
Sales		$200,000.00		$108,990.00		$308,990.00
Cost of sales:						
Materials:						
Purchases	$100,000.00				$100,000.00	
Less inventory, December 31	6,000.00				6,000.00	
Materials used	$ 94,000.00				$ 94,000.00	
Direct labor	90,000.00				90,000.00	
Manufacturing expense, including depreciation	88,000.00				88,000.00	
Total manufacturing cost	$272,000.00				$272,000.00	
Less goods in process, December 31	3,000.00				3,000.00	
Cost of goods manufactured	$269,000.00				$269,000.00	
Goods shipped to London	134,680.00		$134,680.00			
Remainder	$134,320.00					
Less inventory, December 31	5,000.00		51,850.00		56,850.00	
Cost of sales		129,320.00		82,830.00		212,150.00
Gross profit on sales		$ 70,680.00		$ 26,160.00		$ 96,840.00
Expenses, including depreciation		22,000.00		11,833.20		33,833.20
Net profit on operations		$ 48,680.00		$ 14,326.80		$ 63,006.80
Exchange loss ($259.50 + $5.50)				265.00		265.00
Net profit for the year		$ 48,680.00		$ 14,061.80		$ 62,741.80

UNITED STATES COMPANY AND LONDON SUBSIDIARY
Consolidated Balance Sheet Working Papers
December 31, 194-

	United States Company	London Company	Eliminations	Consolidated Balance Sheet
Assets				
Cash	$ 17,720.00	$ 25,925.00		$ 43,645.00
Accounts receivable	10,000.00	10,370.00		20,370.00
London Company current	67,340.00		$ 67,340.00(A)	
Raw materials	6,000.00			6,000.00
Goods in process	3,000.00			3,000.00
Finished goods	5,000.00	51,850.00		56,850.00
Investment in London Company	55,681.80		55,681.80(B)	
Plant less depreciation	57,000.00	34,876.80		91,876.80
	$221,741.80	$123,021.80	$123,021.80	$221,741.80
Liabilities and Net Worth				
Accounts payable	$ 9,000.00			$ 9,000.00
United States Company current		$ 67,340.00	$ 67,340.00(A)	
Capital stock	150,000.00	52,000.00	52,000.00(B)	150,000.00
Surplus:				
United States Company	62,741.80			62,741.80
London Company		3,681.80	3,681.80(B)	
	$221,741.80	$123,021.80	$123,021.80	$221,741.80

Foreign subsidiaries not consolidated. Consolidated statements should not include the accounts of a foreign subsidiary if normal operating relations have been discontinued because of war or other conditions, or if exchange restrictions are such that the current investment in the foreign subsidiary cannot be converted into funds available to the parent company. Under such conditions, no profit should be taken up by the parent company, directly or indirectly, from the subsidiary's operations, and the investment should be reduced, for balance sheet purposes, by the creation of an adequate reserve for losses. The omission of the subsidiary's accounts from the consolidated statements should be mentioned in a footnote or comment.

If the income statement of a foreign subsidiary is consolidated with that of the parent company, consideration should be given to any tax which the foreign government or the United States government might levy on the transfer of profits to the parent company. Provision should be made for such taxes in the consolidated income statement, or a footnote should state that no provision has been made. The absence of such a provision may be warranted if transfers of profits are not contemplated because profits have been invested permanently in foreign assets or for other reasons.

CHAPTER 55

Estates and Trusts

Administration and distribution of an estate. The laws governing the administration and distribution of estates vary to some extent in the different states. The discussion of estates and estate accounting in this text should be understood to be a generalization from a country-wide standpoint, subject to exceptions arising from the differing statutes and court decisions of the several states. For this reason, and because the treatment of the subject in a text devoted to the general field of accounting must necessarily be limited, the two chapters on estates and trusts should be understood to present only a survey of the subject.*

If a person dies intestate—that is to say, without leaving a will, or leaving an invalid will—his estate will be distributed among his distributees in accordance with the laws of descent and distribution, the laws of descent determining the disposition of the real estate to the heirs, and the laws of distribution determining the disposition of the personal property to the next of kin. The administration and disposition of the property is controlled by a court known variously, in different states, as the *probate, surrogate's* or *orphans' court.* The work of dealing with the intestate's assets, paying the debts and charges, and making distribution is placed in the hands of an administrator, who is appointed by the court and to whom the court issues letters of administration evidencing his authority. If a will, although valid, directs the disposition of only a portion of the estate property, a condition of *partial intestacy* exists.

If the decedent leaves a valid will disposing of his entire estate, the laws of descent and distribution will not be operative, and the estate will be distributed in accordance with the wishes of the testator or testatrix, as expressed in this will. (This statement is subject to such exceptions as the widow's option to renounce her rights under the will and claim her elective or distributive share under the law.)

* The author is very greatly indebted to Emanuel Saxe, Ph.D., C.P.A., a member of the New York bar and of the Department of Accountancy, The College of the City of New York, who read the manuscript and offered invaluable suggestions and criticisms. For a more comprehensive treatment of the subject, the reader is referred to Professor Saxe's book, *Estate Accounting.*

Before the will can become operative, it must be admitted to probate, that is, duly proved. A petition is presented to the court, asking that the will be admitted to probate; a date is set for the hearing, and all interested parties are properly notified. At this hearing, the witnesses testify with respect to all significant matters incident to the due and proper execution of the will, including the authenticity of their signatures and that of the decedent. If the witnesses are dead or cannot appear, an attestation clause in the will may help to prove its authenticity; persons familiar with the signatures of the decedent and the witnesses may testify to the genuineness of their signatures. If the court is satisfied that the will is a valid instrument, executed without fraud when the decedent was of age, otherwise competent, and not subject to restraint or undue influence, the will is admitted to probate.

If an executor is named in the will, and if he is competent and willing to serve, he will be granted letters testamentary by the court. If no executor is named in the will, or if one is named but is unwilling or incompetent to serve, the court will appoint an administrator with the will annexed (administrator c. t. a.).

Duties of the executor or the administrator. The executor or the administrator (referred to hereafter by the general term, *fiduciary*) is expected to seek out and take possession of the personal property of the deceased; to keep the estate funds separate from his own; to dispose of perishable property as quickly as possible and, unless authorized by testamentary direction to retain them, of any investments not legally permissible for fiduciaries; to preserve and administer the estate in a prudent manner; to keep excess funds invested to the fullest extent possible; to pay the funeral and administration expenses, the just debts, the estate and inheritance taxes, and all other proper charges; to distribute the estate to the persons entitled thereto; and to account to the court and all interested parties.

If there is a will, the real estate goes to the devisees, and the personal property, through the fiduciary, to the legatees. If there is no will, the administrator distributes the property to those who are next of kin, in accordance with the applicable law of intestacy. The fiduciary does not ordinarily administer or distribute the realty; the heirs take title to it directly from the decedent. The personal representative (fiduciary) of a testate decedent must carry out all of the directions in the will, including the erection of any trusts.

Title to personal property vests in the fiduciary and passes through him to the distributees, except that in many states certain household effects, a limited amount of cash, the decedent's clothes and certain other personal effects may be exempt, title thereto passing directly to the widow or to minor children.

It is only rarely that the fiduciary exercises any control over the real estate, since, by the laws of most states, title vests in the heirs or devisees immediately upon the death of the decedent. If, however, the personal property is not sufficient to pay the debts and charges, the fiduciary generally possesses, or may apply to the court for, authority to sell, mortgage, or lease any parcels of realty in order to obtain funds with which to pay them. Or the will may specifically direct the fiduciary to administer the realty for various purposes. Where the testator has made a contract to sell real estate, the title to the real estate passes to the heir subject to the obligation of the heir to convey title to the vendee; and, since the claim against the vendee is personal property, it passes into the executor's control as part of the inventory.

The proceeds of life insurance policies payable to the estate pass into the hands of the fiduciary and must be accounted for by him; the proceeds of policies payable to specific beneficiaries are payable directly to them and are not part of the decedent's estate.

Inventory of assets.—As soon as the fiduciary is appointed, he should marshal and take possession of the decedent's personal estate. Although the laws differ in the various states, it is desirable, and in some states obligatory, to file an inventory of the assets with the court. This inventory should show items and values; the valuations may be determined by the fiduciary unless the law or practice requires that the valuations be made by independent appraisers. The inventory should include all personal property of the decedent except exempt property.

If a testate decedent has made refundable advances to persons who are beneficiaries of his estate, such advances should be included in the inventory as estate assets, plus the interest thereon (unless a contrary intent appears) from the dates thereof to the date of collection or distribution. The total represents the estate to be divided. In the case of intestacy, the treatment of advancements to the decedent's children is somewhat similar, except that interest is not generally charged. However, if the advancement to such child equals or exceeds his portion of the estate, he is entitled to no further participation, but he is not obligated to return any excess of the advance over his distributable share. If the advancement is less than the child's share, he is entitled to receive the balance of his share.

Income accrued* to and including the day of death is a part of the principal of the estate and should be included in the inventory. If assets are thought to be valueless, they should, nevertheless, be included in the inventory, with a statement that they have no value.

Although real estate titles pass directly to heirs or devisees without passing through the fiduciary, it may be desirable that real estate be inventoried, in order to fulfill the requirements of state inheritance laws and the federal estate tax laws. Moreover, in some states the real estate must be included in the inventory because the inventory, filed with the proper county officer, serves as evidence of the passing of title.

Any assets discovered after the inventory is completed should be reported in a supplementary inventory.

Legacies and devises. A *legacy* (or *bequest*) is a gift of personal property made by a decedent in his will; the recipient thereof is called a *legatee.* A *devise* is a gift of real estate made by a decedent in his will; the recipient of the gift is called a *devisee.*

A *specific legacy* is a gift of some particular property, as a watch, a library, or a specifically described investment.

A *demonstrative legacy* is a legacy payable in cash out of a designated fund.

A *general legacy* is a gift of a sum of money.

A *residuary legacy* includes all personal property remaining after the payment of debts and charges and all other legacies. The residuary legatee receives "all the rest, residue, and remainder" of the personal estate.

Legacies may be paid at any time after the fiduciary takes charge; but unless the estate is clearly sufficient to pay all debts, charges, and legacies, the fiduciary should defer the payment of the legacies at least for the legal executorial period, to enable him to determine the amount of the debts and charges; otherwise he may incur a personal liability to creditors. Any liability owed to the estate by a legatee should be offset against his legacy.

Does accrued income on a specific legacy at the date of the decedent's death belong to corpus or does it go with the gift to the legatee? The law on this subject does not seem to be well settled, and a fiduciary faced with the question should apply to the court for a ruling.

Interest on all unpaid legacies begins to accrue at the end of the executorial period, which varies in different states.

* See subsequent section, "Questions of accrual," for the classes of income which are recognized as accruing in the field of estates and trusts.

Liabilities. In some states it is obligatory, and in all states it is advisable, for the fiduciary to give published notice to creditors of the decedent to present their claims within the legal time limit. Claims will be presented to the fiduciary, or to the court, depending on the law of the state; presentation usually is made to the fiduciary. The fiduciary should include a statement in his accounting to the court showing the nature and extent of the claims filed.

Any claims which the executor considers invalid, he should reject; he is in duty bound to set up all legitimate defenses, including the statute of limitations and the statute of frauds. In some states, creditors whose claims have been rejected may appeal to the probate court; in other states, they must bring suit in the ordinary manner.

The debts and charges must be paid in full before legacies can be paid. If the residuary personal estate is not sufficient to pay the debts and charges, provision for their payment will generally be made in the following order:

By abatement (that is, by scaling down) of legacies, in the following order:
- (a) General legacies (including such part of any demonstrative legacy as is not covered by the fund indicated for the payment thereof).
- (b) Specific legacies.

If the entire personal estate is insufficient to pay the debts and charges, the residuary devises and, lastly, the specific devises will fail.

The fiduciary may sell, mortgage, or lease the decedent's realty to obtain funds for the payment of all proper debts and charges.

Trusts. The testator may provide in his will that all, or some portion, of the principal of the estate shall be placed in the hands of a trustee, or trustees, who shall keep the fund invested, distribute the income to one class of beneficiary during a stated period of time, and eventually turn over the principal of the trust to another class of beneficiary, both being designated in the will. For instance, he may direct that the income shall be paid to his widow during her life and that, at her death, the principal shall be paid to his children or to some institution. Or he may direct that the income shall be distributed in equal parts to his children until the youngest surviving child reaches the age of twenty-five, and that the principal shall then be divided equally among them or their surviving children.

A trust created by a will is called a *testamentary trust.* If the trustee is named in the will, he is called a *testamentary trustee.* The person who is entitled to receive the income during a stated period, and the person who is entitled eventually to receive the principal, or *corpus*, are both beneficiaries of the trust. The income beneficiary is called the *cestui que trust.* The *cestui que trust* is called a *life tenant* if he is entitled to the income during the entire period of his life; if he is entitled to the income for a shorter period, he may be referred to merely as the *income beneficiary;* if the income beneficiary changes from time to time, each beneficiary may be referred to successively as the *present income beneficiary.* The person who is entitled eventually to receive the principal of the trust is called the *remainderman.* The income beneficiary and the remainderman may be the same person; for instance, a child may be entitled to the income of the trust until he attains his majority, and to the corpus of the trust estate at that date.

The trustee does not take over the duties of the trusteeship until the trust property is duly received by him. He takes title to the real estate as of the date of the testator's death, but he does not take title to personal property until it is duly turned over to him. However, the trust takes effect as of the date of death; hence, the income beneficiary is entitled to the income from the trust assets from the date of death.

The trustee's investments must conform to the state laws which prescribe the classes of securities which may be purchased by trustees unless the testator, in the will, authorizes the trustee to go beyond the limits allowed by law. The trustee must exercise diligence and prudence in managing the trust and must keep the funds invested. He is allowed a reasonable time in which to invest cash, after which time he may be charged with interest on uninvested funds.

Principal and income. If a trust is created by the will, the executor and the trustee must keep their records in such a way as to distinguish clearly between the principal and the income. The income beneficiary is entitled to the income (that is, the earnings on principal) during his tenancy, and the remainderman is entitled to the principal (or corpus). Therefore, if cash or property is received, the fiduciary must know, and must indicate in his records, whether the cash or property belongs in the principal account or in the income account. Similarly, a careful distinction must be made between disbursements which are payable out of principal and those which are payable out of income. A strict distinction must be made between principal and income in all accountings for trusts or for an estate in which a trust is involved.

The distinctions between principal and income must be made by the fiduciary in accordance with the law, unless a contrary treatment is prescribed in the will. However, the testator does not have *carte blanche* in his testamentary directions; he must not violate such paramount legal restrictions as, for example, the prohibition against illegal accumulations of income. In cases of doubt about the proper classification of an item as principal or income, the fiduciary should apply to the court for a ruling.

The situations calling for a distinction between principal and income may be broadly classified as follows:

(1) Questions of accrual, or apportionment on a time basis.
(2) Questions of classification.
(3) Questions of impairment.

Questions of accrual. The distinction between the cash basis and the accrual basis of accounting is well understood as applied to ordinary commercial accounts. In the administration of trust estates certain items of income and expense "accrue" and are accounted for, as between the income beneficiary and the remainderman, on an accrual basis, while others are accounted for on a cash basis.

There are two important dates to be noted in connection with the apportionment of items of receipt or expenditure as between the income beneficiary and the remainderman:

The date of the death of the testator.
The date when the tenancy terminates and the remainderman receives the corpus.

Accruable income on trust assets arising prior to the death of the testator belongs to the corpus of the estate, even though it is not collected until a subsequent date; similarly, any such expenses accrued prior to that date are payable out of principal cash.

Such income as accrues after the testator's death up to the termination of the tenancy belongs to the income beneficiary or his estate, regardless of the date of collection; and expenses accrued between these two dates are payable from income cash. Income and expenses accrued after the termination of the tenancy affect the interest of the remainderman. If there are several successive income beneficiaries, accruals must be recognized at the close of each tenancy.

What earnings and expenses accrue* and must be apportioned between principal and income?

* The laws relative to the distinction between principal and income differ somewhat in the several states; therefore, the rules stated in this chapter should be regarded as generalizations, subject to state exceptions.

(1) Interest, in general, accrues from day to day, the interest accrued on receivables and investments to and including the date of death of the testator being principal, and interest accruing during the tenancy being income. Interest expense is similarly accrued. But interest on savings bank deposits is generally not considered to accrue, but is treated as income of the period when it is declared to be available to depositors.

(2) Ordinary cash dividends do not accrue, but are generally considered income of the period when declared. Thus, a dividend declared prior to the testator's death is corpus, even though it is not collected until after his death; and an ordinary cash dividend declared during the tenancy is income, although paid from profits earned prior to the testator's death or paid after the termination of the tenancy. In some states the governing date is that on which the corporation's stock records are closed to determine the stockholders of record to whom the dividends are payable.

A corporation may occasionally elect, instead of paying an ordinary cash dividend, to pay a stock dividend of approximately the same amount in order to preserve the corporation's current position; such dividends are generally treated in the same fashion as ordinary cash dividends.

The rule is not so simple in the case of extraordinary cash and stock dividends, since the laws with respect thereto differ in the various states. In some states such dividends are classified as income, in others they are classified as corpus, and in some states extraordinary dividends are apportioned between income and corpus. In states where apportionment is required, the computation is made by determining the book value per share of stock owned at the date of death (as shown by the paying corporation's books), and the book value per share after the payment of the dividend; if the book value after the payment of the dividend is less than that at the date of death, enough of the dividend must be allocated to corpus so that the book value of the stock after the payment of the dividend plus the dividend so allocated will be equal to the original book value of the stock at the date of the creation of the trust.

If, as frequently happens in connection with property leased by one railroad to another, the lessee company guarantees the dividends on the stock of the lessor company, dividends paid by the lessor from funds received from the lessee in fulfillment of the guarantee partake of the nature of interest and are recognized as accruing.

(3) Rents accrue in most states, although not in all. In the states in which they do accrue, rents earned prior to the death of the decedent are corpus, and the portion accruing during the tenancy is income. A similar rule applies to rents paid.

(4) Taxes on trust property do not generally accrue. Taxes which became a lien on the property before the date of the decedent's death are payable out of principal cash; taxes which became a lien on the property during the tenancy are a charge against income. In many states a specific devisee of realty must pay any taxes thereon accrued before the death of the testator and remaining unpaid at that time. Special assessments for improvements may be chargeable to principal or may be apportioned according to the benefits conferred.

(5) Partnership profits do not accrue. The death of a partner dissolves the partnership; if the books are closed as of the date of his death, the question of accrual does not arise, as the profits to that date will be determined and will be classified as principal. However, the partnership articles sometimes provide that the books shall not be closed until some date subsequent to death; in such cases the profit between the closing date prior to death and the closing date subsequent to death is regarded as principal in some jurisdictions, and as income in others. If interest is allowed on a partner's capital it generally accrues, in accordance with the basic interest rule.

(6) Contract profits do not accrue. A contract for other than personal services entered into by the testator must be completed by the fiduciary, but the profits belong to the principal.

(7) Livestock born during the life tenancy is income, except to the extent necessary to keep the herd intact where such an intention is expressed or implied.

(8) Growing crops are income if the land is part of a trust estate. However, crops growing on the decedent's land at the time of his death are considered to be a part of the principal.

Questions of classification. There are many items which do not involve the question of accrual and apportionment on a time basis, but which involve the equally important question of determining whether the whole amount should be classified as principal or as income.

Increases or decreases in assets forming part of the corpus are classified as corpus; increases or decreases in assets representing undistributed income are classified as income.

The classification of cash receipts and disbursements is discussed below, under the following captions:

(1) Receipts and disbursements applicable to principal.
(2) Receipts and disbursements applicable to income.

Items applicable to principal. In general, it may be said that corpus should be charged with expenditures which represent the payment of obligations incurred prior or incident to the death of the decedent, expenses of administration prior to the setting up of a trust, and, thereafter, those expenditures which result in ultimate benefit to the remainderman. The following are some of the expenditures ordinarily chargeable to principal:

(1) Debts of the decedent, expenses of the last illness, and funeral and administration expenses.
(2) Legal fees and court costs incurred in probating the will, in defending it against a contest, and in interpreting it.
(3) Costs of defending the estate against claims rejected by the fiduciary.
(4) Legal fees incurred in connection with a change in fiduciaries.
(5) Federal estate tax and state inheritance tax (except where otherwise prescribed by law).
(6) Brokerage fees on changes in investments.
(7) Legal fees and other costs of preserving the principal of the estate.
(8) Carrying charges on property which produces no income are usually chargeable to principal; otherwise, the desires of the testator with respect to the income beneficiary might not be fulfilled, because income from other trust assets would be applied to the carrying of unproductive assets for the benefit of the remainderman.

Premiums on fire insurance policies are usually considered to be payable out of income, but in case of loss the proceeds of the policy are considered to be a replacement of principal.

Items applicable to income. All ordinary operating expenses of the estate or the trust are payable out of income. These include such items as:

(1) The fiduciary's commissions for collection and disbursement of income.
(2) Legal fees paid in matters pertaining to the earning of income, as distinguished from matters pertaining to the preservation of the estate.
(3) Wages of clerks, and workmen employed to care for the property.
(4) Costs of caring for and harvesting crops.
(5) Ordinary repairs to trust property.
(6) Interest accrued during the tenancy on mortgages and other liabilities.
(7) Insurance premiums (generally).
(8) Taxes on undistributed income accumulated for the benefit of the income beneficiary.

Repairs and betterments are classified in accordance with the usual accounting rule: ordinary repairs are chargeable to income; extraordinary repairs are chargeable to principal. Replacements and betterments may be apportioned, the portion which makes good wear and tear during the period of the trust being charged to income, and the balance being charged to principal. Although this last mentioned rule is not difficult to state, it is often very difficult to apply.

Special assessments for local benefits may be paid out of principal if the benefits are expected to add lasting value; otherwise, they should be paid out of income. In some cases a portion may be paid from principal, and the remainder from income.

Mortgages and other investments may become delinquent, and for this and other reasons the amount received in liquidation and settlement after foreclosure thereof may be less than the sum of the original value of the investment, the expenses incurred in attempting to preserve and collect the investment, and the uncollected income. Such receipts are generally apportioned between principal and income so that the loss occasioned by the salvage operation will be shared by the income beneficiary and the remainderman without entirely depriving the life tenant of his income during the barren period.

Questions of impairment. If the trust property includes wasting assets (for example, such natural resources as mines, quarries, oil wells and timber; or such other types as leaseholds and copyrights) or assets subject to depreciation (such as a building), the fiduciary must consider whether a portion of any receipts therefrom should be regarded and retained as principal, in order to prevent the impairment of the trust corpus. The intention of the decedent is controlling in these cases and must be sought out carefully. If it appears that the testator intended to give the full, undiminished income to the income beneficiary even though the principal would thereby ultimately be completely exhausted, no deduction from income for the depletion or depreciation factor is permitted. If, however, the express or implied intention to preserve the principal intact appears, the fiduciary is required to retain out of the income such an amount as will be sufficient to maintain the integrity of the original investment.

The same rules apply to income derived from similar investments held in corporate form.

Extraordinary repairs are payable from corpus. Permanent improvements to trust property generally are payable out of corpus; improvements made solely for the purpose of increasing the income-producing power of the property are chargeable to income unless there is strong justification for an apportionment.

Any losses or gains on the realization of assets forming a part of the principal are generally considered to be applicable to principal, for the loss or gain is merely the difference between the estimated or inventory value and the actual value determined by realization. The principal of the estate is composed of the assets left by the decedent, or whatever these assets ultimately realize.

In accordance with this general theory, if bonds left by the decedent are inventoried at a premium, turned over to a trustee, and held by him until maturity, there will be a book loss of the difference between the inventory value and par. But this loss is to be borne by principal, for the principal is not considered to be impaired if it contains the actual assets left by the decedent, or the proceeds of these assets.

Similarly, if bonds left by the decedent are inventoried at a discount, the income beneficiary is not entitled to any income representing accumulation of discount; any discount realized at maturity, or upon disposition of the bonds is regarded as an ordinary gain to be added to the corpus.

With respect to bonds purchased by the fiduciary at a premium or a discount, any desire with respect to amortization expressed by the testator will govern. In the absence of any such expressed desire, it has been held generally that premiums should be amortized, but that discounts should not be; there is, however, a strong minority opinion that discounts also should be amortized. Amortization, when required, may be made by either the straight line method or an actuarial method. If bonds purchased at a premium are disposed of before maturity and the unamortized portion of the premium is not realized, the loss is generally chargeable to corpus; similarly, a gain would be credited to principal.

The right to subscribe for stock is inherent in the stock, which is corpus; if, instead of exercising the rights, the fiduciary sells them, the estate's interest in the corporation is diluted by reason of the reduction of its percentage of stock ownership; therefore, all receipts from the sale of subscription rights, including any profit, should be regarded as principal.

Fiduciary's Accounts

Accounting for the estate principal. The function of estate or trust accounting differs fundamentally from that of commercial or industrial accounting. Commercial or industrial accounting is based on the equation of accounts:

Assets = Liabilities + Net Worth

The books of an industrial concern are opened by debiting asset accounts and crediting liability and proprietorship accounts; and they are kept in such a manner as to show the amounts of, and the changes in, these three elements of financial condition.

A fiduciary is placed in possession of certain assets and his records should show how he has discharged his accountability for them. His accounts, therefore, are based on the following fundamental equation:

Assets = Accountability

The books of an executor or administrator are opened by debiting asset accounts with the valuations shown by the inventory, and crediting a fiduciary accountability account called *estate corpus* or *estate principal.* Liabilities are not recorded until the fiduciary pays them, thus reducing the total assets for which he is accountable. Enough asset accounts should be kept to classify the property adequately. In a small estate, it may be sufficient to keep the asset accounts in one ledger; in a large estate, it may be desirable to maintain controlling accounts in the general ledger, with detailed accounts in subsidiary ledgers. In general, it is desirable to keep separate accounts with assets included in the inventory and similar assets purchased by the fiduciary; for one reason, the nature of the fiduciary's responsibility for losses on assets purchased by him is somewhat different from his responsibility for the difference between the inventory valuation of assets left by the decedent and the amount ultimately realized therefrom; also, bonds included in the inventory and those acquired by the fiduciary may be subject to different amortization procedures.

The fiduciary's accountability is increased if additional assets are discovered after the original inventory is completed; any such subsequently discovered assets should be reported in a supplementary inventory, and should be recorded by debiting asset accounts and crediting an account called *assets subsequently discovered.* This is an accountability account, and is a supplement to the estate corpus account; it is desirable to set up the separate account because the executor, when making his report to the court, should show under separate headings the amount of accountability represented by the original inventory and the amount represented by assets subsequently discovered.

The executor's accountability as to corpus is also increased by any gains on the disposal of assets, because gains increase the total assets of the estate; his accountability is decreased by losses. When an asset is disposed of, the asset account should be credited with the inventory value; gains should be credited to a gain on realization account, and losses should be charged to a loss on realization account. Such gains and losses may be recorded in the journal, or special columns may be provided for them on the receipts side of the cash book. Separate accounts may be set up, if desired, to show the increase or decrease in the valuation of assets not disposed of.

The executor's accountability is also decreased by the payment of funeral and administration expenses. These may be charged to a single funeral and administration expense account if there are only a few expenditures of this nature. If the executor is required to distinguish, for accounting purposes, between funeral and administration expenses, it may be advisable in a large estate to open separate funeral expense and administration expense accounts; and if there are enough expenditures of this nature to warrant doing so, separate accounts may be kept with various classes of administration expenses.

The executor's accountability is also decreased (or, expressed more precisely, discharged) by the payment of liabilities incurred by the decedent. No entry should be made for liabilities until they are paid, thus effecting a decrease in the executor's accountability; when a liability is paid, an entry should be made debiting debts of decedent paid (an accountability account) and crediting cash. The charges to debts of decedent paid account should show, in each instance, the name of the creditor. If there are a large number of creditors, it may be desirable to treat the debts of decedent paid account as a controlling account, and to charge the individual liability payments to subsidiary accounts, such as debts of decedent paid—John Brown.

The executor's accountability is also decreased by the payment of legacies. If there are only a few legacies, one account entitled legacies paid may suffice. If there are numerous legacies, it may be desirable to use several accounts, such as specific legacies delivered, general legacies paid, and so on. If there are a great many legacies or if inheritance taxes are to be charged against the legacies, or if legacies are to be abated in order to pay debts, an account should be kept with each legatee, either in the general ledger or in a subsidiary ledger.

Entries in legacy accounts are illustrated below:

Legacy—John Doe
    Cash
  Payment of inheritance tax.

Cash
    Legacy—John Doe
  Refund from Doe for inheritance tax paid.

Legacy—John Doe
    Bonds of *X Y* Company
  Delivery of legacy to Doe.

The will may direct that the total inheritance tax shall be paid by the estate, thus reducing the residuary legacy.

The accounts with assets subsequently discovered, gain on realization, loss on realization, funeral and administration expense, debts of decedent paid, and legacies are temporary accountability accounts set up to provide information required for the executor's report to the court; after they have served their purpose, they are closed to the estate corpus account, generally after the fiduciary's report is accepted.

Accounting for estate income. All of the income of a small estate may be credited to a single income account; in a large estate it is preferable to open separate accounts with the various classes of income, such as interest income and dividend income.

All expenses deductible from income may be charged to one account called *expense-income;* or separate accounts may be kept with various kinds of expense.

If cash collected as income is paid to beneficiaries, the charges should be made to an account called *distributions to income beneficiaries.* If desired, a separate account may be kept with each beneficiary to whom distributions are made.

Principal and income cash. A fiduciary should keep his records in such a manner as to distinguish between principal cash and income cash. A form of cash book which accomplishes this purpose is illustrated later in the chapter.

Separate bank accounts may be kept with principal cash and income cash, or both may be deposited in one account; if the latter procedure is followed, the amounts applicable to principal and income can be determined from the balances of the cash-principal and cash-income accounts in the ledger.

Summary of estate accounts. As indicated above, a fiduciary's accounts should show the assets and accountability as to corpus, and the assets and accountability as to income. The following trial balance is assumed to have been prepared from the accounts of an executor of an estate involving a trust before the final statement to the court was prepared and the books were closed:

	Debit	Credit
ACCOUNTS AS TO PRINCIPAL:		
Accountability Accounts:		
Estate corpus		$81,050
(The original amount for which the executor was accountable, as shown by the inventory.)		
Assets subsequently discovered		450
(Increase in accountability resulting from discovery of additional assets.)		
Gain on realization		500
(Increase in accountability representing excess of amount realized for assets over inventory value.)		
Loss on realization	$ 300	
(Decrease in accountability resulting from losses on asset disposals.)		
Funeral and administration expense	535	
(Decrease in accountability resulting from disposal of assets in payment of expenses.)		
Debts of decedent paid	3,360	
(Decrease in accountability resulting from payment of debts.)		
Legacies—Mary Henderson	13,000	
Legacy—W. C. Turner	1,000	
(Decreases in accountability resulting from payments to legatees.)		
(The net credit balance of the foregoing accounts is $63,805, representing the executor's accountability for the remaining corpus assets.)		
Asset Accounts (Remaining assets, totaling $63,805, for which the executor is still accountable):		
P Q Co. stock	10,000	
S T Co. bonds	25,000	
L M Co. bonds	5,000	
Cash—principal	23,805	
Total balances of accounts as to principal	$82,000	$82,000

ACCOUNTS AS TO INCOME:

Accountability Accounts:		
Income..........		$ 4,525
(The gross amount for which the executor has assumed accountability to the income beneficiaries.)		
Expense—income..........	$ 250	
(Decrease in accountability as to income, resulting from payment of expenses applicable to income.)		
Distributions to income beneficiaries..........	500	
(Decrease, or discharge, of accountability, resulting from distributions to income beneficiaries.)		
(The net credit balance of $3,775 in these accounts reflects the executor's accountability for the following income assets.)		
Asset Accounts (Remaining income assets, totaling $3,775, for which the executor is still accountable):		
Accrued interest receivable..........	450	
Dividends receivable..........	500	
Cash—income..........	2,825	
Total balances of accounts as to income......	$ 4,525	$ 4,525
Total balances of all accounts, combined....	$86,525	$86,525

Illustration of Fiduciary Accounting

A hypothetical case will be used in the remainder of this chapter and in the following chapter to illustrate:

The entries made in an executor's accounts.
The statements prepared by the executor.
The transfer of trust assets from the executor to a testamentary trustee, involving:
The closing of the executor's books.
The opening of the trustee's books.

George Henderson died on March 31, 1946, leaving a will in which he named W. C. Turner as executor and trustee, without bond, and in which he disposed of his property as follows:

Household furniture and $10,000.00 in cash to his widow.
Stock of *X. Y.* Co., amounting to $1,000.00, to W. C. Turner, in lieu of fees as executor and trustee.
All of the remaining property in trust, the income to be paid to his widow during her life, and at her death the principal to be paid to the Carmody Foundation.
The executor was directed to dispose of the patents and include the proceeds in the trust fund. Amortization prior to disposal was not to be charged against income.

Following is a list of events, with an indication of the books in which they are recorded.

The cash books have been presented in skeleton form, the purpose being merely to indicate the accounts to be debited and credited. To meet the requirements of the reports to be rendered, the cash records should show the names of persons from whom cash was received and to whom it was paid. The cash disbursements book should be provided with a check number column, and both books would normally have ledger folio columns. And, by providing sufficient columns, it would be possible to record on a single line each of several transactions which have required two lines in the illustrative records.

Recorded Event No.	Books	Dates	Events
		April 10	The will was admitted to probate, and letters testamentary were issued to W. C. Turner.
1	J.—C.R.	" 15	The executor filed the following inventory with the court:

Cash	$ 700.00
Life insurance policies payable to estate	20,000.00
X. Y. Co. stock	1,000.00
S. T. Co. bonds, 6%, F. & A.	25,000.00
Accrued interest on *S. T.* Co. bonds	250.00
P. Q. Co. stock—100 shares	10,000.00
Dividend declared on March 10 on *P. Q.* Co. stock, payable April 30	600.00
Patents	19,000.00
Household furniture	3,000.00
Automobile	1,500.00
	$81,050.00

(Exempt property set aside for the widow is not included in the inventory.)

Recorded Event No.	Books	Dates	Events
2	C.R.	" 20	The executor collected the $20,000.00 life insurance policies.
3	C.R.	" 30	Collected the $600.00 dividend on the *P. Q.* Co. stock.
4	C.D.	" 30	The executor purchased $5,000.00 of *L. M.* Co. 6% bonds, F. & A. at par and accrued interest of $75.00.

Recorded Event No.	Books	Dates	Events
5	C.D.	May 20	Paid funeral expenses, $300.00.
6	C.R.	June 5	Sold the automobile for $1,200.00.
7	C.R.	" 15	Discovered a savings bank account with a balance of $450.00. Withdrew this balance and deposited it in the estate checking account.
8	C.D.	July 10	Paid personal property taxes assessed prior to the testator's death, $260.00.
9	C.R.	Aug. 1	Collected a $30.00 dividend on *X. Y.* Co. stock. The stock is a specific legacy and the dividend goes to the legatee.
10	C.R.	" 1	Collected $750.00 interest on the *S. T.* Co. bonds.
11	C.R.	" 1	Collected $150.00 interest on the *L. M.* Co. bonds.
12	C.D.	" 5	Paid $500.00 to the widow out of income.
13	J.	Sept. 10	Dividends of $500.00 were declared on the *P. Q.* Co. stock, payable November 5.
14	C.R.	" 15	Collected royalties on patents, $3,000.00.
15	C.D.	" 30	Paid legal fees incident to collection of royalties, $250.00.
16	C.R.	Oct. 1	Sold the patents for $19,500.00.
17	C.D.	" 10	Paid all liabilities filed against the estate, as follows: John Smith....... $1,000.00; Wm. Green....... 2,100.00; Total.......... $3,100.00
18	C.D.	" 12	Paid administration expense, $235.00.
19	J.	" 15	The executor turned over the household furniture to the widow as a legacy.
20	C.D.	" 18	The executor paid the widow $10,000.00 in cash as a legacy.

Recorded Event No.	Books	Dates	Events
21	J—C.D.	October 20	The executor took the *X. Y.* Co. stock and the $30.00 dividend collected on August 1, in settlement of his legacy.
22	J.	" 31	The executor recorded the accrued interest on the *S. T.* Co. bonds and the *L. M.* Co. bonds. (Since there is no change in the income beneficiary at this date, the transfer from executor to trustee could have been made without recording income accruals.)

The student is advised to post the following journal and cash book entries to skeleton ledger accounts, and compare the balances with those shown in the trial balance.

Executor's Journal

	Date	Account		Debit	Credit
	1946				
(1)	Apr. 15	Insurance policies		$20,000.00	
	as of	*X. Y.* Co. stock		1,000.00	
	Mar. 31	*S. T.* Co. bonds, 6% (F & A)		25,000.00	
		Accrued interest receivable		250.00	
		P. Q. Co. stock		10,000.00	
		Dividends receivable		600.00	
		Patents		19,000.00	
		Household furniture		3,000.00	
		Automobile		1,500.00	
		Estate corpus			$80,350.00
		Assets, per inventory.			
(13)	Sept. 10	Dividends receivable		500.00	
		Income			500.00
		Dividend declared on *P. Q.* Co. stock, payable Nov. 5.			
(19)	Oct. 15	Legacies—Mary Henderson		3,000.00	
		Household furniture			3,000.00
		Satisfaction of specific legacy.			
(21)	20	Legacy—W. C. Turner		1,000.00	
		X. Y. Co. stock			1,000.00
		Specific legacy. See cash book entry for dividend.			
(22)	31	Accrued interest receivable		450.00	
		Income			450.00
		3 months interest on *S. T.* bonds	$375.00		
		3 months interest on *L. M.* bonds	75.00		
		Total	$450.00		

Executor's Cash Receipts

Date	Account Credited	Explanation	Principal: Credit Amount	Principal: Loss	Principal: Gain	Principal: Cash	Income Cash
1946							
(1) Apr. 15	Estate corpus	Cash per inventory	$ 700.00			$ 700.00	
(2) " 20	Insurance policies	Collected	20,000.00			20,000.00	
(3) " 30	Dividends receivable	On *P. Q.* Co. stock	600.00			600.00	
(6) June 5	Automobile	Sold	1,500.00	$300.00		1,200.00	
(7) " 15	Assets subsequently discovered	Savings bank account	450.00			450.00	
(9) Aug. 1	Legacy—W. C. Turner	Dividend on *X. Y.* Co. stock	30.00			30.00	
(10) " 1	Accrued interest receivable	*S. T.* bonds to March 31	250.00			250.00	
(10) " 1	Income	*S. T.* bond interest since March 31					$ 500.00
(11) " 1	Accrued interest receivable	*L. M.* bonds to April 30	75.00			75.00	
(11) " 1	Income	*L. M.* bond interest since April 30					75.00
(14) Sept. 15	Income	Royalties on patents					3,000.00
(16) Oct. 1	Patents	Sold	19,000.00		$500.00	19,500.00	
			$42,605.00	$300.00	$500.00	$42,805.00	$3,575.00

Executor's Cash Disbursements

Date			Account Debited	Explanation	Principal	Income
	1946					
(4)	Apr.	30	*L. M.* Co. bonds, 6%, F & A	Bonds purchased at par	$ 5,000.00	
(4)	"	30	Accrued interest receivable	Purchased on *L. M.* bonds	75.00	
(5)	May	20	Funeral and administration expense	Funeral expense	300.00	
(8)	July	10	Debts of decedent paid	Personal property taxes	260.00	
(12)	Aug.	5	Distributions to income beneficiary	Payment to widow		$500.00
(15)	Sept.	30	Expense—income	Legal fees re. royalties		250.00
(17)	Oct.	10	Debts of decedent paid	John Smith	1,000.00	
(17)	"	10	Debts of decedent paid	Wm Green	2,100.00	
(18)	"	12	Funeral and administration expense	Administration expense	235.00	
(20)	"	18	Legacies—Mary Henderson		10,000.00	
(21)	"	20	Legacy—W. C. Turner	Dividend on *X. Y.* Co. stock	30.00	
					$19,000.00	$750.00

Trial Balance
October 31, 1946
(Before making report to court and before closing books)

Estate corpus		$81,050.00
Assets subsequently discovered		450.00
Gain on realization		500.00
Loss on realization	$ 300.00	
Funeral and administration expense	535.00	
Debts of decedent paid	3,360.00	
Legacies—Mary Henderson	13,000.00	
Legacy—W. C. Turner	1,000.00	
P. Q. Co. stock	10,000.00	
S. T. Co. bonds	25,000.00	
L. M. Co. bonds	5,000.00	
Cash—principal	23,805.00	
Income		4,525.00
Expense—income	250.00	
Distributions to income beneficiary	500.00	
Accrued interest receivable	450.00	
Dividends receivable	500.00	
Cash—income	2,825.00	
	$86,525.00	$86,525.00

In connection with the recording of declared dividends and accrued interest, it should be realized that the cash basis of accounting usually is satisfactory until the executor makes his final accounting, and even then it is acceptable unless the recording of accruals is necessary in order to effect an equitable distribution. In this illustration it would not be essential; the accruals are set up merely to indicate the procedure, which is permissible even though not necessary.

CHAPTER 56

Estates and Trusts (Concluded)

Fiduciary's report to the court. The exact forms of the statements to be rendered by a fiduciary are generally prescribed by the forum to which they are presented. Customary reports include a charge and discharge statement as to principal and a charge and discharge statement as to income.

The fiduciary may also be required to submit a statement of cash transactions, which may be in a prescribed form, or may be a transcript of the cash books illustrated in the preceding chapter.

Charge and discharge statement as to principal. In the "I Charge Myself" section of the following statement, the executor summarizes and totals the elements for which he is charged with accountability; in the "I Credit Myself" section, he indicates the decreases in, and discharges of, accountability. The balance shows the amount for which he still is accountable.

ESTATE OF RICHARD ROE
JOHN DOE, EXECUTOR
Charge and Discharge Statement as to Principal
Period Covered

I Charge Myself with:

Assets per inventory (Schedule *A*) $.......
(The total of the assets listed in the inventory should agree with the credit balance of the estate corpus account.)

Assets subsequently discovered (Schedule *B*)... $.......
(The total of this schedule should agree with the credit balance of the assets subsequently discovered account.)

Gain on assets realized (Schedule *C*)........... $.......
(This schedule should describe the property sold, and should have four money columns, to show inventory or appraised value, price realized, gain on realization, and loss on realization. The total of the gain column is the amount to insert in the charge and discharge statement at this point, and it should agree with the balance of the gain on realization account.)

Total charges................................ $.......
(This total shows the amount of the principal or corpus for which the fiduciary must account. He accounts for the total as shown below.)

Charge and Discharge Statement as to Principal—Continued

Total charges—brought forward $........

I Credit Myself With:

Loss on assets realized (Schedule *C*)........... $........

(See explanation of this schedule above. The amount shown here will be the total of the loss on realization column of Schedule *C*.)

Funeral and administration expense (Schedule *D*) $........

(This schedule will consist of an analysis of the account of the same title in the ledger.)

Debts of decedent paid (Schedule *E*)........... $........

(This schedule will contain a list of the debts paid, as shown by the ledger.)

Legacies paid or delivered (Schedule *F*)........ $........

(This schedule should show the total legacies, the inheritance taxes paid thereon, if any, and payments or deliveries to legatees.)

Total credits.................................. $........

Balance (Schedule *G*)............................ $........

(This schedule should show the assets belonging to the corpus of the estate, still in the fiduciary's possession, and should agree with the total of the open asset accounts.)

Charge and discharge statement as to income. The charge and discharge statement as to income will contain information as indicated below:

ESTATE OF RICHARD ROE
JOHN DOE, EXECUTOR
Charge and Discharge Statement as to Income
Period Covered

I Charge Myself With:

(List all income earned since the decedent's death, classified as interest, dividends, etc. This item may be supported by a schedule showing the names of the parties from whom the income was received, the dates of the transactions, etc. The total should agree with the balance of the income account.)........... $........

Total charges.................................. $........

I Credit Myself With:

Expenses chargeable to income............... $........

(This amount should agree with the balance of the expense-income account; it may be supported by a schedule showing names of payees, dates of disbursements, etc.)

Distributions to income beneficiaries........... $........

(This amount should agree with the balance of the account with the same title. A supporting schedule may show names, dates, and amounts of individual distributions.)........

Total credits.................................. $........

Balance.. $........

If all of the assets have been distributed, or if the residue of the estate has been transferred to a trustee, the charges and credits in the statements will be equal and the charge and discharge statements will show no balances.

If a testamentary trust is not created and the principal and income go to the same beneficiary, the separation of principal and income in the accounts and statements of an executor may not be of great significance, and the report to the court may be made in one charge and discharge statement instead of two.

Illustration continued. The following statements and closing entries are based on the accounts of the estate of George Henderson. The transactions, books of original entry, and trial balance are shown in the preceding chapter.

Statements. The charge and discharge statements and the schedules supporting the charge and discharge statement as to principal are shown below. The schedules for an actual estate should be prepared in accordance with the legal requirements as to form and content (dates, names, and so on) in effect in the state having jurisdiction. The following illustrative schedules are presented in skeleton form; more descriptive data are usually included, and the statements are usually signed by the parties making the accounting.

ESTATE OF GEORGE HENDERSON
W. C. TURNER, EXECUTOR
Charge and Discharge Statement as to Principal
March 31, 1946 to October 31, 1946

I Charge Myself With:		
Assets per inventory (Schedule *A*)	$81,050.00	
Assets subsequently discovered (Schedule *B*)	450.00	
Gain on realization (Schedule *C*)	500.00	
Total charges		$82,000.00
I Credit Myself With:		
Loss on realization (Schedule *C*)	$ 300.00	
Funeral and administration expense (Schedule *D*)	535.00	
Debts of decedent paid (Schedule *E*)	3,360.00	
Legacies paid or delivered (Schedule *F*)	14,000.00	
Total credits		18,195.00
Balance as to Principal		$63,805.00
Consisting of:		
P. Q. Co. stock	$10,000.00	
S. T. Co. bonds	25,000.00	
L. M. Co. bonds	5,000.00	
Cash	23,805.00	
Total	$63,805.00	

Inventory of Assets — Schedule *A*

March 31, 1946

Cash	$ 700.00
Life insurance policies	20,000.00
X. Y. Co. stock	1,000.00
S. T. Co. bonds	25,000.00
Accrued interest on *S. T.* Co. bonds	250.00
P. Q. Co. stock	10,000.00
Dividend declared on *P. Q.* Co. stock	600.00
Patents	19,000.00
Household furniture	3,000.00
Automobile	1,500.00
Total	$81,050.00

Assets Subsequently Discovered — Schedule *B*

Savings bank account	$ 450.00

Assets Realized — Schedule *C*

	Inventory Value	Price Realized	Gain	Loss
Insurance policies	$20,000	$20,000		
Dividends receivable on *P. Q.* Co. stock	600	600		
Accrued interest on *S. T.* Co. bonds	250	250		
Patents	19,000	19,500	$500	
Automobile	1,500	1,200		$300
Total	$41,350	$41,550	$500	$300

Funeral and Administration Expense — Schedule *D*

Funeral expenses	$ 300.00
Administration expenses	235.00
Total	$ 535.00

Debts of Decedent Paid — Schedule *E*

John Smith	$ 1,000.00
Wm. Green	2,100.00
Personal property taxes, due by decedent	260.00
Total	$ 3,360.00

Legacies Paid or Delivered — Schedule *F*

Mary Henderson:		
Household furniture	$ 3,000.00	
Cash	10,000.00	$13,000.00
W. C. Turner:		
X. Y. Co. stock		1,000.00
And $30.00 dividend thereon		
Total		$14,000.00

ESTATE OF GEORGE HENDERSON
W. C. TURNER, EXECUTOR
Charge and Discharge Statement as to Income
March 31, 1946 to October 31, 1946

I Charge Myself With:			
Interest on *S. T.* Co. bonds:			
Collected, August 1	$750.00		
Less accrued at date of death, March 31	250.00	$ 500.00	
Accrued, August 1 to October 31		375.00	$ 875.00
Interest on *L. M.* Co. bonds:			
Collected, August 1	$150.00		
Less accrued at purchase, April 30	75.00	$ 75.00	
Accrued, August 1 to October 31		75.00	150.00
Dividend on *P. Q.* Co. stock:			
Declared but not collected			500.00
Royalty on patents			3,000.00
Total charges			$4,525.00
I Credit Myself With:			
Expenses applicable to royalties		$ 250.00	
Distribution to income beneficiary—widow		500.00	
Total credits			750.00
Balance as to Income			$3,775.00
Consisting of:			
Dividends receivable:			
Declared on *P. Q.* Co. stock		$ 500.00	
Accrued interest:			
On *S. T.* Co. bonds		375.00	
On *L. M.* Co. bonds		75.00	
Cash		2,825.00	
Total		$3,775.00	

Closing the executor's books. After the executor has rendered his final report to the court his books should be closed. If all of the assets have been distributed to the beneficiaries, the asset accounts will have no balances, and only the accountability accounts will remain open. These should be closed in the following manner:

Corpus accountability accounts:

Close to estate corpus account the assets subsequently discovered and gain on realization accounts showing increases in accountability, and the loss on realization, funeral and administration expense, debts of decedent paid, and legacy accounts showing decreases in accountability.

Income accountability accounts:

Close to income account the expense-income and distributions to income beneficiaries accounts showing decreases in accountability.

If, as in the illustration of the estate of George Henderson, assets remain for transfer to a trustee, balances will remain in asset and accountability accounts after making the entries indicated above. These asset and accountability accounts should be closed to an account with the trustee, thus completing the closing of the books.

Illustration continued. The following entries close the accounts of W. C. Turner as executor of the estate of George Henderson.

Executor's Journal

Nov. 1	Assets subsequently discovered.......	$ 450.00	
	Gain on realization..................	500.00	
	Estate corpus..................		$ 950.00
	To close accountability accounts showing increases in corpus.		
1	Estate corpus.......................	18,195.00	
	Loss on realization..............		300.00
	Funeral and administration expense		535.00
	Debts of decedent paid..........		3,360.00
	Legacies—Mary Henderson.....		13,000.00
	Legacy—W. C. Turner..........		1,000.00
	To close accountability accounts showing decreases in corpus.		
1	Income.............................	750.00	
	Expense—income..............		250.00
	Distributions to income beneficiary		500.00
	To close accountability accounts showing charges against income.		
1	Estate corpus......................	63,805.00	
	Income.............................	3,775.00	
	W. C. Turner, trustee..........		67,580.00
	To close the two accountability accounts by transfer to the trustee.		
1	W. C. Turner, trustee...............	40,000.00	
	P. Q. Co. stock................		10,000.00
	S. T. Co. bonds................		25,000.00
	L. M. Co. bonds...............		5,000.00
	To record the transfer to the trustee of corpus assets other than cash.		
1	W. C. Turner, trustee..............	950.00	
	Dividends receivable............		500.00
	Accrued interest receivable......		450.00
	To record the transfer to the trustee of income assets other than cash.		

Executor's Cash Disbursements

			Principal	Income
Nov. 1	W. C. Turner, trustee.	Transfer to trustee	$23,805.00	$2,825.00

The trustee's accounts. Since a trustee is not charged with the responsibility of paying the debts of the deceased and conducting operations incident to administration of the estate, his accounts will be somewhat less numerous than those of the executor. The general nature of his accounts is indicated below; it should be understood that the number of accounts and the desirability of using controlling accounts will depend upon the size and nature of the trust.

Accountability Accounts—Principal:
- Original accountability:
  - Trust principal
    - This account is credited with the original amount of the trust, and to it are closed periodically the following temporary accounts.
- Increases:
  - Gains on sales or other realizations
  - Increases recognized at distribution
    - This account is credited with any excess of the agreed value at which a beneficiary accepts a trust principal asset in distribution over the book value thereof.
- Decreases:
  - Losses on sales or other realizations
  - Decreases recognized at distribution
  - Expense accounts applicable to principal.

Asset Accounts—Principal:
- The nature of the asset accounts will depend upon what assets are owned by the trust.

Accountability Accounts—Income:
- Accounts with interest, dividends, etc., or a single income account.
- Expense accounts in such detail as required.
- Gains on disposal of income assets.
- Losses on disposal of income assets.
- Accounts with income beneficiaries.
  - These accounts are credited with the beneficiaries' distributive shares of income and are charged with any distributions to them.

Asset Accounts—Income:
- Cash
- Accrued interest receivable
- Accounts with any other assets pertaining to income.

Liabilities will not normally exist and therefore no accounts for them have been mentioned; if any must be recorded, accounts can be provided for them.

Illustration continued—Opening trustee's books. The following entries will open the accounts of W. C. Turner as trustee:

Trustee's Journal

1946			
Nov. 1	*P. Q.* Co. stock	$10,000.00	
	S. T. Co. bonds	25,000.00	
	L. M. Co. bonds	5,000.00	
	Trust principal		$40,000.00
	To record the principal assets, other than cash, at the inception of the trust.		

1	Dividends receivable	$ 500.00	
	Accrued interest receivable	450.00	
	Income		$ 950.00
	To record the income assets, other than cash, at the inception of the trust.		

Trustee's Cash Receipts Book

			Principal	Income
Nov. 1	Trust principal	From executor	$23,805.00	
	Income	From executor		$2,825.00

Trustee's reports. The trustee's periodical reports may be prepared in the charge and discharge form. The charges and credits shown therein are the credit and debit balances of the accounts in the trustee's ledger, as indicated by the list on page 471. Two statements should be prepared: one for principal and one for income.

Closing the trustee's books. The trustee's accounts should be closed periodically. The accounts showing increases and decreases in accountability as to principal should be closed to the trust principal account. The accounts showing increases and decreases in accountability as to income are closed to the accounts with the income beneficiaries.

CHAPTER 57

Budgets

Nature of a budget. A budget is an operating and financial program for a future period, based on results attained in prior periods and on data obtained by research and analysis. A budget is developed by:

(1) Making forecasts of such items as:
   (a) Sales.
   (b) Production costs.
   (c) Distribution expenses.
   (d) Administrative expenses.
   (e) Financial expenses.
   (f) Additions to capital assets.

(2) Assembling these forecasts of details into:
   (a) An estimated profit and loss statement for the budget period.
   (b) An estimated statement of cash requirements and sources of receipts to meet such requirements.
   (c) An estimated balance sheet at the end of the budget period.

Length of the budget period. The budget period should be long enough to allow for seasonal fluctuations in operations and in financial requirements, and for the length of the merchandise turnover period and the production period. If the budget covers too long a period, many unforeseeable conditions having a material effect on operations may arise. A more workable plan can be formulated for a three months' period than for a period of a year. However, there is considerable advantage in having at least a skeleton plan for a year in advance. It is sometimes found desirable to prepare a skeleton budget for a year and a detailed budget for three months. The skeleton budget is used primarily as a basis for general plans and policies, whereas the three months' budget is used to control the current operations. When the latter method is used, the yearly plan is revised at the end of each quarter to include a year in advance. A yearly budget divided into twelve months, with monthly comparisons, is usually the most successful plan of operation for smaller organizations.

Chapter outline. In connection with the explanation of budget procedure in this chapter, we shall prepare a budget of The *A B* Company. The company's balance sheet as of December 31, 1946, is presented below; the budget will cover the year 1947.

THE *A B* COMPANY — Exhibit A

Balance Sheet—December 31, 1946

Assets			
Current assets:			
Cash		$ 350,000	
Receivables	$1,840,000		
Less reserve for bad debts	90,000	1,750,000	
Inventories:			
Finished goods	$ 623,000		
Goods in process	150,000		
Raw materials	400,000	1,173,000	$3,273,000
Prepaid expenses:			
Factory supplies		$ 15,000	
Unexpired insurance		18,000	
Prepaid interest		7,000	40,000
Fixed assets:			
Land		$ 500,000	
Buildings	$2,150,000		
Equipment	3,500,000		
Total	$5,650,000		
Less reserve for depreciation	1,350,000	4,300,000	4,800,000
			$8,113,000
Liabilities and Net Worth			
Current liabilities:			
Notes payable—bank loans		$ 750,000	
Accounts payable		180,000	
Accrued taxes—local		35,000	
Accrued taxes—federal income		60,000	
Accrued mortgage interest		6,250	1,031,250
Mortgage payable			500,000
Net worth:			
Preferred capital stock		$1,500,000	
Common capital stock		3,000,000	
Surplus		2,081,750	6,581,750
			$8,113,000

To simplify the illustrations, we shall present only the budget for the year as a whole; it should be understood that, for practical use, the budget should be detailed by monthly or quarterly, periods.

We shall first present the estimates of details, such as sales, production costs, expenses, and capital expenditures, and shall then assemble them in the principal budget statements.

Relation of expense and income to cash. The budget should include a statement of estimated income and expense and a statement of estimated cash receipts and disbursements. These statements will naturally differ because of such matters as depreciation and bad debt reserve provisions, accruals and deferred items, and lags between sales and collections and between purchases and payments. Therefore, the estimate of each operating detail should show the amounts to appear in the operating budget and those to appear in the cash budget.

Budgets of Sales and Collections from Customers

Estimated future sales. In the preparation of a budget, the sales estimate is generally used as the basis, or point of departure, because all of the activities of an enterprise are usually limited by its sales possibilities. However, the sales estimates should not dictate the policies of the general budget program, except in so far as the general budget is limited by the sales possibilities. The sales department sometimes prepares the basic estimates, and all other departments are required to make their programs conform to the sales estimates. However, this procedure does not make for a coördinated program. The original sales estimates should be used as a starting basis only; if the carrying out of these estimates would result in an unbalanced program in the other departments, the sales estimates should be revised.

The sales estimates should be based on:

(1) A study of past results. The sales department should be furnished with reports showing the sales of the last several years, analyzed by products, salesmen, branches, geographical divisions, and so forth. These reports should be prepared on a quantity basis.

(2) A product analysis, showing the extent of the demand for each product, the available gross profit, and the distribution cost; such an analysis may show that some products should be discontinued.

(3) A market survey, based on customer demand and competition in various geographical territories, showing the sales opportunities, and indicating where the future sales can probably be obtained with least resistance.

The first sales estimates should be made by the salesmen. Each salesman should be given information, applicable to his territory, regarding past sales; sales opportunities, as indicated by the product analysis and the market survey; and the amount to be spent for advertising. He should also be told the prices which have been tentatively set.

The salesmen's estimates should then be given to the sales executives, who will decide whether to accept or to revise the quotas. No general ratio of increase over last year should be requested; each individual salesman's quota should be considered separately. Last year's sales should be considered as the base in each case, and the amount of any budgeted increase or decrease should be influenced by the ratio of past sales to sales opportunity. In some cases, it will be found conservative not to anticipate any increases in territory that is well covered; and if customers have been overloaded, it may be necessary to consider the possibility of decreases. No salesman should be permitted to undertake a task that is unreasonable, and he should be able to show definitely how he expects to secure his increase. On the other hand, the sales executives should not be satisfied with quotas which are not progressive.

After the final estimates of sales in quantities have been set by the sales executives, it will be necessary to apply the sales prices to the quantities so that the sales may be expressed in terms of both units and dollars.

As a simple illustration, let us assume that The *A B* Company manufactures a single article which it proposes to sell during 1947 at $50.00 each. The following statement shows the estimates that represent the company's sales budget for the year:

THE *A B* COMPANY Schedule 1

Sales Budget

Year Ending December 31, 1947

Salesman	Units Sold, 1946	1947 Estimates Units	Price	Amount
A	13,500	14,500	$50.00	$ 725,000.00
B	18,500	18,000	50.00	900,000.00
C	20,000	21,500	50.00	1,075,000.00
D	19,500	21,000	50.00	1,050,000.00
E	15,000	16,400	50.00	820,000.00
F	17,500	18,200	50.00	910,000.00
G	15,000	16,000	50.00	800,000.00
Total	119,000	125,600	50.00	$6,280,000.00

Collections from customers. The method of estimating cash receipts from collections will depend upon the type of business. If all the sales of the business were cash sales, the total of the estimated sales as shown by the sales budget would represent the cash collections. However, this is very seldom the case, and an analysis will show that the collections will usually involve some lag on sales. This lag may be determined by scheduling the sales by weekly or monthly periods for several prior years and scheduling the collections for the same periods. A graphical presentation of these facts will show the gap between sales and collections.

Another method of determining the relationship between sales and collections is to determine the number of days' billings included in accounts receivable, based upon past experience, as follows:

Computation for The *A B* Company

Sales, 1946	$5,950,000.00
Accounts receivable, December 31, 1946	1,840,000.00
Per cent of sales uncollected = $1,840,000.00 ÷ $5,950,000.00 =	30.92%
Multiplied by	365
Days' sales uncollected	113

The cash receipts from collections for The *A B* Company will be estimated as follows:

THE *A B* COMPANY — Schedule 2

Statement of Estimated Collections from Customers

Year Ending December 31, 1947

Receivables, December 31, 1946 (Exhibit *A*)		$1,840,000.00
Sales for 1947 (Schedule 1)		6,280,000.00
Total		$8,120,000.00
Deduct:		
Bad debts to be charged to reserve	$ 50,000.00	
Estimated receivables, December 31, 1947: 113/365 of $6,280,000.00	1,944,000.00	1,994,000.00
Accounts collected		$6,126,000.00
Probable discounts taken, based on experience of .75% of accounts collected		46,000.00
Cash collections		$6,080,000.00

The Production Budget

Quantity to be produced. The number of units of finished goods to be produced during the budget period should be determined on the basis of the estimated sales, the desired closing inventory, and the available inventory at the beginning of the period. Assuming that the inventory of The *A B* Company, at the beginning of 1947, contains 18,500 units, and that it is desired to have 20,500 units on hand at the end of the year, the quantity to be manufactured may be determined as follows:

THE *A B* COMPANY — Schedule 3

Estimate of Quantity of Finished Goods to be Manufactured

Year Ending December 31, 1947

Required to meet sales deliveries (per Schedule 1, page 476)	125,600
Desired for inventory, December 31, 1947	20,500
Total	146,100
Available in inventory, January 1, 1947	18,500
Quantity to be manufactured	127,600

So far as possible, the production program should contemplate an even flow of production during the budget period, in order to avoid wastes due to the changing and training of labor, overtime rates, dissatisfied employees, and so forth.

Material purchases budget. After the quantity to be manufactured has been determined, it is necessary to estimate the material purchases which must be made in order to meet the production requirements. A specification sheet will be prepared, showing the different kinds and the amounts of materials required to meet the manufacturing schedule.

The quantities to be purchased will be determined on the basis of these specification sheets, with due consideration of the inventories at the beginning of the period and the desired inventories at the end of the period. One of the major values of a budget lies in the proper coördination of the purchasing program and the manufacturing program for the purpose of avoiding excessive and unbalanced inventories.

The purchase requirements based upon material specifications, spoilage allowances (if any), and material inventory requirements may be modified by the amount of material already in goods in process. However, if the goods in process at the beginning of the period represent a normal inventory and if it is expected that a like amount of goods will remain in process at the end of the period, the allowance for goods in process may be ignored.

Assuming that only one item of raw materials is used by The *A B* Company, that there are 20,000 units of this material in the opening inventory, and that it is desired to have 22,500 units in the closing inventory, the material purchase requirements for the year may be budgeted as follows:

THE *A B* COMPANY Schedule 4

Estimate of Quantity and Cost of Raw Materials to Be Purchased

Year Ending December 31, 1947

Required for finished goods to be manufactured (per Schedule 3, page 477)	127,600
Desired for inventory, December 31, 1947	22,500
Total	150,100
Available in inventory, January 1, 1947	20,000
Quantity to be purchased	130,100
Estimated unit cost	$ 20
Estimated total cost	$2,602,000

The purchases should be apportioned to the various months, with consideration of the factors mentioned on the following page.

(1) Minimum inventory requirement to meet manufacturing program.
(2) Maximum inventory allowable.
(3) Purchasing economies.
(4) Quantity which constitutes an economical buy.
(5) Distance from source of supply.
(6) Available storeroom space.

Estimated payments to material suppliers. The payments to material suppliers are estimated as follows:

THE *A B* COMPANY — Schedule 5

Estimate of Payments on Accounts Payable
Year Ending December 31, 1947

Accounts payable, December 31, 1946 (Exhibit A)	$ 180,000
Purchases (Schedule 4)	2,602,000
Total	$2,782,000
Deduct estimated accounts payable, December 31, 1947, representing estimated December invoices	200,000
Accounts to be paid	$2,582,000
Probable discounts to be taken, based on experience of 1.6% of accounts paid	41,300
Cash payments	$2,540,700

The labor budget. The direct labor cost for the manufacture of 127,600 units (see Schedule 3, page 477) is estimated in the following schedule, on the basis of the estimated labor cost in each of the manufacturing departments.

THE *A B* COMPANY — Schedule 6

Estimated Direct Labor Cost
Year Ending December 31, 1947

Department	Quantity to Be Produced	Standard Labor Cost Per Unit	Total Estimated Labor Cost
1	127,600	$ .90	$115,000.00
2	127,600	1.60	204,000.00
3	127,600	1.12	143,000.00
4	127,600	1.75	223,000.00
5	127,600	1.30	166,000.00
	127,600	$6.67	$851,000.00

It is assumed that the direct labor costs will be paid in full during the year; the cash disbursements will therefore be equal to the operating charge.

The manufacturing expense budget. Certain elements of manufacturing expense are fixed charges which will not vary with production; the amounts of other expenses will vary with the quantity of production. In preparing the manufacturing expense budget, it is necessary to have available information concerning the actual manufacturing expenses during prior periods, the relation of these expenses to quantities produced, and the production schedule contemplated by the budget.

Some of the manufacturing expenses will be paid when incurred. Others will not: Depreciation will be provided by credits to reserves; indirect materials will be charged to stores when purchased, and to expense when used; insurance will be charged to a prepaid expense account and written off on the basis of expirations; taxes will be set up in an accrued account, to which payments will subsequently be charged.

The manufacturing expenses and the cash payments therefor are estimated as follows:

THE *A B* COMPANY Schedule 7

Estimated Manufacturing Expenses

Year Ending December 31, 1947

	1946 Actual	1947 Estimates: Expense	Increase (Decrease*): Inventories	Prepaid Expenses	Accrued Expense	Reserves	Cash
Indirect labor	$180,000	$185,000					$185,000
Indirect material	93,000	112,600	$3,500				116,100
Light, heat, and power	67,000	75,000					75,000
Repairs to equipment	65,000	68,000					68,000
Depreciation	330,000	350,000				$350,000	
Taxes	32,000	36,000			$1,000		35,000
Insurance	25,000	27,000		$2,000			29,000
Factory office expense	18,000	18,000					18,000
Total	$810,000	$871,600	$3,500	$2,000	$1,000	$350,000	$526,100

Budget of Cost of Goods to Be Sold

Estimates already made. Thus far the following items to be used in the statement of the estimated cost of goods to be sold during 1947, appearing on page 481 have been determined:

Manufacturing costs:	
Material purchases (Schedule 4, page 478)	$2,602,000.00
Direct labor (Schedule 6, page 479)	851,000.00
Manufacturing expense (Schedule 7, above)	871,600.00
Raw materials inventories:	
January 1—20,000 units at $20.00 each (Exh. *A*, page 474)	400,000.00
December 31—22,500 units at $20.00 each (Schedule 4)	450,000.00
Goods in process inventories:	
January 1 (Exhibit *A*)	150,000.00
December 31 (assuming no change)	150,000.00
Finished goods inventories:	
January 1—18,500 units (Exhibit *A*)	623,000.00
December 31—20,500 units (Schedule 3, page 477)	?

The value of the December 31 inventory of finished goods is estimated on the basis of manufacturing costs for 1947, as determined by the estimates presented on the foregoing pages and summarized as follows:

Estimate of Inventory Value
December 31, 1947

Materials:	
Inventory, January 1	$ 400,000.00
Purchases	2,602,000.00
Total	$3,002,000.00
Less inventory, December 31	450,000.00
Materials used	$2,552,000.00
Direct labor	851,000.00
Manufacturing expense	871,600.00
Total	$4,274,600.00
Units to be manufactured	127,600
Unit cost	$ 33.50
Units in December 31 inventory	20,500
Inventory value	$ 686,750.00

Forecast of cost of sales. On the basis of this data, the cost of goods to be sold during 1947 may be estimated as follows:

THE *A B* COMPANY — Schedule 8

Statement of Estimated Cost of Sales
Year Ending December 31, 1947

Raw materials:		
Inventory, January 1	$ 400,000.00	
Purchases	2,602,000.00	
Total	$3,002,000.00	
Less inventory, December 31	450,000.00	
Materials cost		$2,552,000.00
Direct labor		851,000.00
Manufacturing expense		871,600.00
Total		$4,274,600.00
Variation of goods in process inventory:		
January 1	$ 150,000.00	
December 31	150,000.00	
Variation		—
Cost of goods manufactured		$4,274,600.00
Variation of finished goods inventory:		
January 1	$ 623,000.00	
December 31	686,750.00	
Increase		63,750.00
Cost of sales		$4,210,850.00

Selling and Administrative Expense Budgets

Fixed and variable expenses. The expenses should be estimated on the basis of the amounts for prior years, modified by any changes which are likely to result from the change in sales. Therefore, in making the estimates, it is desirable to divide the expenses into two groups: Fixed, or expenses that are not likely to be affected greatly by changes in sales; and variable, or expenses likely to increase or decrease with the sales.

Some of the methods of increasing the sales are:

(1) Increasing sales price, quantity of sales remaining the same.
(2) Increasing quantity of sales by:
   (a) Selling more goods to present customers.
   (b) Obtaining new customers.

The methods to be employed in increasing sales volume have a direct bearing on the classification of expenses as fixed and variable, and this fact should therefore be kept in mind when the expense budgets are made up. If it is proposed to increase the sales by increasing sales prices, quantity of sales remaining the same, there should be little variation in salesmen's salaries and traveling expenses, freight out, office expenses, bad debts, and so forth; but advertising and promotion expense may increase, in order to overcome sales resistance. If it is proposed to increase sales by increasing the number of units sold, particularly if this is to be accomplished by adding to the sales force and seeking new customers, most of the selling expenses and some of the administrative expenses will necessarily increase.

Selling expense budget. Following is the estimate of selling expenses of The *A B* Company for 1947. All of these expenses will be paid in the month in which they are incurred, except advertising, which will be paid in the subsequent month; the unpaid advertising bill at the end of 1947 is estimated at $30,000.00.

THE *A B* COMPANY — Schedule 9

Statement of Estimated Selling Expenses

Year Ending December 31, 1947

	1946 Actual	1947 Estimate Expense	1947 Estimate Accounts Payable	1947 Estimate Cash
Sales management salaries	$ 33,000	$ 35,000		$ 35,000
Rent of sales offices	28,000	28,000		28,000
Sales clerical expense	18,000	18,000		18,000
Salesmen's salaries	350,000	375,000		375,000
Delivery expenses	93,000	95,000		95,000
Sales commissions and bonuses	60,000	65,000		65,000
Advertising	215,000	252,000	$30,000	222,000
Traveling expenses	90,000	85,000		85,000
Total	$887,000	$953,000	$30,000	$923,000

In addition to this general budget, a separate budget should be prepared, showing the amount of expenditures allowed each of the sales territories, and the amount allowed the general sales office. The sum of these territorial and general allotments will agree with the aggregate budgeted in Schedule 9. All of these budgets should be apportioned by months, so that frequent comparisons can be made of the budgeted and the actual expenses.

Administrative expenses. The theory of budgetary control can be applied very effectively to the administrative expenses of a business. Control of the administrative expenses within certain bounds very often is the deciding factor in producing a profit. Following is the administrative expense budget of The *A B* Company:

THE *A B* COMPANY — Schedule 10

Statement of Estimated Administrative Expenses

Year Ending December 31, 1947

	1946	1947 Estimate		
	Actual	Expense	Reserves	Cash
Management salaries	$ 90,000.00	$ 95,000.00		$ 95,000.00
Depreciation	31,000.00	35,000.00	$35,000.00	
Rent	25,000.00	25,000.00		25,000.00
Corporate expenses	30,000.00	35,000.00		35,000.00
Office salaries *	82,000.00	85,000.00		85,000.00
Office supplies	14,000.00	14,000.00		14,000.00
Communication	12,000.00	12,000.00		12,000.00
Traveling	7,500.00	9,000.00		9,000.00
Bad debts	52,000.00	60,000.00	60,000.00	
Total	$343,500.00	$370,000.00	$95,000.00	$275,000.00

Additions to Capital Assets

Relation to cash and operating budgets. The contemplated additions to capital assets must necessarily be determined before the budget of cash receipts and disbursements can be prepared, because the additions to capital assets will involve expenditures.

The estimates of capital additions should be made by the plant superintendent and the purchasing department, after a consideration of the production budget and the plans for subsequent expansion.

Following is the summary of the budget of plant additions of The *A B* Company:

THE *A B* COMPANY — Schedule 11

Statement of Estimated Additions to Capital Assets

Year Ending December 31, 1947

Land	$ 100,000.00
Buildings	750,000.00
Equipment	450,000.00
Total—to be paid in cash	$1,300,000.00

Financial Budget

Bank loans and securities. The proposed changes in bank loans, mortgages, and stock issues are shown below:

THE *A B* COMPANY Schedule 12
Estimated Changes in Loans, Mortgages, and Stock
Year Ending December 31, 1947

	Balances, December 31, 1946	Changes: Increases	Changes: Decreases	Balances, December 31, 1947
Bank loans:				
Present..........	$ 750,000		$750,000	
New..............		$ 900,000		$ 900,000
Mortgage:				
On old plant—5%.	500,000			500,000
On new plant—6%.		250,000		250,000
Capital stock:				
Preferred........	1,500,000	500,000		2,000,000
Common..........	3,000,000			3,000,000
	$5,750,000	$1,650,000	$750,000	$6,650,000

Interest. The interest expense for 1947 is estimated as follows:

Notes payable, January 1, 1947..........	$ 750,000.00	
Notes payable, December 31, 1947.........	900,000.00	
Total..................................	$1,650,000.00	
Average notes payable....................	$ 825,000.00	
Interest at 6½%....................		$53,625.00
Mortgage payable—old...................	500,000.00	
Interest at 5%........................		25,000.00
Mortgage payable to be dated March 31, 1947	250,000.00	
Interest at 6%..........................		11,250.00
Total................................		$89,875.00

The interest expense charges and the cash payments therefor will differ because of the prepaid and accrued interest.

THE *A B* COMPANY Schedule 13
Estimated Interest Expenses
Year Ending December 31, 1947

	Expense	Prepaid: January 1	Prepaid: December 31	Accrued: January 1	Accrued: December 31	Cash
Interest on bank loans	$53,625	$7,000	$9,000			$55,625
Interest on mortgages:						
Old..............	25,000			$6,250	$ 6,250	25,000
New..............	11,250				3,750	7,500
Total..........	$89,875	$7,000	$9,000	$6,250	$10,000	$88,125

Dividends and Federal income taxes. The dividend and income tax budgets appear on the next page.

THE *A B* COMPANY — Schedule 14

Statement of Estimated Dividend Payments

Year Ending December 31, 1947

	Par of Stock	Rate	Amount
Preferred	$2,000,000.00	7%	$140,000.00
Common	3,000,000.00	8	240,000.00
Total			$380,000.00

THE *A B* COMPANY — Schedule 15

Estimated Income Tax Payments and Accruals

Year Ending December 31, 1947

Tax accrued for 1946—to be paid	$60,000.00
Estimated tax accrual for 1947	$78,000.00

Assembling the Budgets

Working papers. The opening balance sheet is entered in the working papers (see pages 487 to 492), and the budget estimates are journalized and posted thereto.

Journal Entries

Schedule			
1	Receivables	$6,280,000.00	
	Sales		$6,280,000.00
	Estimated sales.		
2	Cash	6,080,000.00	
	Discount on sales	46,000.00	
	Reserve for bad debts	50,000.00	
	Receivables		6,176,000.00
	Collections, discounts, and write-offs.		
4	Purchases—raw materials	2,602,000.00	
	Accounts payable		2,602,000.00
	Material purchases.		
5	Accounts payable	2,582,000.00	
	Discount on purchases		41,300.00
	Cash		2,540,700.00
	Payments to material suppliers.		
6	Direct labor	851,000.00	
	Cash		851,000.00
	Payments for direct labor.		
7	Manufacturing expense:		
	Indirect labor	185,000.00	
	Indirect material	112,600.00	
	Light, heat, and power	75,000.00	
	Repairs to equipment	68,000.00	
	Depreciation	350,000.00	
	Taxes	36,000.00	
	Insurance	27,000.00	
	Factory office expense	18,000.00	
	Factory supplies (inventory increase)	3,500,00	
	Prepaid insurance (increase)	2,000.00	
	Accrued taxes (increase)		1,000.00
	Reserve for depreciation		350,000.00
	Cash		526,100.00

Schedule			
8	Finished goods	$ 686,750.00	
	Goods in process	150,000.00	
	Raw materials	450,000.00	
	Profit and loss		$1,286,750.00
	Inventories at end of year.		
9	Sales management salaries	35,000.00	
	Rent of sales office	28,000.00	
	Sales clerical expense	18,000.00	
	Salesmen's salaries	375,000.00	
	Delivery expenses	95,000.00	
	Sales commissions and bonuses	65,000.00	
	Advertising	252,000.00	
	Traveling expenses	85,000.00	
	Accounts payable		30,000.00
	Cash		923,000.00
10	Management salaries	95,000.00	
	Depreciation	35,000.00	
	Rent	25,000.00	
	Corporate expenses	35,000.00	
	Office salaries	85,000.00	
	Office supplies	14,000.00	
	Communication	12,000.00	
	Traveling expenses	9,000.00	
	Bad debts	60,000.00	
	Reserve for depreciation		35,000.00
	Reserve for bad debts		60,000.00
	Cash		275,000.00
11	Land	100,000.00	
	Buildings	750,000.00	
	Equipment	450,000.00	
	Cash		1,300,000.00
12	Bank loans	750,000.00	
	Cash		750,000.00
	Payment of present loans.		
	Cash	1,650,000.00	
	Bank loans		900,000.00
	Mortgage payable—new		250,000.00
	Preferred capital stock		500,000.00
	Loans, and securities issued.		
13	Interest on bank loans	53,625.00	
	Interest on mortgages	36,250.00	
	Prepaid interest (increase)	2,000.00	
	Accrued interest (increase)		3,750.00
	Cash		88,125.00
	Interest expense and payments.		
14	Dividends on preferred stock	140,000.00	
	Dividends on common stock	240,000.00	
	Cash		380,000.00
15	Accrued taxes—federal income	60,000.00	
	Cash		60,000.00
	Payment of 1946 tax.		
	Federal income tax	78,000.00	
	Accrued taxes—federal income		78,000.00
	Estimated accrual for 1947.		

THE *A B* COMPANY
Working Papers
Estimated Statement of Cost of Goods Manufactured and Sold
Year Ending December 31, 1947

Sheet 1

	Balances, December 31, 1946		Journal Entries		Statement	
	Debit	Credit	Debit	Credit		
Raw materials:						
Inventory—December 31, 1946	$ 400,000				$ 400,000	
Purchases			$2,602,000(4)		2,602,000	
Total					$3,002,000	
Inventory—December 31, 1947				$ 450,000(8)	450,000	
Materials used						$2,552,000
Direct labor			851,000(6)			851,000
Manufacturing expenses:						
Indirect labor			185,000(7)		$ 185,000	
Indirect material			112,600(7)		112,600	
Light, heat, and power			75,000(7)		75,000	
Repairs to equipment			68,000(7)		68,000	
Depreciation			350,000(7)		350,000	
Taxes			36,000(7)		36,000	
Insurance			27,000(7)		27,000	
Factory office expense			18,000(7)		18,000	
Total manufacturing expense						871,600
Total material, labor, and expense						$4,274,600
Inventory variation—goods in process:						
Inventory—December 31, 1946	150,000				$ 150,000	
Inventory—December 31, 1947				150,000(8)	150,000	—
Cost of goods manufactured						$4,274,600
Inventory variation—finished goods:						
Inventory—December 31, 1946	623,000				$ 623,000	
Inventory—December 31, 1947				686,750(8)	686,750	
Increase						63,750
Cost of goods sold (forward to sheet 2)						$4,210,850
Totals (forward to sheet 2)	$1,173,000	—	$4,324,600	$1,286,750		

Sheet 2

THE *A B* COMPANY
Working Papers
Estimated Profit and Loss Statement
Year Ending December 31, 1947

	Balances, December 31, 1946 Debit	Credit	Journal Entries Debit	Credit	Statement	
Totals (brought forward from sheet 1)	$1,173,000.00		$4,324,600.00	$1,286,750.00		
Sales				6,280,000.00(1)		$6,280,000.00
Cost of goods sold (brought forward from sheet 1)						4,210,850.00
Gross profit on sales						$2,069,150.00
Selling expenses:						
Sales management salaries			35,000.00(9)		$ 35,000.00	
Rent of sales office			28,000.00(9)		28,000.00	
Sales clerical expense			18,000.00(9)		18,000.00	
Salesmen's salaries			375,000.00(9)		375,000.00	
Delivery expenses			95,000.00(9)		95,000.00	
Sales commissions and bonuses			65,000.00(9)		65,000.00	
Advertising			252,000.00(9)		252,000.00	
Traveling expenses			85,000.00(9)		85,000.00	
Total selling expenses						953,000.00
Net profit on sales						$1,116,150.00
Administrative expenses:						
Management salaries			95,000.00(10)		$ 95,000.00	
Depreciation			35,000.00(10)		35,000.00	
Rent			25,000.00(10)		25,000.00	
Corporate expenses			35,000.00(10)		35,000.00	
Office salaries			85,000.00(10)		85,000.00	
Office supplies			14,000.00(10)		14,000.00	
Communication			12,000.00(10)		12,000.00	
Traveling expenses			9,000.00(10)		9,000.00	
Bad debts			60,000.00(10)		60,000.00	
Total administrative expenses						$ 370,000.00
Net profit on operations						$ 746,150.00
Net financial expense:						
Interest on mortgages			36,250.00(13)		$ 36,250.00	
Interest on bank loans			53,625.00(13)		53,625.00	
Discount on sales			46,000.00(2)		46,000.00	
Total					$135,875.00	
Less discount on purchases				41,300.00(5)	$ 41,300.00	
Net financial expense						94,575.00
Net income before federal income tax						$ 651,575.00
Federal income tax			78,000.00(15)			78,000.00
Net income (forward to sheet 3)						$ 573,575.00
Totals (forward to sheet 3)	$1,173,000.00	—	$5,861,475.00	$7,608,050.00		

Sheet 3

THE *A B* COMPANY
Working Papers
Estimated Surplus Statement
Year Ending December 31, 1947

	Balances, December 31, 1946 Debit	Balances, December 31, 1946 Credit	Journal Entries Debit	Journal Entries Credit	Statement	
Totals (brought forward from sheet 2)	$1,173,000		$5,861,475	$7,608,050		
Surplus—December 31, 1946		$2,081,750				$2,081,750
Net income for the year (brought forward from Sheet 2)						573,575
Total						$2,655,325
Less dividends:						
On preferred stock—7%			140,000(14)		$140,000	
On common stock—8%			240,000(14)		240,000	380,000
Balance—December 31, 1947 (forward to sheet 6)						$2,275,325
Totals (forward to sheet 6)	$1,173,000	$2,081,750	$6,241,475	$7,608,050		

Sheet 4

THE *A B* COMPANY
Working Papers
Estimated Statement of Cash Receipts and Disbursements
Year Ending December 31, 1947

	Balances, December 31, 1946 Debit	Balances, December 31, 1946 Credit	Journal Entries Debit	Journal Entries Credit	Statement	
Balance, December 31, 1946	$350,000					$ 350,000
Receipts:						
Accounts receivable			$6,080,000(2)		$6,080,000	
Bank loans			900,000(12)		900,000	
Mortgage on new plant			250,000(12)		250,000	
Preferred stock			500,000(12)		500,000	
Total receipts						7,730,000
Total						$8,080,000
Disbursements:						
Material suppliers				$2,540,700(5)	$2,540,700	
Direct labor				851,000(6)	851,000	
Manufacturing expenses				526,100(7)	526,100	
Selling expenses				923,000(9)	923,000	
Administrative expenses				275,000(10)	275,000	
Interest				88,125(13)	88,125	
Federal income tax—1946				60,000(15)	60,000	
Bank loans—December 31, 1946				750,000(12)	750,000	
Dividends:						
Preferred stock				140,000(14)	140,000	
Common stock				240,000(14)	240,000	
Additions to capital assets:						
Land				100,000(11)	100,000	
Buildings				750,000(11)	750,000	
Equipment				450,000(11)	450,000	
Total disbursements						7,693,925
Balance, December 31, 1947 (forward to sheet 5)						$ 386,075
Totals (forward to sheet 5)	$350,000	—	$7,730,000	$7,693,925		

THE *A B* COMPANY
Working Papers
Estimated Balance Sheet—Assets
December 31, 1947

Sheet 5

	Balances, December 31, 1946 Debit	Balances, December 31, 1946 Credit	Journal Entries Debit	Journal Entries Credit	Statement	
Current assets:						
Cash (brought forward from sheet 4)	$ 350,000		$ 7,730,000	$ 7,693,925		$ 386,075
Receivables	1,840,000		6,280,000(1)	6,176,000(2)	$1,944,000	
Less reserve for bad debts		$ 90,000	50,000(2)	60,000(10)	100,000	1,844,000
Inventories:						
Finished goods			686,750(8)		$ 686,750	
Goods in process			150,000(8)		150,000	
Raw materials			450,000(8)		450,000	1,286,750
Total current assets						$3,516,825
Prepaid expenses:						
Factory supplies	15,000		3,500(7)		$ 18,500	
Unexpired insurance	18,000		2,000(7)		20,000	
Prepaid interest	7,000		2,000(13)		9,000	
Total prepaid expenses						47,500
Fixed assets:						
Land	500,000		100,000(11)		$ 600,000	
Buildings	2,150,000		750,000(11)		2,900,000	
Equipment	3,500,000		450,000(11)		3,950,000	
Total					$7,450,000	
Less reserve for depreciation		1,350,000		{350,000(7) 35,000(10)}	1,735,000	
Total fixed assets						5,715,000
Total assets						$9,279,325
Totals (forward to sheet 6)	$8,380,000	$1,440,000	$16,654,250	$14,314,925		

Sheet 6

THE *A B* COMPANY
Working Papers
Estimated Balance Sheet—Liabilities and Net Worth
December 31, 1947

	Balances, December 31, 1946		Journal Entries		Statement	
	Debit	Credit	Debit	Credit		
Totals (brought forward from sheet 5)	$8,380,000	$1,440,000	$16,654,250	$14,314,925		
Current liabilities:						
Notes payable—bank loans		750,000	750,000(12)	900,000(12)	$ 900,000	
Accounts payable		180,000	2,582,000(5)	2,602,000(4) 30,000(9)	230,000	
Accrued taxes—local		35,000		1,000(7)	36,000	
Accrued taxes—federal income		60,000	60,000(15)	78,000(15)	78,000	
Accrued mortgage interest		6,250		3,750(13)	10,000	
Total current liabilities						$1,254,000
Fixed liabilities:						
Mortgage payable—old		500,000			$ 500,000	
Mortgage payable—new				250,000(12)	250,000	
Total fixed liabilities						750,000
Net worth:						
Capital stock:						
Preferred		1,500,000		500,000(12)	$2,000,000	
Common		3,000,000			3,000,000	
Total					$5,000,000	
Surplus (brought forward from sheet 3)		2,081,750			2,275,325	
Total net worth						7,275,325
Total liabilities and net worth						$9,279,325
Other totals forward from sheet 3	1,173,000		6,241,475	7,608,050		
	$9,553,000	$9,553,000	$26,287,725	$26,287,725		

Analysis of the Budgets

Comparisons and ratios. Before the estimates are finally approved, they should be analyzed by preparing comparative statements and by computing ratios, so that the management may determine whether the contemplated results are satisfactory.

Comparative balance sheet. The comparative balance sheet with accompanying ratios, presented below, might cause the management to reconsider the entire budget. The student should note the changes in the balance sheet items and ratios in comparison with the per cent of change in sales, and the decreases in all of the very significant ratios at the foot of the statement.

THE *A B* COMPANY
Condensed Comparative Balance Sheet
December 31, 1946 (Actual) and 1947 (Estimated)

	December 31		Increase (Decrease*)	
Assets	1947	1946	Amount	Per Cent
Current assets:				
Cash	$ 386,075	$ 350,000	$ 36,075	10.31%
Receivables—net	1,844,000	1,750,000	94,000	5.37
Inventories	1,286,750	1,173,000	113,750	9.70
Total	$3,516,825	$3,273,000	$ 243,825	7.45
Prepaid expenses	47,500	40,000	7,500	18.75
Fixed assets—net	5,715,000	4,800,000	915,000	19.06
	$9,279,325	$8,113,000	$1,166,325	14.38
Liabilities and Net Worth				
Current liabilities	$1,254.000	$1,031,250	$ 222,750	21.60
Fixed liabilities	750,000	500,000	250,000	50.00
Total liabilities	$2,004,000	$1,531,250	$ 472,750	30.87
Net worth:				
Preferred stock	$2,000,000	$1,500,000	$ 500,000	33.33
Common stock	3,000,000	3,000,000	—	—
Surplus	2,275,325	2,081,750	193,575	9.30
Total net worth	$7,275,325	$6,581,750	$ 693,575	10.54
	$9,279,325	$8,113,000	$1,166,325	14.38
Sales	$6,280,000	$5,950,000	$ 330,000	5.55%
Working capital ratio	2.80	3.17	.37*	
Acid test ratio	1.78	2.04	.26*	
Ratio of sales to fixed assets	1.10	1.24	.14*	
Ratio of net worth to fixed assets	1.27	1.37	.10*	
Ratio of net worth to liabilities	3.63	4.30	.67*	

Comparative profit and loss statement. The brief statement on page 494 compares the operations for 1946 with the proposed operations for 1947. Although the statement shows an increase in net income, the management might question the slightly increased

THE *A B* COMPANY
Condensed Comparative Profit and Loss Statement
1946 Actual and 1947 Estimated

	1947 Estimated		1946 Actual		Increase	
	Amount	Per Cent of Sales	Amount	Per Cent of Sales	Amount	Per Cent
Sales	$6,280,000.00	100.00%	$5,950,000.00	100.00%	$330,000.00	5.55%
Cost of goods sold	4,210,850.00	67.05	4,100,000.00	68.91	110,850.00	2.70
Gross profit on sales	$2,069,150.00	32.95%	$1,850,000.00	31.09%	$219,150.00	11.85
Selling expenses	953,000.00	15.18	887,000.00	14.91	66,000.00	7.44
Net profit on sales	$1,116,150.00	17.77%	$ 963,000.00	16.18%	$153,150.00	15.90
Administrative expenses	370,000.00	5.89	343,500.00	5.77	26,500.00	7.71
Net profit on operations	$ 746,150.00	11.88%	$ 619,500.00	10.41%	$126,650.00	20.44
Net financial expense	94,575.00	1.50	73,500.00	1.24	21,075.00	28.67
Net income before federal income tax	$ 651,575.00	10.38%	$ 546,000.00	9.17%	$105,575.00	19.34

ratios of selling and administrative expenses, and particularly the large increase in net financial expense; this latter increase arises largely from increases in fixed expenses, which affect the break-even point and may therefore be dangerous.

Similar comparative statements might be prepared to show the details of manufacturing costs and expenses.

Comparison of actual results with budget estimates. Periodic comparisons of actual results with the budget estimates should be prepared. These comparisons should be made frequently, so that variations may be determined quickly and any improper variations investigated and corrected if possible.

If actual results indicate that it will be possible to operate within the budget estimates for the period, no revisions will be necessary. However, if results from time to time indicate that the budget estimates are considerably out of line, it will be necessary to revise the budget in order to take into consideration the new problems which have arisen as a result of current operating conditions. The budget should not be revised merely because some department is not meeting the budget requirements, but should be revised only when current conditions necessitate changes in the program of operations.

The periodic comparison of actual results with the budget is one of the most important parts of the budget program and is the chief means of enforcing the budget.

Classification of accounts. To make the comparison of the actual results with the budget estimates of greatest value, it is necessary that the classification of accounts used in the budget conform to the classification of accounts used in reporting the actual results.

If the proper control of the business is to be exercised through the accounts, the classification of accounts should be so designed that for every person in the business who has power to requisition materials, labor, or funds, there will be a separate account or group of accounts showing what his requisitions have amounted to. Each expenditure should be charged against the account representing the person who has the power to increase, decrease, or eliminate the expenditure. With such a classification, an intelligent study of operating results can be made, and responsibility for desirable and undesirable results can be definitely placed.

CHAPTER 58
Public Accounts*

Governments and institutions. Public accounts include accounts of (1) governments and subdivisions thereof, such as the national and state governments, counties, cities, villages, and park, drainage, and school districts; and (2) institutions, such as hospitals, libraries, and universities.

Sources of assets. The assets recorded in public accounts are derived from the following principal sources:

(1) Taxes and other revenues, including licenses, fees, fines, franchises, and service charges.
(2) Loans, on bond issues or otherwise.
(3) Assessments against property owners for improvements.
(4) Grants from superior governments.
(5) Gifts.

Funds. The National Committee on Municipal Accounting has defined a *fund* as "a sum of money or other resources (gross or net) set aside for the purpose of carrying on specific activities or attaining specific objectives in accordance with special regulations, restrictions, or limitations, and constituting an independent fiscal and accounting entity."†

The authorizations for the levying of taxes or assessments or for the issuance of bonds, stipulate the purposes for which the funds thus obtained may be used. Grants and gifts are usually received subject to definite limitations regarding the uses to be made thereof.

Since each fund is usually available for one designated purpose, it is imperative that a separate group of accounts be kept for each fund, showing the amount of its assets, the liabilities and commitments payable therefrom, and the amount of its surplus, or the excess of the assets over the liabilities and encumbrances of the fund.

---

* Grateful acknowledgement is made to Professor Lloyd Morey, University of Illinois, who read the manuscript of this chapter and made valued suggestions.

† Municipal Accounting Statements, 1941.

The accounts of each fund constitute a complete accounting unit, from which a balance sheet can be prepared. This segregation of the accounts by funds is an important and peculiar feature of public accounts.

Classification of funds. The following classification of funds is not exhaustive; it merely indicates the nature of different funds:

(I) Expendable funds:
- (1) Revenue funds, derived from taxes or other revenue sources, and used for current operating activities:
  - (a) General fund—expendable for all general operating activities of the government or institution.
  - (b) Special fund—derived from revenues specifically raised for a particular purpose, such as a hospital, a library, or a park.
- (2) Special assessment funds to be expended for local improvements, the cost of which will be charged, in whole or in part, to the owners of the property that is regarded as benefited by the improvement.
- (3) Bond funds, arising from the sale of bond issues, and to be expended for public improvements.
- (4) Sinking funds for the payment of indebtedness.
- (5) Trust funds, if principal as well as income is expendable.

(II) Nonexpendable funds:
- (1) Working capital or revolving funds; although expenditures are made from these funds, their principal is kept intact because they are replenished by receipts from other funds.
- (2) Trust funds, if only the income is expendable.

It will be noted that trust funds may be either expendable or nonexpendable. Trust funds may be obtained from public or other sources, and are held for particular, designated purposes. Endowment funds and cemetery-care funds held by a city as custodian are illustrations.

The nature of these various classes of funds will be clarified by the following discussion and by the illustrations of the accounts reflecting the operations of the funds.

In addition to the accounts with the various funds, a group of accounts should be maintained showing the fixed assets owned and the bond issues that are not direct obligations of particular funds.

If utilities are operated, accounts for them will be maintained similar to those of privately owned utilities.

The budget. The operations of expendable revenue funds are controlled by the budget, which shows, with respect to each fund, the authorized estimated revenues and the approved appropriations for expenditures. A well-prepared budget will usually contain:

Three principal statements (illustrated below):
- A budgct summary.
- A schedule showing the estimated revenues classified by sources.
- A schedule of appropriations classified by departments.

Numerous supporting statements, such as:
- A statement comparing the estimated revenues for the current year and the actual revenues for previous years.
- A statement comparing the appropriations for the current year and the expenditures for prior years.
- A statement for each department, showing the appropriations classified according to the objects of the proposed expenditures, such as salaries, office expense, equipment, and repairs.

Budget Summary

Schedule *A*

	General Fund	Special Fund	Total
Unexpended balance (if any) from preceding year, available for expenditure in current year	$ —	$ —	$ —
Estimated revenues (Schedule *B*)	100,000	30,000	130,000
Total	$100,000	$30,000	$130,000
Appropriations (Schedule *C*)	98,000	29,000	127,000
Unappropriated surplus	$ 2,000	$ 1,000	$ 3,000

Estimated Revenues

Schedule *B*

Sources	General Fund	Special Fund	Total
Taxes	$ 71,000	$25,000	$ 96,000
Licenses, fees, etc	29,000	5,000	34,000
Total	$100,000	$30,000	$130,000

Appropriations

Schedule *C*

Departments	General Fund	Special Fund	Total
General administration	$ 30,000	$20,000	$ 50,000
Police department	25,000	—	25,000
Public welfare	8,000	—	8,000
Other items detailed	35,000	9,000	44,000
Total	$ 98,000	$29,000	$127,000

Outline of illustration. The remainder of this chapter consists of illustrative transactions and general ledger entries therefor, applicable to the following typical funds and accounts of a municipality:

General fund.	Sinking fund.
Special fund.	Special assessment fund.
Stores fund.	Trust fund.
Bond fund.	Property accounts.

Following the explanation of the entries in the general ledger accounts of each fund is a discussion of the subsidiary ledger accounts. Finally, the customary balance sheets and other statements are discussed.

To simplify the illustration, it will be assumed that, at the beginning of the period, there are no balances in any fund accounts, and that the only accounts open on the books of the municipality are the following:

Property (debit balance)	$1,000,000.00
Surplus invested in fixed assets (credit balance)	1,000,000.00

These balances are shown, with the identifying number (1), in the summary (page 523) of the accounts of the property section of the general ledger.

General Fund

Transactions. A summary of the general ledger accounts of the general fund appears on page 504; one column is devoted to each account; debit entries are unstarred; credit entries are starred. The entries for the transactions carry numbers that correspond to the numbers in the following statement of assumed facts:

(2) The total estimated revenues for the general fund for the fiscal year, as shown by the budget on page 499, are $100,000.00. Debit estimated revenues; credit unappropriated surplus.

(3) The total appropriations shown by the budget are $98,000.00. Debit unappropriated surplus; credit appropriations.

(4) The tax levy for general fund purposes is $75,000.00; it is estimated that $3,000.00 of this amount will not be collected. Debit taxes receivable $75,000.00; credit reserve for uncollectible taxes, $3,000.00; credit estimated revenues, $72,000.00.*

* To simplify the discussion in this chapter, the credit is made to the estimated revenues account. By this procedure, the estimated revenues account is credited with reductions in estimated revenues and with definite amounts of revenues collected or determined to be receivable. A more refined procedure is to credit items of the latter class to a revenues account. At the end of the period, the revenues account is closed to the estimated revenues account.

(5) Tax anticipation warrants amounting to $30,000.00 are sold for cash at par. Debit cash; credit tax anticipation warrants payable.

(6) Taxes in the amount of $68,000.00 are collected. Debit cash; credit taxes receivable.

(7) Tax anticipation warrants in the amount of $20,000.00 are paid. Debit tax anticipation warrants payable; credit cash.

(8) A loan of $10,000.00 is made to the special fund. Debit special fund; credit cash. (A contra entry in the accounts of the special fund is described later.)

(9) A fund is established for the purpose of purchasing stores to be furnished to all other funds as required by their operations; $5,000.00 is transferred to this fund to provide it with working capital. Debit stores fund; credit cash. (A contra entry in the accounts of the stores fund is described later.)

(10) Materials are requisitioned from the stores fund; the stores fund charges the general fund $1,000.00 for these materials. Debit appropriations;* credit stores fund. (A contra entry will be made in the accounts of the stores fund.)

(11) Cash is transferred to the stores fund in payment for these materials. Debit stores fund; credit cash. (A contra entry will be made in the accounts of the stores fund.)

(12) Commitments are made in the form of orders and contracts in an estimated amount of $20,000.00. These commitments are encumbrances against the appropriations; that is, they reduce the balance which may be used for other purposes; therefore, a memorandum record should be made of the amount thereof, by debiting appropriation encumbrances and crediting reserve for encumbrances.

(13) Certain materials ordered (see transaction 12) are received; two entries are required:

(a) The estimated cost of the materials was $14,000.00, and the memorandum entries for the commitment should be reversed. Debit reserve for encumbrances; credit appropriation encumbrances.

(b) The invoice price of the materials is $15,000.00, and vouchers for that amount are certified. Debit appropriations; credit vouchers payable.

* To simplify the discussion in this chapter, expenditures are recorded by charges to the appropriations account. By this procedure, the appropriations account is charged with reductions in appropriations and also with expenditures. A more refined procedure is to charge expenditures to an expenditures account, which is closed at the end of the period to the appropriations account.

(14) Vouchers totaling $14,000.00 are paid by warrants issued against the treasury. Practice differs regarding the accounting for warrants; two methods are in use:

First method: When warrants are issued by the accounting or disbursing department, debit vouchers payable and credit cash.

Second method: When warrants are issued, debit vouchers payable and credit warrants payable. When paid vouchers are returned by the treasurer to the accounting department, debit warrants payable and credit cash.

Under the first method of accounting, the cash is regarded as reduced immediately by the issuance of the warrant; under the second method, the cash is not regarded as reduced until the warrant has actually been presented to, and paid by, the treasurer. The first method is used in the illustrative entries.

(15) Some of the equipment owned at the beginning of the year is sold for $2,000.00. This cash receipt is not a revenue receipt, but resulted from the conversion of an asset. It was not included in the estimated revenues for the period, and therefore it should not be credited to estimated revenues. Debit cash; credit surplus receipts. (An entry for the cost of the property disposed of, to be made in the property group of accounts, will be discussed later.)

(16) A cash payment of $6,000.00 was made for the purchase of equipment; two general fund entries are required:

(a) For vouchers certified; debit appropriations; credit vouchers payable.

(b) For warrants issued; debit vouchers payable; credit cash.

(Entries recording the cost of this property will also be made in the property group of accounts.)

(17) A cash contribution of $5,000.00 is made to a trust fund, the nature of which is more fully discussed in the comments relative to the trust fund accounts. Debit appropriations; credit cash. (A contra entry in the trust fund accounts is described later.)

(18) A $2,000.00 payment is made to the sinking fund. Debit appropriations; credit cash. (A contra entry will be found in the sinking fund accounts.)

(19) Cash in the amount of $7,000.00 is received from the special fund, in partial repayment of the loan made to that fund (transaction 8). Debit cash; credit special fund. (Contra entry in special fund accounts.)

It is often desired to prepare balance sheets at interim dates during the period; for the purpose of illustrating such a balance sheet, the balances in the general fund accounts after transaction 19 are shown in the summary of these accounts on pages 504 and 505.

(20) Licenses, fees, and so forth, are collected in the amount of $29,000.00. Debit cash; credit estimated revenues.

(21) Additional vouchers are certified, as follows:

For previous encumbrances:

(a) The original estimate of the encumbrances was $4,000.00; reverse the memorandum entries by debiting reserve for encumbrances and crediting appropriation encumbrances.

(b) The invoices received agree with the estimate; debit appropriations and credit vouchers payable.

(c) For miscellaneous expenses, amounting to $56,000.00, for which no encumbrances had previously been recorded; debit appropriations and credit vouchers payable.

(22) Warrants amounting to $55,000.00 are issued in payment of vouchers. Debit vouchers payable; credit cash.

(23) A special assessment fund (to be discussed in detail later) has been created for a local improvement; most of the cost of this improvement will be charged to the property owners; however, $10,000.00 of the cost is to be paid from the general fund, as that portion of the cost is regarded as a public benefit; of this amount, $5,000.00 is to be paid during the current fiscal year. Provision for this expenditure was made in the budget of the general fund, and the transfer of $5,000.00 in cash to the assessment fund should be recorded by a debit to appropriations and a credit to cash. (Entries are also required in the assessment fund accounts and in the property accounts.)

(24) A transfer of $1,000.00 in cash is made to the stores fund to cover the loss in that fund for the year. Debit appropriations; credit cash. (Entry also required in stores fund accounts.)

The balances of the general ledger accounts for this fund, after these transactions have been recorded, are shown in the summary on pages 504 and 505.

General ledger and subsidiary accounts. Before considering the closing entries to be made at the end of the period, it is desirable to comment on the nature of certain general ledger accounts and the subsidiary accounts which support them.

General Fund
Summary of General Ledger Accounts
(000 Omitted)

	Cash	Taxes Receivable	Reserve for Uncollectible Taxes	Special Fund	Stores Fund	Estimated Revenues	Vouchers Payable	Tax Anticipation Warrants Payable	Appropriation Encumbrances	Reserve for Encumbrances	Appropriations	Surplus Receipts	Unappropriated Surplus
(2) Total estimated revenues—per budget						100							100*
(3) Total appropriations—per budget											98*		98
(4) Tax levy		75	3*			72*							
(5) Tax anticipation warrants sold	30							30*					
(6) Taxes collected	68	68*											
(7) Tax anticipation warrants paid	20*							20					
(8) Loan to special fund	10*			10									
(9) Advance to stores fund	5*				5								
(10) Materials requisitioned from stores fund					1*						1		
(11) Cash transferred to stores fund in payment of materials	1*				1								
(12) Contracts made and orders placed									20	20*			
(13) Liabilities on vouchers certified:													
(a) Estimated encumbrance—reversed									14*	14			
(b) Vouchers certified							15*				15		
(14) Warrants issued	12*						12						
(15) Receipts from sale of equipment	2											2*	

(16) Purchase of equipment:													
(a) Vouchers certified							6*				6		
(b) Warrants issued	6*						6						
(17) Contribution to trust fund	5*										5		
(18) Transfer of cash to sinking fund	2*										2		
(19) Collection from special fund	7			7*									
Balances at a date during the period	46	7	3*	3	5	28	3*	10*	6	6*	69*	2*	2*
(20) Licenses, fees, etc., collected	29					29*							
(21) Additional vouchers certified:													
For previous encumbrances:													
(a) Estimated encumbrances—reversed									4*	4			
(b) Vouchers certified							4*				4		
(c) For miscellaneous expenses							56*				56		
(22) Warrants issued	55*						55						
(23) Payment to special assessment fund for public benefit	5*										5		
(24) Cash transferred to stores fund to cover shrinkage therein	1*										1		
Final balances—before closing	14	7	3*	3	5	1*	8*	10*	2	2*	3*	2*	2*
Closing entries:													
Adjust reserve for uncollectible taxes			1			1*							
Close estimated revenues						2							2*
Close surplus receipts												2	2*
Close unencumbered balance of appropriations											1		1*
Balances after closing—carried to next fiscal year	14	7	2*	3	5	—	8*	10*	2	2*	2*	—	7*

* Credit.

The estimated revenues account is debited at the beginning of the period with the total estimated revenues shown by the budget and credited during the period with revenues accrued (with taxes, when levied; with licenses and so forth, when collected). A debit balance indicates that the estimated revenues exceeded the actual revenues, and that the estimated surplus was thus reduced; a credit balance indicates that the actual revenues exceeded the estimates, and that the estimated surplus was thus increased. This account should be supported by a subsidiary ledger containing accounts with each class of revenue, which should be debited with the estimates and credited with the amounts accrued.

As a possibly desirable refinement, the actual revenues may be credited to a separate account; the net balance of the two accounts would reflect the facts stated above to be shown by the balance of the estimated revenues account.

The appropriations account is credited with the total of the appropriations shown by the budget and debited with expenditures made against the appropriations. Appropriation encumbrances (with a debit balance) and reserve for encumbrances (with a credit balance) are memorandum accounts showing commitments made against appropriations. The appropriations account and the appropriation encumbrances account are supported by a subsidiary ledger containing accounts with each department (general administration, police, public welfare, and so forth) for which appropriations were made in the budget. The following illustration shows the money columns that should be provided; proper columns for date, reference, name, and so forth, should appear at the left.

General Fund Appropriation for Police Department

	Encumbrances			Appropriations		
	Debit	Credit	Balance Dr.—Cr.*	Debit	Credit	Balance Dr.—Cr.*
Budget appropriation....					$25,000	$25,000*
Orders placed...........	$1,000		$1,000			
Vouchers issued.........		$800	200	$ 850		24,150*
Vouchers issued.........				3,000		21,150*

The subsidiary account illustrated shows a balance of $21,150.00 in the appropriation for the police department; this balance is subject to an encumbrance of $200.00; therefore, the net available balance is $20,950.00. The credit balance in the appropriations account in the general ledger should agree with the total of all credit balances in the appropriations section of the subsidiary accounts applicable to the fund; and the debit balance in the appropriation encumbrances account in the general ledger should agree with the sum of the debit balances in the encumbrances section of the subsidiary accounts.

Each departmental appropriations account in the subsidiary ledger is in turn supported by an account in an expenditure analysis ledger, in which the charges against appropriations are classified according to the object of the expenditure. For example, the subaccount with police department appropriations might be supported by the following expenditure account:

General Fund—Police Department

Analysis of Expenditures

	Salaries	Office Expense	Supplies	Etc.	Etc.	Total
January (summary)......	$3,000	$300	$550			$3,850

It will be noted that the total debits of $3,850.00 agree with the total debits in the appropriations account for the police department. These accounts in the expenditure analysis ledger furnish the information for the periodical statements of expenditures.

The nature of the tax anticipation warrants payable and the vouchers payable accounts is obvious; they should be supported by subsidiary registers.

The credit balance in the surplus receipts account represents the increase in surplus arising from sources other than revenues.

The unappropriated surplus account balance shows the (estimated during the period, actual at the end of the period) difference between revenues and appropriations.

Closing the accounts. Entries closing certain accounts of the general fund are shown in the summary on page 505.

The reserve for uncollectible taxes is found to be excessive; as the estimated revenues were therefore understated, the reserve is adjusted by debiting reserve for uncollectible taxes and crediting estimated revenues.

After this adjustment has been made, the estimated revenues account has a credit balance of $2,000,000.00, which shows that the actual revenues were greater than the estimated revenues; therefore, the estimated surplus was understated during the period. Debit estimated revenues, to close; credit unappropriated surplus.

The credit balance in surplus receipts represents an addition to surplus; the account is therefore closed by transfer to unappropriated surplus.

Appropriations not expended or encumbered at the end of the period usually lapse; therefore, the unencumbered balance of appropriations ($3,000.00 credit balance in appropriations, minus $2,000.00 debit balance in appropriation encumbrances) is closed to unappropriated surplus.

The summary on page 505 shows the balances in the general fund accounts after the foregoing closing entries have been made. These balances are carried forward to the accounts for the succeeding period.

Special Revenue Fund

Transactions. The precise nature of this illustrative fund is of no significance; it should be regarded as applicable to some particular operating activity, such as a park or a library. Reference numbers appearing below in other than numerical sequence refer to transactions already mentioned in connection with the general fund. The summary of the general ledger accounts for the special revenue fund appears on page 509.

(25) The total estimated revenue for the special revenue fund for the fiscal year, as shown by the budget on page 499, was $30,000.00. Debit estimated revenues; credit unappropriated surplus.

(26) The total appropriations shown by the budget were $29,000.00. Debit unappropriated surplus; credit appropriations.

(27) The tax levy for special revenue fund purposes is $25,000.00; it is estimated that $1,000.00 of this amount will not be collectible. Debit taxes receivable, $25,000.00; credit reserve for uncollectible taxes, $1,000.00, and estimated revenues, $24,000.00.

(8) A loan of $10,000.00 is received from the general fund. Debit cash; credit general fund. (Contra entry in general fund accounts.)

(28) Tax collections amount to $22,000.00. Debit cash; credit taxes receivable.

(29) Materials that cost $2,000.00 are requisitioned from the stores fund. Debit appropriations; credit stores fund. (Contra entry will be made in stores fund accounts.)

(30) Cash is transferred to the stores fund in payment for the materials. Debit stores fund; credit cash. (Contra entry will be made in stores fund accounts.)

(31) Contracts are made and orders are placed in an estimated amount of $12,000.00. Debit appropriation encumbrances; credit reserve for encumbrances.

(32) Vouchers are certified for liabilities applicable to prior encumbrances.

(a) Estimated amount of encumbrances, $10,000.00; debit reserve for encumbrances and credit appropriation encumbrances.

(b) Vouchers certified, $9,000.00; debit appropriations and credit vouchers payable.

(33) Warrants are issued in the amount of $7,000.00 in payment of vouchers. Debit vouchers payable; credit cash.

(19) A transfer of $7,000.00 is made to the general fund in partial repayment of the loan. Debit general fund; credit cash. (Contra entry in general fund accounts.)

The balances in the accounts at this point are shown in the above summary, and are used in the illustration of a balance sheet prepared during the fiscal period.

Special Revenue Fund
Summary of General Ledger Accounts
(000 Omitted)

	Cash	Taxes Receivable	Reserve for Uncollectible Taxes	Estimated Revenues	Vouchers Payable	General Fund	Stores Fund	Appropriation Encumbrances	Reserve for Encumbrances	Appropriations	Unappropriated Surplus
(25) Total estimated revenue—per budget				30							30*
(26) Total appropriations—per budget										29*	29
(27) Tax levy		25	1*	24*							
(8) Loan from general fund	10					10*					
(28) Taxes collected	22	22*									
(29) Materials requisitioned from stores fund							2*			2	
(30) Cash transferred to stores fund in payment for materials	2*						2				
(31) Contracts made and orders placed								12	12*		
(32) Liabilities on vouchers certified:											
(a) Estimated encumbrances—reversed								10*	10		
(b) Vouchers certified					9*					9	
(33) Warrants issued	7*				7						
(19) Partial repayment of loan from general fund	7*					7					
Balances at a date during the period	16	3	1*	6	2*	3*	—	2	2*	18*	1*
(34) Licenses, fees, etc., collected	5			5*							
(35) Additional vouchers certified:											
For previous encumbrances:											
(a) Reverse encumbrances								1*	1		
(b) Vouchers certified					1*					1	
(c) For miscellaneous expenses					15*					15	
(36) Warrants issued	14*				14						
Final balances—before closing	7	3	1*	1	4*	3*	—	1	1*	2*	1*
Closing entries:											
Close estimated revenues				1*							1
Close unencumbered balance of appropriations										1	1*
Balances after closing—carried to next fiscal year	7	3	1*	—	4*	3*	—	1	1*	1*	1*

* Credit.

(34) Licenses, fees, and so forth, are collected in the amount of $5,000.00. Debit cash; credit estimated revenues.

(35) Additional vouchers are certified, as follows:

For previous encumbrances:

(a) Estimated encumbrances, $1,000.00; debit reserve for encumbrances and credit appropriation encumbrances.

(b) Vouchers certified, $1,000.00; debit appropriations and credit vouchers payable.

(c) For miscellaneous expenses not represented by previous encumbrances; amount of vouchers certified, $15,000.00; debit appropriations and credit vouchers payable.

(36) Warrants are issued in payment of vouchers in the amount of $14,000.00. Debit vouchers payable; credit cash.

Closing entries. The balances before closing are shown in the summary; the following closing entries are made at the end of the fiscal period:

The estimated revenues account has a debit balance of $1,000.00, representing the excess of estimated over actual revenues; this debit balance is closed to unappropriated surplus.

There is a $2,000.00 credit balance in the appropriations account, and a $1,000.00 debit balance in the appropriation encumbrances account; hence the unencumbered balance of appropriations is $1,000.00; as the appropriation now lapses, debit appropriations and credit unappropriated surplus.

The summary shows the account balances after these closing entries have been made; these balances are carried forward to the special revenue fund accounts for the succeeding period.

Stores Fund

Transactions. A fund is established to centralize the purchasing of supplies, which are issued to the other funds upon requisitions. Theoretically, the stores should be issued at cost, including a prorated share of the expense of operation; actually, a surplus or deficit may develop, which should be taken up by the general fund. The receipts and expenditures of the fund cannot be easily estimated; therefore, no budget will be prepared, and the accounts of the fund will not be opened by a debit to estimated revenues and a credit to appropriations.

(9) Cash is transferred to this fund from the general fund, to provide working capital for stores fund operations. Debit cash; credit general fund. (Contra entry in general fund accounts.)

(37) Orders are issued for the purchase of stores. Debit store encumbrances; credit reserve for encumbrances.

(38) Stores are received, and vouchers therefor are certified:

(a) The estimated amount of the encumbrances applicable to these invoices was $4,000.00; reverse the memorandum entries by debiting reserve for encumbrances and crediting store encumbrances.

(b) The actual amount of the invoices was also $4,000.00; debit stores and credit vouchers payable.

(10) Stores are issued to the general fund on requisition. Debit general fund; credit stores. (Contra entry in general fund accounts.)

(29) Stores are issued to the special fund on requisition. Debit special fund; credit stores. (Contra entry in special fund accounts.)

(11) Cash is received from the general fund in payment for the materials. Debit cash; credit general fund. (Contra entry in general fund accounts.)

(30) Cash is received from the special fund in payment for the materials. Debit cash; credit special fund. (Contra entry in the special fund accounts.)

The balances in the accounts at this point are shown in the summary on page 512; they are used to illustrate a balance sheet prepared during the fiscal period.

(39) Vouchers are certified for freight, handling, and other expenses. Since all expenses of operating this fund may be considered costs of the stores issued to the other funds, debit stores and credit vouchers payable.

(40) Additional stores are purchased and received. Debit stores; credit vouchers payable.

(41) A physical inventory shows that the cost of the stores on hand is $1,000.00 less than the balance of the stores account. Debit surplus; credit stores.

(24) The working capital of the stores fund was impaired by the inventory shortage, and cash is received from the general fund to replenish it. Debit cash; credit surplus. (Accompanying entry in general fund accounts.)

The balances in the stores fund accounts, after these transactions have been recorded, are shown in the following summary. There are no closing entries; all balances are carried forward to the next fiscal period.

Stores Fund
Summary of General Ledger Accounts
(000 Omitted)

	Cash	Special Fund	Stores	Stores Encumbrances	Vouchers Payable	Reserve for Encumbrances	General Fund	Surplus
(9) Cash received from general fund for working capital.	5						5*	
(37) Orders issued for stores				6		6*		
(38) Liability for vouchers certified:								
(a) Estimated encumbrances—reversed				4*		4		
(b) Vouchers certified			4		4*			
(10) Stores issued to general fund			1*				1	
(29) Stores issued to special fund		2	2*					
(11) Cash received from general fund in payment for stores	1						1*	
(30) Cash received from special fund in payment for stores	2	2*						
Balances at a date during the period	8	—	1	2	4*	2*	5*	
(39) Freight, handling, and other expenses			1		1*			
(40) Purchases			7		7*			
(41) Adjustment of stores account to physical inventory.			1*					1
(24) Cash from general fund to cover shortage of stores	1							1*
Final balances—carried to next fiscal year	9	—	8	2	12*	2*	5*	—

* Credit.

Bond Fund

Transactions. The accounts of bond funds are intended to show the disposition of the proceeds of bonds issued for capital purposes, such as the construction of a bridge or a building. The bonds are not shown as liabilities of the fund, because they are not to be paid from the proceeds of the bonds; the property constructed is not shown as an asset of the fund, because it is not available for further expenditure. The fixed assets acquired and the bond liability are shown in the accounts in the property section of the general ledger. If bonds are issued for special, non-capital purposes, bond fund accounts should be opened, to show the proceeds of the issue and the disposition thereof.

(42) Bonds of a par value of $100,000.00 are authorized. Debit bonds authorized and unissued; credit unappropriated balance. (See accompanying entry in property accounts.)

(43) Bonds of a par value of $75,000.00 are sold for $78,000.00. If bonds are issued for the construction of assets to be used in some revenue-producing activity, such as a municipally operated utility, the premium should be set up and amortized, so that true interest costs can be charged against the subsequent operations. In other cases the premium may be regarded merely as an addition to the amount available for expenditure, and the effect upon interest costs may be ignored; it is so treated in the illustration. Debit cash,

$78,000.00; credit bonds authorized and unissued, $75,000.00, and unappropriated balance, $3,000.00.

(44) A total of $99,000.00 is appropriated for expenditure for the purpose for which the bonds were issued. Debit unappropriated balance; credit appropriations.

(45) A construction contract is signed; the estimated cost is $90,000.00. Debit appropriation encumbrances; credit reserve for encumbrances.

(46) As the work progresses, progress payments are made:

(a) For the estimated portion of the contract completed: debit reserve for encumbrances; credit appropriation encumbrances.

(b) For vouchers certified: debit appropriations: credit vouchers payable.

(47) Warrants are issued in payment of vouchers. Debit vouchers payable; credit cash.

The balances in the accounts at this point are shown in the summary on page 514; they are used in the illustrative interim balance sheet.

(48) The remaining bonds, of a par value of $25,000.00, are sold for $24,000.00. Debit cash, $24,000.00, and unappropriated balance, $1,000.00; credit bonds authorized and unissued, $25,000.00.

(49) The construction contract is completed:

(a) Close the memorandum accounts with encumbrances; debit reserve for encumbrances and credit appropriation encumbrances.

(b) Record the certification of vouchers; debit appropriations and credit vouchers payable.

(50) Vouchers are certified for other expenses totaling $10,000.00. Debit appropriations; credit vouchers payable.

(51) Warrants are issued in payment of all certified vouchers. Debit vouchers payable; credit cash.

The balances in the general ledger accounts of this fund, after the completion of the contract, are shown in the summary on the following page.

General ledger and subsidiary accounts. The appropriations, appropriation encumbrances, and reserve for encumbrances accounts are similar to those discussed under the general fund, and are supported by similar subsidiary records. The nature of the bonds authorized and unissued account is obvious. The unappro-

Bond Fund
Summary of General Ledger Accounts
(000 Omitted)

	Cash	Bonds Authorized and Unissued	Vouchers Payable	Appropriation Encumbrances	Reserve for Encumbrances	Appropriations	Unappropriated Balance
(42) Bonds authorized		100					100*
(43) Bonds sold at a premium	78	75*					3*
(44) Appropriation for purpose of fund						99*	99
(45) Contract signed				90	90*		
(46) Vouchers certified for progress payments:							
(a) Estimated encumbrance—reversed				45*	45		
(b) Vouchers certified			45*			45	
(47) Warrants issued	40*		40				
Balances before completion	38	25	5*	45	45*	54*	4*
(48) Remaining bonds sold at a discount	24	25*					1
(49) Contract completed:							
(a) Encumbrances reversed				45*	45		
(b) Vouchers certified			45*			45	
(50) Vouchers certified for other expenses			10*			10	
(51) Warrants issued in full payment of vouchers	60*		60				
Balances after completion	2	—	—	—	—	1	3*
Closing entries:							
Close appropriations						1*	1
(52) Transfer remaining cash to sinking fund	2*						2
Balances	—	—	—	—	—	—	—

* Credit.

priated balance account is credited with the par of the bonds authorized, and debited and credited with items which decrease or increase the amount available for expenditure; it is debited with the appropriations; its balance, therefore, represents the unappropriated resources of the fund.

Closing the accounts. As shown by the above summary the appropriations account has a debit balance of $1,000.00, indicating that the expenditures were in excess of the appropriation; this balance is transferred to the debit of unappropriated balance.

(52) The cash account now has a debit balance of $2,000.00, and the unappropriated balance account has a credit balance of the same amount. The unexpended cash is transferred to the sinking fund for the payment of the bonds, and the accounts of the bond fund are closed by debiting unappropriated balance and crediting cash. (Contra entry in sinking fund accounts.)

Sinking Fund

Transactions. The accounts of this group show the provision for, and payment of, the interest and principal of bonds and other funded debt. The illustration relates to the $100,000.00 of bonds dealt with in the preceding discussion of the bond fund.

(53) At the beginning of the period, or at the time of the issuance of the bonds, entries should be made showing the amount which must be provided in the sinking fund during the year, to meet principal and interest* requirements. In the illustration, it is assumed that $10,000.00 must be provided for principal and $6,000.00 for interest. Debit sinking fund requirements, $16,-000.00; credit reserve for retirement of bonds, $10,000.00, and reserve for bond interest, $6,000.00.

(18) A portion of the requirements is met by a transfer of $2,000.00 from the general fund. Debit cash; credit sinking fund requirements. (Contra entry in general fund accounts.)

(54) The special tax levy for sinking fund purposes is recorded by debiting taxes receivable, $14,000.00, and crediting reserve for uncollectible taxes, $1,000.00, and sinking fund requirements, $13,000.00.

(55) Taxes are collected in the amount of $10,000.00. Debit cash; credit taxes receivable.

(56) Securities are purchased. Debit investments; credit cash. If securities are purchased with the intention of holding them until maturity, any premium or discount may be amortized.

(57) Interest in the amount of $1,000.00 is collected on sinking fund investments. Debit cash; credit income.

(58) Securities are sold. Debit cash; credit investments. Any profit or loss on sales of securities may be taken up in the income account.

(59) Bond interest for a half year is paid:

(a) Debit reserve for bond interest; credit appropriations.†

(b) Debit appropriations; credit cash.

The balances in the accounts at this point are shown in the summary, and appear in the illustrative interim balance sheet.

(52) The unexpended cash in the bond fund was transferred to the sinking fund. Debit cash; credit sinking fund requirements. (Accompanying entry in bond fund accounts.)

(60) Bonds of a par value of $5,000.00 are retired:

(a) Debit reserve for retirement of bonds; credit appropriations.†

(b) Debit appropriations; credit cash.

---

* The sinking fund may provide for the payment of principal only, and interest payments may be provided for by appropriations from some revenue fund.

† The appropriations account may be unnecessary. If interest payments are provided for through a revenue fund, no credit to an appropriations account (transaction 59) will be required for interest in the sinking fund accounts. Also the credit,

(Since the bond liability is shown in the property group of accounts, an entry for the retirement of the bonds is also required in that group of accounts.)

The balances in the accounts at the end of the fiscal year, before closing entries are made, are shown in the following summary.

Sinking Fund
Summary of General Ledger Accounts
(000 Omitted)

	Cash	Taxes Receivable	Reserve for Uncollectible Taxes	Investments	Sinking Fund Requirements	Reserve for Retirement of Bonds	Reserve for Bond Interest	Appropriations	Income	Surplus
(53) Requirements for the fiscal year					16	10*	6*			
(18) Received cash from general fund	2				2*					
(54) Tax levy for the year		14	1*		13*					
(55) Taxes collected	10	10*								
(56) Securities purchased	11*			11						
(57) Income on securities	1								1*	
(58) Securities sold	8			8*						
(59) Bond interest paid:										
(a) Appropriation							3	3*		
(b) Payment	3*							3		
Balances at a date during the period	7	4	1*	3	1	10*	3*	—	1*	—
(52) Cash transferred from bond fund	2				2*					
(60) Bonds paid:										
(a) Appropriation						5		5*		
(b) Warrants issued	5*							5		
Balances at end of fiscal year before closing	4	4	1*	3	1*	5*	3*	—	1*	—
Closing entries:										
Close income to sinking fund requirements					1*				1	
Close sinking fund requirements to surplus					2					2*
Balances after closing—carried forward to next fiscal year	4	4	1*	3	—	5*	3*	—	—	2*

* Credit.

General ledger and subsidiary accounts. A debit balance at any time in the sinking fund requirements account shows that resources equal to the requirements for the period have not yet been received; a credit balance indicates that the assets received have exceeded the requirements.

The nature of the cash, taxes receivable, reserve for uncollectible taxes, investments, and income accounts is obvious. The two reserve accounts show the prospective disposition of sinking fund assets during the period; when actual dispositions are made, this account is debited and appropriations is credited.

---

to an appropriations account and the immediately following debit to the same account for the retirement of bonds (transaction 60) may be omitted, the two entries for this transaction shown in the illustration being combined into one entry debiting reserve for retirement of bonds and crediting cash.

If there are several sinking funds, applicable to different bond issues, all of the general ledger accounts should be supported by subsidiary records showing the facts with respect to each fund. If the investments of several funds are pooled, the subsidiary investment record will show the investments in detail, but without allocation by funds.

Closing entries. The income account (see summary on page 516) has a credit balance of $1,000.00; this balance is transferred to the credit of sinking fund requirements, because the income collected helps to meet the sinking fund requirements. After this entry is made, the sinking fund requirements account has a credit balance of $2,000.00, which represents the excess of resources obtained by the fund over its requirements for the period—in other words, the surplus of the fund. Therefore, the balance in the sinking fund requirements account is closed to the credit of surplus.

Special Assessment Fund

Transactions. Special assessment funds, frequently found in the accounts of municipalities, arise generally from the sale of local improvement bonds. The proceeds are expended for the improvement; the cost thereof is charged back to the property owners, or in part to the city as a public benefit; and the bonds and interest are paid from the collections from the property owners and the city. Since the bonds are paid from collections received by the fund, they are shown as a liability of the fund.

(61) A $50,000.00 expenditure for a local improvement is approved. Debit available authorization; credit unencumbered balance.

(62) Bonds of a par value of $50,000.00 are authorized. To record the authorization, debit bonds authorized and unissued; credit bonds payable.

(63) Bonds of a par value of $40,000.00 are sold for $41,000.00; the premium realized increases the available balance of the fund. Debit cash, $41,000.00; credit bonds authorized and unissued, $40,000.00 and unencumbered balance, $1,000.00.

(64) A contract for the improvement is signed; the estimated cost is $45,000.00. Debit unencumbered balance; credit reserve for encumbrances.

(65) Vouchers for miscellaneous costs and expenses, totaling $5,000.00, are certified. Debit unencumbered balance; credit vouchers payable.

(66) Warrants for $3,000.00 are issued against vouchers.

(a) Debit vouchers payable; credit cash.
(b) Since the expenditures from this fund are recoverable by charges to the property owners and the city, debit reimbursable expenditures and credit available authorization.

The balances in the accounts at this point are shown in the summary on page 519, and appear in the illustrative interim balance sheet.

(67) The remaining bonds are sold at par. Debit cash; credit bonds authorized and unissued.

(68) Vouchers are certified for the completed contract, at a cost of $45,000.00. Debit reserve for encumbrances; credit vouchers payable.

(69) Warrants are issued for all certified vouchers.

(a) Record the payment by debiting vouchers payable and crediting cash, $47,000.00.
(b) Record the amount reimbursable by debiting reimbursable expenditures and crediting available authorization, $47,000.00.
(c) The contract is now completed and all expenditures have been made. The unencumbered balance account has a credit balance of $1,000.00, representing the surplus of the fund, and this balance is transferred to surplus. Any losses on, or abatements of, assessments may subsequently be charged against this surplus balance.

(70) The expenditures from the fund totaled $50,000.00; of this amount, $40,000.00 is assessed against property owners, and $10,000.00 is regarded as a public benefit. Debit assessments receivable, $40,000.00, and public benefit, $10,000.00; credit reimbursable expenditures, $50,000.00. This entry closes the last-named account.

(23) A collection of $5,000.00 is received from the general fund to apply against the amount assessed as a public benefit. Debit cash;* credit public benefit. (The accompanying general fund entry is: debit appropriations; credit cash. An entry will also be made in the property account section of the ledger, debiting property and crediting surplus invested in fixed assets, $5,000.00.)

* It may be desirable to maintain two cash accounts: one for funds expendable for construction, and another for the payment of bonds and interest.

Assessment Fund
Summary of General Ledger Accounts
(000 Omitted)

	Cash	Bonds Authorized and Unissued	Reimbursable Expenditures	Available Authorization	Assessments Receivable	Public Benefit	Interest	Vouchers Payable	Bonds Payable	Reserve for Encumbrances	Unencumbered Balance	Surplus
(61) Expenditure approved				50							50*	
(62) Bonds authorized		50							50*			
(63) Bonds sold at a premium	41	40*									1*	
(64) Contract signed										45*	45	
(65) Vouchers certified for expenses								5*			5	
(66) Warrants issued:												
(a) Entry for payment	3*							3				
(b) Reimbursable expenditure			3	3*								
Balances at a date during the period	38	10	3	47	—	—	—	2*	50*	45*	1*	—
(67) Remaining bonds sold at par	10	10*										
(68) Vouchers certified for completed contract								45*		45		
(69) Warrants issued in final payment:												
(a) Entry for payment	47*							47				
(b) Reimbursable expenditures			47	47*								
(c) Close unencumbered balance to surplus											1	1*
(70) Assessment			50*		40	10						
(23) Collection from general fund	5					5*						
(71) Assessments and interest collected	16				15*		1*					
(72) Bond interest paid	3*						3					
(73) Bonds paid	5*								5			
Balances at end of period	14	—	—	—	25	5	2	—	45*	—	—	1*

* Credit.

(71) An assessment installment of $15,000.00, with $1,000.00 interest thereon, is collected. Debit cash, $16,000.00; credit assessments receivable, $15,000.00, and interest, $1,000.00.

(72) Bond interest totaling $3,000.00 is paid. Debit interest; credit cash.

(73) Bonds of a par value of $5,000.00 are paid. Debit bonds payable; credit cash.

The account balances carried over to the next fiscal period are shown in the summary on page 519.

General ledger and subsidiary accounts. It is believed that the nature of all general ledger accounts illustrated is obvious. It should be understood that separate subsidiary accounts should be maintained with each special assessment fund, so that there may be no danger of confusion and misapplication of funds.

If, after a particular fund has been closed by the final payment of the bonds, a balance remains in the surplus account, theoretical propriety would require a distribution of the residue of the fund to the property owners and to the general fund in proportion to the assessment and public benefit charges paid by them. Since such a distribution is usually impracticable, the excess is generally transferred to other assessment funds or to the general fund.

Trust Fund

Transactions. Endowment funds, pension funds, and other trust funds may be received by gift or by appropriation of public funds. Usually only the income is expendable.*

(74) A gift of $45,000.00 is received in cash for the creation of a special-purpose trust fund. The gift is conditional upon the appropriation of an additional $5,000.00 from the public treasury, and only the income from the fund is to be expended. For the $45,000.00 gift: debit cash; credit permanent balance.

(17) Cash in the amount of $5,000.00 is transferred from the general fund. Debit cash; credit permanent balance. (Contra entry in general fund accounts.)

(75) Securities are purchased for the fund:

(a) For vouchers certified: debit investments; credit vouchers payable.

(b) For warrants issued: debit vouchers payable; credit cash.

* As already stated, trust funds may be expendable both as to principal and as to income. This illustration deals with a trust fund which is expendable as to income only.

If securities are purchased at a premium for a fund of which only the income is expendable, the premium should be amortized against income.

(76) Income is collected. Debit cash; credit expendable balance.

(77) Expenditures are made for the purpose for which the fund was created:

(a) For vouchers certified: debit expendable balance; credit vouchers payable.

(b) For warrants issued: debit vouchers payable; credit cash.

The summary of the general ledger accounts is shown below:

Trust Fund
Summary of General Ledger Accounts
(000 Omitted)

	Cash	Investments	Vouchers Payable	Permanent Balance	Expendable Balance
(74) Gift received	45			45*	
(17) Contribution from general fund	5			5*	
(75) Purchase of securities:					
(a) Vouchers certified		45	45*		
(b) Warrants issued	45*		45		
(76) Income collected	3				3*
(77) Expenditures:					
(a) Vouchers certified			2*		2
(b) Warrants issued	2*		2		
Balances at a date during (and also at the end of) the period	6	45	—	50*	1*

* Credit.

General ledger and subsidiary accounts. The nature of all general ledger accounts in the trust fund group is obvious. If there are several trust funds, one group of general ledger accounts will be sufficient, but all of these general ledger accounts should be supported by similar subsidiary accounts for each fund.

Property Accounts

Transactions. The property, fixed assets, or plant capital group of accounts shows the cost of fixed assets owned and not appertaining to any fund; the capital liabilities which are not obligations of particular funds; and the excess of such assets over such liabilities, or the surplus invested in fixed assets.

Fixed assets are customarily carried at cost, and are not subjected to depreciation charges, because: (a) No profit and loss statement is prepared (except for utilities, such as water or light plants operated by a city; fixed assets applicable to such plants should be depreciated). (b) There would be no justification for the charge unless it were desired to create a replacement fund by including a provision therefor in the budget; but this would be undesirable because fixed assets are usually purchased from the proceeds of bond issues, and are paid for by assessments subsequent to acquisition. The inclusion of both the sinking fund requirements and a depreciation fund requirement in the same budget would involve a double charge upon the same taxpayers during the life of the bond issue.

(1) The summary on page 523 shows the condition at the beginning of the period, reflected by the debit balance in the property account and the credit balance in surplus invested in fixed assets.*

(15) Certain property which cost $10,000.00 was disposed of. Debit surplus invested in fixed assets; credit property. (The proceeds of the sale, $2,000.00, were taken up in the general fund. The $8,000.00 loss is nowhere recorded.)

(16) Equipment was purchased with general fund cash. Debit property, credit surplus invested in fixed assets. (Contra entry in general fund accounts.)

(42) Bonds of a par value of $100,000.00 were authorized for a public improvement. Debit improvements in progress; credit bonds payable. (Contra entry in bond fund accounts.)

The balances shown in the accounts at this point are assumed to reflect the condition at the date of the illustrative interim balance sheet.

(23) A payment of $5,000.00, representing the portion of the cost of the local improvement that is regarded as a public benefit, was made from the general fund to the assessment fund. Debit property; credit surplus invested in fixed assets. (Accompanying entries will of course be made in the general fund and assessment fund accounts.)

(78) The public improvement for which bonds were issued (transaction 42) has been completed. Its cost, as shown by the accounts of the bond fund, was $100,000.00. Debit property; credit improvements in progress. Any difference between the cost of the completed improvement and the par of the bonds issued therefor would be recorded in surplus.

* Instead of "Surplus invested in fixed assets," the following title may be used: 'Excess of fixed assets over fixed liabilities."

(60) Bonds of a par value of $5,000.00 (authorized in transaction 42) have been retired by payments from the sinking fund. Debit bonds payable; credit surplus invested in fixed assets. (Accompanying entry in sinking fund accounts.)

The balances at the end of the period are shown in the following summary:

Property Accounts
Summary of General Ledger Accounts
(000 Omitted)

	Property	Improvements in Progress	Bonds Payable	Surplus Invested in Fixed Assets
(1) Opening balances	1,000			1,000*
(15) Cost of property disposed of	10*			10
(16) Cost of equipment purchased with general fund cash	6			6*
(42) Bonds authorized for public improvement		100	100*	
Balances at a date during the period	996	100	100*	996*
(23) Payment by general fund to assessment fund for portion of local improvement cost regarded as public benefit	5			5*
(78) Total cost of improvement paid from bond fund	100	100*		
(60) Bonds paid from sinking fund			5	5*
Balance at end of fiscal period	1,10[illegible]		95*	1,006*

* Credit.

General ledger and subsidiary accounts. Complete subsidiary records should be maintained showing the cost of each separate unit of property, and the amount of liability on each bond issue.

Statements

So many different statements may be prepared to reflect the operation and condition of the various funds, that it is impracticable to attempt to do more than mention and illustrate some of the more important statements.

Statement of realization of revenues. From time to time during, as well as at the end of, the period, it is desirable to prepare a statement showing the relation of revenue accruals to revenue estimates, and of revenue collections to revenue accruals. Such a statement may be prepared in the form illustrated on the following page.

Statement of appropriations. Departmental executive officers should be kept informed of the status of appropriations for their

Statement of Realization of Revenues

From .... To ....

	Estimate Per Budget	Accrued			Not Accrued	Collected	Not Collected
		Total	Reserve	Net			
	(a)	(b)	(c)	(d)	(e)	(f)	(g)
	Amounts shown by debits in subsidiary revenue ledger accounts.	Taxes, from debit to taxes receivable in general ledger; other amounts from credits to accounts in subsidiary revenue ledger.	Amount shown by credit to reserve account in general ledger.	(b) – (c).	(a) – (d).	Shown by cash records.	(d) – (f).
General Fund:							
Taxes							
Licenses							
Etc.							
Total							
Special Fund:							
Taxes							
Licenses							
Etc.							
Total							

departments. This can be most easily accomplished by providing them at intervals with copies of the departmental subsidiary appropriation accounts (general administration, police department, and so forth; see page 507). A summary may be prepared in the form illustrated on the following page.

Balance sheets. A balance sheet may be prepared for each fund and for the property accounts. The illustration on pages 526 and 527 shows a consolidated balance sheet prepared at a date during the period. The illustration on page 528 shows the account balances at the end of the period. Either form illustrated could be used for either an interim or a final balance sheet.

It should be noted that the amount shown as appropriations in each section of the balance sheet is the difference between the credit balance in the appropriations account and the debit balance in the appropriation encumbrances account.

The illustrations do not show the treatment of a funded deficit in a revenue fund. If it becomes necessary to issue bonds because of an accumulated deficit, the entries are: (1) debit cash, credit revenue bonds; and (2) debit funded deficit, credit surplus. The bonds should be shown as a liability of the revenue fund, since they are payable from revenues to be raised by the fund. The

Summary of Appropriations

From..................... To.....................

	Appropriations (a)	Expenditures (b)	Unexpended Balance (c)	Encumbrances (d)	Unencumbered Balance (e)
General fund:	Amounts shown by credits in subsidiary appropriation ledger. (See page 506.)	Amounts shown by debits in subsidiary appropriation ledger. (See page 506.)	(a) − (b).	Amounts shown by debits in encumbrances column of subsidiary appropriation ledger accounts. (See page 506.)	(c) − (d).
General administration					
Police department					
Etc.					
Total					
Special fund:					
General administration					
Etc.					
Total					

condition should be shown in the balance sheet somewhat as follows:

Cash	$20,000		Vouchers payable	$35,000	
Taxes receivable	50,000		Appropriations	40,000	
Estimated revenues	10,000		Unappropriated surplus	5,000	
Subtotal	$80,000		Subtotal	$80,000	
Funded deficit	15,000	$95,000	Revenue bonds	15,000	$95,000

Revenues and receipts; expenditures and disbursements. Revenues may differ from cash receipts, because revenues may have accrued and been credited to revenue accounts, although they have not been collected. Expenditures may differ from disbursements, because an expenditure is made as soon as a liability is incurred.

For these reasons it is desirable to prepare, for each fund and for all of the funds combined, both a statement of revenues and expenditures and a statement of receipts and disbursements. In these statements, the revenues and cash receipts should be classified by sources (taxes, licenses, and so forth); the expenditures

Balance Sheet

(At a Date During the Fiscal Year)

Assets				Liabilities and Surplus			
GENERAL FUND:				GENERAL FUND:			
Cash		$ 46,000		Vouchers payable		$ 3,000	
Taxes receivable	$7,000			Tax anticipation warrants payable		10,000	
Less reserve for loss	3,000	4,000		Reserve for encumbrances		6,000	
Due from other funds:				Appropriations		63,000	
Special fund	$3,000			Surplus:			
Stores fund	5,000	8,000		Unappropriated surplus	$2,000		
Estimated revenues		28,000		Surplus receipts	2,000	4,000	
Total			$ 86,000	Total			$ 86,000
SPECIAL REVENUE FUND:				SPECIAL REVENUE FUND:			
Cash		$ 16,000		Vouchers payable		$ 2,000	
Taxes receivable	$3,000			Due to general fund		3,000	
Less reserve for loss	1,000	2,000		Reserve for encumbrances		2,000	
Estimated revenues		6,000		Appropriations		16,000	
				Unappropriated surplus		1,000	
Total			24,000	Total			24,000
STORES FUND:				STORES FUND:			
Cash		$ 8,000		Vouchers payable		$ 4,000	
Stores:				Reserve for encumbrances		2,000	
Inventory	$1,000			Due to general fund		5,000	
Orders	2,000	3,000					
Total			11,000	Total			11,000
BOND FUND:				BOND FUND:			
Cash		$ 38,000		Vouchers payable		$ 5,000	
Bonds authorized and unissued		25,000		Reserve for encumbrances		45,000	
				Appropriations		9,000	
				Unappropriated balance		4,000	
Total			63,000	Total			63,000

Sinking Fund:			
Cash		$ 7,000	
Taxes receivable	$4,000		
Less reserve for loss	1,000	3,000	
Investments		3,000	
Requirements		1,000	
Total			14,000
Assessment Fund:			
Cash		$ 38,000	
Bonds authorized and unissued		10,000	
Reimbursable expenditures		3,000	
Available authorization		47,000	
Total			98,000
Trust Fund:			
Cash		$ 6,000	
Investments		45,000	
Total			51,000
Property:			
Property		$996,000	
Improvements in progress		100,000	
Total			1,096,000
Grand total			$1,443,000

Sinking Fund:		
Reserve for retirement of bonds	$ 10,000	
Reserve for bond interest	3,000	
Income	1,000	
Total		14,000
Assessment Fund:		
Vouchers payable	$ 2,000	
Bonds payable	50,000	
Reserve for encumbrances	45,000	
Unencumbered balance	1,000	
Total		98,000
Trust Fund:		
Vouchers payable	$ —	
Trust fund balances:		
Permanent	50,000	
Expendable	1,000	
Total		51,000
Property:		
Bonds payable	$100,000	
Surplus invested in fixed assets	996,000	
Total		1,096,000
Grand total		$1,443,000

Balance Sheet

(At the End of the Fiscal Year—After Closing)

Assets	General Fund	Special Revenue Fund	Stores Fund	Bond Fund	Sinking Fund	Assessment Fund	Trust Fund	Property	Total
Cash	$14,000	$7,000	$ 9,000	(Closed at the end of the year)	$ 4,000	$14,000	$ 6,000		$ 54,000
Taxes receivable—less reserve	5,000	2,000			3,000				10,000
Assessments receivable						25,000			25,000
Due from other funds	8,000								8,000
Stores on hand and ordered			10,000						10,000
Investments					3,000		45,000		48,000
Public benefit						5,000			5,000
Interest						2,000			2,000
Property								$1,101,000	1,101,000
	$27,000	$9,000	$19,000		$10,000	$46,000	$51,000	$1,101,000	$1,263,000
Liabilities and Surplus									
Vouchers payable	$ 8,000	$4,000	$12,000						$ 24,000
Tax anticipation warrants payable	10,000								10,000
Reserve for encumbrances	2,000	1,000	2,000						5,000
Due to other funds		3,000	5,000						8,000
Reserve for retirement of bonds					$ 5,000				5,000
Reserve for bond interest					3,000				3,000
Bonds payable						$45,000		$ 95,000	140,000
Surplus:									
Unappropriated	7,000	1,000			2,000	1,000			11,000
Permanent trust fund balance							$50,000		50,000
Expendable trust fund balance							1,000		1,000
Surplus invested in fixed assets								1,006,000	1,006,000
	$27,000	$9,000	$19,000		$10,000	$46,000	$51,000	$1,101,000	$1,263,000

and disbursements should be classified by departments (general administration, police department, and so forth), and, for each department, by objects (salaries, supplies, and so forth).

The statement of receipts and disbursements is made from the cash records. Data for the statement of revenues and expenditures are obtained as follows: revenues—from the subsidiary ledger revenue accounts; expenditures—from the accounts in the subsidiary expenditure analysis ledger supporting the subsidiary appropriations ledger. (See pages 506 and 507.)

CHAPTER 59

Bank Accounting

General ledger accounts. The following trial balance shows the account balances of the general ledger of a commercial bank. It should be understood that many of the accounts are controls, which are supported by subsidiary ledgers or other records.

THE *X* NATIONAL BANK
Trial Balance

Cash on hand	$ 2,463,100	
Federal Reserve Bank—reserve account	78,021,000	
Federal Reserve Bank—transit account	4,833,000	
Due from banks—domestic	35,173,800	
Transit account—domestic	2,031,900	
Due from banks—foreign	552,500	
Transit account—foreign	35,100	
Exchange from clearings	3,735,000	
Coupons and bonds in transit	35,700	
Cash items	19,500	
Sundry holdovers	8,600	
Bills of exchange	397,200	
U. S. Government securities	70,812,000	
Other securities	12,597,600	
Stock in Federal Reserve Bank	600,000	
Call loans	2,800,000	
Brokers' loans	3,597,300	
Federal Reserve funds sold	150,000	
Bankers' acceptances	450,500	
Commercial paper	3,337,800	
Banks' and bankers' loans	2,840,000	
Commercial loans	49,021,500	
Advances on foreign bills	145,000	
Other loans and advances	856,100	
Customers' liability on acceptances executed	240,900	
Acceptances executed		$ 240,900
Funds in anticipation of maturing acceptances		27,300
Prepayments on acceptances		30,000
Acceptances of this bank	40,500	
Customers' liability on letters of credit	418,200	
Letters of credit issued under guarantee		418,200
Payments under letters of credit	12,000	
Letters of credit and travelers' checks sold for cash		26,600
Overdrafts	13,200	
Accrued interest receivable	414,900	
Bank building	1,300,000	
Furniture and fixtures	358,400	
Other resources	94,700	
Prepaid expenses	157,800	

Capital stock		$20,000,000
Surplus		3,000,000
Undivided profits		950,600
Contingent reserve		159,300
Bond reserve		182,100
Taxes reserved and unpaid		408,000
Unearned discount		171,900
Individual deposits—demand		136,803,600
Special deposits		295,000
Garnishee accounts		6,400
Trust department deposits		24,104,000
Bank deposits—domestic		38,200,000
Bank deposits—foreign		2,883,000
Bank money orders		407,000
Cashier's checks		3,172,000
Certified checks		2,101,200
Expense checks		29,900
Clearing house return checks		2,400
Public funds		13,853,000
Savings deposits		28,647,000
Certificates of deposit		210,100
Interest and discount		2,735,300
Exchange		29,000
Foreign exchange		3,600
Trust department earnings		188,600
Rents received		45,000
Other earnings		242,100
Interest paid or accrued	$ 700,600	
Expense	1,307,700	
	$279,573,100	$279,573,100

Nature of the accounts. The nature and operation of the accounts shown in the foregoing trial balance are explained in the following comments:

Cash on hand—$2,463,100.00.

Currency and coins on hand are the only items included as cash in the statements and the accounts of a bank. Checks, money orders, and deposits in banks are segregated in the accounts and the statements. As cash on hand is a non-productive asset, a bank will ordinarily have on hand as little cash as possible; the amount will depend partly on the normal requirements and partly on the bank's accessibility to the Federal Reserve Bank.

Federal Reserve Bank—reserve account—$78,021,000.00.
Federal Reserve Bank—transit account—$4,833,000.00.

Every member bank of the Federal Reserve System is required by law to maintain on deposit with the Federal Reserve Bank of its district a certain percentage of its deposits. The percentages are determined (Regulation D, as amended

October 2, 1942) by the types of deposits and the bank's location, thus:

(A) An actual net balance equal to 6% of its time deposits, plus:

(B) If the bank is not in a reserve or central reserve city, 14% of its net demand deposits;

(C) If the bank is in one of the sixty-four reserve cities, 20% of its net demand deposits, except that a bank located in an outlying district of a reserve city or in a territory added to such city by the extension of the city's corporate limits may be permitted, upon the affirmative vote of five members of the Board of Governors of the Federal Reserve System, to maintain 14% reserves against its net demand deposits;

(D) If the bank is located in a central reserve city, 20% of its net demand deposits, except that a bank located in an outlying district of a central reserve city or in a territory added to such city by the extension of the city's corporate limits may be permitted, upon the affirmative vote of five members of the Board of Governors of the Federal Reserve System, to maintain 14% to 20% reserves against its net demand deposits.

Notwithstanding any other provision of this regulation, the actual net balance which each member bank is required to maintain on deposit with the Federal Reserve Bank of its district in accordance with the foregoing shall be changed by such percentage within the limitations prescribed by law as the Board of Governors of the Federal Reserve System shall prescribe from time to time pursuant to the sixth paragraph of Section 19 of the Federal Reserve Act, as amended, in order to prevent injurious credit expansion or contraction. The amount of the reserve required by such member bank as a result of any such change may not be less than the amount of the reserve specified under Regulation D as amended effective July 14, 1942, nor more than twice such amount. On the aforementioned date, reserves specified for A, B, C, and D above, were 3%, 7%, 10% and 13% respectively.

Items deposited with, or cleared through, the Federal Reserve Bank are ordinarily recorded in the transit account until the credits are reported by the Reserve Bank, when they are transferred from the transit account to the reserve account. The proceeds of paper rediscounted with the Reserve Bank are credited directly to the reserve account.

Due from banks—domestic—$35,173,800.00.
Transit account—domestic— 2,031,900.00.

Banks normally maintain deposits with the correspondent banks through which their out-of-town checks, drafts and collection items are cleared; therefore, a daily settlement for items cleared is not necessary. Such items are charged to the transit account until the credits are reported by the correspondent bank, when they are transferred to the due from banks account.

Due from banks—foreign—$552,500.00.
Transit account—foreign—$35,100.00.

These two accounts are operated in the same manner as the corresponding domestic accounts. They are kept in both foreign and domestic currencies.

Exchange from clearings—$3,735,000.00.

The balance of this account represents cash items on other banks in the same city in process of collection.

Coupons and bonds in transit—$35,700.00.

Coupons and matured bonds presented to the bank by customers for collection are charged to, and carried in, this account until collected; after the coupons and bonds are collected, this account is credited, and due from banks or some other asset account is debited.

Cash items—$19,500.00.
Sundry holdovers—$8,600.00.

These accounts are charged with collection and clearing items received too late to be put through the afternoon clearings. Items received by the tellers after the close of banking hours and held overnight in their cages are charged to cash items; items which have passed through the clearing department are charged to sundry holdovers.

Bills of exchange—$397,200.00.

This account is charged with notes and drafts received from customers for collection.

U. S. government securities—$70,812,000.00.
Other securities—$12,597,600.00.

These two accounts are charged with securities acquired.

Stock in Federal Reserve Bank—$600,000.00.

All banks that are members of the Federal Reserve System are required to subscribe for Federal Reserve Bank stock in an amount equal to 6% of their capital stock and paid-in surplus; only one half of these subscriptions has been called. Stock holders are entitled to 6% cumulative dividends on their paid-up stock.

Call loans—$2,800,000.00.
Brokers' loans—$3,597,300.00.

Both of these accounts are charged with loans to brokers, secured by readily marketable collateral and payable on demand—usually with twenty-four hours' notice. The distinction between the two accounts lies principally in the manner in which the loans are made: Brokers' loans are made by direct negotiation with the brokers; call loans are normally made in the New York call money market through the bank's New York correspondent. The interest rate on call loans varies with the call-loan rate in the stock exchange.

Federal reserve funds sold—$150,000.00.

If a member bank finds itself in need of funds for a short period, say twenty-four hours, it may call its principal correspondent or bank of deposit and ask that bank to authorize the Federal Reserve Bank to charge its account for the amount requested and credit the account of the bank needing the funds. The bank selling the funds will debit Federal Reserve funds sold and credit its Federal Reserve Bank reserve account. The bank buying the funds will debit its Federal Reserve Bank reserve account and credit Federal Reserve funds bought. These entries will be reversed when settlement is made. The bank selling the funds is entitled to interest income on the transaction.

The transaction can also be handled by having the selling bank issue to the bank needing the funds its draft drawn on the Federal Reserve Bank, which the bank requiring the funds will deposit to its reserve account with the Federal Reserve Bank; settlement can be effected by a subsequent issuance of a draft by the bank which had obtained the funds.

Bankers' acceptances—$450,500.00.

This account is charged with the cost of bankers' acceptances purchased in the open market. These drafts usually arise through export and import transactions.

Commercial paper—$3,337,800.00.

This account shows the cost of short-term notes acquired from commercial paper brokers.

Banks' and bankers' loans—$2,840,000.00.

The debit balance in this account shows the amount of loans made directly to other banks and bankers.

Commercial loans—$49,021,500.00.

This account is charged with the amount of direct loans made to customers on their secured or unsecured notes, and of indirect loans made to them by the discounting of notes or acceptances held by them.

Advances on foreign bills—$145,000.00.

This account is charged with payments made to customers on foreign drafts discounted. Because of the greater risk involved in foreign drafts than in domestic drafts, the longer and less definite collection period, the exchange restrictions, and the uncertainty about the charges which will be made by the bank's correspondents, banks frequently advance only a portion, usually about 80%, of the discounted value of the drafts, and make a final settlement with the customer after receipt of the collection advice.

Other loans and advances—$856,100.00.

This account is charged with loans, such as those made on real estate, which do not belong in any of the foregoing classifications.

Customers' liability on acceptances executed—$240,900.00 (debit).
Acceptances executed—$240,900.00 (credit).
Funds in anticipation of maturing acceptances—$27,300.00 (credit).
Prepayments on acceptances—$30,000.00 (credit).
Acceptances of this bank—$40,500.00 (debit).

In the simple acceptance transaction, the bank makes no actual advance of funds; by the act of acceptance, it merely promises to pay the draft at its maturity. The bank's customer, by a corollary agreement, promises to turn over to the bank the necessary funds before the maturity date, or authorizes the bank to charge paid acceptances to his account.

The bank's liability on the acceptance, although a direct liability, is thus offset by the customer's liability to the bank.

The following entry is made by the bank at the time of acceptance:

Customers' liability on acceptances executed...	$xx,xxx.xx	
Acceptances executed....................		$xx,xxx.xx

These two accounts remain on the books until the maturity of the acceptance, when they are reversed.

If the customer pays in the entire amount of the acceptance before its maturity, such payment is credited to the funds in anticipation of maturing acceptances account. Partial payments by customers in advance of maturity are credited to the prepayments on acceptances account. Some banks with a small acceptance business do not keep the two latter accounts, but merely credit customers' advance payments to the customers' liability on acceptances executed account.

When the acceptance has matured, it will be presented to the bank for payment; two entries will be required:

(1) To reverse the accounts set up at the time of acceptance:

Acceptances executed........................	$xx,xxx.xx	
Customers' liability on acceptances executed		$xx,xxx.xx

(2) To record the payment; this entry will vary somewhat according to the circumstances:

(a) If the customer has paid in the entire amount of the acceptance:

Funds in anticipation of maturing acceptances....	$xx,xxx.xx	
Due to banks (bank presenting acceptance)..		$xx,xxx.xx

(b) If the customer has made a partial payment in advance:

Prepayment on acceptances (for amount of payment)................................	$x,xxx.xx	
Customer's deposit account (for balance)..........	x,xxx.xx	
Due to banks............................		$xx,xxx.xx

(c) If the customer has made no payment in advance:

Customer's deposit account....................	$xx,xxx.xx	
Due to banks............................		$xx,xxx.xx

A bank may purchase its own acceptances in the open market before their maturity, just as it may purchase the acceptances of other banks; such purchases will be recorded in the acceptances of this bank account, which appears in the bank's balance sheet under the caption of loans and discounts. Purchased acceptances are eliminated from customers' liability on acceptances executed, and from acceptances executed, on the asset and liability sides of the balance sheet respectively, as shown below. (These eliminations are made to prevent a duplication of the asset, and to remove the liability now nonexistent.)

Resources

Loans and discounts:			
Acceptances of this bank			$ 40,500.00
Customers' liability on acceptances outstanding:			
Customers' liability on acceptances executed		$240,900.00	
Less:			
Funds in anticipation of maturing acceptances	$27,300.00		
Prepayments on acceptances	30,000.00		
Acceptances acquired	40,500.00	97,800.00	143,100.00

Liabilities

Acceptances outstanding:		
Acceptances executed	$240,900.00	
Less acceptances acquired	40,500.00	$200,400.00

The entries to be made at the maturity of an acceptance purchased and carried in the acceptances of this bank account, would be the same as those, already described, to be made at the time of the payment of an acceptance, except that the bank would credit acceptances of this bank instead of due to banks, in entry (2).

Customers' liability on letters of credit—$418,200.00 (debit).
Letters of credit issued under guarantee—$418,200.00 (credit).
Payments under letters of credit—$12,000.00 (debit).
Letters of credit and travelers' checks sold for cash—$26,600.00 (credit).

Commercial letters of credit are documents stating that the issuing bank will honor drafts under certain conditions and within certain limits. They are usually issued with the understanding that the customer's account will be charged, not with the amount of the letter of credit issued, but with the amounts of the drafts drawn against the letter and paid by the bank. Typical entries are shown below:

At the time the letter is issued:

Customers' liability on letters of credit	$xx,xxx.xx	
Letters of credit issued under guarantee		$xx,xxx.xx

When sight drafts drawn against the letter of credit are paid by the bank, the entries are:

Payments under letters of credit (or customer's deposit account)	$x,xxx.xx	
Due from banks (domestic or foreign)		$x,xxx.xx

The account, payments under letters of credit, is charged when, by agreement, the customer is to take up all of the drafts (plus interest) at the exhaustion of the credit, or at a specified future date, rather than at the date of payment by the bank. Otherwise the customer's deposit account is charged.

Letters of credit issued under guarantee..........	$x,xxx.xx	
Customers' liability on letters of credit......		$x,xxx.xx

When time drafts drawn against a letter of credit are accepted by the bank, the following entries are made:

Letters of credit issued under guarantee..........	$x,xxx.xx	
Customers' liability on letters of credit......		$x,xxx.xx
Customers' liability on acceptances executed.....	x,xxx.xx	
Acceptances executed..........................		x,xxx.xx

The payment of the acceptances is recorded in the manner discussed in the preceding section, dealing with acceptances.

When letters of credit or travelers' checks are issued for cash, the bank's entry is:

Cash (or due from banks)......................	$x,xxx.xx	
Letters of credit and travelers' checks sold for cash....................................		$x,xxx.xx

Subsequent payments made by the bank against such letters are charged to the liability account.

Overdrafts—$13,200.00.

When customers' checks are honored in amounts in excess of their credit balances, the resulting debit balances are controlled through this account.

Other resources—$94,700.00.

Any merchandise or other assets that the bank may have taken over in settlement of a loan, or any miscellaneous receivables, are usually classified as other resources.

Capital stock—$20,000,000.00.
Surplus—$3,000,000.00.
Undivided profits—$950,600.00.

At the time of organization, banks very frequently issue their stock at a premium and thus create an immediate surplus. Profits are accumulated in the undivided profits account, and transferred to surplus in round amounts.

Contingent reserve—$159,300.00.
Bond reserve—$182,100.00.
Taxes reserved and unpaid—$408,000.00.

The contingent reserve is intended chiefly as a provision for losses on loans; it is sometimes created by monthly charges to operations, but more frequently by end-of-year provisions. The bond reserve is a provision for declines in the value of bonds and other investments. The tax reserve is a provision for the tax accrual.

Unearned discount—$171,900.00.

This is a deferred credit account, representing discounts deducted in making loans but not yet earned by the expiration of the loan period.

Individual deposits—demand—$136,803,600.00.
Special deposits—$295,000.00.
Garnishee accounts—$6,400.00.
Trust department deposits—$24,104,000.00.
Bank deposits—domestic—$38,200,000.00.
Bank deposits—foreign—$2,883,000.00.

All of these credit balances reflect demand liabilities. Special deposits include such items as deposits in escrow, balances of deceased persons, and deposits under court jurisdiction. Deposits that have been garnisheed by a creditor are not available to the depositor and are controlled by a special account. Trust department deposits represent uninvested funds held by the trust department for various trusts. The nature of the other deposit accounts is obvious.

Bank money orders—$407,000.00.
Cashier's checks—$3,172,000.00.
Certified checks —$2,101,200.00.
Expense checks —$29,900.00.
Clearing house return checks—$2,400.00.

Bank money orders and *cashier's checks* are the bank's own checks issued to its customers as a convenience. *Certified checks* are depositors' checks certified by the bank, and consequently segregated from the depositors' accounts. *Expense checks* are the bank's own checks issued in payment for expenses, and carried as a liability until presented for payment. *Clearing house return checks* are the bank's own checks, issued to other banks to take up clearing house return items.

Public funds—$13,853,000.00.

These accounts represent municipal, state, and Federal deposits.

Banks are frequently required to deposit Government bonds as collateral for such accounts.

At the time of this writing, two additional accounts are of sufficient importance to deserve mention; they are (1) War loan deposit account—U. S. Treasury Department, which is credited with funds received by the bank for sales of war bonds and other government securities sold by it in connection with war bond campaigns; and (2) Withheld taxes—U. S. Treasury Department, which is credited with deposits, by customers of the bank and others who have made arrangements, of amounts deducted from employees' wage or salary payments.

Savings deposits—$28,647,000.00.

These deposits bear interest and are not subject to check. Under ordinary conditions, banks pay such deposits on demand, but the deposit agreement permits the bank to require a thirty-day or a sixty-day notice.

Certificates of deposit—$210,100.00.

These accounts represent interest-bearing time deposits.

Interest and discount—$2,735,300.00.
Exchange—$29,000.00.
Foreign exchange—$3,600.00.
Trust department earnings—$188,600.00.
Rents received—$45,000.00.
Other earnings—$242,100.00.
Interest paid or accrued—$700,600.00.
Expense—$1,307,700.00.

The nature of each of these income and expense accounts is apparent from its title.

Statements. The following statements illustrate how the account balances shown by the trial balance are assembled in the income statement and in the statement of condition, or balance sheet. Two statements of condition are presented: one showing the assets and liabilities in detail, and another which has been condensed by grouping related items.

THE *X* NATIONAL BANK

Detailed Statement of Condition

(Date)

Resources

Cash and due from banks:			
Cash on hand		$ 2,463,100	
Federal Reserve Bank—reserve account		78,021,000	
Federal Reserve Bank—transit account		4,833,000	
Due from sundry banks—domestic		35,173,800	
Transit account—domestic		2,031,900	
Exchange from clearings		3,735,000	
Due from sundry banks—foreign		552,500	
Transit account—foreign		35,100	
Coupons and bonds in transit		35,700	
Cash items		19,500	
Sundry holdovers		8,600	
Bills of exchange		397,200	$127,306,400
Investments:			
U.S. Government securities		$70,812,000	
State and municipal bonds and other securities		12,597,600	
Stock in Federal Reserve Bank		600,000	84,009,600
Loans and discounts:			
Call loans		$ 2,800,000	
Brokers' loans		3,597,300	
Federal reserve funds sold		150,000	
Bankers' acceptances		450,500	
Commercial paper		3,337,800	
Banks' and bankers' loans		2,840,000	
Commercial loans		49,021,500	
Acceptances of this bank		40,500	
Payments under letters of credit		12,000	
Advances on foreign bills		145,000	
Other loans and advances		856,100	63,250,700
Accrued interest receivable			414,900
Customers' liability on acceptances executed		$ 240,900	
Less:			
Funds in anticipation of maturing acceptances	$27,300		
Prepayments on acceptances	30,000		
Acceptances acquired	40,500	97,800	143,100
Customers' liability on letters of credit			418,200
Bank building			1,300,000
Other resources:			
Furniture and fixtures		$ 358,400	
Other resources		94,700	
Overdrafts		13,200	
Prepaid expenses		157,800	624,100
			$277,467,000

Liabilities

Capital, surplus, and undivided profits:		
Capital stock	$ 20,000,000	
Surplus	3,000,000	
Undivided profits	2,185,900	$ 25,185,900
Reserves:		
Contingent reserve	$ 159,300	
Bond reserve	182,100	
Taxes reserved and unpaid	408,000	
Unearned discount	171,900	921,300
Deposits:		
Demand:		
Individual	$136,803,600	
Special deposits	295,000	
Garnishee accounts	6,400	
Trust department deposits	24,104,000	
Bank deposits—domestic	38,200,000	
Bank deposits—foreign	2,883,000	
Certified checks	2,101,200	
Bank money orders	407,000	
Cashier's checks	3,172,000	
Expense checks	29,900	
Clearing house return checks	2,400	
Letters of credit and travelers' checks sold for cash	26,600	
Total	$208,031,100	
Public funds	13,853,000	
Total demand deposits	$221,884,100	
Time:		
Certificates of deposit	$ 210,100	
Savings deposits	28,647,000	
Total time deposits	$ 28,857,100	250,741,200
Acceptances executed	$ 240,900	
Less acceptances acquired	40,500	200,400
Letters of credit issued under guarantee		418,200
		$277,467,000

Note. United States Government and other securities carried at $16,410,000.00 are pledged to secure public and trust deposits and for other purposes as required or permitted by law.

THE *X* NATIONAL BANK
Condensed Statement of Condition
(Date)

Resources		Liabilities		
Cash and due from banks	$127,306,400	Capital stock		$ 20,000,000
U. S. Government securities	70,812,000	Surplus		3,000,000
State, municipal, and other securities	12,597,600	Undivided profits		2,185,900
Federal Reserve Bank stock	600,000	Reserves		921,300
Loans and discounts	63,250,700	Deposits:		
Accrued interest receivable	414,900	Time	$ 28,857,100	
Bank building	1,300,000	Demand	208,031,100	
Other resources	624,100	Public funds	13,853,000	250,741,200
Customers' liability on acceptances outstanding	143,100	Acceptances outstanding		200,400
	$277,048,800			$277,048,800

Notes. United States Government and other securities carried at $16,410,000.00 are pledged to secure public and trust deposits and for other purposes required or permitted by law.

Contingent liability on letters of credit issued under guarantee, $418,200.00.

THE *X* NATIONAL BANK
Statement of Net Earnings
Year Ended——————

Earnings:		
Interest and discount	$2,735,300.00	
Exchange	29,000.00	
Foreign exchange	3,600.00	
Trust department earnings	188,600.00	
Rents received	45,000.00	
Other earnings	242,100.00	
Total earnings		$3,243,600.00
Expenses:		
Interest paid or accrued	$ 700,600.00	
Operating expenses	1,307,700.00	
Total expenses		2,008,300.00
Net earnings		$1,235,300.00

CHAPTER 60

Stock Brokerage*

Broker's services to his customers. The principal services rendered by a stockbroker to his customers are the following:

(1) Acting as their agents in the purchase and sale of securities. The broker is better able to make these purchases and sales for his customers than they are to make them for themselves, because the broker, through his stock exchange memberships and his contacts with other brokers has extensive information regarding the demand for and the supply of securities in which his customers desire to trade. Since he possesses this information, he is in a position to buy and sell a security at the most advantageous price obtainable in various markets.

The broker's service as agent for his customer also includes the guaranteeing of the accounts arising from sales; in other words, the broker acts as a *del credere* agent.

(2) Providing information with respect to the financial status, earnings, and management of the companies whose securities are purchased and sold by his customers, and also information concerning the changes in the price of these securities.

(3) Assisting his customers in the financing of their purchases. The customer may deposit with the broker only a portion of the purchase price. The broker, under such circumstances, advances the remainder of the funds necessary to pay for the securities purchased.

This method of borrowing is a very convenient one for the customer. As no time limit is placed on the loan, it is not necessary for the customer to arrange for renewals. Moreover, the amount of the loan is flexible; it is determined by the customer's changing requirements, and is increased and decreased to conform with them. Such extension of credit must meet the requirements set by

---

* For invaluable assistance in the preparation of this chapter, the author acknowledges his indebtedness to Mr. Herbert Levy, C. P. A., associate of the American Institute of Accountants, general partner in the firm of Paine, Webber, Jackson & Curtis, and lecturer on brokerage accounting at Northwestern University.

the Federal Reserve Board as empowered by the Securities and Exchange Commission Act of 1934. These regulations do not apply beyond the original extension of credit, and from this point on brokers must determine their own marginal requirements, subject to Stock Exchange regulations setting minimum requirements.

The funds loaned by the broker to his customers are obtained in part from the broker's capital investment, in part from customers' free credits, and in part from bank loans. To obtain these bank loans, the broker pledges his own securities or rehypothecates the securities left with him by his customers as collateral to their accounts. Securities belonging to partners, either as part of their capital or in personal accounts, may not be used in a loan commingled with customers' securities.

(4) Providing facilities for safeguarding the securities which his customers leave with him to collateralize their accounts and to facilitate the prompt delivery of securities which they may order him to sell. While the securities are in his possession, the broker renders his customers the further service of collecting the interest and dividends on them. In the long and short record an account is carried on the short side called *box* or *drawer*, which refers to negotiable securities on hand in a brokerage office. Although many brokers do not distinguish between securities available as collateral and those being held in safekeeping on the long and short record, those in safekeeping must be physically segregated from those available for use as collateral.

The stock exchange. The stock exchange provides a convenient place where brokers with orders to sell may meet other brokers with orders to buy. In addition, if a clearing house is operated by the exchange, it greatly facilitates the settlement of transactions. Settlement procedures differ, but the theory of the clearing house may be illustrated as follows:

On a certain day:

Broker Brown sold Broker Jones 2,000 shares of *B* Company stock for $65,000.00.

Broker Jones sold Broker Smith 3,000 shares of *B* Company stock for $97,800.00.

Broker Smith sold Broker Brown 2,000 shares of *B* Company stock for $65,100.00.

Settlements for these transactions require payments of cash and deliveries of securities that may be facilitated by the clearing house, as explained in the following summary:

	Brown	Jones	Smith
Cash receipts and payments*			
If each broker were obliged to make a separate settlement with each other broker:			
Brown would collect from Jones	$65,000	$65,000*	
Jones would collect from Smith		97,800	$97,800*
Smith would collect from Brown	65,100*		65,100
But settlement through the clearing house may be made on the basis of differences, thus:			
Brown pays the clearing house	$ 100*		
Smith pays the clearing house			$32,700*
Jones collects from the clearing house		$32,800	
Security receipts and deliveries*			
If each broker were obliged to make a separate settlement with each other broker, the number of shares delivered would be:			
Brown would deliver to Jones	2,000*	2,000	
Jones would deliver to Smith		3,000*	3,000
Smith would deliver to Brown	2,000		2,000*
But settlement through the clearing house may be made on the basis of differences, thus:			
Brown delivers and receives no shares	—		
Jones delivers to the clearing house		1,000*	
Smith receives from the clearing house			1,000

Thus the three transactions, totaling 7,000 shares and $227,900.00, are settled through the clearing house by the following net payments of cash and deliveries of securities:

	Cash		Shares	
	Received	Paid	Received	Delivered
Brown		$ 100.00	—	—
Jones	$32,800.00			1,000
Smith		32,700.00	1,000	
	$32,800.00	$32,800.00	1,000	1,000

Broker's balance sheet: Principal items. The following illustration shows the items of major importance that appear in a broker's balance sheet:

Balance Sheet—June 30, 1946

Assets

Cash in bank	$ 471,000.00
Customers	12,250,000.00
	$12,721,000.00

Liabilities and Net Worth

Bank loans	$10,000,000.00
Capital	2,721,000.00
	$12,721,000.00

Broker's security position. Although the foregoing balance sheet may be a true picture of the broker's financial condition as shown by his general ledger, the following extremely important questions are not answered by it:

What is the market value of the securities left with the broker by his customers as collateral to the accounts totaling $12,250,000.00? Unless these accounts are adequately secured, the broker may suffer losses in their realization.

How adequately are the bank loans secured by the rehypothecation of securities? Unless the bank loans (whether time or call loans) are adequately secured, they may be called and the broker may be placed in financial difficulties.

What securities remain "in the box"; that is, in the broker's possession?

To give this important information, the foregoing balance sheet may be amplified as follows:

Balance Sheet—June 30, 1946

	Ledger Balances	Market Value of Securities
Assets		
Cash in bank	$ 471,000.00	
Customers	12,250,000.00	$17,600,000.00
	$12,721,000.00	$17,600,000.00
Liabilities and Net Worth		
Bank loans	$10,000,000.00	$15,800,000.00
Securities in the box		1,800,000.00
Capital	2,721,000.00	
	$12,721,000.00	$17,600,000.00

Money and security records. To provide the information required for a balance sheet in the form just illustrated, and also for the broker's control of his daily operations, his records must include:

(1) A double entry system of accounts, similar to that employed by other lines of business, showing the assets, liabilities, income, expense, and capital of the business. The entries in these accounts are, of course, expressed in dollar amounts.

(2) A double entry system of records showing both the location and ownership of each security under the broker's control. Since market values of securities are continually changing, the security entries are made in terms of number of shares and face value of bonds; market values can be applied to these quantities whenever

the determination of market values is required for any purpose.

To show why both of these classes of records are necessary, and how they are both kept on a double entry basis, let us assume that a broker purchases for a customer 200 shares of *Z* Company stock at $20.00 per share. The dollar entries in the ledger accounts will be:

Customer *A*	$4,025.00	
Cash		$4,000.00
Commissions		25.00

The debit to the customer represents the amount which the broker is entitled to collect from him; the credit to cash records the broker's disbursement in payment for the stock purchased; and the credit to commissions shows the broker's earning.

But the broker has received 200 shares of stock, and he has an obligation to deliver this stock to the customer when the customer pays his account. In other words, in addition to debiting the customer for the price of the stock, $4,025.00, the broker must credit the customer with the 200 shares. Also, the broker's records should show the location of the stock. The facts concerning the securities are recorded by the following debit and credit:

Box	200 shares	
Customer *A*		200 shares

As used in connection with security entries, *debit* and *short* are synonymous, and *credit* and *long* are synonymous. The money debit and the security credit to the customer are posted to his account in the manner illustrated below.

Attention is directed to the columns provided for the security entries. It should be noted that the bought or received column is a credit, or long, column, but that it appears at the left of the sold or delivered column, to which the debit, or short, entries will be posted.

Customer *A*

Date	Bought or Received	Sold or Delivered	Description	Debit	Credit	Balance
Aug. 1	200		*Z* Company @ 20.00	4,025.00		4,025.00

The security entry debiting the box and crediting the customer is also posted to the long and short record, or position book, in which a separate sheet or card is devoted to each stock or bond. Various forms of position books are used, but the following illustration will serve our purpose. A debit, a credit, and a balance column are provided for each date, and the dates are shown at the head of these columns. The debit and credit entries for the above-stated transaction, and the resulting long and short balances are shown below:

***Z* Company Stock**

	1			2			3		
Long	Debit	Credit	Balance	Debit	Credit	Balance	Debit	Credit	Balance
Due to customers:									
A....................		200	200						
Short									
Box....................	200		200						

The debit to box shows the receipt of the securities, and the credit to the customer reflects the broker's obligation to account to the customer for the 200 shares. The position book thus shows both the location and the ownership of the stock.

Exchange settlements. Under the rules of some stock exchanges, purchases and sales must be settled on the day following the transaction, except that Friday and Saturday transactions are settled on Monday. The New York Stock Exchange provides for settlement on the second full business day following the transaction. A delay is necessary because the volume of business done by a broker makes it impossible for him, within a single day, to make his purchases and sales on the floor of the exchange, to confirm the transactions with the other brokers, to complete his records, to make any necessary arrangements for obtaining funds required for the payment of his purchases, and to assemble the securities needed to make deliveries. The exchange also requires time to make up its settlement records.

Because of the lapse of one or more days between the purchase and the payment of cash and receipt of the stock, it might seem that the entries for a purchase of stock should be made as follows.

On the day a purchase contract is made with another broker (say July 30):

Money entries:

Customer *A*..................................	$4,025.00	
Clearing house (for broker's liability)........		$4,000.00
Commissions..................................		25.00

Security entries:

Clearing house (for stock receivable)..........	200 shares	
Customer *A*..................................		200 shares

On the settlement day, when the contract is executed by the payment of cash to, and the receipt of stock from, the clearing house (say August 1):

Money entries:

Clearing house (for payment of liability)	$4,000.00	
Cash		$4,000.00

Security entries:

Box (for stock received)	200 shares	
Clearing house		200 shares

However, if the broker purchases stock for his customer on July 30, but does not pay for and receive the stock until August 1, he cannot properly charge the customer until August 1. If the debit to the customer were made under date of July 30, the broker would charge the customer two days' interest to which he would not be entitled. Hence, it is customary to post-date the purchase and sales entries as of the settlement date, so that both the purchase and settlement are recorded as of the same date. The following entries, all under date of August 1, would therefore be made for the foregoing transaction:

Money entries:

Customer *A*	$4,025.00	
Clearing house		$4,000.00
Commissions		25.00
For purchase of stock.		
Clearing house	4,000.00	
Cash		4,000.00
For settlement with the clearing house.		

Security entries:

Box	200 shares	
Customer *A*		200 shares

It will be noted that, in the money entries, clearing house is debited and credited $4,000.00. Since these entries exactly offset each other and are made as of the same date, many brokerage houses merely prove the equality of each day's debits and credits to the clearing house in the books of original entry, without posting them to a clearing house account in the ledger. The posted entries are therefore as follows:

Money entries:

Customer *A*	$4,025.00	
Commissions		$ 25.00
Cash		4,000.00

Security entries:

Box	200 shares	
Customer *A*		200 shares

Principal transactions. The following are the principal transactions affecting a broker's accounts with his customers:

(1) Securities are purchased for the customer.
(2) Securities are sold for the customer.
(3) Cash is received from the customer.
(4) Cash is paid to the customer.
(5) Securities are received from the customer.
(6) Securities are delivered to the customer.

These events may occur in various sequences. For instance, a purchase may be made for a customer; on the settlement date, cash may be received from the customer and the securities delivered to him.

Or, a margin deposit may be received from the customer; securities may be purchased and, at a later date, sold. During the period between the purchase and the sale, the customer occupies a long position in the security.

Or, the sequence of purchase and sale may be reversed. If the customer believes that the price will decline, he may make a margin deposit and order his broker to sell; at a subsequent date, he will make a covering purchase. During the period between the sale and the purchase, the customer occupies a short position in the security.

Illustrative transactions. We shall now consider a number of typical brokerage transactions, which differ in the sequence of the events enumerated in the preceding section. It does not appear desirable, within the limitations of a single chapter, to attempt to describe the books of original entry. Throughout these illustrations, credit entries are indicated by asterisks.

Cash purchase. One of the simplest series of brokerage transactions involves:

On one day:
The purchase of securities for a customer.
On the exchange settlement day:
The payment of cash to, and the receipt of stock from, the clearing house; and
The receipt of cash from, and the delivery of stock to, the customer.

Although these transactions would actually occur on two days, they would be recorded under date of the settlement day. To illustrate the method of accounting for this series of transactions, assume that:

(a) A purchase of 200 shares of *Z* Company stock is made for John White, at $20.00.
(b) Payment is made to the clearing house.
(c) The stock is received from the clearing house.
(d) Collection is received from the customer.
(e) The stock is delivered to the customer.

The following summary of money and security entries is not intended to illustrate the *form* of any book kept by a broker; it merely indicates the debits and credits in dollars and shares, required to record the foregoing transactions.

	Money Entries				Security Entries	
Transaction	John White	Clearing House	Commissions	Cash	Box	John White
(a)	$4,025.00	$4,000.00*	$25.00*			
(b)		4,000.00		$4,000.00*		
(c)					200	200*
(d)	4,025.00*			4,025.00		
(e)					200*	200

* Credit.

The money and security debits and credits to the customer, John White, are posted as follows:

John White

Date	Bought or Received	Sold or Delivered	Description	Debit	Credit	Balance
Aug. 1	200		*Z* Company @ 20.00	4,025.00		4,025.00
Aug. 1		200	*Z* Company		4,025.00	—

The debit and credit to clearing house are not posted.

The security entries are posted to the position book, thus:

***Z* Company Stock**

	1								
Long									
Due to customers:	Debit	Credit	Balance	Debit	Credit	Balance	Debit	Credit	Balancc
John White..........	(e)200	(c)200	—						
Short									
Box..................	(c)200	(e)200	—						

Margin purchase. Instead of paying the cost of the securities, the customer arranges in advance to have the broker carry the account on margin; in other words, the customer makes a margin deposit of cash and/or securities with the broker, and the broker carries the customer's account for the excess of the purchase price and the commission over the amount of the margin deposit. To illustrate, assume the following transactions:

(f) James Black deposits with the broker $4,500.00 as a margin.
(g) The broker purchases 400 shares of *Z* Company stock at $20.00.
(h) The broker pays for the stock.
(i) The stock is received by the broker and held as collateral to the customer's account.

The debits and credits, in dollars and shares, are summarized as follows:

	Money Entries				Security Entries	
Transaction	James Black	Clearing House	Commissions	Cash	Box	James Black
(f)	$4,500.00*			$4,500.00		
(g)	8,050.00	$8,000.00*	$50.00*			
(h)		8,000.00		8,000.00*		
(i)					400	400*

* Credit.

The position book sheet for the *Z* Company stock appears as follows:

***Z* Company Stock**

	1			2					
	Debit	Credit	Balance	Debit	Credit	Balance	Debit	Credit	Balance
Long									
Due to customers:									
John White..........	(e)200	(c)200	—						
James Black.........					(i)400	400			
Short									
Box....................	(c)200	(e)200	—	(i)400		400			

Subsequent sale. In this transaction, James Black disposed of part of his holdings. The Federal tax on sales is paid by the broker, by the application of revenue stamps which the broker purchases for that purpose and carries in an asset account. Assume the following transactions:

(j) The broker sells 100 shares of *Z* Company stock at $22.00.
(k) The broker collects the selling price of the stock through the clearing house.
(l) The stock is delivered to the clearing house.

The debits and credits, in dollars and shares, are as follows:

	Money Entries					Security Entries	
Transaction	James Black	Clearing House	Commissions	Revenue Stamps	Cash	Box	James Black
(j)	$2,178.50*	$2,200.00	$12.50*	$9.00*			
(k)		2,200.00*			$2,200.00		
(l)						100*	100

* Credit.

The customer's account, after these entries have been posted, appears as follows:

James Black

Date	Bought or Received	Sold or Delivered	Description	Debit	Credit	Balance
(f) Aug. 2			Cash margin		4,500.00	4,500.00 Cr.
(g) 2	400		*Z* Co. @ 20.00	8,050.00		3,550.00 Dr.
(j) 3		100	*Z* Co. @ 22.00		2,178.50	1,371.50 Dr.

The customer now has a debit money balance of $1,371.50, and a long security balance of 300 shares. The position book sheet for the *Z* Company stock is continued as follows:

***Z* Company Stock**

	1			2			3		
Long	Debit	Credit	Balance	Debit	Credit	Balance	Debit	Credit	Balance
Due to customers:									
John White..........	(e)200	(c)200	—			—			—
James Black..........					(i)400	400	(l)100		300
Short									
Box..................	(c)200	(e)200	—	(i)400		400		(l)100	300

Short sale. In transactions of this type, the customer orders his broker to sell securities which the customer does not own, and which he must therefore purchase at a later date, hoping to do so at a reduced price. The broker is expected to deliver immediately the stock thus sold short; and we shall assume, in this illustration, that the broker obtains the consent of James Black to use for this purpose some of Black's shares which the broker is holding as collateral. Assume the following transactions:

(m) George Green deposits with the broker $2,500.00 as collateral.

(n) The broker sells 200 shares of *Z* Company stock at $24.00.

(o) The broker collects for the stock.

(p) The stock is delivered to the purchasing broker through the clearing house.

The debits and credits, in money and securities, for these transactions are summarized below:

Transaction	Money Entries: George Green	Money Entries: Clearing House	Money Entries: Commissions	Money Entries: Revenue Stamps	Money Entries: Cash	Security Entries: Box	Security Entries: George Green
(m)	$2,500.00*				$2,500.00		
(n)	4,757.00*	$4,800.00	$25.00*	$18.00*			
(o)		4,800.00*			4,800.00		
(p)						200*	200

* Credit.

The customer's account is shown in the next illustration. The position book entries are shown below.

***Z* Company Stock**

Long	2 Debit	2 Credit	2 Balance	3 Debit	3 Credit	3 Balance	4 Debit	4 Credit	4 Balance
Due to customers:									
John White			—			—			
James Black		(i)400	400	(l)100		300			300
Short									
Box	(i)400		400		(l)100	300		(p) 200	100
Due from customers:									
George Green							(p)200		200
									300

Subsequent purchase. George Green, who occupied a short position in the *Z* Company stock as a result of the preceding short sale, makes a partial covering purchase. Assume the following transactions:

(q) The broker purchases 100 shares of *Z* Company stock at $22.50.

(r) The broker pays for the stock.

(s) The broker receives the stock for Green's account.

The debits and credits, in money and securities, for these transactions are summarized below:

Transaction	Money Entries: George Green	Money Entries: Clearing House	Money Entries: Commissions	Money Entries: Cash	Security Entries: Box	Security Entries: George Green
(q)	$2,262.50	$2,250.00*	$12.50*			
(r)		2,250.00		$2,250.00*		
(s)					100	100*

* Credit.

The position book is continued as follows:

_Z_ Company Stock

	3			4			5		
Long	Debit	Credit	Balance	Debit	Credit	Balance	Debit	Credit	Balance
Due to customers:									
John White			—			—			—
James Black	(l)100		300			300			300
Short									
Box		(l)100	300		(p)200	100	(s)100		200
Due from customers:									
George Green				(p)200		200		(s)100	100
						300			300

The customer's account appears below.

George Green

Date	Bought or Received	Sold or Delivered	Description	Debit	Credit	Balance
(m) Aug. 4			Cash margin		2,500.00	2,500.00 Cr.
(n) 4		200	_Z_ Co. @ 24.00		4,757.00	7,257.00 Cr.
(q) 5	100		_Z_ Co. @ 22.50	2,262.50		4,994.50 Cr.

Sale with failure to deliver. For various reasons a broker may be unable to make immediate delivery of stock sold. He may have none in the box; or the certificates in the box may not be such as to permit the delivery of the exact number of shares required; or the broker may be unable to obtain, from a customer occupying a long position in the stock, consent to use his shares to make the delivery.

Although exchange rules and brokers' practices regarding sales on which deliveries are not immediately made, vary somewhat in different cities, the following illustrations show the principal accounting requirements.

(t) Fred Grey deposits with the broker $3,500.00 as a margin.

(u) The broker sells 300 shares of _Z_ Company stock at $23.00.

(v) The broker finds that he is unable to make delivery of the stock, and he records the "failure" by debiting failed to deliver and crediting clearing house, $6,900.00, thus showing that the proceeds from the sale are not immediately collectible from the clearing house, but are collectible only when the broker is in a position to deliver the stock.

The debits and credits are summarized below:

	Money Entries						Security Entries	
Transaction	Fred Grey	Clearing House	Commissions	Revenue Stamps	Cash	Failed to Deliver	Failed to Deliver	Fred Grey
(t)	$3,500.00*				$3,500.00			
(u)	6,835.00*	$6,900.00	$37.50*	$27,00*				
(v)		6,900.00*				$6,900.00	300*	300

* Credit.

The $6,900.00 debit money balance in the failed to deliver account represents the amount that the broker is entitled to receive from the purchasing broker when the stock is delivered. The credit, or long, security balance in the failed to deliver account reflects the broker's obligation to deliver the 300 shares.

The position book is continued as follows:

***Z* Company Stock**

	4			5			6		
Long	Debit	Credit	Balance	Debit	Credit	Balance	Debit	Credit	Balance
Due to customers:									
John White..........			—			—			—
James Black..........			300			300			300
Failed to deliver.......								(v)300	300
			300			300			600
Short									
Box....................		(p)200	100	(s)100		200			200
Due from customers:									
George Green........	(p)200		200		(s)100	100			100
Fred Grey............							(v)300		300
			300			300			600

When the broker is in a position to deliver the stock, the settlement may be made through the clearing house, but it is usually made directly with the other broker. The money entry for the collection of the sale price will be: debit cash and credit failed to deliver, $6,900.00. The security entry for the delivery of the stock will be debit failed to deliver and credit box, 300 shares.

Purchase with failure to receive. To illustrate the accounting procedure of a broker who has purchased stock from another broker who fails to deliver, assume the following transactions:

(w) The broker receives a margin deposit of $4,500.00 from Henry Brown.

(x) The broker purchases 400 shares of *Z* Company stock at $20.00.

(y) The selling broker fails to deliver.

The debit and credit entries, in money and securities, are summarized as follows:

	Money Entries					Security Entries	
Transaction	Henry Brown	Clearing House	Commissions	Cash	Failed to Receive	Failed to Receive	Henry Brown
(w)	$4,500.00*			$4,500.00			
(x)	8,050.00	$8,000.00*	$50.00*				
(y)		8,000.00			$8,000.00*	400	400*

* Credit.

The $8,000.00 credit balance in the failed to receive account shows the purchasing broker's obligation to pay for the stock when it is received; the debit, or short, security balance reflects his claim against the selling broker for the shares not yet received.

The subsequent settlement may be made through the clearing house, but it is usually made directly between the two brokers involved. In the latter case, the purchasing broker's entries are: debit failed to receive and credit cash, $8,000.00; debit box and credit failed to receive, 400 shares.

The position book prior to the settlement appears below.

***Z* Company Stock**

	5			6			8		
Long	Debit	Credit	Balance	Debit	Credit	Balance	Debit	Credit	Balance
Due to customers:									
John White			—			—			—
James Black			300			300			300
Henry Brown								(y)400	400
Failed to deliver					(v)300	300			300
			300			600			1,000
Short									
Box	(s)100		200			200			200
Due from customers:									
George Green		(s)100	100			100			100
Fred Grey				(v)300		300			300
Failed to receive							(y)400		400
			300			600			1,000

Stock borrowed. A broker who has no available stock with which to make delivery on a short sale may borrow the stock from some other broker. Or, assume that Broker *A* has sold stock to Broker *B* and has failed to deliver; in order to make delivery to his own customer, Broker *B* has a right to buy the stock elsewhere and to charge Broker *A* with the cost thereof. To avoid a possible loss that might result from this threatened "buy-in," Broker *A* may borrow the stock from Broker *C* and deliver it to Broker *B*. When Broker *A* borrows the stock, he gives Broker *C* his check for the market value thereof; he may also give Broker *C* a due bill for the stock, although practice in this respect varies. If the market price of the borrowed stock rises or falls, the cash deposit with Broker *C* is increased or decreased to keep it "marked to the market." To illustrate, assume the following transactions:

(z) William Rose deposits with the broker $3,500.00 as a margin.
(aa) The broker sells 300 shares of *Z* Company stock at $23.00.
(bb) The broker borrows the stock from Broker *C*.
(cc) The selling price is received from, and the stock is delivered to, the clearing house.

The debit and credit entries are summarized as follows:

	Money Entries						Security Entries		
Transaction	William Rose	Clearing House	Commissions	Revenue Stamps	Cash	Stocks Borrowed	Stocks Borrowed	Box	William Rose
(z)	$3,500.00*				$3,500.00				
(aa)	6,835.50*	$6,900.00	$37.50*	$27.00*					
(bb)					6,900.00*	6,900.00	300*	300	
(cc)		6,900.00*			6,900.00			300*	300

* Credit.

These entries differ from preceding entries for sales only in so far as the debits and credits for the borrowed stock are concerned. The debit money balance in the stocks borrowed account represents the broker's right to receive $6,900.00 from Broker *C* when the borrowed stock is returned to him. The credit, or long, security balance in the stocks borrowed account shows the broker's obligation to deliver 300 shares to Broker *C* in return for the stock borrowed. The position book is continued as follows:

***Z* Company Stock**

	6			8			9		
Long	Debit	Credit	Balance	Debit	Credit	Balance	Debit	Credit	Balance
Due to customers:									
John White			—			—			—
James Black			300			300			300
Henry Brown					(y)400	400			400
Failed to deliver		(v)300	300			300			300
Stocks borrowed								(bb)300	300
			600			1,000			1,300
Short									
Box			200			200	(bb)300	(cc)300	200
Due from customers:									
George Green			100			100			100
Fred Grey	(v)300		300			300			300
William Rose							(cc)300		300
Failed to receive			—	(y)400		400			400
			600			1,000			1,300

Stock loaned. A broker who loans stock to another broker and receives a check for the stock thus loaned will make entries as indicated below:

	Money Entries		Security Entries	
Transaction	Cash	Stock Loaned	Box	Stock Loaned
(dd)	$1,150.00	$1,150.00*	50*	50

* Credit.

The credit money balance in the stocks loaned account shows the broker's liability to return the cash to the borrowing broker when the stock is returned. The debit, or short, security balance shows the broker's right to receive the 50 shares of stock.

The position book is continued as follows:

***Z* Company Stock**

	8			9			10		
Long	Debit	Credit	Balance	Debit	Credit	Balance	Debit	Credit	Balance
Due to customers:									
John White			—			—			—
James Black			300			300			300
Henry Brown		(y)400	400			400			400
Failed to deliver			300			300			300
Stock borrowed					(bb)300	300			300
			1,000			1,300			1,300
Short									
Box			200	(bb)300	(cc)300	200		(dd)50	150
Due from customers:									
George Green			100			100			100
Fred Grey			300			300			300
William Rose				(cc)300		300			300
Failed to receive	(y)400		400			400			400
Stock loaned							(dd)50		50
			1,000			1,300			1,300

Transactions settled direct. Some transactions are settled directly by the two brokers involved and do not pass through the exchange and the clearing house. This may occur if the security traded in is not listed on the exchange, or if, although listed, it is so inactive that offset settlements are not made by the exchange. In such instances, each broker may debit or credit the other broker in accounts that are kept in the same way as customers' accounts, or brokers may handle such transactions "ex-clearing," controlled through a separate account in the general ledger designed for this purpose, avoiding opening and posting to an individual ledger account with each broker in the receivable ledger.

As an illustration of the procedure of recording such transactions in the receivable ledger, assume that Broker *C* buys for the account of a customer 100 shares of Blank Company stock from Broker *D*. The entries on the books of Broker *C* are summarized on the next page.

	Money Entries				Security Entries		
Transaction	Customer	Broker *D*	Commission	Cash	Broker *D*	Box	Customer
Purchase	$2,012.50	$2,000.00*	$12.50*		100		100*
Settlement		2,000.00		$2,000.00*	100*	100	

* Credit.

The account with Broker *D* would appear as follows:

Date	Bought or Received	Sold or Delivered	Description	Debit	Credit	Balance
July 9		100	Blank Company @ 20.00		2,000.00	2,000.00
July 11	100		Blank Company	2,000.00		—

Bank loans. In order to be able to carry their customers' accounts, brokers frequently borrow from banks. Bank loans are generally secured by the deposit, as collateral, of securities owned by the broker, or held by him as collateral to his customers' accounts. The money entries to record a bank loan are: debit cash and credit bank loans. The security entries are: debit pledged with banks and credit box. The shares thus pledged will appear as a short item in the position book.

Stock out for transfer. When a broker sends stock to the issuing company's transfer agent for the issuance of new certificates, usually in the broker's name, entries are made in the position book, debiting due from transfer office and crediting box.

Dividends receivable. To reflect the amounts of dividends receivable on stocks under the broker's control, the portions of such dividends that must be paid to other parties, and the portion that can be taken into income, entries are made for dividend amounts determined on the basis of the position shown by the position book on the date when the stock went ex-dividend. To illustrate, assume that the position book showed the following long and short items:

Short

(a) Due from customers.
(b) Due from brokers.
(c) Stocks loaned.
(d) Failed to receive.
(e) Pledged with banks.
(f) Due from transfer office.
(g) Box.

Long

(h) Due to customers.
(i) Due to brokers.
(j) Stocks borrowed.
(k) Failed to deliver.
(l) Stocks owned.

Theoretically, the broker should make the following entry:

Accounts Debited and Credited	For Dividends on Items	
Various customers	(a)	
Various brokers	(b), (c), (d)	
Collectible dividends	(e), (f), (g)	
Various customers		(h)
Various brokers		(i), (j), (k)
Dividends (income account)		(l)

Actually, it may be impossible to determine the amounts to be credited to various customers and to various brokers. Under such conditions, the broker credits customers and brokers with the amounts to which he knows they are entitled; he credits the dividends account with dividends on the stock which he himself owns; and he credits any unallocated remainder to the unclaimed dividends account. The unclaimed dividends account is therefore a suspense account representing a liability to parties who temporarily cannot be determined.

Margin records. In addition to the accounts with customers, showing money and security entries as already illustrated, brokerage concerns must keep margin records, which show whether or not the customers' accounts are adequately margined. Postings to the margin records and to the customers' accounts are made from the same sources. The margin records are of extreme importance, as they furnish the information required by the broker to prevent the losses that might arise from a decline in the market value of securities held as collateral to the account of a customer occupying a long position, or the losses that might be occasioned by a rise in the market value of securities which a customer has sold short. The margin requirement for each stock or bond is separately determined on the basis of then existing regulations.

There are several forms of margin records, but the following illustration shows how they may be maintained. Let us assume that a customer has made a margin deposit of $5,000.00, and that he has purchased 400 shares of *Y* Company stock for $8,800.00 and has been charged with the cost thereof plus $50.00 commission. His ledger account therefore has a debit balance of $3,850.00. Let us assume, also, that a net margin of $2,800.00 is regarded as adequate for this particular stock; that is, no additional margin will be called for unless the customer's equity in the stock decreases below that amount. The margin card at the time of the purchase will appear as follows:

Name		Address	Telephone		
Long	Short	Security	Price	Value	Required
400		*Y* Company	22	$8,800.00	$2,800.00
(Several lines		*are provided for listing other securities)*			
		Market value (total)		8,800.00	
		Balance (of ledger account)		3,850.00	
		Equity		4,950.00	

The amount shown on the balance line is the debit balance of the customer's account. The card shows that the value of the stock is $4,950.00 in excess of the customer's debit balance; in other words, the customer has a $4,950.00 equity in the stock on the basis of its present market value. Since only $2,800.00 is required, the account is adequately margined.

If the customer has purchased several securities, the total market value thereof and the total margin required would be shown on the total line; the balance of the customer's account would be deducted from the total market value; and the remainder, or total equity, would be compared with the total requirement.

Let us assume that the price of the *Y* Company stock drops to $18.00. The entries on the margin card were made in pencil so that they could be easily erased and new figures inserted. The margin card showing the changed margin status appears below:

Name		Address	Telephone		
Long	Short	Security	Price	Value	Required
400		*Y* Company	18	$7,200.00	$2,800.00
		Market value (total)		7,200.00	
		Balance		3,850.00	
		Equity		3,350.00	

The equity is still in excess of the $2,800.00 requirement, but further declines in the market value of this security will have to be very closely watched. A decrease of $1.50 per share would reduce the equity to $2,750.00, which is less than the requirement.

Interest charges to customers. Customers are charged with interest as a consequence of security purchase transactions, but not as a consequence of short sale transactions.* To show the reason for this difference, let us assume the following transactions:

A customer makes a margin deposit of $3,000.00, and purchases securities at a cost of $5,525.00, including commission; his account therefore has a debit balance of $2,525.00, representing the amount of funds advanced by the broker, plus the commission charge. The broker can therefore properly charge interest on $2,525.00.

A customer makes a margin deposit of $2,500.00, and orders his broker to make a short sale that involves a credit to his account in the net amount of $4,657.00. His account therefore has a credit balance of $7,157.00. Obviously, the broker cannot charge his customer any interest, because the broker's capital is not used. Although the broker may be obliged to borrow the stock for delivery and to deposit his own check with the broker who loans the stock, this disbursement is offset by the collection and retention of the proceeds from the sale.

Partners' trading accounts. If purchase or sales orders are executed for individual members of the brokerage firm, the partners virtually become customers of the firm, and the ledger should show the resulting charges and credits to them in accounts that are kept in the same manner as the customers' accounts. The customers' accounts are kept in a subsidiary ledger under the control of a general ledger customers' account. Theoretically, it is undesirable to keep the partners' trading accounts in the subsidiary ledger, but, if machine bookkeeping is used, it may be desirable to do so from the standpoint of convenience. In any event, the partners' trading accounts should be set out as separate items in the periodical statements.

Trading securities account. If a brokerage firm buys securities for its own account, a trading securities account is charged with the cost thereof. When the securities are subsequently sold, entries may be made in either of two ways:

(1) The trading securities account may be credited with the cost of the securities sold, and the profit or loss may be

* New York Exchange rules, under certain circumstances, make technical exceptions to this procedure.

taken up immediately by a credit or debit to the trading profits account.

(2) The trading securities account may be credited with the selling price of the securities sold; at intervals, the unsold securities will be inventoried, and the profit or loss thus ascertained. When the account is operated in this manner, it is similar to an old-fashioned merchandise account.

This account is generally used to record only those transactions that involve the purchase and subsequent sale of securities; the firm's short sales, with subsequent purchases, are usually recorded in the account discussed below.

Short sales account. This account should be credited with the proceeds of short sales made by the firm for its own account, and should be charged with the cost of subsequent purchases. Any profits or losses should be reflected in the trading profits account.

Syndicate securities account. This account should be charged with the cost of securities purchased by the firm as a member of a syndicate, credited with the proceeds of sales, and recharged with the cost of any securities repurchased from the public for the purpose of maintaining the market or for other reasons. Profits may be taken up periodically by inventorying the unsold securities, or the more conservative procedure may be followed of postponing the taking of profit until all of the securities are sold. Profits or losses should be reflected in the syndicate profits account, which may also be credited with any amount received from the syndicate manager as the broker's share of the direct syndicate profit.

If the broker is participating in numerous syndicates, the syndicate securities account in the general ledger should be operated as a controlling account, with subsidiary records reflecting the operations of each syndicate.

Summary of general ledger accounts. The typical general ledger accounts of a brokerage firm are listed below.

<u>Asset Accounts</u>

Cash:

Accounts with cash in banks and on hand are operated in the same manner as similar accounts of other businesses.

Stock clearing funds:

This account shows deposits made with stock exchanges to guarantee the clearing of transactions.

Revenue stamps:

This account is charged with the cost of revenue stamps purchased, and is credited with stamps charged to customers to cover the tax on sales or used in connection with the firm's own trading operations.

Customers:

This account controls a subsidiary ledger containing accounts that may have balances of the following four classes:

(1) Debit balances secured by collateral.
(2) Credit balances resulting from short sales.
(3) Free credit balances payable to customers.
(4) Unsecured debit balances that may develop if a broker does not obtain adequate collateral and does not sell the customer's securities before his margin is exhausted.

The periodical statements should show these four classes of balances, as disclosed by the trial balance of the subsidiary ledger, instead of the net balance of the controlling account.

Other brokers:

These accounts will show amounts receivable from brokers as a result of such transactions as sales to them that are to be settled direct instead of through the clearing house.

Failed to deliver:

The operation of this account was explained on page 557. Its debit balance represents the amount receivable for securities that the broker has failed to deliver.

Stocks borrowed:

The operation of this account was explained on page 559. It is charged with cash deposits made with other brokers to assure the return of securities borrowed from them. It may be operated on a controlling account basis.

Collectible dividends:

The nature of this account was indicated on page 562.

Partners' trading accounts:

These accounts were discussed on page 565. Debit balances should be deducted from the capital accounts in the balance sheet.

Trading securities:

This account was discussed on page 565.

Syndicate securities:

This account was discussed on page 566.

Exchange seat:

This account shows the cost of the broker's seat on the exchange.

Fixed assets and reserves:

Accounts with fixed assets, and the related depreciation reserves, are kept in the usual manner.

Deferred charges:

Accounts with prepaid expenses are kept as in any other business.

Liability Accounts

Notes payable:

These accounts show note liabilities, principally to banks.

Other brokers:

These accounts show amounts payable to other brokers as a result of such transactions as purchases from them that are to be settled direct instead of through the clearing house.

Failed to receive:

The operation of this account was explained on page 558. Its credit balance represents the broker's liability to pay for stocks that will subsequently be received on "failed" transactions.

Stocks loaned:

The operation of this account was explained on page 561. It is credited with the amounts of deposits received from other brokers to assure the return of securities loaned to them.

Unclaimed dividends and coupons:

The credits made to this account in connection with dividends were explained on page 563. Similar credits are made in connection with matured coupons on bonds. When proof of claim is submitted, payment is made and this account is debited.

Short sales:

This account is credited with the proceeds from short sales made by the firm for its own account.

Partners' short sales:

These accounts are credited with the proceeds from short sales made for the partners' individual accounts.

Accrued expenses:

Such accounts are operated as in any other business.

Partners' capital:

These accounts are debited and credited as similar accounts are in any other partnership.

Clearing Accounts

Clearing house:

The debits and credits to this account have been illustrated in the preceding pages. As the debits and credits to this account for each day's transactions should always be equal, brokers frequently omit the postings to the account.

The peculiarities of brokerage accounting arise principally in connection with the asset and liability accounts. The accounting for income and expense is extremely simple.

Income Accounts

Commissions:
Customers' interest:
These accounts are credited with commissions and interest charged to customers.
Trading profits:
Syndicate profits:
These accounts show the profits or losses on the firm's own transactions recorded in the trading securities, short sales, and syndicate securities accounts.
Other interest:
Dividends:
These accounts may be subdivided as much as necessary to furnish the information desired for the operating statements or required for the income tax return.

Expense Accounts

Interest expense:
Salaries:
Rent:
And so forth:
The expense accounts of a brokerage firm do not differ greatly from those of other businesses.

Balance sheet with security values. The balance sheet on page 570 shows ledger balances and related security values. It is generally indicative of the form required by the New York Stock Exchange.

NAME OF COMPANY

Answers to New York Stock Exchange Questionnaire Part I

At April 30, 19—

	Ledger Balance Debit	Ledger Balance Credit	Securities Valuations Long	Securities Valuations Short
Question—1 Bank balances and other deposits:				
Cash on hand and in banks	$ 4,763,000			
Cash in banks—segregated funds	2,500			
Contributions to clearing organizations	175,000			
Drafts deposited for collection	240,000			
Question—2 Money borrowed—banks and brokers:				
Money borrowed from banks and trust companies collateralized by nonexempt securities		$ 4,500,000		$ 6,500,000
Question—4 Other accounts and open items:				
Securities borrowed	80,000		$ 85,000	
Securities failed to deliver	1,400,000		1,380,000	
Customers' securities loaned		300,000		325,000
Customers' securities failed to receive		900,000		875,000
Question—5 Valuation of securities:				
Negotiable securities in box and transfers				17,500,000
Negotiable securities in transit between offices				1,000,000
Question—6 Customers' security accounts:				
Cash accounts	1,300,000	360,000	1,760,000	325,000
Secured accounts	14,000,000	1,200,000	20,000,000	790,000
Unsecured accounts	8,000			
Accounts with credit balances and open contractual commitments		752,500	200,000	
Accounts with free credit balances		11,000,000		
Customers' fully paid for securities not segregated			2,300,000	
Joint accounts (respondent's participation 50%)	64,000		65,000	
Question—9 Partners' accounts:				
Individual accounts of partners		200,000		
Nonexempt securities			500,000	
Exempt securities			25,000	
Question—10 Firm trading and investment accounts:	1,000,000			
Nonexempt securities			560,000	60,000
Exempt securities			500,000	
Question—11 Capital accounts:				
Partnership capital		3,500,000		
Undistributed profit and loss items		200,000		
Reserve for partners' withdrawals		200,000		
Question—12 Other accounts:				
Exchange memberships at book value	100,000			
Sundry accounts receivable and miscellaneous inventory accounts	260,000			
Accrued taxes, various reserves, and sundry accounts payable		280,000		
	$23,392,500	$23,392,500	$27,375,000	$27,375,000

QUESTIONS AND PROBLEMS ON CHAPTER 31

Questions

Question 31-1. Mention the chief points to be observed in reporting upon the accounts of a partnership in which you are acting on behalf of a retiring partner, when the business is to be continued by the remaining partners.

Question 31-2. *A* and *B* are partners, dealing in wholesale drugs. *A* dies. His widow objects to a statement offered by *B*, as a basis of settlement on the ground that the stock of merchandise is listed by *B* at cost, whereas during the six months preceding the death of *A* the average value of the drugs has increased 50% over the original cost. What settlement would you suggest as being equitable, giving your reasons? State how the settlement that you suggest should be dealt with in the books of *B*.

Question 31-3. Assume that, at the time of the withdrawal of a partner, it appeared impractical to attempt to value the accounts receivable. It was therefore decided to adjust the withdrawing partner's account at the end of two years and to make final settlement with him at that time with respect to accounts receivable. What method of accounting would you recommend to facilitate the determination of the subsequent payments to be made to the retiring partner?

Question 31-4. *A*, *B*, and *C* are partners, sharing profits equally. *C* is to retire. The goodwill of the business is valued at $12,000.00. Give journal entries showing two methods of placing the goodwill on the books, and state which method is preferable.

Question 31-5. As bookkeeper for a firm having no articles of partnership, what action would you take on learning of the death of a partner?

Question 31-6. Are there any circumstances under which you would regard it as entirely permissible to defer the closing of the books after the death of a partner until the close of the accounting period?

Question 31-7. If goodwill is placed on the books at the time of a partner's withdrawal, in what ratio should it be divided? Why should this ratio govern?

Question 31-8. It has been argued that when a firm is dissolved losses on liquidation are losses of capital and should be divided in the capital ratio. Answer this argument.

Problems

Problem 31-1. Ruggles, Stanton and Tracy are partners having capitals of $32,174.00, $41,908.00, and $27,635.00 respectively. They share profits as follows: Ruggles, 35%; Stanton, 45%; and Tracy 20%. They sell their assets for a lump sum of $150,000.00. Of the profit made, $24,000.00 was on a patent which has been developed principally by Tracy, and it was agreed that he should have half of that profit, before the remaining profits were divided.

(*a*) Prepare a statement showing the distribution of the cash. Assume there were no liabilities.

(*b*) Give the journal entries to record the sale and the distribution of the proceeds.

Problem 31-2. Upton, Varney, and West were partners having capitals of $34,600.00, $21,300.00, and $12,800.00 respectively. They share profits in the ratio of 3:2:1. Upton wishes to retire, and it is agreed that he shall be paid $40,000.00 for his interest and that the total goodwill of the firm implied by the payment shall be set on the books. Varney and West continue the business for two years, sharing profits in the ratio of 2 and 1. During that period their profits total $33,750.00. Varney withdrew $14,400.00 and West $8,400.00. It was then agreed that the profit and loss ratio should be changed to 3 and 2. In the third year the profits were $21,690.00, and Varney withdrew $7,200.00 and West $4,200.00. At the end of the third year they wrote off the goodwill.

(*a*) Prepare a statement showing the changes in the partners' capital accounts from before Upton's retirement through the third year.
(*b*) How much more or less did Varney lose by the write-off of goodwill than he would have lost had only Upton's share of the goodwill been placed on the books and had it been written off at the end of the first year?

Problem 31-3. Houston, Cass, and Jackson were partners having capitals of $64,300.00, $48,500.00, and $27,500.00 respectively on January 1, 1945. They shared profits in the ratio of 45:35:20.

The articles of partnership provided that, in the event of the death of a partner, the surviving partners need not close the books, but should credit the deceased partner's capital account with an amount computed by applying the fraction of the year since the last closing to the date of death to the average of the partner's share of the profits for the preceding three years. In addition to this, he was to receive as a payment for goodwill, 10% of his capital after the above adjustment for profits and before consideration of any drawings.

The partners were insured for $45,000.00, $35,000.00, and $20,000.00 respectively, the firm being named as beneficiary, and the premiums, although not allowable as a deduction for tax purposes, were paid by the partnership. The policies had no cash surrender values. It was provided that the proceeds of any one of these policies should be used in partial liquidation of the partner's capital account and that any balance in the capital account should be paid one third in cash, one third in a six-months note, and one third in a one-year note.

The profits had been: 1942, $36,850.00; 1943, $47,120.00 and 1944, $52,206.00. Drawings in 1945 prior to Cass's death had been: Houston, $2,200.00; Cass, $1,860.00; and Jackson, $2,400.00.

Cass died on June 15, 1945. (*a*) Prepare a statement showing the computation of his interest. (*b*) Prepare a statement of the partners' capital accounts. (*c*) Give the journal entries to record the dissolution.

Problem 31-4. In the partnership of Morrey and Newton, Morrey's share of the profits was 60% and his capital account had a balance of $74,320.00. The partnership was incorporated. Before the conversion there was a net revaluation of assets amounting to a $21,600.00 increase. Each partner invested enough cash to bring his capital up to a round $500.00 and then received stock with a par value of $100.00 a share for his interest. After two years the corporation paid a stock dividend of 20%. Morrey then sold 200 shares at $95.00 a share.

Assuming that the basis of his investment in the corporation was his original capital plus the cash he invested, how much profit or loss did he realize on the sale?

Problem 31-5. The partnership of Kistler and Maybury decided to incorporate as the Kistler, Maybury Sales Corporation. Its balance sheet prior to incorporation follows:

Assets			Liabilities		
Cash		$ 18,341	Accounts payable	$14,732	
Accounts receivable	$42,165		Notes payable	15,000	$ 29,732
Less reserve for bad debts	3,442	38,723	**Capital**		
Merchandise		26,904	Kistler, capital	$42,137	
Machinery	$22,138		Maybury, capital	38,617	80,754
Less reserve for depreciation	7,620	14,518			
Patents		12,000			
		$110,486			$110,486

The profit and loss ratio was Kistler 55%, Maybury 45%. The assets are to be revalued as follows: Reserve for bad debts is to be $4,000.00; merchandise, $30,000.00; machinery, $28,000.00; reserve for depreciation, $8,000.00; and patents, $20,000.00.

Capital stock of $200,000.00 is authorized, with a par value of $10.00 a share. Capital stock is issued to the partners to the nearest $10.00 below their capitals and the excess is transferred to surplus. Stock with a par value of $30,000.00 is sold to the public at 90.

(*a*) Prepare the journal entries to record the conversion if the partnership books are to be retained.

(*b*) Prepare the balance sheet of the new corporation after all the above transactions have been completed.

Problem 31-6. Using the information shown below, adjust and determine the respective partners' capital accounts as of March 31, 1946, and the amount due and payable yearly per agreement by the surviving partners to the estate of *A*.

A, *B*, and *C* were partners in a merchandising business. The written articles of copartnership provided that profits and losses were to be shared: *A*, 50%; *B*, 30%; *C*, 20%. The articles provided further that in the event of the death of one partner, the survivors were to continue the business, the share of the deceased partner to be paid over to his executor or administrator within three years from day of death in three equal yearly principal installments, 5% interest to be paid on unpaid balance.

The net profits of the firm, certified as correct by the partners, were as follows:

1943	$3,995.00
1944	3,635.00
1945	3,295.00

In January 1946, the copartnership agreement was amended by an addition to the effect that the interest of a deceased partner in the firm was to include his share of the firm's goodwill, this to be the sum of the net profits of the business for three years prior to and ending on the day of death.

A died on March 29, 1946. The survivors and *A*'s representative agreed that the partnership should be considered as terminated, insofar as *A*'s interest was concerned, on March 31, 1946.

The assets and liabilities of the partnership as of December 31, 1945, with resulting net worth, were:

Assets		
Cash		$2,500.00
Notes receivable		2,300.00
Accounts receivable	$2,300.00	
Less reserve for bad debts	100.00	2,200.00
Merchandise inventory		1,665.00
		$8,665.00
Liabilities		
Notes payable	$1,950.00	
Accounts payable	2,415.00	$4,365.00
Net Worth		
A	$1,719.00	
B	1,505.00	
C	1,076.00	$4,300.00

The following summary of operation results covers the months of January, February, and March 1946:

Merchandise inventory, December 31, 1945:	
cost, $1,665.00; retail	$ 2,220.00
Merchandise purchases, three months:	
cost, $10,479.72; retail	13,099.65
Additional mark-on (net)	300.00
Sales (net)	13,300.55
Mark-downs (net)	408.00
Merchandise inventory, March 31, 1946:	
actual, at retail	1,881.10
Notes receivable on hand	2,000.00
Notes receivable under discount at bank	1,500.00
Discount was $15.00	
Customers' balances	2,614.75
Cash payments:	
Salaries and wages	600.00
Rent	225.00
A, drawings	150.00
B, drawings	125.00
C, drawings	100.00
Notes payable	950.00
Accounts payable	5,302.25
Sundry expenses	1,350.00

Problem 31-7. Kelly, Kinsey, Culbertson, and Malone were partners whose capital contributions were $112,500.00, $202,500.00, $45,000.00, and $90,000.00 respectively. Profits were shared in the ratio of initial capital investments.

At the end of the second year of operations, Culbertson died. His estate was paid the sum of $40,700.00 and was released from all liability to the partnership.

At the beginning of the third year, Booth, a former salesman of the firm, was admitted as a partner with a capital contribution of $100,000.00 and with a guarantee against losses of prior periods.

The following drawings were made by the partners during the first three years:

Year	Kelly	Kinsey	Culbertson	Malone	Booth
1	$25,000.00	$60,000.00	$30,000.00	$15,000.00	$ —
2	30,000.00	60,000.00	13,000.00	17,000.00	—
3	20,000.00	55,000.00	—	19,000.00	25,000.00

The profits during the same period were: first year, $270,000.00; second year, $117,000.00; third year, $280,000.00.

After the admission of Booth into the partnership, the profit and loss ratio was:

Kelly	40%
Kinsey	25%
Malone	20%
Booth	15%

After the books were closed at the end of the third year it was discovered that the profits had been misstated by reason of the following facts:

(1) Depreciation of buildings had not been taken into consideration. Depreciation should have been: First year, $45,000.00; second year, $60,000.-00; third year, $45,000.00.

(2) The assets included $75,000.00 of valueless securities purchased with cash contributed by Booth.

Prepare a statement showing the capital accounts of the five partners, after giving effect to the necessary adjustments to correct the books.

Problem 31-8. Jones and Johnson have been partners in a successful business for a number of years. They decide to admit two of their employees on the following basis of profit sharing: Jones, 45%; Johnson, 30%; Jennis, 15%; Jergen 10%.

It is agreed that Jennis and Jergen will not be required to make any capital contributions, but it is provided that in the event of the sale of the business within five years, Jones and Johnson alone shall share in the proceeds of any goodwill.

Three years subsequent to the admission of the employees as partners, an offer of $250,000.00 is received by the partnership for the business. This offer is accepted, the books are closed, and the following balance sheet is drawn off:

Assets	
Cash	$ 20,000.00
Accounts receivable	28,000.00
Notes receivable	35,000.00
Inventory	50,000.00
Automobile	1,020.00
Building	85,000.00
Land	7,980.00
	$227,000.00
Liabilities and Capital	
Accounts payable	$ 15,000.00
Notes payable	12,000.00
Jones, capital	90,000.00
Johnson, capital	75,000.00
Jennis, capital	20,000.00
Jergen, capital	15,000.00
	$227,000.00

The purchasers take the assets at the above values, except as follows:

(*a*) The inventory is taken at $42,000.00.

(*b*) Land and buildings together are taken at $102,000.00.

(*c*) A reserve of $1,500.00 is established for doubtful accounts.

Prepare a statement showing the proper distribution of the $250,000.00 among the four partners.

Problem 31-9. Fisher and Gregg are partners in a manufacturing business, sharing profits in the capital ratio. They, together with their sales manager, Hughes, their factory superintendent, Isaacs, and an outsider, James, have developed plans to form a corporation.

A written agreement, signed by the five parties, contains the following provisions:

The authorized capitalization of the corporation is to consist of enough shares of preferred and common stock, of $100.00 par value each, to meet the requirements stated hereafter.

Hughes and Isaacs are to contribute, in equal parts, sufficient cash to pay the principal of the real estate mortgage which matures January 2, 1945.

James is to furnish sufficient cash to pay the principal of the demand notes.

Preferred stock is to be issued in payment for:

The net worth of the partnership, exclusive of goodwill and cash contributed under this agreement.

Common stock is to be issued for the goodwill of Fisher and Gregg, valued at one half of the net worth of their business.

Fisher and Gregg agree to surrender enough of their shares of the common stock to reduce their holdings to 35% and 25% respectively, of the total common stock issued for goodwill; the shares so surrendered are to be distributed 2/5 to Hughes, 2/5 to Isaacs, and 1/5 to James.

A certified public accountant will make an examination of the accounts as of December 31, 1944, and close the books after providing therein for his fee and reflecting fixed asset values as determined by an appraisal.

The partnership books are to be continued by the corporation.

The accountant submits the following balance sheet:

FISHER AND GREGG

Balance Sheet—December 31, 1944

Assets		Liabilities	
Cash	$ 50,000.00	Accounts payable	$ 65,000.00
Accounts receivable	250,000.00	Demand notes	100,000.00
Notes receivable	150,000.00	Accrued interest on notes	2,000.00
Inventories	250,000.00	Accrued interest on mortgage	5,000.00
Fixed assets	500,000.00	Accrued taxes	13,000.00
		Real estate mortgage	200,000.00
		Reserve for bad debts	15,000.00
		Fisher, capital	500,000.00
		Gregg, capital	300,000.00
	$1,200,000.00		$1,200,000.00

Prepare entries to record the above facts in the manner agreed. The cash contributed by Hughes, Isaacs, and James was used for the purposes designated.

Problem 31-10. *P* and *Q* were partners in a manufacturing concern. On December 31, 1945, they decided to incorporate and do business under the name of the *P Q* Manufacturing Company, with an authorized capital of $750,000.00. The new organization purchased all the assets and assumed all the liabilities of the partnership, as disclosed in the following balance sheet of December 31, 1945:

P Q MANUFACTURING COMPANY

Balance Sheet—December 31, 1945

Assets		Liabilities	
Cash	$ 46,795.00	Accrued wages	$ 2,150.00
Notes receivable	18,000.00	Accounts payable	19,368.00
Accounts receivable	152,716.00	Notes payable	19,421.00
Inventories	161,112.00	*P*, capital	300,000.00
Plant	100,000.00	*Q*, capital	350,000.00
Machinery	212,316.00		
	$690,939.00		$690,939.00

The entire issue of capital stock was taken by *P* and *Q* as consideration. The change in organization was not reflected on the books at the time of incorporation; on December 31, 1946, the trial balance appeared as follows:

Trial Balance, December 31, 1946

Sales		$ 871,608.00
Purchases	$ 321,060.00	
Labor	191,060.00	
Office salaries	40,000.00	
Notes receivable	35,000.00	
Notes payable		56,380.00
Accounts receivable	176,181.00	
Accounts payable		37,382.00
Cash	70,020.00	
Traveling expenses	15,000.00	
Interest received		1,460.00
Interest paid	2,162.00	
Stationery and printing	931.00	
Rent and taxes	26,000.00	
Discounts on purchases		4,280.00
Discounts on sales	3,182.00	
Heat and light	25,150.00	
Insurance	9,800.00	
Freight in	9,290.00	
Commissions	46,172.00	
Advertising	56,810.00	
Inventories, December 31, 1945	161,112.00	
Plant	150,000.00	
Machinery	252,180.00	
P, capital		300,000.00
Q, capital		350,000.00
P, personal	15,000.00	
Q, personal	15,000.00	
	$1,621,110.00	$1,621,110.00

Inventories, December 31, 1946 and 1945, were as follows:

	December 31, 1946	December 31, 1945
Raw material	$52,161.00	$54,270.00
Goods in process	22,380.00	23,015.00
Finished goods	82,690.00	83,827.00

December 31, 1946 adjustments:

Depreciation: plant, 5%; machinery, 10%.

Required reserve for bad debts, $1,986.00.

Accruals: factory payroll, $1,840.00; office salaries, $400.00.

Unexpired insurance, $4,300.00.

P and *Q*, as president and vice-president, are entitled to salaries of $25,000.00 and $18,000.00 respectively, none of which has been charged to operations, all money paid to *P* and *Q* having been charged to their personal accounts.

Distribute certain expenses as follows:

	Manufacturing	Selling	General
Executive salaries................	40%		60%
Rent and taxes..................	95		5
Heat and light....................	98		2
Insurance.......................	90	2%	8

Make the necessary adjusting entries and prepare operating statements and a balance sheet as of December 31, 1946. Submit your working papers.

QUESTIONS AND PROBLEMS ON CHAPTER 32

Questions

Question 32-1. Name three general causes of dissolution of a partnership.

Name four ways in which the acts of the partners may result in a dissolution of a partnership.

Name four causes of dissolution by operation of law.

Name five causes for which a court will dissolve a partnership.

Question 32-2. Does the dissolution of a partnership necessarily involve the discontinuance of the business and the distribution of the assets among the partners? Explain fully.

Question 32-3. What is the order of priority in the payment of equities, in the liquidation of a partnership?

Question 32-4. Why should losses and gains on realization be divided among the partners before any liquidating payments are made to them?

Question 32-5. State two errors frequently committed in dividing the cash among the partners of a liquidating partnership.

Question 32-6. *A* and *B* enter into partnership on January 1, 1946, investing $20,000.00 and $16,000.00 respectively, and making no agreement regarding the division of profits. The business is unsuccessful, and it is decided to liquidate. On November 30, after converting all assets into cash and paying all liabilities, the partners find that they have $27,000.00 in cash to divide. Between January 1, and November 30, 1946 *A* has drawn $2,000.00 and *B* has drawn $1,000.00. A dispute then arises concerning the division of the $27,000.00. *A* claims that the money should be divided in the capital ratio—5/9 and 4/9. *B* contends that, since they made no agreement, they are equal partners, and hence the $27,000.00 should be divided equally. You are asked for your opinion. Write a letter to the partners, showing how you think the $27,000.00 should be divided, and giving your reasons.

Question 32-7. What is meant by "the right of offset" in partnership liquidations?

Question 32-8. *F* and *G* have capitals of $25,000.00 and $3,000.00 respectively. *G* manages the business and is allowed a salary. Two thousand dollars of his salary has not been paid, and it appears as a credit in an account called *G*, salary. All assets have been realized; all liabilities have been liquidated; and there is $22,000.00 of cash for division between the partners. State how this money should be divided.

Question 32-9. How should you distribute the cash on hand in liquidating a partnership, if, after charging off losses:

(*a*) One partner has a credit balance and the other has a debit balance?
(*b*) Two partners have credit balances and one has a debit balance?
(*c*) A partner has a debit balance in his capital account and a credit balance in a loan account?

Question 32-10. Because the profit and loss ratio in a given partnership differed from the capital ratio, some of the partners had debit balances and others had credit balances after all losses were charged off. The assets were not sufficient to pay the liabilities. Could the creditors collect from any partner, or would they have to collect from only those partners who had debit balances, on the theory that the partners with credit balances had equities in the partnership assets similar to those of the creditors?

Question 32-11. If a partnership is insolvent and the partners are individually insolvent, what is the rule for making payments to firm creditors and to individual creditors?

Question 32-12. *A*, *B*, and *C* are in partnership. Their capitals are $4,000.00, $20,000.00 and $34,000.00 respectively. The balance sheet shows assets of $68,000.00 and liabilities of $10,000.00. The partnership is dissolved and the assets are sold for $50,000.00.

A has outside assets of $2,000.00 and owes outside liabilities of $3,000.00; *B* has outside assets of $5,000.00 and owes outside liabilities of $7,000.00; *C* has outside assets of $15,000.00 and owes outside liabilities of $2,500.00.

State the rights of the firm creditors, and of *A*, *B*, and *C*, or their creditors, in the $50,000.00 received from the sale of the partnership assets. Assume that the uniform partnership law does not apply.

Problems

Problem 32-1. The balance sheet of the firm of Allston and Blaine follows.

Assets	$68,000.00	Liabilities	$28,000.00
Blaine, capital	3,000.00	Loan, Blaine	10,000.00
		Allston, capital	22,000.00
		Cabot, capital	11,000.00
	$71,000.00		$71,000.00

Profits were divided as follows: Allston, 50%; Blaine, 30%; and Cabot, 20% The assets were sold for $38,000.00.

(*a*) Prepare a statement showing the distribution of the cash.
(*b*) Prepare the journal entries to record the liquidation.

Problem 32-2. The firm of Howell and Jackson presents the following balance sheet before liquidation

Assets	$83,400.00	Liabilities	$41,420.00
		Howell, capital	24,250.00
		Jackson, capital	6,730.00
		Howell, loan	5,000.00
		Jackson, loan	6,000.00
	$83,400.00		$83,400.00

The assets were sold for $46,000.00. Prepare two statements showing the liquidation of the partnership, one under the assumption that the profit and loss ratio was Howell 65% and Jackson 35%, and the other under the assumption that the profit and loss ratio was Howell 80% and Jackson 20%.

Problem 32-3. The firm of Katchel and Lownes was insolvent. Prepare a statement showing the amounts which creditors of the firm and creditors of the partners may collect under the common law rule, assuming the creditors of the partnership collect on their deficiency from Katchel.

Cash	$49,350.00	Liabilities	$53,620.00
Katchel	17,840.00	Lownes, capital	2,140.00
		Macy, capital	6,430.00
		Macy, loan	5,000.00
	$67,190.00		$67,190.00

Profits were shared as follows: Katchel, 60%; Lownes, 25%; and Macy, 15%. The personal balance sheets of the partners follow:

	Katchel	Lownes	Macy
Assets	$13,125.00	$15,628.00	$36,170.00
Liabilities	8,410.00	16,100.00	1,800.00

Problem 32-4. Owing to the insolvency of Bruce, the firm of Arnold, Bruce, and Camp is compelled to liquidate. They share profits in the ratio of 40:35:25. The balance sheet of the firm follows:

Cash	$ 23,400.00	Liabilities	$ 42,140.00
Accounts receivable	48,650.00	Arnold, capital	63,445.00
Merchandise	37,108.00	Bruce, capital	8,642.00
Fixed assets	38,580.00	Camp, capital	33,511.00
	$147,738.00		$147,738.00

A new firm, Arnold and Camp, is to be formed. It agrees, with the creditors' consent, to assume the liabilities of the old firm, and to take over the assets of the old firm at the following values:

Cash	$ 23,400.00
Accounts receivable	41,300.00
Merchandise	25,200.00
Fixed assets	27,100.00

All creditors are paid 50 cents on the dollar at once and given notes for the the remainder of their claims. Arnold invests $10,000.00 and Camp $5,000.00 in cash to restore the cash position of the firm. The claim against Bruce is to be carried at its realizable value under the common law rule as an asset of the new partnership until settled.

Bruce has personal assets of $7,886.52 and personal creditors of $17,600.00.

(*a*) Prepare a statement showing the changes in capital brought about by the dissolution of the old partnership.

(*b*) Prepare a balance sheet of the new partnership.

Problem 32-5. The affairs of the partnership of Colton and Corning have become involved owing to Colton's habit of mingling his personal and partnership affairs. Colton and Corning began business with capitals of $30,000.00 and $20,000.00 respectively, and share profits in the same ratio. Corning wishes to withdraw, and asks you to determine his interest. A balance sheet prepared from the firm's ledger follows:

Cash	$ 7,320.00	Liabilities	$18,344.00
Other assets	63,170.00	Colton, capital	24,193.00
		Corning, capital	27,953.00
	$70,490.00		$70,490.00

You learn that Colton has paid out of partnership funds certain mortgage notes on properties he owned. These, together with interest, amounted to $18,364.00. In addition to this, Colton sometimes collected accounts and deposited the money in his own account. When the bookkeeper learned of such collections, he would credit the account receivable and debit Colton's capital account. These collections were determined to be $13,580.00, of which $3,460.00 have not yet been recorded on the books.

On the other hand, at one time Colton satisfied a judgment of $21,300.00 against the firm by deeding to the claimant property which had cost Colton $16,420.00 and was valued at $20,000.00 at the time of the settlement. This judgment had never been recorded on the books.

The cash on hand has been proved against the bank account, and the liabilities are correctly stated. Colton offers to take over all the non-cash assets at $50,000.00 and Corning agrees to the offer.

How much will Corning receive in liquidation?

Problem 32-6. The partnership of *C* and *D* is preparing to liquidate. *C* and *D* draw off a trial balance which shows the following balances: Assets, $13,000.00; liabilities, $2,000.00; *C*-capital, $9,000.00; *D*-capital, $2,000.00.

The assets are sold for $11,500.00. Prepare a statement showing the liquidation of the partnership.

Problem 32-7. On January 1, 1944 Alton and Bestor formed a partnership, the terms of which specified that all profits and losses were to be shared equally, and that no interest was to be credited on the investments or charged on the withdrawals.

Alton invested $25,000.00, and Bestor invested $20,000.00. The books had not been closed, but the capital accounts had been charged with drawings.

On August 31, 1946 the partnership was dissolved; the books had been very poorly kept, and, as a result, the following statement was presented to the partners as a basis for settlement and was agreed to by them:

Debits	
Cash	$15,100.00
Expenses	16,700.00
Alton, capital	5,100.00
Profit and loss	8,000.00
Real estate (estimated value)	3,500.00
Credits	
Bestor, capital	$11,200.00
Bank loan (six-month, 6% note due October 31, 1946)	11,000.00

Interest on the bank loan is unpaid.

Alton sold the real estate for $3,300.00 and paid the note when due.

Prepare a statement of the partners' accounts, showing their interests as of August 31, 1946 and at the close of liquidation.

Problem 32-8. Walsh, Andersen, and Graham, all active in the auto business, believed they could operate advantageously as a partnership. On January 1, 1944 the three men accepted, as the basis for organizing a firm, the plan outlined below:

Capital contributions:

Walsh to contribute a garage and a new car agency, valued together at $25,000.00.

Andersen, a mechanic, to sell his repair shop and tools, and invest in the new firm the cash realized by the sale.

Graham to transfer to the firm a bargain lot, including an inventory of used cars, and to receive therefor a capital credit of $21,000.00.

Profits to be shared equally.

Andersen, as agreed, sold his repair shop and tools, obtaining $5,000.00 in cash and $10,000.00 in notes, which the partners accepted as his contribution.

Walsh acted as office manager, and also undertook to keep a double entry system of accounts, but failed to keep them in balance. After 19 months of operations, the partners disagreed over policies and decided to liquidate the business. Therefore, on July 31 Walsh closed the books and drew off account balances as follows:

Cash	$ 15,600.00	
Garage	14,000.00	
Inventory of used cars	12,000.00	
Tools	1,400.00	
Non-interest-bearing note payable		$ 2,000.00
6% first-mortgage payable—interest payable Jan. 31, July 31		8,000.00
Walsh		9,300.00
Andersen	1,300.00	
Graham		11,200.00
Sales		70,000.00
Expenses	61,000.00	
	$105,300.00	$100,500.00

On August 15 the garage, the inventory of used cars, the tools, and the mortgage and accrued interest were taken over by Walsh for $17,000.00, which was charged against his capital account. Interest on the mortgage had not been paid when due on July 31, but was paid on August 5. On August 10 the note was paid in full.

Prepare statements showing the interests of the partners on July 31 and August 15, 1945 and the distribution of all cash on August 15.

Problem 32-9. *C* and *D* are partners sharing profits and losses in the ratio of 55% and 45%.

C's capital investment is $4,500.00 and *D*'s is $3,500.00. It is decided by the partners that the business should be dissolved. The firm has liabilities of $7,200.00, including $900.00 due *D* and $600.00 due *C* on loans. The only asset is cash in the amount of $7,500.00.

Prepare a statement of liquidation.

Problem 32-10. The balance sheet of the firm of Adams and Coleman appeared as follows as of November 30, 1946:

Assets	$42,500.00	Liabilities	$20,000.00
		Adams—capital	12,000.00
		Adams—loan	3,000.00
		Coleman—capital	5,000.00
		Coleman—loan	2,500.00
	$42,500.00		$42,500.00

Adams and Coleman share profits and losses equally. The partnership is dissolved as of the above date, and the assets are sold for $26,500.00 cash.

Prepare a statement showing the proper distribution of the $26,500.00.

Problem 32-11. Bullitt and Crass, upon winding up their partnership, found that their assets had realized as follows:

	Book Value	Realized
Machinery	$ 8,000.00	$3,200.00
Building	12,000.00	5,000.00
Merchandise	10,000.00	2,500.00
Accounts receivable	9,800.00	8,900.00

Unpaid liabilities amounted to $14,800.00.

The partners shared profits and losses equally; Bullitt's capital stood at $16,000.00 and Crass' capital stood at $9,000.00.

You are to divide the proceeds of the realization between the partners after paying off the liabilities; debit them as having been paid the proportion to which each was entitled, and show what amount would be payable by either partner to the other to settle the account.

Problem 32-12. *J*, *K*, and *L* are in partnership, with capitals of $13,000.00, $5,000.00, and $1,500.00 respectively. It is decided to dissolve the partnership; the assets are disposed of, the liabilities are paid, and there is $9,000.00 of cash on hand as the only remaining asset.

The partners share profits in the following ratios:

J	45%
K	35
L	20

How should this cash be divided?

QUESTIONS AND PROBLEMS ON CHAPTER 33

Questions

Question 33-1. Wherein lies the danger of making liquidating distributions to partners before the assets are all realized and the liabilities all paid?

Assume that all partnership liabilities have been paid, but that the partnership assets have not all been realized. How can a liquidator safeguard himself if he wishes to make partial payments to the partners?

Question 33-2. If the liabilities have not all been paid, how may the liquidator safeguard himself in making partial payments to the partners?

Question 33-3. Assume that a partnership is to be liquidated in installments. What consideration, if any, should be given to the partners' loan accounts in determining the amounts which can be paid to them in distribution of the installments?

Question 33-4. Assume that a partner had a loan account and a capital account, and that the sum of the balances of both accounts was less than his possible losses on future realization. The other partner had only a capital account, but its balance exceeded his possible loss. Would it be permissible to waive the rule requiring payments of loans before capital and to make a payment on the second partner's capital account before making any payments on the first partner's loan account?

Question 33-5. You have been appointed liquidator of the firm of *A*, *B*, and *C*, whose balance sheet appears as follows:

Cash	$ 5,000.00	*A*, capital	$30,000.00
Other assets	45,000.00	*B*, capital	15,000.00
		C, capital	5,000.00
	$50,000.00		$50,000.00

State how you would divide the $5,000.00 cash.

Question 33-6. Referring to the preceding question, assume that *B* and *C* insist that the money should be divided in the capital ratio: $3,000.00 to *A*, 1,500.00 to *B*, and $500.00 to *C*. Explain why this division would be unwise.

Question 33-7. You have been appointed liquidator of the firm of *X* and *Y*, whose balance sheet appears as follows:

Cash	$ 5,000.00	*X*, capital	$25,000.00
Other assets	40,000.00	*Y*, capital	15,000.00
		Y, loan	5,000.00
	$45,000.00		$45,000.00

To which partner would you pay the $5,000.00 cash on hand? Or, would you divide it?

Problems

Problem 33-1. Dale, Files, and Garth, partners, decide to liquidate. The balance sheet of the partnership follows.

Assets		Liabilities	
Cash	$ 16,400.00	Mortgage payable	$ 30,000.00
Other assets	101,860.00	Other liabilities	28,450.00
Fixed assets	42,300.00	Dale, capital	64,000.00
		Files, capital	32,100.00
		Garth, capital	6,010.00
	$160,560.00		$160,560.00

The partners shared profits in the ratio of 60:30:10.

During the first month, assets carried at $40,000.00 were sold for $32,000.00, but since the mortgage payments were not due, no payments were made on the mortgage.

During the second month, the mortgagee agreed to take the fixed assets in settlement of the mortgage and to pay $5,000.00 additional consideration. Other assets carried at $26,000.00 were sold for $19,000.00.

During the third month, assets carried at $29,500.00 were sold for $15,000.00, and the remainder of the assets were considered valueless.

Prepare a statement showing the liquidation by months.

Problem 33-2. The partnership of Mason, Nash, and Otis presents the following balance sheet.

Cash	$ 6,230.00	Liabilities	$18,462.00
Nash, capital	3,880.00	Mason, capital	17,144.00
Other assets	74,160.00	Otis, capital	48,664.00
	$84,270.00		$84,270.00

The profits were shared as follows: Mason, 55%; Nash, 30%; and Otis, 15%. During the first month, assets valued at $23,100.00 were sold for $20,600.00, and the cash was distributed.

During the second month, assets recorded at $38,750.00 were sold for $21,460.00, and the cash was distributed.

During the third month, the remainder of the "other assets" were sold for $2,800.00, and it was discovered that no collections could be made from Nash. Mason is fully solvent.

Prepare a statement showing the progress of the liquidation.

Problem 33-3. Prepare a statement of partners' capitals, showing the monthly distributions, for the firm of Quimby, Ross, and Scott, whose balance sheet follows:

Cash	$ 18,640.00	Liabilities	$ 21,365.00
Other assets	97,165.00	Ross, loan	15,000.00
		Scott, loan	10,000.00
		Quimby, capital	23,140.00
		Ross, capital	34,420.00
		Scott, capital	11,880.00
	$115,805.00		$115,805.00

The partners shared profits as follows: Quimby, 60%; Ross, 30%; and Scott, 10%. Assets valued on the books at $26,000.00 were sold for $21,000.00 during the first month. All cash except $2,000.00 was distributed.

During the second month, assets valued at $42,000.00 were sold for $34,000.00. All cash except $2,500.00 was distributed.

In the third month, the remaining non-cash assets were sold for $8,000.00, expenses of $1,800.00 were paid, and the remainder of the cash was distributed to the partners.

Problem 33-4. The partnership of Frost, Flint, and Fraser presented the following balance sheet, prior to its liquidation:

Assets	$93,650.00	Liabilities	$18,430.00
		Frost, capital	34,160.00
		Flint, capital	16,630.00
		Fraser, capital	24,430.00
	$93,650.00		$93,650.00

The profit and loss ratio was 4:4:2.

During the first month, assets carried at $18,500.00 were sold for $15,000.00 and the cash was distributed. During the second month, assets carried at $22,400.00 were sold for $18,000.00. At that time, Flint was anxious to get his money out of the partnership in order to get started in another business. He offered to take $10,000.00 from the second realization as his final payment, releasing the other partners from all other claims. The other partners agreed. All cash was distributed.

During the next three months the remaining assets were sold for $35,000.00.

(*a*) Prepare a statement showing the progress of the liquidation.
(*b*) How much did Frost gain or lose by accepting Flint's offer?

Problem 33-5. Prepare a statement of partners' capitals showing the progress of the following liquidation:

Cash	$ 4,000.00	Liabilities	$12,000.00
Other assets	92,000.00	*Q*, loan	10,000.00
		R, loan	5,000.00
		P, capital	29,000.00
		Q, capital	25,000.00
		R, capital	15,000.00
	$96,000.00		$96,000.00

Profit and loss ratio: *P*, 40%; *Q*, 35%; *R*, 25%.

Realizations	Assets Valued at	Cash Realized	Expenses of Realization
1st month	$14,000.00	$12,000.00	$1,000.00
2d month	24,000.00	21,000.00	1,500.00
3d month	54,000.00	28,000.00	2,000.00

It is to be understood that all cash available is distributed each month.

Problem 33-6. Romean, Julien, Copar, and Dogmen, partners, decide to liquidate their business. All losses on the partial realization of assets to date have been charged off, there are no liabilities, and the partners' capitals are $20,000.00, $13,000.00, $15,000.00, and $18,000.00 respectively.

There is $6,000.00 of cash on hand to distribute to the partners, whose profit and loss sharing ratios are as follows:

Romean	23%
Julien	19
Copar	28
Dogmen	30
	100%

Prepare a statement showing how the cash should be distributed.

Problem 33-7. Samuels, Rosecrans, and McLinden are in partnership: their capital contributions were $85,000.00, $60,000.00, and $40,000.00 resepectively. Profits are shared equally.

During the year, Rosecrans withdrew $12,500.00. The firm incurred a net loss of $18,000.00 during the year, and it is decided to liquidate the business.

Although none of the assets is known to be worthless, it is uncertain just how much they will ultimately realize. The partners agree to distribute the cash realized from the assets in such a manner as to avoid, as far as possible, the possibility of paying any partner cash which he might later have to repay to another.

Assets were realized, and distributions made as follows:

August	$20,000.00
September	17,000.00
October	47,000.00

Nothing more can be collected on the assets. Show the partners' accounts, indicating how the cash should be distributed in each installment.

Problem 33-8. *R*, *S*, *T*, and *U*, partners, decide to liquidate their business. Their capitals and profit and loss sharing ratios are as follows:

	Capital, May 31	Ratio
R	$ 45,000.00	35%
S	24,000.00	25
T	40,000.00	20
U	5,000.00	20
Total	$114,000.00	100%

The liabilities are all paid and the assets are realized as follows:

In June assets having a book value of $39,000.00 are sold for $27,000.00; during July assets carried at a book value of $50,000.00 are sold for $45,000.00; and in August assets valued at $25,000.00 are sold for $18,500.00.

All of the cash realized is distributed to the partners each month.

Prepare a statement of the capital accounts and working papers, showing the distribution of the cash.

Problem 33-9. The following balance sheet was taken from the books of a partnership as of November 30, 1946:

Cash	$ 7,500.00	Liabilities	$ 10,000.00
Other assets	111,500.00	*L*, capital	18,000.00
		L, loan	7,000.00
		M, capital	17,000.00
		M, loan	2,000.00
		N, capital	35,000.00
		O, capital	20,000.00
		O, loan	10,000.00
	$119,000.00		$119,000.00

It is decided to liquidate the partnership. The non-cash assets are realized in three installments, as follows:

	Assets Realized	Loss	Cash Obtained	Expenses Paid	Net Cash Proceeds
First installment	$ 33,010.00	$ 5,000.00	$28,010.00	$1,110.00	$26,900.00
Second installment	47,000.00	8,500.00	38,500.00	1,200.00	37,300.00
Third installment	31,490.00	6,500.00	24,990.00	900.00	24,090.00
	$111,500.00	$20,000.00	$91,500.00	$3,210.00	$88,290.00

All cash available after each periodical realization is distributed. Prepare working papers and statement of partners' accounts showing the distributions.

Losses and gains are shared equally.

Problem 33-10. *R*, *S*, *T*, and *U* enter into partnership, each partner contributing $35,000.00. They are to share profits and losses in the following proportion:

R	40%
S	25
T	15
U	20

At the completion of the first year's business there is a loss of $10,000.00; the partners agree to dissolve the business and to distribute the proceeds of the firm's assets. Partners' drawings have been: *R*, $500.00; *S*, $750,00; *T*, $350.00; *U*, $550.00.

The realization and liquidation lasts four months and the transactions are as follows:

	Total	September	October	November	December
Assets realized—book value	$150,000.00	$45,260.00	$52,186.00	$45,880.00	$6,674.00
Loss on realization	18,200.00	5,000.00	12,000.00	300.00	900.00
Liabilities paid	22,150.00	5,480.00	3,690.00	10,850.00	2,130.00

Prepare a statement showing how much should be paid to each partner on each realization of assets.

Problem 33-11. Four partners who are about to liquidate their business close their books and draw off the following balances:

Cash	$ 12,500.00
Other assets	190,500.00
Frank, capital	43,000.00
Morris, capital	32,000.00
Sherman, capital	50,000.00
William, capital	61,000.00
Liabilities	17,000.00

The partners' profit and loss sharing ratios are: Frank, 25%; Morris, 30%; Sherman, 20%; and William, 25%.

It is mutually agreed that Frank, Morris, and William shall immediately be free to enter other businesses, and that Sherman shall liquidate the business. In consideration of his services, Sherman is to be allowed a commission of 2% of all cash collected. The commission is to be considered a partnership expense and is payable in cash.

Following is a summary of the liquidation:

	Assets Realized	Loss	Cash Collected	Expenses Paid	Liabilities Paid	Balance
First month	$ 49,800.00	$ 1,020.00	$ 48,780.00	$1,000.00	$ 5,800.00	$ 41,980.00
Second month	48,000.00	980.00	47,020.00	1,050.00	6,290.00	39,680.00
Third month	65,720.00	6,390.00	59,330.00	1,900.00	3,800.00	53,630.00
Fourth month	26,980.00	2,110.00	24,870.00	1,250.00	1,110.00	22,510.00
Total	$190,500.00	$10,500.00	$180,000.00	$5,200.00	$17,000.00	$157,800.00

You are to determine the commissions allowable to Sherman, and show the monthly distribution to the partners.

Prepare working papers and a statement of the partners' capital accounts.

Problem 33-12. The capital of the copartnership of Goe & Gettem amounted to $40,000.00, of which Goe contributed $25,000.00 and Gettem $15,000.00. The arrangement with respect to the distribution of profits was that Goe received 60% and Gettem 40%. The capital contributions referred to represented the amount of the capital of the respective partners immediately prior to the admission of Goode as a partner on January 1, 1943.

By agreement among the three partners, the aggregate contributed capital of the new firm at its inception on January 1, 1943 was to continue at $40,000.00, Goode to pay Goe, personally, $10,000.00 for the transfer of a one-quarter interest in Goe's capital account to Goode's capital account and Goode to have a 20% interest in the profits or losses, with the interests in profits and losses of Goe and Gettem 40% each.

The profits for 1943 amounted to $15,000.00, and during the year Goe withdrew $7,000.00, Gettem $5,000.00, and Goode $2,500.00. A loss of $25,000.00, was sustained in 1944, and the withdrawals during that year were: Goe, $4,000.00; Gettem, $3,000.00; Goode, $2,000.00. Goode had advanced $1,000.00 as a loan, and the other liabilities at December 31, 1944 consisted of trade accounts payable.

When it was decided at the end of 1944 to liquidate, the trade creditors were paid in full from the cash on hand and the collections of accounts receivable. Of the then remaining $7,500.00 assets, $6,500.00 were sold for $1,500.00 cash. It was agreed that this cash should be distributed before realization of the sole remaining asset of $1,000.00, the value of which was problematical. Assuming that Goe and Gettem may have to absorb any deficiency on Goode's accounts:

1. How should the $1,500.00 cash be distributed?
2. How should the proceeds from the sale of the doubtful asset be distributed if $800.00 is ultimately realized?
3. How, if $5,000.00 is ultimately realized?
4. What is the amount that should be realized so that Goode's share may exactly reimburse his partners for the deficiency assumed by them?

QUESTIONS AND PROBLEMS ON CHAPTER 34

Questions

Question 34-1. How would you require manufactured goods, shipped to customers for sale to them, as and when used by them, to be stated in a balance sheet you are to certify?

Question 34-2. Discuss the theory which justifies carrying consignment expenses applicable to unsold goods as part of the inventory value instead of closing them out as charges against profits.

Question 34-3. In auditing the accounts of an engineering corporation, you find that a number of engines have been shipped to dealers on consignment, against which the dealers have made deposits of 75% of the invoice price. The engines were invoiced to the dealers at the regular contract prices, which were charged to the accounts receivable; the deposits referred to were credited to the same accounts. How should these items be stated in the balance sheet, and on what basis should they be valued?

Question 34-4. If a consignor desires to keep consignment profits separate from profits on regular sales, how should he record:

(*a*) The shipment of merchandise?
(*b*) Expenses?
(*c*) The proceeds received from the consignee?

If the consignor does not desire to distinguish between profits on consignments and those on regular sales, how should the foregoing items be recorded?

Question 34-5. Assuming that a consignor keeps his accounts in such a manner as to merge the consignment profits with the other profits in the sales account, state whether you consider it advisable for him to credit sales with the net proceeds of consignments or to credit sales with the gross proceeds, and to debit the consignee's charges to expense accounts? Give reasons.

Question 34-6. Assume that a consignee has sold part of the consignment and made remittance after deducting expenses applicable to the consignment as a whole; what adjustments, if any, should the consignor make because of such expenses in preparing a profit and loss statement and a balance sheet?

Question 34-7. The amount of outstanding accounts receivable by a selling house for account of a consignor, whose account is unguaranteed, is $762,000.00; the selling house has advanced thereon to the consignor, $80,000.00. The consignor shows in his balance sheet: "Outstanding accounts receivable, $682,-000.00," as embracing the above. State your opinion of the propriety thereof, and if you would treat the items differently, state how and why.

Question 34-8. How should consignment-in accounts be shown in the consignee's balance sheet?

Assume that the consignee keeps a controlling account with consignments; how should the balance of the controlling account be shown in the balance sheet?

Question 34-9. What adjustments should the consignee make at the end of the accounting period because of consignments on which he has made partial sales without rendering account sales?

Problems

Problem 34-1. The Podlach Novelty Company ships goods on consignment. It bills these goods to the consignees at 50% above cost, and carries consignments in its accounts receivable balance at an amount which represents the billed price less any advances and net remittances. The consignees are allowed to sell the goods at billed prices and deduct 15% for commissions and also expenses paid. The Podlach Company's balance sheet appears as follows:

Cash	$ 11,230.00	Accounts payable	$ 23,400.00
Accounts receivable	52,630.00	Capital stock	75,000.00
Merchandise	27,142.00	Surplus	30,852.00
Other assets	38,250.00		
	$129,252.00		$129,252.00

An examination of the consignment accounts reveals the following information:

	Black	White	Green	Brown
Shipments billed	$21,000.00	$15,000.00	$12,000.00	$9,000.00
Expenses:				
Paid by Podlach	300.00	200.00	100.00	50.00
Paid by consignees	200.00	100.00	100.00	100.00
Advances by consignees	6,000.00		3,000.00	2,000.00
Cash remitted on account sales	2,725.00	5,000.00		5,550.00
Portion of shipment unsold	½	¼	All	None

Required: (*a*) Restatement of balance sheet.
(*b*) Statement of profits made on consignments.
(*c*) Reconciliation of corrected surplus.

Problem 34-2. The Evanston Company consigned five lathes which cost $1,200.00 each to the Louisville Supply Company which was to sell them for a 20% commission on the selling price. The Evanston Company paid trucking charges of $260.00 on the shipment. The Louisville Supply Company paid $400.00 freight and $30.00 drayage on the shipment. At the end of the year the Louisville Supply Company reported that it had sold three of the lathes, two for cash at $2,200.00 each and one on terms at $2,400.00 on which it had collected 25% as a down payment. The Louisville Supply Company remitted all the cash then due.

(*a*) Prepare the account sales.
(*b*) Show the journal entries on the books of the Evanston Company:
(1) If it keeps consignment sales separate from regular sales, uses a perpetual inventory, and takes up net proceeds only.
(2) If it does not keep consignment sales separate from direct sales, uses a periodic inventory, and reports gross proceeds.

Problem 34-3. The Birmingham Company presented the following statements:

Profit and Loss Statement

Sales	$1,072,400.00
Cost of goods sold	854,300.00
Gross profit	$ 218,100.00
Expenses	172,360.00
Net profit	$ 45,740.00

Balance Sheet

Cash	$ 9,230.00	Accounts payable	$ 28,640.00
Accounts receivable	48,038.00	Notes payable	10,000.00
Inventories	63,882.00	Capital stock	100,000.00
Other assets	75,100.00	Surplus	57,610.00
	$196,250.00		$196,250.00

The president is much concerned over the fact that while the sales have expanded, the gross profit, which usually was about 30%, has declined to approximately 20%. This is explained to him as owing to the fact that most of the increase in sales arose from consignment arrangements made with three large brokers; that no entries are made for consignments until the goods are sold by the consignees; and that sales by the brokers were recorded on the books on a net basis after commissions of 20% and expenses which average 4% of sales had been deducted. The president asks you to reconstruct the statements on a basis comparable with prior periods.

You find that the sales by brokers, as recorded on the books, were $456,000.00. You also discover that, of the inventory, $32,400.00 was on consignment and that expenses amounting to $1,200.00 which are applicable to this consignment inventory were charged to expenses instead of being deferred.

Prepare such statements as you deem necessary to clarify the situation.

Problem 34-4. The Moffett Sales Company received a $12,500.00 shipment from the Gainesville Manufacturing Company, for sale on a 10% commission basis. The commission, which was based on the portion of the sales price collected, was deductible at the time of remittance. It was agreed that the merchandise could be sold on credit, 2% in 30 days, and that all cash discounts were deductible from Moffett's remittances, as well as all expenses and cash advanced.

The Moffett Sales Company advanced $5,000.00 on the shipment and also paid expenses of $420.00 chargeable against the shipment. It sold 80% of the shipment for $18,000.00. Of this amount, $14,000.00 less discounts was collected, and Moffett made the necessary remittance.

(*a*) Journalize all transactions on the books of Moffett Sales Company up to the time of closing the books.

(*b*) State how the above facts would be reflected in the balance sheet of Moffett Sales Company.

Problem 34-5. The Barstow Company started business on January 1, 1946 with an investment of $10,000.00 represented by common stock. It was to act as the Pacific coast representative of the Meehan Manufacturing Company of New York. It received merchandise on consignment, which it sold on credit, receiving the regular commission of 15% of sales and an additional 1% for guaranteeing the credit of the accounts sold. Commissions are collectible upon remittance of the proceeds of the accounts.

It wants to keep its records in such a way as to show the loss or gain resulting from its guaranty. It also wants its records to reveal the commissions earned, even though they have not matured.

During the year the Barstow Company made sales of $284,360.00. The outstanding consignment accounts receivable on December 31, 1946 were $43,128.00. Of this amount $2,440.00 were uncollectible and were written off. The expenses of the Barstow Company were $36,380.00 of which $4,074.00 represented items deductible against remittances to the consignor. Deductions already taken amount to $3,250.00. All remittances due have been made.

(*a*) Prepare journal entries to summarize the transactions of the Barstow Company.
(*b*) Prepare a balance sheet of the Barstow Company.

Problem 34-6. In the month of January 1945 John Hopkinson organized a company for the purpose of selling goods consigned to him by the Miller Manufacturing Company. The company issued $25,000.00 of stock, all of which was sold for cash.

The company's agreement with the Miller Manufacturing Company contained the following provision:

Freight charges and a commission of 10% were to be deducted from cash received by him as collections from sales; the remainder would be remitted to the consignor company.

During the year, consigned goods in the amount of $125,000.00 were received from the Miller Manufacturing Company.

The numerous account sales rendered to the consignor during the year may be summarized as follows; sales, $142,000.00; commissions, $14,200.00; freight in, $1,710.00; cash proceeds remitted, $126,090.00.

From the above information and the following trial balance, prepare:

(*a*) Entries in journal form recording the transactions of the year.
(*b*) Profit and loss statement.
(*c*) Balance sheet.

Following is the trial balance of the consignee company as of December 31, 1945:

Capital stock issued		$25,000.00
Accounts receivable	$22,000.00	
Freight in	340.00	
Expenses	8,750.00	
Commissions earned		16,400.00
Cash	30,110.00	
Miller Manufacturing Company		19,800.00
Consignments in—nominal price	14,000.00	
Miller Manufacturing Company—consignors		14,000.00
	$75,200.00	$75,200.00

Problem 34-7. (*a*) From the following information taken from the books of the Hedges Corporation, make any necessary adjusting entries.

The balance in the consignments-out controlling account on August 31, 1946 was $1,912.50, made up of the following balances:

T. R. Keen	$ 150.00
P. B. Smart	712.50
A. R. Orr	1,050.00
	$1,912.50

The account with T. R. Keen contained a debit on August 3 for the cost of merchandise, $750.00 including a freight charge of $25.00; on August 10 the account was credited in the amount of $600.00 for a draft.

The account sales rendered by Keen on August 15, 1946 was:

Sales—⅓ of consignment		$350.00
Deduct: Expenses	$21.00	
Commission—10%	35.00	56.00
Net proceeds		$294.00

The account with P. B. Smart contained the following items:

July 5 Cost (including a $55 freight charge)	$1,080.00	July 9 Draft	$200.00
		August 10 Proceeds	167.50

The reports rendered by Smart are summarized as follows:

Sales—¼ of consignment		$425.00
Deduct: Expenses	$15.00	
Commission—10%	42.50	57.50
Net proceeds		$367.50
Draft (July 9)		200.00
Remittance		$167.50

The expenses deducted in the account sales submitted by Keen and Smart represented total expenses incurred by the consignees to date, and were applicable only to goods sold.

The account with Orr contained only one debit, for $1,050.00, including a freight charge for $50.00. Orr returned all of the goods consigned to him; he had paid the return freight charges, $50.00, and had made other expenditures of $14.00, for which he is to be reimbursed.

You find that in the past the company has closed consignment-out accounts to consignment profit and loss when the entire consignment has been disposed of.

(*b*) The balance sheet of the Hedges Corporation as of August 31, 1946, before adjustment, contained the following items:

Inventory—Finished goods:	
On hand	$13,200.00
On consignment	1,912.50

State the figures which should have appeared in the balance sheet, and state what effect your adjustments will have on the profits of the period.

Problem 34-8. The Hinds Company was organized on January 1, 1945. It manufactures only one product, which is marketed partly by direct sales and partly by consignments. South American sales were billed at an amount which equals 125% of the established price in this country.

Following is the condition of the accounts of the Hinds Company on December 31, 1945:

Accounts receivable	$ 59,836.00
Accounts payable	37,500.00
Selling expenses	21,000.00
Sales	630,000.00
Returned sales	4,970.00
South American consignees	94,500.00
Direct labor	197,000.00
Indirect labor	30,000.00
Rent of factory and equipment	54,000.00
Capital stock	150,000.00
Raw material purchases	278,314.00
Miscellaneous factory expense	55,000.00
General administrative expenses	18,000.00
Cash	1,880.00
Freight on consignments	3,000.00

The account with South American consignees is composed of charges for consignments at the billed price. No goods have been sold by these South American consignees, and no remittances have been received from them.

The inventories on December 31, 1945 were: finished goods (exclusive of consignments), \$83,764.00; goods in process, \$45,000.00; raw materials, \$52,600.00.

A reserve of 5/7 of one per cent of the net sales is to be set up to cover losses on accounts receivable.

Prepare:

(*a*) Balance sheet as of December 31, 1945.
(*b*) Statement of income and expense for the year.

Problem 34-9. Following is the trial balance of the Buell Company, together with certain supplementary data, as of December 31, 1946:

Accounts payable		\$ 20,000.00
Accounts receivable	\$ 11,250.00	
Buildings	28,300.00	
Cash	2,800.00	
Capital stock		60,000.00
Consignment sales		2,700.00
Consignments out—cost plus freight	2,900.00	
Commission on consignments—10%	2,700.00	
Direct labor	48,200.00	
Discount on purchases		575.00
Discount on sales	1,125.00	
Expenses deducted by consignees	280.00	
Freight in	1,175.00	
General and administrative expenses	6,300.00	
Heat, light, and power	3,840.00	
Indirect labor	13,125.00	
Inventories, January 1, 1946:		
Finished goods	8,300.00	
Goods in process	6,625.00	
Raw materials	7,500.00	
Insurance and taxes on factory	2,815.00	
Land	4,700.00	
Machinery	65,000.00	
Miscellaneous selling expenses	4,913.00	
Other factory expenses	7,400.00	
Raw material purchases	52,930.00	
Reserve for bad debts		1,200.00
Reserve for depreciation—buildings		5,700.00
Reserve for depreciation—machinery		12,000.00
Returned purchases and allowances		400.00
Returned sales and allowances	975.00	
Sales		180,000.00
Salesmen's salaries	8,000.00	
Surplus, January 1, 1946		8,578.00
	\$291,153.00	\$291,153.00

Inventories as of December 31, 1946 were as follows:

Finished goods	\$9,250.00
Goods in process	7,813.00
Raw materials	8,943.00

The cost of goods sold on consignment was 15% of the cost of goods sold direct. Depreciation at the rate of 5% should be provided on buildings and 10% on machinery.

From the above information, prepare the following:

(*a*) Balance sheet.
(*b*) Statement of profit and loss.
(*c*) Statement of cost of goods manufactured and sold.

The gross profit in the profit and loss statement should be separated as between that derived from regular sales and that derived from consignment sales.

Problem 34-10. The following consignment accounts are open on the books of the Fairfield Corporation as of December 31, 1945:

	Cost of Goods Shipped	Shipping Charges	Total Charges	Drafts Drawn at Time of Consignment	Net Proceeds	Balance
A	$1,500.00	$ 40.00	$1,540.00	$ 600.00	$285.00	$ 655.00
B	1,000.00	30.00	1,030.00	400.00	—	630.00
C	2,000.00	50.00	2,050.00	350.00	180.00	1,520.00
D	1,300.00	20.00	1,320.00	300.00	325.00	695.00
Total	$5,800.00	$140.00	$5,940.00	$1,650.00	$790.00	$3,500.00

Account sales received from such consignees during 1945 show the following:

	Sales	Commission 10%	Expenses	Total	Balance	Drafts	Cash Remitted
A	$1,000.00	$100.00	$15.00	$115.00	$885.00	$600.00	$285.00
B	400.00	40.00	20.00	60.00	340.00	400.00	
C	600.00	60.00	10.00	70.00	530.00	350.00	180.00
D	700.00	70.00	5.00	75.00	625.00	300.00	325.00

The portion of goods sold by each consignee was: *A*, ⅓; *B*, ⅕; *C*, ⅙; *D*, ¼.

The following financial statement was prepared by the Fairfield Corporation as of December 31, 1945:

Assets		Liabilities	
Cash	$ 20,000.00	Accounts payable	$ 40,515.00
Accounts receivable	21,200.00	Capital stock	150,000.00
Finished goods on hand	22,500.00	Surplus	26,685.00
Finished goods on consignment	3,500.00		
Land, buildings, and machinery	150,000.00		
	$217,200.00		$217,200.00

What adjusting journal entries should be made to correct the books? Prepare a corrected balance sheet as of December 31, 1945.

QUESTIONS AND PROBLEMS ON CHAPTER 35

Questions

Question 35-1. State two general methods which may be used to record the transactions of a joint venture, and state what considerations should determine which method to use.

Question 35-2. Assuming that a separate set of books is to be maintained for a joint venture, describe the record that will be kept on these books and on the books of the participants for:

(*a*) Merchandise contributions.
(*b*) Cash contributions.
(*c*) Expenses paid from the venture funds.
(*d*) Expenses paid by one of the participants.
(e) Sales.
(f) Cash withdrawals.
(g) Closing of books and distribution of profit.
(h) Final cash settlement.

Question 35-3. Assuming that a separate set of books is not to be kept, describe how each participant will record each of the transactions listed in the preceding question.

Question 35-4. How should uncompleted ventures be shown in the balance sheet?

Problems

Problem 35-1. In a certain joint venture, Craig was to supply merchandise, Bass was to provide funds, and Drake was to sell merchandise. Drake was to be allowed commissions of 3% on the gross amount of all collected sales. Craig and Bass were to be credited with interest at 6% on all amounts outstanding.

On May 1, Craig shipped merchandise valued at $12,000.00 to Drake, who received it on May 10, when he paid freight and insurance charges of $450.00 on it. On May 6, Bass sent Drake $10,000.00. On May 26 Drake purchased more merchandise for $9,200.00. Drake made various sales amounting in all to $16,000.00. These were collected less a 2% cash discount on June 20th, with the exception of accounts totaling $1,200.00, one of which, amounting to $960.00, was considered uncollectible and was written off. On June 30, Drake sold more merchandise for $8,000.00, which was collected, less 2%, on July 10. Drake was unable to sell the rest of the merchandise and Craig agreed to take it at $780.00, which he did on July 30. On that day the venture was closed and settlements were made. Drake agreed to accept the uncollected account at its face value.

The first method of keeping joint venture accounts is to be used.

(*a*) Prepare the journal entries, in columnar form, for all sets of books.
(*b*) Show the joint venture account as it will appear on all sets of books.
(*c*) Show the account with each participant as it will appear on the books of the other participants.
(*d*) Show how Craig will present the facts relating to the venture in his balance sheet on June 30.

Problem 35-2. Refer to Problem 35-1. Record the transactions described in that problem, using the second method of accounting for joint ventures.

(*a*) Prepare journal entries, in columnar form, for the four sets of books.
(*b*) Show how each participant will show the facts relating to the venture in his balance sheet on June 30.

Problem 35-3. Rand and Quejado entered a joint venture by which Quejado was to ship coffee to the United States and Rand was to sell it. Arrangements were made with the Bank of North America to pay 90-day drafts drawn by Quejado on Rand for the amount of the invoice on shipments. When the coffee was sold, Rand was to make arrangements to have the bank draw on the buyers, crediting the amounts so realized against Rand's liability on Quejado's drafts, and depositing any excess in Rand's account. At the conclusion of the venture Rand was to make a settlement with Quejado. Profits were to be divided equally.

Quejado drew on the bank for $17,420.00. The bank charged Rand's account for $1,465.00 for freight, customs fees, and insurance. The coffee was sold to various roasters, and the bank drew on them for $22,360.00. These drafts were paid, and the bank charged Rand $224.60 for interest and collection charges. The excess was credited to Rand's account in the bank, and Rand made a statement to Quejado and sent him the proceeds.

(*a*) Prepare the statement sent to Quejado.
(*b*) Submit all journal entries on Rand's books which should show not only Rand's interest in the venture but his liability on the drafts.

Problem 35-4. MacDonald and McQuarrie entered a joint venture to subdivide some acreage. Inasmuch as the venture was likely to extend over a long period of time, separate books were kept. On June 15, MacDonald sent $20,000.00 to McQuarrie, which was to receive 6% until repaid. McQuarrie is to carry on operations and to receive a 5% commission on all sales and 40% of the net profits.

On July 1 he purchased the land for $48,000.00, giving a 6% mortgage for $33,000.00 and cash in payment. Interest is payable semiannually, or upon payment of any installment if paid earlier. On August 1 MacDonald advanced an additional $22,000.00 on the same terms, to be used to pay for improvements. The actual cost of the improvements was $19,000.00. By December 31 sales totaling $52,000.00 had been made and collected in cash. The unsold land at that date was inventoried at cost at $44,100.00. Advertising, office expenses, and other expenses, exclusive of commissions and interest, had been $11,420.00. The mortgage was reduced by $5,000.00 on September 30, $8,000.00 on October 31, $6,000.00 on November 30, and $4,000.00 on December 31; interest was paid for 3, 4, 5, and 6 months on these installments. All commissions earned by McQuarrie were paid to him on December 31; interest was allowed MacDonald for 6½ months on his first contribution and for 5 months on his second contribution; and all cash on hand in excess of $5,000.00 was returned to MacDonald.

MacDonald requests statements showing his share of the profit to date and the financial condition of the venture.

(*a*) Prepare the journal entries for the venture books.
(*b*) Prepare the journal entries for MacDonald's books.
(*c*) Prepare the statements requested by MacDonald.

Problem 35-5. Hilliard, Zinn, and Jeffrey entered a venture to dispose of their holdings of the common stock of the Georgia Timberlands Company.

Gains or losses are to be shared in proportion to the number of shares contributed to the venture.

Hilliard contributes 12,000 shares, which had cost him $42.00 a share; Zinn 15,000 shares, which had cost him $58.00 a share; and Jeffrey 10,000 shares, which had cost him $62.00 a share.

The market value of the shares when the venture began was $82.00 a share. Zinn was to handle the liquidation for a flat fee of $10,000.00 plus his expenses.

During October he sold 9,500 shares at an average price of $79.00 a share.

On November 1 the Georgia Timberlands Company paid a stock dividend of 20%. Zinn sold 8,000 shares, ex-stock dividend, on November 5 for $55.00 a share. On November 15, the company paid a cash dividend of $1.00 a share. On November 22 he sold 10,000 shares for $58.00. The remainder of the shares were sold in December for $60.00 a share. Zinn's expenses totaled $6,700.00. A distribution of the proceeds was made on December 31.

(*a*) Prepare the journal entries as they should be recorded on Hilliard's books.
(*b*) Submit the joint venture account as it appears on all sets of books.
(*c*) What was Hilliard's total gain on his stock from the time he purchased it until he received the proceeds of the venture?

Problem 35-6. Lloyd Freene and Douglas Farblow entered into a joint venture agreement on December 31, 1944.

Each contributed $5,000.00 on January 1, 1945, with which they paid for goods that were shipped on that date to Egbert Walker. Walker, the consignee, is allowed 8% on the cost of the goods and was to sell them at the best price obtainable. Freene advances $500.00 to defray freight and incidental expenses.

On March 1, 1945, on the strength of a report sent by wire, Farblow drew at sight on Walker for $5,000.00 to the order of David Dillon of Jersey City, New Jersey.

On April 1, 1945 Farblow received from the consignee a check for $14,100.00, all of the goods having been sold; on the same day Freene and Farblow settled.

Interest at 6% is allowed on all transactions affecting the parties to the venture.

Prepare journal entries and ledger accounts as they should appear on the books of Freene.

Problem 35-7. Prepare journal entries and accounts with joint venture and S. Newton as they should appear on the books of N. Tabor.

S. Newton and N. Tabor agree to a joint venture in which each is to have an equal interest.

On October 1, 1946 they purchase the necessary commodities and ship them to their agent in Mexico. Newton pays for the goods in cash, $344.00.

Their agent receives the goods, disposes of them immediately, and sends in return to Newton 3,500 cases of commodity *X* and 220 cases of commodity *Y*. He draws on Newton at sight for the equivalent of $240.00, which is the amount of his charges and out-of-pocket expenses over and above the net proceeds received by him from the commodities sent to him by Newton and Tabor. The draft is paid by Newton.

On November 1, 1946 commodities *X* and *Y* are received, charges thereon of $485.50 being paid by Newton. Other charges, amounting to $530.00 are paid by Tabor.

On November 6, 1946 Newton sells 2,350 cases of commodity *X* for $3,525.00. Of this amount, Newton receives $2,600.00 and Tabor receives the remainder. Tabor sells the remainder of commodity *X* for $1,610.00.

On November 8, 1946 Tabor sells 100 cases of commodity *Y* for $210.00.

On November 15, 1946 the remaining cases of commodity *Y* are exchanged for 40 crates of commodity *Z*, which are divided equally between the two men.

Commodities *X* and *Y* now are completely disposed of and Newton presents a bill for miscellaneous charges that he has paid, amounting to $76.32.

Problem 35-8. On April 30, 1945, F. D. Austin and E. C. Miller bought 50 acres of land, and opened a subdivision to be known as Sleepy Hollow. The tract of land cost $3,350.00 per acre, of which one half was paid in cash from funds furnished equally by the participants; a 5% mortgage was given for the balance.

The property was subdivided as follows:

200 lots to sell for $1,000.00 each.
200 lots to sell for $ 675.00 each.

When computing the profit on sales, you may assume the cost of the two classes of lots to be in the same ratio as the selling price. Lots may be released from the mortgage by paying to the trustee under the mortgage cash equal to 125% of the original cost of the lot (computed as indicated above) and the accrued interest on the portion of the mortgage released.

In May and June the property was improved by grading, and so on, at a cost of $33,500.00, which was paid for from funds furnished by Austin.

During July and August, lots were sold as follows:

	Selling Price $1,000.00	Selling Price $675.00
July	85	100
August	55	90

All lots were sold for one half cash, and the mortgage notes received for the balance were indorsed without recourse and sold to the banks at par. The lots were released from the mortgage by payment of the prorata amounts. The releases were obtained and the payments to the trustee were made on the last day of the month in which the sale was made.

Selling expenses were as follows:

Advertising	$10,000.00
Salesman's salary	2,500.00
Miscellaneous selling	1,000.00
Total	$13,500.00

Neither Austin nor Miller is to receive a salary. No allowance is to be made for interest on partners' balances, and the profits are to be divided equally.

Prepare a joint venture account showing the record of the transactions. Also prepare a profit and loss statement and a balance sheet after closing the accounts on August 31, 1945.

Problem 35-9. *A*, *B*, *C*, and *D* held stock, individually, in the Hardwood Lumber Company as follows:

A	8,000 shares
B	6,000 shares
C	5,000 shares
D	1,000 shares

The stock had all been acquired at par, $10.00 per share.

A, *B*, *C*, and *D* formed a pool by contributing their holdings at an equitable valuation, and by purchasing from *Y*, 20,000 shares of the stock of the same company at the market price, $25.00 per share. The parties were to share equally in the purchase from Y, and they were to participate in the joint venture in accordance with the shares originally held plus the purchase from Y, on joint account. The effective date of the venture and the purchase of the shares from Y, was February 1, 1946.

The purchase of the 20,000 shares from Y was effected with funds borrowed at 6% from the Inventors Banking Company, all the shares held in the pool being pledged as security to the loan.

On February 15, 1946 the Hardwood Lumber Company issued rights to buy one share of stock at $15.00 for every four shares owned. The pool borrowed money from the bank on February 25, 1946 and took up its rights, depositing the stock with the bank.

Various circumstances contributed to rapid rises in the value of the stock, and sales of stock were made as follows:

March 6, 1946	8,000 shares @ $30.00
March 9, 1946	8,000 shares @ 32.50
March 16, 1946	12,000 shares @ 35.00
March 20, 1946	10,000 shares @ 30.00

As the proceeds of the various sales were obtained on the dates mentioned, the bank was paid off and the remaining funds were deposited. The bank charged interest for the actual number of days of the loans, but used 360 days to the year in computing interest.

On March 31, 1946 it was decided to wind up the pool and to distribute the stock and cash. Prepare a joint venture account showing the result of the above transactions, and a statement of the division of the cash and of the shares unsold among the participants.

Problem 35-10. Ten men went on a fishing trip. *A, B, C, D, E, F, G,* and *H* were with the party ten days; *J* left at the end of four days, and *K* left at the end of six days. Each was to pay his traveling expenses, fishing license fee, and any personal expenses. The cost of board and room at the resort, guides' fees, bait, tips, and so forth, was to be charged to each member of the party in proportion to the time spent.

The bill rendered by the resort at the end of ten days included the following items:

Fishing licenses—*A, B, J,* and *K*	$ 12.00
Board and room	400.00
Guides	100.00
Packing fish for shipment	5.00
Cigars—*D*	3.00
Long distance telephone—*A*	2.00
Total	$522.00

Cash was contributed for the payment of this bill, as follows:

A	$ 85.00
B	75.00
C	60.00
D	80.00
E	60.00
F	45.00
G	45.00
H	30.00
J	25.00
K	17.00
Total	$522.00

Other payments made by members of the party for group expenses were:

B—Rent of boats at Trout Lake	$10.00
E—Rent of boats at Loon Lake	15.00
G—Rent of launch for pleasure tour—As *A*, *C*, *E*, *J* and *K* were not on this tour, they are not to be charged with any of the expense	30.00
C—Tips	10.00
Total	$65.00

F was asked to prepare a report showing the final settlement. To those who had paid more than their share of the joint expense, he remitted his personal checks; those who had paid less than their share were requested to remit to *F*.

Prepare a report such as *F* might have rendered.

QUESTIONS AND PROBLEMS ON CHAPTER 36

Questions

Question 36-1. You have been called to audit the books of a furniture company which sells on the installment plan. The books have been closed when you reach the office, and you are handed a completed profit and loss statement and balance sheet. The company has been in business one year only.

On investigation you find that all installment sales are credited to an account designated *installment sales.* A controlling account and subledger are kept for the installment customers. You find, also, that the installment sales account has been closed into profit and loss.

All accounts, installment and otherwise, that were known to be uncollectible have been charged off. No reserves against balances due from customers appear on the books.

What criticisms or comments have you to make on the correctness of the balance sheet and the profit and loss statement handed to you?

Question 36-2. Describe three methods of taking up profits on the basis of cash collections, and state the conditions which would justify the use of each method.

Question 36-3. The Farmers' Machine Company sells its product on terms which provide for collection in three equal annual installments. The cost of production for one year is $10,991,468.80; sales, $13,210,900.00; general expenses, $105,000.00. The first year's installments have been collected in full. Compute the profit for the year.

Question 36-4. Why is it desirable to keep the accounts receivable separated by years if profits on installment sales are taken up on the basis of cash collections?

Question 36-5. You are auditing the accounts of an incorporated automobile dealer who sells cars on the partial payment plan and accepts notes that fall due in monthly installments. It appears that all of these notes have been discounted at the bank, because the debit balance of the notes receivable account, $125,648.50, is offset by an equal credit balance in the notes receivable discounted account.

You also find that during the past three months seven cars have been seized because of nonpayment of notes, which were charged back by the bank, together with protest fees. The cars were inventoried at the end of the period at the face of the notes unpaid. State what entries should be made in such instances, and at what values the cars should be inventoried, assuming that none of the notes had been paid but that the initial deposit received at the time of sale equaled the gross profit on the car. (Assume that the cars cost $600.00 and were sold for $900.00.)

Question 36-6. Upon examining the accounts of a furniture dealer, who sells to the retail trade on an installment basis, you find that repossessed furniture (that is, articles sold and replevined because of the customer's failure to pay installments due) is included in the inventory at original cost plus cost of reconditioning. Give your reasons for approving or disapproving of this procedure.

Question 36-7. In 1943 the Economy Installment House sold to Mrs. Brown for $400.00 a dining room suite that cost $200.00. In accordance with her contract, Mrs. Brown made installment payments of $100.00 per year for 1943, 1944, and 1945. In 1946, before any further installments were due, Mrs. Brown departed for Europe and permitted her dining room suite to revert by forfeit, according to the terms of her contract, to the Economy Installment House, which took back the furniture into its stock of merchandise. State what method you would adopt to place a value on the returned furniture for inventory purposes and what entries should be made for each of the four years.

Question 36-8. A large hotel is furnished on the installment plan. Explain, giving reason, whether the question of interest is of importance to (*a*) the seller; (*b*) the buyer.

Question 36-9. Describe two ways, long end and short end, in which interest may be paid on installment sales.

Question 36-10. A manufacturer makes machines at a cost of $500.00 and sells them for $750.00. He also leases them for $120.00 per year, with an understanding that the rent is payable monthly in advance. Persons leasing the machines may, at any time within one year from the date of the lease, elect to purchase, and may apply all rentals against the purchase price. Explain how lease transactions should be recorded.

Problems

Problem 36-1. On July 31, the Apex Motor Company, which maintains a perpetual inventory, sold to Gibson for $1,500.00 a car which cost $1,050.00. Gibson paid $600.00 down and gave twelve equal monthly notes for the balance. All notes were paid as due.

(*a*) Make journal entries to record all transactions on the Apex Motor Company's books up to and including December 31.

(*b*) Prepare a statement summarizing the profit realized during the year.

Problem 36-2. Refer to the preceding problem. Assuming that, instead of giving notes for $900.00, Gibson gave notes for $996.00, the extra $96.00 being $64.74 for interest and $31.26 for cost of insurance.

The company wishes to keep its accounts so as to show the interest earned during the calendar year as well as the profit realized.

Make a journal entry for the books of the Apex Motor Company to record the sale and entries summarizing the collections to the close of the year and the transfers of deferred profit and interest income to profit and loss.

Problem 36-3. The balance sheet of the Nightwine Company on January 1, 1945 follows:

Cash	$ 15,230.00	Accounts payable	$ 16,200.00
Accounts receivable, '43	12,650.00	Notes payable	5,000.00
Accounts receivable, '44	46,860.00	Deferred gross profit, '43	5,060.00
Inventory	36,530.00	Deferred gross profit, '44	16,401.00
Other assets	41,730.00	Capital stock	100,000.00
		Surplus	10,339.00
	$153,000.00		$153,000.00

The trial balance at the end of the year was:

Cash	$ 28,222.00	
Accounts receivable, '43	2,400.00	
" " '44	12,750.00	
" " '45	52,630.00	
Inventory	36,530.00	
Other assets	35,120.00	
Sales		$160,000.00
Purchases	92,150.00	
Repossessions	1,400.00	
Expenses	37,520.00	
Loss on defaults	4,420.00	
Accounts payable		11,342.00
Deferred gross profit, '43		5,060.00
" " " '44		16,401.00
Capital stock		100,000.00
Surplus		10,339.00
	$303,142.00	$303,142.00

The repossessions represent the appraised value of property repossessed. All were made on 1943 accounts at a time when such accounts had balances of $5,820.00. The ending inventory was $30,080.00.

(*a*) Prepare a profit and loss statement for the year.
(*b*) Prepare a balance sheet on December 31, 1945.

Problem 36-4. The Scott Furniture Company had on its books at the beginning of the year an account with C. H. Pope for $480.00. It made two collections of $40.00 each during the year, but was unable to collect any more and repossessed the furniture. At the time of repossession the furniture was appraised at $120.00. The original cost to the company was $360.00 and the original selling price was $680.00.

Show the journal entries to be made if no refund is to be made to the customer.

Problem 36-5. The Carlton Land Company started business with $50,000.00 capital in cash, on June 30, 1946. It purchased furniture and fixtures for $2,000.00 and bought land for $40,000.00. It sold land which cost it $30,000.00 for $54,000.00, retaining title in each case until payment for the land was completed.

It may be considered that all the land was sold at the same mark-up. Payments on contracts of $18,000.00 were made in full and titles were transferred. On sales aggregating $27,900.00 the company had collected $19,400.00. The remainder of the contracts were defaulted after collections of $3,300.00 had been made. Because of the building activity in the area, the property was worth $2,000.00 more at the time of foreclosure than it had cost. The expenses of the company during the period were $14,230.00, of which $1,100.00 are unpaid, and $260.00 was the cost of repossessing land.

(*a*) Prepare a profit and loss statement and a balance sheet on December 31, 1946.
(*b*) State the profit on repossessions as it would be computed for income tax purposes had the sales been made by other than a dealer.

Problem 36-6. A company sells radios for $165.00 on the installment basis. The terms of sale are:

(a) Down payment, \$35.00.
(b) The balance in 13 monthly installments of \$10.00 each.

The radios cost the company \$100.00 each.

A radio is sold on June 1, 1945, and all collections during 1945 are received when due.

Determine the amount to be taken into income for 1945, assuming:

(a) No interest on the debt.
(b) Monthly payments to include interest at 6% computed (1) on the long-end basis; and (2) on the short-end basis (total payment \$10.00 plus interest).

Problem 36-7. From the information presented below, give entries to adjust and close the accounts on December 31, 1945. Prepare a balance sheet and a profit and loss statement, showing profits or losses from various sources.

The trial balance of the Arinoco Company as of the above date is as follows:

Accounts receivable, 1945	\$192,000.00	
Deferred profit, 1944		\$ 65,000.00
Deferred profit, 1943		14,000.00
Repossessed property	15,500.00	
Loss on repossessions	14,000.00	
Sales		375,000.00
Purchases	217,000.00	
Cash	22,500.00	
Accounts receivable, 1944	45,000.00	
Inventory, January 1, 1945	23,000.00	
Accounts payable		37,500.00
Capital stock		75,000.00
Surplus		14,500.00
Expense	52,000.00	
	\$581,000.00	\$581,000.00

The balances in certain accounts on January 1, 1945 were: accounts receivable, 1943, \$30,000.00; accounts receivable, 1944, \$150,000.00; deferred profit, 1943, \$14,000.00; deferred profit, 1944, \$65,000.00.

Repossessions during the year were recorded as follows:

	Dr.	Cr.
Repossessed property—depreciated value	\$15,500.00	
Loss on repossessions	14,000.00	
Accounts receivable, 1943 (unpaid balances)		\$ 9,500.00
Accounts receivable, 1944 (unpaid balances)		12,000.00
Accounts receivable, 1945 (unpaid balances)		8,000.00

The inventory of new and repossessed merchandise, December 31, 1945, was \$38,000.00.

The sales of \$375,000.00 include sales of repossessions, which are made on the installment basis.

Problem 36-8. From the following data prepare a statement of profit and loss for the year and a balance sheet as at December 31, 1945 for the G. Furniture Store:

Trial Balance
as at December 31, 1945

	Debits	Credits
Cash	$ 46,000.00	
Accounts receivable	165,000.00	
Merchandise inventory	15,000.00	
Accounts payable		$ 3,000.00
Unrealized profit, 1944		57,000.00
Capital stock		100,000.00
Surplus		10,000.00
Sales		250,000.00
Expenses	66,000.00	
Purchases	128,000.00	
	$420,000.00	$420,000.00

The accounts receivable account is a controlling account for three subsidiary ledgers which show the following totals:

1944 installment contracts	$ 30,000.00
1945 installment contracts	120,000.00
Charge accounts (terms 60 days net)	15,000.00
	$165,000.00

The gross profit on installment contracts for 1944 was 60% of sales price, on installment contracts for 1945, 50%, and on charge accounts, 40%.

Collections on installment contracts for 1944 total $60,000.00 for the year just closed; on installment contracts for 1945, $80,000.00; on charge accounts, $45,000.00. The charge accounts on the books at the beginning of the year amounted to $10,000.00.

Repossessions for the year were on installment contracts for 1944 on which the unpaid balances at the time of repossession amounted to $5,000.00. Merchandise repossessed was charged to purchases at the amount of the uncollected balance. Appraisal reports show that this repossessed merchandise actually was worth $4,000.00 at time of repossession.

The final inventory of merchandise valued at cost amounted to $13,000.00, including the repossessed merchandise at $5,000.00.

Problem 36-9. Jones Jewelry Corporation was organized on January 1, 1945, and commenced operations on that date in the installment jewelry business.

The following is an analysis of the cash transactions for the two years ended December 31, 1946:

Cash Receipts		Cash Payments	
1945		1945	
Capital stock	$200,000.00	Purchases	$148,278.14
Collections on 1945 installment accounts	50,362.50	Repairs and engraving	3,142.06
Notes payable	10,000.00	Direct labor	1,983.91
		Officers' salaries	7,500.00
		Advertising	8,483.25
		Office expense (state tax included)	31,225.80
		Furniture and fixtures	3,000.00
		Notes payable	10,000.00

1946		1946	
Collections on 1945 installment accounts	$120,447.59	Purchases (all 1946)	$123,261.49
Collections on 1946 installment accounts	147,726.02	Repairs and engraving	3,363.60
		Direct labor	2,248.19
		Advertising	15,652.62
		Officers' salaries	7,500.00
		Office expense (state tax included)	39,797.57

The trial balance of the corporation's books at December 31, 1946 follows:

Cash	$123,099.48	
Furniture and fixtures	3,000.00	
Inventory—January 1, 1946	31,233.05	
Sales		$272,989.19
Purchases	123,261.49	
Repairs and engraving	3,363.60	
Direct labor	2,248.19	
Officers' salaries	7,500.00	
Advertising	15,652.62	
Office expenses	39,797.57	
Depreciation—furniture and fixtures	300.00	
Bad debts	4,326.40	
Unrealized gross profit—1945 sales (December 31, 1945 balance)		116,488.21
Collections on 1945 installment accounts		120,447.59
Collections on 1946 installment accounts		147,726.02
Installment accounts receivable—1945	215,517.70	
Installment accounts receivable—1946	272,989.19	
Reserve for depreciation—furniture and fixtures		600.00
Reserve for bad debts		7,169.00
Deficit—January 1, 1946	23,130.72	
Capital stock		200,000.00
	$865,420.01	$865,420.01

Net sales—1945	$265,880.20
Inventory—December 31, 1946	35,820.60
Bad debts reserve—1945	2,842.60
Depreciation on furniture and fixtures—10% per annum	

Required:

(*a*) Balance sheet as at December 31, 1946.

(*b*) Profit and loss statements for the year ended December 31, 1945, and for the year ended December 31, 1946.

Problem 36-10. In January 1944 the Geneva Park Estates (a common law trust) purchased a 640-acre tract of land on Pine Lake for the sum of $100,000.00. A portion of the tract, to be known as Unit No. 1, and valued at two fifths of the cost of the tract, was immediately subdivided into 200 lots which were equally priced and offered for sale on terms requiring annual payments of 10% of the contract price. The sales prospectus stipulated that the Geneva Park Estates was to lay out roads, install water service, and build a pier on the lake front. Competent engineers estimated that these improvements would cost $10,000.00, and up to and including December 31, 1946 a total of $8,465.73 had been spent thereon, with good prospects of the work being finished for the estimated amount. The improvements conferred equal benefits on each of the 200 lots.

A set of books was opened in January 1944. Lot sales and the profit therefrom were handled according to the "cost-recovery" method whereby cash collections are first applied to the recovery of costs, and after such costs are recovered, further collections are considered as earned gross profit. When a sale was made, the bookkeeper debited accounts receivable, Unit No. 1, and credited unearned gross profit on sales; at the same time he debited unrecovered cost of lots sold, Unit No. 1, and credited inventory of unsold lots, Unit No. 1, for the cost of the lot. At the end of each year a journal entry was made adjusting the accounts of unrecovered cost of lots sold and unearned gross profit on sales, according to the cash collections received during the year.

In 1945 the manager of the trust, believing that it would be more advantageous to accrue income by the "installment" rather than "cost-recovery" method, hands you the following cumulative trial balances together with certain other information and asks you to prepare (1) the necessary adjusting journal entries to effect the change including therein a recomputation of costs based on good accounting practice, (2) a statement of profit and loss in columnar form for the years 1944, 1945, and 1946 respectively, and (3) a balance sheet as of December 31, 1946.

	Cumulative Trial Balance December 31,		
Accounts	1944	1945	1946
Debit balances—			
Cash in bank	$ 1,994.34	$ 1,097.37	$ 2,216.26
Petty cash	50.00	50.00	50.00
Accounts receivable—Unit 1	17,425.00	33,440.00	53,940.00
Sundry receivables	275.00	695.00	1,100.00
Inventory of unsold lots—Unit No. 1	36,000.00	32,000.00	24,000.00
Inventory of unsubdivided acreage	60,000.00	60,000.00	60,000.00
Unrecovered cost of lots sold	1,425.00	1,440.00	1,500.00
Tractor, tools, and implements	700.00	700.00	700.00
Office furniture	300.00	300.00	300.00
Improvements in Unit No. 1	3,500.00	7,385.46	8,465.73
Improvements in unsubdivided acreage	3,500.00	5,040.42	6,825.92
General and administrative expenses	3,349.58	6,698.75	9,345.68
Commissions paid on sale of lots	2,000.00	5,000.00	9,752.50
Interest paid	375.00	1,285.50	1,835.65
Total debits	$130,893.92	$155,132.50	$180,031.74
Credit balances—			
Accounts payable	$ 2,093.67	$ 916.58	$ 1,213.63
Notes payable	10,000.00	17,000.00	10,000.00
Capital account	100,000.00	100,000.00	100,000.00
Earned gross profit on sales	—	—	7,560.00
Unearned gross profit on sales	17,425.00	33,440.00	53,940.00
Interest earned	1,375.25	3,775.92	7,318.11
Total credits	$130,893.92	$155,132.50	$180,031.74

Sales of lots for the three years were as follows:

Year	Particulars	Amount
1944	20 lots at $1,000.00 each	$20,000.00
1945	20 lots at $1,000.00 each	20,000.00
1946	40 lots at $ 900.00 each	36,000.00

Cash collections were:

Year	Particulars	Amount
1944	on 1944 sales	$ 2,575.00
1945	on 1944 sales	$ 985.00
	on 1945 sales	3,000.00
	Total	$ 3,985.00
1946	on 1944 sales	$ 4,000.00
	on 1945 sales	5,000.00
	on 1946 sales	6,500.00
	Total	$15,500.00

In lieu of depreciation on the tractor, tools, implements, and office furniture, the total is to be treated as an additional cost of development and prorated on the basis of the original cost of the tract.

Disregard Federal income tax liability, if any.

Problem 36-11. The Roane Realty Company purchased a 60-acre tract of land (43,560 square feet to an acre) for $24,000.00 and spent $91,620.00 for improvements and expenses. Of the acreage, 701,100 square feet were used for streets, parkways, alleys, and so on.

No sales were made during the first year. During the second year, lots were placed on the market and sales were made based on two classes. One third of the land was placed in a class called "*A*" and the balance was classed as "*B*." The lots were of equal size, containing 12,750 square feet each. The price was 8¢ per square foot for Class *A* and 7¢ per square foot for Class *B* lots, with discount of 10% on all sales for cash.

In the second year, 10 Class *A* and 17 Class *B* lots were sold. Four of the ten sales of Class *A* and six of the seventeen sales of Class *B* were for cash. The other sales were on the basis of 10% cash and nine additional equal payments.

During the third year all the other lots were sold. Ten Class *A* and twenty-five Class *B* lots were sold for cash; the rest, on the ten-payment plan.

Profit is to be considered as earned and unearned. Earned profit is that part of the profit that is realized by actual collection. At the end of the second year (the first year of sales) there was still due on installment sales an average of four installments which were paid in the third year. At the end of the third year there was an average balance on installment sales of three payments, all good and collectible.

State the earned profit for each of the two years in which sales were made. Carrying charges need not be considered.

QUESTIONS AND PROBLEMS ON CHAPTER 37

Questions

Question 37-1. State how to set up and close a fire loss account, explaining what items should be charged and credited to it.

Question 37-2. Explain why the inventory at the date of a fire may be underestimated by the gross profit method, if the inventory at the date of the last preceding closing was written down to a market value below cost or was written down because of depreciation or obsolescence.

Question 37-3. The owners of a large plant operating on highly inflammable material were required to pay prohibitive rates for insurance and therefore installed a sprinkler system in order to reduce the cost of insurance. In consequence of such installation the company was enabled to obtain a full line of insurance, though mostly in mutual companies, at rates far below those previously charged. The company received at the end of the year $1,000.00 as dividends from the mutual insurance companies. To what account should the cost of the sprinkler system be charged and how should the insurance dividend be treated?

Question 37-4. Assume that a fire takes place some time after the annual closing. How would you determine the amount to charge to the fire loss account in respect to fixed assets?

How would you determine the estimated values of the inventories to be charged to the fire loss account?

Question 37-5. Should the fire loss account be charged with the estimated values of the inventories or with the amounts allowed by the adjustor?

Question 37-6. What is meant by the coinsurance clause? How would you proceed to determine the amount which could be collected under a policy carrying the coinsurance clause?

Question 37-7. The stock and plant of the Caroline Manufacturing Company were badly damaged by fire on June 30th. An appraisal of the loss, as made and used as a basis for settlement with the insurance companies, showed: that machinery which had cost $10,000 was destroyed, against which a $3,000 reserve for depreciation had been built up; that the building was damaged to the extent of $8,000; that raw materials were destroyed which had cost $12,000; that finished goods were also destroyed which had cost $18,000 to manufacture. Total settlement with insurance companies was $35,000. Make the necessary entries to establish the loss on the books, and to record properly the fire loss.

State how you would determine the raw materials and finished goods destruction had you been called upon to appraise the damage.

Question 37-8. How would you record the payment of insurance premiums on the life of an officer of a corporation, assuming that the officer's estate is the beneficiary?

How would you record the payment of premiums and the increase in the cash surrender value in case the company is the beneficiary?

Question 37-9. How would you record the collection of an insurance policy by a corporation on the life of a deceased officer?

How would you record the collection of an insurance policy by a partnership if the policy covered the life of one of the partners?

Question 37-10. A company has insured the life of its president for its own benefit, and is carrying on its balance sheet the amount of premiums paid. What position should an auditor take with regard to these premiums?

Question 37-11. The president of the Marshall Company assigned certain patents to the company under a contract whereby the company agreed to pay the premiums (amounting to $3,500.00 per year) on $100,000.00 of insurance on the president's life, his wife and son (the latter also an officer of the company) to be the beneficiaries of the insurance.

The company paid the annual premiums regularly for several years; it failed to pay the 1946 premium, and shortly thereafter the president died.

What recognition would you give to this situation in the preparation of financial statements on December 31, 1946?

Problems

Problem 37-1. The Scranton Coal Company purchased a 10-year old building for $33,350.00 at a bankruptcy sale at the beginning of 1934. At that time its estimated remaining life was 20 years. In January 1942 the company had it appraised and its value was set on the books on the basis of a reproduction cost new of $57,750.00, with a remaining life of 15 years. On April 1, 1946 the building was 60% destroyed by fire. The Company had insured it for $40,000.00 on a policy which had an 80% coinsurance clause. The insurance companies and the Scranton Coal Company agreed that the building was worth $55,000.00 at the date of the fire. The prepaid insurance on the building at that date was $155.00.

Compute the settlement to be made by the insurance companies.
Make the journal entries to record the facts relating to the fire.
Prepare a fire loss account.
State what the actual loss or gain on the fire was, and reconcile it to the loss or gain shown on the books.

Problem 37-2. Gray and Callery, partners, started business on January 1, 1943. On May 1, 1943, they agreed to insure each partner's life for $25,000.00, the premiums to be chargeable against partnership profits, regardless of income tax considerations. In the event of the death of a partner, the proceeds of the insurance were to be paid to the partnership and used to liquidate the deceased partner's capital account.

The total premiums paid were $1,800.00 a year, which was charged as an expense when paid. The total cash surrender values stated by the policies were $1,650.00 at the beginning of the third year and $2,460.00 at the beginning of the fourth year; cash surrender values were never recorded on the books. During the first three calendar years the partners shared profits in the ratio of 70% to Gray and 30% to Callery, but on January 1, 1946 the ratio was changed to equality.

At the beginning of 1946 Gray's capital account had a balance of $29,500.00 and Callery's $17,000.00. Gray died March 1. The bookkeeper closed the books and determined the profit for the two months to be $2,600.00. The policy was collected and the proceeds were credited to the partners' capital accounts in the profit and loss ratio, and Callery offered to settle with the executor on this basis. The executor protested that this was not fair to Gray's estate on the ground that the cash surrender value should have been set on the books at a time when

Gray was receiving 70% of the profits, and had this been done, Gray's capital account would have been larger. Callery agreed to the change. The increase in surrender value during the third policy year was prorated on a time basis.

(a) State the amount Callery first offered to pay.

(b) Submit a schedule showing the determination of the amount paid to Gray's estate.

(c) Submit the journal entries necessary to adjust the books on March 1.

Problem 37-3. Wilmerding and Winter had their inventory insured for $32,000.00 under an 80% coinsurance policy. They had a fire which did damage which they claim amounted to $15,120.00. Their inventory before the fire, they claimed, was $42,000.00. The insurance adjuster contended that the inventory was worth only $38,000.00 and that $800.00 of the $4,000.00 overvaluation was in the part of the inventory destroyed by the fire. How much less was the amount offered by the adjuster than Wilmerding and Winter would have received under their own claim?

Problem 37-4. The Trussell Manufacturing Company had on its books a charge of $2,870.00 for workmen's compensation insurance on December 31, 1945. This amount comprised a charge to make up the deficiency on the prepayment made on March 1, 1944, which was based on the estimated payroll for the fiscal year which began then, and the prepayment made on March 1, 1945. From the data below, correct the account, and state any amounts prepaid or accrued on December 31, 1945.

Classification	Rate per $100.00	Estimate March 1, 1945	Actual payroll for portion of calendar year to March 1, 1945	Actual payroll for portion of calendar year after March 1, 1945
A.....	$1.15	$120,000.00	$23,540.00	$123,700.00
B.....	.90	80,000.00	15,010.00	84,620.00
C.....	.42	24,000.00	4,200.00	28,720.00
D....	.12	18,000.00	3,300.00	19,520.00
E.....	.08	22,000.00	3,800.00	21,640.00

Problem 37-5. The fire insurance account on the books of Pratt and Read for the year 1946 follows:

March 1: 1-year Policy Fireman's LX368—Renewal...	$242.65	
May 15: 2-year Policy Des Moines F582—Renewal....	148.63	
September 15: Cancellation against Fireman's LX368..		$ 38.92
September 15: Cancellation against Des Moines F582..		43.35
September 30: 1-year Policy Globe HC8395—New....	90.40	
December 31: Balance to *P & L*....................		399.41
	$481.68	$481.68

Pratt and Read had a fire on September 15 and the amounts shown above as cancelled represent the portions of the premiums charged into the fire loss account. These amounts bore the same relation to the total unexpired premiums on September 15 that the claims paid by the insurance companies bore to the face amounts of the policies.

Policies LX368 and F582 were renewals of identical policies previously purchased at the same rates.

Correct the account.

Problem 37-6. A company organized January 1, 1944 lost its complete stock of merchandise just before inventory would have been taken on December 31, 1946. From the books you obtain the following facts:

	1944	1945	1946
Purchases	$200,362.51	$262,416.81	$198,998.42
Inventory, beginning of year	71,394.60	52,371.34	50,457.87
Sales	306,342.12	379,144.44	277,176.75
Allowances on purchases	3,297.12	6,848.40	4,313.91
Allowances on sales	6,219.00	8,312.40	5,281.14

(*a*) You are to determine the value of the merchandise destroyed and the amounts recoverable under the following concurrent policies containing an 85% coinsurance clause:

A Co	$13,000.00
B Co	10,000.00
C Co	17,000.00

(*b*) If the merchandise loss had been 75%, what amounts would have been recoverable?

Problem 37-7. Prepare journal entries to record properly the fire loss, the insurance receivable, and the expired insurance premium at March 31, 1946 on the books of the *X Y* Manufacturing Company.

The inventory of finished goods at January 1, 1946 was $21,000.00, and an insurance policy was written at that date in the amount of $14,000.00 for one year at a premium of $280.00 with the usual 80% coinsurance clause. All finished goods were stored in a warehouse which was partially destroyed by fire on the night of March 30, 1946. Immediately after the fire, an inventory of the undamaged goods was taken and showed a total of $13,600.00. The factory cost of the merchandise placed in the warehouse between January 1 and March 31 was $41,000.00, and the sales for the same period were $60,000.00. The statements for 1944 and 1945 showed an average gross profit of 30% and the insurance company agreed to settle on this basis.

Problem 37-8. Using the following information, compute the amount of insurance that can be collected on the loss of each asset, assuming that the insurance policies contain the 80% coinsurance clause.

Opening inventory	$30,000.00
Purchases	25,000.00
Sales	45,000.00
Average gross profit	25% of sales

	Sound Value	Agreed Loss	Insurance
Buildings	$50,000.00	$20,000.00	$45,000.00
Machinery	15,000.00	8,200.00	9,000.00
Furniture	3,000.00	1,500.00	2,100.00
Merchandise	?	Total	15,300.00

Problem 37-9. The *P* Company constructed its own plant and commenced business in 1940. It operates in a state in which a workmen's compensation law is in effect. The company desires to set aside a reserve from its own funds to cover the risk rather than continue to deal with insurance companies, and draws up the following table showing its accident experience and cost of insurance:

	Annual Payroll	Compensation Payments	Insurance Premiums Paid
1940	$1,500,000.00	$ 6,975.00	$ 8,000.00
1941	1,400,000.00	8,625.00	8,500.00
1942	1,375,000.00	8,550.00	9,000.00
1943	1,275,000.00	7,810.00	9,500.00
1944	1,350,000.00	8,920.00	9,500.00
	$6,900,000.00	$40,880.00	$44,500.00

In addition to the above compensation payments, there are awards payable weekly, extending as far as four years from December 31, 1944, on which the insurance companies are liable in an amount of $3,000.00.

What rate per thousand dollars of payroll do you recommend be used to calculate the reserve, and what accounts would be opened to record the new method of providing for the company's liability under the workmen's compensation law?

Problem 37-10. The J. Bowles Company in its tax returns for 1943 and 1944 had reported insurance charged on a cash basis instead of on an accrual basis. This necessitates preparing amended federal income tax returns for 1943 and 1944. Make adjustments to change to the accrual basis, and all other adjustments needed to correct the books, using the following information:

Insurance Account

		Dr.	Cr.
1943:			
May 1	Fire insurance premium on building for the period from May 1, 1943 to April 30, 1947	$ 5,200.00	
June 15	Fire insurance premium on stock, for the period from June 1, 1943 to May 30, 1944	1,600.00	
Aug. 1	Employees' fidelity insurance for the period from Aug. 1, 1943 to July 31, 1946	7,200.00	
Aug. 15	Refund because of reduction in rate of employees' fidelity insurance		$ 675.00
Sept. 1	Fire insurance premium on equipment for the period from Sept. 1, 1943 to August 31, 1947*	7,500.00	
Oct. 1	Due from Atka Insurance Company on shortage of bonded employee	1,400.00	
Dec. 31	Transferred to profit and loss		22,225.00
		$22,900.00	$22,900.00

* 4-year policy containing 85% coinsurance clause.

		Dr.	Cr.
1944:			
Mar. 1	Recovery from Atka Insurance Company on 1943 shortage		$ 1,400.00
Mar. 15	Premium on liability insurance carried on trucks, June 15, 1943 to June 14, 1944*	$ 2,820.00	
June 1	Additional fire insurance carried on building for the period June 1, 1944 to May 31, 1947	1,500.00	
June 15	Fire insurance premium on stock for the period from June 1, 1944 to May 31, 1945	1,500.00	
Nov. 15	Shortage of P. Jones to be paid fully by Superior Insurance Company	200.00	
Dec. 31	Transferred to profit and loss		4,620.00
		$ 6,020.00	$ 6,020.00

* This policy was renewed June 14, 1944, to June 14, 1945, but has not yet been paid. Premium, $2,820.00.

The adjusted insurance expense for 1943 and 1944 should be indicated on your work sheet, as well as the journal entries to bring the books into agreement with the amended tax returns.

Problem 37-11. The Johnson Manufacturing Company suffered a fire loss April 15, 1946. Although the books of account were damaged badly, the information shown below was secured from various sources.

Using the material given below, prepare the following:

(*a*) Balance sheet after the fire.

(*b*) Profit and loss statement for the three and one-half months' period ended after the fire.

JOHNSON MANUFACTURING COMPANY
Balance Sheet
December 31, 1945

Assets		
Cash		$ 38,910.15
Accounts receivable		36,205.00
Merchandise inventory		48,000.00
Machinery and equipment	$50,000.00	
Less depreciation reserve	8,602.30	41,397.70
Automobiles		3,805.35
		$168,318.20
Liabilities		
Notes payable		$ 5,306.40
Accounts payable		3,719.30
Capital stock		100,000.00
Surplus		59,292.50
		$168,318.20

Cash receipts and payments were compiled as follows:

Receipts	
Accounts receivable	$101,206.30
Notes payable	29,483.00
Payments	
Notes payable	$ 1,050.00
Accounts payable	46,785.40
Machinery and equipment	2,500.00
Manufacturing costs	85,416.75
Selling expenses	9,843.60
Administrative expenses	15,194.15

As of April 15, 1946, accounts receivable were $169,896.25; accounts payable were $30,105.60.

Depreciation to April 15, to be considered: machinery and equipment, $1,571.50; automobiles, $805.35.

Merchandise inventory saved from the fire was given a value of $18,500.00.

The inventory was insured for $29,000.00 on an 80% coinsurance policy. The insurance company agreed to accept a before-the-fire inventory calculated on an average gross profit basis of 38%.

Machinery and equipment fire loss was $4,500.00. On this, the insurance company agreed to pay 90%.

Problem 37-12. The plant of the Tamarack Manufacturing Company, engaged in the manufacture of hunting and camping articles, was partly destroyed by fire on the night of September 1, 1945. Practically all books of account were burned, but the data given below were obtained from various sources.

Balance Sheet January 1, 1945

Assets		Liabilities	
Machinery and fixtures....	$ 47,000.00	Notes payable............	$ 4,729.50
Automobiles.............	3,494.40	Accounts payable.........	2,553.60
Bonds...................	10,000.00	Reserve for depreciation...	8,437.50
Customers' accounts......	35,524.00	Capital stock............	100,000.00
Inventory...............	50,000.00	Surplus..................	59,220.90
Cash....................	28,923.10		
	$174,941.50		$174,941.50

An analysis of the check book and cancelled vouchers for the eight-month period revealed the following receipts and payments:

Receipts		Payments	
From customers..........	$ 98,746.70	Notes payable............	$ 917.50
Notes payable...........	34,376.00	Accounts payable.........	42,584.20
Interest on bonds.........	237.50	Machinery...............	3,750.00
		Labor....................	77,366.40
		Administrative salaries....	9,675.28
		Selling expenses..........	11,900.00
		Sundry manufacturing expenses.................	646.62
		Rent.....................	4,000.00
		Office expenses...........	2,418.50
		General expenses.........	2,381.40
	$133,360.20		$155,639.90

A report rendered to the president on September 1, 1945 showed that $172,952.10 was receivable from customers and $24,457.50 was due to creditors (accounts payable).

There should be a charge of $1,012.50 for depreciation to September 1, 1945, and the automobiles should be written down to $3,000.00.

An inventory of the merchandise not burned was valued at $20,000.00. The insurance company agreed to accept the inventory of the company as before the fire if calculated on a basis of average gross profits at 35% of the sales. The company's inventory was insured for $30,000.00 on an 80% coinsurance policy. There was a $5,000.00 loss on machinery and fixtures which the insurance company also agreed to pay; the gross asset value of the destroyed machinery was $7,000.00, and the related depreciation reserve was $2,000.00.

From the foregoing data:

(*a*) Reconstruct the accounts of the company, and show the method followed.

(*b*) Prepare (1) a balance sheet as at September 1, 1945, which is to include the liability of the insurance company and (2) a profit and loss account for the eight months ended on that date, showing details of cost of sales.

QUESTIONS AND PROBLEMS ON CHAPTER 38

Questions

Question 38-1. Give an illustration of an error in computing the profits of one year which will be offset by a counterbalancing error in a subsequent year, thus correcting the surplus but leaving the profits incorrectly stated by years.

Question 38-2. Give an illustration of an error in computing the profits of one year which will not be counterbalanced in a subsequent year.

Question 38-3. Sales aggregating $25,000.00 were entered on the books as of December 31, 1945, but the goods were not delivered until January 25, 1946. What adjustments, if any, would you make in preparing the profit and loss statement and the balance sheet?

Question 38-4. The Wisconsin Manufacturing Company has always followed the practice of inventorying finished goods at selling price. The following statement was prepared on this basis, and you are required to make the necessary corrections on the assumption that the percentage of mark-up for the current year is normal:

Sales			$712,600.00
Raw materials used, at cost		$308,920.00	
Labor and factory expenses		413,631.00	
Total		$722,551.00	
Work in process, at cost:			
Opening	$306,142.00		
Closing	352,325.00	46,183.00	
Cost of goods made		$676,368.00	
Finished goods, at selling—			
Opening	$124,729.00		
Closing	436,929.00	312,200.00	364,168.00
Gross profit			$348,432.00

Question 38-5. You find a bookkeeper's trial balance with the debit footings exceeding the credits by $131.56, which amount you temporarily carry to a suspense account. On audit, you discover that a purchase amounting to $417.50 had been debited to a creditor as $192.94; that $312.50 for depreciation of machinery had not been posted to the depreciation account; that $500.00 withdrawn by the proprietor had been charged to wages account; that a discount of $76.13 allowed to a customer had been posted to the wrong side of merchandise discount; and that the total of the sales returned was footed $5.00 short.

Prepare a schedule showing whether the correction of these errors will bring the books into balance.

Question 38-6. An audit of the *M* Company's records on June 30, 1945 reveals the necessity of making only minor adjustments to book figures, all of which are agreed to by the company's officials. The president of the company, however, states that he has submitted a tentative balance sheet to various creditors and to the company's bank, and requests that, after making the necessary adjustments, you certify to the balance sheet in the form prepared by the company's accounting department.

A review of the company's records reveals the following facts:

(*a*) "Cash" included bank deposits and petty cash; of the latter item, $1,550.00 was made up of I O U's signed by the company's officers.

(*b*) A large number of receivables had been discounted with a finance company. The balance in the individual accounts so discounted represented the 10% cash withheld by the finance company until the accounts had been paid in full.

(*c*) Inventory of finished goods included stock in a warehouse in a distant city, the receipt for which had been deposited with the bank as collateral.

(*d*) The real estate, machinery, and equipment were included at appraised values, and the offsetting credit was included with capital surplus.

(*e*) Principal and accrued interest of a first mortgage loan appeared in a separate classification below current liabilities. A payment of $15,000.00 was due on the principal on April 10, 1946, and interest was payable on April 10 and October 10 of each year.

(*f*) Under the classification of surplus were the following reserves:

Bad debt reserve
Contingent reserve
Sinking fund reserve
Depreciation reserve

Would you certify a balance sheet so prepared, or would you insist that certain alterations of form be made? If you assume the latter attitude on any of the above items, what changes would you make?

Question 38-7. A corporation has been engaged in business for three years, with an investment in machinery totaling $75,000.00 during that time. No depreciation has ever been provided. At the end of the third year, the directors decide that an annual charge of 5% of the cost of the machinery should have been made for depreciation, and they now propose to set up such a reserve. State how the entry should be made.

Question 38-8. For three years the Evasion Company has charged items to the machinery repairs account which should have been charged to the machinery and equipment account. It is agreed that 5% is the correct rate of depreciation and that assets are to be depreciated for one-half (½) year in the year of acquisition.

Items incorrectly charged to the machinery repairs account are as follows:

1944	$6,000.00
1945	7,500.00
1946	8,000.00

Submit journal entries to correct the records as of December 31, 1946, assuming 1946 depreciation on the unadjusted balance of the machinery account has been recorded but that the books have not yet been closed.

Problems

Problem 38-1.

(*a*) The Harrington Company asked you to make the changes in the balance sheets and profit and loss statements which were made necessary by the discovery that during the last three years certain replacement parts which should have been charged to maintenance expense were charged to the machinery account. The company based its depreciation, which was computed at 10% per annum, on the closing balance of the machinery account and credited the amount to a reserve. The balances affected are shown below:

	Balance of Machinery Account December 31	Balance of Reserve for Depreciation December 31	Erroneous Charges to Machinery	Net Profit Reported
1943..........	$232,460.00	$41,732.00		
1944..........	237,850.00	41,747.00	$27,120.00	$56,850.00
1945..........	246,170.00	58,232.00	15,620.00	63,210.00
1946..........	260,320.00	67,829.00	31,170.00	20,750.00

(*b*) Prepare the adjusting entry necessary to record your corrections on the books on December 31, 1946. State the corrected profits for the three years. Include working papers.

Problem 38-2. The Vesley Company presented the following profit and loss statement for 1946:

Sales....................................		$646,320.00
Cost of goods sold:		
Opening inventory......................	$ 87,432.00	
Purchases..............................	531,145.00	
Total................................	$618,577.00	
Less closing inventory.................	135,624.00	482,953.00
Gross profit.............................		$163,367.00
Expenses.................................		131,795.00
Net profit...............................		$ 31,572.00

The president of the company is struck by the fact that the per cents of gross profit, expenses, and net profit do not conform to the usual performance of the business and asks you to investigate. You find that on December 31, 1945, the following matters required attention.

There was on hand and not included in the inventory merchandise amounting to $11,430.00. The liability for this merchandise was on the books at that time. There was omitted from the inventory and the liabilities an amount of $5,430.00 in addition to the amount above.

Accrued expenses of $6,320.00 existing on December 31, 1945 were ignored on that date. On December 31, 1946 there was included in the inventory merchandise costing $7,982.00, for which the liability had not been recorded. Expenses of $2,870.00 should be deferred on December 31, 1946. A sale of $11,700.00 in 1946 had been returned. No entry was made for this return. The goods were included in the inventory at selling price, which was 150% of cost.

Prepare a corrected profit and loss statement and submit the journal entry to make the corrections on the books, which had been closed.

Problem 38-3. From the following trial balance of the Mather Company on December 31, 1946 and the data which follow prepare a balance sheet and a statement of surplus:

Cash.....................................	$ 21,726.00	
Accounts receivable......................	43,640.00	
Inventories..............................	17,159.00	
Plant....................................	42,818.00	
Reserve for depreciation.................		$ 15,284.00
Accounts payable.........................		14,072.00
Capital stock............................		50,000.00
Surplus, January 1.......................		32,628.00
Profit and loss..........................		13,359.00
	$125,343.00	$125,343.00

(*a*) The opening inventory was understated by $7,520.00, which represented a purchase which was recorded but omitted from the inventory.
(*b*) No provision for bad debts was made. It was estimated that 5% of the accounts receivable outstanding at the end of the year were uncollectible. During the period, accounts amounting to $742.00 which were more than a year old were written off.
(*c*) A machine which cost $4,108.00 was sold on January 3, 1946 for $380.00. The sales price was credited to the plant account. The depreciation on this machine to the date of sale was $2,420.00. The company took depreciation at 10% on the closing balance of the plant account.

Submit the journal entries to put your corrections on the books on December 31, 1946.

Problem 38-4. T. W. Fitzgerald, Inc. presented the following statement of surplus:

Balance, January 1, 1946		$ 71,826.00
Add: Profits 1946		27,417.00
Adjustment of 1945 closing inventory		6,382.00
Appraisal increase in value of machinery		18,200.00
Total		$123,825.00
Deduct: Dividends paid	$20,000.00	
Loss on sale of machine	7,200.00	27,200.00
		$ 96,625.00

Omit any items you think are not properly included in the statement, and recast the statement in the light of the following information.

The company had not taken depreciation amounting to $4,200.00 in 1945. Of this amount $2,200.00 applied to the machine which was sold in 1946. Of the increase in value due to appraisal, $5,250.00 applied to this same machine.

Problem 38-5. The president of the Jordon Company claims that there would have been a tax advantage to the company had it kept its books on the accrual basis instead of on the cash basis during the years 1944 and 1945. In 1944 the company reported a profit of $26,520.00, and its income in excess of $23,400.00 was subject to a tax of 95%. In 1945 the company reported a profit of $28,150.-00 and its income in excess of $25,650.00 was subject to a tax of 95%. In both years there was available a postwar refund of 10% of the tax. On the basis of the following data, was his claim correct?

	December 31		
	1943	1944	1945
Accrued expenses	$3,875.00	$5,710.00	$4,870.00
Deferred expenses	4,872.00	5,600.00	3,100.00
Accrued income	3,650.00	1,920.00	4,460.00
Deferred income	2,100.00	2,750.00	6,350.00

His bookkeeper claimed that "it would all come out in the wash," and that over a period of years it would equalize itself. Explain why this contention is true or false.

Problem 38-6. In making an audit of the accounts of a company for the year ended December 31, 1946, you find the following errors in the inventory at that date:

Merchandise on hand; purchase not recorded; not included in the inventory	$12,000.00
Inventory sheets overfooted; several errors totaling	7,849.60
Errors in extensions resulting in a net understatement of	416.35

Upon discovery of these errors you decide to test the inventory of December 31, 1945 (this being your first audit of the accounts), and you find the following errors:

Errors in addition resulting in a net undervaluation of	$4,350.00
An item entered in the inventory after making the closing entries, and hence not included in the inventory account in the ledger	375.00
Merchandise on hand, not recorded in purchases until 1946, and not included in inventory	965.85

Prepare journal entries which should be made to adjust the accounts, assuming that the books had been closed as of December 31, 1946, prior to your audit; also prepare the entries which you will wish to apply to your working trial balance in determining the correct profit for 1946. State the net effect of your adjustments on the profits for 1946, and upon the surplus at the end of that year.

Problem 38-7. You are asked to submit a statement of the profits of a company for the two years ended December 31, 1946. No dividends have been paid in recent years and the surplus balance on December 31, 1946, per the books, amounts to $480,000.00, comprising:

Balance, December 31, 1944	$243,000.00
Profits of 1945	146,000.00
Profits of 1946	91,000.00
Balance, December 31, 1946	$480,000.00

The following matters require consideration as at the respective dates:

December 31, 1944:

Bad debts amount to $15,500.00, for which there was no provision on the books. These accounts were written off in 1945.

Consigned goods (own) are included in the inventory at $148,000.00, which is 25% in excess of cost.

The following liabilities are omitted from the books:

New construction	$38,000.00
Materials included in inventory	4,600.00
Wages	2,850.00
Accrued taxes	1,500.00

December 31, 1945:

Bad debts amount to $12,600.00. No reserve was provided and the accounts were written off in 1946.

Consigned goods (own) amounting to $215,000.00 are valued at 25% in excess of cost.

The following liabilities are omitted from the books:

Goods on hand omitted from inventory	$9,600.00
Accrued taxes	2,400.00

The inventory was overstated $16,800.00 because of an error in recapitulation.

No provision for depreciation was made on the books, and your computation shows that $7,600.00 should be provided.

December 31, 1946:

Bad debts amount to $16,800.00; no reserve has been provided.

Consigned goods (own) amount to $216,000.00, being valued at 20% in excess of cost.

Liabilities omitted from the books:

For purchase of new machinery	$16,300.00
Accrued wages	3,400.00
Accrued taxes	3,200.00

No provision was made on the books for depreciation; you compute same at $10,300.00.

Prepare an adjusted statement of surplus covering the period from December 31, 1944 to December 31, 1946. Also prepare whatever journal entries are necessary to correct the books on December 31, 1946.

Problem 38-8. The unaudited accounts for the year 1944 of the Bilt-Well Furniture Company are as follows:

Balance Sheet—December 31, 1944

Assets:	
Cash	$ 8,000.00
Accounts receivable	50,000.00
Inventory	343,000.00
	$401,000.00
Liabilities:	
Notes payable	$ 25,000.00
Trade creditors	45,000.00
Reserve for bad debts	8,000.00
Capital stock	150,000.00
Surplus	173,000.00
	$401,000.00

Surplus and Profit and Loss Account
Year Ended December 31, 1944

Sales	$230,000.00
Cost of sales	183,000.00
Gross profit	$ 47,000.00
Expenses	$ 72,000.00
Bad debts	16,000.00
	$ 88,000.00
Loss for the year	$ 41,000.00
Surplus at January 1, 1944	214,000.00
Surplus at December 31, 1944	$173,000.00

An examination discloses that at the end of the year 1944 the following adjustments are necessary:

To reduce inventory to market by	$125,000.00
To increase reserve for bad debts by	8,000.00
To set up the liability for:	
Commissions payable to salesmen	5,000.00
Sundry expenses	2,000.00

The examination further reveals the following adjustments at the beginning of the year that were accepted by the company but had not been taken up on the books:

Reduction of inventory to market	$100,000.00
Increase of reserve for bad debts	19,000.00
Provision for:	
Unrecorded liabilities	3,000.00
Commissions due salesmen	1,500.00

Prepare adjusted accounts.

Problem 38-9. The prospective purchasers of The Mason Manufacturing Company have asked you to make an examination of that company's records for the five-year period covered by the statements given below.

Balance Sheets

	December 31,				
	1942	1943	1944	1945	1946
Assets					
Cash	$ 4,365.21	$ 6,785.10	$ 7,110.18	$ 6,975.84	$ 6,435.23
Inventories	40,639.57	42,587.39	43,321.15	41,782.53	43,140.67
Accounts receivable	26,701.15	27,889.33	28,690.28	36,564.63	41,787.19
Plant property	69,000.00	69,850.00	71,690.00	72,973.00	73,784.50
Deferred charges	2,795.35	2,364.10	1,931.49	1,847.15	2,184.75
	$143,501.28	$149,475.92	$152,743.10	$160,143.15	$167,332.34
Liabilities					
Accounts payable	$ 36,427.63	$ 34,698.92	$ 38,146.88	$ 34,814.53	$ 35,246.47
Mortgage payable	30,000.00	30,000.00	30,000.00	30,000.00	30,000.00
Reserve for depreciation	11,520.00	14,812.50	14,812.50	22,081.50	25,620.72
Capital stock	50,000.00	50,000.00	50,000.00	50,000.00	50,000.00
Surplus	15,553.65	19,964.50	19,783.72	23,247.12	26,465.15
	$143,501.28	$149,475.92	$152,743.10	$160,143.15	$167,332.34

Surplus Statements

	Year Ended December 31,				
	1942	1943	1944	1945	1946
Balance at beginning of year	$11,816.68	$15,553.65	$19,964.50	$19,783.72	$23,247.12
Net profits	6,236.97	7,410.85	1,819.22	6,463.40	6,218.03
Total	$18,053.65	$22,964.50	$21,783.72	$26,247.12	$29,465.15
Dividends	2,500.00	3,000.00	2,000.00	3,000.00	3,000.00
Balance at end of year	$15,553.65	$19,964.50	$19,783.72	$23,247.12	$26,465.15

Your examination discloses the following facts:

Depreciation was computed at 5% of the balance in the plant property accounts at the end of each year, except in 1944 when the profits were small and no depreciation was provided. During 1945 the depreciation rate was doubled to provide for the prior omission. The 5% rate is regarded as reasonable.

Except as noted below, the depreciation reserve has been properly charged with accrued depreciation of plant property disposed of in these years. Losses and gains on such property disposals have been properly reflected in surplus, with the exception of the disposal of machinery in 1945. From this sale the company received $1,000.00 on equipment orginally costing $2,500.00, and for which depreciation in the amount of $200.00 had been provided. At the time of the sale the only entry was a $1,000.00 charge to cash and credit to the property account.

A reserve for bad debts was maintained until December 31, 1941. A reserve of 4% of the accounts receivable should have been set up at the end of each year to provide for losses on the receivables written off during each respective succeeding year.

Unexpired insurance in the amount of $385.00 was ignored in closing the books on December 31, 1944.

During 1943, certain equipment was purchased for $650.00 and improperly charged to merchandise purchases. During 1944 the bookkeeper undertook to correct the error by charging plant property and crediting purchases with the cost.

The inventory was overvalued $2,145.00 on December 31, 1941, and undervalued $1,984.00 on December 31, 1944.

Prepare an adjusted surplus statement for the five-year period, an adjusted balance sheet at the end of each year, and a journal entry which will harmonize the books with your balance sheet as of December 31, 1946.

Problem 38-10. From the following trial balance of the Anderson Company and the accompanying data prepare a columnar work sheet showing the adjustments and the segregation of balance sheet and profit and loss items.

ANDERSON COMPANY
Trial Balance
December 31, 1947

	Debit	Credit
Cash in banks	$ 180,000.00	
Petty cash funds	5,000.00	
Customers' notes receivable	80,000.00	
Accounts receivable	900,000.00	
Current advances to subsidiary companies	25,000.00	
Investment in subsidiary companies	500,000.00	
Land	5,000.00	
Buildings	20,000.00	
Machinery and equipment	50,000.00	
Furniture and fixtures	40,000.00	
Reserve for depreciation at January 1, 1947		$ 35,000.00
Life insurance	200,000.00	
Inventory at January 1, 1947	500,000.00	
Trade creditors		220,000.00
Common stock ($100 par) authorized and issued		500,000.00
Surplus at January 1, 1947		960,000.00
Net sales		5,800,000.00
Purchases	3,500,000.00	
Manufacturing expenses	400,000.00	
Selling, administrative, and general expenses	1,150,000.00	
Other income		40,000.00
	$7,555,000.00	$7,555,000.00

During the examination the following facts are disclosed:

1. Checks totaling $10,000.00 in settlement of accounts payable were dated and issued in December, 1947 but not entered in the cash book until January, 1948.

2. Accounts receivable include an amount of $400,000.00 representing capital advances to subsidiary companies. The balance is receivable from customers.
3. It is estimated that 10% of the customers' accounts receivable and 10% of the notes receivable are doubtful of collection. All accounts and notes receivable at the beginning of the year were considered at that time to be collectible.
4. The inventory at January 1, 1947, includes the following:

Machinery and equipment	$200,000.00
Less reserve for depreciation	100,000.00
	$100,000.00

5. The inventory at December 31, 1947 (excluding machinery and equipment and the relative reserve) is as follows:

Inventory on hand	$500,000.00
Inventory in transit for which the liability has not been recorded	10,000.00
	$510,000.00

6. The amount shown as life insurance represents the accumulated premiums which were charged to this account. The premiums paid to December 31, 1946 amounted to $160,000.00 and the premiums paid in 1947 amounted to $40,000.00. An examination of the policies shows that the cash surrender value at December 31, 1946 amounted to $85,000.00 and the cash surrender value at December 31, 1947 amounted to $100,000.00.
7. There has been no change in the various property accounts during 1947. Depreciation should be provided at the following rates:

Buildings	5% per year
Machinery and equipment	10% " "
General office furniture and fixtures	10% " "

8. Insurance premiums, charged to general expenses:

Prepaid at December 31, 1946	$3,000.00
Prepaid at December 31, 1947	2,000.00

9. Taxes, charged to general expenses:

Prepaid at December 31, 1946	$5,000.00
Prepaid at December 31, 1947	8,000.00

10. Commissions, charged to selling expenses:

Accrued at December 31, 1946	$4,000.00
Accrued at December 31, 1947	5,000.00

Inventories, fixed assets, and investments are shown throughout at their cost. Income taxes are not to be considered.

Problem 38-11. The following balance sheet of the Star Manufacturing Company as at December 31, 1943 is presented to you for purposes of revision of form, content, and presentation of items therein, based upon the information hereinafter set forth.

THE STAR MANUFACTURING COMPANY

Balance Sheet, December 31, 1943

Assets

Current assets:		
Cash on hand and in banks	$137,500	
Notes receivable, less discounted notes, $20,000	60,000	
Accounts receivable, less reserve, $8,500	247,800	
U. S. Government bonds and accrued interest, $420	42,350	
Total current assets		$ 487,650
Working and trading assets:		
Raw materials and supplies	$ 92,440	
Work in process	110,700	
Finished goods, including consigned merchandise, $21,670	181,320	
Total working and trading assets		384,460
Investments in the capital stock of other companies		120,000
Capital assets:		
Land and buildings at cost, less depreciation	$440,000	
Machinery and equipment, less depreciation, $162,800	332,000	
Furniture and fixtures, less depreciation, $3,200	15,900	
Total capital assets		787,900
Sinking fund for first mortgage bonds		69,700
Treasury stock		10,000
Prepaid expenses and deferred charges:		
Unexpired insurance	$ 3,300	
Discount on capital stock	15,000	
Prepaid advertising	4,600	
Prepaid interest on notes discounted	1,800	24,700
		$1,884,410

Liabilities

Current liabilities:		
Accounts payable—trade	$273,000	
Accrued payrolls and interest (exclusive of interest on installment notes payable to bank)	15,620	
Reserve for federal income and excess profits taxes	72,000	
Reserve for other taxes	14,300	
Installment notes payable to bank due $12,000 on first of each month beginning January 1, 1944, and accrued interest $4,500	124,500	
Total current liabilities		$ 499,420
Dividends payable January 16, 1944		6,000
Funded debt:		
5% first mortgage bonds due January 1, 1960		350,000
Capital stock and surplus:		
Capital stock:		
Preferred, 2,000 shares authorized; 1,800 shares issued	$180,000	
Common, 3,000 shares authorized; 2,500 shares issued	250,000	
Subscription to common stock, 400 shares	22,000	
Total capital stock	$452,000	

Earned surplus:			
Reserve for employees' pensions...	$ 14,000		
Free and available for dividends...	159,990		
Total earned surplus..................		173,990	
Capital surplus............................		403,000	
Total capital stock and surplus.......			1,028,990
			$1,884,410

Through inquiry and investigation you obtain the following information with respect to items in the foregoing balance sheet:

(1) Cash includes $14,000 in an employees' pension fund.

(2) The U. S. Government bonds represent $42,000 face value 2% Treasury bonds valued at cost plus accrued interest. The market value of such bonds on December 31, 1943 was $44,700.

(3) Accounts receivable include $8,400 of advances to employees.

(4) Accounts receivable also include $15,000 advanced to suppliers of raw materials for materials neither received nor in transit. Since the placement of the orders, which are not subject to cancellation, the replacement cost of the materials has declined to 70% of the commitment price.

(5) Raw materials and supplies are stated at the lower of cost or market and include invoices received, in the amount of $7,000, for materials shipped f.o.b. point of shipment and in the hands of common carriers on December 31, 1943. Excluded are $9,000 of raw materials received on December 28, 1943, for which invoices are dated January 15, 1944. Delivery of this material was accepted in December merely as an accommodation to the seller (whose warehouse was congested), with the understanding that it would not be billed until January.

(6) Work in process is valued at actual cost of direct materials and direct labor, plus a normal charge for manufacturing overhead based upon company experience, which is less than market value.

(7) Finished goods are similarly valued, except for merchandise in hands of consignees, which is priced and billed on memorandum at 110% of cost. Finished goods valued at $140,000 are pledged against installment notes payable to bank.

(8) Of the capital stock investments in other companies, $95,000 represents investments at cost in 50% or more of the stock of subsidiary companies. The realizable values of such investments exceed cost, and income therefrom is recorded as dividends are received.

(9) The remaining investments represent small stock interests considered necessary for business operations, having an aggregate market value of $21,800 at December 31, 1943.

(10) The land and buildings account, when analyzed, discloses the following:

Cost of land..	$ 75,000
Depreciated cost of buildings as at January 1, 1938, established by revenue agent's report dated July 7, 1939, adjusted for subsequent additions and retirements.....................	669,500
Accumulated depreciation since January 1, 1938.............	304,500

(11) The sinking fund consists of $19,700 in cash and $50,000 of the company's own first mortgage 5% bonds.

(12) The treasury stock represents 100 shares of preferred valued at par and acquired for resale to employees.

(13) The preferred stock has a $100 par value. It is cumulative at the rate of 6%, and is callable after July 1, 1945 at 105% of par value plus accumulated and unpaid dividends, if any. The 1,800 shares issued include the 100 shares in the treasury.

(14) The common stock also has a $100 par value. The subscriptions to 400 shares of common stock are stated in the balance sheet net of $18,000 representing receivables from subscribers on their stock subscription contracts.

(15) The reserve for employees' pensions of $14,000 offsets the amount of cash in the employees' pension fund. This fund was set up in 1943 as a result of a contract with employees.

(16) The current earned surplus account dates back to July 1, 1934, on which date a voluntary reorganization served to eliminate an operating deficit.

QUESTIONS AND PROBLEMS ON CHAPTER 39

Questions

Question 39-1. Distinguish between a balance sheet and a statement of affairs.

Question 39-2. For what two general purposes may a statement of affairs be prepared? In what way will statements prepared for these two purposes differ?

Question 39-3. Why is the balance sheet classification of assets usually an illogical one to use in a statement of affairs?

How should the asset side of a statement of affairs be classified?

Can you think of any circumstances under which the balance sheet classification of assets might properly be used in a statement of affairs?

Question 39-4. What are liabilities having priority? Describe the method of showing them in the statement of affairs.

Question 39-5. Explain the methods used in a statement of affairs for:

(*a*) Offsetting fully secured liabilities and the security.
(*b*) Offsetting partially secured liabilities and the security.
(*c*) Indicating the special rights of creditors having priority.

Question 39-6. Do notes payable necessarily rank ahead of accounts payable?

Question 39-7. State two methods of showing valuation reserves in the statement of affairs.

Question 39-8. If additional expenditures must be incurred in order to realize certain assets, how would you show the necessary additional expenditures in the statement of affairs?

Question 39-9. How would you show in the statement of affairs the contingent liability on notes receivable discounted?

Question 39-10. What relation does the deficiency account bear to the statement of affairs?

Question 39-11. A balance sheet is handed you with the request that you prepare a statement of affairs. This balance sheet shows the following items:

Capital stock	$50,000.00
Surplus—January 1	12,000.00
Dividends paid during the year	10,000.00
Loss for the year	19,000.00

How would you show these facts in the statements of affairs and in the deficiency account?

Question 39-12. How could you prepare a statement of affairs for an individual proprietorship or a partnership in order to show the prospective loss to the owner as well as the deficiency to creditors?

Would this form of statement be applicable to a corporation?

Question 39-13. *A* and *B* are in partnership. *A* is the managing partner, and he is allowed a salary of $250.00 per month. The partnership becomes insolvent on December 31, at which time *A*'s salary for December has not been paid. How would you deal with this unpaid salary in the statement of affairs?

Problems

Problems 39-1. You are to write a report on the F. D. Thompson Company, which is financially embarrassed, stating what action you think should be taken, and making any proposals you believe practical which might continue the business as a going concern. Its balance sheet follows.

Cash		$ 12,340.00	Accounts payable	$ 165,320.00
Accounts receivable	$185,420.00		Notes payable	140,000.00
Less reserve for bad debts	4,652.00	180,768.00	Mortgage payable—6%	400,000.00
Inventory		265,402.00	Capital stock	400,000.00
Fixed assets—net		652,490.00	Surplus	105,680.00
Goodwill		100,000.00		
		$1,211,000.00		$1,211,000.00

In your examination of the company you find that of the accounts receivable, $75,400.00 are more than one year old, and a recovery of only $25,000.00 is likely. Of the remainder, $80,000.00 which are considered good are pledged to a finance company for a loan of $60,000.00, carried in the notes payable account. The reserve on the books is considered sufficient to cover losses on accounts not classified as old.

Much of the inventory is obsolete and a portion priced at $84,300.00 would probably bring only $15,000.00 in the market. The company's annual sales average about $650,000.00.

Maintenance charges have been capitalized and the depreciation charged has been inadequate by about $22,000.00 a year. The property is appraised at $420,000.00. The goodwill is valueless.

Included in accounts payable are accrued wages amounting to $2,360.00. Accounts payable also include $30,000.00 owed to the president of the company who is its principal stockholder.

The mortgage must be paid off at the rate of $50,000.00 a year, beginning at the end of two years.

The company has shown a profit of about $15,000.00 for several years, but has not paid any dividends for ten years.

Problem 39-2. The Fowler Transportation Company called a meeting of its creditors and offered a composition of 20 cents on the dollar to the general creditors, payable 10 cents in cash and the balance in six monthly installments. The debtor claims that it can raise $10,000.00 additional capital if the composition is accepted by all unsecured creditors. Attempts to persuade the company to raise its offer failed. You are to submit a report to the general creditors advising them whether it would be better for them to accept this offer or to seek a legal liquidation or reorganization. Its balance sheet follows.

Cash	$ 634.00	Accrued wages		$ 3,150.00
Accounts receivable	28,658.00	Accounts payable		83,170.00
Supplies	1,389.00	Notes on trucks		38,600.00
Trucks	57,540.00	Capital stock	$10,000.00	
Prepaid insurance	1,560.00	Less deficit	45,139.00	
		Capital deficiency		35,139.00*
	$89,781.00			$89,781.00

* Denotes deduction.

Conservative valuations for the assets would be: accounts receivable, $25,000.00; supplies, $500.00; trucks, $45,000.00; and prepaid insurance, $720.00. The trucks are subject to repossession by the finance company if the notes are not paid, but it may be assumed that repossession would be stayed if bankruptcy proceedings were begun. It is estimated that the costs of legal proceedings would be $8,000.00.

Problem 39-3. The Aztec Company, which failed owing its creditors $92,000.00, made a composition with its general creditors at the rate of 40 cents on the dollar. Secured creditors and creditors having priority, whose claims are included in the above amount, were paid $24,500.00. Grohs, a general creditor with a claim of $22,000.00 against the company, learned that a favored creditor had received a fraudulent preference of $14,000.00, prior to the company's failure. Grohs asks you to inform him how much he lost because of this preference.

It is estimated that the legal costs of recovering this preference will be $2,000.00. You may assume that these costs are chargeable against the collection. How much will Grohs gain if the attorneys are successful in recovering the $14,000.00?

Problem 39-4. The Thurston Company has made an assignment for the benefit of creditors. Before taking action they request you to prepare a statement of affairs. You find that the Thurston Company has not maintained good records and has no trial balance, but from various sources you derive the following information:

The Thurston Company has issued capital stock of $60,000.00, but only $40,000.00 has been collected and the remainder is apparently uncollectible.

The cash book shows a balance of $4,632.00; the bank reports a balance of only $864.00, and it is known that two checks, amounting to $534.00, are still outstanding. These checks will not be allowed to clear. There is no cash on hand.

The company's accounts receivable total $34,875.00. Of this amount, accounts totaling $22,800.00 have been assigned to a finance company for an advance of $18,240.00. The finance company has deducted a discount fee of $456.00 against the company's equity and accrued interest of $320.00 on the advance. One of the assigned accounts, amounting to $640.00, is due from a debtor who has made an offer to settle his debts for 60 cents on the dollar. Of the accounts retained by the company, you estimate that $2,000.00 will prove uncollectible.

An inventory was taken and it amounted to $14,320.00 at current market values.

The president of the company has been using company funds to buy himself an annuity. The annuity has cost $22,000.00 and has a cash surrender value of $14,150.00. Since this action was not authorized by the board of directors, the attorneys consider the policy an asset of the company.

The fixed assets are appraised at $18,000.00. They cost $43,165.00 and have never been depreciated although 40% of their average life has expired. They are mortgaged for $15,000.00, and there is $150.00 interest accrued on the mortgage.

Other liabilities comprise accounts payable amounting to $41,680.00 and unsecured notes payable amounting to $12,000.00 with accrued interest of $600.00.

Prepare the desired statement and a deficiency statement.

Problem 39-5. Prepare a statement of affairs and a deficiency account from the following data.

THE BOYLSTON COMPANY

Balance Sheet

December 31, 1945

Assets			
Current assets:			
Cash		$ 1,465.00	
Accounts receivable	$16,275.00		
Less reserve for bad debts	152.00	16,123.00	
Notes receivable		3,500.00	
Accrued interest		70.00	
Inventories:			
Finished goods	$ 3,200.00		
Goods in process	7,400.00		
Raw materials	18,900.00	29,500.00	$50,658.00
Fixed assets:			
Buildings	$34,000.00		
Less reserve for depreciation	5,100.00	$28,900.00	
Machinery	$24,400.00		
Less reserve for depreciation	6,800.00	17,600.00	46,500.00
			$97,158.00
Liabilities			
Current liabilities:			
Accounts payable		$36,328.00	
Notes payable		8,418.00	
Accrued interest on notes payable		89.00	
Accrued interest on mortgage payable		200.00	
Accrued taxes		341.00	$45,376.00
Fixed liabilities:			
Mortgage payable			20,000.00
Capital			
Capital stock		$50,000.00	
Less deficit		18,218.00	31,782.00
			$97,158.00

The reserve for bad debts should be $2,200.00. In addition to the notes receivable recorded, notes receivable of $5,000.00 have been discounted at the bank, and it is expected that all except $200.00 will be collected. The notes on the books are worth their face value. Raw materials carried at $6,600.00 are pledged under a warehouse receipt given to secure the notes payable. These goods are now worth $8,000.00. Raw materials carried at $2,540.00, and currently worth $2,750.00, must be used to complete the goods in process. It is estimated that $4,000.00 must also be paid for labor for this purpose. The goods in process will then be worth $8,000.00. The remaining raw materials are worth $9,200.00. The finished goods may be sold for $2,400.00.

The building is built on leased land which reverts to the owner at the termination of the lease. The mortgagee has offered to pay the Boylston Company $2,000.00 and take over the ground lease in satisfaction of his claim.

The estimated value of the machinery is $8,000.00.

Problem 39-6. Following is the balance sheet of the *C D* Company, a partnership, on October 10, 1945:

Assets	
Cash (including due bills of partners, aggregating $400.00)	$ 2,110.00
Investment bonds—*A* Company—par	20,000.00
Investments—bonds of Segram Company—par	22,500.00
Inventory	27,228.00
Accounts receivable	35,200.00
Notes receivable (all believed good)	6,180.00
Real estate used in business	25,000.00
Machinery and equipment	23,000.00
Total assets	$161,218.00
Liabilities	
Accounts payable	$ 96,133.00
Notes payable	36,000.00
Accrued taxes	500.00
Accrued wages	750.00
Total liabilities	$133,383.00
Capital	
C, capital	$ 16,220.00
D, capital	11,615.00
Total capital	$ 27,835.00

You are asked to prepare a statement of affairs and a deficiency account. The notes payable are classified as follows:

Secured—Second National Bank	$11,000.00
Unsecured	25,000.00

Accounts receivable are classified as follows:

Good	$15,000.00
Doubtful (estimated 50% collectibility)	14,000.00
Bad	6,200.00

The investment bonds are worth par. The bonds of Segram Company are held by the Second National Bank as collateral to loans.

The inventory is expected to realize about two thirds of its book value.

The machinery and equipment are estimated to be worth 15,000.00, and the real estate can be sold for $22,000.00.

Problem 39-7. F. P. Pegg, who has made an assignment for the benefit of his creditors, lists the following assets, together with his creditors and their claims on December 31, 1946:

Assets:
- Building and equipment, $15,000.00; estimated value, $9,000.00.
- Cash, $533.00 (includes petty cash in which there are expense vouchers of $133.00).
- Investments (stock) $20,000.00; estimated value, $16,000.00.
- Raw materials, supplies, and goods in process, book value, $8,500.00; estimated to realize, $6,200.00.

Creditors:

Accounts payable:	
James Jason	$ 7,200.00
Walter Ferrington	11,300.00
Hudson M. Marlingworth	5,200.00

Employees, $600.00 for accrued wages.
Union Eagle National Bank, holding notes of $16,000.00, secured by bonds having a book value of $21,000.00; estimated value, $17,580.00.
Cryhake Distributing Corporation, holding notes cf $10,000.00, unsecured, and notes of $8,500.00, secured by warehouse receipts for finished goods of a book value of $8,000.00; estimated value of $6,000.00.

The creditors' committee asks you to prepare statements showing the payments that can be made to each of the several creditors on the basis of the above information.

Problem 39-8. Following is the balance sheet of the Pelmel Manufacturing Company as of November 30, 1946:

Land	$ 10,000.00	
Buildings	26,000.00	
Reserve for depreciation—buildings		$ 5,000.00
Plant, machinery, and equipment	28,900.00	
Goodwill	15,000.00	
Stock of the Kansas Co	50,000.00	
Advances to the Kansas Co	15,000.00	
Finished goods	13,000.00	
Goods in process	8,900.00	
Raw materials	4,200.00	
Accounts receivable	33,300.00	
Notes receivable	5,400.00	
Accrued interest on notes receivable	81.00	
Reserve for bad debts		300.00
Cash	889.00	
Office supplies	290.00	
Prepaid expenses	170.00	
Capital stock		60,000.00
Surplus		45,320.00
Reserve for contingencies		10,000.00
Mortgage on land and buildings		12,000.00
Notes payable		38,000.00
Accounts payable		36,000.00
Accrued taxes		150.00
Accrued wages		3,200.00
Accrued interest on mortgage		120.00
Accrued interest on notes payable		1,040.00
	$211,130.00	$211,130.00

The advances to the Kansas Co. are unsecured. This company has gone into the hands of a receiver, and it is expected that it will pay its creditors at the rate of thirty-five cents on the dollar.

The Pelmel Corporation is thereby financially embarrassed, and its creditors call upon you to prepare a statement of affairs.

The land is expected to be sold for $9,000.00; the building will realize about $15,000.00; and the plant, machinery, and equipment, $13,500.00.

The inventories are expected to realize as follows:

	Book Value	Estimated Value
Finished goods	$13,000.00	$10,000.00
Goods in process	8,900.00	5,000.00
Raw materials	4,200.00	3,900.00

The accounts receivable are classified as follows:

Good	$25,000.00
Doubtful (estimated 50% collectible)	5,000.00
Bad	3,300.00

The notes receivable and accrued interest are considered collectible. A note discounted at the Third State Bank will probably be uncollectible; the amount of this note is $1,200.00.

The deferred charges are valueless except for the office supplies, which can be sold for $50.00.

The notes payable consist of one note for $30,000.00 with accrued interest of $240.00, and three other notes aggregating $8,000.00, on which $800.00 interest has accrued. The holder of the $30,000.00 note also holds the Kansas Company stock as collateral.

Of the $8,000.00 notes payable mentioned above, one note for $3,000.00, on which $320.00 interest has accrued, is secured by notes receivable of $5,000.00, on which $75.00 interest has accrued. The note for $4,000.00 with accrued interest of $480.00 thereon is secured by warehouse receipts for raw material having a book value of $4,200.00 and an estimated realizable value of $3,900.00.

The remaining note for $1,000.00 is unsecured.

Problem 39-9. The Clark Manufacturing Company is being operated by a committee of its creditors, and you are called in to prepare financial statements, at an interim date, for information of the creditors. Your examination reveals the following:

1. After the creditors' committee had taken charge, but before the date of your examination, a fire occurred causing an estimated damage of $80,000.00, made up as follows:

Machinery and equipment (Book value less depreciation)	$50,000.00
Inventories	20,000.00
Customers' merchandise on hand for work to be done thereon	10,000.00
	$80,000.00

(The building occupied was leased, not owned.)

The company has accepted from the insurance companies $57,080.00 in full settlement for the loss, and this amount is still on deposit at the date of your examination. The cost of clearing the debris and obtaining the equipment considered necessary would be $47,250.00.

2. There is $130,112.00 in accounts and notes payable to creditors, parties to an agreement whereby each creditor has accepted a note of the corporation, due October 31, 1945 and bearing interest at 5% per annum. The notes are secured by mortgage on all plant property and by all the issued capital stock. The latter is held in escrow. There will be $13,348.00 interest accrued on the notes at maturity.
3. Expenses have accrued to the amount of $1,532.00.
4. There is due to the president $30,000.00 for salary and cash advances, for which the corporation has given him a demand note. A part of the agreement with the creditors is a covenant by the president to take capital stock for this note at par. The president cannot surrender the note, however, because he has used it as collateral to secure a personal loan. The stock has therefore not yet been issued.

5. There is a corporation note dated February 1, 1939, payable on demand to the widow of the former treasurer, for $6,900.00. She has agreed to subordinate her claims to those of the other creditors.
6. The liabilities incurred since the creditors entered into the agreement aggregate $15,699.00.
7. There are $17,400.00 notes payable for equipment purchased prior to the creditors' agreement, due in monthly installments of $2,175.00 each and secured by chattel mortgage on the equipment.
8. Balances aggregating $3,066.00 are due employees under an arrangement whereby they received 90% of their earnings in cash and 10% in scrip payable October 31, 1945.
9. Accrued interest on all outstanding obligations of the corporation at the interim date is $7,506.00. This amount has been recorded by the corporation and is included in the loss from operations since the date of the creditors' agreement.
10. A deficit of $178,032.00 existed at the date of the creditors' agreement. The subsequent loss from operations is $8,942.00, before adjustment of the fire loss.
11. The authorized capital stock is 150,000 shares of $10.00 each, of which 50,000 shares are issued and outstanding and placed in escrow for the benefit of creditors. Of the unissued 100,000 shares 5,350 were subscribed in 1936 but the subscriptions were never paid. They are of doubtful status and are given to the creditors' attorney for collection.

From the foregoing data prepare the liabilities side of the balance sheet as you would submit it to your client, together with footnotes to the balance sheet which in your opinion are necessary for a clear understanding of the corporation's financial position.

Problem 39-10. On the petition of principal creditors, receivers in bankruptcy were appointed for the Skihigh Liquor Company on September 30, 1946. Appraisers appointed by the court took a physical inventory on the morning of October 1, 1946, finding the following merchandise on the premises:

	Cases of 12 Bottles
Spirits:	
Old Mahogany rye	40
Filibuster Special bourbon	10
Old Bluebottle	5
Wines:	
Sparkling muscatel	20
Beers:	
The Brewers Own	60

Accountants appointed by the receivers on October 1, 1946 found that the books had not been posted since September 15, 1946, when accounts had been prepared for the purpose of obtaining a bank loan. The trial balance of that date was as follows:

	Dr.	Cr.
Cash in bank	$ 500.00	
Petty cash	100.00	
Accounts receivable	7,609.66	
Accounts receivable—assigned	12,000.50	
Note receivable	190.00	
Note receivable—officer	300.00	
Advances to salesmen	6,000.00	

Inventories:		
Spirits	$ 3,180.00	
Wines	360.00	
Beers	375.00	
Inventories—assigned	10,006.54	
Insurance, taxes and rent prepaid to Sept. 30, 1946	1,866.66	
Life insurance policy	4,000.00	
Notes payable—president		$ 2,000.00
Accounts payable		55,100.90
Accrued sales taxes		900.12
Capital stock		10,000.00
Deficit	21,512.66	
	$68,001.02	$68,001.02

On the basis of these accounts a loan of $5,000 was obtained from the bank on the agreement that accounts receivable collections (after September 15th) be deposited in a special account at the bank, amounts to be withdrawn therefrom only as approved by the bank. Cash transactions from September 15 to 30, 1946 were as follows:

Collections:	
Accounts receivable deposited in special bank account	$ 2,005.00
Accounts receivable—assigned—deposited in special bank account	12,000.50
Note receivable	190.00
Advances to salesmen	500.00
Proceeds of bank loan of $5,000	4,900.00
Total	$19,595.50
Disbursements:	
President's note payable	$ 2,000.00
Accounts payable	5,000.00
Liquor license for year to September 30, 1947	1,000.00
Advances to salesmen	1,000.00
Petty expenses (paid from petty cash)	100.00
Total	$ 9,100.00

An amount of $7,000 had been transferred from the special account to the regular drawing account as approved by the bank.

There were no purchases from September 15 to September 30, 1946. Verified sales during the period, all on credit, were as follows:

	Cases	Per Case (Net)	Total
Spirits:			
Old Mahogany rye	10	$30	$300
Filibuster Special bourbon	5	20	100
Old Bluebottle	5	12	60
Wines:			
Sparkling muscatel	10	15	150
Beers:			
The Brewers Own	40	2	80
			$690

The perpetual stock records showed the following goods on hand at the close of business September 15:

	Cases of 12 Bottles	Cost per Case
Spirits:		
Old Mahogany rye	100	$24.00
Filibuster Special bourbon	40	18.00
Old Bluebottle	10	6.00
Wines:		
Sparkling muscatel	30	12.00
Beers:		
The Brewers Own	250	1.50

Among the accounts payable of September 15, 1946 is a debt of $21,007.04 to a distillery, representing two successive shipments of $11,000.50 and $10,006.54. The first shipment had been sold for $12,000.50, and the customer's account pledged to the distillery as security. The second shipment had been stored in a bonded warehouse, but the title to the goods was passed back to the distillery on September 28, 1946.

The life-insurance policy (surrender value at September 15, 1946, $2,500) was on the life of the president of the company, but it had been assigned to his wife some years ago.

The receivers expect that the bank will attempt to attach all balances at September 30, 1946, and that other creditors will also assert that their claims are preferential.

The attorneys appointed by the receivers request that you prepare at once a balance sheet of September 15, 1946 on a going concern basis and a tentative balance sheet of September 30, 1946 for purposes of a discussion on October 2, 1946. A report or memorandum containing full notes should accompany the balance sheets so that the attorneys may be informed about the facts so far determined.

QUESTIONS AND PROBLEMS ON CHAPTER 40

Questions

Question 40-1. What factor will determine whether an assignee, a receiver, or a trustee will open new books or record his transactions on the old books?

Question 40-2. An assignee has been appointed for an insolvent manufacturing corporation whose liabilities and assets consist of its capital stock, notes and accounts payable, unpaid wages, cash, notes and accounts receivable, raw materials, supplies, finished goods, stock in process, plant, and balances against branches. The assignee is temporarily to handle the property as a going concern. What are the first steps he should take relative to (*a*) assets, (*b*) liabilities?

Question 40-3. State briefly how you would proceed to open a set of books for the receiver of a small manufacturing concern, the court having issued an order that the receiver should continue manufacturing.

Question 40-4. When a receiver in equity takes charge of a business, why is it advisable for him to leave the liabilities on the old books?

Question 40-5. Describe the receiver's method of recording the payment of liabilities which existed before the receivership. What entries should be made on the old books to record the payments on prior liabilities by the receiver?

Problems

Problem 40-1. The Kennedy Hotel Company is unable to meet the interest on its bonds, and the court appoints a receiver in equity to operate the business until such a time as its affairs are brought into order. The balance sheet of the company follows:

THE KENNEDY HOTEL COMPANY
Balance Sheet
June 30, 1945

Cash	$ 3,264.00	Accounts payable		$ 34,642.00
Accounts receivable	16,134.00	Accrued interest on bonds		7,500.00
Inventories—supplies	6,853.00	Bonds payable—6%		250,000.00
Land	60,000.00			
Buildings—net	420,000.00	Capital stock	$500,000.00	
Equipment	148,360.00	Less deficit	137,531.00	362,469.00
	$654,611.00			$654,611.00

The receiver takes title to all assets except land and buildings.

During the first year of operations the receiver collects $10,480.00 on the accounts receivable, and writes off the rest of the accounts as uncollectible. The total revenues from operations are $244,675.00 of which all but $8,240.00 is collected. A reserve of $1,240.00 for bad debts is set up against these balances.

The operating expenses, exclusive of bad debts, losses on realization and depreciation charges were recorded as $188,435.00, of which $12,165.00 remains unpaid. This total gives no consideration to expense inventories.

Supplies carried at $2,550.00 in the beginning balance sheet are sold for $2,000.00. The closing inventory of supplies was $4,200.00.

Much of the equipment is obsolete or no longer usable. Equipment carried at

$53,650.00 is sold for $18,500.00, and new equipment costing $12,400.00 is purchased. Depreciation at 10% per annum is taken on the equipment, on the basis of the closing balance, and is adjusted for half a year's depreciation on the additions.

The receiver pays the accounts payable, accrued interest on bonds and bond interest for the year, and his fee of $12,000.00. The company provides $13,800.00 depreciation on the building.

Prepare entries in journal form for the books of the receiver and the company to record the stated facts and to close the books. Also prepare working papers for a balance sheet on June 30, 1946.

Problem 40-2. The accountant for a receiver is unable to reconcile the reciprocal accounts between the receiver and the company in receivership. The two trial balances follow. From them and the following data, you are to prepare a statement reconciling the reciprocal accounts and showing adjusted trial balances. The receivership has been in operation for one year, ending October 31, 1945.

	Receiver's Books		The Morley Company In Receivership	
Cash	$ 40,533.00			
Accounts receivable—new	48,160.00			
Accounts receivable—old	3,572.00			
Reserve for bad debts	3,220.00			
Inventory	32,414.00			
Fixed assets	62,000.00		$400,000.00	
Reserve for depreciation		$ 7,400.00		$120,000.00
Accounts payable		29,520.00		83,650.00
Bonds payable—6%				200,000.00
Accrued interest, October 31, 1944				7,500.00
Capital stock				500,000.00
Surplus			363,321.00	
G. M. Crane—receiver			147,829.00	
Sales		522,000.00		
Purchases	424,650.00			
Expenses	128,050.00			
The Morley Company—in receivership		183,679.00		
	$742,599.00	$742,599.00	$911,150.00	$911,150.00

The receiver wrote off old accounts receivable amounting to $8,460.00 against the reserve for bad debts and provided $4,000.00 for bad debt losses on the new accounts receivable. The rest of the old accounts receivable are considered collectible. At the end of the year he sold fixed assets carried at $42,000.00 for $12,000.00 crediting this amount to the fixed asset account. The reserve for depreciation on the receiver's books represents the amount provided by the receiver on the assets transferred to him, computed at 10%. The fixed assets retained by the company should have been depreciated at 10%.

The receiver paid a 30% dividend on the accounts payable existing prior to receivership, and debited this amount to accounts payable on his own books. The reduction of the liability has been recorded on the company's books. In addition to this he paid the interest for one year on the company's bonds, which he charged to expense. The company has made no record of this payment.

The receiver, with the approval of the court, paid himself a fee of $10,000.00 which has been charged to expenses.

Problem 40-3. A receiver asks your advice on how the following situations should be handled on his books and on the books of the company in receivership. Show the journal entries you would submit to him.

(*a*) Among the assets the receiver took over was certain machinery which the company purchased on a conditional sales contract under which the vendor had the right of repossession upon default of any installment. The contract price was $22,460.00, and certain carrying charges were to be paid. The company had paid $10,680.00 on this contract, which it had debited to the liability account originally set up; but it was ascertained that $1,432.00 of this payment represented carrying charges not included in the face of the contract. The company had depreciated the asset by 30%, which seems adequate.

The receiver made an arrangement with the vendor under which the vendor agreed not to repossess and to settle the remainder of the face of the contract at a discount of 10%, provided all installments are met promptly in the future.

(*b*) One creditor, to whom $27,000.00 is owed, has agreed to settle his claim by accepting the immediate delivery to him of certain merchandise carried on the books at $32,450.00. This creditor claims the merchandise is worth, at market value, only $24,000.00. The other creditors have agreed to this arrangement and it has been executed.

Problem 40-4. The receiver of the Gunnison Company has among the assets to which he has taken title a deposit at the Security State Bank for $14,230.00. The Gunnison Company owed the bank $8,200.00 on a loan. While it is expected that the Gunnison Company will eventually prove fully solvent, there is little hope that the bank will pay over 80 cents on the dollar. The Gunnison Company is denied the right to offset its liability against its deposit. The bank ultimately pays a dividend of 72 cents on the dollar, deducting the loan from the balance due the company before making the remittance.

(*a*) Show the entries to record these facts on the receiver's books.

(*b*) In some jurisdictions the right of offset is allowed. Show the entries on the receiver's books under such circumstances (ignoring any consequent reduction in the 72% dividend).

Problem 40-5. The Reed and Henley Company is unable to meet its obligations. Its balance sheet follows:

REED AND HENLEY COMPANY
Balance Sheet
December 31, 1946

Cash	$ 3,246.00	Accounts payable		$ 82,465.00
Accounts receivable	48,534.00			
Inventory	75,620.00	Capital stock	$150,000.00	
Fixed assets	124,340.00	Surplus	19,275.00	169,275.00
	$251,740.00			$251,740.00

A. D. Echardt is appointed receiver. He finds that the fixed assets have never been depreciated, no bad debts have been written off, and obsolete merchandise is included in the inventory at cost. To avoid showing these overvaluations as losses incurred in his receivership, he insists that the company set up a reserve for depreciation of $63,190.00, a reserve for bad debts of $6,420.00, and write the inventory down to $42,460.00 before he takes title to the assets.

During the following year he collects $39,400.00 on the accounts receivable and decides the remainder are uncollectible. He purchases $423,200.00 worth of merchandise, and pays all but $22,000.00 of the liabilities for it. His sales are $562,140.00, of which all but $34,680.00 is collected, and he sets up a reserve of $1,250.00 against this amount. His expenses were $94,365.00, of which $12,414.00 is unpaid at the end of the year. His closing inventory is $37,140.00. He charges 6% depreciation on the fixed assets. He collects his fee of $12,500.00, and pays a dividend of 80% to the creditors having claims before the receivership. He then returns the business to its owners.

Journalize these transactions on the receiver's books and on the company's books, and prepare the balance sheet after the close of the receivership.

Problem 40-6. The Rossiter Corporation, finding that its working capital was insufficient to continue operations, applied for a receiver. The following balance sheet, as prepared by the company on December 31, 1944, was given to R. R. Ernst, the receiver, who was granted permission to operate.

Assets		Liabilities and Net Worth	
Cash	$ 10,695.00	Accounts payable	$295,672.00
Accounts receivable	135,607.00	Capital stock	200,000.00
Inventory	244,172.00	Surplus	169,802.00
Fixed assets (net)	275,000.00		
	$665,474.00		$665,474.00

At the request of the receiver, the company wrote down the accounts receivable to $96,702.00 and the inventory to $197,800.00. The receiver took over the assets as shown at the balance sheet figures except as noted.

By June 30, 1946 he had made sales on account amounting to $365,750.00, collecting all but $36,800.00, which is carried as accounts receivable. All of the old accounts receivable were collected but at an additional loss of $5,635.00. He paid $193,000.00 on old accounts payable and receiver's expenses of $102,520.00. He made purchases of $95,755.00 during the period, which were paid in full. He returned the business to the stockholders on the above date after writing off $25,600.00 as depreciation. The inventory amounted to $153,875.00.

Prepare all entries which should appear on the company's books and on the receiver's books, and submit a balance sheet and analysis of surplus of the company after the business was returned to the stockholders.

Problem 40-7. On August 31, 1946 Grange and Co. made a general assignment to B. Britton for the benefit of creditors. The assignee intended to continue operations and opened a new set of books. The assignor's balance sheet on August 31 was:

Assets		Liabilities	
Cash	$ 2,000.00	Accounts payable	$26,250.00
Notes receivable	10,000.00	First mortgage bonds, 6%	25,000.00
Accounts receivable	19,000.00	Accrued interest on bonds	750.00
Due from officers	3,000.00	Capital stock	20,000.00
Inventories	13,000.00	Surplus	5,000.00
Equipment	30,000.00		
	$77,000.00		$77,000.00

By October 1, 1946 the assignee had determined that the assets were not worth their book values and that continued operations and a reorganization was impracticable. He decided to liquidate.

October 6—Inventories sold for $8,000.00.
October 17—Accounts receivable, excluding officers' accounts, sold for $10,000.00.
October 18—Officers paid $425.00 in full settlement of their accounts.
November 15—Notes receivable for $8,000.00 collected, and one for $2,000.00 settled for $750.00.
November 30—Equipment sold to bondholders for $26,500.00. Interest on mortgage paid to November 30.
November 30—25% dividend paid on accounts payable.
December 15—The assignee paid his fee and expenses amounting to $3,600.00 and made a final dividend payment to creditors.

Make journal entries in parallel columns to show how the transactions should be recorded on the books of the receiver and on the books of the company, and to close the two sets of books.

Problem 40-8. The Eastern Manufacturing Co. was unable to pay interest on its bonds due September 30, 1945, and was placed in the hands of E. A. Kelly, as receiver. Kelly took over the assets on the date of the following balance sheet:

Balance Sheet—September 30, 1945

Cash	$ 2,500.00	Accounts payable	$ 57,523.00
Accounts receivable	63,400.00	Notes payable	75,000.00
Finished goods	32,600.00	Accrued bond interest	3,000.00
Goods in process	20,900.00	First mortgage 6% bonds	100,000.00
Raw materials	40,000.00	Reserve for depreciation:	
Land	50,000.00	Buildings	32,500.00
Buildings	112,500.00	Machinery and equipment	25,400.00
Machinery and equipment	98,280.00	Reserve for bad debts	2,580.00
		Capital stock	100,000.00
		Surplus	24,177.00
	$420,180.00		$420,180.00

The receiver operated the business until the close of the fiscal year, March 31, 1946; during this period his transactions were as follows:

Purchases of raw materials	$ 79,000.00
Payments on above purchases—cash	63,670.00
Discounts taken on above	1,330.00
Expense payments:	
Direct labor	49,000.00
Indirect labor	8,725.00
Factory expenses	15,000.00
Selling expenses	23,280.00
Administrative expenses	15,670.00
Sales on account	250,000.00
Collections on sales (excluding discounts of $1,500.00)	198,000.00
Collections on old accounts receivable	59,750.00
Payments on old accounts payable	51,810.00
Bond interest paid to March 31, 1946, and interest accrued on notes payable to same date at 6½ per cent.	

The books were closed on March 31, 1946; depreciation was provided in the following amounts:

Buildings	$ 2,812.50
Machinery and equipment	12,285.00

The following inventories were set up:

Finished goods	$25,000.00
Goods in process	10,000.00
Raw materials	33,000.00
Total	$68,000.00

On April 1, 1946 an offer was received and accepted for the sale of the business other than cash, on the following basis:

Land	$39,000.00
Buildings	83,000.00
Machinery and equipment	79,000.00
Inventories—110% of values stated above	
Accounts receivable:	
Old accounts—50% of book figure	
New accounts—99% of book figure	

The purchaser assumed the mortgage, and paid the remainder of the purchase price in cash.

The receiver then paid all the remaining liabilities and turned the remaining cash back to the corporation, which distributed it to its stockholders and dissolved.

Prepare journal entries in parallel columns as they would appear on the books of the corporation and on the books of the receiver.

Problem 40-9. On June 30, 1945 a receiver in equity was appointed by the court to take over the assets and operate the business of Jones, Wilson & Co. The balance sheet published as of that date appears below:

Assets		Liabilities	
Cash	$ 3,200.00	Accounts payable	$ 70,000.00
Accounts receivable	35,000.00	Notes payable	60,000.00
Finished goods	27,000.00	Reserve for depreciation:	
Work in process	15,000.00	Buildings	45,000.00
Raw materials	30,000.00	Machinery	36,500.00
Land	30,000.00	Reserve for bad debts	1,500.00
Buildings	120,000.00	Capital stock	150,000.00
Machinery	85,000.00		
Deficit	17,800.00		
	$363,000.00		$363,000.00

The receiver operated the business for one year, during which time the following transactions occurred:

Purchases of raw materials on account	$ 75,750.00
Sales of finished goods	328,000.00
Collections thereon	298,000.00
Payments on accounts payable for raw material purchases	63,000.00
Collections on old accounts receivable	25,000.00
Payment for direct labor	58,750.00
Payment for indirect labor	12,500.00
Payment for manufacturing expense	22,600.00
Payment for selling and general expense	27,000.00

It appears that, of the remaining old accounts receivable, $2,500.00 are uncollectible.

The receiver provided depreciation at the rate of 4% on buildings and 10% on machinery. A reserve amounting to ¾ of 1% of sales was set up on new accounts receivable.

All old liabilities were paid together with interest amounting to $2,200.00. Inventories at the end of the year were:

Raw materials	$20,600.00
Goods in process	3,500.00
Finished goods	15,500.00

Make all the necessary entries on the books of the company and of the receiver to record:

(1) The transfer of the business to the receiver.
(2) The operations during the receivership.
(3) The return of the business to the owners.

Prepare, in addition, a profit and loss statement for the year and a balance sheet showing the condition of the business as returned to the stockholders.

Problem 40-10. Adams and Company were unable to meet their current obligations, and Robert Wilcox was appointed receiver. The post closing trial balance on June 30, 1944 shows the following:

	Debits	Credits
Cash	$ 750.00	
Accounts receivable	95,400.00	
Reserve for bad debts		$ 4,750.00
Notes receivable	3,500.00	
Raw materials	12,500.00	
Goods in process	25,000.00	
Finished goods	45,000.00	
Land	10,000.00	
Buildings	100,000.00	
Furniture and fixtures	6,000.00	
Machinery and equipment	50,000.00	
Tools	5,000.00	
Reserve for depreciation		28,000.00
Accounts payable		85,250.00
Notes payable		74,500.00
Accrued interest—notes payable		2,000.00
Accrued interest—bonds payable		750.00
Accrued taxes		1,400.00
6% first mortgage bonds		75,000.00
Capital stock		75,000.00
Surplus		6,500.00
	$353,150.00	$353,150.00

The transactions for the first year of the receivership are summarized as follows:

Collections on old accounts receivable:		
Total accounts		$ 95,400.00
Less: Discounts allowed	$ 790.00	
Bad debts	5,875.00	6,665.00
Net		$ 88,735.00
Collections on old notes receivable		$ 3,500.00
Settlement of old notes payable:		
Total notes		$ 74,500.00
Receiver's certificate issued		50,000.00
Paid in cash		$ 24,500.00

Settlement of old accounts payable:		
Total accounts		$ 85,250.00
Receiver's certificate issued		65,000.00
Paid in cash		$ 20,250.00
Sales on account		$390,000.00
Provision for bad debts ½ of 1% of sales		
Less: Returns and allowances	$ 2,700.00	
Discounts	2,500.00	
Charged to reserve	450.00	
Cash received	336,350.00	342,000.00
Balance		$ 48,000.00

Cash disbursements:	
Purchase of raw material	$93,650.00
Labor	94,500.00
Factory expense	51,360.00
Salesmen's salaries	27,500.00
Selling expense	15,750.00
Receiver's expenses	21,625.00
Bond interest (one year)	4,500.00
Taxes—prior year	1,560.00
Taxes—current year	1,200.00
Interest on notes payable	4,000.00

Prepare journal entries as they should appear on the company's books and the receiver's books, and trial balances of both sets of books.

Adjustments are required for the following matters prior to preparing statements on June 30, 1945:

Inventories:		
Raw materials		$10,500.00
Goods in process		7,800.00
Finished goods		32,200.00
Accrued taxes		1,250.00
Accrued bond interest		750.00
Accrued interest on receiver's certificate		550.00
Depreciation:		
Buildings	2%	
Machinery and equipment	10	
Furniture and fixtures	10	
Tools	20	

Prepare working papers and the following statements:

Balance sheet
Profit and loss and surplus statement
Statement of cost of goods sold

QUESTIONS AND PROBLEMS ON CHAPTER 41

Questions

Question 41-1. Distinguish between a statement of affairs and a realization and liquidation account, between a deficiency account and a realization profit and loss account.

Question 41-2. Explain why the realization and liquidation account, which shows facts regarding assets, liabilities, income and expense, has a balance representing profit or loss.

Question 41-3. In preparing a realization and liquidation account, how would you show:

(*a*) Depreciation reserve at the beginning of the period, depreciation charge for the period, and depreciation reserve at the end of the period?
(*b*) Discounts allowed to customers?

Question 41-4. John Smith made a composition with his creditors by which it was agreed that all accounts and notes would be settled by payments of sixty cents on the dollar. He owed $15,000.00 of notes and $10,000.00 of accounts. A trustee was put in charge, and new notes were given for the reduced amounts agreed upon. Payments of forty cents on the dollar were made by the time the trustee presented a realization and liquidation account to the creditors. Show how these facts would be set out in the realization and liquidation account.

Question 41-5. The realization and liquidation account with its supporting statements should be prepared by a process of journalizing in the statements. Explain what the offsetting debit and credit entries would be with respect to the following:

(*a*) Assets, liabilities, and capital at the beginning of the period.
(*b*) The discovery of additional assets.
(*c*) The sale of merchandise.
(*d*) The collection of accounts receivable at a loss.
(*e*) The collection of interest on notes.
(*f*) The payment of expenses.
(*g*) The payment of liabiliaties.

Problems

Problem 41-1. Lester Keith was appointed the trustee in bankruptcy for the Acme Woolen Company, whose balance sheet on June 28, 1945 appeared as follows:

Assets		Liabilities and Net Worth		
Cash	$ 600.00	Accounts payable		$ 8,200.00
Merchandise	7,200.00	Notes payable		7,000.00
Accounts receivable	5,300.00	Accrued interest		140.00
Investments	1,200.00	Total		$15,340.00
Land	4,000.00			
Building	7,000.00	Capital stock	$30,000.00	
		Less deficit	20,040.00	9,960.00
	$25,300.00			$25,300.00

Keith's cash account at the termination of the receivership, on May 15, 1946, appeared as follows:

Cash Account

Balance—June 28, 1945......	$ 600.00	Accounts payable...........	$7,700.00
Merchandise..............	7,500.00	Notes payable.............	7,000.00
Accounts receivable.........	4,900.00	Interest expense..........	210.00
Land and building...........	8,500.00	Receiver's expenses.........	200.00

The receiver requested a fee of $2,000.00, which has not yet been paid. The merchandise creditors accepted the $7,700.00 as payment in full. The only assets not realized were the investments, which are not readily marketable.

Prepare: (*a*) A realization and liquidation account.
(*b*) Memorandum capital account.
(*c*) Realization profit and loss account.

Problem 41-2. Refer to the facts cited in Problem 41-1 and prepare a statement of realization, liquidation, and operations.

Problem 41-3. Ray Howard started his receivership of the Kelsey Tool Company on March 27, 1945, when a statement was drawn up as follows:

Assets		Liabilities and Net Worth		
Cash....................	$ 860.00	Accounts payable.........		$ 56,000.00
Accounts receivable.......	42,300.00	Bank loans—unsecured....		30,000.00
Raw materials............	11,265.00	Mortgage payable........		22,000.00
Work in process..........	43,872.00	Accrued interest on mortgage...............		330.00
Finished goods...........	1,400.00			
Land....................	8,000.00	Total..................		$108,330.00
Building.................	34,000.00			
Machinery...............	12,000.00	Capital stock.	$50,000.00	
Goodwill................	15,000.00	Surplus......	10,367.00	
		Total.................		60,367.00
	$168,697.00			$168,697.00

The company's credit was exhausted, but it was believed that the receiver could complete the goods in process and liquidate all liabilities in full.

In order to do this he made operating expenditures as follows:

Raw materials—purchased on account....................	$ 3,000.00
Direct labor paid....................................	18,000.00
Factory expenses paid................................	6,000.00

He collected $39,000.00 in cash on the old accounts receivable, after allowing discounts of $370.00. A reserve for bad debts of $1,900.00 was set up against the remaining accounts. He made sales of $92,650.00. Of this amount he collected all but $12,400.00, after allowing discounts of $1,264.00.

At this point, being doubtful of his ability to pay the liabilities in full, he induced the unsecured creditors to accept 90 cents on the dollar, which he paid. The liability for raw materials purchased was paid in full. The mortgagee agreed to extend the mortgage provided installments in arrears amounting to $6,000.00 were paid, together with the interest, which, by this time, had accrued to $660.00. These payments were made.

The receiver provided depreciation of $1,020.00 on the buildings and $1,000.00 on the machinery. He was directed to write off the goodwill as worthless. He submitted a bill of $7,200.00 for his services and expenses, which was paid. There were raw materials valued at $400.00 and finished goods valued at $1,310.00 still on hand on January 12, 1946.

Prepare:

(*a*) A realization and liquidation account.
(*b*) A cash account.
(*c*) A realization and liquidation profit and loss account.

Problem 41-4. Refer to the facts cited in Problem 41-3 and prepare a statement of realization, liquidation, and operations based on them.

Problem 41-5. On July 1, 1944 the liquidation of The Superal Co. was begun. The condition of the company as of that date was as follows:

Assets		Liabilities and Net Worth		
Cash	$ 235.00	Notes payable		$ 9,700.00
Notes receivable	1,200.00	Accounts payable		40,610.00
Accounts receivable	4,300.00	Accrued salaries		1,950.00
Raw materials	10,364.00	Unpaid taxes		95.00
Work in process	27,620.00	Interest on mortgage		210.00
Co. *A* bonds	11,200.00	Mortgage on land and building		13,000.00
Land	2,000.00	Net worth:		
Building	18,641.00	Capital stock	$60,000.00	
Machinery	16,320.00	Less deficit	33,685.00	26,315.00
	$91,880.00			$91,880.00

The transactions for the year ended June 30, 1945 are detailed below.

Expenses amounted to $2,935.00; accounts receivable collections were $2,-700.00; the remainder of the accounts receivable, with the exception of $425.00, were written off. Co. A bonds were sold for $12,000.00, and interest of $60.00 was collected. Notes receivable were all collected.

The work in process was completed by the use of raw materials valued at $7,320.00, together with labor costs of $9,100.00, and the finished goods were then sold for $40,500.00. The sale of the balance of the raw material brought $2,400.00.

The land and building were sold for $16,000.00. The mortgage of $13,000.00 and the interest on the mortgage as of July 1, 1944, plus the additional interest of $75.00, due at date of settlement, were paid with the proceeds. The sale of machinery valued at $12,000.00 brought $10,500.00.

Payments on the liabilities as of June 30, 1944 were made as follows: salaries, $1,950.00; notes payable, $5,600.00; accounts payable $30,605.00; taxes, $95.00.

Taxes, amounting to $40.00, accrued subsequent to July 1, 1944 were also paid.

Prepare the following statements:

Realization and liquidation account, realization profit and loss statement, cash account, and balance sheet as of June 30, 1945.

Statement of realization, liquidation, and operations.

Problem 41-6. The balance sheet of the partnership, Hause and Smith, on December 31, 1944 was as follows:

Assets

Current assets:		
Cash		$ 720.00
Accounts receivable	$20,650.00	
Less reserve for doubtful accounts	710.00	19,940.00
Notes receivable	$27,000.00	
Less notes receivable discounted	8,000.00	19,000.00

Inventories:			
Finished goods..............	$11,732.00		
Goods in process............	5,741.00		
Raw materials...............	4,266.00	$21,739.00	
Accrued interest on notes receivable		550.00	$61,949.00

Fixed Assets:

	Cost	Depreciation Reserve	Net Book Value	
Land............	$ 15,000.00	—	$15,000.00	
Buildings........	42,000.00	$ 7,900.00	34,100.00	
Machinery.......	50,500.00	12,400.00	38,100.00	
Equipment......	10,500.00	2,400.00	8,100.00	
Total.......	$118,000.00	$22,700.00		95,300.00
				$157,249.00

Liabilities and Net Worth

Current liabilities:		
Accounts payable......................	$18,750.00	
Notes payable.........................	42,500.00	
Accrued interest on notes payable..........	740.00	
Accrued taxes.........................	1,175.00	$ 63,165.00
Fixed liabilities:		
Mortgage on land and buildings..........	$40,500.00	
Mortgage on machinery and equipment.....	20,000.00	60,500.00
Net worth:		
H. Hause, capital.....................	$16,159.00	
R. Smith, capital.....................	17,425.00	33,584.00
		$157,249.00

On January 1, 1945 the partners realize that they cannot meet the demands of the creditors, and they consent to the appointment of a creditors' committee. This committee operates the business for a year.

From the information given, prepare a realization and liquidation account, profit and loss statement, cash account, statement of partners' capitals for the year, and a balance sheet as of December 31, 1945.

Also prepare a statement of realization, liquidation, and operations.

The activities of the committee with regard to the assets and liabilities taken over by it, resulted in the following:

Accounts receivable—collected in full, accounts totaling $19,200.00; charged $175.00 against the reserve.

Notes receivable—collected in full, together with interest of $950.00.

Notes receivable discounted—of the discounted notes, those which had to be paid by the partnership, because of uncollectibility from the makers, amounted to $3,500.00, plus interest and protest fees of $210.00. Consider these notes as a total loss.

Liabilities paid in full: accounts payable; accrued taxes; notes payable, together with $1,275.00 interest.

During the year, additional expenditures were made as follows: raw materials, $20,700.00; factory expenses, $19,600.00; office expenses, $510.00; factory labor $37,710.00; office salaries, $2,300.00; creditors' committee expenses, $3,000.00; interest for 1945 at the rate of 6% on the two mortgages.

Depreciation rates used were, buildings 3½%, machinery 6%, and equipment 5%.

Sales during the year totaled $135,000.00. Of this amount, cash collections totaled $129,000.00; to take care of any doubtful accounts in the balance remaining, a reserve for $750.00 was set up.

During the year, each partner was permitted to withdraw $2,800.00.

Additional information as of December 31, 1945:

Accrued taxes	$1,290.00
Finished goods inventory	8,200.00
Goods in process inventory	3,473.00
Raw materials inventory	3,050.00

Problem 41-7. The stockholders of the Howarth Corporation, at a meeting held January 3, 1945, voted to dissolve the corporation and authorized the directors to proceed on a plan so that the windup of the affairs of the corporation could be accomplished without too great a loss to the stockholders. The balance sheet of the company on December 31, 1944 was as follows:

Assets

Current assets:			
Cash		$ 7,500.00	
Accounts receivable	$ 43,240.00		
Reserve for doubtful accounts	2,162.00	41,078.00	
Inventories		17,000.00	$ 65,578.00
Bond sinking fund			93,000.00
Notes receivable—employees			2,150.00
Fixed assets:			
Land		$ 25,000.00	
Building	$310,000.00		
Reserve for depreciation	87,000.00	223,000.00	
Machinery and equipment	$148,000.00		
Reserve for depreciation	72,000.00	76,000.00	324,000.00
Goodwill			50,000.00
Deferred charges:			
Prepaid expenses		$ 2,250.00	
Unamortized bond discount		2,300.00	4,550.00
			$539,278.00

Liabilities and Net Worth

Current liabilities:		
Notes payable	$ 23,000.00	
Accounts payable	42,000.00	
Accrued bond interest	1,875.00	$ 66,875.00
First mortgage, 6% bonds		100,000.00
Rentals collected in advance		250.00
Net worth:		
Capital stock:		
Preferred—1000 shares	$100,000.00	
Common—1000 shares	100,000.00	
Reserve for contingencies	25,000.00	
Reserve for sinking fund	93,000.00	
Surplus	54,153.00	372,153.00
		$539,278.00

On March 31, 1945 the assets had been realized and the liabilities liquidated as follows:

Accounts receivable produced $40,000.00.
The inventories were sold for $15,300.00.
All notes receivable from employees were collected.
The machinery and equipment were disposed of for $50,000.00.
The sinking fund trustee was paid additional cash to buy in all the outstanding bonds at 100 plus accrued interest to December 31, 1944.

The bond liability having been liquidated and the mortgage eliminated, the land and buildings were sold for $200,000.00. The purchaser, however, would not take the property subject to the lease, which was held by a tenant who occupied a portion of the building and whose prepaid rental was reflected in the balance sheet of December 31, 1944. In order to consummate the sale of the plant, it was necessary to effect a cancellation of the lease. This was accomplished by paying the tenant the advance rental and an additional $1,500.00.

All other liabilities were paid.

Liquidation proceedings were completed during March, and the directors notified the stockholders to surrender their stock certificates for cancellation as of March 31, 1945. The preferred stock was cumulative and entitled to receive dividends at the rate of 7% per annum, payable on the last day of March, June, September, and December. In the event of voluntary dissolution the preferred stock was to be retired at 115 plus cumulative dividends. Dividends on preferred stock had been paid to December 31, 1944.

On March 31, 1945, all stock certificates having been received, the cash remaining, after payment of expenses during the liquidation period, in the amount of $3,750.00, was distributed and the certificates were canceled.

From the foregoing information prepare a realization and liquidation account, a realization profit and loss account, a cash account, and a statement of capital.

Also prepare a statement of realization and liquidation.

Problem 41-8. The partnership of Coulson, Cambell, and Weir was placed in the hands of a receiver on July 1, 1946, at which time the assets and liabilities were as follows:

	Dr.	Cr.
Cash	$ 300.00	
Accounts receivable	28,000.00	
Merchandise	32,000.00	
Unexpired insurance	500.00	
Bonds of Hoad Co	12,000.00	
Land	8,000.00	
Buildings	65,000.00	
Reserve for depreciation		$ 7,000.00
Accounts payable		45,000.00
Accrued interest on mortgage		175.00
Unpaid taxes		600.00
Notes payable (secured by Hoad Co. bonds)		17,000.00
Mortgage on land and buildings		35,000.00
Coulson		21,380.00
Campbell		11,975.00
Weir		7,670.00
	$145,800.00	$145,800.00

The receiver placed the following estimated values on the assets:

Accounts receivable:	
Good	$12,000.00
Doubtful—estimated to be 75% collectible	12,000.00
Bad	4,000.00
Merchandise	21,000.00
Unexpired insurance	100.00
Bonds of Hoad Co	12,000.00
Land	7,000.00
Buildings	35,000.00

Prepare a statement of affairs and a deficiency account.

The liquidator completed his work on August 15, 1946; the following transactions took place:

Assets realized:	
Accounts receivable	$24,000.00
Merchandise	26,000.00
Land and buildings	62,000.00
Bonds of Hoad Co	12,000.00
Unexpired insurance	80.00
Interest on bonds	60.00
All liabilities liquidated	
Interest accrued after July 1, 1946, paid	85.00
Expenses of liquidator paid	250.00

Prepare a realization and liquidation account, a profit and loss account, and a cash account.

How should the cash on hand be distributed to the partners? Assume that it is so distributed, and prepare a statement of the partners' accounts.

Also prepare a statement of realization, liquidation, and operations. Do not include the distribution of cash to the partners.

QUESTIONS AND PROBLEMS ON CHAPTER 42

Questions

Question 42-1. Discuss the theoretical distinction between an agency and a branch in respect to the following particulars:

(*a*) Amount of stock carried.
(*b*) Shipments of merchandise.
(*c*) Passing of credits.
(*d*) Billing of merchandise and handling of accounts receivable.
(*e*) Cash and cash records.

Question 42-2. Why is it sometimes considered desirable to bill merchandise to a branch at an arbitrary figure in excess of cost?

In what way, if at all, would the procedure of closing the branch books be affected by this practice?

In what way, if at all, would the procedure of closing the home office books be affected?

Question 42-3. Describe a good method of internal check for handling branch receipts and disbursements.

Question 42-4. State what entry is made by the home office in taking up the profit of a branch, and explain the theory underlying this entry. State, and explain the reason for, the entry taking up a branch loss.

Question 42-5. Assume that the branch fixed assets are carried on the home office books. How will fixed asset purchases by the home office be recorded, and how will fixed asset purchases by the branch be recorded?

If fixed assets at the branch are carried on the branch books, how will purchases be recorded?

Question 42-6. If expenses are incurred by the home office on account of the operations of the branch, how are such expenses to be recorded, and how should the accounts be closed out?

Question 42-7. A company having several branches desires to charge each branch with interest on the average capital invested in the branch. State how these entries will be made on the home office books. What effect will such entries have on the branch profits, and on the profits of the concern as a whole?

Question 42-8. Outline the instructions you would give to afford the main office of a company adequate control over expenditures at its various plants for additions and replacement repairs, and to insure uniform and correct accounting treatment thereof.

Question 42-9. A firm having several branches maintains an account in its ledger with each branch, and charges to such accounts all goods sent to the branches for stock. At the end of the year the balance of each branch account is treated as an ordinary account receivable, and is included in the balance sheet with the general debts owing to the firm. If you see any objection to this method, state it, and state also how you would deal with the accounts.

Question 42-10. A trading and mining company maintains five general stores at five separate stations, and concentrates its supplies each year at Station *A*, which is the only station accessible by railway; distribution is made from this station by means of wagon and pack trains. The cost of goods laid down at Station *A* is 10% above the invoice prices at the company's general office in Montana, and the agent at Station *A* is instructed to rebill all shipments to Station *B* at 20%, to Station *C* at 35%, to Station *D* at 40%, and to Station *E* at 50% above original invoice cost, since the experience of several years bears out the general manager's statement that such additions are approximately correct and cover actual cost of transportation.

In auditing the accounts for the purpose of certifying the annual balance sheet, you ascertain that certain goods at Station *D*, amounting to $10,000.00, are inventoried by the agent at that point at 70% above the original invoices, which you have examined at the home office. He states that Station *E*, being overstocked, shipped him several lots of merchandise at the price billed out to *E* by Station *A*, plus 10% for estimated cost of handling and repacking at *E*; and to this amount *D* legitimately added 10% for cost of transportation from *E* back to *D*.

In your visits to other stations you find many similar instances in which goods have been moved back and forth, and each time the shipping station has added 10% for handling and repacking. Of a total inventory at all stations of goods originally costing $200,000.00, the summary shows final extensions of values aggregating $325,000.00, of which not more than $75,000.00 is covered by the cost of direct transportation, leaving approximately $50,000.00 represented by internal charges added between the different stations.

Review the foregoing statement, and give your method of handling such accounts.

Problems

Problem 42-1. The Yankie Drill Company established agencies in Wichita, Dallas, and Tulsa. During the year the following transactions took place:

	Home Office	Wichita	Dallas	Tulsa
Sales	$458,108.00	$62,744.00	$134,390.00	$265,117.00
Expenses:				
General	42,388.00			
Selling, other than samples	38,156.00	8,545.00	11,038.00	18,225.00
Cost of samples	4,682.00	5,102.00	3,742.00	6,640.00

The total cost of goods manufactured was $756,453.20, and you may assume no changes in the inventories.

Prepare in columnar form a statement of profit and loss showing the operating results of each unit and the totals, together with percentage comparisons. Use any logical method for allocating the costs to the sales.

Problem 42-2. The Ware Tea and Coffee Company had branches in many cities. The fixed assets of all these branches were carried on the home office books. Each branch had an imprest fund of $1,000.00 and was reimbursed periodically for its expenses. All merchandise was billed to the branches at an advance of 20% over cost. All collections were deposited in a bank account against which only the home office could draw. Certain expenses were paid by the home office and charged against the bank.

The branch office current account for Nashville follows.

Nashville Branch Current Account

January 1, balance	$26,600.00	Collections	$74,427.00
Shipments to branch	50,400.00		
Advertising	2,600.00		
Depreciation	1,400.00		
Reimbursement of expenses.	17,200.00		
Net profit	7,062.00		

The opening inventory at this branch was $9,600.00, and the branch reported sales of $78,752.00, but of this amount $450.00 had proved uncollectible. The branch inventory at the end of the year was $9,960.00.

(*a*) From an analysis of the account, together with the above data, reconstruct the profit and loss statement submitted by the Nashville branch to the home office.

(*b*) State what the correct profit of the branch was, after elimination of all unrealized profit.

(*c*) Assuming the branch had no liabilities and only those assets indicated by the problem, reconstruct the closing balance sheet of the Nashville branch.

Problem 42-3. In making the annual audit of the Maxon Stores the auditor attempted to reconcile certain reciprocal accounts. He found the following balances on the books:

Home office:	
Darby branch current account	$57,620.00 Dr.
Riverside branch current account	27,120.00 Dr.
Darby branch:	
Home office current account	55,520.00 Cr.
Riverside branch current account	2,080.00 Dr.
Riverside branch:	
Home office current account	22,220.00 Cr.
Darby branch current account	4,600.00 Dr.

He ascertained the following facts. Merchandise was billed to the branches at 10% above cost. A bank draft of $4,600.00 sent by the Darby branch to the home office was in transit. The home office had charged advertising to the branches as follows: Darby, $4,300.00; Riverside, $3,200.00. Neither branch had taken these charges into its records. Merchandise which cost $5,000.00 was in transit from the home office to the Riverside branch. At the direction of the home office, the Riverside branch had billed merchandise to the Darby branch at $4,600.00, which included the freight from the home office to Riverside. After the Darby branch had paid the freight from Riverside, the merchandise cost $100.00 more than it would have cost if shipped from the home office. It billed this $100.00 back to the Riverside branch, but that branch has never recognized the claim. The home office instructs the Riverside branch to accept the charge and rebill it to the home office, which will charge it to an expense account. Both branches have credited their book profits to the home office, Darby at $6,800.00 and Riverside at $5,200.00; the profits have not been taken up by the home office. Merchandise billed at $6,580.00 is in transit from the Darby branch to Riverside, at the direction of the home office. Cash is in transit from the Riverside branch to the home office in the amount of $1,400.00.

Show how the reconciliations were made.

Problem 42-4. The Speedex Company sold its product directly and also through a branch opened at the beginning of the year. Its profit and loss statement, in condensed form, follows:

Sales	$284,000.00
Cost of goods sold	198,800.00
Gross profit	$ 85,200.00
Expenses	57,650.00
Net profit	$ 27,550.00

Its balance sheet follows:

Cash	$ 16,000.00	Accounts payable		$ 21,000.00
Accounts receivable	38,000.00			
Inventory	23,000.00	Capital stock	$75,000.00	
Fixed assets	41,000.00	Surplus	22,000.00	97,000.00
	$118,000.00			$118,000.00

The account with the branch was treated as an ordinary account receivable. Shipments to the branch were billed at 20% above cost by credit to sales account. When the branch made a sale, a duplicate sales invoice was forwarded to the home office, which took up the receivable on its own books, giving the branch credit for it, and then made the collection itself. A petty cash fund of $500.00 was kept at the branch, and its closing inventory was $19,200.00. No other assets or liabilities were kept on the branch books.

Prepare working papers to correct the two statements.

Problem 42-5. The Ryder Building and Supply Company has had a branch at Bay City for several years. All expenses are paid out of a petty cash fund which is periodically reimbursed by the home office. No other cash balance is maintained by the branch. The following data relate to this branch:

Petty cash fund	$ 500.00
Sales	58,000.00
Returned sales	1,200.00
Bad debts written off	600.00
Shipments from home office	32,000.00
Accounts receivable, Jan. 1	14,600.00
Accounts receivable, Dec. 31	15,350.00
Inventory, Jan. 1	8,750.00
Inventory, Dec. 31	9,300.00
Expenses paid	16,805.00

From this information, prepare the following:

(*a*) The branch balance sheet at January 1.
(*b*) The branch profit and loss statement.
(*c*) The branch balance sheet at December 31.
(*d*) The branch current account on the home office books.
(*e*) The journal entry to take up the branch profit on the home office books.

Problem 42-6. The Soft Shoe Company of Chicago operates a branch in Detroit. Merchandise shipped to the branch by the home office is billed at 140% of cost. Following is a trial balance of the branch's general ledger at the close of 1945:

Home office, current account		$20,935.00
Inventory, January 1, 1945	$11,200.00	
Merchandise from home office	68,600.00	
Accounts receivable (increased from $5,000.00 on January 1)	6,250.00	
Sales		70,175.00
Expenses	4,910.00	
Working fund cash	150.00	
	$91,110.00	$91,110.00

All cash receipts, with the exception of reimbursements of the working fund, are deposited intact in a Detroit bank, subject to check by the home office. Expenses are paid from the working fund, which is replenished by check from the home office on an imprest basis. The inventory on December 31, 1945 at billed prices is $7,250.00.

Prepare:

(*a*) Journal entries in parallel columns, for the transactions of the branch for the year, as they should be recorded on the branch and the home office books.

(*b*) Entries to close the branch books.

The home office trial balance on December 31, 1945 is:

Capital stock		$ 25,000.00
Accounts receivable	$ 16,562.50	
Branch current account	20,935.00	
Cash	13,100.00	
Accounts payable		5,475.00
Purchases	147,500.00	
Sales		125,095.00
Inventory, January 1, 1945	25,000.00	
Shipments to branch		68,600.00
Expenses	11,300.00	
Surplus		10,227.50
	$234,397.50	$234,397.50

Inventory, December 31, 1945, $26,625.00

Prepare:

(*c*) Entries to close the home office books.

(*d*) Consolidated profit and loss statement and balance sheet, with working papers.

Problem 42-7. The Coldpack Meat Company of Chicago operates branches in St. Louis, Louisville, and Memphis. Each branch keeps its own accounts receivable and remits its collections, intact, to the home office. Each branch pays all its own expenses from a working fund which is reimbursed by draft on the home office.

On December 31, 1945 the branches submit the following information, applicable to the year then ended, to the home office:

	St. Louis	Louisville	Memphis
Sales (on account)	$374,000.00	$342,000.00	$326,000.00
Returned sales	5,000.00	2,800.00	—
Expenses paid	77,000.00	73,900.00	73,500.00
Bad debts	—	2,500.00	1,200.00
Cash collected from customers	337,000.00	325,200.00	307,000.00
Accounts receivable—December 31, 1944	190,000.00	171,000.00	140,000.00
Accounts receivable—December 31, 1945	222,000.00	182,500.00	157,800.00
Working fund	5,000.00	5,000.00	5,000.00
Inventory, December 31, 1944	70,000.00	78,000.00	73,000.00
Inventory, December 31, 1945	86,000.00	94,000.00	90,000.00
Goods received from main office	270,000.00	236,000.00	247,000.00

From these details, prepare:

(*a*) A statement of branch assets on December 31, 1944, and balances of current accounts.
(*b*) The closing entries for the St. Louis branch.
(*c*) The home office current account on the St. Louis books.
(*d*) The journal entry on the home office books, taking up the St. Louis branch profit; and the St. Louis branch current account on the home office books.
(*e*) A combined branch profit and loss statement.
(*f*) A statement of branch current accounts on the home office books; and lists of assets represented by balances on December 31, 1945.

Problem 42-8. The Handy Auto Accessory Manufacturing Company of Toledo operates a retail sales branch in Miami. Goods shipped to the branch are billed at cost. All cash receipts from customers are remitted to the home office. Fixed assets, other than furniture and fixtures, are carried on the home office books at a value of $150,000.00, which is being depreciated at the rate of 5% per annum. The home office purchases and pays for all additions to furniture and fixtures. A working fund is maintained at the branch from which branch expenses are paid; reimbursements thereof are made by draft on the home office.

On December 31, 1945 the following statements were rendered to the home office by the branch:

Comparative Balance Sheet

	December 31, 1944	December 31, 1945
Assets		
Cash working fund	$ 2,000.00	$ 3,000.00
Accounts receivable	63,880.00	62,630.00
Merchandise	152,750.00	173,200.00
Furniture and fixtures	10,000.00	11,000.00
Deferred charges	400.00	500.00
	$229,030.00	$250,330.00
Liabilities		
Accrued salaries	$ 600.00	$ 500.00
Reserve for doubtful accounts	1,700.00	2,050.00
Reserve for depreciation	3,000.00	4,200.00
Home office current	223,730.00	243,580.00
	$229,030.00	$250,330.00

Profit and Loss Statement
Year Ended December 31, 1945

Sales		$542,340.00
Deduct:		
Returned sales and allowances	$ 2,090.00	
Freight out	1,720.00	3,810.00
Net sales		$538,530.00
Deduct cost of goods sold:		
Inventory, January 1, 1945	$152,750.00	
Merchandise from home office	462,540.00	
Total	$615,290.00	
Less inventory, December 31, 1945	173,200.00	442,090.00
Gross profit on sales		$ 96,440.00
Deduct:		
Salaries	$ 30,650.00	
Depreciation of buildings	7,500.00	
Depreciation of furniture and fixtures	1,200.00	
Provision for bad debts	1,050.00	
Interest charged by home office	9,000.00	
Other expenses	3,600.00	
Home office overhead charged to branch	10,000.00	63,000.00
Net profit		$ 33,440.00

Prepare: (1) an analysis of the home office current account for the year, which should accompany the foregoing statements; and (2) all entries (in journal form) on the home office books during the year affecting the branch current account.

Problem 42-9. On January 1, 1945, the Fibre Products Manufacturing Company of Seattle opened a retail sales branch in Dallas. The branch was placed under the management of I. M. Boss. Goods were billed to Boss at 130% of cost; one sixth of the amount thus added to cost represented expenses of shipping to the branch. Proceeds of sales and collections of accounts receivable were remitted to the home office intact; branch expenses were paid from a working fund which was maintained at $250.00 by drafts on the home office when reimbursements were necessary. Under Boss's management agreement he was to receive 30% of the net profit as shown by the branch books at the end of the year. Throughout the year the home office sent Boss a check for $125.00 monthly as an advance on his share of the profits. In computing the profit, the monthly advances to Boss were not to be considered as expenses, but any difference between his share of the profit and the amount thus advanced would constitute the balance to be paid to Boss or the amount to be refunded by him to the company.

On December 31, 1945, Boss submitted the following statements to the home office:

Branch Profit and Loss Statement, 1945

Sales		$82,500.00
Less cost of goods sold:		
Merchandise received	$91,000.00	
Less inventory, December 31, 1945	22,100.00	68,900.00
Gross profit		$13,600.00
Expenses		9,000.00
Net profit		$ 4,600.00

Branch Assets

Cash	$ 250.00
Accounts receivable	6,000.00
Merchandise	22,100.00
Total	$28,350.00

The home office statements for the year were as follows:

THE FIBRE PRODUCTS MANUFACTURING COMPANY
Profit and Loss Statement
Year Ended December 31, 1945

Sales:		
To I. M. Boss	$ 91,000.00	
Other	317,500.00	$408,500.00
Less cost of goods sold:		
Inventory, January 1, 1945	$ 52,500.00	
Cost of goods manufactured	339,000.00	
Total	$391,500.00	
Less inventory, December 31, 1945	55,000.00	336,500.00
Gross profit		$ 72,000.00
Expenses		24,000.00
Net profit		$ 48,000.00

THE FIBRE PRODUCTS MANUFACTURING COMPANY
Balance Sheet
December 31, 1945

Assets		Liabilities	
Cash	$ 7,825.00	Accounts payable	$ 20,000.00
Accounts receivable:		Capital stock	200,000.00
I. M. Boss	25,250.00	Surplus	41,575.00
Other	17,500.00		
Inventories	55,000.00		
Plant—depreciated value	156,000.00		
	$261,575.00		$261,575.00

The books have been closed. Give journal entries to adjust the company's books to a proper basis. Prepare an adjusted profit and loss statement with columns for home office, branch and combined, and a balance sheet.

Problem 42-10. The following is the trial balance of George T. Day, a sole trader, as of December 31, 1945:

	Dr.	Cr.
Cash	$130,190.16	
Bonds	58,300.00	
Inventory, finished goods, January 1, 1945	7,865.56	
Machinery and tools	20,857.29	
Reserve for depreciation, machinery and tools		$ 5,885.89
Shop supplies inventory, January 1, 1945	1,937.13	
Furniture	6,697.73	
Reserve for depreciation, furniture		3,338.70
Real estate and buildings	75,026.35	
Reserve for depreciation, buildings		10,263.90
Insurance	890.03	

Contingent profit (Philadelphia branch inventory, January 1, 1945)		$ 6,034.25
Miscellaneous investments	$ 1,223.93	
Accrued interest	2,734.64	
Accounts receivable	32,173.78	
Accounts payable		6,254.34
George T. Day, capital		293,998.24
George T. Day, withdrawals	50,000.00	
Sales		332,343.74
Raw materials	21,612.81	
Manufacturing supplies	103,330.88	
Labor	45,542.48	
Shop supplies	4,141.63	
Salaries	42,515.73	
Employees' profit sharing	19,096.96	
Advertising	8,401.72	
Traveling expense	2,430.06	
Taxes	1,866.06	
Donations	514.35	
Miscellaneous expense	15,689.99	
Interest		3,710.01
Philadelphia branch accounts:		
Inventory, January 1, 1945	12,068.50	
Shipments from home office	14,017.60	
Sales		27,531.58
Accounts receivable	7,818.47	
Furniture	691.57	
Cash	1,725.24	
	$689,360.65	$689,330.65

The shipments to the Philadelphia branch are credited to the home office sales account. The shipment price includes a profit of 50%.

The inventories December 31, 1945 are as follows: Finished goods, $5,242.65; raw materials, $5,025.06; manufacturing supplies, $28,196.80; Philadelphia branch merchandise, $3,229.06; unexpired insurance, $34.77.

Depreciation for the year is as follows: Buildings, $3,034.00; machinery and tools, $445.00; furniture, $105.00.

Prepare profit and loss statement and balance sheet. Set out the Philadelphia branch transactions as a separate division of the profit and loss statement, to show the gross profit of the branch.

QUESTIONS AND PROBLEMS ON CHAPTER 43

Questions

Question 43-1. What is the purpose of a consolidated balance sheet? How does a consolidated balance sheet differ from the parent's balance sheet?

Question 43-2. Assume that the subsidiary had a surplus at the date of acquisition of its stock by the parent company, and that the parent company bought all of the stock, paying exactly book value for it. What eliminations would be made in preparing a consolidated balance sheet at the date of acquisition?

Question 43-3. Assume that the subsidiary had a deficit at the date of acquisition, and that the parent company bought all of the stock, paying par less the deficit. What accounts should be eliminated in making a consolidated balance sheet at the date of acquisition?

Question 43-4. If the parent company pays more than book value for the subsidiary stock, how is the excess shown on the consolidated balance sheet? Justify this treatment.

Question 43-5. Assume that the parent company acquired 98% of the stock of the subsidiary, and that a consolidated balance sheet is to be made at the date of acquisition. Assume also that the parent company paid exactly book value for its holding, as shown by the books of the subsidiary. State how the eliminations should be made and how the minority interest should be determined in each of the following cases:

(*a*) The subsidiary had no surplus.
(*b*) The subsidiary had a surplus.
(*c*) The subsidiary had a deficit.

Question 43-6. State the amount of the goodwill and of the minority interest in the following case and explain how you obtained your figures. The subsidiary has a capital stock of $100,000.00 and a surplus of $50,000.00. The parent company acquired 90% of the stock and paid $140,000.00 for it. A consolidated balance sheet is to be made at the date of acquisition.

Question 43-7. The *A* Company's balance sheet on December 31, 1945 contained the following accounts:

Capital stock authorized	$200,000.00
Unissued stock	30,000.00
Treasury stock (50 shares—par $100.00) cost	7,500.00
Surplus	24,500.00
Premium on stock (issued at $110)	17,000.00
Reserve for sinking fund	35,320.00
Reserve for extension of plant	20,000.00

On the same date the *B* Company bought 90 per cent of the outstanding stock at 170 and acquired the treasury stock and the unissued stock at 150.

Compute, for consolidated balance sheet purposes, the goodwill arising from the transactions.

Question 43-8. Among the Mississippi Company's accounts receivable, which aggregate approximately $1,000,000.00, you find the following:

Account of $50,000.00 for sales during the previous month to the Jonesboro Dry Goods Company, 75% of whose capital stock is owned by the Mississippi Company. Sales to this company are settled promptly in thirty days.

Account of $130,000.00 representing principally advances to the Memphis Metal Company (95% of whose capital stock is owned by the Mississippi Company) to enable it to make additions to its plant. A considerable part of the output of the Memphis Company is sold to the Mississippi Company, at prices advantageous to the latter, for use in its manufacturing operations.

Account of $25,000.00 for advances to the Bluestone Sales Company, all of whose capital stock is owned by the Mississippi Company, but which has a bonded debt of $100,000.00 to others than the Mississippi Company. The advances were made principally to enable the Bluestone Company to continue in business in spite of losses sustained for several years past.

Account of $28,000.00 for advances to the president of the company, who expects to pay it off during the next two years out of the percentage of the company's profits which is payable to him (if earned) under contract.

What treatment would you give these accounts in stating the balance sheet of the Mississippi Company if it is (*a*) a consolidated balance sheet, or (*b*) a non-consolidated balance sheet?

Problems

Problem 43-1. Prepare a consolidated balance sheet for the Barbour Company and its subsidiary, the Blair Company, from the following balance sheets:

	Barbour Company	Blair Company
Assets:		
Cash	$ 35,300.00	$14,300.00
Accounts receivable	62,400.00	27,175.00
Merchandise	43,630.00	17,720.00
Investment in Blair Company—2,700 shares	55,000.00	
Fixed assets	41,708.00	12,365.00
	$238,038.00	$71,560.00
Liabilities:		
Accounts payable	$ 32,690.00	$18,322.00
Notes payable	20,000.00	5,000.00
Capital stock (1,500 shares)	150,000.00	
(3,000 shares)		30,000.00
Surplus	35,348.00	18,238.00
	$238,038.00	$71,560.00

Among the accounts payable of the Blair Company is $12,000.00 due to the Barbour Company.

Problem 43-2. From the following data prepare a consolidated balance sheet of the Mercer Company and its subsidiary, the Northern Company.

	Mercer Company	Northern Company
Assets:		
Cash	$ 17,250.00	$ 6,290.00
Accounts receivable	35,870.00	17,910.00
Inventory	41,705.00	21,742.00
Investment in Northern Company—85%	42,000.00	
Fixed assets	58,324.00	7,194.00
Deficit		17,180.00
Goodwill		5,000.00
	$195,149.00	$75,316.00
Liabilities:		
Accounts payable	$ 6,840.00	$ 5,316.00
Mortgage payable	20,000.00	
Capital stock	100,000.00	70,000.00
Surplus	68,309.00	
	$195,149.00	$75,316.00

Problem 43-3. Compute the total goodwill and the minority interests of the Lorain Company and its subsidiaries from the following data:

Lorain Company:	
Goodwill	$ 50,000.00
Investment in the Savannah Co. 800 shares	114,000.00
Investment in the Norfolk Co. 650 shares	50,000.00
Investment in the Roanoke Co. 6,300 shares	283,500.00
Savannah Co.:	
Capital stock—1,000 shares	100,000.00
Surplus	36,273.00
Norfolk Co.:	
Capital stock—750 shares	18,750.00
Surplus	35,472.00
Roanoke Co.:	
Capital stock—10,000 shares authorized. Outstanding 7,524 shares	376,200.00
Deficit	26,334.00

Problem 43-4. The Parker Precision Tool Company had filed a claim for damages of $18,000.00 against the Stoddard Shear Company. The Stoddard Company had never recognized this claim. The Parker Company then bought 82% of the stock of the Stoddard Company for $53,000.00. Immediately before the purchase, the balance sheets of the two companies were as follows:

	Parker Precision Tool Company	Stoddard Shear Company
Current assets	$132,828.00	$47,149.00
Claim against Stoddard Shear Company	18,000.00	
Fixed assets	82,140.00	24,633.00
Total	$232,968.00	$71,782.00
Current liabilities	$ 21,078.00	$11,635.00
Capital stock	150,000.00	50,000.00
Surplus	61,890.00	10,147.00
	$232,968.00	$71,782.00

Immediately upon acquiring control of the Stoddard Company, the Parker Company ordered that its claim against the Stoddard Company be recognized by that company by setting up a liability for it.

Prepare a consolidated balance sheet, giving effect to this action.

Problem 43-5. Prepare a consolidated balance sheet for the Pratt Company and its two subsidiaries, whose balance sheets at the date of acquisition follow:

	Pratt Company	Abbott Company	Baker Company
Cash	$ 29,478.00	$23,501.00	$ 16,990.00
Accounts receivable	53,107.00	26,635.00	27,132.00
Merchandise	41,756.00	21,075.00	43,958.00
Investments:			
Abbott Company (4,700 shares)	68,000.00		
Baker Company (9,100 shares)	85,000.00		
Fixed assets	46,122.00	18,738.00	31,250.00
	$323,463.00	$89,949.00	$119,330.00
Accounts payable	$ 28,455.00	$23,612.00	$ 19,853.00
Capital stock:			
5,000 shares	250,000.00		
5,000 shares		50,000.00	
10,000 shares			100,000.00
Surplus	45,008.00	16,337.00	523.00*
	$323,463.00	$89,949.00	$119,330.00

* Deficit.

The accounts receivable of the Pratt Company include $2,100.00 owed by the Abbott Company and $5,300.00 owed by the Baker Company. The liability of the Baker Company to the Pratt Company is stated on its books at $4,900.00. The discrepancy is due to a commission charge which the Baker Company has not yet recorded.

Prepare a consolidated balance sheet.

Problem 43-6. Prepare consolidated balance sheet working papers in each of the three following cases:

	Case A		*Case B*		*Case C*	
Assets	Co. *S*	Co. *T*	Co. *S*	Co. *T*	Co. *S*	Co. *T*
Investment in Co. *T* (85%)	$56,000.00	$ —	$53,000.00	$ —	$61,000.00	$ —
Cash	28,000.00	48,000.00	32,000.00	62,000.00	12,000.00	50,000.00
Goodwill	10,000.00	8,000.00	—	8,000.00	10,000.00	8,000.00
	$94,000.00	$56,000.00	$85,000.00	$70,000.00	$83,000.00	$58,000.00
Liabilities						
Accounts payable	$45,000.00	$ 2,000.00	$15,000.00	$ 2,000.00	$ 6,000.00	$10,000.00
Capital stock	65,000.00	50,000.00	65,000.00	50,000.00	65,000.00	50,000.00
Surplus or deficit*	16,000.00*	4,000.00	5,000.00	18,000.00	12,000.00	2,000.00*
	$94,000.00	$56,000.00	$85,000.00	$70,000.00	$83,000.00	$58,000.00

The information shown is as of the date on which the holding company acquired the stock of the subsidiary.

Problem 43-7. On October 30, 1945, Jones Company purchased 90% of the stock of Jackson Company. Immediately after the purchase, the trial balances of the two companies appeared as follows:

Debits	Jones Company	Jackson Company
Cash	$ 9,651.82	$ 3,200.09
Accounts receivable	35,562.18	38,921.04
Notes receivable	6,000.00	12,000.00
Inventories	78,312.91	57,818.96
Investment in Jackson Company	110,000.00	—
Machinery and equipment	50,000.00	46,810.04
Deferred charges	780.00	1,011.66
Goodwill	25,000.00	15,000.00
	$315,306.91	$174,761.79
Credits		
Accounts payable	$ 42,130.16	$ 12,807.16
Reserve for bad debts	2,100.00	1,897.00
Reserve for depreciation	25,616.00	21,918.00
Capital stock	125,000.00	100,000.00
Surplus:		
Earned	95,460.75	32,460.16
Donated	25,000.00	5,679.47
	$315,306.91	$174,761.79

Prepare a consolidated balance sheet.

Problem 43-8. On December 31, 1945 American Company acquired (direct from the holders) all of the stock of Little Company, a customer. The American Company made the purchase for $96,000.00, paying 20% in cash and giving a six-month note for the balance. The balance sheets of the two companies on December 31, 1945, before giving effect to the stock purchase, were as follows:

	American Company	Little Company
Current assets	$200,000.00	$ 90,000.00
Fixed assets	80,000.00	41,000.00
Investments	12,000.00	6,000.00
Other assets	8,500.00	10,000.00*
	$300,500.00	$147,000.00
Current liabilities	$ 40,000.00	$ 50,000.00
Capital stock	100,000.00	75,000.00
Surplus	160,500.00	22,000.00
	$300,500.00	$147,000.00

* Including a claim of $6,500.00 against American Company for overcharge on purchases, never recognized or set up by the latter company.

Prepare consolidated balance sheet working papers after the acquisition.

Problem 43-9. The balance sheet of G. M. Co. on December 31, 1945, appeared as follows:

Assets		
Cash		$ 15,000.00
Accounts receivable:		
The W. C. Company	$ 20,000.00	
Others	18,000.00	38,000.00
Inventories		56,000.00
Fixed assets:		
Cost	$ 92,000.00	
Reserve for depreciation	23,000.00	69,000.00
Deferred charges		3,000.00
		$181,000.00

Liabilities and Net Worth

Accounts payable		$ 25,000.00
Notes payable		24,000.00
Capital stock—authorized, 2,000 shares; in treasury, 1,000 shares; outstanding, 1,000 shares	$100,000.00	
Surplus	32,000.00	132,000.00
		$181,000.00

On December 31, 1945 a large block of the outstanding stock of the above company was acquired by The W. C. Company at 140; the books of The W. C. Company then contained the following balances:

Cash	$ 6,000.00	
Accounts receivable	57,000.00	
Inventories	50,000.00	
Investment in G. M. Co	126,000.00	
Plant, machinery, and equipment	225,000.00	
Accounts payable		$ 51,000.00
Due to G. M. Co		20,000.00
Notes payable (secured by G. M. Co. stock)		80,000.00
Reserve for depreciation		92,000.00
Preferred stock		126,140.00
Common stock		175,000.00
Surplus	80,140.00	
	$544,140.00	$544,140.00

Prepare a consolidated balance sheet as of December 31, 1945.

QUESTIONS AND PROBLEMS ON CHAPTER 44

Questions

Question 44-1. Describe the method that a parent company may use in recording the profits, losses, and dividends of a subsidiary. Explain why this is a proper procedure.

Question 44-2. A subsidiary has capital stock of $100,000.00 and surplus of $50,000.00. The parent company buys 90% of the stock and pays $138,000.00 for it. What eliminations should be made in preparing a consolidated balance sheet at the date of acquisition, and what is the amount of the goodwill and the minority interest?

Assume that, during the first year after purchase, the subsidiary makes a profit of $20,000.00. What entries should be made to take up the profits?

What would be the balances of the investment account on the parent company's books, and the surplus account on the subsidiary's books, at the end of the first year of ownership?

State what elimination should be made and the amounts of goodwill, minority interest, and surplus to be shown in the consolidated balance sheet prepared at the end of the year.

Question 44-3. Refer to the preceding question and assume that during the second year the subsidiary lost $10,000.00. State how the parent company should take up the loss. Also state the balances in the investment account and the subsidiary's surplus account at the end of the second year.

How would you make the elimination in preparing a consolidated balance sheet, and what would be the amount of the goodwill and the minority interest? How would you determine the amount of the surplus to appear on the consolidated balance sheet?

Question 44-4. Continuing the preceding question, assume that, just prior to the close of the second year, the subsidiary declared a dividend of $9,000.00 payable the following year. What entry should be made by the parent company?

What are the balances of the investment account and the subsidiary's surplus account?

Explain how eliminations would be made in preparing a consolidated balance sheet, and state the amount of the goodwill and the minority interest.

State how the surplus to be shown in the consolidated balance sheet would be determined, and whether the declaration of the dividend by the subsidiary would alter the amount of surplus to be shown in the consolidated balance sheet.

Question 44-5. Assume that a parent company purchased stock at a time when a dividend had been declared but not paid. The purchase was made before the date on which the stock records were to be closed to determine the stockholders of record. How should the parent company record the purchase of the stock?

Question 44-6. In the process of consolidating several competing establishments, Corporation *A*, the parent company, acquired $98,000.00 of a total of $100,000.00 of the capital stock of Company *B*. At the time of the purchase, the balance sheet of Company *B* showed surplus and undivided profits of $50,000.00. Corporation *A* bought the stock of *B* at 200%. Almost immediately after the purchase, Company *B* paid a cash dividend of 25%. In what way would the payment of this dividend affect:

(*a*) The balance sheet of *B*?
(*b*) The balance sheet of *A*?
(*c*) The consolidated balance sheet of *A* and its subsidiaries?

Problems

Problem 44-1. The Whiting Company acquired an 82% interest in the Redding Company for $12,000.00 less than its book value. Since that time the Redding Company has made profits aggregating $93,000.00 and paid dividends of $40,000.00. The minority interest at the conclusion of the period was $36,900.00.

(*a*) What was the cost of the investment?
(*b*) At what price was the investment carried at the conclusion of the period?
(*c*) Prove the goodwill deduction at the conclusion of the period.

Problem 44-2. The Lincoln Company acquired, for $350,000.00, a 95% interest in the Decatur Company, represented by 1900 shares of its $100.00 par value stock. The price paid anticipated a dividend of $40.00 per share, which had been declared prior to acquisition and which was paid two weeks after the acquisition. The Decatur Company made a profit of $39,000.00 during the first year of ownership. At the beginning of the second year the Lincoln Company sold a 15% interest at a profit of $7,200.00 based on its book value. What did it get for the stock it sold?

Problem 44-3. The balance sheets of the Pittsburgh Company and its subsidiary, the Scott Company, follow:

	Pittsburgh Company	Scott Company
Cash	$ 12,675.00	$13,855.00
Accounts receivable	36,530.00	22,742.00
Inventories	29,178.00	16,330.00
Fixed assets	40,432.00	22,400.00
Investment in Scott Company (90%)	63,500.00	
	$182,315.00	$75,327.00
Accounts payable	$ 27,452.00	$17,843.00
Capital stock (par $100.00)	100,000.00	50,000.00
Surplus	54,863.00	7,484.00
	$182,315.00	$75,327.00

When the Pittsburgh Company bought control of the Scott Company, it took into consideration the fact that the depreciation taken by the Scott Company had been inadequate to the extent of $12,000.00. Now that the Pittsburgh Company controls the Scott Company, it directs its accountant to correct the depreciation provision.

Prepare consolidated working papers before this adjustment is made and another set of consolidated working papers after this adjustment is made.

Prepare a reconciliation of the amounts shown as goodwill on the two sets of working papers.

Assuming that the contention of the Pittsburgh Company is correct, which consolidated balance sheet would you certify?

Problem 44-4. The Pontiac Company bought control of three companies.

From the following data prepare schedules showing the computation of the nonreciprocal elements where complete working papers are omitted. The Pontiac Company's surplus balance was $183,400.00. The investments are carried at cost.

	The South Company	The Stacey Company	The Soo Company
Per cent owned	95%	90%	80%
Price paid	$165,000.00	$165,000.00	$90,000.00
Profits since acquisition	72,000.00	68,000.00	12,000.00*
Dividends paid	None	60,000.00	18,000.00
Capital stock	100,000.00	150,000.00	75,000.00
Surplus at acquisition	22,000.00*	42,000.00	34,000.00

* Loss or deficit.

Prove the goodwill amounts by a separate computation.

Problem 44-5.

(*a*) The Wright Company purchased 25,000 of the 27,300 outstanding shares of $100.00 par value stock of the Westfield Corporation, at $135.00 a share. During the first year the Westfield Corporation made a profit of $218,400.00 and paid dividends totaling $81,900.00. Journalize the facts pertaining to the subsidiary on the Wright Company's books.

(*b*) The accountant for the Wright Company observed that the increase in the carrying value of the investment exactly equaled the goodwill. What was the minority interest in the Westfield Company at the date of the consolidated balance sheet?

(*c*) Prove the goodwill by two computations, one at the date of acquisition, and another at the date of the consolidated balance sheet.

Problem 44-6. Prepare three-column working papers in each of the following cases to determine the goodwill and minority interest. It is assumed that the holding company owns 90 per cent of the stock of the subsidiary, and that it has taken up its proportion of subsidiary gains and losses since acquisition. Neither the holding company nor the subsidiary has paid any dividends. The holding company has no source of income other than its investment in the subsidiary stock.

State the amount of consolidated surplus in each case.

	Company *S*		Company *P*	
	Capital Stock	Surplus	Investment Account	Surplus
Group I:				
Case *A*—at acquisition	$150,000.00	$30,000.00	$165,000.00	$22,500.00
Case *B*—end of 1 year (*S* gain—$15,000.00)	150,000.00	45,000.00	178,500.00	36,000.00
Case *C*—end of 2 years (*S* loss—$22,500.00)	150,000.00	22,500.00	158,250.00	15,750.00
Case *D*—end of 3 years (*S* loss—$37,500.00)	150,000.00	15,000.00*	124,500.00	18,000.00*
Group II:				
Case *E*—at acquisition	150,000.00	30,000.00	172,500.00	22,500.00
Case *F*—end of 1 year (*S* gain—$30,000.00)	150,000.00	60,000.00	199,500.00	49,500.00
Case *G*—end of 2 years (*S* loss—$42,000.00)	150,000.00	18,000.00	161,700.00	11,700.00
Case *H*—end of 3 years (*S* loss—$30,000.00)	150,000.00	12,000.00*	134,700.00	15,300.00*

	Company S		Company P	
	Capital Stock	Surplus	Investment Account	Surplus
Group III:				
Case *I*—at acquisition.....	$150,000.00	$15,000.00*	$125,000.00	$22,500.00*
Case *J*—end of 1 year (*S* gain—$12,000.00)....	150,000.00	3,000.00*	135,800.00	11,700.00*
Case *K*—end of 2 years (*S* gain—$21,000.00)....	150,000.00	18,000.00	154,700.00	7,200.00
Case *L*—end of 3 years (*S* loss—$45,000.00).....	150,000.00	27,000.00*	114,200.00	33,300.00*

* Deficit.

Problem 44-7. The La Salle Company owns 90% of the stock of the Adams Company and 100% of the stock of the Wells Company; it takes up through its investment accounts the profits, losses, and dividends of the subsidiaries.

On December 31, 1945 the accounts of the three companies contain the following balances:

	La Salle Company	Adams Company	Wells Company
Debits			
Investment in Wells Company..	$121,000.00		
Goodwill....................	20,000.00	$30,000.00	
Surplus.....................	30,000.00	30,000.00	
Credits			
Investment in Adams Company.	3,500.00		
Capital stock................	750,000.00	50,000.00	$50,000.00
Surplus.....................			60,000.00

What amounts of goodwill, minority interest, and surplus will appear in the consolidated balance sheet as of December 31, 1945?

Problem 44-8. The following facts are submitted relative to Company *P* and its subsidiaries, Companies *X*, *Y*, and *Z*, whose stocks were acquired by Company *P* on January 1, 1946:

	Company *P*	Company *X*	Company *Y*	Company *Z*
Par value of stock outstanding..............	$300,000.00	$50,000.00	$100,000.00	$200,000.00
Portion of stock owned by Company *P*...........		80%	85%	90%
Surplus, January 1, 1946..	65,000.00	15,000.00	90,000.00	75,000.00
Cost to Company *P* of stock acquired........		70,000.00	170,000.00	260,000.00
Profit (loss*) 1946........	35,000.00	10,000.00	10,000.00*	40,000.00
Dividends paid, 1946.....	12,000.00	4,000.00	5,000.00	20,000.00

The $35,000.00 profit of Company *P* is its own profit before subsidiary profits and loss are taken up.

Prepare a statement of the parent company's investment accounts and its surplus accounts for the year, including therein the entries for the parent company's interests in subsidiary profits and loss.

Also determine the amounts which should appear in a consolidated balance sheet on December 31, 1946 for:

Goodwill.
Minority interests.
Consolidated surplus.

Problem 44-9. The net worth of the *A* Company on December 31, 1944 appeared as follows:

Capital stock—$100.00 par value:	
Authorized, $100,000.00; issued	$ 80,000.00
Surplus	35,000.00
Net worth	$115,000.00

On January 1, 1945, a 5% dividend was declared, payable February 1 to holders of record January 15.

Also on January 1, 1945 after the dividend had been declared, the *B* Company acquired 90% of the outstanding stock of *A* at 125.

The *A* Company made a profit of $18,000.00 during the six months ended June 30, 1945, and on July 1, 1945, the directors authorized the sale of the unissued stock at 120 to stockholders in amounts proportionate to their holdings as of June 30. The stock was sold in accordance with the authorization.

A dividend of 4% was declared July 15 payable August 15.

The *A* Company made a profit of $9,500.00 during the last half of 1945.

The *B* Company took up its prorata share of the profits on June 30 and December 31, 1945 respectively, by credit to surplus.

(1) Prepare journal entries made by the *B* Company in respect to the foregoing.

(2) Compute the amounts of goodwill and minority interest in consolidated balance sheets prepared on:

(*a*) January 1, 1945, immediately after the first stock purchase.

(*b*) July 1, 1945, immediately after the second stock purchase.

(*c*) December 31, 1945.

Problem 44-10. Ninety per cent of the capital stock of Company *A* and 85% of the capital stock of Company *B* is owned by the holding Company *C*. Company *C* purchased the above stock of Company *A* at 125 on January 1, 1945, on the basis of the following balance sheet as of that date:

Assets		Liabilities	
Real estate, plant, etc.	$125,000.00	Capital stock	$200,000.00
Merchandise	100,000.00	Notes payable	85,000.00
Accounts receivable	80,000.00	Surplus	50,000.00
Cash	30,000.00		
	$335,000.00		$335,000.00

During the year 1945, Company *A* made a net profit of $12,000.00, and the directors declared and paid a dividend of 5% as of March 15, 1946.

The stock of Company *B* owned by Company *C* was purchased on January 1, 1945 at 150, on the basis of the following balance sheet as of that date:

Assets		Liabilities	
Real estate, plant, etc.	$ 500,000.00	Capital stock	$ 500,000.00
Patents	50,000.00	Bonded indebtedness	200,000.00
Merchandise	255,000.00	Accounts payable	75,000.00
Accounts receivable	170,000.00	Surplus	250,000.00
Cash	50,000.00		
	$1,025,000.00		$1,025,000.00

During the year 1945 Company *B* made a net profit of $100,000.00, and the directors declared and paid a dividend of 10% as of February 1, 1946.

Draw up all the necessary entries in respect to the purchase of the stock of the two companies, their earnings and dividends as they should appear on the books of Company *C*, the holding company.

QUESTIONS AND PROBLEMS ON CHAPTER 45

Questions

Question 45-1. A parent company carries its investment in a subsidiary at cost. To what extent will its account balances differ from those which would result from taking up subsidiary profits, losses, and dividends through the investment account?

Question 45-2. Assume that a holding company does not take up profits, losses, and dividends through the investment account, but carries the stock at cost. How would you determine the elimination to be made from the investment account and the subsidiary's capital stock and surplus in making a consolidated balance sheet?

Question 45-3. A corporation owns 85% of the stock of one company, and three shares out of a total of one hundred shares of another company. In what way, if at all, should its records differ in regard to profits earned and dividends paid by the two companies?

Problems

Problem 45-1. Below are the balance sheets of a parent company and its subsidiary three years after the date of acquisition:

	Prescott Company	Salem Company
Miscellaneous assets	$125,643.00	$63,780.00
Investment in Salem Company (at cost)	65,000.00	
	$190,643.00	$63,780.00
Capital stock—Prescott Company	$150,000.00	
—Salem Company		$50,000.00
Surplus—Prescott Company	40,643.00	
—Salem Company		13,780.00
	$190,643.00	$63,780.00

Prepare a consolidated balance sheet under each of the following assumptions:

(*a*) The parent company owns 100% of the stock of the subsidiary, which it acquired when the subsidiary had a surplus of $7,840.00.
(*b*) The parent company owns 90% of the stock of the subsidiary, which it acquired when the subsidiary had a surplus of $18,620.00.
(*c*) The parent company owns 80% of the stock of the subsidiary, which it acquired when the subsidiary had a deficit of $3,250.00.

Problem 45-2. The Drake Company acquired an 82% interest in the Fullerton Company at a price which was $15,400.00 below its book value. The Drake Company carries this investment at cost. At the date of the consolidated balance sheet, the subsidiary's surplus had declined by $30,000.00 since the date of acquisition and the minority interest was stated at $33,840.00.

(*a*) What did the investment cost the Drake Company?
(*b*) Make the journal entry necessary to change the investment to book value.
(*c*) Submit a schedule showing the computation of the eliminations and nonreciprocal elements, as used when no formal working papers are prepared, using such amounts as are available.

Problem 45-3. Prepare a schedule in which you compute the nonreciprocal elements for the following four companies.

			Subsidiary's		
Company	Per Cent Owned	Cost	Capital Stock	Surplus (Deficit*) at Acquisition	Surplus (Deficit*) at Date of Consolidated Balance Sheet
A	90%	$85,000.00	$60,000.00	$30,000.00	$50,000.00
B	85	75,000.00	50,000.00	40,000.00	25,000.00
C	80	27,500.00	40,000.00	8,000.00*	10,000.00*
D	75	55,000.00	75,000.00	6,000.00*	22,000.00

Problem 45-4. The *X* Company purchased its interest in the *Q* Company on January 1, 1946. Prepare a consolidated balance sheet on December 31, 1946 based on the following information:

	X Company	*Q* Company
Assets	$ 920,000.00	$600,000.00
Investment in *Q* Company	576,000.00	
Goodwill		40,000.00
	$1,496,000.00	$640,000.00
Capital stock—*X* Company	$1,000,000.00	
—*Q* Company		$500,000.00
Surplus—*X* Company	496,000.00	
—*Q* Company		140,000.00
	$1,496,000.00	$640,000.00
Surplus, January 1	$ 486,000.00	$130,000.00
Profits for 1946	81,500.00	40,000.00
Dividends from the *Q* Company	28,500.00	
Totals	$ 596,000.00	$170,000.00
Dividends	100,000.00	30,000.00
Surplus, December 31	$ 496,000.00	$140,000.00

Problem 45-5. The Dunlap Company has owned a 92% interest in the Westmore Company for five years and has taken up its share of the subsidiary's profits, losses, and dividends. When its accountant prepared the usual consolidated balance sheet, he observed that the goodwill resulting from consolidation was higher than at the beginning of the year, when it was $4,000.00. Since he understood that the goodwill should remain unchanged, if there is no change in the per cent of ownership, he asked you for an explanation, and to prepare such adjustments as will remedy the situation.

Investigation revealed that the Westmore Company's accountant had reviewed its records for three years prior to the current year and had made adjustments to correct the profits of those years. The Dunlap Company made no entry for these adjustments. The Westmore Company reported a profit for the current year amounting to $18,000.00 and paid $10,000.00 in dividends. At the end of the year the Dunlap Company, after giving recognition to the current year's results, was carrying the investment at $140,160.00, and the subsidiary's net worth, as reported by its accountant, was $132,500.00.

(*a*) What was the net effect of the adjustment of the profits of prior years on the subsidiary's surplus?

(*b*) Show the adjustment that should be made on the parent company's books.

Problem 45-6. Prepare consolidated balance sheet working papers to determine the goodwill, minority interest, and consolidated surplus in each of the following cases. The holding company owns 90% of the subsidiary's stock and carries the investment at cost.

	Company *A*		Company *B*	
	Investment Account	Surplus	Capital Stock	Surplus
Case *A*—at acquisition....	$175,000.00	$30,000.00	$150,000.00	$40,000.00
Case *B*—end of 1 year....	175,000.00	30,000.00	150,000.00	70,000.00
Case *C*—end of 2 years...	175,000.00	30,000.00	150,000.00	20,000.00
Case *D*—end of 3 years...	175,000.00	30,000.00	150,000.00	10,000.00*
Case *E*—end of 4 years...	175,000.00	30,000.00	150,000.00	15,000.00
Case *F*—at acquisition....	155,000.00	25,000.00*	150,000.00	35,000.00
Case *G*—end of 1 year....	155,000.00	25,000.00*	150,000.00	65,000.00
Case *H*—end of 2 years...	155,000.00	25,000.00*	150,000.00	45,000.00
Case *I*—end of 3 years....	155,000.00	25,000.00*	150,000.00	5,000.00
Case *J*—end of 4 years....	155,000.00	25,000.00*	150,000.00	10,000.00*

* Deficit.

Problem 45-7. Following are balances of the accounts of Company *A* and Company *B* on December 31, 1945:

	Company *A*	Company *B*
Accounts payable..........................	$412,500.00	$163,000.00
Accounts receivable.......................	675,000.00	85,000.00
Cash......................................	112,500.00	53,000.00
Capital stock.............................	750,000.00	300,000.00
Plant property............................	762,500.00	700,000.00
Investment in Company *B*..................	475,000.00	—
Inventory.................................	600,000.00	170,000.00
Dividends paid............................	187,500.00	—
Profit for 1945...........................	480,000.00	90,000.00
Surplus, January 1, 1945..................	570,000.00	180,000.00
Notes payable.............................	600,000.00	275,000.00

On May 31, 1945 Company *A* acquired 2,700 shares of the capital stock of Company *B* at a cost of $475,000.00.

Capital stock outstanding:
Company *A*—7,500 shares
Company *B*—3,000 shares

Profits may be assumed to have been earned in equal monthly proportions. Prepare a consolidated balance sheet as of December 31, 1945.

Problem 45-8. On January 1, 1945 Company *A* purchased 95% of the capital stock of Company *B* at $160.00 per share, and 90% of the stock of Company *C* at $75.00 per share.

From the balance sheets of the three companies on June 30, 1945, prepare a consolidated balance sheet of the *A* Company and its subsidiaries at that date.

COMPANY *A*

Current assets	$ 850,000.00	Capital stock	$2,250,000.00
Property	900,000.00	Current liabilities	175,000.00
Investments in subsidiary companies	1,283,000.00	Surplus, January 1, 1945.	475,000.00
		Net profit to June 30	133,000.00
	$3,033,000.00		$3,033,000.00

COMPANY *B*

Current assets	$ 80,000.00	Capital stock—$100 par.	$ 400,000.00
Property	400,000.00	Current liabilities	20,000.00
Goodwill	300,000.00	Surplus, January 1, 1945	225,000.00
		Net profit to June 30	135,000.00
	$ 780,000.00		$ 780,000.00

COMPANY *C*

Current assets	$ 200,000.00	Capital stock—$100 par.	$1,000,000.00
Property (as appraised January 1, 1945)	1,130,000.00	Current liabilities	260,000.00
		Surplus, January 1, 1945	35,000.00
		Net profit to June 30	35,000.00
	$1,330,000.00		$1,330,000.00

There were no changes in the capital stock or surplus accounts during the six months.

Problem 45-9. Company *A*, a nonoperating holding company, owns 90% and 80% respectively of the outstanding capital stock of operating companies *B* and *C*.

From the following data prepare consolidated balance sheet working papers as of December 31, 1947:

Balance Sheets—December 31, 1947

	Company *A*	Company *B*	Company *C*
Cash	$ 50,000.00	$ 60,000.00	$ 40,000.00
Accounts receivable		105,000.00	80,000.00
Inventories		90,000.00	65,000.00
Investment in subsidiaries:			
Company *B*	300,000.00		
Company *C*	260,000.00		
Plant and equipment		200,000.00	150,000.00
	$610,000.00	$455,000.00	$335,000.00
Accounts payable	$ 35,000.00	$ 75,000.00	$ 60,000.00
Capital stock	500,000.00	250,000.00	250,000.00
Surplus	75,000.00	130,000.00	25,000.00
	$610,000.00	$455,000.00	$335,000.00

Analysis of Surplus—Year Ended December 31, 1947

	Company *A*	Company *B*	Company *C*
Balance, January 1, 1947	$125,000.00	$110,000.00	$ 75,000.00
Net profit (loss*) for the year	10,000.00*	70,000.00	35,000.00*
Total	$115,000.00	$180,000.00	$ 40,000.00
Dividends paid	40,000.00	50,000.00	15,000.00
Balance, December 31, 1947	$ 75,000.00	$130,000.00	$ 25,000.00

Company *A* has recorded all dividends received from the subsidiaries by credits to the investment accounts. All subsidiary profits and losses except those for the year 1937 have been taken up through the investment accounts.

Problem 45-10. Company *A* acquired 95% of Company *B*'s stock and 90% of Company *C*'s stock on January 1, 1945 at the costs indicated on its balance sheet.

Prepare a consolidated balance sheet.

COMPANY *A*

Balance Sheet—June 30, 1945

Cash	$ 37,500.00	Accounts payable	$ 18,000.00
Accounts receivable	55,000.00	Notes payable	36,000.00
Inventories	20,000.00	Capital stock	350,000.00
Plant property	135,000.00	Surplus, January 1, 1945	63,500.00
Investment in subsidiaries:		Net profit six months ended	
Company *B*	146,000.00	June 30, 1945	20,000.00
Company *C*	94,000.00		
	$487,500.00		$487,500.00

COMPANY *B*

Balance Sheet—June 30, 1945

Cash	$ 8,000.00	Accounts payable	$ 37,000.00
Accounts receivable	26,000.00	Capital stock	150,000.00
Notes receivable	5,000.00	Surplus	6,000.00
Inventories	9,000.00	Net profit six months ended	
Plant property	150,000.00	June 30, 1945	5,000.00
	$198,000.00		$198,000.00

COMPANY *C*

Balance Sheet—June 30, 1945

Cash	$ 3,000.00	Accounts payable	$ 5,000.00
Accounts receivable	9,000.00	Capital stock	60,000.00
Inventories	3,000.00	Surplus, January 1, 1945	35,000.00
Plant property	85,000.00	Net profit six months ended	
Goodwill	6,000.00	June 30, 1945	6,000.00
	$106,000.00		$106,000.00

QUESTIONS AND PROBLEMS ON CHAPTER 46

Questions

Question 46-1. A parent company holding notes receivable from a subsidiary company to the extent of $100,000.00 indorses and discounts these notes with its bankers, thus creating a contingent liability thereunder. State how and where the liability would appear, if at all, in a consolidated balance sheet of the two companies.

Question 46-2. The *A* Company, in San Francisco, paid a dividend on December 30 and mailed it to the *B* Company in New York. How would you handle this matter on the balance sheet of each company and on a consolidated balance sheet?

Question 46-3. State how you would treat the following item in preparing a balance sheet of the parent company, and a consolidated balance sheet: "Dividends declared and receivable on stock of a subsidiary company."

Question 46-4. Mention a number of adjustments which may have to be made on the books of one company at the close of the period in order to bring the accounts into a condition where proper elimination of intercompany receivables and payables can be made.

Question 46-5. Company *A* owns 88% of the stock of Company *B*. Company *B* has outstanding an issue of $50,000.00 first mortgage bonds which it sold to Company *A* at 95. How would these facts be expressed on the consolidated balance sheet?

Suppose that Company *B* had sold the bonds to outsiders at 90, and that Company *A* had later acquired them at par. How would these conditions be shown on the consolidated balance sheet?

Question 46-6. Assume that a subsidiary issues bonds at par and that the holding company later acquires the bonds at a premium. How would you deal with this condition in the working papers, and how would you show the fact in the consolidated balance sheet?

Question 46-7. Assume that a subsidiary issues a stock dividend. State how you would record the stock dividend, if at all, on the parent company's books, under the following conditions, and give your reasons:

(*a*) The parent company carries its investment at cost.
(*b*) The parent company takes up the subsidiary profits, losses, and cash dividends.

Question 46-8. To what extent, if at all, will the method of making eliminations be affected by the fact that the holding company holds subsidiary stock of no-par value?

Question 46-9. Assume that, at the date of preparing the consolidated balance sheet, the subsidiary has a deficit. Should the minority interest be shown at the par value of the minority stock or at the par value minus a portion of the deficit?

Problems

Problem 46-1. Prepare a consolidated balance sheet for the Avery Company and its subsidiary, the Brighton Company. The Avery Company owns 80% of the subsidiary, and it carries its investment at book value. The parent company's share of the subsidiary's profit for the current year has already been taken into account.

	Avery Company	Brighton Company
Cash	$ 27,324.00	$16,523.00
Accounts receivable	72,416.00	34,906.00
Inventory	45,925.00	19,234.00
Due from Brighton Company	18,700.00	
Investment in Brighton Company	53,406.00	
Fixed assets	84,320.00	18,432.00
	$302,091.00	$89,095.00
Accounts payable	$ 27,514.00	$10,342.00
Due to Avery Company		19,000.00
Capital stock	200,000.00	50,000.00
Surplus	74,577.00	9,753.00
	$302,091.00	$89,095.00

The discrepancy between the reciprocal accounts is explained in the following manner:

(*a*) The Avery Company billed the subsidiary for its share of an advertising campaign in the amount of $2,200.00. The subsidiary has not yet taken this amount up on its books.

(*b*) The Avery Company billed the subsidiary for $1,500.00 for merchandise which is still in transit. The Brighton Company has not recorded the liability nor has it included the merchandise in its inventory.

(*c*) The subsidiary paid a dividend of 10% just before the close of the year. Instead of sending the parent company a check, it credited the dividend payable to the parent company to the reciprocal account.

Problem 46-2. The Hill Company has owned 90% of the Foss Company and 80% of the Staley Company for several years. The Staley Company issued $100,000.00 of 10-year 6% bonds at 102. After the bonds had been outstanding for four years the Foss Company bought $40,000.00 par value of these bonds for 94.

(*a*) State how much the Hill Company will realize for its stockholders as a result of the amortization of the discount and the premium on the intercompany bonds.

(*b*) Show how you would report the premium and discount on the balance sheet at the end of the fifth year. Assume that the bonds were issued on January 1.

Problem 46-3. The Field Company owns 80% of the 7% preferred stock and 95% of the common stock of the Minot Company. The preferred stock, which is cumulative but nonparticipating, was acquired when the subsidiary had a deficit of $18,000.00 and was two years in arrears on its dividends. The common stock was acquired three years later when the Minot Company had a surplus of $32,210.00, but no dividends had been paid in the meantime. During the next four years the Minot Company earned $36,440.00, and paid five years' dividends on the preferred stock. Both investments are carried at cost. Prepare a consolidated balance sheet for the two companies.

	Field Company	Minot Company
Current assets	$220,130.00	$110,830.00
Investment in preferred stock	32,000.00	
Investment in common stock	50,000.00	
Fixed assets	67,420.00	122,640.00
Goodwill	100,000.00	
	$469,550.00	$233,470.00
Current liabilities	$ 74,160.00	$ 32,320.00
Preferred stock—7%		50,000.00
Common stock	350,000.00	100,000.00
Surplus	45,390.00	51,150.00
	$469,550.00	$233,470.00

Problem 46-4. The Phillips Company owns 94% of the Shackford Company. The subsidiary had a surplus of $32,000.00 at the date of acquisition. The Phillips Company followed the practice of carrying the investment at cost, but once added $40,000.00 arbitrarily to the investment account, and when it received a 50% stock dividend, it charged the investment account with the par value of the dividend. Prepare a consolidated balance sheet for the two companies.

	Phillips Company	Shackford Company
Current assets	$372,424.00	$158,910.00
Investment in Shackford Company	220,000.00	
Fixed assets	163,984.00	36,539.00
	$756,408.00	$195,449.00
Current liabilities	$101,875.00	$ 24,365.00
Capital stock	500,000.00	150,000.00
Surplus	154,533.00	21,084.00
	$756,408.00	$195,449.00

Problem 46-5. The Bradford Company carries its 90% investment in the Carver Company at book value. The Carver Company finances its operations by borrowing money from the Bradford Company and by discounting its customers' notes either with the Bradford Company or with finance companies. The Bradford Company sometimes rediscounts these customers' notes and sometimes discounts its own customers' notes. Prepare a consolidated balance sheet reflecting the conditions listed on page 684:

	Bradford Company	Carver Company
Cash	$ 47,564.00	$ 12,832.00
Accounts receivable	48,753.00	24,649.00
Notes receivable	85,463.00	41,400.00
Inventories	64,547.00	38,170.00
Investment in Carver Company	80,443.00	
Fixed assets	79,974.00	42,565.00
	$406,744.00	$159,616.00
Accounts payable	$ 32,148.00	$ 17,646.00
Notes payable		15,000.00
Dividends payable		5,000.00
Notes receivable discounted	58,630.00	38,700.00
Capital stock	250,000.00	50,000.00
Surplus	65,966.00	33,270.00
	$406,744.00	$159,616.00

The Bradford Company has recorded its share of the profits of the Carver Company for the current year, but not the dividends.

The notes payable are all owed to the Bradford Company. Of these the Bradford Company had rediscounted $5,000.00.

Of the notes receivable discounted on the Carver statements, $25,000.00 were discounted with the Bradford Company, and the remainder with finance companies. Of the $25,000.00, the Bradford Company had rediscounted $20,000.00.

Problem 46-6. Prepare a consolidated balance sheet from the following data:

COMPANY *P*
Balance Sheet—December 31, 1945

Assets

Cash	$100,000.00
Investment in Company *R*—7,600 shares, profits taken up annually, dividends credited as received	470,250.00
Investment in Company *Q*—1,600 shares, at cost, 1/1/1945	200,000.00
	$770,250.00

Liabilities

Current liabilities	$ 25,000.00
Notes payable due, 1951	225,000.00
Capital stock:	
Preferred—1,000 shares, par value $100.00	100,000.00
Common—15,000 shares, no-par value	300,000.00
Surplus	120,250.00
	$770,250.00

COMPANY *Q*
Balance Sheet—December 31, 1945

Assets

Cash	$ 60,000.00(1)
Receivables	200,000.00
Inventories	100,000.00
	$360,000.00

Liabilities

Current liabilities		$ 90,000.00
Capital stock, 2,000 shares, $100.00 par value		200,000.00
Surplus—Balance, January 1, 1945	$20,000.00	
Profit for year 1945	50,000.00	70,000.00
		$360,000.00

COMPANY *R*

Balance Sheet—December 31, 1945

Assets		
Cash		$ 95,000.00
Receivables		185,000.00(2)
Inventories		175,000.00
Land, buildings, and equipment as appraised by Appraisal Company of America, December 31, 1945 at sound value of		140,000.00
		$595,000.00
Liabilities		
Current liabilities		$125,000.00(3)
Capital stock, 8,000 shares, par value, $50.00		400,000.00
Surplus:		
Balance, January 1, 1945	$ 30,000.00*	
Profit for the year 1945	150,000.00	
Total	$120,000.00	
Dividends	50,000.00	70,000.00
		$595,000.00

* Deficit.

Notes:

(1)After remitting $10,000.00 to Company *P* as an advance on December 30, 1945; the check was not received by *P* until January, 1946.
(2) Includes $35,000.00 due from Company *Q*.
(3) Includes $25,000.00 dividend payable on January 5, 1946.

Problem 46-7. At the close of business December 31, 1946, there was submitted to you as accountant of a holding company, the trial balances of its three subsidiaries, the No. 1, No. 2, and No. 3 companies, together with a statement of the assets and liabilities of the holding company, from which you are to prepare a consolidated balance sheet for the holding company, showing all the necessary detail, including the percentage of outstanding stock of No. 3 company. Trial balances after closing are as follows:

NO. 1 COMPANY

Debit Balance		Credit Balances	
Cash	$ 25,700.00	Bills payable	$ 64,300.00
Mortgage interest receivable	16,800.00	Accrued lease rentals	1,400.00
Inventories, merchandise held for sale, and supplies	612,000.00	Capital stock	2,700.00
Accounts receivable	20,800.00	Surplus	74,800.00
Advances and miscellaneous contracts	65,500.00	Holding company's account	4,308,000.00
No. 2 Company account	14,800.00		
No. 3 Company account	100.00		
Mortgage receivable	63,600.00		
Property, plant, and equipment (less reserve)	3,528,800.00		
Deferred charges	103,100.00		
	$4,451,200.00		$4,451,200.00

NO. 2 COMPANY

Cash	$ 900.00	No. 1 Company account	$ 14,800.00
Inventories and supplies	105,100.00	Bills payable	6,300.00
Accounts receivable	50,500.00	Holding company's account	2,896,500.00
Property, plant, and equipment (less reserve)	3,175,700.00	Bonds	1,115,400.00
Deferred charges	600.00	Capital stock	1,010,000.00
Deficit	1,710,100.00		
No. 3 Company account	100.00		
	$5,043,000.00		$5,043,000.00

NO. 3 COMPANY

Cash	$ 11,300.00	Holding company's account	$ 14,300.00
Accounts receivable	14,100.00	Bonds (all held by parent company)	323,700.00
Property, plant, and equipment (less reserve)	1,015,000.00	Capital stock	600,000.00
Deferred charges	300.00	Surplus	200,000.00
Bills receivable (loan to the parent company)	97,500.00	No. 1 Company account	100.00
		No. 2 Company account	100.00
	$1,138,200.00		$1,138,200.00

The following is a statement of the assets and liabilities of the parent company:

Assets

Cash	$ 19,400.00
Accounts receivable	2,400.00
Property, plant, and equipment (less reserve)	27,700.00
Claim against the Government	1,017,400.00
Deferred charges	132,800.00
Securities and open accounts of subsidiaries:	
Open accounts:	
Company No. 1	4,308,000.00
Company No. 2	2,896,500.00
Company No. 3	14,300.00
Bonds of subsidiaries:	
Company No. 2	1,115,400.00
Company No. 3	323,700.00
Stock of subsidiaries—acquired at dates of organization:	
Company No. 1, 27 shares, par value $100.00 per share	
Company No. 2, 10,100 shares, par value $100.00 per share	
Company No. 3, 5,250 shares, par value $100.00 per share	

Liabilities

Bills payable	$ 107,200.00
Income notes	2,375,000.00
Accrued interest	285,000.00
Suspense	4,700.00
Capital stock, 60,000 shares no-par value	

Problem 46-8. On January 1, 1945, Company *P* acquired all of the 5,000 outstanding shares of capital stock of Company *S*, with a stated value of $87.50 per share, in exchange for 3,500 shares of its own 7% preferred stock, par value $100.00 per share. At that date the net worth of Company *S* was $387,500.00.

The balances shown by the books of Company *P* and Company *S* on December 31, 1946 were as follows:

Company P:

Cash, $200,000.00; accounts receivable, $150,000.00, of which $10,000.00 represents cash withheld by commercial paper houses to secure payment of customers' notes discounted by *P*; notes receivable, $85,000.00, of which $65,-000.00 are secured by chattel mortgages, and of this amount $50,000.00 are pledged as security for *P*'s bank loans; the total of customers' notes discounted amounting to $50,000.00 has been credited to notes receivable; advances to *S*, $45,000.00; inventories, $190,000.00; prepaid expenses, $5,000.00; investments, $500,000.00, of which $350,000.00 represents *P*'s investment in Company *S*; fixed assets, less reserve for depreciation, $200,000.00, including land and buildings, depreciated value, $110,000.00, subject to mortgage of $75,000.00; accounts payable, $150,000,00, including $15,000.00 due to *S*; notes payable $250,000.00, including $100,000.00 given to *S* ($75,000.00 endorsed and discounted by *S*) and $75,000.00 to banks secured by $50,000,00 notes receivable; accrued expenses, $10,000.00; mortgage payable on land and buildings, $75,000.00; capital stock, 7% preferred ($100.00 par value) $350,000.00, common (no-par value) $350,000.-00 (representing 500 shares); surplus, $190,000.00.

Company S:

Cash, $25,000.00; accounts receivable, $125,000.00, including $15,000.00 due from *P*; notes receivable, $25,000.00; inventories, $210,000.00; prepaid expenses, $1,500.00; fixed assets, less reserve for depreciation, $325,000.00; accounts payable, $90,000.00; notes payable, $100,000.00, consisting of $75,000.-00 to trade creditors and $25,000.00 to banks; advances by *P*, $45,000.00; capital stock—common (stated value $87.50 per share), $437,500.00; surplus, $39,000.00.

It has been the practice of Company *P* to pay portions of its obligations to Company *S* with its own customers' notes, duly indorsed; these notes are discounted by *S* within a short period. *P* also discounts notes received from *S* on the same basis. At the close of the year, in addition to the customers' notes under discount mentioned above, *P* had endorsed and turned over to Company *S* customers' notes totaling $30,000.00 maturing after December 31, 1946, which were discounted by the subsidiary, and *P* had discounted $20,000.00 received from *S*. Both of these transactions were handled through the advance accounts.

Company *P* has an unrecorded dividend liability of $15,000.00, and Company *S* one of $7,500.00. Company *S* has been assessed an additional tax of $1,500.00 for the year 1942; the company will sign the closing agreement when received.

Prepare a consolidated balance sheet.

Problem 46-9. The Consolidated Manufacturing Company purchased 16,-000 shares of the common capital stock of The Acme Manufacturing Company as of December 31, 1943 at a cost of $2,400,000.00. On June 30, 1944, it acquired 5,400 shares of the common capital stock of Marblehead Machines, Inc. for $200.00 per share. The balance sheets of the two companies at the dates of acquisition were as follows:

THE ACME MANUFACTURING COMPANY

Balance Sheet—December 31, 1943

Assets	
Cash	$ 413,000.00
Accounts receivable	900,000.00
Notes receivable	450,000.00
Inventories	950,000.00
Land	175,000.00
Buildings	350,000.00
Machinery and equipment	1,100,000.00
Prepaid expenses	10,500.00
	$4,348,500.00
Liabilities	
Notes payable	$ 100,000.00
Accounts payable	400,000.00
Federal income taxes payable	70,000.00
Accrued interest	1,000.00
Other accrued expenses	5,000.00
Reserve for depreciation	250,000.00
Reserve for bad debts	85,000.00
Capital stock:	
Preferred—5,000 shares (par value $100.00)	500,000.00
Common—20,000 shares (no-par value)	2,400,000.00
Surplus	537,500.00
	$4,348,500.00

MARBLEHEAD MACHINES, INC.

Balance Sheet—June 30, 1944

Assets	
Cash	$ 100,000.00
Customers' notes and accounts	400,000.00
Inventories	250,000.00
Land	250,000.00
Buildings	350,000.00
Machinery and equipment	540,000.00
Discount on first mortgage bonds	21,000.00
Prepaid expenses	5,000.00
	$1,916,000.00
Liabilities	
Notes and accounts payable	$ 150,000.00
Federal income taxes payable	16,000.00
Accrued interest:	
First mortgage bonds	7,500.00
Notes payable	1,000.00
Twenty-year 6% first mortgage bonds, due June 30, 1957	500,000.00
Reserve for depreciation	55,000.00
Reserve for bad debts	20,000.00
Capital stock:	
Preferred—3,000 shares (par value $50.00)	150,000.00
Common—6,000 shares (par value $100.00)	600,000.00
Surplus	416,500.00
	$1,916,000.00

On October 1, 1944 Consolidated Manufacturing Company purchased through brokers $150,000.00 par value of the Marblehead Machines, Inc. first mortgage bonds at 90 and on January 1, 1945, purchased $50,000.00 more at 92. A total of $650,000.00 of these bonds was originally issued as of June 30, 1937 at 95, with interest payable March 31 and September 30.

The balance sheets of the three companies on December 31, 1946, were as follows:

	Consolidated Manufacturing Company	Acme Manufacturing Company	Marblehead Machines, Inc.
Assets			
Cash	$ 300,000.00	$ 350,000.00	$ 50,000.00
Customers' notes and accounts	2,125,000.00	1,500,000.00	350,000.00
Inventories	1,600,000.00	1,010,000.00	560,000.00
Advances to subsidiaries	550,000.00		
Investments:			
$200,000.00 par value of Marblehead Machines, Inc. bonds	181,000.00		
Capital stock of subsidiaries	3,480,000.00		
Land	250,000.00	175,000.00	250,000.00
Buildings	500,000.00	400,000.00	350,000.00
Machinery and equipment	2,000,000.00	1,250,000.00	600,000.00
Discount on first mortgage bonds			18,000.00
Prepaid expense	20,000.00	15,000.00	7,000.00
	$11,006,000.00	$4,700,000.00	$2,185,000.00
Liabilities			
Notes and accounts payable	$ 500,000.00	$ 400,000.00	$ 435,000.00
Federal income tax payable	80,000.00	20,000.00	—
Accrued interest:			
First mortgage bonds			7,500.00
Notes payable	10,000.00	2,000.00	7,000.00
Accrued expenses	15,000.00	8,000.00	
Due to Consolidated Manufacturing Company		200,000.00	340,000.00
Twenty-year 6% first-mortgage bonds			500,000.00
Reserve for depreciation	500,000.00	470,000.00	105,000.00
Reserve for bad debts	165,000.00	75,000.00	15,500.00
Capital stock:			
Preferred		500,000.00	150,000.00
Common	8,000,000.00	2,400,000.00	600,000.00
Surplus	1,736,000.00	625,000.00	25,000.00
	$11,006,000.00	$4,700,000.00	$2,185,000.00

There were 80,000 shares of capital stock of Consolidated Manufacturing Company outstanding on December 31, 1946. There has been no change in the outstanding stock of the subsidiaries.

The preferred stocks of the subsidiaries are cumulative at the rate of 6½% per annum, but nonparticipating. The dividends of Acme Manufacturing Company are payable semiannually on May and November 1 and have been paid regularly since the inception of the corporation. Preferred dividends on Marblehead Machines, Inc. are payable quarterly on March, June, September, and December 1, all dividends having been paid to September 1, 1945.

The parent company takes up interest on its bond holdings only as received from Marblehead Machines, Inc.

On December 30, 1946, Marblehead Machines, Inc. remitted to Acme Manufacturing Company $10,000.00 for the account of Consolidated Manufacturing Company. This was not taken up by Acme Manufacturing Company.

Prepare a consolidated balance sheet of the Consolidated Manufacturing Company and its subsidiaries, making computations to the nearest dollar.

Problem 46-10. The following is a summary of an analysis of the "investment in subsidiary companies" account in the ledger of the *P* Company as at June 30, 1945:

Company	Class of Stock	Number of Shares Issued and Outstanding	Number of Shares Owned	Amount at Which Shares Are Carried	Last Dividend Paid or Declared for the Period Ended
A Company	7% first preferred........	5,000	4,000	$ 200,000.00	June 30, 1942
	7% second preferred......	5,000	4,900	245,000.00	June 30, 1942
	Common................	10,000	9,990	100,000.00	Sept. 30, 1939
B Company	7% cumulative preferred..	10,000	8,000	800,000.00	June 30, 1943
	Common................	10,000	10,000	1,000,000.00	June 30, 1943
C Company	6% cumulative preferred..	5,000	4,500	450,000.00	Sept. 30, 1944
	Common................	5,000	5,000	500,000.00	Sept. 30, 1944
				$3,295,000.00	

The certificate of incorporation of the *A* Company stipulates that in the event of dissolution the 7% first preferred stock shall be entitled to $75.00 per share before any distribution is made to holders of any other class of stock, and no more. It further provides that after $75.00 per share has been distributed to the holders of the 7% first preferred stock, the holders of the 7% second preferred stock shall be entitled to receive $62.50 per share before any distribution is made to the holders of the common stock, and no more. The balance is to be distributed to the holders of the common stock.

The certificate of incorporation of the *B* Company stipulates that, in the event of liquidation or winding up, the 7% cumulative preferred stock shall be entitled to $105.00, plus all dividends, before any distribution is made to the holders of the common stock, and no more. The balance is to be distributed to the holders of the common stock.

The certificate of incorporation of the *C* Company stipulates that after providing for all unpaid dividends on the 6% cumulative preferred stock the holders of the preferred and common stocks shall, in the event of dissolution, liquidation, or winding up, be entitled, share and share alike, to all remaining assets.

A condensed summary of the assets and liabilities of the several companies as at June 30, 1945 follows.

	A	*B*	*C*	*D*	*P*
Current assets	$450,000.00	$1,000,000.00	$1,200,000.00	$150,000.00	$ 100,000.00
Treasury stock:					
600 shares of *D* Company common				6,250.00	
Investments:					
1,000 shares of *B* Company 7% cumulative preferred	50,500.00				
9,000 shares of *D* Company common			112,500.00		
Per analysis					3,295,000.00
Fixed assets, less depreciation	200,000.00	1,200,000.00	200,000.00	17,000.00	
Other assets	9,500.00	165,000.00	27,500.00	250.00	25,000.00
Total assets	$710,000.00	$2,365,000.00	$1,540,000.00	$173,500.00	$3,420.000.00
Current liabilities	$ 85,000.00	$ 165,000.00	$ 240,000.00	$ 26,250.00	$ 70,000.00
Mortgages payable		300,000.00			
Capital stock:					
7% first preferred	250,000.00				
7% second preferred	250,000.00				
7% cumulative preferred		1,000,000.00			
6% cumulative preferred			500,000.00		
Common	100,000.00	1,000,000.00	500,000.00	100,000.00	3,000,000,00
Surplus or deficit*	25,000.00	100,000.00*	300,000.00	47,250.00	350,000.00
Total liabilities	$710,000.00	$2,365,000.00	$1,540,000.00	$173,500.00	$3,420,000.00

Prepare a schedule of the minority interest, assuming liquidation at book value.

QUESTIONS AND PROBLEMS ON CHAPTER 47

Questions

Question 47-1. Why is it necessary to create a reserve for intercompany profits on goods in the inventory of one company which were acquired from another company in the group? How should the reserve be shown on the balance sheet?

Assume that the subsidiary has a 10% minority interest. What do you think should be the amount of the reserve for intercompany profits on goods:

(*a*) In the holding company's inventory, purchased from the subsidiary?
(*b*) In the subsidiary's inventory, purchased from the holding company?

Question 47-2. Company *X* owns 90% of the stock of Company *Y*, and 85% of the stock of Company *Z*; *X* has owned this stock for several years. A consolidated balance sheet is to be prepared, on December 31, 1946, at which time there are goods in Company *Z*'s inventory which were acquired from Company *Y*. The cost to Company *Y* was $20,000.00, and the selling price to Company *Z* was $25,000.00. How should this condition be dealt with?

Question 47-3. On January 1, 1946, Company *A* acquires 90% of the stock of Company *B* and 80% of the stock of Company *C*. Included in Company *C*'s inventory are goods produced by Company *B* at a cost of $10,000.00 and billed to Company *C* at $12,000.00. How should this condition be shown in a consolidated balance sheet prepared on January 1, 1946?

Question 47-4. A company owns all of the capital stock of another company. The subsidiary company has outstanding an issue of bonds not guaranteed by the company holding the stock. The assets of the subsidiary company are deemed insufficient to cover the bonds, so that its capital stock has no value. The parent company desires the auditor to prepare its balance sheet, setting up the assets of this subsidiary company, as well as other assets directly owned, and the bonds as liabilities. Under the circumstances, is the auditor justified in preparing such a balance sheet? Give reasons for your answer.

Question 47-5. Assume that a company had a capital stock of $40,000.00 and a surplus of $10,000.00. Additional stock of a par value of $160,000.00 was issued to another company which had hitherto owned none of the stock. This company paid $230,000.00 for the stock. State the amount of goodwill which would appear in the consolidated balance sheet and the amount of the minority interest.

Question 47-6. What difficulty exists in connection with the establishment of a reserve for intercompany profits in construction which does not exist in connection with intercompany profits in inventories?

Problems

Problem 47-1. The Prince Company carries its 88% investment in the Sharon Company at cost. The Sharon Company's surplus at the date of acquisition was $30,300.00. At the date of the balance sheets given below, the Prince

Company had on hand merchandise which it had purchased from the Sharon Company for $48,000.00. The cost to the Sharon Company was $42,000.00. Owing to market declines this merchandise had been written down 5%. Included in the payables of the Prince Company is $13,466.00 owed to the Sharon Company. Prepare a consolidated balance sheet.

	Prince Company	Sharon Company
Cash	$ 43,756.00	$ 24,562.00
Accounts receivable	96,517.00	58,342.00
Inventories	115,620.00	94,685.00
Investment in Sharon Company	160,000.00	
Fixed assets	123,320.00	74,729.00
	$539,213.00	$252,318.00
Accounts payable	$ 73,456.00	$ 32,056.00
Capital stock	350,000.00	150,000.00
Surplus	115,757.00	70,262.00
	$539,213.00	$252,318.00

Problem 47-2. The Poole Company, which owns 95% of the stock of the Speare Company, has a building which was constructed for it by the Speare Company for $125,000.00. The Speare Company made a profit of $15,000.00 on this price. The building was constructed three years before the date of the balance sheets below, but after the Poole Company had acquired its interest in the Speare Company. The Poole Company has depreciated the building at 3% per annum without regard to the intercompany profit. It carries its investment in the Speare Company at book value. Prepare a consolidated balance sheet.

	Poole Company	Speare Company
Cash	$ 52,391.00	$ 27,602.00
Accounts receivable	74,956.00	38,752.00
Inventories	65,027.00	44,468.00
Investment in Speare Company	115,860.00	
Building, less depreciation	113,750.00	23,650.00
Other fixed assets	32,164.00	18,488.00
	$454,148.00	$152,960.00
Accounts payable	$ 43,615.00	$ 33,174.00
Capital stock	300,000.00	75,000.00
Surplus	110,533.00	44,786.00
	$454,148.00	$152,960.00

Problem 47-3. The Pray Fabrics Company bought $200,000.00 par value of the stock of the Santee Plastics Company directly from that company. The Pray Company carries this investment at its cost of $270,000.00. The Santee Company had a surplus of $32,000.00 immediately prior to the Pray Company's purchase. In addition to other dividends, the Santee Company subsequently paid a stock dividend of 25%. Prepare a consolidated balance sheet.

	Pray Fabrics Company	Santee Plastics Company
Investment in the Santee Company	$270,000.00	
Other assets	717,196.00	$542,675.00
	$987,196.00	$542,675.00

Liabilities	$ 52,654.00	$ 43,175.00
Capital stock	750,000.00	375,000.00
Surplus	184,542.00	124,500.00
	$987,196.00	$542,675.00

Problem 47-4. The Port Company has owned 85% of the Starboard Company for several years, and it carries its investment at book value. The stock was acquired at a time when the subsidiary had a surplus of $4,800.00. Just prior to the date of the balance sheets below, the Starboard Company sold $25,000.00 of stock to its employees at par value. The Starboard Company earned $12,600.00 during the current year, but the Port Company had not taken up its share of this profit at the time the balance sheet below was prepared. Prepare a consolidated balance sheet. No dividends were paid during the current year.

	Port Company	Starboard Company
Investment in Starboard Company	$225,575.00	
Other assets	559,309.00	$306,300.00
	$784,884.00	$306,300.00
Capital stock	$500,000.00	$225,000.00
Surplus	284,884.00	81,300.00
	$784,884.00	$306,300.00

Problem 47-5. The Powers Company has owned 90% of the stock of the Shaw Company and 80% of the stock of the Shields Company for 5 years. It carries its investments in these companies at book value. Four years ago the Shields Company constructed some special machinery for the Shaw Company. The cost of this machinery was $42,000.00, and it was billed to the Shaw Company at $55,000.00. Its estimated life was 12½ years. Prepare a consolidated balance sheet making the proper provision for the intercompany profit on this machinery.

	Powers Company	Shaw Company	Shields Company
Investment in the Shaw Company	$ 360,100.00		
Investment in the Shields Company	384,200.00		
Machinery	153,700.00	$ 75,000.00	$150,000.00
Other assets	642,000.00	380,000.00	424,000.00
	$1,540,000.00	$455,000.00	$574,000.00
Accounts payable	$ 83,750.00	$ 42,000.00	$ 38,000.00
Reserve for depreciation	74,600.00	24,000.00	62,000.00
Capital stock	1,000,000.00	200,000.00	350,000.00
Surplus	381,650.00	189,000.00	124,000.00
	$1,540,000.00	$455,000.00	$574,000.00

Problem 47-6. The Holding Company owns all the stocks of Companies *A*, *B*, and *C*. The gross profit of Companies *A* and *C* is 10% of cost, and the gross profit of Company *B* is 25% of sales. The income statement of Company *A* shows that it produced goods during the period costing $100,000.00, of which 50% was sold to Company *C*, 30% to outsiders, and 20% is on hand. The income statement of Company *C* shows goods produced at a cost of $200,000.00, of which

$55,000.00 was purchased from Company *A*, $5,000.00 from Company *B*, $105,000.00 from outsiders, and other costs of $35,000.00. Company *C* sold 80% of its produced goods to outsiders and the balance is on hand. Company *B*'s cost amounted to $3,750.00.

What should be the amount of the reserve for intercompany profit in inventories?

Problem 47-7. The balance sheets of Company *A* and its subsidiaries on December 31, 1945 were as follows:

	Company			
Assets	*A*	*X*	*Y*	*Z*
Cash	$ 40,000.00	$ 50,000.00	$ 60,000.00	$ 70,000.00
Accounts receivable		300,000.00	200,000.00	100,000.00
Company *X*	50,000.00			
Company *Y*	70,000.00			
Inventories		625,000.00	550,000.00	310,000.00
Fixed assets		890,000.00	750,000.00	380,000.00
Investments in subsidiaries:				
Company *X*—60%	850,000.00			
Company *Y*—80%	900,000.00			
Company *Z*—90%	350,000.00			
	$2,260,000.00	$1,865,000.00	$1,560,000.00	$860,000.00
Liabilities				
Accounts payable	$ 10,000.00	$ 505,000.00	$ 150,000.00	$285,000.00
Notes payable	275,000.00	20,000.00	60,000.00	250,000.00
Company *A*		40,000.00	70,000.00	
First mortgage bonds			230,000.00	
Capital stock	1,800,000.00	1,000,000.00	750,000.00	350,000.00
Surplus (deficit*)	175,000.00	300,000.00	300,000.00	25,000.00*
	$2,260,000.00	$1,865,000.00	$1,560,000.00	$860,000.00

The investments were acquired on January 1, 1945.

The surplus accounts of the four companies for 1945 are detailed below:

	Company *A*	Company *X*	Company *Y*	Company *Z*
Balance, December 31, 1944	$ 50,000.00	$280,000.00	$270,000.00	$50,000.00*
Net profit	54,000.00	100,000.00	90,000.00	25,000.00
Dividends received	96,000.00	—	—	—
Write-up of stock of Company *X*	50,000.00	—	—	—
Total	$250,000.00	$380,000.00	$360,000.00	$25,000.00*
Dividends paid	75,000.00	80,000.00	60,000.00	—
Balance, December 31, 1945	$175,000.00	$300,000.00	$300,000.00	$25,000.00*

Part of the plant of Company *X*, carried at $50,000.00, was destroyed by fire in November, 1945. The account was credited with the salvage of $10,000.00 and no other entries were made pending the insurance settlement. The claim was settled for $37,500.00 and a check was received on December 31, 1945, but entry was not made until January 3, 1946.

The inventory of Company *X* includes $80,000.00 of merchandise purchased from Company *Y*. The cost to Company *Y* was $60,000.00.

Part of the fixed assets of Company *Z* were manufactured by Company *X*. These were purchased by *Z* for $100,000.00 and cost *X* $75,000.00.

The difference between the intercompany accounts of *A* and *X* is represented by a check mailed by *X* on December 31, 1945 and not received by *A* until January 2, 1946.

Prepare a consolidated balance sheet.

Problem 47-8. You have completed an audit as of June 30, 1945 of the Temple Candy Co. and its subsidiaries. From the following data which you have gathered, prepare a worksheet showing the adjustments of the various accounts for the purpose of consolidation and also submit a consolidated balance sheet:

Balance Sheets—June 30, 1945

	Temple Candy Co.	Sweets Candy Co.	Candy Shops, Inc.
Assets			
Cash	$ 10,000.00	$ 6,000.00	$ 2,500.00
Notes receivable	7,000.00	3,000.00	
Accounts receivable	36,000.00	15,000.00	7,500.00
Merchandise inventories	20,000.00	10,000.00	5,000.00
Investments:			
Sweets Candy Co	30,000.00	—	
Candy Shops, Inc	28,000.00	—	—
Land	18,000.00	—	5,000.00
Buildings, plant, and equipment	76,000.00	35,000.00	35,000.00
Deficit	—	—	4,000.00
Total	$225,000.00	$69,000.00	$59,000.00
Liabilities and Capital			
Notes payable	$ 12,000.00	$ 6,000.00	$ 8,000.00
Accounts payable	18,000.00	7,500.00	9,000.00
Bonds payable	50,000.00	15,000.00	—
Reserves for depreciation	25,000.00	9,000.00	7,000.00
Capital stock	100,000.00	25,000.00	35,000.00
Surplus	20,000.00	6,500.00	—
Total	$225,000.00	$69,000.00	$59,000.00

The holding company acquired 90% of the capital stock of the Sweets Candy Co. July 1, 1942 at a cost of $28,000.00 and later arbitrarily increased the book value of this asset to $30,000.00, crediting the increase to surplus. 80% of the capital stock of the Candy Shops, Inc. was acquired at a cost of $28,000.00 when that company was organized, July 1, 1943.

In June 1945 the Candy Shops, Inc. sold to the Sweets Candy Co. for $1,000.00 cash, plant equipment which cost the former company (after depreciation) $500.00.

The intercompany accounts at June 30, 1945 were as follows:

The Temple Candy Co. held notes of the Sweets Candy Co. for $3,000.00 and the Candy Shops, Inc. for $4,000.00.

The Sweets Candy Co. held a note of the Candy Shops, Inc. for $3,000.00.

The Temple Candy Co. owed an open account to the Sweets Candy Co. of $4,000.00 and to the Candy Shops, Inc. of $2,500.00.

The inventories of the subsidiary companies contain goods (the Sweets Candy Co. $3,000.00 and the Candy Shops, Inc. $1,000.00) purchased from the holding company on which the latter made a profit of 10%.

The surplus accounts of the subsidiary companies, were as follows:

	Sweets Candy Co.	Candy Shops, Inc.
Balance, July 1, 1942	$4,000.00	
Profit—1942–43	3,000.00	
Balance, July 1, 1943	$7,000.00	$ —
Profit or loss—1943–44	1,500.00*	5,000.00*
Balance, July 1, 1944	$5,500.00	$5,000.00*
Profit or loss—1944–45	1,000.00	1,000.00
Balance, June 30, 1945	$6,500.00	$4,000.00*

* Designates losses or deficit.

Problem 47-9. Company *A* owns 80% of the capital stock of each of the companies *B* and *C*. Company *B* owns 90% of the capital stock of Company *D*. Company *C* owns 95% of the capital stock of Company *E*. Company *D* sells to Company *E* real estate costing $100,000.00 for $150,000.00 cash.

On the assumption that there was justification for the sale of the real estate and that the selling price was the fair market value at the time of the sale, show how the profit of $50,000.00 is to be treated in the consolidation of:

(1) Company *B* and its subsidiary, Company *D*.
(2) Company *C* and its subsidiary, Company *E*.
(3) Company *A* and its subsidiaries, Companies *B* and *C*.

Problem 47-10. From the following data prepare a consolidated balance sheet of the Alpha Company and subsidiaries as at December 31, 1946:

	Alpha Co.	Beta Co.	Gamma Co.
Cash in banks and on hand	$ 30,000.00	$ 10,000.00	$ 15,000.00
Customers' notes and accounts	90,000.00	50,000.00	60,000.00
Inventories	70,000.00	60,000.00	50,000.00
Investments at cost:			
Stock of Beta Company—75%	100,000.00		
Stock of Gamma Company—80%	200,000.00		
Property, plant, and equipment, less reserve for depreciation	500,000.00	200,000.00	120,000.00
Investment at cost—stock of Beta Company—15%			30,000.00
Deferred charges	10,000.00	5,000.00	5,000.00
	$1,000,000.00	$325,000.00	$280,000.00
Notes payable	$ 60,000.00	$ 50,000.00	$ 30,000.00
Accounts payable	40,000.00	45,000.00	20,000.00
Mortgage on plant			90,000.00
Capital stock—par value $100 a share	500,000.00	200,000.00	100,000.00
Surplus	400,000.00	30,000.00	40,000.00
	$1,000,000.00	$325,000.00	$280,000.00
Surplus:			
Earned surplus at December 31, 1945	$ 280,000.00	$ 10,000.00	$ 50,000.00
Income for year 1946	70,000.00	20,000.00	30,000.00
Increase on appraisal of land as at January 1, 1946	100,000.00		
	$ 450,000.00	$ 30,000.00	$ 80,000.00
Dividends paid	50,000.00		40,000.00
Surplus at December 31, 1946	$ 400,000.00	$ 30,000.00	$ 40,000.00

The Alpha Company acquired its holdings in "Beta" and "Gamma" on December 31, 1945. The Gamma Company's holding of Beta Company stock was purchased at an earlier date at par, which was also the book value.

QUESTIONS AND PROBLEMS ON CHAPTER 48

Questions

Question 48-1. Assume that a holding company buys a subsidiary's stock at less than its book value at the date of acquisition. Discuss different methods of dealing with the excess of the book value over purchase price, and state what you regard as the proper disposition of it.

Question 48-2. A parent company owns the stock of a subsidiary company, for the purchase of which it issued two shares of its own stock for each share of the subsidiary company's stock. The assets of the subsidiary company were sold, and after the debts of such subsidiary company were liquidated, the remaining balance was paid in cash to the parent company. How should the cash so received be treated on the books of the parent company?

Question 48-3. The Republic Stone Corporation has a number of subsidiaries, each one of which has net tangible assets either equal to or in excess of the value at which its stock is carried on the books of the parent company. The Jameson Quarry Company has net tangible assets, the fair going value of which is established by audit and appraisal to be $100,000.00. The Republic Corporation succeeds in buying all the capital stock of the Jameson Company from its various stockholders for an aggregate of $75,000.00. The directors of the Republic Corporation instruct its accounting officer to carry the Jameson stock at a value of $100,000.00 and to credit $25,000.00 to the Republic Corporation's surplus as representing the profit made on a fortunate purchase. If called upon to certify the consolidated balance sheet of the Republic Corporation, what would be your attitude toward this matter?

Question 48-4. The Excel Corporation is a holding company which owns all or a majority of the stock of several steel manufacturing companies.

On June 30, 1946 the Excel Corporation consummated the purchase of 95% of the outstanding shares of the Miller Steel Works, giving two shares of Excel Corporation common stock for one of Miller Steel Works stock.

On the date of this purchase the common no-par value stock of Excel Corporation was carried on the books at a stated value of $37,170,000.00 with 495,600 shares outstanding. The market price was $93.00 per share.

The Miller Steel Works at the same time had 65,000 shares outstanding, which were reflected on the books of the company at a value of $6,500,000.00; there was also an undistributed earned surplus of $4,226,891.58. Miller Steel Works stock was not quoted on the market, but counter sales of several hundred shares had been made early in the year at $155.00 per share.

The legal, accounting, and underwriting costs attributable to completing the stock transfers were $184,251.60, which was charged to surplus on the books of the Excel Corporation. The value of the investment in Miller Steel Works stock taken up on the books of the Excel Corporation was, by authority of the board of directors, $10,000,000.00.

In preparing a consolidated balance sheet of the Excel Corporation and its holdings at the close of the year, what adjustments should be made before eliminating the investment in Miller Steel Works?

Question 48-5. You are to certify the balance sheet and income statement of the *X* Holding Company on a nonconsolidated basis. In the course of the audit you find that its income account includes dividends from two wholly owned subsidiary companies which you do not audit. Concerning the latter you learn the following facts:

That Subsidiary *A* had a net loss for the year but has had sufficient earned surplus since the date of acquisition to cover the loss and the dividend paid; and

That Subsidiary *B* had sufficient earned surplus at the date of acquisition to cover the dividend paid, but has suffered an earned-surplus deficit since, as well as a net loss for the year.

State in what manner, if at all, you will adjust the *X* Holding Company's balance sheet or income statement, or how you will disclose the information you obtained. Give your reasons in full.

Problems

Problem 48-1. The Paddock Company purchased 80% of the stock of the Surrey Company at a price which was $180,000.00 above the book value of the stock. This excess payment represented a recognition of the fact that the Surrey Company owned mines which were worth substantially more than the amounts at which they were carried on its books. Of the depletion shown on the Surrey Company's balance sheet, $90,000.00 has accrued since the date of acquisition.

The Paddock Company carries its investment at cost. From the statements below prepare a consolidated balance sheet:

	Paddock Company	Surrey Company	
Investment in Surrey Company	$415,200.00		
Cost of mine		$300,000.00	
Less allowance for depletion		190,000.00	$110,000.00
Other assets	260,200.00		264,000.00
	$675,400.00		$374,000.00
Capital stock	$500,000.00		$200,000.00
Surplus	175,400.00		174,000.00
	$675,400.00		$374,000.00

Problem 48-2. The Parsons Company purchased a 90% interest in the Sterry Company for $118,440.00. The parent company wants the consolidated balance sheet to show the surplus legally available for dividends separately from the remaining element of economic surplus. The surplus of the Sterry Company at the date of acquisition was $31,600.00, and it has since paid a stock dividend of 20% and cash dividends of $36,000.00. You are to assume that the stock dividend did not result in the creation of legal surplus for the Parsons Company.

Prepare a consolidated balance sheet.

	Parsons Company	Sterry Company
Investment in Sterry Company	$118,440.00	
Other assets	432,652.00	$188,400.00
	$551,092.00	$188,400.00

Capital stock	$400,000.00	$120,000.00
Surplus	151,092.00	68,400.00
	$551,092.00	$188,400.00

Problem 48-3. Five years ago the Penny Company bought an 85% interest in the Sprackling Company, which it carries at book value. The Sprackling Company has decided to record an appraisal of its fixed assets. Its fixed assets were purchased at $80,000.00 at one time, and they have been depreciated at 5% per year. The appraisal states that the replacement value (new) is $120,000.00 and that the life of the assets was 25 years from the date of acquisition. It may be assumed that the increase in value has occurred evenly over the life of the fixed assets, and that it was taken into consideration by the Penny Company in making its purchase of the stock of the Sprackling Company.

From the balance sheets below, made before the appraisal was recorded, prepare a consolidated balance sheet which reflects the appraised values.

	Penny Company		Sprackling Company	
Investment in Sprackling Company		$180,800.00		
Fixed assets	$142,000.00		$80,000.00	
Less reserve for depreciation	48,000.00	94,000.00	36,000.00	$ 44,000.00
Other assets		359,650.00		154,000.00
		$634,450.00		$198,000.00
Capital stock		$500,000.00		$150,000.00
Surplus		134,450.00		48,000.00
		$634,450.00		$198,000.00

Problem 48-4. Three years ago the People's Trading Company purchased a 90% interest in the Snow Sales Company. The purchase price was considerably below the book value of the stock and reflected in part the fact that the Snow Sales Company's inventory was overstated by $12,000.00, and its fixed assets were believed to be overstated by $50,000.00, although no attempt was made to restate the value of the fixed assets. The fixed assets were being depreciated at 10% a year.

The People's Trading Company has taken its share of the profits and dividends of the Snow Sales Company into the investment account.

Based on the following balance sheets, prepare a consolidated balance sheet.

	People's Trading Company		Snow Sales Company	
Investment in Snow Sales Company		$250,000.00		
Fixed assets	$260,000.00		$220,000.00	
Less reserve for depreciation	115,000.00	145,000.00	110,000.00	$110,000.00
Other assets		444,430.00		240,000.00
		$839,430.00		$350,000.00
Capital stock		$500,000.00		$200,000.00
Surplus		339,430.00		150,000.00
		$839,430.00		$350,000.00

Problem 48-5. The Paige Company purchased a 92% interest in the Spencer Company for $90,000.00. At that time the Spencer Company's surplus was $25,600.00. From the balance sheets below prepare two consolidated balance sheets showing two different treatments of the excess of book value over cost.

	Paige Company	Spencer Company
Cash	$ 38,825.00	$ 32,154.00
Accounts receivable	62,143.00	47,563.00
Inventories	41,709.00	21,906.00
Investment in Spencer Company	90,000.00	
Fixed assets	81,523.00	41,528.00
Goodwill	10,000.00	
	$324,200.00	$143,151.00
Accounts payable	$ 42,146.00	$ 17,624.00
Capital stock	200,000.00	80,000.00
Surplus	82,054.00	45,527.00
	$324,200.00	$143,151.00

Problem 48-6. The balance sheets of two companies appeared as follows on May 31, 1945:

	Alpha Company	Beta Company
Assets		
Cash	$150,000.00	$ 30,000.00
Accounts and notes receivable	32,000.00†	10,000.00
Inventories	52,000.00	31,000.00
Land and buildings	60,000.00	42,000.00
	$294,000.00	$113,000.00
Liabilities		
Accounts payable	$ 21,000.00	$ 32,000.00†
Reserve for depreciation	15,000.00	8,400.00
Reserve for bad debts	650.00	200.00
Capital stock	100,000.00	75,000.00
Surplus (deficit*)	157,350.00	2,600.00*
	$294,000.00	$113,000.00

†Includes $9,000.00 due from Beta Company to Alpha Company.

The fixed assets of the companies are appraised as follows:

	Alpha	Beta
Reproduction cost—new	$100,000.00	$ 72,000.00
Accrued depreciation (per appraisal)	25,000.00	18,000.00

The stockholders of Beta Company agree to sell their stock to Alpha Company for $125,000.00, and to use a portion of the cash thus obtained to pay off all the liabilities of Beta Company.

Prepare entries to be made on the books of both companies to reflect the appraisals and the stated transactions, and prepare consolidated balance sheet working papers.

Problem 48-7. On March 31, 1946 Company *A* acquired for cash at a cost of $150,000.00, 950 shares of the capital stock of Company *B*. On December 31, 1946 trial balances after closing the operating accounts of the two companies appeared as follows:

	Company *A* Debit	Company *A* Credit	Company *B* Debit	Company *B* Credit
Accounts receivable	$ 235,000.00		$ 30,000.00	
Accounts payable		$ 160,000.00		$ 81,000.00
Capital stock—$100.00 par value		700,000.00		100,000.00
Cash	25,000.00		6,000.00	
Company *A*				65,000.00
Company *B*	65,000.00			
Dividends paid	200,000.00			
Inventories	265,000.00		63,000.00	
Investment in Company *B*—at cost	150,000.00			
Machinery and equipment	265,000.00		237,000.00	
Profit and loss—earned proportionately through the year		250,000.00		40,000.00
Surplus, January 1, 1946		95,000.00		50,000.00
	$1,205,000.00	$1,205,000.00	$336,000.00	$336,000.00

Prepare a consolidated balance sheet as of December 31, 1946.

Problem 48-8. The balance sheets of Companies *X*, *Y*, and *Z*, as at December 31, 1946, were as follows:

	Company *X*	Company *Y*	Company *Z*
Cash	$ 50,000.00	$ 25,000.00	$ 25,000.00
Accounts receivable	375,000.00	60,000.00	25,000.00
Notes receivable	25,000.00		
Inventories	300,000.00	175,000.00	140,000.00
Investments:			
Capital stock of Company *Y*	250,000.00		
Capital stock of Company *Z*	100,000.00		
Land	85,000.00	10,000.00	5,000.00
Buildings	600,000.00	150,000.00	100,000.00
Machinery and equipment	300,000.00	90,000.00	30,000.00
Deferred charges	15,000.00		
Goodwill	1,000,000.00	200,000.00	
Deficit			50,000.00
	$3,100,000.00	$710,000.00	$375,000.00
Accounts payable	$ 50,000.00	$170,000.00	$168,000.00
Notes payable	135,000.00	55,000.00	50,000.00
Accrued liabilities	10,000.00	3,000.00	900.00
First mortgage 6% bonds	500,000.00		
Reserve for depreciation—buildings	60,000.00	18,000.00	4,000.00
Reserve for depreciation—machinery and equipment	45,000.00	14,000.00	2,100.00
Capital stock—7% preferred	1,000,000.00		
Capital stock—common	1,000,000.00	150,000.00	150,000.00
Surplus	300,000.00	300,000.00	
	$3,100,000.00	$710,000.00	$375,000.00

Company *X* acquired a 95% interest in Company *Y* and a 90% interest in Company *Z* on January 1, 1946, at which time Company *Y* had a surplus of $240,000.00 and Company *Z* a deficit of $60,000.00.

Immediately thereafter Company Z purchased factory buildings from Company X for \$100,000.00; the cost of the buildings to Company X was \$80,000.00. Company Z provided for depreciation at the rate of 4% on buildings and 7% on machinery and equipment.

The X company's inventories at December 31, 1946 contained goods purchased from the Y and Z companies, on which those companies made profits of \$10,000.00 and \$5,000.00 respectively.

The accounts receivable of Company X include \$150,000.00 due from Company Y and \$100,000.00 due from Company Z. The accounts receivable of Company Y include \$20,000.00 due from Company Z.

On the basis of the above information prepare a consolidated balance sheet at December 31, 1946. Submit your working papers relative thereto.

Problem 48-9. The Universal Patent Corporation acquired 700 shares of the capital stock of the General Development Company as follows:

Date Acquired	Number of Shares	Purchase Price
January 2, 1945	600	\$300,000
June 30, 1945	100	46,000

The audited balance sheets of the General Development Company are given below:

	Jan. 1 1945	June 30 1945	Dec. 31 1945
Assets			
Cash	\$ 30,000	\$ 78,000	\$ 40,000
Royalties receivable	60,000	65,000	50,000
Patent	60,000	57,000	54,000
	\$150,000	\$200,000	\$144,000
Liabilities			
Federal income tax payable	\$ 20,000	\$ 19,000	\$ 25,000
Sundry liabilities	5,000	6,000	4,000
Capital stock—1,000 shares	100,000	100,000	100,000
Earned surplus	25,000	75,000	15,000
	\$150,000	\$200,000	\$144,000

Adequate provision was made for amortization of the patent by a straight-line method and for all liabilities, including taxes. On December 30, 1945 a dividend of \$150,000 had been paid.

On that same date the shareholders of the General Development Company ordered the liquidation of the company as at the close of December 31, 1945. The shareholders were to receive a prorata assignment of their interest in the patent on January 2, 1946. The collection of royalties receivable, payment of liabilities, and distribution of available cash was to be effected not later than February 15, 1946, and \$1,000 was appropriated for the estimated expenses in the period of liquidation.

From the foregoing information determine the amount which the Universal Patent Corporation should charge to its patent account to record the amortized cost of its interest in the patent on the date of assignment.

PROBLEMS ON CHAPTER 49

Problems

Problem 49-1. Purchases of stock were made by a major parent and its subsidiaries as follows:

January 1, 1942 Company *A* purchased 1,600 shares of Company *B* at $ 80.00 a share.
Company *A* purchased 1,200 shares of Company *C* at $150.00 a share.

January 1, 1943 Company *A* purchased 100 shares of Company *D* at $125.00 a share.
Company *B* purchased 700 shares of Company *D* at $130.00 a share.

January 1, 1944 Company *C* purchased 150 shares of Company *D* at $140.00 a share.
Company *A* purchased 200 shares of Company *B* at $ 90.00 a share.

All shares have a par value of $100.00.

The surplus accounts of the companies may be summarized as follows:

	Company *A*	Company *B*	Company *C*	Company *D*
Balance, January 1, 1942	$342,000.00	$20,000.00*	$60,000.00	$20,000.00
Profits (losses*), 1942	80,000.00	10,000.00*	30,000.00	15,000.00
Dividends received 1942	16,000.00			
Dividends paid 1942	50,000.00*		20,000.00*	10,000.00*
Balances, January 1, 1943	$388,000.00	$30,000.00*	$70,000.00	$25,000.00
Profits 1943	110,000.00	20,000.00	40,000.00	20,000.00
Dividends received 1943	17,500.00	10,500.00		
Dividends paid 1943	50,000.00*		20,000.00*	15,000.00*
Balances, January 1, 1944	$465,500.00	$ 500.00	$90,000.00	$30,000.00
Profits (losses*), 1944	130,000.00	30,000.00	10,000.00*	25,000.00
Dividends received 1944	27,000.00	14,000.00	3,000.00	
Dividends paid 1944	100,000.00*	10,000.00*	20,000.00*	20,000.00*
Balances, December 31, 1944	$522,500.00	$34,500.00	$63,000.00	$35,000.00

The balance sheets of these companies may be summarized as follows:

	Company *A*	Company *B*	Company *C*	Company *D*
Investment in *B*	$ 146,000.00			
Investment in *C*	180,000.00			
Investment in *D*	12,500.00	$ 91,000.00	$ 21,000.00	
Goodwill	50,000.00	10,000.00	5,000.00	
Other assets—net	1,134,000.00	133,500.00	187,000.00	$135,000.00
	$1,522,500.00	$234,500.00	$213,000.00	$135,000.00
Capital stock	$1,000,000.00	$200,000.00	$150,000.00	$100,000.00
Surplus	522,500.00	34,500.00	63,000.00	35,000.00
	$1,522,500.00	$234,500.00	$213,000.00	$135,000.00

(*a*) Prepare a consolidated balance sheet on December 31, 1945.
(*b*) Prove the amount of the goodwill shown on your consolidated balance sheet by an independent computation.

Problem 49-2. The Adams Company purchased stock in the Bushnell Company as follows:

February 1, 1944	60% for $85,000.00
March 1, 1945	30% for $55,000.00

On January 1, 1946 the Bushnell Company offered its stockholders rights to purchase one new share at par value, $100.00, for each five old shares held. The Adams Company exercised all of its rights, but only half of the minority stockholders' rights were exercised.

The surplus account of the Bushnell Company follows:

January 1, 1944 balance		$28,000.00
Profits, 1944		24,000.00
Dividends paid in December 1944	$10,000.00	
Profits, 1945		36,000.00
Dividends paid in December 1945	15,000.00	
Loss, 1946	10,000.00	
Dividends paid in December 1946	20,000.00	
Balance, December 31, 1946	33,000.00	
	$88,000.00	$88,000.00

Assume that all earnings were realized evenly throughout the year.

Prepare a consolidated balance sheet based on the balance sheets below, dated December 31, 1946.

	Adams Company	Bushnell Company
Investment in Bushnell Company	$167,000.00	
Current assets	215,132.00	$155,900.00
Fixed assets	300,165.00	95,630.00
Goodwill	30,000.00	
	$712,297.00	$251,530.00
Current liabilities	$ 62,384.00	$ 40,030.00
Capital stock	500,000.00	178,500.00
Surplus	149,913.00	33,000.00
	$712,297.00	$251,530.00

Problem 49-3. The Newhall Company bought 825 of the 1,000 shares of $100.00 par value stock of the Chaney Corporation for $132.00 a share on January 1, 1945. On January 1, 1946 the Newhall Company purchased another 100 shares at the same price.

The Newhall Company wants to sell 100 shares of this stock on January 1, 1947 at the market price of $112.00 a share. It has kept the investment at book value, and it wants to select the stock to be sold from the purchase which will reduce the recorded loss to a minimum. (No question of tax saving is involved.)

The surplus account of the Chaney Company follows:

Balance, January 1, 1945		$48,000.00
Profit, 1945		24,000.00
Dividends, 1945	$20,000.00	
Loss, 1946	14,000.00	
Dividends, 1946	5,000.00	
Balance, December 31, 1946	33,000.00	
	$72,000.00	$72,000.00

(*a*) Out of which purchase should it make the sale?
(*b*) How much will it reduce its loss?
(*c*) What will be the carrying value of the investment after the sale?

Problem 49-4. The Wellington Company owns 80% of the stock of the Dunning Company. The Wellington Company carries this stock at book value, and the balance of the investment account is currently $260,000.00. The net worth sections of the balance sheets of the two companies follow:

	Wellington Company	Dunning Company
Capital stock (par value $100.00 a share)...	$600,000.00	$200,000.00
Surplus..................................	60,000.00	120,000.00

A large stockholder offers to sell a 20% interest in the Wellington Company at $130.00 a share. The Wellington Company is anxious to purchase the stock. Would it be to the advantage of the Wellington Company to buy this stock out of its own funds, or to have the Dunning Company purchase it? Prepare statements to support your conclusion.

Problem 49-5. The balance sheets of a parent company and its subsidiary follow:

	Wilcox Company	McClure Company
Investment in McClure Company..........	$171,000.00	
Goodwill................................	30,000.00	
Other assets—net........................	773,360.00	$370,000.00
	$974,360.00	$370,000.00
Capital stock (par value $100.00)..........	$800,000.00	$250,000.00
Surplus..................................	174,360.00	120,000.00
	$974,360.00	$370,000.00

You are to prepare a consolidated balance sheet based on the following information: The Wilcox Company originally bought 1,800 shares of the McClure Company at $115.00 a share. At that time the McClure Company's surplus was $30,000.00. Later the McClure Company paid a 25% stock dividend and thereafter the Wilcox Company sold 250 shares of the stock at $144.00 a share. The investment is carried at cost less the proceeds of the sale.

Problem 49-6. Phoenix Smelting Company (Co. *A*) has agreed to purchase the minority interest in Phoenix Mining Company (Co. *B*). Their balance sheets show:

	(Co. *A*) Phoenix Smelting Co.		(Co. *B*) Phoenix Mining Co.
Assets			
Tangible assets.....	$3,764,513.00		$2,264,718.00
Goodwill..........	500,000.00		
91,000 shares of Co. *B*	1,270,000.00	5,373 shares Co. *A*	622,443.00
	$5,534,513.00		$2,887,161.00
Liabilities			
Creditors..........	$ 367,423.00		$ 133,675.00
Capital stock 40,000 shares..........	4,000,000.00	100,000 shares	2,500,000.00
Surplus............	1,167,090.00		253,486.00
	$5,534,513.00		$2,887,161.00

The stock is to be acquired at asset value, but in the computation the goodwill of either company is not to be considered. How much should be paid to the minority stockholders per share of Company *B*? Do not carry your computation further than whole cents per share.

Problem 49-7. From the information following, prepare a consolidated balance sheet of *H* Co. and subsidiaries, *A* Co. and *B* Co., as at Dec. 31, 1944.

H Co., an operating company, acquired 90% of the outstanding stock of *B* Co. on March 31, 1944 for $162,000.00. Previously, *H* Co. acquired 30% of the outstanding stock of *A* Co., on January 1, 1943, for $25,000.00. On July 1, 1944 *H* Co. purchased an additional 40% of the outstanding stock of *A* Co. for $42,000.00 thereby gaining effective control of *A* Co. as at that date. In order further to increase its stockholdings in *A* Co. without impairing working capital, *H* Co. sold 100 shares of *B* Co. stock on October 1, 1944 for $20,500.00 and immediately used $13,800.00 of the proceeds to secure an additional 15% of *A* Co. outstanding stock.

The balance sheets of the respective companies as at December 31, 1944 are set forth as follows:

Assets	*H* Co.	*A* Co.	*B* Co.
Cash in banks	$ 86,000	$ 12,500	$ 35,000
Notes receivable	18,000	6,000	8,000
Accounts receivable (less reserve)	52,000	13,000	34,000
Inventories	89,500	16,000	51,000
Investment in Company *A* (at cost)	80,800		
Investment in Company *B* (at book value)	149,320		
Plant and equipment (less reserves)	225,000	56,500	101,000
	$700,620	$104,000	$229,000
Liabilities			
Notes payable	$ 9,000	$ 8,000	$ 12,000
Accounts payable	73,600	22,400	46,200
Accrued liabilities	5,320	2,600	4,800
Capital stock—common, $100 par	400,000	60,000	100,000
Earned surplus	212,700	11,000	66,000
	$700,620	$104,000	$229,000

A summary of earned surplus (deficit) from January 1, 1943 to December 31, 1944 is as follows:

	H Co.	*A* Co.	*B* Co.
Balance at January 1, 1943	$150,000	($10,000)	$40,000
Net profit or (loss)—1943:			
1st quarter	7,000	(2,000)	3,000
2nd quarter	9,000	1,000	4,000
3rd quarter	15,000	3,000	6,000
4th quarter	12,000	6,000	5,000
Total	$193,000	($ 2,000)	$58,000
Dividends declared and paid on July 1, 1943	12,000		3,000
Balance at January 1, 1944	$181,000	($ 2,000)	$55,000
Net profit or (loss)—1944:			
1st quarter	6,000	2,500	4,500
2nd quarter	11,500	3,000	7,000
3rd quarter	13,000	3,600	6,200
4th quarter	16,200	5,900	5,300
Total	$227,700	$13,000	$78,000

Total (brought forward)	$227,700	$13,000	$78,000
Dividends declared June 1, 1944 and paid on June 15, 1944	15,000		12,000
Dividends declared December 1, 1944 and paid on Dec. 15, 1944		2,000	
Balance, December 31, 1944—Surplus	$212,700	$11,000	$66,000

Net profit of *H* Co. for the fourth quarter of 1944 includes an amount of $2,500 representing the gain on the sale of 100 shares of *B* Co. stock. (Proceeds $20,500, less March 31, 1944 cost, $18,000.)

Inventories at December 31, 1944 include intercompany items as follows:

	Company		Amount	
Date of Transaction	Purchaser	Seller	Inventory	Seller's Cost
April 5, 1944	*H*	*A*	$ 3,600	$ 3,000
August 15, 1944	*H*	*B*	5,000	4,500*
October 5, 1944	*H*	*A*	10,000	9,000
May 15, 1944	*A*	*B*	7,000	6,200
September 26, 1944	*A*	*B*	6,000	4,800
November 12, 1944	*B*	*A*	16,000	14,000

* Acquired on July 20, 1944 by *B* from *A*, *A*'s cost then being $4,200.

Problem 49-8. From the following data prepare a consolidation of the balance sheets of the Top Holding Company and its subsidiaries:

Balance Sheets

	Top Holding Co.	Subsidiaries *R* Co.	Subsidiaries *S* Co.
Assets			
Current assets	$150,000	$30,000	$118,110
Property, less reserves	47,000	5,500	130,000
Investment *R* Co. stock:			
90%	18,000		
10%			2,500
Investment *S* Co. stock:			
75%	45,000		
15%		9,000	
Investment *S* Co. bonds	41,500		
	$301,500	$44,500	$250,610
Liabilities			
Current liabilities	$ 80,000	$23,000	$ 70,000
Bonds payable			100,000
Capital stock	200,000	30,000	50,000
Surplus at acquisition		1,500	5,000
Earned surplus (deficit)	21,500	(10,000)	25,610
	$301,500	$44,500	$250,610

The investments in *R* Co. stock are carried at cost less subsequent net losses; the investments in *S* Co. stock at cost. The bonds were acquired at $1,500 discount and are held for cancellation.

Problem 49-9.

Company *A* owns 40% of the capital stock of Company *B*
" *A* " 30% " " " " " " *C*
" *B* " 10% " " " " " " *A*
" *B* " 50% " " " " " " *C*
" *C* " 10% " " " " " " *A*
" *C* " 40% " " " " " " *B*

Each company has 10% of its capital stock in its treasury, and all stocks are carried on the books at cost.

The assets of the three companies are:

	A	*B*	*C*
Investment in *A*	$ 10,000.00	$12,000.00	$15,000.00
" " *B*	20,000.00	4,000.00	10,000.00
" " *C*	30,000.00	15,000.00	2,000.00
Other assets (net)	100,000.00	50,000.00	30,000.00
	$160,000.00	$81,000.00	$57,000.00

Determine the respective amounts of net assets belonging to the outside shareholders of companies *A*, *B*, and *C*. Do not consider fractions of dollars in any of the calculations.

Problem 49-10. Prepare a consolidated balance sheet on the basis of the following facts:

	X	*Y*	*Z*
Assets	$200,000.00	$100,000.00	$100,000.00
Stock of *Y* (par)	40,000.00	—	5,000.00
Stock of *Z* (par)	40,000.00	5,000.00	—
Deficit	—	15,000.00	—
	$280,000.00	$120,000.00	$105,000.00
Liabilities	$100,000.00	$ 70,000.00	$ 25,000.00
Capital stock	150,000.00	50,000.00	50,000.00
Surplus	30,000.00		30,000.00
	$280,000.00	$120,000.00	$105,000.00

The three companies were organized on the same date, and the stock acquisitions were made at par on the date of organization.

Problem 49-11. From the following information prepare a work sheet showing the consolidation of the balance sheets of Top Company and its subsidiaries as at June 30, 1945:

Balance Sheets—June 30, 1945

	Top Company	Black Company	White Company	Red Company
Assets				
Cash	$ 10,000.00	$ 80,000.00	$ 60,000.00	$ 25,000.00
Accounts receivable		100,000.00	200,000.00	80,000.00
Inventories		200,000.00	300,000.00	100,000.00
Fixed assets	1,000.00	900,000.00	1,000,000.00	500,000.00
Prepaid expenses	500.00	5,000.00	6,000.00	3,000.00
Investments:				
Black Company—$300,000.00 bonds	275,000.00			
Black Company—10,000 shares	300,000.00			
White Company—6,000 shares	690,000.00			
Red Company—800 shares	80,000.00			
Intercompany accounts	300,000.00	12,000.00	15,000.00	
	$1,656,500.00	$1,297,000.00	$1,581,000.00	$708,000.00

	Top Company	Black Company	White Company	Red Company
Liabilities and Capital				
Accounts payable....	$ 10,000.00	$ 95,000.00	$ 94,000.00	$150,000.00
Accrued taxes.......	5,000.00	10,000.00	18,000.00	4,000.00
Accrued interest.....		6,750.00		
Intercompany accounts..........		10,000.00		310,000.00
Notes payable to Top Company.........			200,000.00	
Reserve for depreciation..............	500.00	400,000.00	350,000.00	250,000.00
6% mortgage bonds, due October 1, 1954		450,000.00		
Capital stock—$100.00 par............	1,500,000.00		800,000.00	100,000.00
Capital stock—10,000 shares, no par.....		300,000.00		
Earned surplus (deficit*)............	141,000.00	25,250.00	119,000.00	106,000.00*
	$1,656,500.00	$1,297,000.00	$1,581,000.00	$708,000.00

An analysis of Top Company's investment in subsidiaries shows the following:

	Date of Transaction	Shares or Bonds Acquired or Sold*	Cost or Proceeds*	Surplus or Deficit* of Subsidiary at Date of Transaction
Black Company bonds (bought for the sinking fund)...............	Sept. 30, 1940	$ 80,000.00	$ 76,000.00	$ 25,000.00
	Nov. 30, 1942	200,000.00	180,000.00	15,000.00*
	Dec. 29, 1944	20,000.00	19,000.00	12,000.00
Black Company stock...	July 1, 1936	10,000 shs.	300,000.00	
White Company bonds..	July 1, 1940	$ 50,000.00	40,000.00	10,000.00*
	Oct. 1, 1943	50,000.00*	50,000.00*(Redeemed)	
White Company stock...	July 1, 1937	8,000 shs.	1,000,000.00	100,000.00
	Dec. 1, 1944	2,000 shs.*	300,000.00*(Sold)	100,000.00
Red Company stock.....	Sept. 1, 1936	600 shs.	70,000.00	20,000.00
	Sept. 1, 1940	200 shs.	10,000.00	5,000.00*

The Top Company was incorporated in 1934. In the same year it incorporated a wholly-owned subsidiary, the Green Company, with paid-in capital of $300,000.00. On July 1, 1936, the net assets of Green Company, in the amount of $250,000.00, were transferred to Black Company in exchange for its capital stock, which had a stated value of $300,000.00. The difference between this stated value and the net assets taken over was added to the fixed assets of Black Company as representing goodwill. This goodwill amount has been amortized by Black Company by charges to operations at the rate of 5% per annum. Green Company was dissolved, the stock of Black Company being turned over to Top Company as a liquidating dividend.

There has been no change in the share capital of the subsidiaries since their incorporation.

On June 29, 1945, White Company drew a check to the order of Top Company for $2,000.00. This check was received and recorded by Top Company on July 1, 1945.

On June 3, 1945, Black Company shipped White Company merchandise in the amount of $5,000.00. White Company's accounting department did not receive the invoice for these goods and did not record the liability therefor. However, when the physical inventory was taken on June 30, 1945, this merchandise was included at the value of $5,000.00.

On June 30, 1942, Black Company sold Red Company certain machinery for $80,000.00. Red Company has provided depreciation on this amount for the years ended June 30, 1943, 1944, and 1945, at 10% per annum on the basis of an estimated useful life of ten years after the date of purchase. This machinery had cost Black Company $75,000.00, and that company had provided a depreciation reserve of $25,000.00 to June 30, 1942, on the basis of 6⅔% per annum. Black Company took the $30,000.00 book profit and eliminated from its accounts the cost of the machinery, as well as the accrued depreciation.

Inventories on June 30, 1945 included the following amounts purchased from affiliated companies:

Company	Purchased from	Amount
Red Company	White Company	$25,300.00
Red Company	Black Company	16,500.00
White Company	Black Company	86,000.00

White Company sold its products to affiliated companies at 15% and Black Company at 25% above cost.

On June 30, 1945, Top Company had discounted at the bank $200,000.00 of notes receivable from White Company.

Top Company has guaranteed the liabilities of the Red Company.

Problem 49-12. The following balances appear on the books of a parent company and its subsidiary on the dates stated:

	Jan. 1 1944	Dec. 31 1944	Dec. 31 1945	Dec. 31 1946
Parent company:				
Investment in subsidiary	$128,000	$128,000	$119,000	$140,000
Surplus	135,000	160,000	148,000	155,000
Subsidiary:				
Capital stock	100,000	100,000	100,000	100,000
Surplus	50,000	62,000	70,000	80,000

The subsidiary's capital stock consists of 1,000 shares of $100 each. The parent company purchased 800 shares on January 1, 1944, sold 50 shares on January 1, 1945, and purchased 100 shares on January 1, 1946. The investment account was charged with the cost of stock purchased and credited with the proceeds from the stock sold. The parent company has made no other entries in the investment account and has credited income with all dividends received from the subsidiary.

Prepare statements showing the composition of the amounts of goodwill, surplus, and minority interest that would appear on the consolidated balance sheets at December 31, 1944, 1945, and 1946.

QUESTIONS AND PROBLEMS ON CHAPTER 50

Questions

Question 50-1. Explain why the three conditions described in this chapter as facilitating conditions simplify the preparation of the consolidated statements.

Question 50-2. Why is it unnecessary to detail the end-of-period inventories by companies in the consolidated working papers?

Question 50-3. Why is it desirable to have separate surplus and minority columns in the working papers?

Question 50-4. In the case of purchases and sales between a parent company and its subsidiary, how should such transactions be shown on the books of each company and on the consolidated profit and loss statements?

Problems

Problem 50-1. From the following trial balances prepare consolidated statements of profit and loss and surplus for the year ended December 31, 1945, and a consolidated balance sheet. There were intercompany sales of $32,400.00 during the year. The closing inventory of the Pensacola Company was $62,148.00 and of the Savannah Company, $37,460.00. The Pensacola Company charged the Savannah Company $18,200.00 for advertising, by charging the current account and crediting the expense account.

	Pensacola Company	Savannah Company
Cash	$ 91,756.00	$ 44,750.00
Accounts receivable	103,244.00	94,150.00
Inventories—December 31, 1944	48,174.00	35,170.00
Savannah current account	21,430.00	
Investment in Savannah Company—85%	120,591.00	
Purchases	406,103.00	193,632.00
Expenses	143,824.00	129,348.00
Dividends paid	25,000.00	15,000.00
	$960,122.00	$512,050.00
Accounts payable	$ 32,176.00	$ 15,600.00
Pensacola current account		21,430.00
Capital stock	200,000.00	100,000.00
Surplus—December 31, 1944	164,426.00	32,460.00
Sales	563,520.00	342,560.00
	$960,122.00	$512,050.00

Problem 50-2. From the following trial balances prepare consolidated statements of profit and loss and surplus for the year ending December 31, 1945 and a consolidated balance sheet. The advertising income represents amounts collected from the Colonial Theatre Company for space paid for by the Indiana Theatre Company.

	Indiana Theatre Company	Colonial Theatre Company
Cash	$ 32,740.00	$ 28,550.00
Land, building, and fixtures	104,840.00	52,000.00
Investment in Colonial Theatre Company—80%	51,800.00	
Expenses	43,720.00	12,450.00
Dividends paid	25,000.00	15,000.00
	$258,100.00	$108,000.00
Accounts payable	$ 4,360.00	$ 2,600.00
Dividends payable		5,000.00
Capital stock	125,000.00	50,000.00
Surplus, December 31, 1944	42,400.00	16,400.00
Ticket sales	82,140.00	34,000.00
Advertising income	4,200.00	
	$258,100.00	$108,000.00

The Indiana Theatre Company has owned its stock in the Colonial Theatre Company for several years.

Problem 50-3. The Palmer Company bought 95% of the stock of the Sturgis Company for $135,000.00 on January 1, 1945. Both companies keep their books on a perpetual inventory basis. During the year the Palmer Company purchased $48,000.00 of merchandise from the Sturgis Company. From the following trial balances prepare consolidated statements of profit and loss and surplus and a consolidated balance sheet for the parent company and its subsidiary.

	Palmer Company	Sturgis Company
Cash	$ 56,410.00	$ 19,500.00
Accounts receivable	72,650.00	76,200.00
Inventories	58,090.00	26,450.00
Fixed assets	110,730.00	42,000.00
Cost of goods sold	433,240.00	287,500.00
Expenses	92,085.00	36,370.00
Dividends	20,000.00	10,000.00
Investment in Sturgis Company	127,875.00	
	$971,080.00	$498,020.00
Accounts payable	$ 23,160.00	$ 15,600.00
Capital stock	300,000.00	100,000.00
Surplus, December 31, 1944	83,720.00	40,000.00
Sales	564,200.00	342,420.00
	$971,080.00	$498,020.00

Problem 50-4. The Pritchard Company has owned 95% of the stock of the Sherman Company for several years. The Sherman Company maintains perpetual inventories, whereas the Pritchard Company uses periodic inventories. The closing inventory for the Sherman Company on December 31, 1944 was $32,410.00, and the inventory for the Pritchard Company on December 31, 1945 was $73,084.00. There were intercompany sales of $107,450.00 during the year. From the trial balances for the year ended December 31, 1945, which follow, prepare consolidated statements of profit and loss and surplus and a consolidated balance sheet. **The Pritchard Company wants the statement on a periodic inventory basis.**

	Pritchard Company	Sherman Company
Cash	$ 78,404.00	$ 19,400.00
Accounts receivable	153,179.00	92,650.00
Inventories:		
December 31, 1944	68,375.00	
December 31, 1945		35,744.00
Purchases	842,563.00	
Cost of goods sold		605,390.00
Expenses	471,068.00	168,442.00
Investment in Sherman Company	151,160.00	
Other investments	2,800.00	23,400.00
Fixed assets	344,290.00	36,172.00
Dividends paid	50,000.00	10,000.00
	$2,161,839.00	$991,198.00
Accounts payable	$ 24,835.00	$ 17,248.00
Capital stock	500,000.00	100,000.00
Surplus—December 31, 1944	164,320.00	62,400.00
Gain on sale of fixed assets	6,100.00	
Sales	1,466,416.00	810,350.00
Dividends received	168.00	1,200.00
	$2,161,839.00	$991,198.00

Problem 50-5. From the following information prepare consolidated working papers for 1946.

	Company *P*	Company *S*
Debits		
Cash	$ 21,848	$ 17,960
Accounts receivable:		
Company *S*	8,000	
Other	36,275	18,355
Notes receivable:		
Company *S*	5,000	
Other	6,500	3,000
Inventory—December 31, 1945	59,330	29,860
Purchases	273,725	123,250
Expenses	71,215	31,115
Interest expense	1,250	
Investment in Company *S*—95%	40,627	
Land and buildings	80,000	
	$603,770	$223,540
Credits		
Sales	$375,000	$169,200
Accounts payable:		
Company *P*		8,000
Other	33,650	
Notes payable:		
Company *P*		5,000
Other	20,000	
Reserve for depreciation	8,375	
Reserve for bad debts	1,200	680
Mortgage on land and buildings	25,000	
Capital stock	100,000	30,000
Surplus	40,545	10,660
	$603,770	$223,540
Inventories, December 31, 1946	$ 55,625	$ 31,225

Sales by Company *P* to Company *S* during 1946, $26,500.00.
The facilitating conditions described in Chapter 50 exist.

Problem 50-6. This problem is based on the same facts as Problem 50-5 except that it is now assumed that both companies declared dividends on December 31, 1946, and made the following entries:

Company *S*:		
Dividends	$ 3,000	
Dividends payable		$ 3,000
To record declaration of dividend		
Company *P*:		
Dividends receivable	2,850	
Investment in Company *S*		2,850
To record 85% of dividend declared by subsidiary		
Dividends	10,000	
Dividends payable		10,000
To record declaration of dividend		

Apply these entries to the trial balances in Problem 50-5, and prepare consolidated working papers for the year.

Problem 50-7. From the following data prepare consolidated statements for the year ended December 31, 1946. All facilitating conditions exist.

	Manufacturing Company	Selling Company
Debits		
Cash	$ 38,620	$ 9,680
Accounts receivable—customers	16,850	58,260
Notes receivable	10,000	
Accrued interest receivable	150	
Dividends receivable	4,500	
Land	20,000	
Factory building	75,000	
Tools and equipment	18,000	
Sales office (used by subsidiary):		
Land	5,000	
Building	25,000	
Equipment		10,000
Inventories—December 31, 1945:		
Finished goods		61,400
Goods in process	15,000	
Raw materials	35,000	
Purchases:		
Raw materials	190,000	
Merchandise		505,000
Direct labor	151,250	
Depreciation:		
Factory assets	5,750	
Sales office assets	1,250	1,000
Other manufacturing expenses	115,000	
Selling expenses		21,200
Management fees		7,500
Other general expenses	48,440	9,870
Sales allowances	1,300	1,260
Discount on sales	4,600	5,900
Bad debts		2,000

Debits (continued)	Manufacturing Company	Selling Company
Mortgage interest	$ 2,000	
Rent of office building		$ 3,500
Interest on notes payable		600
Investment in selling company	72,806	
Dividends	20,000	10,000
	$875,516	$707,170
Credits		
Accounts payable—suppliers	$ 23,720	$ 16,850
Notes payable		10,000
Accrued interest payable		150
Mortgage payable	40,000	
Dividends payable	20,000	5,000
Reserve for depreciation	19,300	2,500
Reserve for bad debts		2,980
Sales	505,000	578,450
Discount on purchases	1,700	4,600
Purchase allowances	1,950	1,300
Rent of office to subsidiary	3,500	
Management fee	7,500	
Interest income	600	
Capital stock	200,000	50,000
Surplus—December 31, 1945	52,246	35,340
	$875,516	$707,170
Inventories—December 31, 1946:		
Finished merchandise		$ 59,750
Goods in process	$ 14,720	
Raw materials	33,780	

Problem 50-8. On January 1, 1946 the *F* company purchased 90% of the stock of Company *G* and 80% of the stock of Company *H*. Wishing to acquire the remaining stock of the more profitable company (Company *H*), Company *F* on June 30, 1946 disposed of 200 shares of its holdings in Company *G* at a price of $160 per share, and on that date was successful in acquiring an additional 10% of the stock of Company *H* in exchange for the entire proceeds of the sale of Company *G* stock.

The investment accounts on the books of Company *F* are carried at cost except the account representing the investment in capital stock of Company *G*; this account has been credited with the proceeds of the 200 shares sold.

From the following post-closing trial balances of the three companies at December 31, 1946 prepare:

1. A consolidated balance sheet.
2. A statement of consolidated earned surplus.
3. A statement of goodwill.

Assets	*F*	*G*	*H*
Current assets	$152,500	$150,000	$105,000
Investment in subsidiary companies:			
Company *G*:			
Capital stock	220,000		
Advances	25,000		
Company *H*:			
Capital stock	214,000		
Advances	40,000		
Buildings and equipment		170,000	235,000
	$651,500	$320,000	$340,000

Liabilities

Capital stock:			
Company *F*—3,000 shares	$300,000		
Company *G*—2,000 shares		$200,000	
Company *H*—1,000 shares			$100,000
Due to parent company		25,000	40,000
Accounts payable	235,000	40,000	25,000
Surplus at beginning of year	166,500	60,000	145,000
Profit for the year	20,000†	15,000	40,000
Dividends (paid Dec. 31, 1946)	70,000*	20,000*	10,000*
	$651,500	$320,000	$340,000

* Deduction.
† Dividends received from subsidiary companies, less expenses of parent company.

It is assumed that the profits of the companies for the year 1946 were divided equally between the two six months' periods.

QUESTIONS AND PROBLEMS ON CHAPTER 51

Questions

Question 51-1. Company *A* owns 90% of the stock of Company *B*. During the year Company *B* has sold to Company *A* goods which cost $100,000.00, and which were billed to Company *A* at a profit of 25% on cost. At the end of the year there remain in Company *A*'s inventory goods billed to it at $10,000.00. How will these matters affect the consolidated profit and loss statement?

Question 51-2. Referring to the preceding question, assume that the goods were sold by Company *A* to Company *B*, and that goods of a billed price of $10,000 remained in Company *B*'s inventory. Would this change in the facts cause any change in the consolidated profit and loss statement?

Question 51-3. Each of the following cases involves one or more variations from the facilitating conditions mentioned in the chapter. In each instance, identify the variation or variations by number, and state the adjusting entries to be made with respect thereto on December 31, 1946.

(*a*) The parent company acquired a 90% interest in the subsidiary on January 1, 1944. The investment account has been debited with the parent company's share of the subsidiary profits by credit to profits from subsidiary, and credited with its share of the subsidiary dividends for 1944, 1945, and 1946. The subsidiary profits for the three years were $9,800.00, $10,350.00, and $11,200.00. The subsidiary paid $6,000.00 of dividends during each of the three years.

(*b*) The parent company is carrying its 90% interest in the subsidiary at cost. The stock was acquired on January 1, 1942. The subsidiary surplus balances were as follows:

Jan. 1, 1942	$15,000.00
Dec. 31, 1942	19,000.00
Dec. 31, 1943	24,500.00
Dec. 31, 1944	29,000.00
Dec. 31, 1945	32,000.00
Dec. 31, 1946	45,000.00

(No dividend paid in 1946)

(*c*) The parent company has debited the investment account with its share of subsidiary profits to December 31, 1945 and with all dividends received to December 31, 1946. It has debited its surplus account during 1946 with dividends paid in the amount of $10,000.00 and with a loss of $35,000.00 on the sale of an abandoned plant. The subsidiary has debited its surplus account during 1946 with $6,000.00 of dividends paid, and has credited the account with a $22,500.00 profit on sales of investments.

(*d*) The parent company acquired a 90% interest in the subsidiary on January 1, 1945. It has debited the investment account with its share of the subsidiary profits for the two years since acquisition by direct credit to surplus; the subsidiary profits for the two years were $23,650.00 and $19,870.00. It has also credited the account with $18,000.00 of dividends received in each year; the subsidiary has charged surplus with all dividends paid.

(*e*) The parent company acquired a 90% interest in the subsidiary on January 1, 1942 and is carrying it at cost, $125,000.00. The increase in the subsidiary's surplus between January 1, 1942 and December 31, 1945 was $30,000.00. The subsidiary's profit for 1946 was $16,000.00. Dividends paid by Company *S* annually for the years 1942 to 1946 inclusive were credited to surplus by the parent company. The annual dividend was $10,000.00.

Problems

Problem 51-1. The Pennland Company bought 75% of the stock of the Shoreland Company for $122,000.00 at a time when the Shoreland Company's surplus was $42,400.00. On January 1, 1945 it purchased 15% more for $32,000,00 and on September 30, 1945 (after three of the quarterly dividends had been paid), 5% more for $15,000.00. Profits were earned evenly throughout the year. Intercompany sales during the year were $34,540.00. The Shoreland Company's inventory on January 1, 1945 included merchandise on which the Pennland Company had made a profit of $2,300.00 and its inventory at December 31, 1945 included merchandise on which the Pennland Company had made a profit of $3,400.00. From the trial balances below prepare consolidated statements.

	Pennland Company	Shoreland Company
Cash	$ 41,365.00	$ 14,175.00
Accounts receivable	72,016.00	32,360.00
Inventories	48,295.00	27,652.00
Investment in Shoreland Company	169,000.00	
Fixed assets	81,887.00	157,375.00
Purchases	412,876.00	240,968.00
Expenses	139,162.00	84,650.00
Dividends—paid quarterly	15,000.00	12,000.00
	$979,601.00	$569,180.00
Accounts payable	$ 31,760.00	$ 18,260.00
Capital stock	300,000.00	120,000.00
Surplus—January 1, 1945	46,520.00	86,300.00
Sales	584,371.00	344,620.00
Rent collected from Shoreland Company	6,000.00	
Dividends received	10,950.00	
	$979,601.00	$569,180.00
Inventories, December 31, 1945	$ 52,948.00	$ 31,657.00

Problem 51-2. The Patterson Company purchased an 85% interest in the State Machinery Company on January 1, 1945 for $125,000.00 and an additional 10% at $25,000.00 on July 1, 1945. The State Machinery Company made $18,000.00 during the first six months and lost $4,000.00 during the second six months. All dividends were paid in December 1945.

The following tabulation gives certain data pertaining to inventories:

	Intercompany Profits		Inventories	
	In Patterson Company Inventory	In State Company Inventory	Patterson Company	State Company
January 1, 1945	$4,500.00	$3,000.00	$56,174.00	$32,310.00
June 30, 1945	2,400.00	1,400.00	52,345.00	24,926.00
December 31, 1945	5,600.00	4,400.00	58,170.00	16,530.00

Intercompany sales during the year were $63,000.00.

From the following trial balances at December 31, 1945 prepare consolidated statements of profit and loss and surplus and a consolidated balance sheet:

	Patterson Company	State Machinery Company
Cash	$ 53,907.00	$ 13,735.00
Accounts receivable	64,783.00	44,172.00
Inventories	56,174.00	32,310.00
Investment in State Machinery Company	140,500.00	
Fixed assets	144,150.00	97,248.00
Purchases	412,864.00	248,600.00
Dividends paid	25,000.00	10,000.00
Expenses	129,373.00	51,081.00
	$1,026,751.00	$497,146.00
Accounts payable	$ 34,179.00	$ 21,365.00
Capital stock	250,000.00	100,000.00
Surplus, December 31, 1944	168,420.00	46,320.00
Sales	574,152.00	329,461.00
	$1,026,751.00	$497,146.00

Problem 51-3. The Pendexter Company has owned 90% of the Switzer Company for several years. At the close of 1946 the Pendexter Company had in its inventory, which totaled $73,640.00, merchandise which it had purchased from the Switzer Company at $24,000.00 below cost to that company. The closing inventory of the Switzer Company was $31,920.00.

Condensed profit and loss statements of the two companies follow:

	Pendexter Company	Switzer Company
Sales	$638,420.00	$372,480.00
Cost of goods sold	524,320.00	344,120.00
Gross profit	$114,100.00	$ 28,360.00
Expenses	60,400.00	36,360.00
Net profit (loss*)	$ 53,700.00	$ 8,000.00*

A minority stockholder claims that the loss is fictitious and that the Switzer Company really earned $16,000.00. The directors of the Pendexter Company claim that the merchandise was sold to it at its market value. Your investigation bears out this contention.

Intercompany sales were $123,440.00.

(*a*) Prepare partial working papers showing a consolidated profit and loss section.

(*b*) Write a statement to be submitted to the minority stockholder explaining the situation to him.

Problem 51-4. The Post Company has owned 80% of the Sun Company for several years. An analysis of the surplus accounts of the two companies follows:

	Post Company		Sun Company	
Balance, January 1, 1945		$68,430.00		$32,600.00
Dividends from Sun Company		3,200.00		
Adjustment of error in inventory on December 31, 1944			$ 3,000.00	
Dividends paid	$10,000.00		4,000.00	
Balance, December 31, 1945	61,630.00		25,600.00	
	$71,630.00	$71,630.00	$32,600.00	$32,600.00

The balance of the surplus account of the Sun Company at the date of acquisition by the Post Company was $8,400.00.

From the trial balances below prepare consolidated statements.

	Post Company	Sun Company
Cash	$ 18,548.00	$ 13,140.00
Accounts receivable	43,726.00	29,320.00
Inventories, December 31, 1945	26,153.00	11,175.00
Investment in the Sun Company	100,060.00	
Other assets	155,893.00	80,205.00
Expenses and costs	417,980.00	65,320.00
	$762,360.00	$199,160.00
Accounts payable	$ 32,410.00	$ 15,420.00
Capital stock	200,000.00	80,000.00
Surplus	61,630.00	25,600.00
Revenues	468,320.00	78,140.00
	$762,360.00	$199,160.00

Problem 51-5. You find among other balances on the consolidated working papers of the Pasco Company and its subsidiary, the Streeter Company, the following:

	Pasco Company	Streeter Company
Debits:		
Investment in Streeter Company (80%)	$174,400.00	
Fixed assets	142,000.00	$ 94,000.00
Expenses	96,486.00	38,974.00
Dividends paid	15,000.00	8,000.00
Credits:		
Capital stock	$300,000.00	$160,000.00
Surplus	124,370.00	46,000.00
Reserve for depreciation	63,000.00	26,000.00

The Pasco Company is carrying the investment at book value. Its own books show a profit for the calendar year of $48,280.00, before consideration of any of the following matters. Prepare partial working papers showing the adjustments and eliminations made necessary by the following matters, and state the adjusted consolidated net profit and the consolidated surplus. State and prove, by an independent computation, the goodwill to appear on the consolidated balance sheet.

(*a*) You discover that the surplus of the Streeter Company was overstated at the date of acquisition by $8,000.00, and at the beginning of the current year by an additional $6,000.00, because of an error in the method of computing depreciation.

(*b*) The Streeter Company paid a dividend of $4,000.00 on June 15. Thereafter the Pasco Company sold one ninth of its holdings at a profit of $1,500.00 above the book value then on the books. This profit was taken directly into the surplus account.

(*c*) The Streeter Company reported a loss of $7,200.00 for the year. This loss failed to take into consideration a charge of $2,000.00 for advertising, made by the Pasco Company.

Problem 51-6. The Mitchell Distributing Corporation owns 85% of the stock of Willard & Co. and takes up its share of the subsidiary's profits, losses, and dividends through its investment account.

Trial balances of the two companies on December 31, 1946 appear below:

	Mitchell Distributing Corporation	Willard & Co.
Debits		
Cash	$ 47,050.00	$ 4,170.00
Accounts receivable	123,250.00	71,180.00
Notes receivable	15,000.00	—
Inventory, December 31, 1946	61,310.00	46,840.00
Advances to Willard & Co	38,000.00	—
Land and buildings	140,850.00	—
Delivery equipment	73,000.00	141,680.00
Goodwill	42,000.00	—
Investment in Willard & Co.:		
Stock	64,200.00	—
Bonds—at par	15,000.00	—
Sinking fund trustee		5,000.00
Cost of sales	537,400.00	201,880.00
Selling expenses	101,150.00	30,050.00
General expenses	51,480.00	16,600.00
Interest expense	7,740.00	5,470.00
Dividends paid	16,000.00	3,000.00
Loss of Willard & Co	11,560.00	—
	$1,344,990.00	$525,870.00
Credits		
Accounts payable	$ 58,710.00	$ 79,630.00
Mitchell Distributing Corporation	—	24,000.00
Reserve for depreciation	79,990.00	46,440.00
Bonds payable	150,000.00	50,000.00
Preferred stock	75,000.00	—
Common stock	150,000.00	100,000.00
Surplus, January 1, 1946	37,860.00	14,600.00*
Sales	793,430.00	240,400.00
	$1,344,990.00	$525,870.00

* Red.

The $14,000.00 difference in the intercompany accounts results from the following debits on the books of Mitchell Distributing Corporation:

December 31—Sinking fund deposit made for Willard & Co on guaranteed bonds of the latter	$ 5,000.00
December 31—Sale to Willard & Co.—merchandise shipped this date. Cost to Mitchell Distributing Corporation $7,500.00	9,000.00
Total	$14,000.00

Prepare consolidated working papers and statements.

Problem 51-7. The Dime Company owns 85% of the stock of the Quarter Company, and takes up its share of the subsidiary's profits, losses, and dividends through its investment account.

Trial balances of the two companies on December 31, 1946 appear below:

	The Dime Company	Quarter Company
Debits		
Cash	$ 62,000.00	$ 8,400.00
Accounts receivable	231,000.00	87,000.00
Quarter Company	7,000.00	
Inventory, December 31, 1945	75,000.00	58,000.00
Land and buildings	175,000.00	
Machinery and equipment	136,000.00	139,400.00
Goodwill	25,000.00	
Investment in Quarter Company	185,000.00	
Purchases	431,000.00	325,000.00
Selling expenses	82,500.00	73,200.00
General expenses	115,000.00	96,800.00
Dividends paid	50,000.00	10,000.00
	$1,574,500.00	$797,800.00
Credits		
Accounts payable	$ 157,500.00	$ 55,300.00
The Dime Company		4,500.00
Reserve for depreciation	79,500.00	52,000.00
Capital stock	500,000.00	125,000.00
Surplus, December 31, 1945	116,250.00	60,000.00
Sales	700,000.00	501,000.00
Profit of Quarter Company	21,250.00	
	$1,574,500.00	$797,800.00
Inventories, December 31, 1946	$ 61,000.00	$ 77,000.00

The $2,500.00 difference in the intercompany accounts results from a payment by The Dime Company on December 31, 1946, which was not received by the Quarter Company until January 3, 1947.

Prepare consolidated working papers and statements.

Problem 51-8. The Smith Company acquired 70% of the stock of the Jones Company at 124 on January 1, 1946, and an additional 25% at 130 on March 31, 1946. The trial balances of the two companies on December 31, 1946, appear as follows:

	Smith Company	Jones Company
Debits		
Cash	$ 15,000.00	$ 71,500.00
Accounts receivable	72,900.00	65,000.00
Notes receivable	60,000.00	15,000.00
Inventory, December 31, 1945	29,300.00	34,700.00
Investment in Jones Company	54,900.00	
Furniture and fixtures	17,000.00	10,900.00
Purchases	375,000.00	184,400.00
Freight in	12,400.00	5,600.00
Returned sales	40,200.00	13,000.00
Wages	62,700.00	39,100.00
General expenses	31,400.00	24,300.00
Bad debts	3,800.00	2,900.00
Depreciation		1,000.00
Interest expense	2,500.00	1,200.00
Dividends paid (May, 1946)		5,000.00
	$777,100.00	$473,600.00

	Smith Company	Jones Company
Credits		
Accounts payable	$ 25,000.00	$ 55,500.00
Notes payable	15,000.00	
Notes payable—Smith Company—due January 2, 1947		25,000.00
Notes receivable discounted	25,000.00(2)	15,000.00(1)
Reserve for depreciation	5,100.00	2,300.00
Capital stock—$100.00 par	100,000.00	50,000.00
Surplus, January 1, 1946	33,500.00	6,300.00
Sales	572,300.00	319,500.00
Interest earned on Jones Company notes paid during the year	1,200.00	
	$777,100.00	$473,600.00
Inventories, December 31, 1946	$ 31,600.00	$ 27,900.00

(1) Discounted with the Smith Company.
(2) The note payable of the Jones Company, discounted the day received.

Accrued interest on $15,000.00 intercompany note, not set up by either company, $400.00.

The Smith Company recorded no depreciation for the year; rate, 10%.

Assuming that the Jones Company profit has been earned evenly through the year, prepare consolidated working papers, statement of profit and loss, statement of surplus, and balance sheet.

Problem 51-9. The annual report of the Major Corporation for 1946 contained statements prepared from the following trial balance:

Debits	
Cash	$ 100,000.00
Accounts receivable	876,000.00
Inventory, December 31, 1945	142,000.00
Fixed assets—net	254,000.00
Purchases	1,486,000.00
Expenses	387,000.00
Investment in Minor Company—90%	852,000.00
Advances to Minor Company	198,000.00
Dividends paid	90,000.00
	$4,385,000.00
Credits	
Accounts payable	$ 425,000.00
Notes payable	75,000.00
Sales	1,996,000.00
Interest income	8,000.00
Estimated profits of Minor Company (90% of $110,000.00)	99,000.00
Capital stock	1,000,000.00
Surplus	701,000.00
Dividends received from Minor Company:	
Stock	45,000.00
Cash	36,000.00
	$4,385,000.00
Inventory, December 31, 1946	$ 157,000.00

The president's letter in the report contains the following statement: "In past years the investment in Minor Company has been carried at cost, and income has been taken up only as dividends have been received. However, with the purchase of an additional 30% interest on January 1, 1946, we have adopted the policy of taking up a proper share of Minor profits as soon as they are earned. The dividends received during the past year were taken into income because they represented distributions out of past surplus; future dividends will not appear in the income account. The stock dividend has been taken into income at par, although its book value is estimated to be considerably in excess of par."

You find that the surplus of Minor Company was $294,000.00 at the date of acquisition of the original holdings.

The general ledger trial balance of Minor Company on December 31, 1946 appears below:

Debits	
Cash	$ 73,000.00
Accounts receivable	374,000.00
Inventories, December 31, 1945	76,000.00
Fixed assets—net	104,000.00
Goodwill	40,000.00
Purchases	868,000.00
Expenses	137,000.00
Dividends paid:	
Cash (January 15, 1946)	40,000.00
Stock (July 15, 1946)	50,000.00
Surplus	67,000.00
	$1,829,000.00
Credits	
Accounts payable	$ 39,000.00
Advances from Major Corporation	190,000.00
Sales	1,081,000.00
Capital stock	450,000.00
Reserve for decline in market value of inventory	69,000.00
	$1,829,000.00

Inventories on December 31, 1946, were $207,000.00.

An analysis of the surplus account is given below:

Balance, January 1, 1946		$ 14,000.00
Deduct:		
Discount on sale of stock to Major Corporation—1,200 shares at $10.00	$12,000.00	
Provision to reduce inventories on December 31, 1946, from cost to market	69,000.00	81,000.00
Balance (deficit), December 31, 1946		$ 67,000.00

Minor Company has not taken up a charge of $8,000.00 for interest due Major Company for the year.

Prepare working papers and statements.

QUESTIONS AND PROBLEMS ON CHAPTER 52

Questions

Question 52-1. Company *X* acquired 90% of the stock of Company *Y* on January 1, 1945, and 80% of the stock of Company *Z* on January 1, 1946. The inventories of the three companies on December 31, 1945 contained goods purchased from other companies in the group, on which profits had been made as follows:

	Profit Made by		
	Company *X*	Company *Y*	Company *Z*
On goods in inventory of:			
Company *X*.............	—	$1,500.00	$1,200.00
Company *Y*.............	$1,000.00	—	400.00
Company *Z*.............	2,000.00	1,800.00	—
Totals.................	$3,000.00	$3,300.00	$1,600.00

What adjustments should be made for intercompany profits in inventories in the consolidated working papers for the year ended December 31, 1946? How will the adjustments affect the statements for 1946?

Question 52-2. Continuing the preceding question, the intercompany profits in inventories on December 31, 1946 were:

	Profit Made by		
	Company *X*	Company *Y*	Company *Z*
On goods in inventory of:			
Company *X*.............	—	$1,900.00	$1,500.00
Company *Y*.............	$1,200.00	—	900.00
Company *Z*.............	2,500.00	2,000.00	—
Totals.................	$3,700.00	$3,900.00	$2,400.00

What adjustments should be made for intercompany profits in inventories in the consolidated working papers for the year ended December 31, 1946? How will the adjustment affect the consolidated statements for 1946?

Question 52-3. Referring to the two preceding questions, state what effect the two adjustments will have upon the consolidated net income for the year 1946?

Question 52-4. Company *A* has owned all of the stock of Company *B* for several years. On December 31, 1945 Company *A* sold Company *B* certain real estate, as follows:

	Cost to Company *A*	Selling Price Company *B*
Land................................	$ 20,000.00	$ 30,000.00
Building............................	100,000.00	120,000.00
Total...............................	$120,000.00	$150,000.00

What reserve for intercompany profit in fixed assets should be created in the consolidated balance sheet of December 31, 1945?

Question 52-5. Continuing the preceding question, during 1946 Company *B* provided depreciation on the building at the rate of 5% on cost ($120,000.00). What adjustment of the consolidated income for 1946 is required, and what reserve for intercompany profit should appear in the consolidated balance sheet as of December 31, 1946?

Question 52-6. What limitations detract from the value of consolidated financial statements?

Problems

Problem 52-1. The Pennstate Plastics Company owns 90% of the stock of the Strout Company, 80% of the Sadler Company, and 70% of the Southboro Company. The Strout Company owns 10% of the Sadler Company and 15% of the Southboro Company. The Sadler Company owns 8% of the Southboro Company.

The Southboro Company produces the primary material and ships it to the Sadler Company at 25% above cost. After further fabrication the Sadler Company sends it to the Strout Company at 20% above total cost to the Sadler Company. The Strout Company sells much of this material to outsiders, but some is shipped to the Pennstate Company at 10% above the total cost to the Strout Company. In each case the manufacturing costs other than raw material costs are equal to the cost of the raw material, and the profits referred to above are based on this total cost.

The closing inventories contain merchandise as follows:

The Pennstate Company has merchandise purchased from the Strout Company for $46,200.00.

The Strout Company has merchandise purchased from the Sadler Company for $60,000.00.

The Sadler Company has merchandise purchased from the Southboro Company for $55,000.00.

No work has been done on any of these inventories by the companies owning them.

Compute the intercompany profit to be eliminated from the closing inventories.

Problem 52-2. You are requested to prepare such partial consolidated working papers, using the alternative form, as the following facts permit:

	Parent Company	Subsidiary *A* (90% Owned)	Subsidiary *B* (80% Owned)
Sales, 1945	$4,320,000.00	$2,400,000.00	$856,000.00
Sales returns	84,200.00	16,500.00	9,400.00
Inventory, December 31, 1944	240,740.00	120,080.00	64,370.00
Purchases	1,446,000.00	899,300.00	225,170.00
Purchase returns	48,110.00	23,400.00	12,060.00
Direct labor	1,085,620.00	364,800.00	347,650.00
Factory expenses	935,650.00	462,420.00	84,870.00
Inventory, December 31, 1945	220,900.00	123,200.00	59,000.00
Other expenses	581,000.00	483,500.00	156,600.00
Surplus, December 31, 1944	401,660.00	84,320.00	35,160.00
Dividends paid	200,000.00	50,000.00	15,000.00

(*a*) In the beginning inventories there were intercompany profits of $32,000.00 made by the parent company, $12,000.00 made by Subsidiary *A*, and $7,200.00 made by Subsidiary *B*.

(*b*) In the ending inventories there were intercompany profits of $54,200.00 made by the parent company, $10,600.00 made by Subsidiary *A*, and $17,080.00 made by Subsidiary *B*.

(*c*) The intercompany sales and purchases during 1945 were $356,400.00.

(*d*) The purchase returns on Subsidiary *A*'s books included merchandise purchased for $12,300.00 in 1944 from the parent company, on which the latter made a profit of $2,500.00. The merchandise had been included in the beginning inventory of Subsidiary *A*. The sales returns on Subsidiary *B*'s books included merchandise purchased during 1944 from the parent company for $8,500.00. The parent company made a profit of $1,900.00 on the sale of this merchandise to the subsidiary.

Problem 52-3. The trial balances and other data pertaining to the Padre Wine Company and its subsidiary, the Sonora Vineyards Company, are given below. Prepare consolidated working papers.

	Padre Wine Company	Sonora Vineyards Company
Debits:		
Inventories, December 31, 1945	$ 152,400.00	$ 31,410.00
Other current assets	321,200.00	125,740.00
Fixed assets	346,520.00	48,320.00
Investment in subsidiary—90%	183,124.00	
Purchases	483,520.00	44,650.00
Other expenses	1,742,640.00	392,140.00
	$3,229,404.00	$642,260.00
Credits:		
Current liabilities	$ 104,159.00	$ 27,810.00
Sales	2,364,530.00	465,190.00
Capital stock	500,000.00	100,000.00
Surplus	260,715.00	49,260.00
	$3,229,404.00	$642,260.00
Inventories, December 31, 1946	$ 163,480.00	$ 34,200.00
Surplus analysis:		
Balance, December 31, 1945	$ 332,644.00	$ 69,260.00
Profits of subsidiary, 1946	28,071.00	
	$ 360,715.00	
Dividends	100,000.00	20,000.00
	$ 260,715.00	$ 49,260.00

Intercompany profits, all made by Sonora Vineyards Company:

In inventory on December 31, 1945	$13,400.00
In inventory on December 31, 1946	17,280.00

Problem 52-4. From the following facts, prepare a consolidated surplus statement for the Producers Corporation and its subsidiary, the Schofield Company.

Surplus: Producers Corporation, December 31, 1946	$362,370.00
Schofield Corporation, December 31, 1946	33,250.00
Dividends: Received by Producers Corporation from the Schofield Corporation and recorded in the Producers Corporation's surplus account	24,000.00
Profits from operations: Reported by the Producers Corporation, 1946	122,650.00
Reported by the Schofield Corporation, 1946	64,320.00
Intercompany profits, made by the Schofield Corporation, in inventories on,	
December 31, 1945	14,230.00
December 31, 1946	11,200.00
Dividends paid: By Producers Corporation	40,000.00
By Schofield Corporation	30,000.00
Surplus of Schofield Corporation at the date of acquisition	32,450.00

Problem 52-5. From the following data prepare a consolidated statement of cost of goods manufactured and sold for the Patton Company and its 90% owned subsidiary, the Simpson Company and its 80% owned subsidiary, the Spicer Company.

	The Patton Company	The Simpson Company	The Spicer Company
Inventories, December 31, 1945:			
Raw materials	$ 48,390.00	$ 36,142.00	$28,110.00
Goods in process	106,380.00	72,370.00	14,800.00
Finished goods	52,660.00	46,000.00	33,100.00
Inventories, December 31, 1946:			
Raw materials	47,240.00	32,060.00	24,500.00
Goods in process	93,075.00	78,780.00	16,415.00
Finished goods	39,020.00	41,100.00	28,640.00
Purchases:			
From the Patton Company		22,340.00	16,300.00
From the Simpson Company	82,820.00		
From the Spicer Company	16,400.00	8,320.00	
From others	212,840.00	160,134.00	78,450.00
Direct labor	218,455.00	120,075.00	76,354.00
Factory expenses	163,217.00	108,546.00	56,397.00
Factory expenses include charges made by the Patton Company for rent		20,000.00	12,000.00
Intercompany profits in inventories:			
On December 31, 1945:			
In raw materials:			
Made by Patton Company		1,200.00	800.00
Made by Simpson Company	4,200.00		
Made by Spicer Company	700.00	400.00	
In goods in process:			
Made by Patton Company		1,400.00	1,100.00
Made by Simpson Company	3,600.00		
Made by Spicer Company	800.00	600.00	
In finished goods:			
Made by Patton Company		1,050.00	1,300.00
Made by Simpson Company	3,800.00		
Made by Spicer Company	2,400.00	200.00	

	The Patton Company	The Simpson Company	The Spicer Company
On December 31, 1946:			
In raw materials:			
Made by Patton Company........		$ 1,400.00	$ 700.00
Made by Simpson Company......	$ 3,700.00		
Made by Spicer Company........	800.00	500.00	
In goods in process:			
Made by Patton Company........		1,600.00	900.00
Made by Simpson Company......	4,100.00		
Made by Spicer Company........	1,000.00	400.00	
In finished goods:			
Made by Patton Company........		1,700.00	600.00
Made by Simpson Company......	3,200.00		
Made by Spicer Company........	1,450.00	300.00	

Problem 52-6. The Allen Company acquired a 90% interest in the Barber Company and an 80% interest in the Coleman Company on January 1, 1946.

From the trial balances and other information submitted, you are requested to prepare a worksheet and consolidated statements.

	Allen Company	Barber Company	Coleman Company
Debits			
Cash................................	$ 15,000.00	$ 5,000.00	$ 11,000.00
Accounts receivable................	70,000.00	21,000.00	40,000.00
Notes receivable....................	30,000.00	5,000.00	5,000.00
Plant and machinery................	100,000.00	60,000.00	80,000.00
Investment in Barber Company—at cost.	100,000.00	—	—
Investment in Coleman Company—at cost....................	125,000.00	—	—
Inventory, January 1, 1946..........	15,000.00	10,000.00	15,000.00
Raw material purchases..............	60,000.00	40,000.00	50,000.00
Labor................................	43,000.00	35,000.00	35,000.00
Manufacturing expenses..............	22,000.00	17,000.00	16,000.00
Selling expenses....................	10,000.00	6,000.00	10,000.00
Administrative expenses..............	25,000.00	10,000.00	10,000.00
Dividends paid......................	45,000.00	10,000.00	20,000.00
	$660,000.00	$219,000.00	$292,000.00
Credits			
Accounts payable....................	$ 22,000.00	$ 10,500.00	$ 36,000.00
Notes payable........................	5,000.00	9,500.00	9,000.00
Capital stock........................	400,000.00	50,000.00	80,000.00
Surplus, January 1, 1946............	48,000.00	29,000.00	34,000.00
Sales................................	160,000.00	120,000.00	133,000.00
Dividends received..................	25,000.00	—	—
	$660,000.00	$219,000.00	$292,000.00

Provide 10% depreciation on total plant and machinery.

The inventories on December 31, 1946 were as follows:

Allen Company..	$40,000.00
Barber Company......................................	20,000.00
Coleman Company....................................	25,000.00

One half of the Allen inventory on December 31, 1946 represented goods purchased from the Barber Company, which were billed at cost plus 25% **and so** carried as accounts receivable by Barber Company. No other intercompany sales were made during the year.

Notes receivable of the Allen Company included money advanced to Barber and Coleman Companies in the amounts of $9,500.00 and $9,000.00 respectively.

Problem 52-7. Following are the trial balances of Company *A* and its subsidiary on December 31, 1945:

	Company *A*	Company *B*
Debits		
Cash	$ 75,000.00	$ 50,000.00
Notes receivable	200,000.00	60,000.00
Accounts receivable	350,000.00	190,000.00
Inventory, raw materials, January 1, 1945	150,000.00	105,000.00
Purchases	650,000.00	400,000.00
Labor	450,000.00	320,000.00
Manufacturing expense	190,000.00	190,000.00
Selling expenses	85,000.00	40,000.00
Administrative expenses	45,000.00	25,000.00
Inventory, goods in process, January 1, 1945	80,000.00	70,000.00
Inventory, finished goods, January 1, 1945	90,000.00	65,000.00
Plant and equipment	900,000.00	400,000.00
Investment in stock of Co. *B*	875,000.00	
	$4,140,000.00	$1,915,000.00
Credits		
Capital stock	$1,800,000.00	$ 500,000.00
Notes payable	110,000.00	80,000.00
Accounts payable	100,000.00	65,000.00
Bonds payable	500,000.00	—
Premium on bonds	5,000.00	—
Reserve for depreciation	100,000.00	60,000.00
Sales	1,400,000.00	1,050,000.00
Surplus	125,000.00	160,000.00
	$4,140,000.00	$1,915,000.00

The inventories on December 31, 1945, were:

	Company *A*	Company *B*	Total
Raw material	$280,000.00	$175,000.00	$455,000.00
Goods in process	95,000.00	80,000.00	175,000.00
Finished goods	135,000.00	145,000.00	280,000.00

Company *A* purchased the entire stock of Company *B* on January 1, 1945 at the price shown in the trial balance. During the year each of the two companies declared and paid a 5% dividend. Company *A* took up its dividend from Company *B* by a credit to surplus. The entries for dividends were the only entries affecting the surplus accounts during the year.

During 1945, Company *B* sold goods to Company *A* at a cost of $300,000.00 and at a selling price of $375,000.00. Company *A* made cash advances totaling $400,000.00 to Company *B* during the year. The sales just mentioned were charged against the advances account, the $25,000.00 balance of which is included in Company *B*'s accounts payable.

The inventories on December 31, 1945 include intercompany profits as follows·

	Raw Material	Goods in Process	Finished Goods
In inventory of Company *A*.......	$20,000.00	$5,000.00	$4,000.00

Company *A*'s bonds were issued July 1, 1945. They bear 5% interest, payable semiannually, and mature in five years. No interest has been paid.

Allow depreciation at 5% per annum on cost of fixed assets.

Prepare the following consolidated statements:

(*a*) Statement of cost of goods manufactured and sold.
(*b*) Profit and loss statement.
(*c*) Surplus statement.
(*d*) Balance sheet.

Problem 52-8. From the following trial balances and supplementary data, prepare consolidated statements as follows: cost of sales, profit and loss, surplus and balance sheet.

	Trial Balances, December 31, 1946		
	Co. *X*	Co. *Y*	Co. *Z*
Investment in common stock:			
Co. *Y*, 90%..............	$ 110,000.00		
Co. *Z*, 95%..............	110,000.00		
Investment in preferred stock:			
Co. *Y*, 40% (par and cost)......	10,000.00		
Investment in bonds:			
Co. *Y*....................	50,000.00		
Co. *Z*....................	49,050.00		
Land, buildings, and machinery—depreciated value...........	367,000.00	$ 225,000.00	$ 250,000.00
Inventories....................	80,000.00	50,000.00	70,000.00
Accounts receivable...........	50,000.00	40,000.00	50,000.00
Cash..........................	40,000.00	20,000.00	35,000.00
Bond discount..................		5,000.00	
Raw material purchases.........	418,000.00	260,000.00	300,000.00
Direct labor...................	365,000.00	240,000.00	210,000.00
Manufacturing expense..........	215,000.00	190,000.00	160,000.00
Depreciation (for the year)......	12,550.00	9,000.00	8,000.00
Selling and general expense......	80,000.00	50,000.00	60,000.00
Bond interest (see note).........		3,000.00	4,125.00
	$1,956,600.00	$1,092,000.00	$1,147,125.00
Capital stock:			
Common.....................	$ 400,000.00	$ 50,000.00	$ 50,000.00
Non-participating 6% preferred, non-voting..................	100,000.00	25,000.00	50,000.00
Bonds payable—10-year issues...		50,000.00	75,000.00
Accounts payable..............	62,500.00	80,000.00	90,000.00
Sales..........................	1,215,000.00	800,000.00	825,000.00
Bond interest..................	3,000.00		
Surplus........................	176,100.00	87,000.00	53,750.00
Bond premium...................			3,375.00
	$1,956,600.00	$1,092,000.00	$1,147,125.00

Company *X*'s investments in subsidiaries are further commented upon as follows:

Common stock of Company *Y*, acquired January 1, 1945, and carried at cost.
Common stock of Company *Z*, acquired January 1, 1946, and carried at cost.
Preferred stock of Company *Y*, acquired January 1, 1946, and carried at cost; no dividends in arrears at date of acquisition.
Bonds of Company *Y*, acquired from Company *Y* at 90 on the date of issue, January 1, 1946.
Bonds of Company *Z*, issued January 1, 1946 at 105; $50,000.00 par value acquired by Company *X* on July 1, 1946 for $49,050.00.

On December 31, 1945 Company *X*'s inventory contained finished goods on which profits had been made by Companies *Y* and *Z* in the respective amounts of $2,000.00 and $3,000.00.

The surplus accounts of the three companies are analyzed as follows:

	Co. *X*	Co. *Y*	Co. *Z*
Balance, January 1, 1945	$128,750.00	$63,000.00	$26,650.00
Common stock dividend from Co. *Y*	2,700.00		
Net profit from operations	87,500.00	33,000.00	39,100.00
Total	$218,950.00	$96,000.00	$65,750.00
Dividends paid:			
Common stock	$ 24,000.00	$ 3,000.00	$ 3,000.00
Preferred stock		1,500.00	3,000.00
Total	$ 24,000.00	$ 4,500.00	$ 6,000.00
Balance, December 31, 1945	$194,950.00	$91,500.00	$59,750.00
Dividends received:			
Co. *Y*: Common	2,700.00		
Preferred	600.00		
Co. *Z*: Common	2,850.00		
Discount on Co. *Y* bonds purchased	5,000.00		
Total	$206,100.00	$91,500.00	$59,750.00
Dividends paid, December 31, 1946:			
Common	$ 24,000.00	$ 3,000.00	$ 3,000.00
Preferred	6,000.00	1,500.00	3,000.00
Total	$ 30,000.00	$ 4,500.00	$ 6,000.00
Balance, December 31, 1946	$176,100.00	$87,000.00	$53,750.00

The accounts receivable and accounts payable include, on December 31, 1946, intercompany accounts as follows:

	Per Books of		
	Co. *X*	Co. *Y*	Co. *Z*
Due from Co. *Y* to Co. *X*	$14,250.00	$14,250.00	
Due from Co. *Z* to Co. *X*	11,500.00		$13,000.00

Company *Y* has paid its bond interest for the year; Company *Z* has paid its interest to outside bondholders and has credited Company *X* with the interest due that company for the year. This has not, however, been taken up by Company *X*.

Intercompany purchases and sales during the year ended December 31, 1946 were:

	To Company		
	X	*Y*	*Z*
By Company			
X		$25,000.00	$35,000.00
Y	$40,000.00		20,000.00
Z	60,000.00	50,000.00	

Summary of Inventories

	Co. *X*	Co. *Y*	Co. *Z*
December 31, 1945:			
Raw materials	$30,000.00	$15,000.00	$10,000.00
Goods in process	25,000.00	20,000.00	30,000.00
Finished goods	25,000.00	15,000.00	30,000.00
	$80,000.00	$50,000.00	$70,000.00
December 31, 1946:			
Raw materials	$25,000.00	$12,000.00	$15,000.00
Goods in process	30,000.00	17,000.00	25,000.00
Finished goods	20,000.00	31,000.00	25,000.00
	$75,000.00	$60,000.00	$65,000.00

Unrealized profit in inventories on December 31, 1946:

	Profit Made by Company		
	X	*Y*	*Z*
Raw materials	$3,000.00	$1,000.00	$2,000.00
Goods in process	2,000.00	1,000.00	1,500.00
Finished goods	1,500.00	3,000.00	2,500.00
Total	$6,500.00	$5,000.00	$6,000.00

Problem 52-9. Refer to Problem 51-7 and prepare consolidated working papers in the alternative form.

Problem 52-10. Company *A* conducts a retail coal business. It was organized January 1, 1945, and on that date purchased a 90% interest in the stock of Company *B* for cash in the amount of $136,200.00, this price being the book value of the stock at the time of purchase plus an allowance to reflect the true value of the coal acreage.

Coal acreage owned by Company *B* contained 1,000,000 tons of coal when acquired, of which 100,000 tons have been mined each year.

Until the mine is exhausted, all coal is to be sold to Company *A* at "cost plus 10% profit." Included in such cost for 1945, by mutual agreement, was an item of $12,000.00 set aside to purchase new equipment.

Company *A* purchases all its coal from Company *B* and the inventory of coal on hand at retail yards on December 31, 1945, priced at cost, was $28,050.00.

From the following trial balances on December 31, 1945, prepare consolidated work sheets in both forms and statements.

COMPANY *A*

	Debits	Credits
Cash	$ 20,600.00	
Retail yards equipment	183,000.00	
Reserve for depreciation		$ 12,000.00
Coal purchased	187,000.00	
Investment in Company *B*	136,200.00	
Administrative and selling expenses	15,000.00	
Delivery expense	35,000.00	
Depreciation	12,000.00	
Bonds of Company *B* (bought at par)	10,000.00	
Accounts payable—Company *B*		20,000.00
Common stock		150,000.00
Paid-in surplus		136,200.00
Sales		280,000.00
Bond interest		600.00
	$598,800.00	$598,800.00

COMPANY *B*

Coal acreage	$100,000.00	
Plant and equipment	70,000.00	
Cash	30,000.00	
Reserve for new equipment		$ 12,000.00
Sales		187,000.00
Reserve for depreciation		30,000.00
Reserve for depletion		40,000.00
Account receivable—Company *A*	20,000.00	
Depreciation	7,000.00	
Depletion	10,000.00	
Mining expense	153,000.00	
Interest paid on bonds	3,000.00	
Capital stock		60,000.00
Surplus, January 1, 1945		14,000.00
Bonded debt		50,000.00
	$393,000.00	$393,000.00

Problem 52-11. From the following balance sheets, profit and loss accounts, and other data, prepare columnar worksheets showing the consolidation of the accounts, minority interests, earned surplus at beginning, and profit and loss.

Balance Sheets, December 31, 1945

	Phoenix Co.	Eastern Airports Inc.	Potomac Airport Co.
Assets			
Cash	$ 428,000	$ 14,500	$ 500
Accounts receivable		45,000	8,500
Prepayments and supplies	5,000	26,500	
Investment in U. S. Airlines Co. stock	630,000		
Investment in Eastern Airports Inc. stock	270,000		
Loans to Eastern Airports Inc.	370,000		
Investment in Potomac Airport Co. common stock		180,000	
Land		284,000	215,500
Buildings and equipment		310,000	
Reserve for depreciation		50,000*	
	$1,703,000	$810,000	$224,500
Liabilities			
Accounts payable		$ 10,000	
Taxes and other accruals	$ 15,000	24,000	
Due Phoenix Co.		370,000	
Due Potomac Airport Co.		8,500	
Capital stock—preferred			$ 40,000
Capital stock—common	500,000	225,000	200,000
Paid-in surplus	500,000	150,000	
Earned surplus	688,000	22,500	15,500*
	$1,703,000	$810,000	$224,500

* Deductions.

Profit and Loss Accounts—1945

Income:			
Rent			$ 8,500
Profit on sales of securities	$165,000		
Revenue from port activities		$ 75,000	
Dividends	25,000		
Interest	48,000		
	$238,000	$ 75,000	$ 8,500
Expenses:			
Interest		$ 18,000	
General, including taxes	$ 75,000	46,000	$ 2,000
Loss on sale of hangar			3,000
	$ 75,000	$ 64,000	$ 5,000
Net income	$163,000	$ 11,000	$ 3,500

Other Data

(1) Phoenix Co. owns 36,000 shares of the stock of Eastern Airports, Inc. Of this holding, 21,000 shares were acquired by subscription at time of issue (January 1, 1942) at $10.00 per share. Additional 3,000 shares of Eastern Airports, Inc. stock were purchased on December 31, 1943 at $20.00 per share; at this time the stock equity of Eastern Airports, Inc. stood as follows:

Capital stock—stated value ($5 per share)	$150,000.00
Paid-in surplus	150,000.00
Earned surplus	100,000.00
	$400,000.00

As of January 1, 1944 Eastern Airports, Inc. declared a stock dividend of $75,000.00 (15,000 shares at $5.00 per share), which was appropriated from earned surplus.

(2) Eastern Airports, Inc. owns 90% of the common stock of Potomac Airport Co. acquired on December 31, 1943 at a total cost of $180,000.00. At this time the accumulated operating deficit of Potomac was $14,000.00 but preferred dividends had been paid to date.

(3) No dividends were paid by Phoenix Co. in 1945.

(4) No dividends (other than the stock dividend referred to above) were declared by Eastern Airports, Inc. during the years 1944 and 1945.

(5) No dividends were declared on the preferred stock of Potomac Airport Co. for the two years, 1944-1945. This is a 6% cumulative stock.

(6) The interest charge on the books of Eastern Airports, Inc. is entirely applicable to the advances made by Phoenix Co.

(7) All of the revenues of Potomac Airport Co. for 1945 are based on charges to Eastern Airports, Inc. not yet collected.

(8) All investment accounts shown are recorded on a cost basis, with no adjustments for intercompany profit, loss, or dividends.

(9) The preferred stock of Potomac Airport Co. entitles its holders in liquidation to par, without cumulative dividends in arrears except to the extent of any surplus.

QUESTIONS AND PROBLEMS ON CHAPTER 53

Questions

Question 53-1. Distinguish between a consolidation and a merger.

Question 53-2. What is the essential difference between a consolidation and a holding company?

Question 53-3. In a report upon a proposed amalgamation of two companies, state how you would treat the following points in arriving at the earning power of each concern. Give reasons for your treatment.

(*a*) Anticipated profits on contracts in process.
(*b*) Insurance of any description.
(*c*) Wages paid general workmen.
(*d*) Salaries paid officers and directors.
(*e*) Depreciation of plant and equipment.
(*f*) Bad debt reserve.
(*g*) Repairs, renewals, and replacements of plant and equipment.

Question 53-4. A client comes to you for assistance in accounting matters involved in the consolidation of five manufacturing companies. He informs you that it has been decided that each concern should send him a balance sheet as at the close of its last fiscal year, and profit and loss statements for each of the past five years, so that a preliminary statement may be prepared showing the approximate amount of common and preferred stock of the new corporation to be turned over to each of the five companies in settlement for its net assets, and so forth.

The plan outlined for consolidation includes the giving of preferred stock for all tangible assets less liabilities, and common stock for the goodwill based upon past profits. The client asks you to prepare for him a letter to be sent to each of these five companies, requesting such further information as might not ordinarily appear on a balance sheet and profit and loss account, all of which information it would be necessary for you to have in order to prepare the preliminary figures referred to above. Outline the information which you would request in such a letter.

Question 53-5. Why is it usually not practicable to effect a consolidation of several companies by issuance of common stock only?

Question 53-6. In a statement of the earnings of a business to be sold on the basis of its earning capacity, how should the question of interest paid on accounts payable, on bills payable, and on loans be treated?

Question 53-7. In a balance sheet to be used for financing, to what extent, if any, should an auditor give effect to transactions or developments occurring subsequent to the balance sheet date?

Question 53-8. During 1946 the *B* Company disposed of 30,000 shares of its Class *A* no-par common stock to the bankers at $15.50 a share. A prospectus issued by the bankers advertised the stock as a new issue, the proceeds of which, arising from the sale to the public, were to be applied by the company in the acquisition of new fixed assets necessary in adding certain products to its regular line of merchandise. The prospectus stated further that the dividend rate had been established at $2.00 per share per annum payable at intervals of six months.

You are auditing the books of the company ten months after the issue has been sold to the public by the bankers at an average price of $24.00 per share. No dividend has been declared or paid on the stock, and a statement of application of funds reveals that more than $150,000.00 of the proceeds has been applied to the payment of dividends in arrears on certain 7% $100.00 par value preferred stock, that the balance has been applied in the payment of past-due accounts of trade creditors from whom merchandise has been purchased, and that no new equipment has been acquired.

Do these facts demand any qualifications on the balance sheet or in your certificate?

Question 53-9. The *X* and *Y* Companies, competing enterprises, merge and form the *Z* Company. Their net worths on the day of the merger are as follows:

Particulars	*X* Company	*Y* Company
Preferred stock—300 shares	$ 30,000	
Common stock—500 shares	50,000	
Common stock—1,000 shares		$100,000
Earned surplus	760,000	300,000
Total net worths	$840,000	$400,000

Immediately before the merger the preferred stock of the *X* Company is retired and a cash dividend of 20% and a dividend of 300% payable in common stock are declared on the common stock. In this manner the book value of each share of outstanding stock of both companies is fixed at $400 per share. The merger is then effected, 3,000 shares (par $100) of the stock of the newly-formed *Z* Company being exchanged, par for par, for the stock of the old companies.

Your opinion is solicited on the correct disposal of the two earned surplus accounts in opening the books of the *Z* Company.

Problems

Problem 53-1. The Copeland Company presents the following balance sheet and statement of average income as a basis for negotiations for a merger:

Cash	$ 42,356.00	Accounts payable	$ 42,100.00
Accounts receivable	68,450.00	Capital stock	250,000.00
Inventories	55,309.00	Surplus	67,669.00
Fixed assets	142,654.00		
Patents	51,000.00		
	$359,769.00		$359,769.00

Average net earnings for past three years, $37,460.00.

After the adjustments below, the Copeland Company is to receive: 50% of the value of its fixed assets, to the nearest $1,000.00, in 5% bonds; 6% preferred stock for the remainder of its net assets, computed to the nearest $100.00; and common stock with a par value of $10.00 to the nearest full share computed by capitalizing its earnings in excess of bond interest and preferred dividend requirements at 15%. Any debit or credit resulting from rounding these amounts is to be closed to the goodwill account.

Expenditures which should have been charged to maintenance and repairs during the past three years have been charged to fixed assets in the amount of $11,154.00. Depreciation on these items was computed at 10%. It may be assumed that these expenditures were made in equal amounts in each year.

The patents were purchased five years ago and are carried at cost. One seventeenth should have been written off each year.

The inventories contain obsolete stock amounting to $8,500.00 which has been accumulating during the last two years. The salvage value of this stock is $400.00.

The accounts receivable include $3,450.00 of uncollectible accounts which should have been written off during the past three years.

Prepare a statement showing the amounts of bonds, preferred stock, and common stock to be issued to the Copeland Company in payment for its assets.

Problem 53-2. The Seeley Company, which has a net worth of $540,000.00 and has reported an average profit for the past three years amounting to $108,020.00, is contemplating entering a merger. The terms of the merger are that the Seeley Company is to receive 5% bonds for 40% of its net assets, 7% preferred stock for the remainder of its net assets, and common stock determined by capitalizing its earnings in excess of the bond interest and preferred dividend requirements at 20%. However, it is contended that the depreciation charged over the past 5 years should have averaged 10% instead of 8%, or $6,000.00 more per year.

The Seeley Company agrees to this proposal, provided the rate on the preferred stock is reduced to 6%, and the rate used to capitalize profits is reduced from 20% to 15%. How much more or less common stock to the nearest $10.00 would the Seeley Company receive under its proposal than under the original proposal?

Problem 53-3. Three companies propose to merge. The following amounts have been accepted by all parties as correctly setting forth the condition of each company:

	Company *A*	Company *B*	Company *C*
Net assets	$600,000.00	$450,000.00	$300,000.00
Net profits (losses*) (five-year average)	72,000.00	90,000.00	12,000.00*

You are asked to submit a plan for combination, giving consideration to asset values, earnings, and voting control. Accompany your statement with an explanation of why you think your plan gives proper consideration to all these factors.

Problem 53-4. Company *A* is contemplating purchasing Company *B*'s assets and goodwill and merging Company *B*'s business with its own. The following statements present the financial condition and average results of operations of the two companies:

	Company *A*	Company *B*
Current assets	$ 400,000.00	$ 300,000.00
Fixed assets	350,000.00	300,000.00
	$ 750,000.00	$ 600,000.00
Current liabilities	$ 120,000.00	$ 100,000.00
Capital stock	500,000.00	400,000.00
Surplus	130,000.00	100,000.00
	$ 750,000.00	$ 600,000.00

Sales	$1,200,000.00	$1,000,000.00
Cost of goods sold	840,000.00	750,000.00
Gross profit	$ 360,000.00	$ 250,000.00
Selling expenses	210,000.00	150,000.00
Net profit on sales	$ 150,000.00	$ 100,000.00
General expenses	80,000.00	60,000.00
Net profit	$ 70,000.00	$ 40,000.00

You are required to compute the prospective earnings of Company *A* after the purchase, provided all the assumptions made below are correct.

It is believed that if Company *B*'s competition were eliminated, selling prices would average 5% higher. Of Company *A*'s manufacturing cost, 35% is factory overhead. Since much of this is fixed, it is estimated that the increased volume would increase the factory overhead expenses by only 40%. Other manufacturing costs would retain their ratio to sales volume.

By the elimination of duplication of sales effort it is believed that at least one third of Company *B*'s selling expenses could be eliminated and that the remainder would be added to Company *A*'s selling cost. Company *A*'s general and administrative expenses are expected to rise 25%.

Problem 53-5. Company *X* and Company *Y* propose a merger. Their statements may be condensed as follows:

	Company *X*	Company *Y*
Net assets	$600,000.00	$400,000.00
Preferred stock—8%	$100,000.00	
Preferred stock—6%		$ 50,000.00
Common stock	300,000.00	250,000.00
Surplus	200,000.00	100,000.00
	$600,000.00	$400,000.00
Average net earnings	$120,000.00	$ 20,000.00

Both preferred stocks are cumulative and preferred as to assets, but not participating.

Submit a plan for merger, giving consideration to the existing rights of the preferred stockholders, asset values, earnings, distribution of securities between the various classes of stockholders, and control.

Problem 53-6. Prepare a statement showing an equitable basis of allotting stock in a new company to be organized for the purpose of consolidating the following three companies:

	A Company	*B* Company	*C* Company
Capital stock	$50,000.00	$75,000.00	$100,000.00
Surplus	10,000.00	5,000.00	—
Deficit	—	—	10,000.00
Average net profit per annum	4,800.00	9,600.00	5,600.00

It is expected that, through increased economies made possible by the consolidation, the combined net profit per annum after the organization of the new company will be $25,000.00.

Problem 53-7. *G* and *H* are domestic companies whose audited balance sheets of December 31, 1944 are as follows:

	G	H
Assets		
Cash	$ 15,000	$ 2,500
Accounts receivable—good and collectible	14,000	19,000
Marketable securities:		
Owned by Company *G* (market value $10,000)	18,000	
Owned by Company *H* (market value $27,000)		27,000
Investment in Company *K* (wholly owned) represented by 5,000 shares—at cost (market value $1,000,000)	500,000	
Investment in *H*—book value (120 shares)	1,200	
Investment in *G*—book value (800 shares)		80,000
	$548,200	$128,500
Liabilities		
Accounts payable	$ 15,000	
Capital:		
6,000 shares, par value $100	600,000	
10,000 shares, par value $10		$100,000
Surplus		28,500
Deficit	66,800*	
	$548,200	$128,500

Under a plan of reorganization the Companies *G* and *H* are to be merged at December 31, 1944 to form a company *J* with an authorized capital of $2,000.-000.00 representing 20,000 shares of $100.00 each. All shareholders agree to the merger except *X*, who owns 100 shares of *G* and 2,000 shares of *H*. However, *X* will accept for his interest in the two companies an equivalent amount of Company *K* shares at their market value. He will receive cash for any fractional part of a Company *K* share.

The other shareholders will receive Company *J* shares at their par of $100.00 each. They will pay or receive cash in lieu of fractional *J* shares, and it is intended to pay out the smallest possible amount of cash to each of the two groups of Company *G* and *H* shareholders.

1. How many shares of Company *K* and how much cash are distributable to *X*?
2. How many shares of Company *J* and how much cash are distributable to each of the two groups of shareholders *G* and *H*?
3. Prepare the opening balance sheet of Company *J*.

Problem 53-8. The Eastern Company, the Southern Company, and the Western Company are consolidated by the following method:

1. A new corporation, the Northern Company, is formed.
2. The Northern Company takes over all the assets and assumes all the liabilities of the three consolidating companies, paying for them as follows: To the preferred stockholders of the old companies, first mortgage bonds of the new company at par. The total authorized bond issue is $400,000.00. To the holders of common stock:

   In the Eastern Company—30 shares of new stock for each share of old stock.

   In the Southern Company—10 shares of new stock for each share of old stock.

   In the Western Company—20 shares of new stock for each share of old stock.

3. The new company (the Northern Company) is capitalized at $1,000,000.-00. (100,000 shares of a par value of $10.00 each.)
4. All properties are to be taken over at their book values.
5. The old companies are to be dissolved.

On the date of consolidation the balance sheets of the three combining companies were as follows:

	Eastern Company	Southern Company	Western Company
Assets			
Land	$ 600,000	$ 30,000	$ 20,000
Buildings	20,000	100,000	25,000
Machinery and equipment	250,000	125,000	10,000
Inventories	75,000	100,000	20,000
Notes receivable	10,000		
Accounts receivable	165,000	325,000	160,000
Cash	30,500	35,000	15,000
Prepaid insurance, etc	2,500	1,500	500
	$1,153,000	$716,500	$250,500
Liabilities and Net Worth			
Preferred stock—par $100	$ 300,000	$ 50,000	$ 50,000
Common stock—par $100	200,000	300,000	50,000
Notes payable	50,000	50,000	
Accounts payable	69,000	158,500	70,500
Accrued taxes	5,000	3,000	1,000
Unpaid wages	20,000	10,000	2,000
Reserve for depreciation:			
Buildings	4,000	20,000	5,000
Machinery and equipment	30,000	45,000	2,000
Surplus	475,000	80,000	70,000
	$1,153,000	$716,500	$250,500

The Western Company owed the Southern Company $24,000.00 on open account.

The $10,000.00 notes receivable of the Eastern Company represent notes of the Southern Company.

Prepare the balance sheet of the Northern Company after the consolidation has been effected.

Problem 53-9. The American Manufacturing Company has a deficiency of working capital. In order to provide the necessary working capital, it is proposed to reorganize. The balance sheet and plans for reorganization follow:

Balance Sheet—December 31, 1946

Assets

Current assets:		
Cash in banks and on hand		$ 25,000.00
Accounts receivable—trade—less reserve		150,000.00
Notes and acceptances receivable		200,000.00
Inventories		750,000.00
Total current assets		$1,125,000.00
Prepaid expenses		15,000.00
Fixed assets:		
Land—appraised value	$2,500,000.00	
Buildings and machinery—appraised sound value	3,250,000.00	5,750,000.00
Goodwill		500,000.00
		$7,390,000.00

Liabilities and Net Worth

Current liabilities:		
Notes payable—banks		$ 750,000.00
Notes and acceptances payable—trade		200,000.00
Accounts payable		250,000.00
Accrued taxes		70,000.00
Accrued expenses		35,000.00
Total current liabilities		$1,305,000.00
Funded debt:		
First mortgage, 6% bonds	$1,650,000.00	
Debentures—5%	500,000.00	2,150,000.00
Net worth:		
Capital stock—authorized and issued:		
Preferred—20,000 shares, 6% cumulative—par $100.00	$2,000,000.00	
Common—15,000 shares—par $100.00	1,500,000.00	3,500,000.00
Surplus:		
Earned	$ 85,000.00	
From appraisal	350,000.00	435,000.00
		$7,390,000.00

Plan of Reorganization

(1) The authorized stock to consist of 50,000 shares of 6% cumulative preferred, par value $50.00 per share, and 100,000 shares of no-par common.

(2) The preferred stock now outstanding to be exchanged: for each share of present preferred, one share of new preferred, one share of new common, and a warrant entitling to purchase, prior to July 1, 1947, one-half share of new common at $30.00 per share.

The common stock now outstanding to be exchanged: each share of present common to receive two shares of new common and a warrant entitling to purchase, prior to July 1, 1947, one-half share of new common at $30.00 per share.

(3) A branch plant to be sold for a cash consideration of $600,000.00. The 5% debentures to be paid out of the proceeds. The plant to be sold is carried on the books as follows:

Land	$250,000.00	
Buildings and machinery (appraised sound value)	375,000.00	$625,000.00

(4) $1,000,000.00 of 5% debentures to be issued and sold at 95, the sale carrying with it a bonus of 5,000 shares of no-par value stock.

(5) The proceeds of the proposed financing to be applied to reduce bank loans by $500,000.00, notes and acceptances payable by $100,000.00, and accounts payable by $150,000.00, and to increase the cash balance.

(6) By resolution of the directors, goodwill is to be written off, and the surplus accounts are to be merged in the stated value of the no-par common stock.

Prepare a balance sheet, as of December 31, 1946, after giving effect to the transactions set forth in the foregoing plan of reorganization.

Problem 53-10. The *A* Corporation had planned to acquire the *B* Corporation by the purchase of its common stock in the open market. After 20,000 shares of the stock had been acquired at prices ranging from $28.00 to $50.00 per share and averaging $37.00, the market price rose to such an extent that this plan of purchase was discontinued. The *A* Corporation had, in addition, acquired 10,000 shares by exchange for its treasury stock, one-half share of the preferred, and one share of the common of the *A* Corporation being given for each share of *B* stock.

Negotiations were then opened with the *B* Corporation to purchase all the assets, except cash. This was agreed to on December 31, 1945 on the following basis:

(1) Current assets and prepaid expenses at 90% of book value, less the amount of current liabilities, which are to be assumed by the *A* Corporation, are to be paid for in cash.

(2) For sound value of fixed assets, to be determined by appraisal, the *B* Corporation is to receive 10% in cash and 90% in preferred stock of the *A* Corporation, at par, $100.00 per share.

(3) The *B* Corporation is to receive common stock of the *A* Corporation (par value $50.00 per share) as payment for goodwill, including all intangibles, the amount to be determined by capitalizing at 20% the average net earnings for the five years 1941 to 1945 inclusive, in excess of $2.00 per share on 100,000 shares of outstanding stock.

In determining such net profits, adjustments are to be made to bring such items as depreciation and capitalization of fixed asset charges in the several years to the basis to be determined by a retrospective appraisal. Administrative salaries are to be adjusted to $25,000.00 for each year in which greater amounts were paid.

An audit of the *B* Corporation, made before the preceding adjustments, discloses the following facts:

	Net Profits	Administrative Salaries	Depreciation Charges	Net Addition to Fixed Asset Accounts
1941	$ 85,000.00	$18,000.00	$195,000.00	$ 35,000.00
1942	190,000.00	30,000.00	205,000.00	15,000.00
1943	175,000.00	23,000.00	218,000.00	205,000.00
1944	315,000.00	70,000.00	235,000.00	275,000.00
1945	295,000.00	65,000.00	250,000.00	85,000.00

The audit also discloses that profits included gains from sales of fixed assets over depreciated values, as follows:

1942	$15,000.00
1943	17,500.00
1944	2,000.00

The appraisal report shows the following:

	Proper Additions to Fixed Assets	True Depreciation
1941	$ 57,000.00	$ 140,000.00
1942	21,000.00	140,500.00
1943	263,000.00	146,000.00
1944	272,000.00	157,500.00
1945	92,000.00	165,000.00

Reproduction value of fixed assets—December 31, 1945	$6,200,000.00
Depreciation	2,800,000.00
Sound value	$3,400,000.00

The true depreciation shown by the appraisal is presumed to be sufficient to absorb all of the cost of an asset during the years of its use, with no profit or loss at time of sale or retirement.

The condensed balance sheet of the *B* Corporation, December 31, 1945, is as follows:

Assets		
Cash		$ 102,000.00
Receivables		60,000.00
Inventories		560,000.00
Prepaid expenses		6,000.00
Mortgage sinking fund		350,000.00
Plant	$4,000,000.00	
Less depreciation	2,500,000.00	1,500,000.00
Organization expense		72,000.00
Patents and trade-marks		1,000,000.00
		$3,650,000.00
Liabilities		
Notes and accounts payable		$ 175,000.00
Long-term notes		75,000.00
Mortgage on plant, due January 1, 1949		800,000.00
Common stock—100,000 shares, no-par value		2,000,000.00
Surplus		600,000.00
		$3,650,000.00

The *A* Corporation has sufficient shares of capital stock, authorized but unissued, to comply with the terms of settlement, but in order to meet cash requirements, it issues 5% debentures amounting to $1,000,000.00, which are taken by a syndicate for cash at 98.

After the deal is consummated, the *B* Corporation immediately liquidates all liabilities, pays the cost of liquidation of $25,000.00, and distributes all assets to stockholders.

You are required to prepare:

(*a*) A tabulated statement showing the determination of amounts needed for settlement purposes.

(*b*) All journal entries to give effect to the above transactions on the books of the *B* Corporation.

(*c*) All journal entries to give effect to the above transactions on the books of the *A* Corporation.

QUESTIONS AND PROBLEMS ON CHAPTER 54

Questions

Question 54-1. Distinguish between par rates of exchange and current rates.

Question 54-2. If two countries are on a gold basis, what may affect the par rate between the two countries?

Question 54-3. If one country is on a gold basis and one is on a silver basis, what additional factor may change the mint par rate?

Question 54-4. What is meant by a *banker's bill?* By a *commercial bill?* Distinguish between a *short bill* and a *long bill;* between a *documentary bill* and a *clean bill.*

Question 54-5. An Illinois corporation manufactures goods in which it uses raw material purchased in England. Invoices are stated in pounds sterling. An invoice of £1,000 is purchased at a time when the rate is 4.65. The invoice is finally paid with a draft purchased at 4.58. What disposition would you make of this element of exchange?

Question 54-6. What entries should be made on the two sets of books to record goods sent by the home office to the foreign branch, and what exchange rate should be used for the conversion?

Question 54-7. If cash is remitted by a foreign branch to the home office, payable in foreign currency, how should the transaction be recorded on the two sets of books, and what rate of exchange should govern the conversion?

If the remittance was payable in dollars, what entries would be made on the two sets of books, and what rate would govern the conversion?

Question 54-8. Assuming that fixed asset accounts are kept on the foreign branch books, how would the branch record a purchase of fixed assets paid for in foreign currency?

How would the branch and the home office record a shipment of machinery from the home office to the branch?

Why is it desirable to keep the branch fixed asset accounts on the home office books? If the fixed asset accounts are kept in the home office books, what entries should be made to record a shipment of machinery by the home office to the branch? What entries would be made to record the acquisition of fixed assets by the branch, paid for in foreign currency?

Question 54-9. In the case of a foreign branch, it is advisable to keep the fixed asset accounts on the home office books. This is, of course, impossible in the case of a foreign subsidiary. How would you recommend that the subsidiary's fixed asset accounts be kept?

Question 54-10. The *XYZ* Company is an American corporation and has as its principal asset an industrial plant, purchased many years ago and located in Mexico. It also has capital locked up in current inventories, accounts receivable, and so forth, incidental to the operation of the Mexican plant. For many years the Mexican accounts were reflected on the head office books on the basis of $2.00 Mex. to $1.00 U. S. A. Do you consider this proper at a time when Mexican exchange stands at $1.00 Mex. equals 18¢ U. S. A.?

Question 54-11. At what rates should the various accounts in the trial balance of a foreign branch be converted into dollars?

Question 54-12. How is the branch trial balance after conversion brought into balance, and what disposition is made of this balancing figure on the home office books?

Question 54-13. Assume that a parent company sells goods to, or purchases goods from, its foreign subsidiary, payable in dollars. Explain how the parent company's and the subsidiary company's current accounts would be kept, state what exchange adjustment might be necessary at the time of settling for the goods, and explain on which set of books such exchange adjustment would be made.

Question 54-14. If a holding company owns all of the stock of a foreign subsidiary, at what value should it carry its investment?

Question 54-15. When the foreign subsidiary's balance sheet is being consolidated with the parent company's balance sheet, how should the foreign company's capital stock account be converted? How should the foreign subsidiary's surplus account be converted?

Question 54-16. Assume that the parent company follows the method of taking up its share of the foreign subsidiary's profits and recording dividends through the investment account. How would a dollar value of such profits and dividends be determined, and what entries would be made to record them?

Question 54-17. Assume that the parent company does not own all of the foreign subsidiary's stock. How would you determine the dollar value of the minority interest for purposes of a consolidated balance sheet?

Problems

Problem 54-1. A merchant in St. Louis purchased merchandise for £8,642-15s.-6d. at a time when the exchange rate was 4.62. When the liability became due, the following rates were quoted.

Pounds	$4.685
Canadian dollars	.915

Pounds were quoted in Toronto in Canadian dollars at $5.085.

Disregarding commissions, would it pay the merchant to buy direct exchange or indirect exchange through Canada? How much would he save by his election? Give the journal entries for the purchase and settlement.

Problem 54-2. At the beginning of the year the T. H. Powers Company opened a branch office in Mexico. The branch receives all merchandise from the home office, and all proceeds of sales are deposited in an account against which the home office draws from time to time. An imprest fund for expenses was established at $1,000.00, and this fund is reimbursed by the home office as required.

The Mexican branch submits the following trial balance at the end of the year:

	Pesos	
Petty cash	4,320	
Accounts receivable	62,145	
Sales		367,542
Shipments from home office	324,625	
Expenses	87,406	
Home office current		110,954
	478,496	478,496

The rate of exchange at the end of the year was $.232. The inventory at the branch was computed at 28,640 pesos. The trial balance of the home office follows:

Cash	$ 16,496.00	
Accounts receivable	85,320.00	
Inventory	44,265.00	
Fixed assets	32,410.00	
Branch fixed assets	2,242.00	
Reserve for depreciation		$ 3,455.00
Accounts payable		12,422.00
Shipments to branch		81,424.00
Remittances from branch		53,724.00
Remittances to branch	19,236.00	
Sales		375,120.00
Cost of goods sold	314,246.00	
Expenses	38,626.00	
Capital stock		100,000.00
Surplus		8,120.00
Branch current account	81,424.00	
	$634,265.00	$634,265.00

Prepare combined statements for the home office and the branch.

Problem 54-3. A. Callahan has made the following export sales to O. Sorensen of Sweden:

Date	Amount	Exchange Rate at Date of Sale
March 4	$3,800.00	$.2562
April 6	5,000.00	.2502
May 10	6,500.00	.2618

Sorensen paid the entire bill on June 14, at which date the exchange rate was $.2581.

Make entries in journal form and also show the personal accounts as they would appear on the books of both parties assuming:

(a) Billings were in U. S. dollars.
(b) Billings were in Swedish kronor on the basis of the exchange rates prevailing at the date of shipment.

Assume that exchange rates were the same between dates of shipment and arrival of goods and between making and receiving remittances. In your solution drop fractions of a Swedish krona.

Problem 54-4. The trial balances of the Pellissier Company and its fully owned subsidiary at the end of a calendar year follow:

	Pellissier Company		Seine Company (Francs)	
Cash	$ 15,465.00		621,342	
Accounts receivable	62,532.00		1,906,175	
Inventories, January 1	48,175.00		634,242	
Fixed assets	71,245.00		1,214,715	
Investment in Seine Company (book value, January 1)	117,940.00			
Dividends paid	10,000.00		60,000	
Seine Company—current account	15,724.00			
Accounts payable		$ 22,176.00		71,466
Pellissier Company—current account				463,214
Dividends received		1,644.00		
Capital stock		200,000.00		3,000,000
Surplus, January 1		74,432.00		410,480
Sales		652,248.00		8,123,746
Purchases	437,254.00		5,624,908	
Expenses	172,165.00		2,007,524	
	$950,500.00	$950,500.00	12,068,906	12,068,906
The closing inventories are:	$ 49,650.00		688,880	

The following rates of exchange are given:

Date of acquisition	$.0354	
January 1	.0303	
December 31	.0269	
Average during year	.0282	
Conversion value of fixed assets		$31,750.00

You are required to prepare:

(a) Consolidated statement of profit and loss.
(b) Consolidated statement of surplus.
(c) Consolidated balance sheet.

Problem 54-5. A merchant in New York purchased goods in London which were billed to him at £638:8:4 at a time when the rate of exchange was 4.715. Two weeks later, fearing an adverse move in the exchange rate, he arranged with his bank to buy future exchange for the amount of the bill at the then current rate of 4.725. A commission of $\frac{1}{20}$ of 1% was charged. When the bill became due, the rate of exchange was 4.575.

(a) Give all journal entries necessary to record these facts on the merchant's books.
(b) How much did he save or lose by the purchase of future exchange?

Problem 54-6.
(1) Make the following conversions at the rates indicated:

(*a*) £526-5-4 to dollars.	Rate	497.30 cents.
(*b*) Fr. 735,000 to dollars.	Rate	2.66 cents.
(*c*) $1,230.00 to reichmarks.	Rate	19.60 cents.
(*d*) $936.50 to belga.	Rate	13.20 cents.

(2) Convert $16,000.00 at the following rates (value in cents) quoted as current:

(*a*) London cables	498.37
(*b*) London cheques	497.87
(*c*) Paris cables	2.78
(*d*) Paris cheques	2.61
(*e*) Brussels cheques	15.35

(3) Convert 16,000 units of the respective foreign moneys to dollars at the rates in (2).

Problem 54-7. Compute the interest on £735-17-6 for 73 days at 5%, using (*a*) 360 days to the year; and (*b*) 365 days to the year.

Problem 54-8. John Smith borrowed 2,000,000 francs in Paris for 150 days at 3%, interest in the United States being at 5% (interest payable on due date of loan). The rate of exchange was $.06 on the date the loan was made and was $.061 on the date of repayment. Commission on purchase or sale of exchange was 1/20% for each transaction. The cable charge for each transfer of funds was $20.00.

How much did Mr. Smith save or lose by borrowing abroad at the lower interest rate? Submit the worksheet supporting your answer.

Problem 54-9. The Goodwear Corporation, having its main office in New York City, received from its Paris branch the following trial balance as of the close of business, December 31, 194—.

	Francs Dr.	Francs Cr.
Cash	76,252	
Notes receivable	78,000	
Purchases	2,512,500	
Accounts payable		96,012
Sales		3,518,750
Inventory	318,000	
Discount on sales	85,000	
Discount on purchases		52,500
Jean Maurier, drawing account	50,000	
Salaries and wages	307,500	
Bad debts	8,750	
Repairs to furniture and fixtures	30,500	
Sundry expenses	200,000	
Suspense	62,500	
Furniture and fixtures	341,600	
New York control		2,650,000
Remittances	1,865,060	
Accounts receivable	381,600	
	6,317,262	6,317,262

Inventory at close, francs 288,000

Jean Maurier, the branch manager, has an agreement with the corporation whereby he receives as compensation in addition to his salary 20% of the net profits, the salary being included on the trial balance in the salaries and wages account. The drawing made by him was made on December 31, 194—, against his share of the profit for the year.

Rates of exchange (value in cents)	
Beginning of year	3.33⅓
Current rate—end of year	4.16⅔
Average rate for year	4.00
Rate when fixtures were purchased	3.57 1/7

On the main office books the Paris branch control and the remittance from the Paris branch appear as $103,000.00 and $77,620.00 respectively. However, in reconciling the transactions it is disclosed that:

(*a*) The suspense account of the Paris branch trial balance consists of an authorized advance to the president of the corporation while in Paris, at a time when the rate of exchange was 4.00. This he repaid to the home office, which treated it as a remittance from the branch.

(*b*) There was a remittance in the amount of francs 120,000 forwarded by the branch before the close of business on December 31.

(*c*) Early in December, the Paris branch had asked the main office to purchase in New York and pay for a special lot of merchandise. On December 31, the New York office paid $6,350.00 for this merchandise and on the same day it was billed and shipped to the Paris branch.

After making the necessary adjustments, journalize on the New York books the results of the Paris branch transactions for the year, and show the Paris control account.

Problem 54-10. The Southern and General Manufacturing Company of Pennsylvania disposes of part of its product at its branch in Rio de Janeiro.

On December 31, 1938 a trial balance of the home office books is prepared as follows:

	Debit	Credit
Accounts payable		$ 23,000.00
Accounts receivable	$ 15,000.00	
Capital stock		100,000.00
Cash	22,000.00	
Raw material inventory, January 1, 1938	20,000.00	
Raw materials purchased	400,000.00	
Work in process inventory, January 1, 1938	12,000.00	
Productive labor	275,000.00	
Manufacturing expenses	195,000.00	
Finished goods inventory, January 1, 1938	10,000.00	
Manufacturing plant	53,000.00	
Reserve for depreciation—plant		14,000.00
Reserve for depreciation—Rio furniture and fixtures		1,000.00
Rio account current	32,000.00	
Rio remittances to home office		35,000.00
Merchandise shipped to Rio		30,000.00
Reserve for exchange fluctuations		2,000.00
Surplus		59,000.00
Selling and general expenses	30,000.00	
Sales		800,000.00
Totals	$1,064,000.00	$1,064,000.00

The inventories on hand at the home office on December 31, 1938, are as follows:

Raw materials	$60,000.00
Work in process	15,000.00
Finished goods	36,000.00

The trial balance on December 31, 1938, forwarded from the Rio office, is stated in the local currency, namely milreis, as follows:

	Debit	Credit
Home office accounts		550,000 milreis
Remittance account	580,000 milreis	
Merchandise received from home office	500,000	
Cash	70,000	
Accounts receivable	50,000	
Inventory, January 1, 1938	40,000	
Furniture and fixtures	30,000	
Accounts payable		10,000
Sales		740,000
Expenses	30,000	
Totals	1,300,000 milreis	1,300,000 milreis
Inventory, December 31, 1938	50,000 milreis	

Exchange rates to be applied:

Date of purchase of furniture	$.0500
January 1, 1938	.0590
December 31, 1938	.0570
Average for the year (use in conversion of nominal accounts)	.0565

From the foregoing information, prepare:

(*a*) Closing entries on the branch books.

(*b*) Statement converting the branch trial balance and December 31, 1938 inventory to the dollar values at which the various items should appear in the statements.

(*c*) Branch profit and loss statement for the year, from branch account balances, expressed in both currencies.

(*d*) Branch balance sheet, expressed in both currencies.

(*e*) Journal entries on the home office books taking up branch profit or loss. Adjust the exchange gain or loss through the reserve account.

(*f*) Journal entries closing the home office books, allowing $1,500.00 depreciation on the plant and $150.00 depreciation on the branch furniture and fixtures.

(*g*) Transcript of the Rio branch current account on the home office books.

(*h*) Combined balance sheet working papers.

QUESTIONS AND PROBLEMS ON CHAPTER 55

Questions

Question 55-1. What is the difference between a *residuary legatee* and a *remainderman?*

Question 55-2. Define *corpus* and *income,* and state why the distinction is maintained in the accounts of a decedent's estate.

Question 55-3. State in what respects (*a*) the rights and (*b*) the duties of an executor and an administrator differ.

Question 55-4. What is the distinction between a *devisee* and a *legatee?*

Question 55-5. The following items do not require apportionment on an accrual basis in estate accounting, but are treated wholly as principal or wholly as income. Which items are to be regarded as principal items and which as income items?

(*a*) Debts of decedent.
(*b*) Expenses of last illness.
(*c*) Proceeds of fire insurance policies.
(*d*) Commissions paid for collection of income.
(*e*) Funeral expenses.
(*f*) Court costs in probating the will, defending it against contests, and interpreting it.
(*g*) Legal fees in matters pertaining to income as distinguished from the preservation of the estate.
(*h*) Wages of bookkeepers and workmen employed to care for the property.
(*i*) Costs of defending the estate against claims rejected by the executor.
(*j*) Costs of caring for and harvesting crops.
(*k*) The proceeds of the sale of subscription rights.
(*l*) Trustee's commissions for collection and disbursement of income.
(*m*) Ordinary repairs of trust property.
(*n*) Legal fees incurred in effecting a change of executors or trustees.
(*o*) Federal estate tax and state inheritance tax.
(*p*) Interest accrued during the life tenancy on mortgages and other liabilities.
(*q*) Brokerage fees on changing an investment.
(*r*) Insurance premiums.
(*s*) Legal fees and other costs of preserving the principal of the estate.

Question 55-6. Are losses and gains on realization of trust assets regarded as principal or income, if the assets have been left by the decedent?

Is the rule any different if the assets have been purchased by the trustee?

Question 55-7. When are ordinary cash dividends, interest, and rents treated as principal?

Question 55-8. What disposition should be made by a trustee of an amount received by him for the sale of the rights to subscribe to stock? Give reasons for your answer.

Question 55-9. State three rules that have been applied in different states for the classification of stock dividends as between principal and income.

Question 55-10. *A* is a purchasing and sales factor, carrying on a foreign business. *A* dies on January 15. The auditor finds that orders to purchase were received prior to January 15, and were executed but not shipped until after January 15, since no steamship was in port to receive the goods. The business is to be carried on by the executor. How are the orders to be regarded with respect to the distribution between corpus and income of the estate?

Problems

Problem 55-1. C. A. Adamic died on June 1, 1946. His estate contained $10,000.00 of Atlantic Company 7% bonds due June 1, 1950, inventoried at 106. Interest was payable June 1 and December 1.

By the terms of his will, the income from the estate was to be held in trust for his widow; it was further provided that premiums on bonds purchased by the trustee should be amortized in such a way that the corpus would not be impaired.

One year after the death of Adamic, $5,000.00 more of the same bonds were purchased by the trustee on a 5% basis.

Prepare a statement showing the income payable to the widow from June 1, 1947 to the maturity of the bonds.

The present value of 1 due 6 periods hence at 2½% is $.86229687.

Problem 55-2. A widower left $375,000.00 to be divided equally among his three children: Jane, 23; Howard, 16; and Robert, 13. The shares of minor children were to be placed in trust until they were 21. The trustee was able to realize 4% on his investments. At the beginning of the third year the trust suffered a $10,000.00 loss of principal. The maintenance of the two minor children and the fees and charges of the trustee amounted to $7,200.00 per annum, which may be assumed to be chargeable equally against the income of the two beneficiaries. Sums not used were reinvested, as of the close of the year. At the end of the fourth year, Robert died, and his estate was divided between Jane and Howard. The expenses of settling his estate were $2,720.00. The expenses of maintenance and the trustee's expenses for the fifth year totaled $4,350.00. A year later the trustee terminated the trust and distributed the assets to the beneficiary.

Prepare a schedule showing your computation of the interests of the three children for the five-year period.

Problem 55-3. R. J. Pullman died on October 10, 1946. E. H. Padgett, who was named executor, filed with the probate court the following inventory:

Bonds—*R* Co.—D & J, 4%	$12,000.00
Bonds—*G* Co.—J & J, 4½%	10,000.00
Accrued interest on bonds	?
Stock of *B* & *S* Co	50,000.00
Dividend declared on *B* & *S* Co. stock	750.00
Notes receivable—non-interest-bearing	1,000.00
Cash	1,850.00

On November 1, 1946, Padgett discovered a bond of $10,000 of the Canadian Pacific R. R.—6%—M & N. Cash collections were as follows:

1946		
Oct. 15	—Dividend on *B* & *S* Co. stock	$ 750.00
Nov. 1	—Interest—Can. Pac. R. R. bond	300.00
	Notes receivable	600.00

Dec. 1—Interest on *R* Co. bonds	$	240.00
15—Notes receivable (balance uncollectible)		300.00
1947		
Jan. 1—Interest on *G* Co. bonds		225.00
15—Dividend on *B* & *S* Co. stock		500.00

Cash disbursements were as follows:

1946		
Oct. 20—Physician's bill	$	450.00
Nov. 15—Funeral expenses		1,250.00
Dec. 1—Miscellaneous debts		1,350.00
1947		
Jan. 15—Administrative expense—executing the will		375.00

All interest collections were turned over to the widow on the day received. Also on January 20 the executor sold the *R* Co. bonds for $12,250.00 and accrued interest, and paid special bequests to Raymond Downer—$3,500.00, and Esther Pullman—$7,500.00.

Record all of the foregoing facts on the books of the executor.

Problem 55-4. Record in a journal and cash book for an executor such of the following matters as he should record. Prepare a trial balance prior to closing at June 30, 1945.

Matthew Hill died on January 15, 1945. The will was admitted to probate and Harry Hill was approved as executor. The decedent owned the following assets at the date of death:

Cash	$ 4,100.00
Home	17,500.00
Household furniture	900.00
Northwest Power 5's, M and S (par $40,000.00)	42,200.00
Accrued interest on bonds	750.00
Idaho Power and Light 6% Pfd. (par $25,000.00)	26,500.00
Apex-Mutual (500 shares)	Nominal
Dividends receivable	375.00
Automobile	1,450.00

There was a life insurance policy of $25,000.00, payable directly to the widow. The home was left to the widow, Charlotte, who was also to have the income of the remainder of the estate during her life, after which it was to be divided among the children.

February	10	The executor filed an inventory, and opened his books.
	25	Paid the funeral expenses, $620.00.
	26	Paid medical bills, $210.00.
March	1	Collected the interest on the bonds.
	5	Paid $200.00 to the widow.
	10	Collected the dividend.
	15	Paid income taxes of deceased, $1,360.00.
	30	Discovered stock of Great Bear Company, value $2,940.00.
April	15	Sold Great Bear stock for $3,200.00.
	20	Paid taxes assessed in 1944 on home, $420.00.
	25	Children waived claim to automobile which was given to widow.
	28	Home was transferred to widow.

May	10	Collected dividend on Idaho Power and Light Pfd., $375.00.
	15	Paid widow, $400.00.
	31	Paid estate taxes, $1,245.00.
June	25	Collected own fee, $1,000.00.
	26	Sold Apex-Mutual shares for total of $50.00.

Problem 55-5. The following problem involves the abatement of legacies. While the solution would vary from state to state, it is to be solved following the general rules set forth in the text.

George Howe died on March 31, 1945. His will provided legacies as follows:

To the First Baptist Church, $10,000.00 in cash.
To the Mercy Hospital, $10,000.00 in cash payable from a savings account.
To his son, Henry, *AB* Bonds, $40,000.00 par value.
To his son, Walter, stock of the *Q* Company, $40,000.00 par value.
To his two daughters, Helen and Ruth, equal shares in the residue.

The inventory of his estate was:

Cash, general account	$ 1,430.00
Cash, savings account	8,748.00
AB Bonds, par value $40,000.00	41,040.00
Accrued interest thereon	410.00
Other bonds	8,640.00
Accrued interest thereon	106.00
Stock, *Q* Company, $40,000.00 par value	36,220.00
Other stocks	5,310.00

Liquidation produced the following results:

Funeral and administration expenses	$ 2,760.00
Debts of decedent	7,250.00
Other bonds sold for	8,710.00
Other stocks sold for	4,405.00

Prepare a schedule showing the amounts to be paid to each legatee.

Problem 55-6. The income of the estate of John B. Lewis was payable to his widow for life; the principal was to be held in trust for his grandchildren. The will stipulated that, to avoid impairing the corpus of the estate by the purchase of bonds at a premium, such premiums were to be amortized over the remaining life of any bonds so purchased.

At the time of Lewis's death, March 1, 1945, the estate contained $10,000.00 of 6% bonds due July 1, 1955, which were inventoried at 105.

On July 1, 1945, the trustee purchased $5,000.00 more of these bonds on a 5% basis.

Compute the price paid by the trustee; the present value of 1.00 due 20 periods hence at 2½% is .61027094. Also prepare a statement showing the income payable to the widow on July 1, 1945, January 1, 1946, and July 1, 1946 from the above bonds.

Problem 55-7. Earl Paige died on April 1, 1946, leaving an estate of $400,000.00. The will provided that the widow was to receive the income from the estate for life and upon her death the principal was to be distributed equally among three children.

Upon examination, it was found that there was included in the above amount $45,000.00 constituting a trust fund established by his previous wife on October

1, 1932 for the benefit of the oldest child, and consisting of $25,000.00 in 6% bonds, interest payable April 1 and October 1, and $20,000.00 in cash. This child had never received anything from the trust.

Prepare a statement showing the portion of the estate on which the widow is entitled to income.

Allow 5% simple interest, the legal rate, on all cash held by the father as trustee.

Problem 55-8. On October 1, 1945, Charles Denby, executor of the estate of Robert Burns, files his final account, after paying all debts, expenses, and special legacies in accordance with the terms of the will.

Funds totaling $255,000.00 remain for division among the residuary legatees.

Following is a statement showing the basis of distribution stipulated by the will and the amounts and dates of advances made to certain of the legatees. Interest at 4% per annum is charged on these amounts, which are required by the testament to be included in the estate.

		Advances	
Beneficiary	Share	Amount	Date
Anna Burns	40%	$25,000.00	January 1, 1945
John Burns	25%	15,000.00	March 1, 1945
Rosa Burns	25%	—	
Charles Denby	10%	2,000.00	July 1, 1945

Prepare a statement showing how the $255,000.00 should be divided.

Problem 55-9. On May 15, 1945 you are engaged by Adam Smith, executor for the estate of Robert Smith, who died on January 10, 1945, to assist him in preparing his accounts.

No records have been kept, with the exception of a list of receipts by the executor, which you are given together with bank statements, canceled checks, and a copy of the inventory filed with the probate court.

The list shows the following receipts:

Receipts

1945:			
January	20	—Dividends on Apex Mining Co. stock declared January 10, 1945	$1,000.00
February	1	—Note and interest dated August 1, 1944 paid—6% interest	5,150.00
	10	—Bank account discovered	500.00
	15	—Cash rent on farm for ensuing year	400.00
March	1	—Interest for 1 year on mortgage	300.00
	10	—Sale of *Q.R.R.* Co. bonds inventoried at $7,500.00	7,750.00
		Accrued interest thereon from November 10, 1944, at 4%	125.00
April	1	—Dividends on Arco Mfg. Co. stock:	
		Cash	400.00
		Stock—par value	1,000.00
	15	—Sale of subscription rights on Electric stock	100.00
	20	—Sale of 4 cows	800.00
		and 3 2-month-old calves	60.00
May	1	—Profits for fiscal year from partnership in the firm of Smith and Jacobs as per partnership agreement	1,750.00

Show how the above should be recorded by the executor.

Problem 55-10. *A* died on March 20, 1945, leaving an estate consisting of the following:

Household goods, $2,500.00.
5% City of Chicago bonds, J & J, $10,000.00.
Cash in bank, $12,345.00.
Cash in home, $255.00.
Real estate mortgages, 6% per annum—payable semiannually, collected to November 1, 1944, $15,000.00.
Horton Steel Co., preferred, 7%, quarterly, par $20,000.00, market March 20, 1945, 105.
Real estate $12,250.00, net rental $900.00 annually, payable monthly in advance.
Share of *A.B.C.* partnership, $50,000.00.

The will provided that the three executors, who were also the trustees, should receive $1,000.00 each; the widow, $10,000.00 cash and household goods; two sons, George and Richard, one half each of the Horton Steel stock; the residue was to be paid to a trust fund, the income of which was to be paid to the widow quarterly for life and the principal distributed to the sons equally. The will also provided that the income of the estate undistributed at the date of transfer of assets to the trustees should be paid to the trustees, to be added to the trust.

Liabilities, $4,500.00.

The executors paid, April 1, 1945, the debts of the decedent and funeral expenses, $875.00. In addition to the legacies, lawyers' and accountants' fees of $1,250.00 were paid on October 1, 1945.

Consider the income collected on the days due and, with the exception of income on willed property, paid to the widow quarterly beginning June 30.

The executors realized $47,500.00 as *A*'s share of the liquidation of the partnership, September 20, 1945.

All legacies were paid or distributed on October 31.

Write up the journal and cash book for the estate.

Problem 55-11. Under the terms of the will of J. J. Bullard, who died in 1943, the beneficiaries were:

Mary Bullard, widow of testator, who was left a special bequest of $50,000.00 payable immediately, and in addition a life interest in one half of the residuary estate, with the right of appointment.
Kathlyn Bullard, his daughter, who was left one fourth of the residuary estate. One half of this was left outright and the other half to remain in trust, with the right of appointment.
Jenny Bullard, his daughter, who was left a life interest in one eighth of the residuary estate, with the right of appointment.
John Bullard, his son, who was also left a one eighth interest in the residuary estate, to be paid to him outright.

The testator specified that, on account of the unsatisfactory market conditions, the trustees have the power and right to defer liquidation of any of the assets until, in their opinion, conditions are favorable and may, in their discretion, make intermediate distributions of principal from the funds so realized to the beneficiaries who are entitled thereto. The income from the estate was to be distributed annually in the proportion of the beneficiaries' interests.

On December 31, 1945, the following advances were made on account of principal:

Kathlyn Bullard	$150,000
John Bullard	100,000

but the special bequest to Mary Bullard had not yet been paid.

The trustees rendered their first accounting to the surrogate as at December 31, 1945, on which date all income, after paying therefrom all expenses applicable to income, was paid to the beneficiaries.

The surrogate's decree on the accounting of December 31, 1945, specified that (1) in considering the distribution of future income, all intermediary payments of principal should be treated as advances to the beneficiaries, and (2) in order to make a fair and equitable division of income, interest at 6% per annum should be charged and credited.

The income of the year 1946 amounted to $450,000.00, after all expenses applicable to income had been paid. No further distribution of principal had taken place.

Prepare a statement showing the amounts payable to each beneficiary on December 31, 1946.

QUESTIONS AND PROBLEMS ON CHAPTER 56

Questions

Question 56-1. Name the various classes of items that might appear in a charge and discharge statement as to principal.

Name the various classes of items that might appear in a charge and discharge statement as to income.

Question 56-2. What is the difference between an executor's intermediate and final account?

Question 56-3. Explain the method of closing the books of an executor, showing the final distribution of the estate.

Problems

Problem 56-1. James S. Overman was appointed executor of the estate of Phillip Sutphen who died on March 20, 1945. On December 27, 1945, Overman completed his executorship and turned the assets over to the trustee. From the following trial balance,

1. Prepare the charge and discharge statements.
2. Make the journal entries to close the executor's books and to transfer the assets to the trustee. Provide for accrued interest.

Trial Balance, December 27, 1945

Estate corpus		$162,420.00
Assets subsequently discovered		3,415.00
Bonds—Indiana Water Co. 3½s, F. & A.	$ 12,100.00	
—Illinios Traction, 4s, M. & S.	9,200.00	
—Iowa Mortgage Co. 5s, A. & O.	8,100.00	
Stocks—Sutphen Development Company	72,148.00	
—Sutphen Trading Corporation	32,465.00	
—*S* and *S* Company	5,120.00	
Loss on realization	3,716.00	
Gain on realization		2,840.00
Funeral and administration expense	2,314.00	
Debts of decedent	1,776.00	
Legacies paid	10,000.00	
Income		7,320.00
Expense—income	1,120.00	
Distributions of income cash	5,000.00	
Cash—principal	11,736.00	
Cash—income	1,200.00	
	$175,995.00	$175,995.00

Problem 56-2. Prepare statements of charge and discharge and cash account for the executor of the estate of Anthony Glembin (widower), who died October 12, 1947, leaving the following:

Life insurance	$ 10,000.00
Household effects, appraised	1,250.00
Real estate, appraised	35,000.00
Bank account	8,500.00
Investments, market value	70,250.00
Total	$125,000.00

The executor paid current debts at time of death, $1,800.00; funeral expenses, $750.00; legal fees and inheritance taxes, $8,350.00.

The securities were sold for $72,500.00; household effects netted $1,500.00. Special bequests (tax free) were $2,500.00.

The residue was to be divided equally among three sons: Anthony Jr., Albert, and Allen, who were required to consider as part of their shares, without interest, advances made to them at various times, to wit: $16,500.00, $12,250.00, and $7,500.00 respectively. Any one of the sons was given the option of taking the real estate at a valuation of $37,500.00; the option was taken by Albert.

Problem 56-3. The estate of William Van Duzen, who died on February 4, 1945, comprised the following assets:

Cash	$ 12,135.00
Government bonds	145,385.00
Other bonds	224,180.00
Accrued interest	3,240.00

His will provided that one half of his net estate should be placed in trust for the benefit of his widow during her life, and upon her death should be divided equally among his three children: Alice, Ruth, and Edward. The other half was to be divided as follows: $5,000.00 to Emerson University, $5,000.00 to the Union Church, and the remainder in equal shares to his three children. He directed his executor, Wallace B. Coffman, to deduct any advances to any of his children plus simple interest at 5% from the date of the advance. (Compute exact interest on basis of 365 days per year.)

The executor ascertained that the following advances had been made:

Alice	$12,000.00	January 1, 1932
Edward	30,000.00	April 10, 1939

Inheritance taxes totaled $43,215.00. The executor's fee was $10,000.00. Funeral and administrative expenses, other than above, were $2,254.00. Debts of the decedent amounted to $442.00. Bonds included in "Other bonds," which were carried at $48,400.00, were sold for $48,650.00 to provide funds to pay the charges. The accrued interest was collected.

Prepare a charge and discharge statement as to principal for the period ended November 12, 1945, the date of closing the estate.

Problem 56-4. Perry Updyke died May 5, 1945. His will provided that two thirds of his estate should go to his widow, Priscilla, and one third to his son, Matthew. An inventory of his estate follows:

Cash	$ 3,120.00
Stocks	22,005.00
Bonds	7,840.00

His will provided that advances to his son in the amount of $15,000.00 were to be regarded as part of the estate, but that, if the advances exceeded his third of the estate, no collection was to be required of him.

Debts of the decedent were $3,844.00. Funeral and administration expenses were $1,408.00. Stocks carried at $5,370.00 were sold at a loss of $465.00. The executor, Frank Harris, distributed the assets and made his final accounting to the court on January 15, 1946.

(a) Compute the amount due, if any, to each legatee.
(b) Prepare the charge and discharge statement as to principal, showing any amounts distributed to the legatees separately.

Problem 56-5. Arthur B. Crane died on May 5, 1945, and his brother, David Crane, was appointed executor. He filed an inventory as follows:

Cash	$ 452.00
Securities	9,685.00
Real estate	6,344.00

The decedent carried $20,000.00 life insurance, which was payable directly to his widow, Marcia. After a legacy of $1,000.00 in cash to his daughter, Dora, he left the rest of his estate to his widow.

Shortly before his death, a judgment of $18,000.00 was given against him. Other debts totaled $1,465.00. Funeral and administration expenses, which may be treated as preferred claims, were $962.00. The securities were sold at a loss of $145.00 and the real estate at a loss of $344.00.

Attempts to get the judgment creditor to compromise his claim at an amount less than he could legally collect failed. The executor completed liquidation of the estate on February 16, 1946, and made his report to the probate court.

(a) Give the entries, in journal entry form, which should be made on the executor's books.
(b) Prepare a charge and discharge statement as to principal.

Problem 56-6. Charles Wilson was appointed on May 20, 1945 administrator of the estate of John Allen, who died April 30, 1945, and assumed his duties immediately. On June 1, 1945, he filed with the probate court the following inventory of assets:

Cash	$ 450
Life insurance, payable to estate	50,000
Bonds—*A.B.* Co., 4%, J & J	24,000
Bonds—*C.D.* Co., 6%, A & O	15,000
Accrued interest on bonds	?
Real estate (home)	17,500
Household furnishings	3,500

On July 1, 1945 the administrator found a savings account amounting to $1,147.50, which was withdrawn and deposited in the checking account.

On August 15, 1945 the bonds of *C.D.* Co. were sold at a premium of 2%, plus accrued interest. The *A.B.* Co. bonds were sold September 15, 1945 at 99½ plus accrued interest.

On July 15, 1945, the administrator paid.

Debts of decedent	$ 750
Dr. Philip Holmes—last illness	175
A. J. Ferguson—funeral	1,225
Aetna—fire insurance (chargeable to income)	85

The administrator paid the widow, Ellen Allen, $300.00 out of income cash and turned over to her the household furnishings and a cash legacy of $5,000.00 on October 1, 1945. The proceeds of the life insurance policy were collected.

Journalize the foregoing and prepare a trial balance, as of October 31, 1945.

The administrator made his report on November 1, 1945, was allowed a fee of $450.00, and was discharged from his administratorship. He turned over to the widow the balance of the income cash, and the balance of the estate was turned over to the trustees as required by the will.

Prepare journal entries closing the estate.

Problem 56-7. The following trial balance was taken from the books of C. O. Webber, executor for the estate of his brother, H. A. Webber, on December 31, 1946. Webber was appointed executor March 15, 1946.

Bonds	$25,000	
Stock	15,000	
Loss on realization	750	
Gain on realization		$ 1,200
Funeral	950	
Administration expense	625	
Debts of decedent paid	2,225	
Legacy paid—Laura Frederick	5,000	
Income		3,600
Expense—income	150	
Distributions to income beneficiaries	3,000	
Cash—income	450	
Cash—principal	11,350	
Estate corpus		57,875
Assets not inventoried		1,825
	$64,500	$64,500

Prepare proper statements (without supporting schedules) and make closing journal entries.

Problem 56-8. William Hamilton died March 1, 1945, leaving 60% of his property outright to his wife, the balance to be held in trust; the income from this trust was to go to the wife during her lifetime and the principal was to go to various hospitals.

The estate was appraised as follows:

6% bonds—J. & J.	$100,000.00
Accrued interest	1,000.00
1,000 shares Western Steel 7% preferred	110,000.00
10,000 shares Dalton Company	147,500.00
2,000 shares Henderson, Inc.	30,000.00
4% bonds—M. & S.	150,000.00
Real estate	75,000.00
Cash in banks	12,500.00
Total	$626,000.00

One quarterly dividend on each stock had been declared at the time of Hamilton's death.

Income on common stocks and real estate was:

Dalton Company	12½¢ quarterly
Henderson, Inc.	30¢ quarterly
Real estate	6% per annum, payable quarterly

Debts and expenses were:

Miscellaneous accounts payable	$5,700
Funeral expenses	1,200
Doctor and hospital	1,600
Executor's commission on principal	½ of 1%
Executor's commission on income	5%

The executor paid the income to the widow as received, and the balance, if any, on March 1, 1946. The principal was distributed at appraised values.

Prepare statements of charge and discharge as to principal and income, and executor's cash account.

Problem 56-9. C. D. Morton died on January 1, 1945, leaving an estate consisting of:

Cash	$ 1,500.00
6% bonds—J. & J.	75,000.00
5% bonds—M. & S.	70,000.00
Life insurance	40,000.00
Real estate	250,000.00
Preferred stocks	10,000.00
Sundry accounts receivable	750.00

None of the income due on January 1, 1945 had been collected by Morton. The executors collected the insurance and the accounts receivable. They also made the following disbursements:

Sundry claims	$ 8,300.00
Funeral expenses	950.00
Bequests	25,000.00

The will provided that the bonds, stocks, and real estate were to be held in trust (the executors were also named as trustees) and that 50% of the income should be distributed to the widow, that 25% should go to the older son, that the younger son should receive $250.00 per month and that the remainder of his 25% of the income should be held by the same trustees in a separate trust to be paid to him upon the attainment of his majority. The principal assets not transferred to the trust were payable to the widow.

On June 30, 1945, the executors closed the estate and distributed the assets in accordance with the terms of the will. Income collected by them prior to that date was immediately transferred to themselves as trustees. Distributions of income cash were made on June 30 and December 31.

Assume that the preferred stocks paid dividends of $600.00 on August 25, and that the real estate was rented for $15,000.00 per year, payable in equal quarterly amounts in advance.

Prepare statements for the executors, for the trustees of the general trust fund, and for the trustees of the minor son.

Problem 56-10. You are visited during the morning of December 31, 1945 by Mrs. Yolande Zeno, executrix and sole beneficiary of the estate of her deceased husband, X. Y. Zeno. She submits the following statements:

ESTATE OF X. Y. ZENO
Trial Balance
December 30, 1945

Cash	$ 2,850.00	
The Xenophon Corporation stock—4,375 shares	28,000.00	
N. Y. Central R. R. stock—120 shares	4,800.00	
U. S. Sorghum Company stock—2,000 shares.	32,000.00	
U. S. Treasury notes—$56,000 face value	56,000.00	
Allowed claims—including interest accrued to December 31, 1945:		
First National Bank—loans to testator		$ 48,000.00
County treasurer—taxes		4,000.00
Yolande Zeno—loans to testator		300,000.00
Theophilus Zeno—loans to testator		24,000.00
The Xenophon Corporation—loans to testator		96,000.00
The Xenophon Corporation—funds advanced for funeral expenses		6,000.00
William Jones—merchandise sold to testator		12,000.00
Smith & Brown—services as counsel to executrix		54,000.00
Deficiency	420,350.00	
	$544,000.00	$544,000.00

THE XENOPHON CORPORATION
Trial Balance
December 30, 1945

Cash	$ 2,750.00	
Lima Bean Company stock—3,600 shares	85,394.73	
Claims against estate of X. Y. Zeno	102,000.00	
Capital stock—5,000 shares		$100,000.00
Surplus		89,794.73
Accounts payable—Smith & Brown		350.00
	$190,144.73	$190,144.73

Mrs. Zeno is the president of The Xenophon Corporation and the owner of 625 shares of its stock and states that during the morning the following transactions took place:

First: The court administering the estate of her deceased husband ordered her:

1. To accept certain offers, namely:
   $2,400.00 for 120 shares N. Y. Central R. R.,
   $123,650.00 for 2,000 shares U. S. Sorghum,
   $56,400.00 for $56,000.00 face value treasury notes, and deliver these securities for cash;
2. To pay in full the indebtedness to Xenophon Corporation and the preferred claims against the estate;
3. To submit to the court at its next session a charge and discharge statement, showing also the payments to be made to the other creditors of the estate and reserving an amount sufficient to pay 12½ % profits tax in the event that the court finds the estate liable therefor despite its insolvency.

Second: The Xenophon Corporation sold its 3,600 shares of Lima Bean stock for $8,000.00 cash and, pursuant to appropriate resolution of its stockholders and directors, paid its debts and credited its shareholders with their proportion of the net worth.

Mrs. Zeno states that she has complied with the first two requirements of the court order, and asks your assistance with the third. You may assume that the only tax provision necessary is 12½% of the net gain from realization of the assets listed in the trial balance.

Prepare the required charge and discharge statement, together with the worksheets showing the position of the estate after complying with the court orders and the position of the Xenophon Corporation after crediting the shareholders with their proportion of the net worth.

Problem 56-11. John Gibbon died January 1, 1940, and left his property in trust to his daughter, Ethel. The income was to be paid to her as long as she lived and at her death the trust was to go to his nephew, William Gibbon. He appointed John Doe trustee at a fixed fee of $5,000.00 per annum. All expenses of settling the estate were paid and accounted for by the executor before the trustee took it over.

Ethel died on September 30, 1943, and left all her property in trust to her cousin, Joseph Hart. John Doe was appointed executor and trustee of her estate, and he agreed not to make any additional charges for these services. All income was to be paid to Joseph Hart. The estate, which consisted solely of Ethel's unexpended income from the John Gibbon trust, was immediately invested in 4% certificates of deposit.

The property received under the will of John Gibbon on January 1, 1940, was:

10,000 shares of the *KO* Corporation, valued at $100.00 each.
$300,000.00 bonds of the *KO* Corporation, paying interest on June 30 and December 31 at 6% per annum.

In the five years ended December 31, 1944 the trustee received the following dividends on the stock:

February 1, 1940	$ 40,000.00
February 1, 1941	40,000.00
February 1, 1942	40,000.00
February 1, 1943	60,000.00
February 1, 1944	60,000.00

and he made the following payments:

Expenses:		
$100.00 a month, totaling		$ 6,000.00
Trustee's fees:		
$5,000.00 per annum, totaling		25,000.00
To beneficiaries:		
Ethel Gibbon		
1940	$27,250.00	
1941	35,000.00	
1942	25,000.00	
1943	37,000.00	124,250.00
William Gibbon		
1943	$17,000.00	
1944	46,000.00	63,000.00
Joseph Hart		
1944		3,000.00

The surplus income was left on deposit in the bank and drew no interest.

Prepare trustee's charge and discharge statements covering the five years ended December 31, 1944, showing the beneficiaries' interests.

Problem 56-12. Samuel Gifford died on July 18, 1945. The executor, having paid all debts, bequests, and expenses, and expecting no more transactions after June 30, 1946, desired to ask the court for his discharge and for an order to turn the remaining assets of the estate over to the trustee named in the will.

An inventory had been filed with the court on August 15, 1945, consisting of the following items:

Cash in First National Bank	$ 4,533.12
Cash in closed bank	2,050.50
Real estate, valued by court appraiser at	38,750.00
Home furnishings	6,824.00
Stocks, at market:	
AB Company preferred	22,865.00
AB Company common	3,738.20
Parkhurst Transit Co. common, at nominal value	100.00
U. S. Savings Bonds, dated April 1, 1945, due April 1, 1955, in the amount of $50,000	37,500.00
Accrued interest at 2.9%	326.25
	$116,687.07

In the latter part of September, 1945, discovery was made of another checking account, in the Second National Bank, with a balance of $2,500.00, and of $125.50 cash in the office safe. Insurance was collected in the amount of $58,000.00; also a dividend of $1,250.00 on the *AB* Company preferred which had been declared on June 1, 1945.

On June 15, 1946, the executor sold one half of the *AB* Company preferred stock for $13,500.00 and the Parkhurst Transit Company common for $200.00. Other receipts during the executor's administration consisted of rents, $4,526.00; dividends, including those declared before the testator's death, $4,025.00; collection on deposit in closed bank, $465.00. All receipts were deposited by the executor in the First National Bank.

Property taxes, accrued at date of death, were $1,575.20; and household debts on that date amounted to $2,111.00. The executor paid $20,000.00 bequests and $1,000.00 executor's fee as specified in the will; also $18,262.50 estate tax, $3,336.95 property taxes including those accrued at date of death, $750.00 funeral expenses, $88.50 court costs, as well as the household debts. The widow received allowances to the aggregate sum of $4,800.00 as directed by the court.

The accrued interest on U. S. Savings Bonds, $326.25, and the annual rate of 2.9% are assumed to be correct.

From the foregoing information prepare charge and discharge statements and supporting statements.

QUESTIONS AND PROBLEMS ON CHAPTER 57

Questions

Question 57-1. Based on the following facts, you are to prepare a statement showing, by months, the cash requirements of an installment dealer for the first year's operations:

(1) Cost of article, $50.00.
(2) Sales price, $90.00.
(3) Selling expense, $15.00.
(4) Overhead, $15.00.
(5) Profit, $10.00.
(6) Sales during the first month, 100 articles.
(7) Sales during the second month, 200 articles.
(8) Sales during subsequent months, 300 articles per month.
(9) Merchandise to be paid for in the month following the sale.
(10) Expenses to be paid during the month of sale.
(11) Payments are received at the rate of $10.00 down and $10.00 per month until paid.

Assume that there were no irregularities.

Problems

Problem 57-1. The Tunniecliff Company has requested you to express an opinion on the results of the budget for manufacturing expense shown below. The company estimated that it would produce 18,000 units during June, but owing to the sudden termination of an important contract, the actual production was only 12,000 units.

THE TUNNIECLIFF COMPANY
Report on Budget of Manufacturing Expenses
For the Month of June, 1945

Account	Budget	Actual	Over	Under
Indirect labor	$ 950.00	$ 750.00		$200.00
Superintendence	600.00	600.00		
Social security expense	450.00	302.00		148.00
Indirect materials	960.00	780.00		180.00
Power, heat, and light	450.00	375.00		75.00
Repairs	540.00	380.00		160.00
Taxes	154.00	172.00	$ 18.00	
Compensation insurance	450.00	316.00		134.00
Depreciation, machines	800.00	800.00		
Fire insurance	145.00	145.00		
	$5,499.00	$4,620.00	$18.00	$897.00
				18.00
Net under				$879.00

The superintendent, in referring to the report, stated that it showed a *saving* from the budget of $879.00. The president contended that actually a *loss* might be indicated.

(*a*) Explain the probable basis for the president's contention.
(*b*) State the method by which you would determine whether the company was above or below a standard performance for the work it did.
(*c*) Draw a form to be used in preparing future budgets of manufacturing expense so that this difference of opinion will not arise.

Problem 57-2. The budget director requests you to prepare a schedule showing the variation in unit costs at different sales levels, at $50,000.00 intervals from $800,000.00 to $1,000,000.00 inclusive. The fixed costs are $300,000.00, and the variable costs are 60% of the selling price. The unit selling price is 40 cents.

(*a*) Prepare such a schedule.
(*b*) Compute the break-even point.
(*c*) Comment on whether you think the schedule is typical of actual business conditions.

Problem 57-3. The Dahl Company has the following items, among others, in its balance sheet, on January 1, 1946:

Cash	$ 18,000.00
Accounts receivable	91,262.00
Inventory (35,000 units)	140,000.00
Accounts payable	162,000.00

Most of the accounts payable are past due and the company seeks a six months' 5% bank loan of $150,000.00 to be used to liquidate the past due accounts. The loan committee at the bank requests the company to prepare a budget showing how the company proposes to retire the debt, and suggests that the company plan to retire $20,000.00 on February 28, 1946 and $20,000.00 monthly thereafter until June 30, 1946, when the entire balance should be paid. Interest is payable on each installment as retired.

The Dahl Company has firm contracts for the sale of 10,000 units a month for the next six months at a gross profit of $2.00 each. The receivables arising from these sales will be collected, less 1% discount, in 30 days. Commercial overhead is estimated at $16,000.00 a month, of which $700.00 is for depreciation. Depreciation charged to manufacturing expenses is $1,000.00 a month. Its inventory can be reduced uniformly during the six months to 11,000 units.

The old accounts receivable will be collected as follows: 60% in 30 days and subject to 1% discount; 35% in 60 days net; and 5% will probably be lost. The company expects to pay for all purchases and expenses during the month incurred. The old accounts payable to be paid in January will be liquidated at a discount of 1%. Thereafter, they will be paid without discount.

If the loan is granted, the bank will require the company to increase its deposit to $30,000.00 and maintain it there.

Prepare the required budget. Assume that production is scheduled for equal monthly accounts.

Problem 57-4. For budgetary purposes, compute the cash required to pay for selling expenses for the year 1946 based on the data given below. It may be assumed that all expenses are incurred in equal monthly amounts.

Actual Expenses Charged in 1945		Expected Increase in 1946
Salaries—executive	$ 20,000.00	None
Salaries—salesmen	148,240.00	None
Commissions—salesmen	12,600.00	50%
Commissions—brokers	22,800.00	10%
Traveling expense	73,684.00	5%
Rentals	12,300.00	None
Warehousing charges	18,348.00	10%
Samples	6,230.00	5%
Stationery	8,880.00	15%
Advertising	90,000.00	33⅓%
	$413,082.00	

Salaries are paid monthly on the last day of the month. Commissions to salesmen are paid on sales above certain amounts. They are determined and paid 15 days after the close of each month. Because of a large return, one salesman has been overpaid by $420.00, which will be deducted from future commissions. Commissions to brokers are computed and paid at the end of the month following the sale.

Salesmen's traveling expenses are paid weekly for the expenses of the preceding week. The company plans to advance to each of its 24 salesmen an imprest fund of $200.00 which will be reimbursed semimonthly, on the 30th and 10th of the month for the first and second halves of the month respectively.

Rentals are payable monthly in advance, on the 15th of the month. Warehousing charges are billed to the company for each month on the tenth of the following month and are paid within ten days.

Samples are sent to salesmen and brokers whose reports reveal to whom they are given. From these reports it was ascertained that there were $2,000.00 of samples in the hands of salesmen and brokers on December 31, 1945. This inventory is expected to increase to $3,000.00 during 1946.

The inventory of office forms on December 31, 1945 was $4,650.00. The company wants to reduce this to $2,000.00 during the year 1946.

Advertising is payable the 10th of the following month.

Problem 57-5. *X* desires to engage in business as a retail distributor of refrigerators, which he proposes to market on an installment basis. The refrigerators will be sold for $150.00 each; $15.00 will be collected at the time of sale, and the balance of the sale price will be collected in nine monthly installments of $15.00 each.

X can obtain the refrigerators on a consignment basis, under an agreement to remit at the end of each month, at the rate of $90.00 each, for all refrigerators sold during the month. Salesmen are to be allowed a 20% commission, payable at the end of the month of sale. Overhead expenses are estimated at $26,400.00, and interest, credit, and collection expenses, at $12,000.00. (For purposes of this problem, it may be assumed that these expenses will be incurred in equal monthly amounts, payable at the end of the month.) Recoveries and repossessions are expected to offset losses on bad accounts.

X budgets his first year's sales as follows:

	Units		Units
January	75	July	300
February	125	August	200
March	150	September	150
April	200	October	100
May	400	November	75
June	400	December	150

X does not have sufficient capital to finance his business, and he carries his plans to his banker. The bank extends *X* a line of credit, secured by a pledge of his entire accounts receivable, on the following basis:

(1) At the end of each month the bank will honor a draft drawn by the manufacturer in any amount up to 60% of *X*'s accounts receivable at that date.

(2) *X* is to maintain at all times a bank balance of not less than 15% of his bank loan, with a minimum of $5,000.00.

(3) On January 1, *X* is to invest in the business the maximum amount of cash he will require (in addition to the bank loan) at the peak point of the year, and is to make no withdrawals of this capital during the year.

(4) Borrowings from, and repayments to, the bank are to be made in units of $1,000.00.

Compute the amount of *X*'s initial investment, to the nearest thousand dollars, and make a schedule of monthly borrowings and repayments.

Problem 57-6. You are engaged by Cavanaugh Company to prepare a forecast of its operations for the period from April 1 to July 31, 1947. From the information given, prepare a monthly cash statement, a monthly income and expense statement in columnar form, and a balance sheet as of July 31, 1947.

Balance Sheet—March 31, 1947

Assets

Cash on deposit	$ 24,820.00
Accounts receivable	69,600.00
Inventory of raw material	27,000.00
Buildings, machinery, and equipment	135,000.00
Prepaid insurance	3,300.00
	$259,720.00

Liabilities and Net Worth

Note payable (special 6% loan)	$ 30,000.00
Accounts payable	51,850.00
Accrued pay roll	11,950.00
Accrued interest and taxes	3,300.00
Depreciation reserve	2,700.00
Capital stock	150,000.00
Surplus	9,920.00
	$259,720.00

Income and Expense—Three Months Ended March 31, 1947

Sales		$180,000.00
Material consumed	$60,000.00	
Direct labor	36,000.00	
Overhead	36,000.00	132,000.00
		$ 48,000.00
Administrative expense	$15,000.00	
Selling expense	9,000.00	24,000.00
		$ 24,000.00
Cash discounts	$ 1,080.00	
Depreciation	2,700.00	
Interest	300.00	4,080.00
Net profit		$ 19,920.00
Organization expense		10,000.00
Surplus		$ 9,920.00

All buildings and equipment are used in manufacturing. In July, $15,000.00 of new machinery will be purchased. Depreciation charges will be as follows: April, May, and June, $1,000.00 each; July $1,060.00.

Thirty per cent of sales are collected during the month of shipment and 2% cash discount is allowed; 60% are collected during the following month; 8%, in the next month; and the balance may be considered uncollectible.

Accounts payable for all purchases and expenses, including administrative and selling, are due on the 10th of the following month. Pay rolls are payable on the 5th and 20th of each month for preceding half-calendar-month periods.

Cavanaugh Company's credit permits loans in multiples of $5,000.00 for full calendar months only, with interest deducted at 6% per annum. In computing monthly cash requirements, you may disregard the actual date of receipts and disbursements and consider that the full month's receipts are available to apply on the disbursements of the same month.

The special term note outstanding March 31 is dated February 1, due in four months.

The following summary shows actual sales and production for the first three months of the year and estimated sales and production for the succeeding five months:

	Units	
	Sales	Production
January (actual)	10,000	10,000
February "	20,000	20,000
March "	30,000	30,000
April	20,000	30,000
May	25,000	40,000
June	30,000	35,000
July	65,000	60,000
August	50,000	50,000

Cost of finished product sold should be based on the average of the opening inventory and the current month's production costs. It is expected that the selling price of $3.00 a unit can be maintained and that selling expense will retain a fixed relation to sales. Administrative expenses will remain unchanged during the period covered by your investigation.

Direct labor and material costs have a constant relation to production. Overhead expenses are at a minimum of $10,000.00 a month when production is at 10,000 units or less, and increase with production at the rate of $1.00 for each $3.00 expended for direct labor. Fifty per cent of such expenses consists of indirect labor and fixed monthly charges for insurance and taxes, and 50% comprises various other manufacturing expenses, exclusive of depreciation.

Insurance was taken out on January 1, for three years, at a cost of $3,600.00. Taxes of $12,000.00 per annum are payable June 20 and December 20 for current semiannual periods.

It is desired that a raw materials inventory sufficient only for the following month's requirements be maintained throughout the period.

At a directors' meeting to be held during April, a dividend of 10% will be declared, payable May 15.

Income taxes may be disregarded.

Problem 57-7. In January, 1947 the Northern Oil Company prepared a budget covering the six months from January 1 to June 30, 1947, the main purpose being an endeavor to forecast the company's *cash position* as of June 30, 1947.

The figures used in compiling the budget and the actual figures for the six months are given below.

From these and the data following, you are required to prepare a statement for presentation to the board of directors, showing a comparison between estimated and actual results and, in addition, a brief but comprehensive report, to be read in conjunction with the statement, explaining the differences.

The figures given below cover all sources of revenue and expense. Cash on hand on January 1, 1947 is $310,500.00.

NORTHERN OIL COMPANY

	Estimated	Actual
Sales of crude oil	$4,000,000.00	$3,610,000.00
Sales of refined products:		
Gasoline	4,400,000.00	4,200,000.00
Kerosene	420,000.00	406,000.00
Others	1,555,200.00	1,580,400.00
Purchases of refined products:		
Gasoline	315,000.00	380,000.00
Others		102,000.00
Operating expenses:		
Direct charges	1,620,000.00	1,560,000.00
Materials and supplies from warehouses	180,000.00	170,000.00
Marketing expenses	2,290,400.00	2,222,240.00
General and administrative expenses	900,000.00	800,000.00
Capital additions:		
Direct charges	2,000,000.00	1,800,000.00
Materials and supplies from warehouses	1,500,000.00	1,500,000.00
Interest on bonds	60,000.00	60,000.00
Bond sinking fund	50,000.00	50,000.00
Preferred stock dividend	350,000.00	350,000.00
Preferred stock sinking fund	200,000.00	200,000.00
Accounts receivable:		
January 1	900,000.00	900,000.00
June 30	1,200,000.00	1,100,000.00
Accounts payable:		
January 1	700,000.00	700,000.00
June 30	800,000.00	750,000.00
Inventories of materials and supplies:		
For operating purposes, January 1	50,000.00	50,000.00
For operating purposes, June 30	50,000.00	50,000.00
For new construction, January 1	500,000.00	500,000.00
For new construction, June 30	500,000.00	400,000.00

There are no marketing expenses on crude oil sales.

Purchases of materials and supplies are paid for within the month received

Statement of Quantities

	Purchases	Production	Sales
Crude oil (barrels):			
Estimated		4,000,000	2,000,000
Actual		3,800,000	1,900,000
Refined products (gallons):			
Gasoline:			
Estimated	3,000,000	50,400,000	40,000,000
Actual	4,000,000	47,880,000	42,000,000
Kerosene:			
Estimated		8,400,000	6,000,000
Actual		7,980,000	5,800,000
Others:			
Estimated		21,000,000	19,440,000
Actual	1,200,000	19,950,000	17,560,000
Refinery loss:			
Estimated		4,200,000	

Note: 1 barrel equals 42 gallons.

Problem 57-8. A corporation, engaged in manufacturing and wholesaling two principal products, has called upon you for advice on their sales policy for the coming year.

In prior years selling expenses were 18% of the sales, of which one third was for advertising. Administrative expenses were 5% of the sales.

Two propositions are now under consideration by the management by either of which they hope (1) to increase the volume of sales, (2) to decrease unit production costs, and (3) to reduce relative selling expenses. These propositions are outlined to you by the management as follows:

Proposition 1.—Premium Stamp Books

Premium stamp books will be widely distributed to consumers who will obtain stamps from the packaged products. When a book is filled with stamps (100 stamps to each book) it may be returned to the corporation and will be redeemed by the award of a prize or premium described under the unbroken seal attached to the book and intact at the time of presentation. A schedule of such prizes and premiums which the management proposes in this plan is as follows:

Number of Books	Prize Each	Amount
1	$150.00	$ 150
5	50.00	250
14	20.00	280
50	10.00	500
160	5.00	800
1,020	1.00	1,020
8,750	0.40	3,500
10,000		$6,500

Every 10,000 books distributed will provide for prizes in accordance with the above schedule. This is definitely fixed and not subject to alteration or modification.

The cost of this plan will be as follows:

Books, including expense of distribution............	$ 15 per	*M* books
Stamps..	1 "	*M* stamps
Prizes, according to schedule......................	650 "	*M* books

It is proposed that each package of product *A* shall contain 8 premium stamps and each package of product *B*, 4 premium stamps. The premium stamp book plan is intended to take the place of all previous advertising, which will be immediately discontinued if this proposition is adopted. Selling prices previously established will be maintained without change.

Proposition 2.—Reduced Selling Prices

Under this plan it is proposed to reduce selling prices of product *A* by 8⅓% and of product *B* by 5% and to continue all previous advertising with some increase therein. This proposition is being considered as an alternative of proposition 1, and if adopted, no use will be made of premium stamp books.

	Product *A*	Product *B*
Facts regarding previous operations:		
Average quantity sold per annum......	200,000 units	600,000 units
Production costs, per unit............	40¢	30¢
Selling prices, per unit...............	60¢	40¢
Expected changes:		
Increase in unit sales volume:		
Proposition 1........................	50%	50%
" 2..................................	40%	25%

	Product *A*	Product *B*
Decrease in unit production costs:		
Proposition 1	5%	10%
" 2	7½%	6⅔%
Advertising:		
Proposition 1	None	None
" 2	8% of sales	7% of sales
Other selling expenses:		
Proposition 1	15% of sales	12% of sales
" 2	12% " "	12% " "
Premium book expenses:		
Proposition 1	(As indicated)	
" 2	None	None
Administrative expenses:		
Proposition 1	4% of sales	4% of sales
" 2	Same amount as prior years.	

In proposition 1 it is assumed that premium stamp books and stamps will be distributed in exactly sufficient quantities to supply every customer under the proposed schedule of sales and that all such books and stamps will be redeemed.

Prepare a schedule, such as you would submit to the management, giving a comparison of the operations in previous years with those under both propositions accompanied by statistical data and analysis. Arrange the schedule so that it will permit an easy appraisal of the advantages and disadvantages of the proposals, and show whether or not the desired results in respect of increased sales, decreased cost, and decreased selling expenses are attained. Your conclusions must be apparent from the comparisons submitted.

Problem 57-9. A manufacturer wishes to enter the hosiery knitting business but lacks sufficient capital. Hoping to obtain the necessary additional funds from temporary bank loans by indicating substantial potential profits, he has requested that the following projected statements or budgets be prepared by quarters, starting with the third quarter in 1945 and ending with the quarter in which it is estimated that all bank borrowings have been liquidated:

(*a*) Statements of cash receipts and disbursements.
(*b*) Balance sheets.
(*c*) Statements of profit and loss.

Prepare these statements. The statements are to be based upon estimates and assumptions furnished by the manufacturer as listed below:

1. It is proposed that the corporation will begin business on July 1, 1945, with a cash capital of $100,000.00, all paid in.

2. Knitting machinery consisting of eight units costing $170,000.00 will be ordered at once; delivery will require one month; and payment will be made as follows:

10% in cash with order.
10% in cash on delivery.
80% by notes dated August 1, 1945, maturing quarterly in equal amounts over two years, the first note falling due at the end of the 1st quarter of 1946. Interest at 6% will be paid at the end of each quarter on unpaid notes.

3. Auxiliary machinery will cost $8,000.00; factory furniture, fixtures, and so on, will cost $2,000.00; both items will be purchased at once for cash.

4. Borrowings in units of \$25,000.00 each, 6% interest (payable at the end of each quarter), will be made as required at the beginning of quarters; repayments of not less than \$25,000.00 each will be made when possible at the end of quarters. Cash balances must be budgeted never to be less than \$20,000.00.

5. Quarterly production of hosiery will be as follows:

4th quarter of 1945	4,000 dozen
1st quarter of 1946	6,000 "
Quarterly thereafter	24,000 "

6. Costs of production will be as follows:

Direct costs per dozen pairs of hosiery produced:	
Thrown silk (purchased on terms of 90 days net)	\$ 3
Direct labor, dyeing, etc	2
Factory overhead, by quarters:	
Starting at once	2,000
4th quarter of 1945	4,000
1st quarter of 1946	9,000
Quarterly thereafter	15,000

Depreciation of fixed assets at a composite rate of 8% per annum will be provided starting with the 4th quarter of 1945.

7. Selling expenses will be \$20,000.00 each quarter, starting at once.

8. General and administrative expenses by quarters will be as follows:

Starting at once	\$3,000
4th quarter of 1945	5,000
Quarterly thereafter	6,000

9. Hosiery manufactured will be sold at the following prices:

80% firsts at	\$12.00 per dozen
20% seconds at	2.00 " "

With every four dozen firsts, one dozen seconds will be sold.

10. Customers' terms will be 30 days net. It will be assumed that payments will be received when due, that there will be no bad debts, and that each month's sales will equal one third of the quarter's sales.

11. Inventories of thrown silk will be one half of the consumption in the succeeding quarter.

12. Inventories of finished hosiery (it will be assumed that hosiery in process will be finished at the ends of quarters) will be as follows:

End of 4th quarter of 1945	1,000 dozen
End of 1st quarter of 1946	1,000 "
End of each quarter thereafter	4,000 "

13. Inventory valuation of finished hosiery will be based upon cost at maximum production.

14. Provision for Federal income taxes will be made only at the close of the calendar years, and will not be considered in the preparation of the projected statements.

QUESTIONS AND PROBLEMS ON CHAPTER 58

Questions

Question 58-1. A municipality obtained a tax levy as follows:

	Mills
For general fund purposes	8.44
For sinking fund purposes	4.9
Total	13.34

On the basis of this levy, $25,000.00 was collected during a certain month of the fiscal year. What part of this $25,000.00 belongs to the general fund and what part to the sinking fund?

Question 58-2. A municipality derives its revenues from taxation. The valuation of its assessable property is as follows:

Real property	$40,350,000.00	
Personal property	4,100,000.00	
Total valuation		$44,450,000.00

The estimated expenses for 1947 are as follows:

Police department	$96,975.00	
Fire department	96,000.00	
Street department	48,500.00	
Sewer department	39,400.00	
Health department	15,000.00	
Other departments	37,500.00	
Total		$333,375.00

In addition to meeting these expenses, the city must provide for the interest on its bonded debt of $1,333,350.00, which bears 5%; and must, according to the stipulation in its charter, levy one half of a mill tax for each park and library, and one mill tax for a sinking fund for the redemption of its bonds.

Prepare a statement giving the tax levy in mills and amounts necessary to produce sufficient money for the following funds:

General fund
Interest fund
Park fund
Library fund
Sinking fund

Question 58-3. A municipality sells its bond issue of $100,000.00 for water works purposes, receiving par, 2% premium, and $500.00 accrued interest. How much of the proceeds can the municipality use for water works purposes? Give reasons for your answer.

Question 58-4. In auditing the accounts of the city of Cook, the following balance sheet under the heading of "Capital Fund" was submitted to you for verification:

Cash	$ 5,000.00	Vouchers payable	$ 1,000.00
Properties	2,500,000.00	Capital surplus	1,504,000.00
		Funded debt	1,000,000.00
	$2,505,000.00		$2,505,000.00

Of the funded debt, $25,000.00 was incurred on account of a current deficit. Prepare a corrected statement for use in your audit report.

Question 58-5. In auditing the annual report of the town of *X*, you find all the following items of receipts stated under the general heading of "Revenues":

1. Taxes received.
2. Loan from Bank of *X*.
3. Dog licenses.
4. Municipal court fines.
5. Bequest from the estate of *A* to establish town library.
6. Street assessments collected from owners of property.
7. Permits for parades.
8. Sale of worn-out equipment.
9. State grant for upkeep of a state highway within town limits.
10. Deposit by *B* to cover cost of extra sewer connection.
11. Interest on bank deposits.
12. Donation from *C* toward repairs on his street.
13. Annual payment under franchise by *X* Street Railway Company.
14. Fees turned in by town clerk.
15. Rent of city dock to steamboat company.
16. Assessments on members of police force for pension fund.
17. Received from *B*: balance of cost of extra sewer connection (see 10).
18. Newsstand privilege in city hall.
19. Proceeds of paving bonds sold at 110.

Show true revenues and indicate how the other items should be treated.

Question 58-6. The town of *X* erects a school building from the proceeds of bonds issued for the purpose. It is estimated that the building will last twenty years. The bonds also mature in twenty years and contain a sinking fund clause to provide the funds for their payment at maturity. The school board takes no provision for depreciation on the building in the annual tax rate, and a controversy arises in the town about whether such a provision should be made. Discuss briefly both sides of this question.

Problems

Problem 58-1. In the city of *B*, a tax levy for a special fund was made on January 1, 1946, in the amount of $3,225,195.00. The receipts for this purpose to May 31, 1946 totaled $1,264,849.00, which sum was the balance in the fund on June 1, 1946. Receipts for the succeeding months were as follows: June, $664,750.00; July, $410,165.00; August, $342,982.00; September, $284,340.00; October, $120,722.00; November, $13,693.00; and December, $9.00. The December receipts were the final possible collections from this levy.

An appropriation of $3,150,000.00 was made on June 1 from this fund, vouchers were certified against the appropriation, and warrants were issued as follows: June, $65,133.00; July, $129,300.00; August, $156,875.00; September, $205,900.00; October, $301,642.00; and November, $375,200.00.

During the month of December vouchers were certified to the amount of $396,427.00, for which warrants were issued to the amount of $170,553.00.

The total amount of warrants paid by the treasurer during the seven months ending December 31 was $1,084,752.00; no warrants were outstanding on June 1.

Set up a statement of the accounts of the special fund, and a balance sheet of the fund as of December 31.

Problem 58-2. You are engaged to audit the accounts of a city for the year 1945. The books show the following information as to the general fund:

Surplus at beginning of year	$332,011.00
Taxes assessed	184,400.00
Other revenues collected	56,841.00
Expense, per vouchers approved	227,642.00
Surplus at end of year	345,610.00

On investigation, you discover the following additional facts:

(*a*) The assets of the fund include the inventory of general stores—$23,812.00. A continuous inventory of about this amount is maintained, the council having authorized such an inventory up to $25,000.00.

(*b*) The assets of the fund also include book value of permanent property, which on January 1 totaled $269,362.00 and on December 31, $286,-962.00. The difference represents capital expenditures for the year charged direct to fixed asset accounts.

(*c*) On December 31, orders and contracts were outstanding estimated to cost $4,350.00, payable out of the appropriations of the year 1945.

(*d*) Taxes for the year were due May 1, but only 82% had been collected at December 31. Estimates indicate further collections of not over 8%.

(*e*) Amounts due the sinking fund from the general fund for the year totaled $9,212.00. of which $6,000.00 was paid and included in expense.

(*f*) On January 2, 1946, a public benefit installment of $3,178.00 is due the assessment fund. A similar installment, due January 2, 1945, was paid in 1945 and entered as an expenditure of that year.

(*g*) Included in the expense of the year under audit are the following sums paid for departments entirely supported by special funds: library, $1,687.00; parks, $2,143.00.

1. Does the surplus as stated at the beginning and the end of the year correctly indicate the amount available for appropriation and expenditure on those dates? If not, prepare working papers to indicate the adjustments you would consider necessary in each amount.
2. Present also a correct statement of general fund revenue, expenditures, and available surplus for the year.

Problem 58-3. The following is a balance sheet of the City of Croix at December 31, 1945:

CURRENT FUND

Assets

Cash	$ 15,482.34
Taxes receivable:	
Year 1942	1,917.66
Year 1943	7,308.14
Year 1944	8,133.11
Year 1945	123,170.65
Deferred charges:	
Overexpenditures of 1945 appropriations	437.10
Taxes canceled—1945	850.00
	$157,299.00

Liabilities

Tax revenue notes:	
Year 1943	$ 7,000.00
Year 1944	8,000.00
Year 1945	123,000.00
Accounts payable	17,601.00
Surplus revenue	1,698.00
	$157,299.00

CAPITAL FUND

Assets

Cash	$ 17,810.95
Improvements in progress	39,152.62
Deferred charges to future taxation for cost of completed improvements	25,380.00
	$ 82,343.57

Liabilities

Serial bonds	$ 26,000.00
Notes payable	49,000.00
Accounts payable	7,343.57
	$ 82,343.57

The governing body of the city adopted the following budget for 1946:

Appropriations

Department of public works	$ 275,450.00
Department of revenue and finance	48,500.00
Department of public safety	535,375.00
Department of public affairs	190,000.00
Department of parks and public property	60,000.00
Interest on bonds	3,500.00
Retirement of bonds	7,000.00
Interest on notes	4,500.00
Overexpenditures of 1945 appropriations	437.10
Taxes canceled—1945	850.00
	$1,125,612.10

Anticipated revenues

General licenses	$ 10,700.00
Liquor licenses	63,000.00
Interest on taxes	22,000.00
City clerk's fees	700.00
Building permits	2,500.00
Bureau of health fees	5,400.00
Police court fines	3,000.00
	$ 107,300.00
Amount to be raised by taxation	1,018,312.10
	$1,125,612.10

The actual amount of taxes levied for the year 1946 was $1,018,603.75.

During the year 1946, improvements in progress costing $30,000.00 were completed. The notes payable issued to finance the improvements were retired from the proceeds of a serial bond issue which was sold at par.

A statement of receipts and disbursements for the year 1946 follows:

Receipts:		
1942 taxes	$ 1,012.75	
1943 taxes	5,475.63	
1944 taxes	6,125.47	
1945 taxes	115,245.78	
1946 taxes	787,375.62	
General licenses	10,754.00	
Liquor licenses	63,125.00	
Interest on taxes	21,900.00	
City clerk's fees	725.00	
Building permits	2,530.00	
Bureau of health fees	5,350.00	
Police court fines	2,925.00	
Miscellaneous fees	250.00	
Tax revenue notes—1946	215,000.00	$1,237,794.25
Serial bonds		30,000.00
		$1,267,794.25

Disbursements:		
Department of public works		$ 270,680.00
Department of revenue and finance		47,350.00
Department of public safety		525,250.00
Department of public affairs		187,325.00
Department of parks and public property		59,100.00
Interest on bonds		3,500.00
Retirement of bonds		7,000.00
Interest on notes		4,300.00
Tax revenue notes—1943		7,000.00
Tax revenue notes—1944		6,000.00
Tax revenue notes—1945		114,000.00
Accounts payable—current fund		16,751.00
		$1,248,256.00
Improvements in progress	$ 5,900.00	
Notes payable	30,000.00	
Accounts payable—capital fund	7,343.57	43,243.57
		$1,291,499.57

The following bills applicable to the year 1946 were unpaid at December 31, 1946:

Department of public works	$4,000.00
Department of revenue and finance	1,000.00
Department of public safety	9,500.00
Department of public affairs	2,000.00
Department of parks and public property	700.00

From the foregoing prepare a worksheet showing (1) the balance sheet on December 31, 1946, (2) the changes in revenue surplus, (3) journal entries, and (4) cash transactions.

Problem 58-4. A Governmental authority was constituted about July 1, 1945 to carry out certain recreational activities for which the authority was to buy or construct the equipment.

It was decided that the accounts of the authority will show budgetary estimates as well as actual income and expenditures in an approved manner, and that the transactions will be recorded in the following funds:

General operating fund
Working capital fund
Sinking fund for redemption of bonds
Property fund

From the following information, prepare a columnar worksheet recording the transactions of the authority so as to show the asset, liability, and budgetary accounts for the year ended June 30, 1946:

(1) An advance of $50,000.00 was made by the government creating the authority to finance the initial construction and activities, to be repaid out of operating revenues.
(2) From the working capital fund thus created, $10,000.00 was transferred to the general fund for current operating expenses until revenues could be realized.
(3) A budget of recreational activities for the year was adopted as follows:

Revenues		
Licenses	$ 50,000.00	
Fees	100,000.00	
Sales	30,000.00	
Miscellaneous	10,000.00	$190,000.00
Expenditures		
Administration	$ 10,000.00	
Bathing pavilion	65,000.00	
Boating	25,000.00	
Park maintenance	54,000.00	
Interest on bonds	6,000.00	
Sinking fund requirements	20,000.00	$180,000.00

(4) Purchases of supplies were made for central stores to the amount of $36,000.00 and paid in full.
(5) A bond issue of $200,000.00 for improvements was authorized as of July 1, 1945, bearing interest at 3 per cent per annum, payable semi-annually. It was disposed of on August 1 at par and accrued interest of $500.00.
(6) Contracts amounting to $165,000.00 were let for improvements. Work was completed and contracts were paid to the extent of $156,000.00, which included $1,000.00 extras, leaving $10,000.00 in progress on June 30, 1946.
(7) Additional construction work was supplied through the working capital fund to the extent of $34,000.00, which included $18,000.00 labor paid in cash, $14,000.00 material from stores at cost, and $2,000.00 overhead. The working capital fund was reimbursed in full for this service.
(8) Other services (labor only) supplied to authority activities and paid for by the working capital fund were as follows, including 10 per cent, or $920.00, for overhead:

Bathing pavilion	$3,300.00	
Boating	1,100.00	
Park maintenance	5,720.00	$10,120.00

Of the above, $2,200.00 for park maintenance was incomplete and not billed as of June 30, 1946. Otherwise, reimbursement to the working capital fund was completed.

(9) Revenues collected during the year were as follows:

Licenses	$ 48,500.00	
Fees	101,400.00	
Sales	29,200.00	
Miscellaneous	9,400.00	$188,500.00

In addition there were $1,600.00 of licenses billed but not collected, on which possible losses should not exceed 20 per cent.

Of the fees collected, it was necessary to refund $210.00.

Of the licenses collected, $500.00 represented advance payments on account of the following year.

(10) Supplies were issued to authority departments by the central stores as follows, the figures in each case including 10 per cent or a total of $1,050.00 for working capital fund overhead:

Administration	$ 330.00	
Bathing pavilion	2,640.00	
Boating	1,650.00	
Park maintenance	6,930.00	$11,550.00

Transfers were made to the working capital fund to the amount of $10,600.00 on account of these items.

(11) Contracts and orders issued during the year for operating expenses totaled $83,000.00. These were liquidated to the extent of $81,160.00, leaving $1,200.00 for bathing pavilion, and $640.00 for boating, or a total of $1,840.00 outstanding at June 30th.

(12) Vouchers approved during the year for payrolls, invoices, and miscellaneous, including those covering contracts and orders liquidated, as well as other items, were as follows:

Administration	$ 9,450.00	
Bathing pavilion	59,160.00	
Boating	21,600.00	
Park maintenance	41,000.00	
Interest	6,000.00	$137,210.00

Treasury warrants were issued and paid in settlement of these items to the amount of $135,610.00.

(13) Transfer was made to the sinking fund for $18,000.00 of the amount due it from the general fund, leaving the remainder as still owing. Securities costing $18,000.00 were purchased for this fund, and income thereon was realized to the amount of $300.00. Among the securities purchased were $5,000.00 bonds of the authority, which were immediately retired.

(14) The sum of $5,000.00 was repaid to the working capital fund on the advance made to the general fund.

(15) Purchases of office and general equipment to the amount of $20,000.00 were made from the working capital fund. This equipment is to be written off by charges to overhead at the rate of 5 per cent per year, beginning with the current year.

(16) Overhead expense of the working capital fund paid for the year was $2,600.00. The physical inventory of stores at the end of the year was $12,300.00. Stores and overhead surplus were carried to the

surplus account of the fund. The sum of $1,000.00 was repaid to the central government to apply on the advance made to the authority.

(17) Among the invoices paid during the year from the general fund were items totaling $16,540.00 for park maintenance equipment.

Problem 58-5. The City of Jonesville classifies its accounts under four different funds. The balances in the accounts of those funds on January 1, 1946, and on December 31 of the same year, before closing, were as follows:

	January 1	December 31
General fund:		
Cash	$ 25,552.00	$ 29,495.00
1945 taxes receivable	19,876.00	16,743.00
Accounts receivable	4,232.00	4,987.00
Stores	13,475.00	13,650.00
Permanent property	4,250,335.00	4,250,335.00
1946 taxes receivable		76,984.00
Estimated revenue from taxes		250,000.00
Estimated revenue from miscellaneous sources		50,000.00
Appropriation expenditures for current purposes		235,000.00
Appropriation expenditures for capital additions		10,650.00
Appropriation expenditures for payment of bonds		30,000.00
Appropriation encumbrances (1946)		7,500.00
	$4,313,470.00	$4,975,344.00
Accounts payable	$ 4,276.00	$ 4,664.00
Reserve for 1945 taxes	15,896.00	14,896.00
Reserve for orders and contracts	5,355.00	7,500.00
Reserve for stores	14,000.00	14,000.00
Current surplus	19,806.00	19,975.00
Bonds payable	330,000.00	300,000.00
Capital surplus	3,924,137.00	3,952,179.00
1946 tax anticipation notes payable		27,000.00
Reserve for 1946 taxes		30,000.00
Revenue from taxes		256,730.00
Revenue from miscellaneous sources		47,250.00
Appropriations		290,000.00
Estimated budget surplus		10,000.00
Sale of old equipment		1,150.00
	$4,313,470.00	$4,975,344.00
Water fund:		
Cash	$ 8,780.00	$ 3,469.00
Accounts receivable	9,542.00	7,432.00
Stores	15,496.00	19,617.00
Investments of replacement fund	28,000.00	31,250.00
Permanent property	253,955.00	256,745.00
Labor and material expense		126,931.00
Interest on bonds		3,000.00
Depreciation charge		14,000.00
Accounts of prior years written off		1,324.00
Expended for additions to plant		15,125.00
	$315,773.00	$478,893.00

	January 1	December 31
Accounts payable	$ 5,133.00	$ 4,785.00
Customers' deposits	2,100.00	2,300.00
Replacement fund reserve	28,000.00	31,250.00
Operating surplus	25,650.00	25,650.00
Bonds payable	75,000.00	60,000.00
Capital surplus	179,890.00	182,680.00
Services billed		170,753.00
Deposits lapsed		75.00
Interest on investments		1,400.00
	$315,773.00	$478,893.00
Assessment funds:		
Improvement No. 19:		
Cash	$ 6,392.00	$ 3,527.00
Assessments receivable	63,396.00	52,509.00
Delinquent assessments receivable	5,247.00	3,478.00
Public benefit receivable	7,320.00	5,972.00
Interest on bonds		4,500.00
	$ 82,355.00	$ 69,986.00
Bonds payable	$ 75,000.00	$ 60,000.00
Surplus	7,355.00	7,355.00
Interest on assessments		2,631.00
	$ 82,355.00	$ 69,986.00
Improvement No. 20:		
Cash		$ 1,584.00
Assessments receivable		31,175.00
Public benefit receivable		3,500.00
		$ 36,259.00
Bonds payable		$ 35,000.00
Surplus		475.00
Interest on assessments		784.00
		$ 36,259.00
Trust funds:		
Cash	$ 4,543.00	$ 2,436.00
Investments	110,500.00	115,475.00
Premium on investments		600.00
Accrued interest purchased		320.00
Cemetery maintenance		1,237.00
Cemetery expense		3,325.00
Policemen's pensions paid		4,800.00
Firemen's pensions paid		3,200.00
	$115,043.00	$131,393.00
Cemetery endowment fund reserve	$ 70,000.00	$ 70,000.00
Policemen's pension fund reserve	22,842.00	22,842.00
Firemen's pension fund reserve	18,932.00	18,932.00
Cemetery maintenance fund reserve	3,269.00	3,269.00
Profit on sale of investments		1,100.00
Undistributed income		5,200.00
Policemen's pension fund contributions		6,300.00
Firemen's pension fund contributions		3,750.00
	$115,043.00	$131,393.00

It has been the practice of the city to close out the unencumbered balance of appropriations of the general fund at the end of each year. Depreciation on the general property of the city is not entered, and accrued interest on investments and outstanding bonds is disregarded. Income and profit on trust fund investments are distributed as follows: 65% to cemetery fund; 20% to policemen's pension fund; and 15% to firemen's pension fund, in round dollars.

The cemetery maintenance fund consists of the income from the cemetery endowment fund and is used for cemetery expense. Excess of receipts over disbursements of pension funds is closed to reserve accounts of the respective funds at the end of each year.

Attention is directed to the following facts and conditions at the close of the year 1946:

(1) The reserve for 1945 taxes is to be increased to the total of such taxes.
(2) The reserve for 1946 taxes is to be increased 65%.
(3) Invoices on all orders and contracts outstanding at the beginning of the year were paid with a saving of $169.00, which amount was credited to current surplus.
(4) The old property sold during the year was carried in the accounts at a value of $7,500.00.
(5) Permanent property valued at $2,350.00 was discarded during the year.
(6) Replacements of water-department equipment costing $7,960.00 were made from the replacement fund during the year at a cost of $10,750.00.

On the basis of all of the above information prepare:

(a) A balance sheet of all funds after closing the books on December 31, 1946.
(b) A statement of the current surplus of the general fund for the year, showing revenues and expenditures.
(c) A statement of income and expense of the water department for the year.

Problem 58-6. Following is a summary of the endowment funds of the State University:

Aggregate of the funds at July 1, 1943		$5,500,000
Increases: Sept. 1, 1943	$ 15,000	
Oct. 1, 1943	50,000	
Jan. 1, 1944	85,000	
Mar. 1, 1944	100,000	
May 1, 1944	25,000	275,000
Aggregate at June 30, 1944		$5,775,000

Included in the endowment funds is a fund for the Dowd Chair of Chemistry, namely:

Balance of fund at July 1, 1943		$ 75,000
Increases: Oct. 1, 1943	$ 5,000	
Jan. 1, 1944	15,000	
May 1, 1944	10,000	30,000
Aggregate at June 30, 1944		$105,000

The total income for the year ended June 30, 1944, earned from the investment of all the funds, is $275,750.00.

If we assume that the securities in which the funds are invested are pooled:

1. What is the average rate of income earned during the year ended June 30, 1944?

2. What amount of the income must be applied toward the expenses of the Dowd Chair of Chemistry?

Problem 58-7. From the following municipal trial balance at the close of a fiscal year but before closing the books, prepare a balance sheet, properly subdivided into funds, after giving effect to necessary entries of the general fund and the sinking fund as of the close of the year and to settlements of all inter fund balances other than permanent advances:

	Debit	Credit
Accounts receivable general fund	$ 3,321.74	
Appropriation balances (unencumbered), general fund		$ 1,117.09
Assessments receivable	72,621.70	
Bond fund cash	2,005.60	
Bond fund balance (unencumbered)		678.00
Bonds payable, general capital account		250,000.00
Bonds authorized and unissued	8,000.00	
Contracts payable, bond fund		4,700.00
Due stores fund from bond fund		1,227.60
Due stores fund from general fund		1,593.96
Due stores fund from other funds	2,821.56	
Estimated revenues	1,500.00	
Fixed property	897,640.00	
Fixed property (income producing, trust fund)	62,000.00	
General fund cash	1,842.10	
Income account, sinking fund		1,960.00
Interest account, special assessments	620.00	
Loan from general to stores and service fund	25,000.00	
Public benefit receivable (assessment fund)	6,400.00	
Reserve for encumbrances, general fund		2,827.10
Reserve for working capital		25,000.00
Reserve for retirement of bonds		160,000.00
Reserve for uncollectible taxes		2,875.00
Sinking fund cash	1,450.00	
Sinking fund investments	160,000.00	
Sinking fund requirements	1,000.00	
Sinking fund surplus		490.00
Special assessment bonds		80,000.00
Special assessment fund cash	1,872.65	
Stores and service fund working capital (loan from general fund)		25,000.00
Stores and service fund cash	1,408.22	
Stores inventory	15,942.80	
Surplus receipts, general fund		896.00
Surplus, special assessment fund		1,514.35
Surplus invested in fixed assets		647,640.00
Taxes receivable, general fund	6,972.61	
Temporary loans, general fund		3,000.00
Trust fund balance		96,320.00
Trust fund cash	6,820.00	
Trust fund investments	27,500.00	
Vouchers payable, bond fund		3,400.00
Vouchers payable, general fund		1,327.30
Work in process, stores and service fund	4,827.42	
	$1,311,566.40	$1,311,566.40

PROBLEMS ON CHAPTER 59

Problems

Problem 59-1. From the following trial balance of the Inland National Bank on December 31, 1946, prepare a condensed statement of condition and a statement of net earnings for the year.

INLAND NATIONAL BANK
Trial Balance
December 31, 1946

Cash on hand	$ 1,463,290.00	
Federal Reserve Bank—reserve account	14,128,700.00	
Due from banks	18,540,800.00	
Transit account	1,666,444.00	
U. S. Government securities	12,150,110.00	
Other securities	3,039,531.00	
Stock in Federal Reserve Bank	60,000.00	
Call loans	1,450,000.00	
Commercial paper	12,320,500.00	
Other loans	421,560.00	
Overdrafts	1,440.00	
Bank building	120,500.00	
Furniture and fixtures	42,000.00	
Prepaid expenses	22,000.00	
Capital stock		$ 2,000,000.00
Surplus		300,000.00
Undivided profits		162,340.00
Contingent reserve		22,440.00
Taxes reserved and unpaid		32,850.00
Interest collected but not earned		37,750.00
Individual deposits—demand		38,870,550.00
Trust department deposits		4,753,800.00
Cashier's checks		420,180.00
Certified checks		164,500.00
Public funds		7,200,000.00
Savings deposits		11,340,175.00
Interest and discount		312,650.00
Exchange		7,210.00
Trust department earnings		37,650.00
Safe deposit rentals		8,224.00
Other earnings		7,556.00
Interest paid or accrued	56,360.00	
Expenses	194,640.00	
	$65,677,875.00	$65,677,875.00

U. S. Government bonds, valued at $8,000,000.00, were deposited as security for the public funds.

Problem 59-2. From the following data prepare a trial balance of the Tri-City National Bank and from the trial balance prepare a condensed statement of condition on December 31, 1946 and a statement of net earnings for the year then ended.

Interest and discount, $96,563.47; time loans, $431,650.00; cashier's checks, $38,659.75; unearned discount, $4,345.19; furniture and fixtures, $1.00; exchange from clearings, $105,784.63; expense, $51,637.45; interest paid, $4,324.64; building, $75,000.00; certificates of deposit, $12,450.00; capital stock, $250,000.00; exchange, $2,165.84; due banks, $557,345.86; depositors, $783,450.17; undivided profits, $224,657.75; other earnings, $9,745.23; stock in Federal Reserve Bank, $7,500.00; securities owned, $146,041.87; cash, 565,050.23; surplus, $75,000.00; demand loans, $37,500.00; customers' loans, $606,917.43; due from banks, $51,340.15; transit items, $72,306.47; savings deposits, $100,670.61.

Problem 59-3. Make the journal entries for the following transactions, and show how the results of these transactions should be reflected in the balance sheet of the bank after (*a*) and after (*b*).

(*a*) The Merchants National Bank made arrangements to accept drafts as follows:

For J. B. Roberts and Company	$40,000.00
For T. V. Powers Company	60,000.00
For Harrison, Trelawney Company	80,000.00

(*b*) Before maturity

J. B. Roberts and Company paid in	$40,000.00
T. V. Powers Company paid in	30,000.00

The bank acquired $20,000.00 of Harrison, Trelawney Company's acceptances.

(*c*) All acceptances were presented to the bank at maturity and paid.

Problem 59-4. The transactions of The Central National Bank for the month of October 1946 may be summarized as follows:

The bank was organized on October 1, with paid-in capital of $650,000.00, of which $500,000.00 represented capital stock, par value $100.00.

The bank purchased fixtures for $20,000.00.

The bank subscribed for stock in the Federal Reserve Bank at $15,000.00 and paid its subscription.

The bank sent a deposit of $100,000.00 to the Federal Reserve Bank to cover its current reserve requirements. The bank received notification from the Federal Reserve Bank that this amount had been credited to its account.

The bank received deposits from regular customers as follows:

Currency	$ 15,650.00
Checks	1,564,320.00
Coupons	2,860.00

Of the checks, $182,450.00 were on this bank. The remainder were sent to the clearing house. At the end of the month all checks and all but $240.00 of the coupons had been collected.

The bank arranged with customers to accept drafts drawn against it in the sum of $180,000.00. The bank lent $280,000.00 to borrowers, all of which was credited to their accounts. Interest was collected in advance on these loans in the sum of $3,200.00. At the end of the month, $1,254.00 of this interest had been earned.

The bank sold cashier's checks in the sum of $68,000.00 and collected fees of $190.00 for this service. At the end of the month $54,000.00 of these had been presented for payment, by out-of-town banks.

The bank certified checks totaling $54,350.00 during the month. Fees of $140.00 were charged for this service. Of the $54,350.00, $2,300.00 was paid in currency, $38,720.00 came through the clearing house, and the remainder was outstanding.

The bank rented safe deposit boxes for $800.00, of which $148.00 was earned during the month.

Checks were presented through the clearing house in the amount of $432,-645.00, which includes the certified checks referred to above. Of the checks deposited by customers and sent to the clearing house, checks for $1,450.00 were returned unpaid. Charges of $28.00 were made against the bank's customers for this service.

Service charges amounting to $420.00 were made against the accounts of customers whose balances were below required amounts.

A customer for whom the bank had accepted a draft instructed the bank to charge his account for the amount, $15,000.00, when it was presented, as it was. The charge on this was $10.00.

The bank bought $100,000.00 of U. S. Government bonds. Interest of $175.00 accrued on these bonds during the month. Of these bonds, $80,000.00 were pledged to obtain public deposits of $75,000.00

One of the borrowers instructed the bank to charge his loan of $15,000.00 against his account when due.

The bank's expenses during the month were $1,356.00.

Prepare a trial balance, a statement of condition, and a statement of net earnings.

Problem 59-5. The following items appear in the trial balance of the Tidewater National Bank. From them, compute the reserve which the bank must have with the Federal Reserve Bank. The bank is in a central reserve city and is required to maintain the reserves effective July 14, 1942. Not all the items listed below are needed in arriving at a solution.

Cash	$ 2,133,200.00
Due from banks	31,365,450.00
U. S. Government bonds	15,645,820.00
Overdrafts	14,135.00
Individual deposits—demand	111,459,540.00
Trust department deposits	18,643,105.00
Bank deposits	33,257,200.00
Bank money orders	236,610.00
Cashier's checks	2,145,302.00
Certified checks	1,802,145.00
Public funds	8,123,450.00
Savings deposits	22,540,976.00
Certificates of deposit	314,500.00

Problem 59-6. From the items following, prepare a detailed statement of the condition of the City Bank and Trust Company as at the close of business on December 31, 1946:

Acceptances anticipated	$ 50,000.00
Acceptances outstanding	445,000.00
Bank premises	1,225,000.00
Bonds—other than U. S. Government	2,700,000.00
Capital stock	3,000,000.00
Cash on hand	650,000.00
Certificates of deposit	225,000.00
Certified checks	100,000.00
Christmas clubs	221,000.00
Commercial deposits	6,300,000.00
Coupon deposits	15,000.00
Customers' liability for acceptances executed	445,000.00

Demand collateral loans	$ 2,350,000.00
Discounts	4,750,000.00
Dividend payable—January 1, 1947	60,000.00
Due from Federal Reserve Bank	1,000,000.00
Due from sundry banks	300,000.00
Due to banks	730,000.00
Exchanges for clearing house	225,000.00
Federal Reserve Bank stock (50% of subscription)	100,000.00
Furniture and fixtures	90,000.00
Interest receivable accrued	7,500.00
Letters of credit—customers' liability	60,000.00
Letters of credit executed for customers	60,000.00
Miscellaneous real estate	80,000.00
Official checks	48,000.00
Overdrafts	5,000.00
Real estate loans	6,350,000.00
Rediscounts	1,600,000.00
Reserve for contingencies	240,000.00
Reserve for interest, taxes, and other expenses	70,000.00
Savings deposits	9,000,000.00
Stock—other than Federal Reserve Bank stock	195,000.00
Surplus	1,600,000.00
Time collateral loans	3,225,000.00
Undivided profits (balance to be determined)	
Unearned discount	50,000.00
United States Government bonds	1,400,000.00
United States Government bonds pledged	400,000.00

Problem 59-7. You have been asked to make an examination of the accounts of a national bank as at the close of its fiscal year and render a report to its board of directors.

A statement of the bank's earnings and expenses as published is as follows:

Earnings	
Discount earned	$1,000,000
Interest on investments	1,750,000
Profit from sales of securities after considering a previous charge-off in the value of such securities to reserve for contingencies of $150,000	50,000
	$2,800,000
Expenses	
Expenses	$1,200,000
Interest on time accounts	500,000
Taxes (Federal and state)	250,000
Uncollectible loans	50,000
Reserve for contingencies	500,000
	$2,500,000
Net earnings	$ 300,000

In addition, you find that there has been (1) an appropriation or transfer of $2,000,000.00 from undivided profits to reserve for contingencies, (2) a write-down of $1,000,000.00 in the value of securities charged against that reserve, and (3) a further charge of $1,000,000.00 against the reserve to cover actual loans considered worthless during the year.

In preparing your report, what would you state to be the year's net earnings or loss which you would certify? Prepare a summary of the earnings statement.

QUESTIONS AND PROBLEM ON CHAPTER 60

Questions

Question 60-1. Why do a broker's records contain a double entry system of security entries as well as a double entry system of dollar amounts?

Question 60-2. Illustrate the money and security entries required to record a purchase and subsequent sale of securities.

Question 60-3. Illustrate the money and security entries required to record a short sale and subsequent purchase of securities.

Question 60-4. What is the position book, and what is its purpose?

Problem

Problem 60-1. From the following post-closing trial balance of a stock exchange house, prepare a balance sheet with relative security valuations. Merely list the items without grouping them under side captions.

Name of Account	Debits
Cash	$ 11,242.75
Customers' long trading accounts, fully secured (market value of long securities in above, $325,048.88)	248,973.64
Customers' debit balances, unsecured	16,625.97
Brokers' debit balances, fully secured (market value of long securities in above, $276,130.00; market value of short securities in above, $472,108.88)	171,969.20
Firm investments, long stocks at market value	10,400.00
Partner *A* trading account, debit balance (market value of long securities in above, $19,000.00)	19,773.07
Partner *B* trading account, debit balance (market value of long securities in above, $140,120.00)	34,641.13
Furniture and fixtures (not depreciated) new	2,480.75
Total	$516,106.51

	Credits
Customers' short trading accounts (market value of short securities in above, $42,590.00)	$ 46,005.46
Customers' free credit balances	34.52
Stocks failed to receive (market value of securities in above, $11,800.00)	11,853.50
Stocks loaned (market value of securities in above, $6,000.00)	6,500.00
Firm short trading account, at market value	228,600.00
Interest payable to partner *A*	625.00
Capital, partner *A*	166,866.08
Capital, partner *B*	55,621.95
Total	$516,106.51

Note: Securities in the firm's safety deposit box at market value, $9,600.00.

Index